To the most attractive
woman
(since

CW00867328

The Socialist League in the 1930s

Best wishes in your
future career
from the author.
film fanatic Mike

x

The Socialist League in the 1930s

Michael Bor

ATHENA PRESS
LONDON

The Socialist League in the 1930s
Copyright © Michael Bor 2005

ISBN 1 84401 043 0

First Published 2005 by
ATHENA PRESS
Queen's House, 2 Holly Road
Twickenham TW1 4EG
United Kingdom

Printed for Athena Press

To my four children,
Joseph, Jethro, Samuel and Maximillian,
and their future as dynamic active citizens
using their talents to the full.

'*I think that capitalism, wisely managed, can probably be made more efficient for attaining economic ends than any alternative system yet in sight, but that in itself it is in many ways extremely objectionable.*'

John Maynard Keynes

CONTENTS

Preface   11

A Summary of the Socialist League's Activities   15

Chapter 1

**Socialist League Origins from Previous Socialist Parties,
and Research Organisations**   25

The S.L.'s Inheritance From the I.L.P. (1920s)
and the Labour Movement (1929–1932)   34

(A) The I.L.P. (1920s)   34
(B) The Labour Movement (1929–1932)   40

Chapter 2

Intellectuals, Politics and the Socialist League   55

(A) The Influence of Marxism on the Socialist League   64

(B) The Russian Revolution, Leninism,
Stalinism, and the Socialist League   70

Chapter 3

The Membership and Function of the Socialist League   78

(A) The Leading Members of the Socialist League   80

(B) The S.L. as a National Organisation –
Its Function and Outlook
Through Pamphlets and Lectures   92

Chapter 4

**The Socialist League's Annual Conferences and
Policy Resolutions**   106

(A) S.L. Policy: the Constitutional Issue,
the Monarchy and Parliament   114

(B) S.L. Policy: Democracy, the Press and
Free Speech   123

(C) S.L. Policy: Fascism and Dictatorship   128

(D) S.L. Policy: Economics, Capitalist Planning,
and Public Ownership   135

Chapter 5

Unemployment, Professionals and Class Struggle   143
(A) The S.L. and Unemployment   143
(B) The S.L. and the Professional Worker   148
(C) The S.L. and Class Struggle   153

Chapter 6

Socialist League Local Branches   161
(A) Local Government and the Labour Party   161
(B) Local Activities   166
(C) Local Agitation Against the Unemployment Act,
     and the 'Mass Resistance Against War' Conferences   176
(D) The S.L. and the Labour League of Youth   182
(E) Local S.L.s, Constituency Labour Parties, and
     The Left Book Club   185
(F) A Socialist League Branch in Action   193

Chapter 7

The Socialist League and the Labour Party   201
(A) S.L. Leaders and Labour Party Leaders   205
(B) Socialist League Successes (1932–1933)   209
(C) 'Forward to Socialism' or 'For Socialism and Peace'
     (1934)?   217
(D) The Southport Conference and the S.L.'s 75 Amendments   221
(E) The General Election (1935)   226
(F) Ambiguities at the Edinburgh Conference (1936)   237
(G) Labour's Immediate Programme or The Unity
     Campaign (1937)?   242

Chapter 8

The Socialist League and the Trade Union Movement   247
(A) E. Bevin and W. Citrine or G. Lansbury and S. Cripps?   250
(B) The S.L. and Union Leaders (1932–1934)   252
(C) The S.L. and Union Leaders (1935–1937)   257
Appendix: The S.L. and the Co-operative Movement   265

Chapter 9

Labour and Communism   269
(A) The Labour Party, the C.P. and the S.L.   270
(B) The Labour Party's 'Democracy and Dictatorship' (1933)   271
(C) The Labour Party, the S.L. and the Unity Campaign   276

Chapter 10

The Socialist League and Foreign Affairs   279

(A) The S.L. and the Empire   281

(B) The S.L. and India   285

(C) The S.L. and the League of Nations   290

(D) The S.L. and German Politics   305

(E) The S.L. and the Spanish Civil War   313

Chapter 11

**The Socialist League and Origins of the 'United Front'
(1932–1936)**   326

(A) I.L.P./C.P. 'United Front' and the Labour Party (1933–1934) 327

(B) The S.L., the C.P. and the I.L.P. on Unemployment,
Fascism and War (1935)   337

(C) The S.L.'s Seven Point Resistance Plan to Rearmament
(April 1936)   346

(D) Edinburgh Conference Decisions   351

Chapter 12

The Socialist League and the Unity Campaign (1937)   356

(A) The S.L. Special Conference, (January 1937)   359

(B) The C.P., the S.L. and the Labour Party   367

(C) Labour's Immediate Programme   370

(D) The N.E.C. Disaffiliates the S.L. (March 1937)   373

(E) Dissolution of the Socialist League   379

Conclusion   389

Bibliography   404

Preface

'The beam that illuminates the dark regions of our past is the spotlight of our conscience.'

Agnes Heller, qu. E. Florescano,
'The Social Function of History', in ed. F. Bédarida,
The Social Responsibility of the Historian, Diogènes No. 168, 1994, p.45.

One of the functions of the intellectual is to raise to consciousness the ambiguities inherent in the professed ideals of society, and to make clear the meaning of the social forces implicit in the actions of society which contradict those ideals. We have failed to see that the ugly violence of our society is not an aberration of an otherwise sound and healthy society, but the unintended and unforeseen consequences of our most cherished ideals. We must act on our ideals or change our minds. 'The struggle', to use Barrington Moore's words, concerns contemporary capitalist democracy's capacity to live up to its noble professions, something no society has ever done... As one peers ever deeper to resolve the ambiguities of history, the seeker eventually finds them in himself and his fellow men as well as in the supposedly dead facts of history. We are inevitably in the midst of the ebb and flow of these events and play a part no matter how small and insignificant as individuals, in what the past will come to mean for the future.

John William Ward, Introduction to Alexander Berkman,
Prison Memoirs of an Anarchist, 2002 edn., p.xxviii

...even in the assault on the investment bank, he thought there was something theatrical about the protest, ingratiating even, in the ... tactical coup of reprogramming the stock tickers with poetry and Karl Marx. He thought Kinski was right when she said this was a market fantasy. There was a shadow of transaction between the demonstrators and the state. The protest was a form of systemic hygiene, purging and lubricating. It attested again, for the ten-thousandth time, to the market culture's innovative brilliance, its ability to shape itself to its own flexible ends, absorbing everything around it.

Don DeLillo, *Cosmopolis*, 2003, p.99

The 1930s witnessed the decisive moment of the Twentieth Century, an historical paradox in the relations of capitalism and communism, in alliance against Fascism until 1945.[i] The 1930s was also the decade in which the forces of hope and despair fought on the streets of cities; it ended when the world was plunged into another war, accompanied by barbarities which put the slaughter of 1914–1918 in the shade.[ii] What intrigued me was the response of the Labour Left to mass unemployment, Fascism, the Soviet Union, 'economic planning', propaganda, Marxism and peace movements.

I have been goaded by Thomas Pynchon's introduction to George Orwell's *1984*,

---

[i] E. Hobsbawm, *Age of Extremes: The Short Twentieth Century 1914–1991*, 2002 edn., pp.7–8.
[ii] C. Harman, *A People's History of the World*, 2002 edn., p.470. In the 1930s, 5% owned 79% of the wealth; the richest 1% owned 56%, J. E. Meade, *Efficiency, Equality and Ownership of Property*, 1964, p.27.

in which he comments: 'there is always some agency like the Ministry of Truth to deny the memories of others, to rewrite the past. It has become a commonplace, circa 2004, for government employees to be paid more than most of the rest of us to debase history, trivialise truth and annihilate the past on a daily basis. Those who don't learn from history used to have to relive it, but only those in power could find a way to convince everybody, including themselves, that history 'never happened', or happened in a way best serving their own purposes – or that it doesn't matter, except as a dumbed-down TV documentary cobbled together for an hour's entertainment.'[i]

Eric Hobsbawm remarked that where governments have enough to distribute to satisfy all claimants and most citizens' standard of life is rising, democratic politics rarely rises to fever pitch. However, between the Wars, the capitalist world economy appeared to collapse and the Socialist League (S.L.) was born at the worst period of the slump (1932–1933), when twenty-two percent of the British labour force was unemployed, unemployment relief was non-existent or meagre, it was the potentially mortal wound in the body politic, and there seemed no solution within the framework of the liberal economy. Socialism seemed superior to capitalism and destined to replace it, yet there were no signs of a significant electoral shift to the Left.[ii] However, the slump convinced the S.L. that the final agony of the capitalist system was occurring; 'capitalism' could no longer even afford the luxury of ruling through parliamentary democracy or liberal freedoms. Faced with insoluble economic problems, wouldn't governments fall back on force, coercion or even fascism? Wasn't the choice, as John Strachey put in his 1932 *The Coming Struggle for Power*, between Socialism and Barbarism? But was the S.L. embarking on a Sisyphean task?

The Socialist League endorsed anti-fascist unity, and the efficient champions of that, at the time, were Communists, while Western intellectuals were the first social stratum mobilised en masse against fascism in the 1930s,[iii] yet never supported the military measures required, such as rearmament and conscription. What drew Labour Left intellectuals into the Soviet sphere of influence was the trauma of the slump, because one country seemed immune to that – the Soviet Union. While liberal Western capitalism partially 'stagnated', the U.S.S.R. was engaged in rapid industrialisation with no unemployment (mass repression and the brutality of collectivisation being side-lined). Whatever its faults, Stalinism had found a way of escaping from the crises which beset market capitalism.[iv] The slump had broken traditions and certainties; intellectuals turned to Marx, having lost faith in social democracy. 'How capitalism worked', capitalist 'exploitation', fluctuations of capitalist economies, or 'causes of unemployment', enhanced Marxist interpretations, as did the 'solution', based on the socialisation of the means of production, distribution and exchange – and planning.[v] Nirvana.

Marxism advanced in the 1930s regardless of Liberal/Labour leaders, trade unionism and cooperatives, because capitalism *was* in crisis, fascism *was* advancing, and there *was* the direct appeal of the Soviet Union; the Marxist case against liberal bourgeois democracy was that the latter was endangered by fascism:[vi]

---

[i] T. Pynchon, introduction to Plume (Penguin US) edition of George Orwell's *1984*, 2003
[ii] E. Hobsbawm, op. cit., pp.86, 93–5, 131, 149.
[iii] Ibid., pp.136, 147, 150.
[iv] C. Harman, op. cit., p.478. E. Hobsbawm, op. cit., p.96.
[v] E. Hobsbawm, *Revolutionaries*, 1999 edn., pp.28, 31, 122.
[vi] Ibid., p.130.

Marxism gave life a pattern. During the 1930s it had explained the abject behaviour of British Conservatives as Hitler gobbled one country after another. It explained the bumbling slowness of the Labour Party in the face of these events.[i]

This is the zeitgeist in which the Socialist League battled within the Labour movement from 1932 to 1937, epitomised by the experience of one of the great Socialists of the time:

J. T. Murphy was threatened with expulsion from the Communist Party in 1932; rather than be thrown out, he left. As the party organiser in Sheffield, he had been moved by the sufferings of the unemployed, and had suggested that they might be alleviated by trade with the Soviet Union, which would also reduce the danger of war. The Political Bureau said: 'J. T. Murphy's childish argument that international trading relations reduce the danger of war is nothing but vulgar capitalist propaganda.'[ii]

That's why the Socialist League would play a useful rôle, and its history deserves to be recorded as fully as possible. Ivan Olbracht opined: 'Man has an insatiable longing for justice. In his soul he rebels against a social order which denies it to him and whatever the world he lives in, he accuses either that social order or the entire material universe of injustice. Man is filled with a strange, stubborn urge to remember, to think things out, and to change things.[iii] Or as Andrew Rawnsley ends *Servants of the People: The Inside Story of New Labour*:

The most important thing was changing the future.[iv]

However, for those readers requiring a brief introduction to Britain in the 1930s:

There were no family allowances, no universally available free medical treatment, no free secondary education except for a handful of children, no free milk in schools except for a tiny minority. There were still relatively few council houses. Old age pensions were a pittance... It was the demonstrations, the exposures of malnutrition, the hunger marches, which helped to create and focus a demand for state guarantees against poverty which no subsequent government could ignore... Far-reaching political questions – such as racialism, militarism, national independence and fascism – became mass issues, and the subject of intense discussion within the Labour movement... The unspoken belief that the rich and expensively educated had a natural right to rule and manage was deeply shaken by their manifest inability to deal either with unemployment or with Hitler.[v]

Part of what was at issue was *why* the Socialist movement, which constituted the most lively and intellectually formidable attempt to promote causes of equality and justice, was so overwhelmed in the 1930s that it never succeeded in reconstituting itself in a politically efficacious and ideologically-convincing fashion. Two historians explain the mood inherited by the S.L. Elie Halévy announced in 1919:

[i] Alison Macleod, *The Death of Uncle Joe*, 1997, p.12.

[ii] Ibid., p.172.

[iii] Ivan Olbracht, qu. in E. J. Hobsbawm, *Bandits*, 1972 edn., p.133–4.

[iv] A. Rawnsley, 2001 edn., p.501.

[v] N. Branson, M. Heinemann, *Britain in the Nineteen Thirties*, 1973 edn., pp.349–351.

Now the time for class war has come... we shall see the class struggle, acclimatized on English soil, adapting itself to the traditional party system... Has not the English political culture of compromise and adaptability come to mean simply a mediation of conflict at all costs, an avoidance of the harsh measures which were necessary to meet changing world conditions and the serious decline of British power?[i]

And, in 1930, E. H. Carr assessed a faltering Labour Government:

The Government of the day has so little faith in its capacity to tackle the major problems of our generation... we have no convictions beyond a vague sort of fatalism... We shall ... find creeds worth defending, causes worth fighting for, missions worth fulfilling. The fashion of indifference and the cult of futility will pass away; and we shall cease to be defeatists. But in the meanwhile we need a faith.[ii]

To revive the flagging spirits of Socialist activists, the S.L. would eventually provide a sustained *critique* of the 'inefficient capitalist system' (through its 27 pamphlets and monthly journals). It would query whether English law was dedicated to the provision of 'liberties for all', debate the limits of Constitutionalism and Parliamentarianism, campaign for a general strike to resist another war, question the mechanisms of power in the State, challenge lukewarm Labour and union policies, produce a comprehensive plan for a Socialist Government, and, in 1937, acknowledge the disparity between Socialist intentions and minimal achievements during the most extraordinary decade of the twentieth century.

[i] Quoting Anthony Hartley, 'Elie Halévy and England Now', *Encounter*, January 1975, p.43.
[ii] E. H. Carr, in J. Haslam, 'E. H. Carr 1892–1982', *History Today*, August 1983, p.37.

A Summary of the Socialist League's Activities

On the whole I am sick of the Girondins. To confess the truth, I find them extremely like our present set of respectable Radical members. There is the same cold clean-washed patronising talk about 'the masses' (a word expressive of a thing, which I greatly hate); the same formalism, hidebound pedantry, superficiality, narrowness, barrenness. I find that the Mountain [the Jacobins] was perfectly under the necessity of flinging such a set of men to the Devil; whither also I doubt not *our* set will go.

> Thomas Carlyle to J. S. Mill, 9/10/1836
> qu. Simon Heffer, *Moral Desperado: A life of Thomas Carlyle,*
> 1996 edn., p.162

In the Thirties there existed among politicians, writers, intellectuals in Britain and in Europe, a culture of paranoia, a feeling of being haunted by a spectre of catastrophe, of a final settling of accounts that was to come.

> Stuart Hampshire
> qu. in *The First and The Last* by Isaiah Berlin, 1999, p.98

Probably few people now remember the beginnings of the Socialist League, or of its relations with the Labour Party in the Britain of the early 1930s. It never became in itself an effective body... but its history is significant for the story of the Labour Party and for the role of the intellectuals in it... in spite of much underground ferment, the 1930s were a depressing period for the British Left... The Socialist League with Cripps, the Left Book Club with Laski and Strachey and various pacifist groups, all stood well to the left of the new party leadership and of the trade unions, now increasingly dominated by Bevin's massive conservatism.

> E.H. Carr, *From Napoleon to Stalin and Other Essays,* 1960, p.220

In the 1930s there were two main divergent strands in Labour politics: the unions who possessed large membership and funds, and the Socialist Societies who offered direction and enthusiasm.[i] Having drawn very different conclusions from the results of the Labour Government of 1929–1931 and the crisis of 1931 (union leaders emphasising 'loyalty' to the Movement, the Left wing of the Party stressing militancy and class struggle in a 'capitalist crisis'), these two elements polarised, as political events required increasingly urgent responses. One of the distinctive features of the 1930s was the participation of intellectuals in the battleground of political interests, particularly apparent in the relation of the intellectual to socialism'.[ii] With little positive reappraisal of programme, policy or leadership (except by the I.L.P.) the general intellectual inertia of the 1920s Labour Movement was transformed in the 1930s into various forms of vigorous commitment. The Socialist League represented a transformation within the Labour Party, although 'militant elements' were in a small minority, as in the wider Movement. It had always been the rôle of the Left wing of

---

[i] Dean McHenry, *His Majesty's Opposition: Structure and Problems of the British Labour Party (1931–8)*, 1939, p.3.
[ii] Neal Wood, *Communism and British Intellectuals*, 1959, p.15. For the view at the time, A. Sturmthal, *The Tragedy of European Labour 1918–1939*, 1943, L.B.C.

the Party to provide criticism (and idealism), and as the Party and unions grew more constitutional, Parliamentary and officially responsible, so the Left wing became a safety-valve for frustrated Socialist spirits. R. H. S. Crossman explained the relationship, that the Labour Party liked to have a Left wing to challenge those in authority and the Left had always received as much affection as anger from the rank and file. A Left may be fanatical and Utopian, but it must never be dull!

From its inception, the Socialist League defined itself more as a series of short-term campaigns than a political strategy, despite its 'Forward to Socialism' policy document of 1934 and its 'policy in themes' gathered in 'Problems of a Socialist Government' (1933) and 'Problems of the Socialist Transition' (1934). For each of its five years in existence, a different and intensive activity coloured its work. This was forced upon the S.L. by its equivocal position in the Labour Party, and its counter-balancing position in a Movement which had many diverse influences at work in its counsels. The Socialist League had to change the form and direction of its agitation and propaganda, because it was anxious to avoid the mistake of the I.L.P. (that is, to allow the Labour Party Executive to compel the S.L. to disband or secede from the Party). The S.L.'s raison d'être was to keep open the channels of communication between itself and other groups on the Left. It would be wrong to dismiss the S.L. by concluding that, in seeking to shape the policies of the Labour Party, it failed to learn from the history of the I.L.P[i]. Its position became untenable, but this was not because of lack of historical awareness; most of its leading members *were* ex-I.L.P.'ers and understood the rôle which the new organisation should adopt. J. T. Murphy, S.L. General Secretary in 1934, clarified this: 'The Socialist League has consequently become the focus of the new demand for a change of policy in the Labour Party. It has now passed beyond the stage of repeating the history of the I.L.P.'[ii]

One of the problems within the S.L., as in all Left-wing pressure groups, was its reliance upon personalities; an advantage while strengthening its following, it became a handicap when those personalities left the S.L. over 'matters of policy'. Prominent individuals, especially 'intellectuals', can always attract considerable attention in a British political Party. They have a 'curiosity value' for onlookers interested in 'characters' and in the 1930s, the Labour Party could utilise knowledge generated by such members. What soured the friendship were inexplicable 'disloyalties' and unexpected 'betrayals' over certain issues, when the Party sought to present a united party to the country and intellectual waverers stood by their individual principles. There could be no reconciliation when what appeared as 'apostasy' to the Party was 'integrity' for individual Socialists.

The Socialist League progressed through tabling militant resolutions for Party Conferences; campaigning for the election of Cripps, Laski and D. N. Pritt to the National Executive Committee; calling on 'Left' MPs to be loyal to their Socialism, making demands on the National Council of the Party for an immediate change of strategy or tactics, and fighting for the unity of the whole Labour Movement. Originally, the S.L. set out to forward Socialist research work in local Labour groups, Co-operative Societies and local union organisations. Only later did it seek to convert and re-channel (through the democratic process) the Labour Party into radical paths. Despite the Press's manufactured image of the S.L.'s 'revolutionary predilections'

---

[i] Eric Estorick, *Stafford Cripps*, 1949, p.121.
[ii] J. T. Murphy, *Preparing for Power*, 1934, p.272.

(later used to damn the S.L. in Labour Party and union circles), all S.L. actions were based on the strategy of giving political priority to Labour in Parliament, and of thinking strategically in terms of the existing structure of the Labour Party.[i]

In practice, the S.L. was a shadow reproduction of the whole Labour Party and its perspectives. Concessions had to be made to function effectively on any level because the Party was a compromise between working-class objectives and existing power structures and the S.L. could not extricate itself from a position of compromise on its Socialist aims in order to retain an influential position within the structure of the Party. Alternately, it chose between electoral campaigns within the Party and independent political agitations on immediate issues (such as the Means Test, rallies on behalf of the Spanish Republicans, and Unity Campaign activities). When the S.L. became involved in electoral campaigns (at any level), it was necessarily implicated in 'machine politics'. Entangled in these political tactics, the S.L. could not be treated as a purely 'Socialist pressure group'. To the extent that it dug its own grave, it could have opposed the bureaucratic tendencies in the Movement instead of manoeuvring for a little more political influence and directing energy into the very machines and methods which Socialists should have questioned. However, it would be unfair to deduce that '*the Left preached and argued but did not lead*'[ii] (for the Left organised and led the United and Popular Front movements), but it was true that the Left was revolutionary in outlook, though not in method.

Inheriting the outlook and style of different Socialist organisations the S.L.'s position in the Labour Movement was ambiguous. It expounded its ideas on educational research, Party programmes, and actual campaigns to differentiate itself from those official policies with which it disagreed. It also had to comply with Labour Party Standing Orders to retain and preserve associations within the Labour Movement. The Party had suffered from the humiliating apostasy of its leaders in 1931. More disciplinary procedures would be enforced and the S.L. received most censure for overstepping 'Party loyalties'. Any reconciliation between the benefits of Party membership and concessions to Party electioneering and pragmatism were not expected in the S.L. On the issue of 'power' within the Labour Movement, the S.L.'s choice of freedom of action or continued association with the Party became hypothetical. There *was* no alternative once the S.L. National Conference at Leeds (May 1934) urged upon its members a more politicising and active rôle. Outside the Labour Party, it would have clashed with the C.P. and the I.L.P. There was only one viable tactic: to continue working *within* the Labour Party. This strategy reached breaking point in 1937, exposing the illogicality and balancing-act in which the S.L. had become entangled. Some of the S.L.'s leading members spoke of it as 'the conscience' of the Labour Party, but it had to surrender its principles for organisational connections with either the Labour Party or (in 1937) the I.L.P. and Communist Party in the Unity Campaign. This was in the peculiar circumstances of the late 1930s, when the need to 'fight Fascism' immediately, on as wide a front as possible, seemed to be the wisest policy, but a Procrustean diktat in 1937 ended that strategy.

Political 'presentations' of issues have always been nurtured by Parties and pressure groups. In most cases, once entrenched in people's minds, an image takes on a life of its own, bearing little resemblance to any kind of political reality, and becomes the

[i] Raymond Williams (ed.), *May-Day Manifesto*, 1968, pp.172–173.
[ii] A. J. P. Taylor, 'Confusion on the Left', *The Baldwin Age*, ed. J. Raymond, pp.68–69.

vehicle for projecting fantasies, or idealisations. With the Socialist League, the press latched on to some of its phraseology and presented it as an 'undemocratic', 'dictatorial', and 'Republican' organisation. Perhaps the S.L. deserved these reactions; at times it seemed enigmatic in its teachings, cryptic in its pronouncements, for, during its short history, it stood for a variety of contradictory aims, professing belief in Parliamentarianism, the 'dictatorship of the working class', social democracy, revolutionary socialism, and anti-Fascism. Indeed, Cripps presaged the S.L.'s stance by demanding a 'peaceful revolution',[i] a 1990s' 'New Labour' paradox which the S.L.'s history exemplified. Its mixed inheritance (from the political attitudes of previous Socialist groups) helps explain the complexities of S.L. policies and its awkward position within the Labour Party, as well as suspicions in the I.L.P. and the Communist Party towards the S.L. The latter's tight-rope walking is intelligible when one considers how it was vehemently attacked in the official Party *and* in most of the Press from its arrival to departure, and was ridiculed for its 'democratic status' by the S.D.F. the disaffiliated I.L.P., and the C.P.

Throughout the 1930s, there was a search for non-Party actions to offset established political parties and tentative policies. The S.L. contained within itself elements of other groups which evolved in response to the political and economic problems in these years. For example, it concurred with the British Union of Fascists' national economic plan, anxiety over the failure of the economy to improve, and disenchantment with the National Government; both wanted abolition of the House of Lords, 'rapid legislation', and the techniques of the Party rally. (Cripps infuriated Labour leaders for his 'Mosley-like' behaviour.) Both failed because of their active or proposed methods, and through resignations, splits over policy, and differences between the London Group and the provinces. (Ironically, one of the break-away groups from the B.U.F. called itself the National Socialist League![ii]) The *'Political and Economic Planning'* research organisation, the *'Next Five Years Group'*, and the *Social Credit Movement* were all campaigning for controlled economic development and the need to 'master international anarchy',[iii] and the S.L. mirrored their views to accentuate the economic basis of society (in its policies and pamphlets). It followed the *Peace Pledge Union* in its technique of enrolling members by means of a card pledge, and a renunciation of war; it joined in the pressure group activity of Hunger Marches, and in research work reflected the sociological activities of Madge and Harrison's *'Mass Observation'*. The Socialist League was also a forerunner to the *Left Book Club*. Its pamphlets exemplified a 'Left Pamphlet Club'; while both groups had discussion groups, rallies, weekend and summer schools, which soon overlapped, because all sections of the Left were represented in both organisations. [iv] They both sought to enlighten, educate, supply relevant information and theoretical analysis of problems, and dealt with the related problems of Fascism, the threat of war and poverty.[v] Eventually they merged officially in one form, *Tribune* overlapping with the Left Book Club Weekly, Gollancz on the editorial board of *Tribune* and *Tribune* membership (of both paper and Left Book Club). Both expressed the aspirations, the indignations, the

---

[i] Sir Stafford Cripps, 'The Future of the Labour Party', *New Statesman and Nation*, September 3rd, 1932.
[ii] Cf. Colin Cross, *The Fascists in Britain*, 1961.
[iii] N.F.Y.G., *Next Five Years*, p.2.
[iv] John Lewis, *The Left Book Club*, 1970, p.13.
[v] Ibid., p.14.

questioning and convictions; they represented 'the voice of the times'.[i]

Epitomising a period of intense political engagement, the S.L. played a leading part in crystallising into short-term campaigns that feeling of unrest in the Labour Party, which was evolving from a federation of political and industrial groups into an alliance of the union movement with a unitary political organisation. Ironically, the S.L.'s most obvious 'effect' would be to reveal the failures of the Labour Movement, politically, industrially, locally and nationally, by the S.L.'s policies and actions, and the S.L.'s history proved there was little future in the Labour Party for an organisation of practising militant socialists. The Labour Party's powers were increasingly concentrated within a permanent leadership, automatically re-elected, with policies mechanically endorsed; any crisis could be weathered by the use of the block vote, and the Executive became more powerful. Official leaders found more reasons for preventing or undermining Left-wing criticisms as chances of electoral success for an alternative Government appeared. Over this difference in approach, the clash between the Labour Party Executive and the S.L. was played out and, with the demise of the S.L. in 1937 (over its United Front agitations), the Labour Party isolated any positive opposition.

The fluid political situation made it inevitable that the Left would be noticed, even if it was not strengthened. Why was the S.L. able to capture attention more effectively than other pressure groups before the Left Book Club? It was not better organised, but it was good 'news value'. Some of its utterances were 'sensational' (in Press terminology), especially Cripps' speeches on 'the Monarchy', 'dictatorship', 'Emergency Powers', 'abolition of the House of Lords', and the Unity Campaign, all of which presented news reporters with headlines for days, if not weeks. The media have always been fascinated by the fallibilities and self-dramatisation of politicians to the point of finding integrity and sincerity rather pedestrian! The S.L. had personalities in its ranks who attracted such attention. Containing 'Marxists' within its membership lessened its impact in the union movement, and allowed the Press to gain political capital from its presentation of the S.L. as 'the thorn in the side' of the Labour and union movement. Thus, Labour's *Daily Herald* criticised the S.L. for its irresponsibility, tactlessness and vacillation, lauding the importance of *loyalty*.

It will be a theme of this book that the Socialist League was a scapegoat for the inadequacies of the wider Movement, but that, like all hounded scapegoats, it drew attention to itself to demonstrate how different it was, and was subsequently chastised for its individuality by the misinformed majority; it was at a disadvantage when calls were made for 'Party loyalty', 'support for agreed Party policy', and 'reasonable party discipline', however 'reasonable' was interpreted. The S.L.'s heyday lasted less than two years, after which its freedom of expression was curtailed, and it never won a single Party Conference resolution or altered one part of the policy of the Party (though some diluted versions of S.L. policies were incorporated into Party programmes).

Following the 1931 'defection' of MacDonald, Snowdon and Thomas, much of the Christianity, brotherhood and utopianism of the Party hardened into a more militant Socialism[ii] and the S.L. took this opportunity to submit their strongly-worded resolutions to Party Conferences. Their early successes in 1932 and 1933 were by-

---

[i] Ibid., p.132.
[ii] Kingsley Martin, *Harold Laski*, 1953, p.82.

passed, muted, or (in the case of the 'joint-stock banks amendment for nationalisation') ignored. However, most members of the S.L. would have accepted J. T. Murphy's formulation that *'the Socialist League is working for the transformation of the Labour Party into the Party of the working-class revolution'*.[i] It produced intelligently-written pamphlets (orientated towards economic problems), stimulating lectures, often to packed halls, augmented by a perceptive monthly paper (and in 1937 *Tribune*); the main influence was in London (where its material was published) and in ex-I.L.P. strongholds, Gateshead, Bristol and South Wales. This was extended beyond ex-I.L.P. areas during the Unity Campaign when the S.L. was absorbed into a wider grouping. In summary the S.L.'s most effective activity occurred in its first two years, *and* in its last five months, when public responses were more emotional and engagé.

From the formation of the group in October 1932, S.L. policies reflected or hinted at discontent or frustration with *Parliamentary* methods, and the way in which the S.L. expressed itself on this matter was one of the chief issues between it and the Executive of the Party, as well as a recurrent theme in the Press. The Labour Movement lived under the cloud of the 1931 débâcle, and this was reiterated as a threat to those offering 'divisive alternative policies' in the Party. The 'lesson of 1931' hung over the S.L.'s activities and governed much of its relations to other sections of the Movement, and was the main reason why the S.L. judged the influence of 'power politics' and 'capitalist interests' as endangering a social and democratic Labour Party.[ii]

Another aspect of this book will show that the 'leftward swing' in the Labour Movement after 1931 has been over-emphasised when viewed in the context of the strengthening of Labour and union bureaucracy. The underlying gradualism and stolidity of the Movement as a whole became more entrenched, as the S.L. became less influential. Finding itself in an increasingly compromised position, the S.L.'s 'leftward swing' was partly manufactured by S.L. members and the *New Clarion* to boost morale, but it obscured rather than clarified the S.L.'s fundamentally untenable position. Labour leaders, such as Dalton, Morrison and Bevin, would have expelled the S.L. before 1937 had it threatened electoral prospects, even had the S.L. not presented an easy target by its own inconsistencies, as it moved into the realm of broader political activism.

It was when the S.L. had become a more disciplined organisation, after its special November Conference of 1934, that it was attacked most harshly. After its adoption of its *'Forward to Socialism'* policies and the defeat of most of its seventy-five amendments to Party policy *'For Socialism and Peace'*, at Southport, when the S.L. had sharpened the process of transforming its branches *from research groups into active political units*,[iii] it was treated with increasing suspicion by the official Executive. There was resentment, by those Labour leaders preoccupied with the heavy responsibilities of official policy, of the S.L.'s well-dramatised activities and apparent cavalier attitude towards Party traditions. Nothing so emphasised this divergence as the S.L.'s *style* of agitation in contrast with the Party's ploddingly scrupulous investigations between 1935 and 1937, yet, despite its attempts to override Party caution and respectability, the S.L. never rejected conventional Party methods. It claimed the rights over much of the

---

[i] J. T. Murphy, 'Why I Joined the Socialist League', *New Clarion*, April 15th, 1933.
[ii] Whereas the National Government was likely to see 'a Red under the bed', the Socialist League was likely to envisage 'a Fascist under the mattress'.
[iii] J. T. Murphy, 'The Year in Review', *Socialist Leaguer*, May 1935.

propagandist activity and political education in the Labour Party, but could not hope to alter the moderate national policies of the Party Executive.

After Hitler's rise to power, international affairs galvanised the S.L., and dominated its thinking. Tinged with Marxist phraseology, its diagnosis of foreign issues could be prescient. It understood the Fascist dangers (in Germany, Italy, and Austria), was prophetic in its views on Spanish democracy, and in its campaign for a vigorous opposition to the National Government. It analysed British problems in international rather than insular terms, an outlook which led to definitions of the League of Nations as 'Imperialist', some ideological jargon to describe British conditions, and an unusual transference of European analogies to decipher British politics, but in its Messianic rôle as the 'conscience of the Labour Party', it sought to expose 'bourgeois democracy' and 'Fascist authoritarianism' and defined itself as a child of its times. Subjugation was the theme linking European governments, so the S.L. dubbed the National Government as 'repressive', (with its household Means Test, its Incitement to Disaffection Bill, even its laissez-faire foreign policy), the National Government depicted as 'National Fascist', the counterpart of European dictatorships. Here, the S.L. exhibited its a priori assumptions concerning capitalist society and the economics of an Imperialist power. Yet, in its reaction to each foreign issue, the S.L. was internally divided over policy, and many of its intellectuals had reservations about categorical political commitments: 'Every Party intellectual has a breaking point beyond which he will not go. If he has no such point, he has ceased to be an intellectual. He ceases to be a creator of ideas and becomes a retailer of the ideas of others and a manufacturer of slogans'.[1]

The S.L. was divided over its position on the Abyssinian crisis (1935); support for defence of a small nation clashed with a suspicion of the Government's use of armaments there. This distrust of the use of deterrents was extended to the issue of war against Fascism but, by then, the S.L. had disintegrated because of issues in the United Campaign of 1937, over questions with the I.L.P., the C.P., (and some Liberals) on the strategy of Peace campaigns. By the time of the S.L.'s dissolution at its Whitsun Conference of 1937, news of the Moscow trials and dissension in the Left in Spain were adversely affecting the United Front campaign, and would, in all probability, have increased divisions within the S.L. During such internal arguments over policy, the S.L. lost the services of some of its best brains, G. D. H. Cole (1933), J. T. Murphy and Sir Charles Trevelyan (1935) and William Mellor (1937).

The quality of the S.L.'s political and economic thinking suffered whenever a crisis arose in the wider Labour Movement, because it had imposed on itself the rule that membership of the Party was the *prime* consideration. Therefore, the S.L.'s relevance and political perception as a group, deteriorated. It could not make an objective appraisal and act upon its conclusions when it was attempting to appease the Labour Party, the I.L.P. *and* the Communist Party, especially in the last six months of its existence. This situation derived from its inheritance of the social democratic tradition of Fabianism and its embodiment in the Party Constitution, with the example of the Russian Revolution and Marxist ideology. This contradictory rôle into which the S.L. was placed has been described as: '*not to be a rival, but the means of recapturing the spirit of*

---

[1] Neal Wood, *Communism and British Intellectuals*, 1959, pp.219–220. Yet realisation of the historical contingency of the existing order was a potent aspect of Marxism in the 1930s, 'endorsing the convert with a wider social awareness and sense of mission, a new enthusiasm, a purpose in life', D. J. Davies, *Daily Worker*, 16/2/32, qu. S. Macintyre, *A Proletarian Science; Marxism in Britain 1917–1933*, 1980, p.109.

the pioneers of militant, idealistic, yet Fabian socialism.[i] The lauded flexibility of the S.L. became a handicap and bowing to the Party Executive on matters of 'Party discipline and loyalty', while accepting C.P. criticisms of 'capitalist democracy', the S.L.'s appeals for 'unity' were exploited by both parties. The strength of the S.L.'s challenge was undermined from within as much from these outside sources of friction.

This book hopes to explain the untenable position of the militant Socialist in the Labour Party. The integrity of the individual rebel was not respected, and was dismissed by those Labour leaders who were antagonistic towards 'abstract ideology' and hostile to 'non-empirical judgements'. Nevertheless, I believe the S.L. enriched the Labour Party by questioning the possibility of achieving *any* kind of Socialist society in Britain through gradual means and it brought to the surface doubts as to the possibility of working towards Socialism through a Parliamentary Party. On the local level, its formation helped to keep many I.L.P. members in the Party, where they could contribute to discussions on new Labour programmes. S.L. local branches did a great deal of community work on local councils on behalf of the unemployed, keeping up morale, presenting a positive outlook to the disillusioned. Contacts were made with local Communist Parties, I.L.P.s and *Unemployed Workers' Associations* to pressurise councils to provide amenities. Research work into local problems was one of the main activities suggested by the S.L.'s national organisation, and this gave a new dimension to local politics, as well as giving a basis of 'facts for Socialist pronouncements' for the needs of a locality.

Gradually, the S.L. developed an independent outlook in conflict with the official programme of the Party, and acquired the characteristics of a political pressure group. It organised *Anti-War Conferences*, recruiting some of the most able speakers in the Labour Movement, and attempted to ignore I.L.P./C.P. squabbles, which rendered ineffective Left-wing action groups, except the *National Unemployed Workers' Movement*. However, the S.L. helped to educate and enliven local Labour organisations and in the protest 'demonstrations for Peace', and in Unemployed Marches, helped to modify British prejudices towards radical minorities. It also drew attention to the diversity of opinion within the Labour Party. Although Party constitutional devices were used to soften radical ideas, and resulted in some union leaders' relative indifference to the 'crisis in capitalism' (from the point of view of a Socialist solution), the S.L. mirrored the dissatisfaction of many Socialists. Its main disagreement with the Party was over the *pace* of reform, and the *priorities* of a Socialist Party remained vital for the Party in power from 1945 to 1950.

In 1932, the Party Executive donated the S.L. a short spill with which to light the dead wood of the research section of the Party. Instead, the S.L. began behaving, in official eyes, like a pyromaniac. If the S.L. was to play more than a passive rôle it needed a considerable degree of independence within the Party; its activities were extended in the *Left Book Club*, the *Constituency Party Associations*, and the *Popular Front Movement* and the *Left Book Club* incorporated Socialist viewpoints in its campaigns against Fascism, for an egalitarian social and economic system, the dissemination of progressive ideas, and extended the S.L.'s attempts to form a Left identity. The *Constituency Party Association* (1936–37) presented radical views in local Labour Parties, and succeeded in altering the Party Constitution to include more local representation on the National Executive, and allow the choice of Party candidates by constituencies,

---

[i] Eric Estorick, *Stafford Cripps*, 1949, p.120.

while the *Popular Front* of 1938 and 1939 attempted to continue the unification of progressives into an awareness of political consequences of a laissez-faire attitude towards Fascism and War, and underlined the S.L.'s interest in stimulating the militant who might have no Parliamentary ambitions. Not far away is Gramsci's concept of 'hegemony' wherein class control in a capitalist society is ideological and cultural, and in which only the working class, 'educated' by radical intellectuals (such as the S.L.'s leadership) could 'see through' bourgeois propaganda. That was also a legacy left by the S.L., as was the questioning of liberalism, constitutionalism, the rule of law, democracy, free markets (even the separation of church and state) which, in the 21st century, have little resonance in Islamic, Confucian, Japanese, Hindu or Buddhist cultures.[i]

---

[i] Samuel Huntington, qu. F. Wheen, *'How Mumbo-Jumbo Conquered the World': A Short History of Modern Delusions*, 2004, p.305.

Chapter One

Socialist League Origins from Previous Socialist Parties, and Research Organisations

It is capitalism which is out of control and socialism which seeks to restrain it. It is capitalism, as Marx recognised, which is revolutionary to its roots, one extravagant thrust of Faustian desire, and socialism which recalls us to our humble roots as labouring, socialising, materially limited creatures. The postmodern fashion for perpetual reinvention is thus the least radical of attitudes, however it may see itself.

Terry Eagleton, *The Gatekeeper: A Memoir*, 2001, p.84

Despite our potential for the production of meaning, what it is possible for us to think and do at a particular time is actually quite limited. This is because the rules that shape what we think and do are in large part the product of power relations in society... repressive and permissive procedures determine how knowledge is applied, distributed, valued and rejected. History tells of a constant struggle between different powers, which try to impose their own 'will to truth'.

Michel Foucault, 'The Order of Discourse'
in ed. R. Young *Untying the Text: A Post-Structuralist Reader*,
1981, pp.55–68

As far as much of New Labour is concerned the past may be another country, but for all the dexterity of the party's spin-doctors it will not be expunged.

David Powell, *What's Left? Labour Britain and the Socialist Tradition*, 1998, p.16

A strength and weakness of British Socialism is that it fed on contradictory sources, the fons et origo of Chartist Radicalism, Owenite optimism, Christian Socialism, William Morris romanticism, Fabianism and Marxist materialism.[i] The S.L. contained elements of all these traditions, although it was the Webbs' political thought and philosophy of gradualism (from the 1918 Labour Party Constitution) which dominated the Party in the 1930s. Bertrand Russell noted that the Webbs did great work in giving intellectual backbone to British Socialism, and the Labour Party would have been more wild and woolly if they had never existed.[ii] Since its birth, and heterogeneous origins, the Labour Party had preserved an anti-theoretical, anti-doctrinal basis, despite R. H.

---

[i] K. Martin, *Harold Laski*, 1953, London, p.82.
[ii] Bertrand Russell, quoted by Hugh Dalton, *Call Back Yesterday: Memoirs (1887–1931)*, 1953, p.198.

Tawney's espousal in *'Labour and the Nation'* (1928) that the Labour Party's Socialism is 'neither a sentimental aspiration for an impossible Utopia nor a blind movement of revolt against poverty and oppression... It is a conscious, systematic and unflagging effort to use the weapons forged in the victorious struggle for political democracy to end the capitalist dictatorship'.[i] In Britain, 'Socialism' derived less from systematised thought than from empirical action, and it was comparatively easy to see what 'Socialism' meant to its advocates in the context of the 1930s; it meant protest against poverty, physical hardship and demoralisation, which the system of 'capitalism' produced; passionate concern for those in desperate need; belief in the 'classless society'; for the worker a responsible and dignified status at work; protest against inefficiencies and inequalities of capitalism as an economic system; an ethical view of society, and a belief in certain moral values. However nebulous these aspects, they linked Socialists.

Within the Labour Party, the Socialist League carried forward, in its own way, the traditions of the Social Democratic Federation, the Fabian Society and the I.L.P. The S.L. mouthed some of the S.D.F. philosophy, with its emphasis on class warfare and suspicion of 'Parliamentarianism', but it did not incorporate S.D.F. insistence upon industrial action as the quickest road to social change. Yet, the S.L.'s militant tone seemed to some Labour leaders 'echoes of the S.D.F.'

Another seminal influence on the S.L. was *Lansbury's Labour Weekly*, which campaigned for a number of Left-wing demands subsequently paraded on S.L. platforms, such as abolition of the House of Lords, State control of foreign trade; drastic improvement in wages, hours of work, housing and education; Dominion status to all parts of the Empire; disarmament by agreement; and settlement of international differences by arbitration.[ii] The S.L. did not inherit the paper's desire for Britain to remain in the League of Nations (to defend the rights of oppressed nationalities), because by 1933 there was a far more sceptical attitude towards the League of Nations, reflected in the S.L.'s critique of it as 'an imperialist organisation'. Apart from this, the S.L.'s programme was similar to that of *Lansbury's Labour Weekly*, demanding the next Labour Government should, by the use of an Emergency Powers Act, take all necessary means to remove obstacles standing in the way of the immediate application of fundamental Socialist measures (such as socialisation of the banks, industry and land).[iii] The programmes of Left-wing groups in the inter-war years often overlapped and the two newspapers which most influenced the S.L.'s own policies and 'style', were amalgamated in 1927 under James Maxton's editorship, the reason given that *Lansbury's Labour Weekly* was close in policy to the I.L.P.'s *New Leader*.[iv]

No Socialist group which has lasted in Britain had been unaffected by Fabian teachings, even if only to emphasise the dissimilarities. Many Socialist League members were members of the *New Fabian Research Bureau* or the *Fabian Society*, before the Bureau was formed in 1931. Aiming to transform society by the conversion of middle-class administrators and to awaken the political consciousness of the working class, the Fabians' practicality stemmed from reducing questions of principle to questions of *fact*: 'Fabianism means reform without resentment, social reconstruction

---

[i] *Labour and the Nation*, 1928, pp.5–6.

[ii] Cf. J. T. Murphy, *Preparing for Power*, 1934, p.249.

[iii] Ibid., pp.272–273.

[iv] Raymond Postgate, *Life of George Lansbury*, 1951, p.243.

without class war, political empiricism without dogma or fanaticism'.[i] In its determination to remain within the Labour Party the S.L. followed some Fabian precepts, but, in 'ideology' (principles, programmes, policies, methods, tactics) the S.L.'s fragmented history was one long critique of the Fabians. Margaret Cole enumerated the contributions which Fabianism made to the Labour Movement; breaking the 'spell of Marx', it still sought the use of the State as an instrument of the working class, taught intellectuals to be Socialists 'without the jargon', prevented the break-up over doctrinal disputes, and established tolerant discussion within Socialist circles.[ii] Its adverse effects were to deprive the Movement of a discernible philosophy and discourage discussion of fundamentals. The S.L. reacted against this Fabian style of political combat in its attempts to redirect Labour policies, to pressurise the Party into a 'more Socialist' approach, and carve out a niche as the indispensable conscience of the Movement. A later assessment of the Fabians' influence confirmed that of the Socialist League: 'The Fabians refused to expound any general conception of things, failed to propose anything more stirring than the Webbs' minimum national standard of living, paralysed ideological debate within the Labour Movement, and channelled its energies into the backwaters of dreary practicality. They saw the State, not as an apparatus of power to be reconstructed, but as a neutralist instrument'.[iii]

The Socialist League originated from other sources – *I.L.P. affiliationists*, the *Society for Socialist Inquiry and Propaganda* (S.S.I.P.) and the *New Fabian Research Bureau* (N.F.R.B.). There were other factors in the formation of Socialist organisations: reactions to the record of the Labour Party and its political failures by I.L.P. MPs in the Second Labour Government (1921–1931); the need to find centres of socialist activity and socialist discussion, which the formal organisation of the Labour Party prevented (c.f. S.S.I.P. and N.F.R.B.); and reactions of Socialists to political events elsewhere in the world[iv] (the World economic depression and the crisis in capitalism).

S.S.I.P. began in 1930, when the economic depression was gathering momentum and the Labour Government seemed to have little idea of coping with it. A group of Socialists, on the initiative of G. D. H. Cole, Margaret Cole, C. M. Lloyd (of the *New Statesman and Nation*), H. L. Beales, G. R. Mitchison and W. R. Blair (of the C.W.S.) met at Easton Lodge in Essex to organise S.S.I.P. meetings. The nickname of 'Loyal Grousers' indicated its relation with the Labour Party.[v] This organisation was to counter-balance lack of purpose and ignorance of facts[vi] which (it was felt) made the Labour Government ineffectual. S.S.I.P. recruited its membership from many sources, including a group of ex-University Socialists.[vii] Nine of its twenty most prominent members joined the Socialist League as pamphleteer, adviser or active S.L. member on its National Council. S.S.I.P. gathered some of the most enlightened and aware minds in the Labour Movement (apart from Margaret Cole, C. M. Lloyd, H. L. Beales, G. R. Mitchison, and W. R. Blair, there was Hugh Gaitskell, George Lansbury, Raymond Postgate, Clement Attlee, William Mellor, Sir Stafford Cripps, Ellen Wilkinson, Frank

[i] William Ebenstein, *Today's Isms: Communism, Fascism, Capitalism & Socialism*, 1970, pp.233–34.

[ii] Margaret Cole, *The Story of Fabian Socialism*, 1961, Stanford, pp.327–28.

[iii] Giorgio Fanti, 'The Resurgence of the Labour Party', *New Left Review*, No. 30, March–April 1965.

[iv] R. Williams, ed., *May-Day Manifesto*, 1968, p.168.

[v] G. D. H. Cole, *The History of Socialist Thought: Socialism and Fascism (1931–39)*, pp.67–68.

[vi] Margaret Cole, op. cit., pp.223–225.

[vii] Ibid.

Horrabin, H. N. Brailsford, R. H. Tawney, Arthur Pugh, D. N. Pritt,[i] and W. H. Thompson, with G. D. H. Cole as Vice Chairman and Ernest Bevin as Chairman). All sections of Labour were represented, and there grew within the organisation a conviction of being united for Socialist objectives: 'We discussed all sorts of Socialist problems,' said D. N. Pritt,[ii] and he added (ironically, given the circumstances of the 1929–1931 Labour Government) 'plus periodical shadow cabinet meetings in George Lansbury's room'. As Bevin noted, S.S.I.P. evolved because *'we had despaired of getting much done in this Parliament'*, and nothing seemed to be developing in the Labour Party's thinking for a future Government. He denied that S.S.I.P. was a ginger group to the Party; he saw its purpose as studying and projecting ideas and policy, and an attempt to work out problems and give the new generation something to grip. It would function as a new kind of Fabian Society, with, an avoidance of 'dogma', and an attempt to replace the stalemate in thought in the Labour Movement.[iii]

The S.S.I.P.'s inaugural meeting was held at Transport House on June 15th, 1931, to carry on the work of research within the Labour Party and examine aspects of socialisation.[iv] S.S.I.P. pamphlets included *Facts and Figures for Labour Speakers*, *National Planning* by Colin Clark; and six *Study Guides* (for Labour and Socialist Study Circles) by G. D. H. Cole. (Others submitted reports on economic planning, public control of nationalised industries, banking policy, reform of the Cabinet, and reorganisation of Government Departments). Despite Bevin's interpretation of its objectives, S.S.I.P. set about establishing Socialist 'ginger groups' within local Labour Parties, organising a corps for a more constructive Socialist programme of the Left.[v] It lasted for one and a half years, had 14 branches, several Study Groups, gave Sunday-night lectures in Transport House (to which Lansbury, E. F. Wise, A. L. Rowse and J. M. Keynes contributed), held conferences, and published 12 pamphlets and a cyclostyled bulletin. The Socialist League inherited this programme of activities from S.S.I.P., which had provided a fillip to Socialists who had been near to leaving the Labour Movement in despair at its sterility.[vi]

Concerned with propagandist activity throughout the country, S.S.I.P. became a body putting forward its own Socialist programme'[vii], to secure the adoption of *a well-constructed Socialist policy*.[viii] S.S.I.P. made use of the researches and publications of the *New Fabian Research Bureau*, formed after the 1931 crisis. (Post-mortem discussions took the view that the causes of defeat lay in the absence of any defined policy and programme for the 1929–1931 Labour Government, and that, if Labour returned to office, it must not be without such a programme. One of these discussions led to the formation of the N.F.R.B.[ix] This organisation was formed largely out of the same elements as the S.S.I.P., but devoted itself to 'purposeful' research of the kind pursued

[i] D. N. Pritt, *From Right to Left*, Autobiography Vol. 1, 1965, pp.34–35; Pritt adds Hugh Dalton and Colin Clark to the list.
[ii] Ibid.
[iii] Ernest Bevin in a letter to J. R. Bellerby, May 23rd, 1931, quoted Alan Bullock, *The Life and times of Ernest Bevin, Vol. 1, (1881–1940)*, 1960, p.501. (My italics.)
[iv] *New Clarion*, July 1931.
[v] Francis Williams, *Ernest Bevin*, 1952, p.176.
[vi] M. Cole, op. cit., p.225.
[vii] C. Cooke, *The Life of Richard Stafford Cripps*, 1957, London, p.141.
[viii] G. D. H. Cole, *The History of the Labour Party Since 1914*, 1948, London, p.282. (My italics.)
[ix] G. D. H. Cole, *The History of Socialist Thought*, op. cit., p.66.

by the Fabian Society in its prime. *New Fabian* was chosen to emphasise the continuity of tradition with a programme of research in international, political and economic sections.[i] The N.F.R.B., with C. M. Lloyd (Vice Chairman), G. D. H. Cole (Honorary Secretary) and G. R. Mitchison (Treasurer), had to justify its existence; it saw the Movement as requiring constant expansion and adaptation of policy (in the context of a changing environment) to be achieved by accurate research and collation of 'all the facts'.

In practice, the two functions (of N.F.R.B. and S.S.I.P.) became blurred.[ii] Originally, the S.S.I.P. was to be the 'talking body' with a wide membership and branch organisations, doing propaganda work and dealing with quotidian propositions on Socialist lines, while the N.F.R.B. was to limit itself to 'hard thought and study',[iii] a research-oriented organisation developing a constructive Socialist programme. S.S.I.P. devoted its time to the diffusion of the results of the work of the N.F.R.B., and the former's small, active local branches undertook valuable educational work in the wider Labour Movement, helped Labour groups formulate policy on local councils, and attempted to organise in support of 'Socialist principles' and a 'Socialist assessment' of events. Yet, the S.S.I.P.'s involvement in research and propaganda (to give a basis from which the Labour Party could generate reforms as a Government or as a Parliamentary Opposition) was achieved without formulating the alternative programme and strategy which might bring it into disfavour with the official leadership'.[iv] S.S.I.P.'s function, planned and begun before the Labour Government's débâcle, would have had to alter its perspective, with the National Government in power. Its oppositional and critical rôle was unnecessary once the Labour Party set up its own policy-making organisation in 1932. Neither S.S.I.P. nor N.F.R.B. were created to take *any* part in Parliamentary politics, or seek formal affiliation to the Labour Party.

As the initiator of both organisations, G. D. H. Cole regarded both as designed to work as independent auxiliaries, with freedom to discuss and advance policies without committing the Labour Party. This enabled the two research groups to plan with less regard to expediency or the existing state of union or Labour Party sentiment.[v] This flexible relationship could not last if S.S.I.P. and N.F.R.B. pressed their ideas on the Movement; they remained without official Labour Party contacts and without power to move resolutions at Party Conferences, seeking simply 'to influence', with their flavour of Hampstead, Bloomsbury and University Labour Clubs, even while they acted as ancillaries to the Labour Party. As Labour regained its confidence, it became less inclined to accept leadership from such 'intellectuals'. In terms of the future S.L. within the Labour Party, the most important factor was that the income to initiate both research groups was provided largely by Sir Stafford Cripps, D. N. Pritt and G. R. Mitchison,[vi] all S.L. members. Behind the formation of S.S.I.P. and N.F.R.B. was an attempt to revive something of the climate of the early days of the Labour Movement when the I.L.P. had acted as a crusading body to spread a concept of socialism supported intellectually by the research and theoretical analysis of the Fabian Society.[vii]

---

[i] Ibid., p.68.

[ii] Alan Bullock, op. cit., p.50.

[iii] M. Cole, op. cit., p.231.

[iv] Michael Foot, *Aneurin Bevan*, Vol. 1, 1962, p.153.

[v] Cf. G. D. H. Cole, *The History of the Labour Party Since 1914*, 1948, p.283.

[vi] Cf. M. Cole, op. cit., pp.227, 231.

[vii] F. Williams, op. cit., pp.176–77.

The difference was that the two later groups had no intention of becoming, as the I.L.P. had done, a rival force to the Labour Party.

What changed these alignments was the disaffiliation of the I.L.P. from the Labour Party at the Bradford I.L.P. Conference (July 1932). I.L.P. members not wishing to go into the political wilderness conceived the idea of amalgamating with the S.S.I.P. and N.F.R.B. into a new Socialist organisation which would seek affiliation to the Labour Party. They were not discouraged by Labour leaders who in their unenthusiastic or sceptical fashion were understood 'not to be opposed to the idea'. The former I.L.P. MP, J. F. Horrabin (later editor of the *Socialist Leaguer* and the *Socialist* – the S.L. monthly organs) acted as go between.[i] The two most notable I.L.P. affiliationists, E. F. Wise and H. N. Brailsford, saw the S.S.I.P. as offering a springboard for a new campaign[ii] which could also benefit the S.S.I.P. by giving it a prominent place in Labour counsels. Most sympathisers for the proposed amalgamation stressed the elimination of overlapping functions and programmes which were so prevalent in Left-wing groups. In working towards the end of unnecessary and unfruitful competition, S. Cripps and D. N. Pritt felt more akin to I.L.P. affiliationists',[iii] and E. F. Wise was proposed by the I.L.P. Affiliation Committee as Chairman of the new body, and, after long debate, this was accepted by a majority. S.S.I.P. opponents to the merger were outmanoeuvred and niggling resentments remained. It had been over the personal issue of E. Bevin or E. F. Wise as Chairman that negotiations nearly broke down. G. D. H. Cole regarded it as indispensable to bring Bevin into the new body as the outstanding union figure capable of rallying union opinion behind it';[iv] Bevin suggested the new group include the remnant of the old S.D.F. As it was, he distrusted the ex-I.L.P. faction and took no part in the negotiations. The new body might have strengthened the Movement at one of its most vulnerable points – the gap which separated intellectuals from trade unionists, but the determination to oust Bevin (and the choice of Wise as Chairman) deepened, in the unionist's mind, the conviction (implanted by the behaviour of Oswald Mosley and Ramsay MacDonald) that 'intellectuals of the Left... stabbed you in the back'.[v]

Holding to its purpose as an objective research agency and refusing to become involved in politics outside this sphere, the N.F.R.B. maintained its separate existence. S.S.I.P., a propagandist body with branches, had been placed in a dilemma. After the negotiations, I.L.P. affiliationists and the S.S.I.P. organisation became allied on the terms that the combined body would become an active political organisation affiliated to the Labour Party presenting its views in the Party and, as opportunity permitted, in Parliament. It was for just these reasons that opponents of this unification had fought. As far as they could assess, any group would inevitably be deflected from inquiry and propaganda into active political and parliamentary considerations.

Held on the Sunday before Labour's Annual Conference at Leicester (Oct. 1932), the inaugural meeting of the new amalgamated organisation decided upon its basic policy: to carry out research work, propaganda and Socialist education.[vi] The decision of the I.L.P. affiliationists had afforded an opportunity for extending S.S.I.P.'s activities. The new Socialist League's objectives would be to make Socialists and to further by propaganda

[i] Cf. M. Cole, op. cit., pp.228–230.
[ii] F. Williams, op. cit., pp.176–77.
[iii] Cf. M. Cole, op. cit., pp.228–230.
[iv] G. D. H. Cole, op. cit., 1948, p.284.
[v] Alan Bullock, op. cit., pp.515–516.
[vi] *New Clarion*, October 8th, 1932 (S.L.'s Provisional Draft Constitution).

and investigation the adoption by the Movement of an advanced programme and a Socialist outlook. A feeling of elation exuded from this meeting; E. F. Wise denied that they were forming a new party; they were anxious to serve the Labour Party as a vigorous ally. Fred Henderson said the Socialist League was to provide continuous research work on fundamentals; Susan Lawrence spoke of the rank and file hungering for socialist propaganda; Pat Dollan saw the S.L. as a new Socialist fellowship, and others hoped for a disinterested group of propagandists supplying the Labour Party with new ideas, working in harmony with the Party (but hoping it would not drift into the position of the old I.L.P). G. D. H. Cole commented that they were 'Socialists in a hurry', and the *New Statesman and Nation* described the S.L. as 'the most interesting thing that happened at Leicester. Its origin was unlike any previous Socialist organisation; it had the approval of the official Labour Party and might encourage realistic thinking and the growth of an intelligent socialism.[i] But it mentioned the recriminations within the S.S.I.P.; that some members feared amalgamation would mean subordination of the research work of S.S.I.P. to political activities. However, safeguards against this had been introduced into the Socialist League's Constitution.[ii]

This supposition did not delve into deeper reasons for disenchantment. S.S.I.P. members had, in many cases, been informed of the action of their Executive only two or three days before; had a brief, stormy meeting among themselves an hour before the inaugural meeting of the Socialist League, where they were presented with a 'fait accompli', and had expressed considerable differences of opinion between S.S.I.P. members and I.L.P. delegates. They saw nothing in the Socialist League Constitution about local branches being pledged to open research offices, and the 4d per month member subscription (for the branch affiliation fee to the S.L. National Council) that suggested the main function was 'co-ordination of research'. Was it going to play the rôle of the old I.L.P.?; whereas the S.S.I.P. had been an admirable method for the dissemination of ideas, the S.L. would be 'an inadequate substitute'? It would be a larger, more highly organised body, acting much more as a unit within the party, putting its views on party policy formally. Even if its policy was sound, its influence on the Party would be minimised, while, locally, if its branches were strong, they would create friction. Research, with a view to propaganda for future action was the most urgent work before the Party. S.S.I.P. and its energetic branches had been beginning to perform this function.[iii] What would happen in the Socialist League?

S.S.I.P. was swallowed up. Margaret Cole (Hon. Sec. of S.S.I.P.) took a positive attitude. Clauses in the Constitution enabled the S.L. in certain cases to promote Parliamentary candidates for adoption by local Labour Parties to meet the difficulties of certain branches (where 'loyal' I.L.P.'ers had played a part recognised as valuable in local electoral machinery and where a break in this tradition at this moment would be unfortunate).[iv] She pointed out that the S.L. constitution stated that political activity was *not* to be the primary object of the S.L. The S.S.I.P. Executive was to lend the S.L. house-room and secretarial support. No S.S.I.P. activities had been curtailed. She asked that the S.L. be looked upon as helping to create an *informed and vigorous body of Socialist opinion*, because the new body would bring in the wider public, who belonged to neither S.S.I.P.

---

[i] *New Statesman and Nation*, October 8th, 1932.

[ii] Ibid.

[iii] Cf. Letters to *New Statesman and Nation*, October 15th, 22nd and 29th, 1932.

[iv] Cf. E. A. Radice (General Secretary of the S.L.), 'The S.L. does not propose to form an electoral machine of its own' (letter to *N.S. & N.*, October 15th, 1932).

nor the I.L.P.[i] E. F. Wise corroborated Cole's comments, stating the S.L. Constitution expressly debarred the S.L. from responsibility for running electoral machinery or financing candidates. The rate of subscriptions was fixed so the expenditure of the S.L. might be covered by regular membership fees, rather than by special campaigns for funds which distracted efforts from the tasks of Socialist research and educational propaganda. Funds could not be used for electoral purposes.[ii] The other complaint which emerged with the S.L's formation, and which existed within the Labour Movement, was of 'intellectual snobbery'. This arose because of the lack of 'mixing' at the inaugural meeting. Members who had the privilege of a University education had the duty, not only to devote their attainments to the service of comrades, but to cultivate relations of fraternal equality.[iii] J. F. Horrabin[iv] retorted that not all S.L. members were labouring under the disadvantage of a University education, and that by no means all Parliamentary candidates at the inaugural meeting came to join the S.L. (a number of orthodox Right-wing Labourites attended to keep a disciplinary eye on the new organisation and insisted on putting on the S.L. Executive Committee three men as guarantors of a safe and moderate policy. One of the three was Sir Stafford Cripps!)[v] Horrabin asserted that if the S.L. did not include 10 workers for every one University educated members he would not be in it, yet the people with University education who had joined up were most emphatically of the kind that believed in devoting their attainments to the service of their comrades.

According to Constance Borrett (member of the S.L. National Council), the name 'Socialist League' was suggested by Winifred Horrabin.[vi] No one disputed the statement. The new organisation took the name in reminiscence of William Morris' Socialist League (which had split from the S.D.F. in 1884). As if to emboss the connection, the new S.L. was seen as a potential rival to the S.D.F. of 1932, fulfilling a similar function in the Labour Party, on a more radical platform. The S.D.F. was hostile from the start, having been rebuffed in its invitation to the I.L.P. Affiliation Committee to join ranks. To augment this animosity towards the new S.L., the I.L.P. disaffiliationists expressed scepticism that the only groups which would participate were the insignificant number which had already put themselves outside the I.L.P.[vii] The S.L. denied any suggestions that it was exceeding its limited aims. Its formation had only been made possible by the determination of its members that the only political organisation which held *any hope* for working people was the Labour Party. It repeated its functions as primarily those of research, education and propaganda (among local Labour Parties, unions and Co-operative Societies).[viii] The S.S.I.P., finding its work duplicated by the S.L., and despite Margaret Cole's pleas, disbanded in November 1932, most of its personnel and activities already absorbed in the S.L.

So, while union leaders were on the defensive, and Labour Party leaders dispirited, the small group who regarded the situation as a challenge formed themselves into the S.L. with the object of radicalising the Party. In the Labour Movement, educational work

---

[i] Cf. Margaret Cole (letter on 'Socialist League'), *New Statesman and Nation*, October 22nd, 1932.

[ii] Cf. E. F. Wise letter to *New Statesman and Nation*, October 29th, 1932.

[iii] 'Dormouse' on 'Unsocial Socialists', *New Clarion*, October 15th, 1932.

[iv] J. F. Horrabin, *New Clarion*, October 29th, 1932.

[v] Patricia Strauss, *Cripps: Advocate and Rebel*, 1943, London, p.63.

[vi] C. Borrett, 'New Beginnings', *Socialist Leaguer*, No. 7, December 1934.

[vii] *New Leader*, September 28th, 1932.

[viii] S.L. Notes, 'Down to Business', *New Clarion*, October 15th, 1932.

had been a constant theme since the end of the Labour Government in 1931: 'We must consider the taking of steps by literature, by meetings and by the spread of knowledge in every possible way in order to get the principles of socialism more deeply rooted in the hearts of the people...'[i] Ernest Bevin spoke for the movement: Was there any way in which an organised political party could retain the *inspiration* necessary to win a crusade? Stafford Cripps saw the answer as of vital importance to the future of the Party: 'the time for vague and general programmes has passed, and with the necessity for more precision and definition, there is a tendency to great caution... in the approach of the Labour Party in the future it must be clear and definite in the purpose of its actions.'[ii] He wanted the Party to stand for a fundamental change of the whole economic system, not 'organised state charity'.

By the time of the formation of the S.L., there was a weekly *Plain Man's New Statesman*[iii] called the *New Clarion* (begun on June 11th, 1932), and the S.L. was given a column of its own (from October 8th, 1932 to March 10th, 1934). Socialist Leaguers (and sympathisers) contributed to the paper's main sections. Eventually, Laski had submitted 27 articles; G. D. H. Cole, H. N. Brailsford and A. L. Rowse 20 each, while E. F. Wise and S. Cripps wrote often. I.L.P. affiliationists brought into the S.L. general political analysis and some prominent Socialists and, with S.S.I.P. members, the S.L. was not only an amalgam of many tendencies but a galaxy of intellectual talent. It became that spearhead of much needed Socialist agitation within the Labour Party, if only for a short while. The S.L.'s Executive Committee encompassed every shade and nuance of the Left from barely left of centre to near Communist.[iv] In fact, its membership was so flexible as to present instability. Its heterogeneity was revealed in its first National Council, which consisted of E. F. Wise (Chairman), F. Wynne Davies and G. R. Mitchison (Joint Treasurers), H. N. Brailsford, G. D. H. Cole, S. Cripps, J. F. Horrabin, David Kirkwood, W. Mellor, F. W. Pethick-Lawrence, Arthur Pugh, Dr. Alfred Salter, Sir Charles Trevelyan, and E. A. Radice (Gen. Sec.) Others had tenuous connections (a pamphlet written, a speech made, a platform shared with the Socialist League). These included C. R. Attlee, Ellen Wilkinson, D. N. Pritt and Aneurin Bevan, although J. T. Murphy (the S.L. General Secretary 1933–1935) and unionists like Harold Clay (of T.G.W.U.) and H. L. Elvin played a more prominent rôle. The three leading academic figures of the Labour Party,[v] G. D. H. Cole, H. Laski, and R. H. Tawney, although attracting a great deal of attention to the S.L., played little part in its work after the first year.

The Socialist League became an organisation of Socialist opinion which caused the Labour Party much trouble,[vi] but in 1932 it was a loosely-formed body, a grouping of Left Socialists for propaganda in the Party with a view to giving a more Socialist character to Party policy. The formation remained a direct sequel to the protests within the Labour Party against the policy pursued by the Labour Government of 1929–1931.[vii] It was also the outcome from the I.L.P. of the 1920s and its clashes with the Labour Government's outlook and activities.

---

[i] Ernest Bevin, General Secretary's Quarterly Report, November 1931, quoted by A. Bullock, op. cit., p.503.

[ii] S. Cripps, 'The Future of the Labour Party', *New Statesman and Nation*, September 3rd, 1932.

[iii] A. Bullock, op. cit., p.505 (G. Lansbury also wrote regularly and he had an immense influence upon S. Cripps, Chairman of the S.L. 1933–36).

[iv] Ralph Miliband, *Parliamentary Socialism*, 1961, p.196.

[v] R. Miliband, op. cit., p.197.

[vi] C. Cooke, op. cit., p.141.

[vii] J. T. Murphy, *New Horizons*, 1941, p.308.

The S.L.'s Inheritance From the I.L.P. (1920s) and the Labour Movement (1929–1932)

(A) The I.L.P. (1920s)

There is no better way of putting S.L. policies and functions in perspective than relating them to the I.L.P. of the 1920s. This is not surprising; the S.L. was its offspring and many I.L.P. personnel (especially two I.L.P. policy formulators, E. F. Wise and H. N. Brailsford) created the S.L. in conjunction with the S.S.I.P. Every friction, tension and difficulty in the I.L.P. of the 1920s and the S.L. of the 1930s sprang from the same difficult position vis-à-vis the rest of the Labour Movement. The S.L. inherited the I.L.P.'s central position in the development of the Labour Left. It was the I.L.P.'s raison d'être which the S.L. attempted to continue; the 1922 I.L.P. Constitution had adumbrated 'a socialist organisation (which) has for its object the establishment of a Socialist Commonwealth... in which land and capital are communally owned and the processes of production, distribution and exchange are social functions.... dissemination of Socialist principles: to obtain control of national and local governing bodies on socialist lines... [and] ...in the transition from Capitalism to Socialism to work for legislative and industrial changes which contribute to its final aim'.[i]

The I.L.P. and later the S.L. responded to 'direct action' as a political weapon (for a 'general strike' to prevent any future war), and both saw war as an extension of the capitalist market economy. (The I.L.P. became an anti-war barometer within the Labour Movement, and the S.L. accentuated this rôle after 1934). The I.L.P.'s association with a group not formally connected to the Labour Party (the U.D.C. in 1914–18) was reflected in the S.L.'s Unity campaign with the I.L.P. and the C.P. in 1937. Respectively, the I.L.P. and S.L. fought against domination of the Movement by the Party Executive and union leaders, and were eventually restricted to a policy of exposing the inadequacy of the Labour Party's conception of Socialism (the I.L.P. in the Labour Government 1929–1931, and the S.L. in Party Conferences 1932–37). Consisting of many intellectuals, a majority recruited from London, both regarded their rôle as the catalyst within the Party; such intellectuals brought to both a spirit of disinterested social enquiry. The S.L. continued propaganda tours and helped with organisational problems in the localities, attempting to effect a closer liaison between central and local organisations. Local branches were advised to form evening classes, and were supplied with socialist study material from HQ: both organisations extended weekly study circles, weekend and summer schools (to discuss policies), and were financed by substantial individual contributions, affiliation fees, and quotas from the branches.

Possessing the 'advanced' policies in the Party, the I.L.P. and the S.L. believed they would bring to the party an enthusiasm and energy it was lacking. Beneath their

---

[i] R. E. Dowse, *Left in the Centre*, 1966, p.34.

apparent successes were unresolved contradictions stemming from the diversity of opinion within their ranks which hampered the growth and influence of the Left. One I.L.P. difficulty was the lack of political discipline within its own organisation.[i] This became a feature of the S.L.; both groups could only be buttressed when they became equipped with a distinctive policy, (the I.L.P.'s *'Socialism in our Time'* and the S.L.'s *'Forward to Socialism'*); both insisted they were no rival to the Labour Party, viewing themselves as just a vital focal point, agitating and educating the electorate along Socialist lines. Both concluded that British foreign policy was a misguided attempt to rectify problems which were consequences of the defects of capitalism; these had to be abolished as a preliminary to peace and international co-operation. Given the circumstances, nothing proved to be more unrealistic than I.L.P. and S.L. proclamations on immediate needs in foreign policies, despite, and perhaps because of, their unwavering assessment of the 'evils of British Imperialism'.

In its policy statements and pamphlets, the S.L. extended the view which the I.L.P. held as to the possibility of 'armed resistance' to a Socialist Government, believing the Press constructed a negative image of the Labour Left pronouncing 'irresponsible' and 'violent' measures to undermine Parliamentary authority. It was partly because of such presentations that both these organisations experienced a crisis in relations with the official Labour Party. The only alternative to this was iconoclasm or the panacea of a changed alliance. It is axiomatic that, in this situation, the S.L. would inherit from the I.L.P. belief in the existence of a midway position between dogmatic communism and social democratic empiricism, an expression of an equivocal position within the British political spectrum'.[ii] Both attempted to meet the C.P. and Labour Party by counter-balancing one against the other, but the C.P. and L.P. were too suspicious to pursue any unifying theme to its logical end. The S.L. (and the I.L.P. of the 1920s) *could* have become a new kind of opposition, centred around a different type of training in politics. Instead, they could only pacify Labour and Communist Parties as to their intentions, and become isolated as misfits, safety valves or pressure groups working in a vacuum. Such labels are never enviable; for the I.L.P. and the S.L. they become intolerable.

Both groups remained between the political positions of Labour and Communist Parties, approving much of the C.P.'s 'ideology' and principles, and accepting Labour's platforms and basis in the Labour Movement, criticising both C.P. dependence on 'Moscow', and Labour's lack of a philosophy applicable to all situations. This rôle was tenuous: 'The democratic revolutionary synthesis lays itself open to the charge of prevarication and confusion',[iii] although both the I.L.P. and the S.L. saw the valuable space between Labour's empiricism and C.P. dogmatism, and searched for a radical yet democratic set of policies. The C.P.'s attitude towards the position of such groups as the I.L.P. and S.L. was ideologically expressed by R. Palme Dutt: 'The unity of the working class in the fight against capitalism can only be effectively realised if the influence of Social Democracy, of Labourism and Left Labourism is actively fought... The whole propaganda of Left Social Democracy consists of the endeavour to create this illusion of the imaginary middle line, of the imaginary 'third alternative' which in practice is found to consist of the use of empty revolutionary phrases to cover the old

---

[i] R. E. Dowse, op. cit., p.43.

[ii] Ibid., op. cit., p.55.

[iii] Ibid., op. cit., p.74.

reformist practice and programme'.[i] So, both groups came under the C.P. jibe that they were 'not really Socialist', were merely adopting 'militant Socialist postures', were a Left-wing smokescreen, while the Labour Party accusation was that groups such as the I.L.P. and S.L. were scaring away the marginal voter, did not accept the limitations of Parliamentary government, and exhibited 'irresponsible', 'idealistic' political behaviour. J. R. Clynes put it thus: 'the place for critics is within the Party, where their plans for better strategy will always be given a hearing'.[ii] The S.L. wanted more than a hearing.

The I.L.P. of the 1920s and the S.L. of the 1930s needed a tighter organisation if they were to withstand such criticisms and be the militant Socialist heart of the Labour Party. They were uncompromising in their demands for prompt and principled action in Parliament, but this had led to I.L.P. disillusionment with the Labour Government's financial orthodoxy and failure to tackle unemployment. It led to the adoption of theories of Socialist tactics to dissociate themselves from 'gradualism' and obtain their own distinctiveness.[iii] In I.L.P. and S.L. policy statements,[iv] similar in intent, both based their outlook and strategy upon the apocalyptic conviction in 'capitalism's economic collapse', deficiencies of Parliamentary gradualism, and the empiricism of the Labour Party. They condemned lack of urgency detected in their Labour colleagues. Yet Ramsay MacDonald called these proposals[v] 'flashy futilities'[vi] and 'millstones... round the neck of the Movement'.[vii] Both the S.L. and the I.L.P. were critical of the weakness of the Labour Party; its lack of a philosophy of action, and attributed political shortcomings of the Parliamentary Labour Party to 'weak theory'.[viii] They justified their existence by formulating a radical programme, as ginger groups bringing to the public a realisation of the need for changes which Socialism represented and to influence the Labour Party in a rapid direction.[ix] Both failed to impress the union movement by their policy statements. In fact, they exacerbated the relationship: criticism of Labour Party policy was interpreted as an attack on the whole Movement. I.L.P. and S.L. claims to be working for Socialism in a constructive, challenging spirit within the Party served as a further irritant, and even the motives (to give the Party principles upon which to act as a Government) were regarded as suspect.

Another attempt to enhance the Socialist momentum, the 'Cook-Maxton Manifesto' (1928), influenced the 'tone' of the Socialist League. As a counter blast to the Mond-Turner union/employer negotiations and 'class collaboration', the Manifesto had proclaimed 'war against Capitalism', for a working-class Labour Party to abandon 'reformism'.[x] 'We can no longer stand by and see thirty years of devoted work destroyed in making peace with Capitalism and compromises with the philosophy of

---

[i] R. Palme Dutt, 'The Burning Question of Working-class Unity', *Labour Monthly*, Vol. 14, No. 7, July 1932.
[ii] J. R. Clynes, *Memoirs 1924–1937*, autobiography, 1937, p.284.
[iii] R.E. Dowse, 'The Left-wing Opposition During the First Two Labour Governments', *Parliamentary Affairs*, Vol. XIV, No. 1, 1960–61, p.91.
[iv] I.L.P.'s 'Socialism in Our Time', 1926, in S.L.'s *Forward to Socialism*, 1934.
[v] N.A.C. introduction to *Socialism in Our Time*.
[vi] John Paton, *Left Turn*, 1936, p.235.
[vii] *Socialist Review*, March 1926, p.9.
[viii] N.A.C. Report, 1926, p.8.
[ix] N.A.C. statement in I.L.P. Annual Conference Report, 1926, p.28.
[x] Allen Hutt, *The Postwar History of the British Working-class*, 1937, p.192.

our Capitalist opponents'.[i] The Cook-Maxton *Our Case for a Socialist Revival* (1928), for abolition of the monarchy, nationalisation without compensation, taxation of all wealth over £5000 was as much a reaction to Labour Party compromise as were S.L. pronouncements on the House of Lords, bankers, and 'constitutional monarchy'. Eventually, the I.L.P. (of the 1920s) and later the S.L., were asked to *confine* their work to propaganda and not meddle in active political changes. They both suffered in their propaganda rôle from small membership and diversity of opinion; dichotomy between educational and political functions led to rebuffs as that 'propagandist' body and attacks on a 'political action group'; and both groups failed to unify around a single policy. Even so, had they achieved such cohesion, Labour leaders would not have been prepared to allow them opportunity to develop as a leading force in the Party.

During the 1929–1931 Labour Government, the I.L.P.'s strategies helped to shape the S.L.'s future policies and reactions to the events of those years, and determined the S.L.'s position vis-à-vis the official Party. How the S.L. of 1932 assessed, diagnosed and interpreted the 'lessons to be learnt' from the events of that Labour Government (and especially the 1931 crisis) shaped its subsequent views. The I.L.P. showed its radical temper from the beginning of the Labour Government and it was unrepresented in the Government.[ii] It feared that Party pragmatism was obscuring Socialist principles in relation to unemployment and an agreement with the Liberals. In reaction to the King's speech, an I.L.P. amendment sought nationalisation of key sources of industrial power and opposed the 'not genuinely seeking work' clause in the Unemployment Insurance Bill. By March 1930 (at a P.L.P. meeting), the I.L.P.'s 'lack of discipline' was denounced, and pressure was put on I.L.P. candidates to swear allegiance to the P.L.P., but an increasingly enlarged section of the Parliamentary I.L.P. had become a separate entity in opposition to the Government, and the memory of their 'awkwardness' rankled in Labour circles, when S.L. activities branched out or were embellished.

John Paton voiced what was to become the S.L. position on gradualism and the capitalist crisis: 'We believe the timid policies of the Government do not spring from their minority position, but from the adoption of wrong views on policy. The partial collapse of capitalism has found both political and industrial Labour without a plan to cope with it. For both, the Socialist principles and policies on which the power of the movement was built have come to be regarded as of merely theoretic importance'.[iii] The I.L.P. (and later the S.L.) believed the root of the problem was 'bad' political philosophy, but an I.L.P. amendment criticising the Government's timidity and vacillation in refusing to apply Socialist remedies was defeated at the Labour Conference (1930). The question of disaffiliation was debated at the I.L.P. Conference (1931) and rejected by 173 votes to 37, but this possibility of disaffiliation had been 'in the air' throughout the Labour Government's existence. Cripps felt that if the I.L.P. decided to remain affiliated, a new Left-wing party might be formed of 'the discontents'. In the House of Commons they spent time attacking the Labour Party in speeches, but voting with them; not a satisfactory method.[iv]

---

[i] I.L.P. Conference Report, 1929, Appendix 11, p.32.

[ii] R. E. Dowse, 'Left-wing Opposition During the First Two Labour Governments', *Parliamentary Affairs*, Vol. XIV, No. 2, Spring 1961, p.232.

[iii] *New Leader*, April 3rd, 1931, cf. J. P. in *New Leader*, December 12th, 1930.

[iv] Cripps Papers (at Nuffield College), Cripps on 'Future of Political Parties,' at Bridlington, February 20th, 1931.

The I.L.P.'s position became more circumspect. At the Scarborough Labour Conference (1931), Arthur Henderson expounded the Executive's objection to the 'organised conscience' of bodies like the I.L.P., and New Standing Orders tightening Party discipline were adopted.[i] The Executive was determined to muzzle I.L.P. criticisms by demanding a pledge from endorsed candidates that they would obey Standing Orders (which forbade a member voting in Parliament against policies laid down by the Labour Party); behind this was, indeed, a difference of interpretation over the means of achieving socialism.[ii] The Labour Party refused to relax its position, and the I.L.P. contended: 'The issue is whether in this economic situation the Labour Movement is to make futile attempts to rebuild capitalism or whether it is to accept the challenge of the failure of capitalism by boldly determining to lay the foundation of the new social order'.[iii] After this rift, the Labour Party was glad to release the I.L.P. from its control. Within a few weeks, the I.L.P. was accusing defected Labour leaders of 'a form of sleepy sickness called gradualism [which] ... is perhaps the most pernicious theory a workers' movement has ever had to contend with'.[iv] The S.L.'s vehemence towards the Second Labour Government was a continuance of this I.L.P. revulsion against MacDonald's meticulous observation of constitutional conventions and excessive concentration on details of Parliamentary and court etiquette.

The I.L.P. choice was working in the Labour Party, agitating to the point of being disciplined by the Party and yet keeping contact with the wider Movement, or gaining more freedom through independent agitation, with the risk of isolation, sectarianism and possible impotence outside Party ties. Meanwhile, the C.P.'s attitude was blatant: 'the only alternatives are Social-Democracy (defence of Capitalism) and revolutionary Socialism (Communism)... there is really no change in the I.L.P. leaders... but only Social Democratic Parliamentarianism with an occasional revolutionary shout'.[v] Within the I.L.P., disunity prevalent in the Labour Party culminated in the issue of continual affiliation to the Party. Maxton, Brockway and Paton led the disaffiliationists'; Wise, Brailsford, Pat Dollan and David Kirkwood supported continued affiliation. The arguments used by both sides were unrealistic, coming from such trenchant minds as leading I.L.P. members. At a time when the deliquescence of the Labour Government and rout at the subsequent Election had ended any talk of 'hopes for Socialism' in the Movement, let alone the wider public, I.L.P. leaders were arguing in terminology that suggested a healthy Socialist consciousness in the rank and file! E. F. Wise posed the question 'can the I.L.P. hope to obtain Governmental power in open conflict with the Labour Movement?'[vi] This argument was countered; the 'Governmental power' for the Left had been a myth in the last Labour Government.

For I.L.P. disaffiliationists, the argument was that to accept the Labour Executive's conditions of entry would be sacrificing all possibility of exercising influence in the Labour Movement. An isolated but free I.L.P. would have greater opportunities to make its position clear than a restricted and frustrated section within the Labour Party: 'The I.L.P. would only consider it necessary to leave the Labour Party if its liberty of action was so restricted as to prevent it from representing working-class principles or

[i] Allen Hutt, op. cit., pp.208–209.

[ii] C. L. Mowat, *Britain Between the Wars*, 1955, Chicago, p.547.

[iii] *New Leader*, August 14th, 1931.

[iv] *New Leader*, September 4th, 1931.

[v] N. C. Soderland, *Labour Monthly*, January 1932.

[vi] *New Leader*, January 15th, 1932.

expressing Socialism, or if it became clear the policy of the Party was not serving the interests of the working class or gave no hope of attaining socialism'.[i] This statement could equally be challenged, since the Left was not able effectively to 'represent working-class principles' outside the Labour and union Movement, and the Labour Party had not 'served the interests of the working class' in the last Labour Government, so it was important to stay *inside* to change this state of affairs.

Most I.L.P. members were placed in a dilemma, and reflected their confusion by voting for 'conditional affiliation' at the I.L.P. Conferences in January 1932.[ii] The I.L.P. adopted a new Statement of Policy, announcing the impending downfall of capitalism, calling for a new militancy, noting inadequacy of parliamentary methods, demanding 'mass industrial action', and voicing faith in internationalism to prepare the workers for a critical struggle,[iii] but the I.L.P. was disaffiliated by 241 to 142 votes in July 1932.[iv] As an ex-I.L.P.'er observed of the Bradford Conference speeches; 'there runs through them a deep note of repugnance for what the Labour Party machine has become... there is not, and cannot be, any middle ground between the evolutionary and revolutionary position'.[v] The Socialist League was formed a month later to discover whether this was true or not. As if to sound a warning for I.L.P. disaffiliations, H. Pollitt for the C.P. stated: 'Bradford does not mean a break with the whole practice and policy of reformism';[vi] Palme Dutt dubbed the I.L.P. Programme of 1932 'our old friend Parliamentary Democracy plus IF',[vii] and J. R. Campbell saw in the I.L.P. 'only some new phrases hiding the old reformist policy.[viii] Clearly, the I.L.P. affiliationists forming the Socialist League could not be in a more difficult situation. Between July 1932 and November 1932, the I.L.P. closed 203 branches out of 653.[ix]

It had been the decision of the Bradford Conference to opt out of relations with the Co-operative Movement, opt out of paying the levy on unionists to the Labour Party, and to detach itself from Trades Councils, local authorities and union branches. The effect was to drive out of the I.L.P. every member of local influence[x] and it was to become one of the functions of newly-formed local S.L. branches to bring back into the Labour Party many of these people. The S.L. took over the I.L.P.'s wider strategy of politics, both ideological and active, but in attempting to fill the I.L.P.'s place as the major propagandist influence in the Labour Movement, the S.L. did not have a formidable parliamentary group of MPs (as did the I.L.P. 1929–1931). However, this allowed the Socialist League to build extra-parliamentary agitation when 'parliamentary politics' was anathema in the wider Labour Movement. The Socialist League inherited from the I.L.P. the latter's over-estimation of 'capitalist rigidity', *and* the I.L.P.'s structural position in the Party, which left little room for manoeuvre, but the issues which led to the S.L.'s major confrontation with the official policy of the Party were 'international' rather than 'domestic' struggles between the Labour Party

[i] James Maxton quoted in John McNair, *James Maxton: The Beloved Rebel*, 1955.
[ii] I.L.P. Conference Report, 1932.
[iii] Ibid.
[iv] *New Leader*, August 5th, 1932.
[v] An ex-I.L.P.'er, 'The Future of the I.L.P.', *Labour Monthly*, Vol. 14, No. 9, September 1932.
[vi] H. Pollitt, *Labour Monthly*, Vol. 14, No. 8, August 1932.
[vii] P. Dutt, 'The I.L.P. and Revolution', *Labour Monthly*, Vol. 14, No. 9, September 1932.
[viii] J. R. Campbell, 'The I.L.P. – Has it Really Changed?', *Labour Monthly*, Vol. 14, No. 9, September 1932.
[ix] N.A.C. Minutes, December 12th, 1932, R. E. Dowse, op. cit., p.185.
[x] J. Paton, op. cit., p.398.

and pre-1932 I.L.P. The S.L. membership, the majority of whom were ex-I.L.P.'ers, remained conscious of the I.L.P.'s decline after 1932, which haunted all would-be disaffiliationists.[i] As a result, S.L. strategies were sensitive to any possibility of further dispersal of the Left from the Labour Party, a Left which had fragmented into Mosley's group, I.L.P. disaffiliationists, some to the Communist Party. The void left by the departure of the I.L.P. could hopefully be filled by the Socialist League; 'unity of the Movement' was to become its justification.

(B) The Labour Movement (1929–1932)

The Socialist League had its own interpretation of the collapse of the Labour Government of 1929–1931. That exegesis revealed for the S.L. the necessity of a comprehensive plan for the transition to Socialism, because it claimed the Government had not outlined a practical Socialist economic policy, nor possessed a strategy for Socialist aims. For the Left, in particular, that failure was the turning point in Britain's history between the wars.[ii] It determined the politics of the following decade'.[iii] There was little 'Socialism' in the programme announced in the King's Speech on July 2nd, 1929. Dalton commented: 'From their first day in office some Ministers were in full retreat from their election pledges. The first King's Speech… was a mere travesty of '*Labour and the Nation*', even if we exclude as impracticable in the circumstances all large measures of socialisation'.[iv] The responsibility for the failure lay upon everyone in the Government: 'We should have kicked up more row, been less loyal to leaders and more *loyal to principles*.'[v] Always the issue with Labour Governments. The Socialist League drew the same conclusion: 'So many Labour MP's followed the "tentative, doctrineless socialism"'[vi] which Labour theoreticians formulated in 1928, and Labour leaders attempted in 1929. The Socialist League embodied the reaction against the dissociation from any logical outcome of a trend of policy which the T.U.C. and the Parliamentary Labour Party had accepted before the crisis. The tone of the S.L.'s 1932 message carried commitment and convictions in contrast with the vacillation and confusion in Parliamentary Labour ranks between 1929 and 1931.

The Labour Government's rank and file MPs came in for most criticism for their quiescence. It was the 'behaviour of the solid rows of decent, well-intentioned, unpretentious Labour back-benchers' who seemed to have 'done the most deadly damage'.[vii] Partly because of the 'loyalty' principle in the Party, and lack of experience in Government, the majority of Labour MP's 'would see nothing, do nothing, listen to nothing that had not first been given the seal of MacDonald's approval'.[viii] A minority

---

[i] Patrick Seyd, review of Haseler's *The Gaitskellites (1951–64)*, *Society for the Study of Labour History*, bulletin 21, Autumn 1970.

[ii] C. L. Mowat, *Britain Between the Wars*, 1955, p.356.

[iii] R. Skidelsky, *Politicians and the Slump*, 1967, p.387.

[iv] H. Dalton, *Practical Socialism for Britain*, 1935, pp.21–22.

[v] Ibid. (My italics.)

[vi] *Labour and the Nation*, 1928.

[vii] Jennie Lee, *This Great Journey*, 1942, p.112.

[viii] Ibid. The apathy was shown by habitual Labour voters who had lost faith and their crusading spirit, cf. N. Branson, M. Heinemann, op. cit., 1973, p.29.

of I.L.P. Parliamentarians were prepared to oppose the Government, but the rest did not wish to embarrass Ministers. As a result, the Socialist League decided to make every effort to cause 'embarrassment' to the Labour Right and would be ostracised for its inconvenient and awkward pronouncements, especially in the Party's *Daily Herald*. Hugh Dalton, vehement in his denunciation of Socialist League 'personalities', remained aware of failures of the Labour Government: 'We brought in no bold measures, and we cold-shouldered and irritated the Liberals... we lacked positive decisions (because of)... the operation of personal timidities, vanities and jealousies.'[i] In its own criticisms of the Government, the Socialist League (justifying its relevance) was apt to dwell on 'palliatives' in Labour Government policies, the defeatism, lack of any Socialist convictions, and withdrawal from the consequences of its policies. Yet, S. Cripps, later the leading S.L. member, gave a glowing account of the Labour Government as late as July 18th, 1931: 'The Labour Government has achieved wonders, has re-established England, brought disarmament into practical politics, has handled India with sympathy and imagination and prevented British extremists from a brutal policy of arrogance; has made vast and useful public works, and has had a sympathetic treatment of the unemployed. It has minimised hardship and suffering as in no other country in the world, and has made great achievements in housing, town planning, education, London traffic, agriculture, Land Tax and the Coal industry'.[ii] His only regrets: progress had been slow because of the 'minority position' and the House of Lords' power to veto, which had to be curtailed.

The main source of disillusionment within the S.L. would be the Government's unemployment policy, a Government 'far too half-hearted and apologetic in fighting the battles of the poor'.[iii] This became the reason for the S.L.'s preoccupation with formulation of a Socialist economic policy. While it diagnosed the 'sickness of Labourism',[iv] Labour leaders analysed the Government's 'misfortune' in entering office as the illness of the British economy took a desperate turn brought on by 'the widening world depression.'[v] Although the S.L. evolved during this 'crisis in capitalism', it concentrated much of its attention upon gradualist policies of the Party in its three years in office, and impracticability of Fabianism during a World economic depression. Once more a Labour Government found itself engrossed in the task of administering capitalism in the midst of increasing difficulties: 'Having accepted the policy of gradualism they were committed to reviving capitalism before they could give any attention to their programme of promises'.[vi] This taunt about Labour Party 'philosophy' from the S.L.'s General Secretary, J. T. Murphy, was not conducive to empathising with the ex–Government's problems. Socialists found it easy to explain the past and foresee possibilities, yet had to make compromises for the present. Thus the S.L. was in a unique position, formed close to the events of 1929–1931, not responsible for any 'failures', yet *within* the Party (which had exhibited its uncertainties in Government). Critics could thrive. The Labour Party had governed (without conviction) a system it did not believe in but saw no real prospect of changing;[vii]

---

[i] H. Dalton, op. cit., 1935, p.21.

[ii] Cripps Papers, Nuffield College, Oxford, Cripps' speech at Birmingham, July 18th, 1931.

[iii] Jennie Lee, op. cit., 1942, p.130.

[iv] Phrase by Miliband, op. cit., 1961, p.318.

[v] J. R. Clynes, *Memoirs 1924–37*, 1937, p.193 and C. L. Mowat, op. cit., 1955, p.356.

[vi] J. T. Murphy, *Preparing for Power*, 1934, pp.256–257.

[vii] R. Skidelsky, op. cit., 1967, p.395.

awareness of this could only increase friction between a Socialist League bent upon stating truths within the context of its membership of a defeated Party.

Labour leaders felt helpless as the crisis had sharpened and unemployment figures mounted, but the question was not one of 'making up their minds to prevent economic collapse'. That was an interpretation put on their behaviour by later commentators.[i] Lack of any strategy and an atmosphere of bewilderment were paramount in the Government's counsels; failures arose from confusion rather than from deceitful leadership or insincerity. It was not just a failure of a Government, its individuals and a Party. It was, as the Socialist League attempted to explain, failure of tentative doctrineless socialism; the Labour Government followed half-measures and 'Socialism' was not so much the cause for inaction as the victim of the actions taken without regard to it; there were no heroic gestures, no attempts to bargain or explore less orthodox paths'.[ii] Reactions to the resignations of Oswald Mosley and Sir Charles Trevelyan, and criticism of the few I.L.P. rebels in the Government, were that these weakening aspects in a Government were caused by the Party's lack of commitment to Socialism. This S.L. assessment was to govern *its* behaviour in the Party, for, at every occasion, the S.L. stressed that the Government had fallen a victim of its own shortcomings, the other parts being the 'bankers' ramp' and Conservative political manoeuvrings.

The chief failure of the Government was deemed to be unemployment policy; and the S.L. never ceased to expose this irony in a Labour Government: 'What was the Government to do? ... They had inveigled against capitalism and now found themselves its legatees, like prohibitionists unexpectedly made responsible for the management of a derelict brewery'.[iii] *Mosley's Memorandum*[iv] and its programme of action exemplified the quandary in the Government; Party 'loyalty' resulted in his motion (for an alternative unemployment policy) to be defeated. It was tragic for the future of the Left that the Mosley episode could be sanctimoniously dismissed by Party leaders as 'a disreputable piece of buccaneering by an incorrigible careerist'.[v] Later efforts by the S.L. to revivify Party policies on unemployment issues (and others) were denounced with equal self-righteousness. Understandably, suspicion within the Party towards 'Left-wingers' was confirmed by Mosley's resignation (seen as that 'stab in the back' by the Party). In fact, neither side benefited from Mosley's defection which, done so brusquely and ineptly, blunted the effect of what might have been serious exposure of the gangrene affecting the Party.[vi] Mosley's tactics were later emulated by Stafford Cripps, and were just as easily side-tracked by the Party. Both submitted a 'radical' Memorandum and counselled for support; both Memoranda were denounced and defeated at Party Conference, both left the Party, Mosley by resignation, Cripps by expulsion.

Recriminations and suspicions which clouded relations between the S.L. and Labour leaders stemmed from events in this Government. In the related problems of unemployment insurance and relief, the attack from within the Party from Maxton and the minority of the I.L.P. was vociferous: 'The cry of disloyalty drowned most

---

[i] J. T. Murphy, *Preparing for Power*, 1934, pp.256–257.
[ii] S. Pollard, 'The Great Disillusion' (a review of R. Skidelsky's *Politicians and the Slump*), *Society for the Study of Labour History*, Bulletin 16, Spring 1968.
[iii] M. Muggeridge, *The Thirties*, 1940 (1967 edn.), p.123.
[iv] Sent to R. MacDonald, January 23rd, 1930, qu. by R. Skidelsky, op. cit., p.170.
[v] Quoted by Kingsley Martin, *Harold Laski*, 1953, p.79.
[vi] M. Foot, *Aneurin Bevan*, Vol. 1, 1962, p.133.

attempts to question the course which the Government was treading.[i] These aspects, the I.L.P. pressure group and the cry of disloyalty, reappeared after the formation of the Socialist League. Sir Charles Trevelyan spoke of the crisis requiring 'big Socialist measures',[ii] his resignation from the Government regarded as 'disloyal' by the Party. Suspicions were not lessened when he joined the S.L. and gave the first public lecture: 'The Challenge to Capitalism', on January 22nd, 1933. He helped to create the image of the S.L.: 'working out the details and implications of the accepted policy of the Labour Party',[iii] and this increased the resentment of an insecure Party leadership. It was also from the experience of this Labour Government that the S.L. decided to incorporate into its programme a 'general strike' (in the event of a possible war). This originated from the Syndicalists of 1910–1914 when there had been a similar wave of disillusionment and anti-Parliamentarianism in the Movement, and specifically from the Government's Bill (1930) to amend the Trade Disputes Act (1927), the Bill aiming to legalise the sympathetic but not the general strike. S.L. attitudes towards that Labour Government were complemented by union militants: 'The workers in many industries found themselves exposed to the full blast of the crisis-urged attack of the employers; nor were they to get any protection from the MacDonald Government'.[iv] As with Labour members of the Government, union leaders made it hard for themselves to pursue any opposition to the Government's policy by their tenacious support of Mondism.

A crucial part of S.L. thinking emerged from its interpretation of the financial crisis of 1931. The bankers' remedy (a balanced budget to restore confidence and to 'save the pound') gave the crisis that flavour of 'conspiracy' which formed an integral feature of the S.L.'s response to events of August/November 1931. Respected political commentators, Tawney and G. D. H. Cole, reacted to the events with an over-dramatised prognosis of 'capitalism's inherent contradictions'. They wrote pamphlets on the 1931 crisis which became the bedrock of the S.L.'s view. G. D. H. Cole commented: 'The Labour Government of 1931 was brought down... despite its exceedingly moderate and non-Socialist policy, by a flight from the pound. There is much more reason to fear a financial crisis as the sequel to the return to power of a Government pledged to an immediate Socialist policy'.[v] The S.L.'s attitude is understandable; the experiences of 1931 destroyed the Labour Party as a political force for a decade.

Ramsay MacDonald had feared the worst: 'the power of the financier is to be that by which Labour Parties and Labour Governments are likely to be brought to grief... the class which is the creditor class can bring to its knees any public movement with which it disagrees'[vi] (this connection, full of foreboding and premonition, corresponds with Baldwin's 'the bomber will always get through').[vii] The Labour Party's attitude

---

[i] M. Foot, op. cit., p.112.

[ii] The Times, March 3rd, 1931.

[iii] Socialist League Statement, October 1932.

[iv] Allen Hutt, Postwar History of the British Working Class, 1937, pp.204–205 The Mond-Turner industrial negotiations of 1928 proved union leaders' belief in the resilience of capitalism and added fuel to the militants' fire.

[v] G. D. H. Cole, A Study Guide on Socialist Policy, August 1933 (S.L. pamphlet prepared for National Council of S.L.).

[vi] R. MacDonald in Laski's Papers, quoted by K. Martin, Harold Laski, August 1931, p.80.

[vii] Baldwin in House of Commons, July 30th, 1934, quoted by A. W. Baldwin, My Father: The True Story, 1955, p.182.

underwent a change between the downfall of the Government and the General Election (October 27th, 1931); the failure of the Government was secondary to financial interests 'engineering the crisis' and having brought a 'bankers' ramp,' (launched by the *Daily Herald* on August 25th, 1931 under the headline 'Surrender to the City'.[ii]) The S.L. incorporated those reactions to 1931, though it was not a positive response to deduce from the 'failures' of 1924 and 1929–1931 talk of 'sell-outs' and 'betrayals'.[iii] The Labour Government's attempt to place the unemployment problem on a non-party basis was the wisest formula for a 'National' Government to tackle the issue, although interpretations upon the events of 1931 by Tawney, Cole and Laski were attempts to understand wider implications of the crisis for the Labour Movement. Laski broached the issue from a conspiratorial perspective: 'Finance-capital will not permit the ordinary assumptions of the constitution to work if these operate to its disadvantage'.[iv] He drew the conclusion, later adopted by the S.L., that Socialist measures were not obtainable by constitutional means: 'Whenever a party in office seeks by legislative action to alter seriously *the distribution of wealth*, finance-capital will not accept the rule of Parliamentary governments.'[v] The implications were alarming.

The initial premise of a 'bankers' ramp' left much fantasising. To describe the bankers as engaged in a deliberate plot to destroy 'potentially Socialist policy' was an evasion of a situation in which a Labour Government had possessed little 'Socialist policy', and the Labour Left (including the I.L.P.) had little influence. The *only* hope was for the Left to re-channel the Party into more militant paths. By challenging Labour leaders, the Left wanted to show that a tough approach was required to deal with the crisis: 'the highest point of capitalist crisis in Britain between the wars'.[vi] Aneurin Bevan typified this approach: 'If a weak and innocuous minority Government can be broken by a conspiracy of finance capitalists, what hope is there for a majority Government which really threatens the bankers' privileges? What will a future Labour Government do? Drop its gradualism and tackle the emergency on Socialist lines? Or drop its Socialism in the hope of reassuring private enterprise to get a breathing space?… The policy of the Labour Party needs to be drastically overhauled.'[vii]

Reactions to 1931 in the Labour Movement led to odd excuses for those events. J. R. Clynes described the Labour Government as 'a long distance runner with a heavy weight (the Liberals) chained to his leg';[viii] Allen Hutt took the opposite view, that every point in the record of the second Labour Government was a pioneering of social disaster…: 'the whole outlook of the Cabinet was hidebound; the limits of orthodox capitalist precept and practice were their limits'.[ix] (Both of those views were expressed six years later.) The S.L.'s analysis took the middle road, even if the conclusions its policy-makers drew were apocalyptic in tone, and preoccupied with intrigues of power politics. This was apparent in an article by R. H. Tawney (*'The Choice before the Labour*

---

[i] J. R. Clynes, *Memoirs 1924–37*, 1937, p.209.

[ii] R. Bassett, *Nineteen Thirty-one*, 1958, p.173.

[iii] J. R. Clynes, op. cit., p.197.

[iv] H. Laski, 'Some Implications of the Crisis', *Political Quarterly*, October–December 1931.

[v] Ibid. (My italics.)

[vi] R. Miliband, op. cit., 1961, p.172.

[vii] M. Foot, op. cit., 1962, p.150.

[viii] J. R. Clynes, op. cit., 1937, p.112.

[ix] A. Hutt, op. cit., 1937, p.200.

44

Party').[i] His consciousness of the intrigues (cultivated in all Left-wing thinking) sheds light on S.L. attitudes regarding the 'plot': 'If the privileged classes' position is seriously threatened they will use every piece on the board, political and economic, the House of Lords, the Crown, the Press, disaffection in the army, financial crises, international difficulties, and even, as newspaper attacks on the pound in 1931 showed, the émigré trick of injuring one's country to protect one's pocket – in the honest conviction that they are saving civilisation'.[ii] Cripps paraphrased those arguments in a lecture for the S.L. on January 29th, 1933, positing the ruling class would go to any lengths to defeat Parliamentary action, if the issue was continuance of financial and political control.[iii] The dangers of 'sabotage' and anti-Socialist manoeuvrings was further entrenched in S.L. mythology with G. D. H. Cole in *A Study-Guide on Socialist Policy*[iv] for the S.L.'s first Conference, which stated: 'The Socialist League realises that a Socialist Government attempting to carry out its immediate programme must be prepared to face *sabotage by vested interests* or a financial panic, to overcome the consequences of which it will require wide emergency powers'. Socialists were living in a fool's paradise if they thought a majority in Parliament would suffice; Socialist legislation would meet with resistance from the aristocratic, plutocratic, financial and capitalist classes generally.[v] That was the S.L.'s credo.

R. H. Tawney was also practical, diagnosing the Labour Party's ills and suggesting healthy remedies: 'What Labour most needs is not self-commiseration but a little cold realism… they (the Labour Ministers) retard the recovery of the Party by concealing its malady… the Labour Party is the author of its own misfortunes… What was tried and found wanting in 1929–1931 was not merely two years of a Labour Cabinet, but a decade of Labour politics.' The S.L. embraced his analysis as the basis of its programme. Its awareness of 'the gravest weakness of the Party, its lack of a creed', came from Tawney. He saw a Party *'hesitant in action because divided in mind'*, and the S.L. took as its own raison d'être his statement that the Party needed 'clear convictions of its own meaning and purpose.' The programme of the Party needed to be modernised, its organisation overhauled; it was the S.L. which strove to emphasise *these* aspects of the Party structure.

Although the S.L. reflected, the turmoil in the Labour Party, part of its function would be to explain *why* so little had been achieved by the Labour Government. William Mellor posed it bluntly: 'The Labour Party is attempting to transform capitalism by encroachment and will be building the new with the foundations and superstructure of the old still standing'.[vi] With the experience of a two-year Labour Government, the S.L. took I.L.P. observations further. It deduced that the Party, for all its Socialist theories, plans and policies, could not apply them. Its conclusions were that the Party was born from the same political culture as Conservative and Liberal Parties; the Party could not 'think radically' because it remained trapped in this body of thought. It had, as a Government, bought power by offering conformity. The S.L. would present a firm detailed outline of how to achieve a future Socialist Government, to boost the spirits of the temporarily disillusioned. As well as creating a theory of

---

[i] *Political Quarterly*, July–September 1932, an S.L. pamphlet, August 1933.

[ii] Ibid.

[iii] Cripps, *Can Socialism Come by Constitutional Methods?*, S.L. pamphlet, January 29th, 1933 lecture.

[iv] July 29th, 1933.

[v] F. Brockway, *Inside the Left*, 1942, p.240. (My italics.)

[vi] W. Mellor, February 19th, 1933, S.L. lecture, 'The Claim of the Unemployed'.

'power politics' out of Socialist reactions to 1931, the S.L. evolved an economic 'solution' to Snowden's 'orthodox' policies. It would be a mixture of nationalisation, Parliamentary Socialism, and class struggle, mirroring the views in the Movement after the débâcle of 1931. The Party had inherited the optimistic deductions of Liberalism concerning progress and amelioration but, the Labour Government had offered timid measures to deal with unemployment and a weakening trade balance: 'The Cabinet has no plans and drifts along helplessly. The real defect is a lack of moral courage'.[i] That became the supposition. The S.L, sensitive to the pitfalls of Labour in Parliament, [ii] aware of uncertainties as to a peaceful transition to Socialism, construed that the situation fatal for Parliament was 'helplessness in face of economic difficulties'. Warnings as to the danger of following economic orthodoxy were heeded after the Government's collapse. The task of the Labour Party, if it was to be effective, was to become emancipated as to what was economically sound.[iii] Keynes' view was followed by Leonard Woolf, who threatened: 'The future will be equally disastrous if the Party of the Left continues to have no internal economic policy of its own or not sufficient courage to stand or fall by it'.[iv]

Every Left-wing member of the Labour Party attributed the crisis to the fact that the Cabinet had not provided sufficient directives to finance and industry, and should have concentrated on national ownership, reorganisation and planning. The crisis was that industries were neither conducted on capitalist nor socialist lines; the country laboured under the disadvantages of both, and the advantages of neither.[v] This crisis provided the psychological snap which led to acceptance of the need for economic planning. The old mechanism which served when markets were expanding naturally was no longer adequate.[vi] Economic policies and resolutions of the S.L. would be based on the axiom that 'War, Unemployment and Poverty are the children of Capitalism... plan to end the parent's rule'.[vii] Or in Cripps' words, the Socialist League stood for 'Socialism not State capitalism... the key point is economic power'.[viii] (Cripps was one of the few people MacDonald contacted to join the 'National' Government to deal with the emergency, but he refused: 'My own personal hope is that the rift in the Party may be quickly healed'!)[ix] The S.L. would be less bothered by the departure of MacDonald, Thomas and Snowden than attempts of the Party to dissociate itself from the results of its Government and the bankers' and the King's rôle in the crisis. The normally laconic Attlee wrote of MacDonald: 'He perpetrated the greatest betrayal in the political history of this country'.[x]

The myth of the 'leftward swing' in the Party began at the Scarborough Party Conference (October, 1931). It merits 'myth' because there was little desire among

---

[i] Quoting Kingsley Martin, *Harold Laski*, 1953, p.78.

[ii] Cf. E. F. Wise, 'The Alternative to Tariffs', *Political Quarterly*, April–June 1931 (Wise proposed the alternative of Import Boards).

[iii] J. M. Keynes, 'The Dilemma of Modern Socialism', *Political Quarterly*, April–June 1932.

[iv] L. Woolf, 'A Constitutional Revolution', *Political Quarterly*, October–December 1932.

[v] W. A. Robson, 'The Past and the Future', ibid.

[vi] H. Macmillan, *Reconstruction*, 1935, p.18.

[vii] Editorial, 'Socialist Democracy – Forward to Socialism', *Socialist Leaguer*, June–July 1934.

[viii] Cripps, May 20th, 1934, address by Chairman to opening of S.L. Annual Conference at Leeds. (My italics.)

[ix] Cripps to R. MacDonald, August 28th, 1931, Cripps Papers.

[x] C. Attlee, *As It Happened*, 1954, p.74.

remaining Labour and union leaders to probe into the reasons for the Government's failures. With the desertion of the best known Labour leaders, Left-wing Socialists began questioning the Party's 'philosophy', although for the majority of the Party, the break with MacDonaldism was more instinctive than rational;[i] 'MacDonaldism' remained the guiding force in the Party because reactions in the Party to the S.L. were based on MacDonald's tenets of the 'responsible' Labour Party, the mixed economy, the Parliamentary approach. The Conference of 1931 sat in an atmosphere of challenge with Arthur Henderson noting the 'breakdown of capitalism' and refusal to 'tinker with its inadequacies'; F. W. Pethick-Lawrence spelt out the quandary: 'The one thing that is not inevitable now is gradualness ... the unemployment problem is one of the main symptoms of the breakdown of capitalist organisations ... measures and maintenance are mere hospital work and *we are not here to do hospital work for the juggernaut of Capitalism* ... the time has come when we can no longer try with one hand to patch up the old building of Capitalism and with the other to build Socialism'.[ii] This is the approach used later by the S.L. in its assessments. In Cripps' speeches and letters between the end of the Labour Government and the Election of 1931 can be traced a theme for the S.L.: to *expose* the overwhelming odds against the Labour Party in Parliamentary electioneering and the *unusual* circumstances of the Election which led to suspicions about 'Parliamentarianism'. As the Election Campaign proceeds, hesitancy and defensiveness mingle with accusations; interpretations of the failure of the Government and need for 'Socialist measures' take on 'Marxist' overtones. Towards the day of the Election, desperation appears in reference to the 'panic' and 'class' campaign of the 'National' Government. After the rout of the Labour Party, hope for the future is inculcation of Socialist principles into Labour's propaganda. This is the background to the S.L.'s outlook. Through Cripps' electioneering is mirrored the gradual 'leftward' development with the Socialist League. On September 1st, 1931, Cripps noted the rank and file's attitude as dangerous because of 'the use of half-digested slogans in place of arguments'.[iii] To reiterate 'vague, non-constructive statements' would be fatal to the Party, because it would not distinguish Labour policies from those of the 'National' Government, (except details as to how to raise the money to balance the Budget). Cripps expressed rejection of compromise and acceptance of a 'slap-up Socialist policy' for dealing with the whole industrial and financial situation.[iv] Within a few days, he turned to the 'crisis in Capitalism'; the Labour Party somehow had to 'eliminate' the privileged classes and those who carried out industry for private profit; the sources of finance and trade had to be 'controlled'; the fight was 'between the Workers and the Capitalists' and his stand would be on Labour's programme outlined in '*Labour and the Nation*'.[v]

On October 1st, at a Labour meeting, Cripps rashly announced that workers would probably 'withdraw their labour' if the 'National' Government returned to power.[vi] Later, public ownership was the only answer: 'the reorganisation of industry had to be tackled immediately and taken out of the control of private enterprise, perhaps by

---

[i] G. D. H. Cole, *Short History of the British Working-class Movement*, 1962 edn., p.x.

[ii] Ibid. (My italics.)

[iii] Cripps to W. Graham in Cripps Papers, quoted by Eric Estorick, op. cit., p.93 and C. Cooke, op. cit., p.130. Cripps was himself accused of 'sloganising', by other Labour leaders.

[iv] Ibid.

[v] *Bristol Times* (Conservative local paper), September 5th, 1931 (in Cripps Papers).

[vi] *Bristol Times*, October 1st, 1931.

direct nationalisation',[i] the country was suffering from 'a complete lack of planning in industry and finance', tariffs would not solve the problem'; what needed to be 'controlled' were banks and credit (through Parliament) and the flow of investments in industries.[ii] Cripps, prophesised: 'there was bound to be a clash between Capital and Labour',[iii] and he was seen as 'one of the leading advocators of national ownership and control of the banking and credit system'[iv] and challenged under the headline 'Socialists and the Banks.'[v]

By mid-October, Cripps was making accusations about the 'National' Government's 'class' campaign and 'opportunism': 'If the right atmosphere of panic could be produced about the risk of going off the gold standard or as to the awful effect of an unbalanced Budget, then the country might be made to swallow these cuts as an act of patriotism without any realisation of their true significance'.[vi] He warned that the Government was obscuring Election issues with a 'smokescreen of fear and panic'; there were other ways of 'saving money' than by reducing unemployment benefits.[vii] His change of emphasis during the Election campaign was an expression of frustration in the Party at the way the Election had been developing. Labour's Manifesto mirrored Party concerns about the 'minority position' of the Labour Government, political intrigues, class-conscious hostility of the House of Lords, and undermining by business interests.[viii] With its 'call to action',[ix] the Manifesto represented that so-called 'leftward swing' in the Party (which the S.L. alone continued). Paradoxically, the fiercest critic of the S.L. (Hugh Dalton) reacted similarly to Cripps in 1931: 'For the future, slogans were not enough. We must hammer out a firm, detailed policy of Socialist reconstruction in industry and finance'.[x] This matured fourteen years later.

The main influence upon subsequent reactions by the S.L. was the 'National' Government's Election campaign, which affected the future tone and approach of the S.L. The election of 1931 was not fought on programmes or doctrines, nor on the issue of 'Socialism', and the S.L. would lose faith in Labour's possibilities of forming a majority Government *because* of peculiarities of the campaign. The Conservatives timed the date of the Election, dictated its theme, and had on their platform the three Labour leaders! Despite doubts that the campaign was created in panic[xi], it was the shortest, strangest, most fraudulent election[xii] so far. Given the manner in which the Government was formed, its composition and programme, it had to be[xiii]; this 'National' Government confused voters with myriad voices, augmented by an appeal to voters' fears if Labour were victorious',[xiv] and it remains one of the peculiarities of Parliamentary procedures

[i] *Bristol Times*, October 12th, 1931.
[ii] *Western Daily Press*, October 13th, 1931, on Cripps' speech at Ruskin Hall, Brislington, Bristol.
[iii] *Bristol Times*, October 13th, 1931.
[iv] *Bristol Times*, October 14th, 1931.
[v] *Bristol Times*, October 17th, 1931.
[vi] Patricia Strauss, *Cripps: Advocate and Rebel*, 1943, p.50.
[vii] Cf. Patricia Strauss, op. cit., p.52.
[viii] *Labour Party Annual Conference Report*, 1932, pp.319–322.
[ix] Carl Brand, *The British Labour party*, 1964, Stanford, California, p.160.
[x] Hugh Dalton, *Call Back Yesterday (Memoirs 1887–1931)*, 1953, p.279.
[xi] R. Bassett, *Nineteen Thirty-one*, 1958, pp.311–312.
[xii] J. R. Clynes, *Memoirs 1924–37*, 1937, p.209, and *Manchester Guardian*, October 28th, 1931.
[xiii] R. Miliband, op. cit., p.189.
[xiv] Cf. C. L. Mowat, op. cit., p.409.

that, though intended to ensure issues should be clarified and all information of public importance made available, its effect was to spread confusion.[i] This mystification of the public was seized upon by the S.L., as expressed (wildly) by Cripps: 'The 1931 Election was essentially Fascist in nature ... The cry for the 'elimination of party', 'we must all pull together', 'equality of sacrifice' and such slogans, the fantastic claim of the Government to the title 'National', wild and lying accusations against Social Democrats – all were evidence of the frantic efforts of the capitalists to induce the workers by fair means or foul to return to power a solid capitalist block'.[ii] Every objection which Cripps made to the campaign is an answer, point by point, to Snowden's broadcast on behalf of the Government on October 17th.[iii] Upon this reaction, S.L. leaders constructed a neo-'Marxist' analysis which claimed Labour had been 'bought' by the 'pound in danger', the Capitalist press, the Post Office Savings scare, and unscrupulous use of the wireless. The theory was not developed further than that, because, to the S.L., it was sufficient to comment that 'blatant calumny and misrepresentation were used against us by press, pulpit and wireless... Our business is to prove ourselves an efficient, active body, and to make the Labour Party 'more Socialist'.[iv] The struggle would be against press, pulpit and wireless for the foreseeable future.

The reason for the S.L.'s refusal to take its conclusions further was that it wished to work *within* the Labour Party. The S.L. became conscious of the fact that the Party's lack of a detailed policy on domestic issues damned the Party as much as Conservative 'intrigues', and the S.L. was not to be so naïve in its approach to 'Parliamentary democracy' as to believe (as Labour leaders had) that the electorate could distinguish between what was and was not due to the actions of the Labour Government.[v] Despite this, the S.L. developed a one-dimensional outlook in its criticisms of both 'Capitalist economics' and 'Parliamentary Socialism', both of which stemmed from its assessment of the events of 1931. So profound were the crisis conditions, so clearly defined were the 'class' issues (in measures proposed to deal with them) that Labour leaders began to speak the language of 'class war', but only the S.L. *within* the Party continued that. The radical mood lasted until the Party had redefined its policy and tactics in 1934, because it had to reassess its old values, following the Election; the plea was for a 'bold Socialist policy', 'no more gradualism', an awareness that social reform under the 'capitalist system' had limitations; Labour leaders were to 'put Socialism first', 'abandon palliatives', 'purify' the Party. Again, far from disloyalty, the S.L. was the only organisation in the Party which followed this through. The first reaction of the Party, post-1931, that it had parted with its worst 'non-Socialists,' was a pretence. There were bitter dissensions in the Party, and the S.L would be ostracised for exposing them.

The moralistic position towards the Party after the Election débâcle was begun in Labour's intellectual circles by Beatrice Webb: 'I rejoice in the crisis as I think it will clear the issue and purify the Party... As I want the Labour Party to have more time for thought about the future, I am not keen on it taking office for another five years'.[vi] No chance of that. And Lord Ponsonby took a lofty attitude and flight in metaphor: 'The Party had been saved for Socialism; although some of its spectacular blooms have

[i] M. Muggeridge, *The Thirties*, 1940, pp.129–130.

[ii] S. Cripps, *'National' Fascism in Britain*, Socialist League pamphlet, 1935.

[iii] Quoted in full, R. Bassett, *Nineteen Thirty-one*, 1958, pp.444–49.

[iv] George Lansbury, circular to Labour MPs, November 18th, 1931, Lansbury's Papers at the L.S.E.

[v] Cf. R. B. McCallum, 'The Future of Political Parties', *Political Quarterly*, April–June 1932.

[vi] B. Webb, *Diaries (1924–1932)*, 1956, ed. M. I. Cole; October 20th, 1931.

gone, the tree is all the healthier for being pruned of what turned out to be a spurious growth.[i] Although there was an understandable reluctance to embark upon a searching examination, such a study would have enabled the party to attain a clearer perspective. The S.L. would provide that inspection in 1933 and 1934 through its lectures 'Crisis in Capitalism' and Socialist Programme pamphlets, (the first of which dealt with where the points of resistance were likely to arise),[ii] while Sidney Webb echoed this need for 'faith and loyalty' within the Party, which, 'more than ever definitely Socialist in policy, is not "smashed" but rather consolidated and purified'.[iii]

Underlining their own political position, Socialist commentators found a purpose and meaning in the 1931 crisis. Some witnessed the whole system and outlook of 'MacDonaldism' coming to its logical conclusion and a whole stage in the development of the Labour Movement coming to an end.[iv] The inadequacies of social democracy had been revealed; there was a dichotomy between the picture of the Socialist future which Labour MPs had prophesied and the realities they found at Westminster; 'the "new Jerusalem" vision faded when the MP became an accepted member of an excellent club, and was courteously received by those he had been denouncing as "grinders" of the faces of the poor!'[v] The S.L. would be mid-way between these two reactions, exemplified by H. Laski, to whom the crisis had awakened the Labour Party to announce: 'the purpose of Socialists is Socialism ... the experience of two attempts to rule upon the principles and by the methods of its opponents has made it obvious that disaster is the inevitable consequence of a policy of quarter-measures. Its objective has necessarily become the capture, by Parliamentary means, of the citadel of economic power; this it must now attempt with a completeness as rapid as the technical obstacles will permit'.[vi] Still relevant in the 21st century.

Socialist League hopes were high that '1931' would be a learning process for the Party, but the experience caused no major transformations. Arthur Henderson expressed the official position: 'nothing had happened to the Party or to our electoral position to warrant any scrapping of our programme, or policy, or the revolutionising of our methods'.[vii] Labour leaders were prepared to accept a long-term programme to mollify the rank and file, and wait until they had a majority in Parliament, This did not deter a leading member of the S.L., Sir Charles Trevelyan, from declaring, in the first S.L. Lecture (January 1933) that the defeat of 1931 could have done 'nothing but good if it leads the Party to determine that it will put the country into a position where it is required to make a choice between the continuance of the present system and a Socialist Commonwealth'.[viii] The defeat also clarified for S.L. members the belief that any future Socialist Government would meet resistance of an unconstitutional nature from defenders of the 'old regime.' This theme was extrapolated in Cripps' 'Can

[i] Lord Ponsonby, 'The Future of the Labour Party', *Political Quarterly*, January–March 1932.
[ii] G. D. H. Cole and G. R. Mitchison, *The Need for a Socialist Programme*, December 31st, 1932 (S.L. pamphlet) and *New Clarion*, December 31st, 1932.
[iii] Sidney Webb, 'What Happened in 1931: A Record', *Political Quarterly*, January–March 1932.
[iv] Allen Hutt, op. cit., 1937, p.214.
[v] Kingsley Martin, *The Editor (1931–45)*, Vol. 2, 1968, p.53.
[vi] H. J. Laski, *The Labour Party and the Constitution*, Socialist Programme Series No. 2, February 11th, 1933 (S.L. pamphlet).
[vii] A. Henderson, *Labour Party Annual Conference*, 1932.
[viii] Sir Charles Trevelyan, *The Challenge to Capitalism*, January 22nd, 1933, S.L. pamphlet.

Socialism come by Constitutional Methods?", and the policies necessary to deal with such a situation were tabulated in Laski's *'The Labour Party and the Constitution'*[ii] (his pamphlet proposed 'how to deal with the House of Lords, the judiciary, the civil service and all other constitutional barriers to the enforcement of a Socialist programme).[iii]

It was natural for the S.L. to expect such a confrontation. There had been the 1924 Red Letter hoax and the General Strike 1926 as examples of 'media manipulation' by Conservatives; the crisis in the second Labour Government precipitated secessions of Mosley, MacDonald, and (in 1932) Maxton and the I.L.P., and the Election campaign had been shrouded in 'intrigue'. Therefore, the S.L. intended a future Labour victory to represent more than a change of government; a Labour government would be *pledged to eradicate privilege, title and property ownership*. The S.L. also anticipated (from its understanding of events mentioned above) that counter-measures would be invoked. Perversely, this approach was implying its own disbelief in 'Socialism coming through the Labour Party',[iv] which was bound to bring intractable conflicts (of personality and ideology) in the Labour Party and a theme of this book is that the S.L. had a major responsibility for its own demise which resulted in Labour's Procrustean enforcement of conformity.

However, in 1932, the S.L. represented a new resolve in the Labour Party. It interpreted the 'Crisis' as having decisively altered the relations of all Parties, as having brought nearer a confrontation of Parties on class lines[v] and this 'class' analysis within the Labour Party would cause friction with official leaders and union hierarchy, but would be a response to unique conditions of mass unemployment and threat of Fascism and War: 'This crisis... enables us to see which are the real forces in conflict. The class struggle is now between the investing class who have lent capital... and the mass of employed and unemployed people'.[vi] The S.L. propounded three assumptions which were to be challenged throughout its existence; that there was a place within the Labour Party for a group with sharply-defined Socialist views; that the slump was most propitious for political activity (and the class struggle); and if confidence in political democracy was to be sustained, political freedom had to arm itself with economic power.

By December 1931, the Labour Party was without effective leadership in Parliament or country and there were now the empty gestures[vii] of opposition to the Government's policies. While the Labour Party prepared to battle on two fronts, (to reorganise its forces and to continue its dispute with the I.L.P.), Cripps did not see among its leaders that sense of urgency he felt.[viii] Again, in tracing Cripps in speeches and letters from December 1931 to October 1932, further understanding of the ambiguities in the Socialist League emerge. The theme during these months (in which Cripps became identified as a 'militant') was revulsion against Party 'gradualism'. In December, Cripps wrote to Lansbury: 'Arthur Henderson is terribly worried about the

---

[i] S.L. pamphlet, January 29th, 1933.

[ii] S.L. pamphlet, February 11th, 1933.

[iii] *New Clarion*, February 11th, 1933.

[iv] See R. Lyman, 'The British Labour Party: The Conflict Between Socialist Ideals and Practical Politics Between the Wars', *Journal of British Studies*, Vol. 5, No. 1, November 1965.

[v] J. T. Murphy, *Preparing for Power*, 1934, p.262.

[vi] Kingsley Martin, 'This Crisis', *Political Quarterly*, October–December 1932.

[vii] G. D. H. Cole, *History of the Labour Party Since 1914*, 1948, p.274.

[viii] Patricia Strauss, *Cripps: Advocate and Rebel*, 1942, p.62.

Party. He feels Labour is in the wilderness for a long period unless we can trim our sails... he is not anxious for us to be too definite about Socialist measures as our first objective... the Movement he has done so much to foster will perish if once again it gets lost in the morass of opportunism'.[i] Cripps was now living the experience of sitting on the Opposition benches where administrative capacity took second place to political argument.[ii] The *Bristol Labour Weekly* (Cripps' local mouthpiece from 1932 to 1939) described Cripps as 'presenting Labour's case in reasoned language and without rhetorical display'![iii] He was already recognised as the "orator of the Party" and more than fulfilled his rôle, his verbal pyrotechnics prolific.[iv] His speeches became abundant with metaphor, resonant with optimism, tense with impatience, and a letter to Lansbury typifies this: 'It is sometimes very difficult to see the wood for the trees, but I am sure it is vitally important to carry that picture of the wood as we should like it to be in our minds even though we have to consider in detail which trees to fell and how best to fell them. I attach a great deal of importance to 'the show we put up' (in the House of Commons) for the sake of the cause in the country ... there is a very clear necessity in my mind to amend rather drastically the machinery of Democracy ... to make it effective. The present machinery seems to me to put a premium upon 'laggardliness' ... we must try and get rid of the futility and delay of Parliament.'[v]

Despite his genuine fervour for a 'classless society,' Cripps displayed in the early 1930s an ignorance of the complexity of issues. Several times during these years, he described what could evolve as nothing other than violent revolution in the misleading guise of 'a change-over to Socialism', as if a facile gesture would suffice for the transformation of society: 'The longer we try to patch up this system (of capitalism) the greater will be our difficulty in effecting the changeover to Socialism ... We must now definitely put out of our heads any idea of the possibility of a gradual changeover ... the more critical circumstances become the more necessary is it to effect the change with rapidity'.[vi] This simplicity of analysis (and conclusions) were due in part to an excessive concern for 'order'. Capitalism was all that was "untidy and chaotic", Socialism was to be the model of planning and control: 'On economic grounds, the case for Socialism is unanswerable at the present time. It is the disordered competition of the profit-seeker that had brought our difficulties ... we must plan production for the benefit of the consumers and regulate our finances for the benefit of the State.'[vii] War was the symbol of disorder within capitalist society: 'The chaos of war is typical of the system of private enterprise ... an example of lack of orderliness and control inevitable in a free-for-all society'.[viii] Here's the paradox, Cripps calling for an inevitably violent conflict in the language of the paternalistic lawyer: 'The final collapse of capitalism will depend upon the vigour with which the workers insist upon their right to a higher standard of life'.[ix]

Cripps' assessment of the economy was also characteristically oversimplified. The

[i] Lansbury Papers (L.S.E.), also quoted in R. Postgate, *Life of G. Lansbury*, pp.279–280.
[ii] C. Cooke, op. cit., p.127.
[iii] *Bristol Labour Weekly*, June 4th, 1932, Cripps Papers.
[iv] By June 27th, 1932, Cripps had spoken 190 columns of Hansard since November, Cripps Papers.
[v] Cripps to Lansbury, January 13th, 1932, Lansbury Papers.
[vi] *Bristol Labour Weekly*, January 16th, 1932, Cripps Papers.
[vii] Cripps, *Bristol Labour Weekly*, June 25th, 1932, Cripps Papers.
[viii] Cripps, 'War on War and Capitalism', *Social Democrat*, February 1932, Cripps Papers.
[ix] Cripps, article for *New Leader*, February 1932, Cripps Papers.

'need for a fundamental reorganisation, social, political and industrial, to obtain prosperity for all'[i] was too vague. He was extremely concerned about 'dictatorship', ironical when considering his Press image throughout the history of the Socialist League. He wrote: 'with establishment of a large Government majority, there will be a danger of a virtual dictatorship by the Cabinet, backed by the Commons and Lords which will merely register the approval of Cabinet decisions without any effective debate or discussion.'[ii] One wonders what he would have proposed to counteract Prime Ministerial government today? Meanwhile for Cripps: 'political power must be sufficiently strong to override the vested interest of individuals and classes in the financial and industrial framework of the country'. During the Labour Government, 'the forces of Capitalism were effective to put a stop even to the initiation of any wide measures of a Socialist character'.[iii] And Cripps represented the S.L., especially after he had become Chairman in December 1933. In his own speeches and letters (from December 1931 to October 1932) he mirrored the Socialist League; its authoritarian simplicity, desire for order, oratorical approach to problems; its meticulousness (understandable in a research group which began 'to educate and organise'); its confidence in a Socialist future, and impatience with tentative Labour Party approaches.

Throughout its history, the S.L.'s interpretation of the events of 1929–1931 coloured its relationship to the *whole* Labour Movement. Its essence became its questioning of assumptions underlying Parliamentary gradualism. This gave S.L. pamphlets their 'Marxist' tone, and S.L. policy resolutions at Party Conference their militant content. With most of the media closed to Socialist views, Labour's best opportunities to carry its messages to the country were through Party meetings and leaflet propaganda.[iv] Here, S.L. lectures and pamphlets,[v] by prominent figures in the Movement, helped to retain a spirit of militancy within the Party. Most of the pamphlets were on the necessity for the Party to return to basic principles and ideology. Alfred Zimmern's query that R. H. Tawney wanted the Labour Party to escape from its commitments by closing its ranks, expelling its doubters and the lukewarm, and welding itself into a body of zealots[vi] prompted the reply: 'It is a mistake for a Labour Government to make the retention of office *its principal objective*, and for that purpose to abandon measures to which it has repeatedly committed itself'.[vii] This concentration on 'basic principles' became an integral part of the political armour of the S.L.: 'Whenever the Labour Party has made a mistake, it has not been in consequence of pursuing its principles too roughly or too far, but by making too many concessions to conventional opinion'.[viii] Therein lay the S.L.'s cutting edge. In a catechism, Philip Noel-Baker asked how the Party could overcome the handicap

[i] Cripps, 'The Alternative to Capitalism', *Bristol Labour Weekly*, February 13th, 1932, Cripps Papers.

[ii] C. Cooke, op. cit., p.132, quoted Cripps.

[iii] Cripps, 'Should Labour Ever Again Take Office as a Minority: Sir Stafford Cripps Says No!', *Bristol Labour Weekly*, September 10th, 1932, Cripps Papers.

[iv] Dean McHenry, op. cit., 1938, pp.162–180.

[v] Cf. the series of S.L. lectures published in *Problems of a Socialist Government* , 1933 and *Problems of the Socialist Transition*, 1934, plus pamphlets.

[vi] R. H. Tawney, 'The Choice Before the Labour Party', *Political Quarterly*, April–June 1932, S.L. pamphlet 1933.

[vii] R. H. Tawney, *Political Quarterly*, October–December 1932. (My italics.)

[viii] Aneurin Bevan, *In Place of Fear*, 1952 edn., p.126.

which lack of money imposed upon it; only by intensive political education and propaganda.[i] This was the final illusion. All the S.L.'s work in politicising Party members in localities and national Party level, had little effect in altering Labour Party's *practice*. The importance of the radicalising function of 'education and propaganda', the raison d'être of the S.L. in its first two years, was 'a new form of 'attentisme'[ii] for Labour leaders.'

To conclude, the S.L. evolved its outlook and style from the inordinate disillusionment at failures of the second Labour Government, fear of the power of the Press and wireless to influence events; a scepticism towards Parliamentary Elections and electoral 'stunts'; a 'conspiratorial' awareness which accentuated intrigues of power politics;[iii] indignity and bitterness engendered by the Means Test and economic collapse which gave the S.L. a 'cause'; and lack of faith in the newly elected 'National' Government and its 'manufactured' Parliament. As in most of its pronouncements, the S.L.'s anti-Parliamentarian' arguments were ambiguous, because, if (as it analysed) such deadly blows could be struck at the power of the Labour Movement and working-class standards by Parliamentary leaders, then Parliament *was* an essential arena in the pursuit of power. In its revulsion from 'MacDonaldism' the S.L. leant too far towards a catastrophic view to address the conditions of crisis. Its 'agitatory' style, so successful while the Party recovered, grew less relevant and more irksome in an Election-conscious Party. Nevertheless, at the Leicester Conference of 1932, the S.L. had arrived, full of the unbounded optimism that Cripps exhibited: 'The Labour Party will undoubtedly continue with a policy of definite immediate Socialism, having finally abandoned the theory of "the inevitability of gradualness"'.[iv] So began a struggle in the Labour Movement outside Parliament in which the S.L. sought to capture the mind of the Labour Party and secure it for a militant Socialist economic policy.[v] The aims derived from collective ideals, but the struggle would become a desperate one, and the obstacles not easily surmountable.

---

[i] P. Noel-Baker, 'The Future of the Labour Party', *Political Quarterly*, January–March 1932.

[ii] R. Miliband, op. cit., 1961, p.194.

[iii] C. Brand, 'The British Labour Party', op. cit., p.167, 'Cripps and the S.L. were so firmly convinced of the inevitability of this adamantine resistance (by Capitalist interests) that they advocated the enactment of an Emergency Powers Act by the next Labour Government in order to overcome it.'

[iv] Cripps, 'The Next Election', 'The Future of the Political Parties', *Political Quarterly*, January–March 1932.

[v] E. Estorick, op. cit., p.108.

Chapter Two

Intellectuals, Politics and the Socialist League

The story of the 1930s is a stampede of liberal and left intellectuals into the Soviet camp.

E. H. Carr, *From Napoleon to Stalin and Other Essays,*
1986 edn., p.266

All of us carry around a mixture of principle, prejudice and habit which shapes our political decisions. Sometimes indeed the habit has hardened into a crusty shell that repels any argument, any thesis, any fact which upsets any cherished assumptions.

Dennis Potter, qu. by Humphrey Carpenter,
Dennis Potter, pp.147–48

The role of the intellectual in modern society is not to offer prescriptive analysis but to lay bare the mechanisms of power: *The intellectual no longer has to play the role of an adviser. The project, tactics and goals to be adopted are a matter for those who do the fighting. What the intellectual can do is to provide instruments of analysis... a topological and geological survey of the battlefield – that is the intellectual's role.*

Jeffrey Weeks, 'Foucault for Historians',
in *History Workshop Journal,* Autumn 1982, No. 14, p.117

Society in the 1930s exhibited signs of having suffered a mental wound.[i] José Ortega y Gasset in *The Revolt of the Masses* (1929) had depicted the 20th century as dominated by the mediocrity of the masses, and argued for the vital rôle of intellectual élites (in averting the slide into the barbarism of Fascism or Communism). It was in this atmosphere that intellectuals joined Left-wing organisations, including the Socialist League. Disillusionment, scepticism, political indifference, part of the intellectual environment in the earlier 20th century, evolved into political militancy and commitment. It had been a Marxist axiom that radical politics flourished in a seed-bed of economic and political catastrophe, and in the 1930s, poverty, malnutrition, the dole, and the mass protest of the Hunger Marches, were realities. The principal result of the 1931 crisis for the intelligentsia was its return to politics.[ii]

After the advent of Hitler in Germany, the movement to the Left among intellectuals became more widespread, intensity of commitment deepened,

---

[i] A. Marwick, *Britain in the Century of Total War,* 1968, p.62.
[ii] D. Mirsky, *The Intelligentsia of Great Britain,* 1935, London, p.40.

manifestations of revolt more overt, the political implications more direct. Fascism was the target: 'Chaos and bewilderment were created in the minds of the intelligentsia as they came gradually to realise that war could come again'.[i] It resulted in the 'ending of bright hopes', the beginnings of 'feelings of guilt', the 'sickening discovery of what democracy could do'.[ii] And those intellectual Socialists who joined the S.L. attacked traditional ideas, established principles and parliamentary institutions, *because* of the collapse of two Labour Governments, and failure of Western democracies to deal with the economic crisis. Socialist Leaguers questioned the premise that democratic action through Parliament provided the *best* method for radical reform, especially in an age of ideologies. The S.L.'s intellectual objections to capitalist democracy became its most distinguishing feature as a pressure group, and played a large part in provoking friction vis-à-vis Labour and union leaders.

It was a unique feature of the S.L. that it attracted so many prominent Labour intellectuals into its ranks. They formulated S.L. policies, which implied 'necessary, drastic political measures' to deal with the political and economic conditions of the 1930s. This was an attempt by a second post-War generation 'to escape from the Wasteland',[iii] to escape the loneliness of their isolation 'from the shipwreck of Western values, and the desire for a refuge.'[iv] For the S.L. militant intellectual, 'involvement' was the catchword motivated by the indignity of 'starvation in the midst of plenty', which could be remedied by the application of Marxism, humanism and a dose of Soviet economics. This revival of political interest was accompanied by theory: a thirst for replacing the shattered hulk of British empiricism.'[v] In the S.L. this took the form of a renewed interest in Marxian analyses, expressed in lectures, pamphlets, and resolutions to Labour Conferences. *Adelphi* published new translations of writings by Marx, Engels and Lenin, and Trotsky's autobiography *My Life* (1930) and *History of the Russian Revolution.*[vi]

From its inception, the S.L. defined the division between Government and Opposition as a choice between accepting the inevitability of booms and slumps; unemployment and periodic wars, and the vision of a planned Socialist economy, elimination of unemployment, and an international foreign policy which could prevent war. This might seem an impractical, even irrelevant reaction on the part of a frustrated, powerless pressure group minority, but the S.L.'s attitude was a sincere, spontaneous expression of an optimism which grew out of disillusionment, the first time in British history when a *large* section of middle-class intellectuals became radicalised: 'Politics became a by-word among intellectuals',[vii] and S.L. intellectuals were the only non-integrated social group in the Labour Movement who, by virtue of their privileged position, could have pierced the ideological mystification of political indoctrination, but it did not work out like that.

Although it is one of the themes of this book that the Labour Party did not become

---

[i] M. Cole, 'In the Past', *Political Quarterly*, Vol. 40, No. 4, October–December 1969.

[ii] Ibid.

[iii] Julian Bell letter to *New Statesman and Nation*, December 9th, 1933, p.731.

[iv] R. H. S. Crossman, ed., *The God That Failed*, 1952, New York, pp.4–7, quoting N. Wood, op. cit., p.102.

[v] D. Mirsky, op. cit., p.243. Aldous Huxley took the opposite stance: 'Idealism is the noble toga that political gentlemen drape over their will to power.'

[vi] B. Pearce, 'The Establishment of Marx House – a Comment', *Society for the Study of Labour History*, Bulletin 16, Spring 1968, pp.20–22.

[vii] N. Wood, op. cit., p.37.

'more consciously Socialist' after 1931, S.L. members did attempt to invoke a new element of ideology in the Movement. The new development was a revolt of social conscience by intellectual members,[i] and policies were a field in which the previously apolitical intellectual could put into practice his or her thoughts; what began as a political awakening became a radicalisation'.[ii] Through the propaganda work of the S.L. the struggle was to *redefine* the rôle of the Party intellectual; Cripps clarified that his use of 'workers' covered all who made a living from their brain or hand, and not out of their property; the S.L. had a preparatory function: it was the duty of Socialist intellectuals to provide the Movement with a tangible philosophy and a framework in which to approach problems. The pamphlets, lectures, discussion groups and policy resolutions were means to train an opposition, and expose the Government's policies and its anti-Socialist activities and legislation. Another of the functions of the S.L. was to counteract the 'anti-theory' prejudices in the Labour Party and unions and adumbrate the need for radical thinking. It was not only the intellectual's function to describe change and advocate it. He/she had to be seen as the *'prophet of an intelligent radicalism'*.[iii] In this age of crisis, when a social conscience motivated so many to work for radical changes, S.L. leaders applied themselves to the examination and solution of historical, economic, political and sociological problems.[iv] Had the circumstances of its formation and position in the Movement been different, the S.L. could have functioned as a radical agency of change.[v]

From its formation at Leicester, the S.L. was viewed by numerous Labour supporters as an organisation for which 'earnest Socialists' were looking. In hoping that *'the Nobodies will rally to a Blazing Socialist Faith'*,[vi] 'Gex' saw the possibility the new S.L. would be an organisation to which Party and union leaders could turn, as a loyal group which could be relied upon to 'put the cause first', and be ready to render organised aid in any emergency: 'We want nothing short of *a religion of Socialism*. It may be that the S.L. will renew in us that spirit.'[vii] Certainly, Socialist Leaguers saw themselves as militants inducing class-consciousness in the Labour Movement. This is apparent through their writings; they viewed themselves as 'agitators' revitalising a Labour Party which had become *subdued* by the propaganda of Press, wireless and Parliament. Inside the Party they were to be the 'saviours of Socialism', they were to feel the moral compulsion of rebels; a community which did not produce rebels was in danger of decay, for they were the antidotes to sloth, to conformity and to corruption.'[viii] This is why the S.L. continued the educational and research work from the I.L.P.

These professional radicals appointed themselves as observers to the Movement; they believed there had been a failure of the Labour Party to develop a coherent philosophy; S.L. leaders reiterated Marxist theories (and added slogans) and organising and administrative abilities in the localities. In discussing the function of the S.L. and local groups, there was an air of confidence and certainty of purpose: 'The National

---

[i] A. J. P. Taylor, *English History (1914–1945)*, 1965, pp.346–47.

[ii] N. Wood, op. cit., p.37.

[iii] Cripps in letter, December 11th, 1934, Cripps Papers.

[iv] Cf. James Weinstein, 'Socialist Intellectuals', *Studies on the Left*, Vol. 6, No. 5, September–October 1966.

[v] Cf. Robert Wolfe, 'Intellectuals and Social Change', *Studies on the Left*, Vol. 2, No. 3, 1962, p.64.

[vi] 'Gex', *New Clarion*, November 5th, 1932.

[vii] Ibid. (My italics.)

[viii] Amber Blanco White, *The New Propaganda*, 1939, p.363.

Council and the Central Office's primary task is to *initiate*. Members of the S.L strive to equip themselves in advance for their activities in the wider Movement by getting down to a realistic examination of the problems which face it. The foundations are laid by the National Council, which surveys and selects the ground to be covered. To do this, it has set to work a series of committees of *experts* and others with specialised knowledge whose conclusions are placed before the branches as the basis of their work'.[i] All very honourable, but this overt confidence hid another feature between the S.L. and Labour and union leaders, a battle between extremist and moderate in which suspicions of ambition and self-seeking fell on those who spoke too freely and too often of their own ideas. The resentment against 'the Party intellectual' was ingrained in the Movement; the 'dogmatism' of the intellectual socialist, his/her impatience with the practical details of a subject, and seeming contempt for the parochialism of 'proletarian comrades,' and bourgeois manners and speech, set him apart from workers'.[ii] Nevertheless, such differences were accentuated to undermine the validity of the S.L.'s case in Party conferences; there was a prejudice among some Labour and union leaders against a Party intelligentsia (personified in the S.L.) which had pretensions to be a catalyst of historical change. (Marcuse noted that this prejudice against intellectuals was an essential factor in the development of capitalist as well as Socialist societies in weakening the opposition.)[iii]

Coming to political consciousness in response to their view of the crisis in capitalism, S.L. intellectuals looked to the old Bolsheviks for inspiration. Here they purported to find that combination of ideological commitment, all-embracing philosophy of certainty, propensity for strong action, sensitive morality, toughness, wide intellectual horizon, and devotion to economic planning and technology.[iv] S.L. leaders sought to combine intellectual analysis with practical action yet behind rejection of Parliamentary gradualism there was a special frustration in the S.L.; it would try to shatter the halo of propriety and smug righteousness with which the National Government surrounded its activities.[v] Marxism filled the void for the S.L.; Marxism had the authority, logic, relevance to an understanding of (and answer to) economic depression, and put real demands on Socialists; its message filtered into the Labour Party through campaigners like J. T. Murphy, William Mellor, J. F. Horrabin, E. F. Wise and H. N. Brailsford. [Only Cripps in this group of S.L. leaders had come into politics late, in 1929]. They tried to bridge the gap between the intellectual and politician; they stood for State Socialism, application of scientific thinking to politics, public accountability for State action; to build an efficient and non-acquisitive society! (The Webbs had epitomised this approach: 'They wished first to analyse society, and then so marshal and publicise the facts and the policy arising from them that argument and opinion would eventually defeat the vested interests.)[vi]

One of the causes of tension between the S.L. and Party and union leaders was that the S.L., by its dramatisation of issues, attracted public attention to *itself*. With the S.L.'s ideological 'crisis in capitalism', it attracted many outstanding Party personalities who

---

[i] S.L. Notes, 'National Council at Work', *New Clarion*, July 29th, 1933. (My italics.)

[ii] N. Wood, op. cit., p.17.

[iii] Herbert Marcuse, 'Liberation from the Affluent Society', *The Dialectics of Liberation*, David Cooper, ed., 1970, pp.187–88.

[iv] J. P. Nettl, *The Soviet Achievement*, 1967, p.63.

[v] Margaret George, *The Hollow Men*, 1965, p.242.

[vi] K. Martin, *The Editor Vol. 2 (1931–45)*, 1968, pp.74–75.

accepted a common field of action and rejected some conventional methods of propaganda (which clashed with Party gradualism, caution and respectability). However, there were inherent uncertainties as to the S.L.'s pretensions as a pressure group. It was hoped in the Party that the S.L. would maintain the spirit of fraternity which characterised the old I.L.P., (and not as the I.L.P. had been during the 1929–1931 Labour Government, 'a chosen superior, group'); 'if the S.L. is to succeed there must be no room in it for persons so superior to ordinary Trade Unionists or Party members that to them alone is infallibly revealed *Socialist truth*, or for persons *too middle-class* to put their head to the humdrum teamwork of the Party'.[i] Nevertheless, it would be pointless if the S.L. became a refuge for elderly gentlemen interested in economics or for 'harmless Party workers'.[ii]

Suspicions and resentments towards the newly formed Socialist League (and Socialist intellectuals) was expressed by Ernest Bevin, whose hostility had been reinforced by the choice of E. G. Wise as Chairman, instead of himself.[iii] Bevin belittled the work of the S.L. and, as stated, dubbed intellectuals 'people who stabbed honest Trade Unionists in the back'.[iv] For Bevin, S.L. leaders did not place the same value upon *organisational loyalty*; they had a habit of creating a purely subjective and fictitious picture of the working class and its political ambitions,[v] presumably unlike Bevin's vision. As he saw it, the S.L. demanded a political attitude that would settle difficulties in general, painful decisions could be obviated and dilemmas evaded, if only the Labour Movement hit on the right *theoretical* approach. Much of the factionalism in the Party could be traced to this crude division between 'working-class' unionists and 'middle class' Socialists, but then the very composition of the Party, its diverse and sometimes antipathetic emotional and intellectual compulsions, which brought people to 'visualise a Socialist society', made periodic clashes endemic.

In its first year, the S.L. concentrated on first principles. Progress in political outlook had stemmed from this pressure of forward-looking militant sections of the Party, whether Fabians, political malcontents or intellectual theorists. There were doubts as to whether the S.L. was not too close to William Morris's original S.L. despite the positive similarities (brilliant sponsors, similar constitutions, flaming enthusiasms, and a membership of extraordinary diversity).[vi] Party and union leaders were irritated by S.L. criticism of Party resolutions in Conferences, which seemed to be telling unions and Party officials what they ought to do.[vii] The intellectual was thus stigmatised as 'unreliable' and 'irresponsible'; Cripps was aware of this image of the Party intellectual but, though he recognised that 'it is always a difficult problem how Socialists should act within a Capitalist State';[viii] he felt it was 'not one of very great importance compared with the necessity for working for the change'.[ix]

Although intellectuals in the S.L. had made some personal sacrifice, inability to fit into conventional Party politics implied to official leaders they were more concerned

---

[i] 'Gex', *New Clarion*, November 5th, 1932. (My italics.)

[ii] Ibid.

[iii] Kingsley Martin, op. cit., Vol. 2, p.49.

[iv] M. Cole, *The Story of Fabian Socialism*, 1961, p.233.

[v] F. Williams, *Ernest Bevin*, 1952, p.176.

[vi] Constance Borrett, 'New Beginnings', *Socialist Leaguer*, No. 7, December 1934.

[vii] F. Williams, op. cit., p.177.

[viii] Cripps to a L.P. Constituency member, February 11th, 1935.

[ix] Ibid.

to be 'noticed' in a militant minority. Dalton voiced this opinion, that new arrivals in the Party nearly all made their entry from the Left, that much that looked and sounded left was in manner, not matter: 'The Left is sometimes only a mystique, a snobbism.'[i] Bevin led, with Citrine, most unionists against the Socialist programme of the S.L. at Party Conferences, because for them the S.L. lacked an appreciation of *loyalty to Party decisions*, and as a body was *unreliable as an intellectual guide*: 'They were too volatile, haring off after new ideas and new enthusiasms.'[ii] For Bevin, the Party had been littered with abandoned initiatives by Socialist intellectuals; they suffered from an opposition mentality and thought politics was a perpetuation of University Labour Clubs in which nothing more serious was at stake than a resolution.[iii] Bevin's half-truths were typical of the response towards the S.L.'s functions, which, by its mere existence, implied shortcomings in the Labour and union leadership, although his comments reveal more about him than about the people he criticises: *'When we have tried to associate with the intellectuals, our experience has been that they do not stay the course very long ... the difference between the intellectuals and the trade unionists is this. You have no responsibility, you can fly off at a tangent as the wind takes you ... we, however, must be consistent and we have a great amount of responsibility'.*[iv] However, it was the inertia in the Labour and union leaders itself which roused the S.L.; many whose lives were spent in political discussion were attracted to the S.L.'s 'Marxist' approach. The middle-class Socialist was difficult to ignore in political and Parliamentary circles. He was used to 'good manners', less affected by them or by the social pressure upon working-class Labour Parliamentarians,[v] although, the gentlemanly and 'amateur' tradition in British politics made S.L. National Council leaders suspect as advocates of Labour policies.

There was an underlying prejudice in some working-class Labour circles against middle-class Socialist Leaguers from the London area.[vi] The S.L. membership remained small (c. 3000), with an image of a literary clientèle with 'bourgeois tastes'. Occasionally, in the pages of the S.L. monthly journal, there erupts the old resentment against 'those people who imagined that they could abolish class distinctions without making any uncomfortable change in their own habits and ideology' and there was a little truth in the description of the middle-class Socialist enthusing over the proletariat and running Summer Schools 'where the proletariat and the repentant bourgeois are supposed to fall upon one another's necks and be brothers for ever.'[vii] There had always been this paradox in the Labour Left, but it had never really affected its overall strategy. The ambiguity or contradiction lay much deeper in a combined hostility to authority with elements of authoritarianism in its ideology, humanitarianism with State collectivism, idealism with materialism, the belief in determinism yet in individual moral responsibility.

The Labour Party sought intellectual allies among those who had been trained to state a case, but although leading S.L. members trusted that research, education and pamphleteering could *change* Party policies, political activities became circumscribed when the S.L. branched out into agitations on behalf of the unemployed and Left-wing

---

[i] H. Dalton, *Call Back Yesterday Memoirs 1887–1931*, 1953, pp.199–200.

[ii] A. Bullock, op. cit., 1960, p.53. (My italics.)

[iii] A. Bullock paraphrasing Bevin, op. cit., p.532.

[iv] Bevin to Cole, December 31st, 1935, G. D. H. Cole Papers, Nuffield College.

[v] Cf. D. McHenry, *His Majesty's Opposition 1931–38*, 1938, p.168.

[vi] Cf. chapter on 'Local Branches of the Socialist League'.

[vii] G. Orwell, *The Road to Wigan Pier*, 1966 edn., pp.118–119. See p.380 for the refutation.

'unity'. Throughout the S.L.'s short life, the Party and union national approach was one of compromise and conciliation to present a united Parliamentary alternative. Vacillation on issues such as unemployed demonstrations and a united front (and pragmatism in daily affairs) conflicted with the S.L.'s search for definitive answers to the problems of the age. The S.L.'s dilettantism, indecisiveness, and what union leaders in the 1930s called 'anarchistic tendencies' accentuated this divergence in approach. Its policy resolutions tended to be piecemeal in scope and character, whereas Party and union leaders were dealing with the temporal changes in politics and practical minutiae; platitudes and slogans had to be Party currency if it sought office by appealing to all strata of society; this depended upon political compromise, guile, opportunism, not the S.L.'s extemporised, 'irresponsible but imaginative' modus operandi. The S.L. was not assimilated into that political environment in which bold, independent policies were cloaked in mild-seeming phraseology. This attitude was unrealistic in the 1930s, as I.L.P.'er Clifford Allen stated: 'Day after day, I meet progressive person after progressive person, all having the right ideas, but none of them willing to do anything else other than enjoy their own superiority or caustically criticise their fellow progressives.'[i]

It was a feature of S.L. leaders that they could not accept that anyone opposing the Labour Movement could do so without having 'corrupt motives', or an ignorant belief that Socialism 'would not work', or a fear of the discomforts of the 'revolutionary' period before Socialism had been established. (The conflicts engendered by the Spanish Civil War later began to teach S.L. members about the realities of power politics. At first, that Civil War was a rallying-point for Left-wing intellectuals, but by June 1937 there had been dissensions in the Left in Spain, policy clashes between the I.L.P. and C.P., and knowledge of Soviet trials of old Bolsheviks.) S.L. remonstrations over Austria (1934), Abyssinian independence (1935), the League of Nations (1932–37), Republic support in Spain, against the inadequate treatment for the unemployed, and the 'Fascism' of the National Government – all failed to galvanise official Labour on the lines of the S.L.'s programme. Widespread feeling of ineffectiveness led to disenchantment in the mass Movement; the S.L.'s aspirations represented that 'abortive revolution of the spirit, a false dawn of history'.[ii] For intellectuals it was purgatory. They learnt that the politician was the manipulator, a broker of power, the middleman who bought ideas cheaply and sold demagogy dearly.[iii] The predominant features of S.L. leaders emerged; their essential motivation was 'action', a hypertrophied sense of the need for 'efficiency', a moral dedication blended with ethical idealism, and an acute realisation of what Labour empiricism meant in practice.

---

[i] Clifford Allen Papers, letter to Mr. Curry, December 31st, 1932, quoting Marwick, *Clifford Allen*, 1964, p.142.
[ii] Arthur Koestler, *The Invisible Writing: An Autobiography*, 1954, London, p.241.
[iii] N. Wood, op. cit., p.229. However, as John Strachey noted in *The Theory and Practice of Socialism* (1936), p.457: "for the accomplishment of social change, knowledge is indispensable, but not enough. It is by the courageous, persistent *action* of those who know, that the world can be remade. By wisdom and courage, by patience and audacity … we shall conquer."

DISARMAMENT SITUATION

June 27, 1932

The Disarmament Conference began. The U.S.A. suggested if European nations disarmed they would be better able to pay their debts. European nations replied that if they did not have to extract debts from each other they could disarm. Britain (which had a navy) objected to cutting navies, but didn't mind cutting down armies. France (which had an army) objected to cutting down armies, but didn't mind cutting down navies. Proposals for government control of arms production were defeated – Britain produced a plan for disarmament, Germany remained disarmed.

NEXT BIG FLIGHT

February 20, 1933

Air disarmament was found to be difficult unless the principle of internationalism and the idea of an air police force were accepted. 'Patriotic' interests in various countries opposed both, but expressed their willingness to hope that in future wars no one would drop bombs.

Hitler   EUROPEAN CLOTHES-LINE   Mussolini

May 9, 1933

Signs were early that Nazi Germany had designs on Austria.

CIVILIZATION, 1933

August 1, 1933

A World Economic Conference met to abate the world slump by international collaboration. The Conference asked the U.S.A. to support a reformed gold standard. U.S.A. said no but asked the rest of the world to relax its hidebound nationalism. The Conference ended. After that, all nations dug in for a long winter.[i]

---

[i] All cartoons and comments hereafter by David Low, published by Penguin Books, 1940, *Europe Since Versailles*. Original copyright holder: *London Star, Evening Standard*, Cresset Press Ltd, London; Jonathan Cape Ltd, London; Allen & Unwins Ltd, London; and Simon & Schuster, New York.

(A) The Influence of Marxism on the Socialist League

The Soviet Union's achievements were, to S.L. leaders, a tangible demonstration of Marxist theories in action; two implications of Marx's vision of Socialism were accepted by the S.L. as already part of Soviet structure – absence of the ethics of private property, and belief in dialectical materialism as a guide to thought and practice. In Labour's S.L. the only generation to be *dominated* by Marxism came to political maturity. It was contrary to Labourism's rejection of political theorising, and reluctance to examine its contradictions, but the factors which compelled the S.L.'s allegiance to Marxism were economic depression, two million plus unemployed, thwarting of industrial action, the disappointment of two Labour Governments; rise of Fascism, and exclusion from power of Socialists.[i]

There were specific reasons why it was Marxism which was integrated into the S.L.'s political thinking. It gave systematic coherence, dogmatic comprehensiveness, had a universal applicability, 'it possessed an appropriate response to capitalist society.'[ii] Ideologies were under constant discussion. After the discrediting of gradualist theories of social change S.L. policy-makers turned to the pioneers (Keir Hardie, the Chartists, the Marxists) for their inspiration, and the S.L. was sceptical that Socialism could be achieved through Parliamentary channels and constitutional means; that was an essential aspect of the S.L.'s outlook, an important facet of the intellectual and ideological stirrings of the time.'[iii]

The prominent figures in the Labour Party who were 'Marxist' in outlook joined the S.L.; the working man was the chosen instrument of history, and the rise of Fascism appeared an accurate fulfilment of Marxist prophecy.[iv] Some of the S.L. leaders had been Marxists or neo-Marxists before the 1930s. Others who had been Christian Socialists or Secular Fabians began to question their earlier assumptions concerning Parliamentary democracy and British 'freedoms'. J. T. Murphy (future General Secretary of the S.L.), founder member of the British C.P., had always interpreted political events through a Marxist framework. In *'Why I have joined the S.L.'* he explained it was 'because I am a revolutionary Marxist who is convinced that the working class of this country is facing an oncoming revolutionary crisis in which the Labour Party, of which the S.L. is a part, will be called upon to play a deciding rôle... an ever-increasing number of people of the working class, the middle class and intellectuals are ceasing to have faith in the durability of capitalism.'[v] (The renaissance of 30's Marxism saw a shift from self-educated J. T. Murphy-style workers to university-based intellectuals.)

Marxism exerted a powerful influence on the S.L.'s outlook not only on account of economics and the labour theory of value radically changing society, but also as

---

[i] Cf. B. Magee, *The New Radicalism*, 1962, pp.86–89. G. D. H. Cole wrote in 1933, 'To look around on the world of today with seeing eyes is to be a Marxist, for Marxism alone explains what is going on,' *Plebs* XXV (1933), p.65, qu. S. Macintyre op. cit., 1980, p.94.

[ii] G. Barraclough, *An Introduction to Contemporary History*, 1964, p.208.

[iii] R. Miliband, op. cit., 1961, p.198.

[iv] M. Foot, *A. Bevan – A Biography*, Vol. 1, 1962, p.196.

[v] J. T. Murphy, *New Clarion*, April 15th, 1933. On May 10th it was reported Nazis were burning 'Marxist books'.

providing a philosophy for S.L. idealists *and* S.L. disciplinarians. These two types of S.L. member fused in their appreciation of Marxism. For the idealists, Marxist socialism was a formula for implementing ideals, yet they were also aware that the Marxist view of social structure diagnosed the faults that provoked discontent, poverty, oppression, and industrial decay. By unmasking inconsistencies in British 'democracy' and 'freedom', it looked to the future positively. For the disciplinarians, Marxism was a method of analysing class, state and politics and a technique, the most important machine 'to think with' that Socialists could have at their disposal.[i] It was also a stick with which to beat Labour empiricists: 'We have been opportunists too long and we need a vital stiffening of doctrine… Such a discipline for Socialists can begin only with Marx,'[ii] opined S.L. leader, H. L. Elvin. S.L. policy-makers lauded the importance of Marxism as a science of human change. One S.L. reviewer claimed S.L. members should study John Strachey's *The Nature of Capitalist Crisis* because it gave a 'brilliant and crystal exposition of Marx's labour theory of value, and passed through the illusions of capitalist recovery.[iii] Illusions! Another S.L. member asserted that clearing the road to Socialism demanded a political science; a guide to action, of the experience of the working class; a knowledge (such as economics and history could give) of the growth and development of human society, of the way in which it had solved its past problems, of its failures and successes, and the forces at work within society: 'We need to make the utmost use of those who have *hammered out on the anvil* of a struggle, industrial, political and theoretical, the principles which should guide the actions of the world's workers in the colossal struggle for Socialism'.[iv]

Marxism was a 1930s contribution by the S.L. to the Labour Party; Marxism, the key to social action, the tool of politics, with a group inside the Party who posited the notion of a 'class struggle' if a Socialist transformation was to be realised. The S.L.'s views were taken seriously, as can be observed by the C.P.'s frenetic attempt to render its impact ineffective. Palme Dutt reflected on the S.L.'s *'Marxism in Caricature'*: 'The reformist illusions of the 'inevitability of gradualness' came a heavy crash in 1931. The vindication of Marxism is established with greater power at every turn of history. The Labour theorists now all 'recognise' Marx and 'adapt him'.[v] However, 1932 to 1937 remains the only period before the 1960s (with the Socialist Labour League, the Young Socialist Movement, and the prospect of a Marxist Party) when the C.P. feared competition from a rival revolutionary Marxist Party. Much of the C.P.'s activity in these years represented the aggregate of measures to prevent this possibility from becoming a reality.

What was there in Marxist works which compelled the S.L. to cling so strongly to theories founded more than 60 years before, endeavouring, as it appeared to the uncommitted, to make a 19th century ideology fit 20th century facts? The S.L. believed in the vision of a New Jerusalem; Marxism *was* a philosophy for a time of *crisis*, and justified the S.L.'s raison d'être, an attempt to give the Labour Party principles and

[i] H. L. Elvin (S.L. National Council member), reviewing G. D. H.Cole's 'What Marx Really Meant', *Socialist Leaguer*, No. 2, July–August 1934.

[ii] H. L. Elvin, ibid. The hallmark of Marxist tradition is a stubborn intransigence, rejection of mores and institutions of the existing social order, and suspicions about the respectable path to social reform, cf. S. Macintyre, op. cit., 1980, p.3.

[iii] D. R. Davies, *Socialist Leaguer*, No. 11, May 1935.

[iv] 'Jacques', 'Science, Not Rule of Thumb', *Socialist*, No. 1, September 1935. (My italics.)

[v] P. Dutt, *Labour Monthly*, Vol. 16, No. 7, July 1934.

faith with which to oppose the Government. L. A. Fenn[i] argued the Movement had never attended carefully to its fundamental aims: 'A movement with lots of ideals and no adequate philosophy is like a motor-car with a powerful engine and no steering gear. It proceeds at high speed, but with complete indifference to direction';[ii] only critical appraisal of Socialist ideals in the light of 'general principles' would suffice for the Party. He expressed a basic S.L. tenet: 'the working Socialist needs to cultivate fundamental ideas as a guide to action and an anchor to keep him steady in a crisis'.[iii] The S.L.'s journal, the *Socialist Leaguer,* saw structural organisation and conditions of production as determinants of class relationships, simplified class attitudes into 'owners versus workers', and diagnosed a scarcity economy ruling lives by relentless pressure of material needs and deprivation. Social relations were determined mainly by the growth or stagnation of production, status of property ownership, with economic 'interests' as the stratifying influence. It was from Marxist analysis (before Foucault) that the S.L inherited the belief that since all economic relationships were central, society was governed by 'naked power'. The S.L. judged that Marx anticipated economic dislocations (such as the crisis of 1931) where the market operated in an unplanned economy; he had 'proved' that, in politics, economics was the key. For the S.L. such a theory made sense when applied to conditions in the 1930s and brought an optimism in its corollary, that the historical development of capitalism *produced* conditions which paved the way for a Socialist society. Through S.L. policies and pamphlets runs the refrain that the soul of capitalist production (the drive for profit) could never be stabilised. It had to expand or die.

'Historical materialism' was incorporated into the S.L.'s Weltanschauung to explain major political and cultural changes in terms of the development in the mode of economic production. Although this conflicted with the interpretation of the Soviet Union's economic changes (which had been achieved through political action), Marxism was the most notable attempt to work out evolutionary ideas in the realm of social science.[iv] The S.L. saw positive aspects of Marxist interpretations; man as the active agent in the historical process; the working class able to paralyse the economy by a general strike, social inequalities 'eliminated' by socialisation of instruments of production; the chief actors in the drama of history were economic classes, society was a moral organism – these became the S.L.'s credo, illustrated in Cripps' book *Why this Socialism?* (1934), highly moral in tone. Cripps here discussed the need to build a 'conscious, all-inclusive, working-class party,'[v] because there was no real freedom until economic equality was in operation,[vi] while the cause of internal strife was economic. He attacked unplanned savings, the haphazard exchange of commodities, myth of over-production and the scarcity of planning in 'capitalism', classifying war as the outcome of economic competition, 'Capitalist Imperialism' responsible for war[vii] and

---

[i] A member of the S.L. National Council.

[ii] L. A. Fenn, 'We Must Use Our Heads', *New Clarion*, February 10th, 1934.

[iii] Ibid.

[iv] A. L. Rowse, *The Use of History*, 1963 edn., p.103. The historical materialist view that ideology was socially produced was inconsistent with the conspiratorial view that it was class produced, cf. S. Macintyre, op. cit. (1980), pp.106–126.

[v] Cripps, *Why This Socialism?*, 1934, p.14.

[vi] Ibid., p.16–69, 'Marxism was oppositional, dwelling on the defects of the existing order. Its reputation was that of the troublemaker, the rebel, the hardcase', S. Macintyre, op. cit. p.58.

[vii] Ibid., p.41.

class antagonism a product of the social and economic structure of the capitalist system.[i]

Marxism implied for the S.L. the public ownership and control of large-scale industry and finance necessary for the taming of 'naked power', the message implicit in the theory that a point was reached in every society that was not a Socialist society in which the existing economic structure hampered the full use of the productive forces existing within it and the monopoly of capital became a fetter upon the mode of production.[ii] Leading S.L. member William Mellor saw this primary issue as the *problem of power*, of uprooting the power of those class-interests which blocked the road to progress, of storming their key-positions and dislodging them[iii] (not unlike the Bolsheviks storming the Winter Palace). The S.L. judged social institutions by their effects on everyday working lives. The Communist Manifesto, with its understanding of the history of all hitherto-existing society as the history of class struggles, and capitalism as the last expression of class rule, was reflected in the S.L.'s watchword of 'class struggle': 'The working class fight against imperialist war must not be separated from the whole gamut of the class struggle. War is the continuation of politics by other means... the struggle against war is the struggle against the classes which rule society and which hold under their control all the productive forces and all the weapons of destruction.'[iv] The Marxist asked: Which class was conducting the war? In whose hands were the weapons? The S.L. member concluded that only when the means of production and of State power were in the hands of workers, would the creation of forces for defence be supported by revolutionary Socialists.[v]

Endeavouring to play its part in the daily work of the Movement, the S.L. thus demanded a consideration of *how* to transform a defensive struggle with capitalism into a relentless challenge to the existing order.[vi] J. T. Murphy summed up the effect of Marxist teaching on the S.L. in reviewing *'Dialectics – the Logic of Marxism'* by T. A. Jackson. Murphy explained that it was upon the S.L.'s understanding of dialectical materialism that depended the reading of history, and that upon these depended S.L. policies. He concluded that capitalism would be 'smashed', because the 'contradictions' within it had become incompatible with the further development of society, and because, by the very development of its contradictions, the revolutionary class within it becomes incapable of ending the system and synthesising the contradictions in Socialism.[vii] Whatever that meant in practice.

All the books which emerged on Marx, his philosophy, his 'message' were reviewed in the S.L. monthly journal, and similar conclusions were drawn. In a review of H. R. G. Greaves' *Reactionary England*, stress was on the 'fundamental Marxist thesis' it illustrated.[viii] H. N. Brailsford described Marx as the greatest human creative force of

---

[i] Ibid., p.44.

[ii] Karl Marx, *Capital*, 1961 edn., Moscow, Vol. 1, Chapter 32, p.763. The S.L. grounded its Marxism in a mechanical version of the materialist conception of history which 'demonstrated' the dominance of the 'economic factor', cf. S. Macintyre, op. cit., 1980, p.17.

[iii] Mellor reviewing Maurice Dobb's *Social Credit Discredited*, *Socialist*, No. 6, April 1935.

[iv] 'Jacques', 'A Marxist Looks at War and Its Causes', *Socialist*, No. 6, April 1936.

[v] Ibid.

[vi] S.L. News, 'Who Said Archangels?', *New Clarion*, August 26th, 1933.

[vii] J. T. Murphy, *Socialist*, No. 8, June 1936.

[viii] D. R. Davies, review, *Socialist*, No. 9, July–August 1936.

his century:[i] Marx had delineated the rôle of the intellectual in the Socialist Movement; it was partly for that he was the inspiration for the S.L. Marxism was envisaged as a religion, Socialism adhered to as a cause and a faith, just as the revolutionary character of Christ was upheld against the institutionalised church: 'It is only by a social revolution which clears the way to a new order that the Church can be true to its own Founder.... Communism is the declared enemy of institutionalised religion, but the strongest ally of the human spirit.'[ii] Discuss! So, 'Marxism' provided the S.L. with a general ideological outlook, its theories, its comprehensive approach to problems. This led to suspicion and subsequent denigration of the S.L. The Movement aimed to create a social service State, a greater equalisation of wealth through economic planning but only the S.L. within the Party assented to these aims, thinking them unattainable within 'the existing economic framework'. Anti-doctrinal theories and electoralism prevented Labour leaders from countenancing the S.L.'s plea for a thorough-going analysis to explain the catastrophe (which was engulfing the market economy). Yet, the Party's pragmatism was a philosophy[iii]; what perturbed the Labour Party was use of Marxist language which would bring 'unpopularity' to the Party,[iv] which would lose votes.

For Labour theorists, the only alternative to the Party programme was the use of 'half-baked Marxian jargon and elaboration of revolutionary proposals without the organisation of a revolutionary force'.[v] This, for E. F. M. Durbin, was a sickening intellectual spectacle[vi], while Milne-Bailey regarded the habit of expressing everything in Marxian terminology as a conventional gesture, a concession to good form; wearing the old Marxian tie, they were nevertheless Social-Democrats![vii] G. B. Shaw, writing to F. Brockway, expressed what many Party officials felt, but did not say, when he complained that the jargon which resulted from attempts to translate Marx into English haunted Socialist literature: 'You feel bound to use the old Marxian catchword 'revolutionary' as often as possible. When you have frightened off enough people with it, you will have to explain that it means just nothing?'[viii]

The problem in the S.L.'s Marxist stance was that British politics had become more complex; political theory, transformed into ideology, was a rationalisation of economic interest, ideas became tools of manipulation for propagandists, and Party criticism of Marxist economic doctrine was that it had been elaborated when the science of economics was in an imperfect state (and could not appeal to the electorate in the 1930s). Douglas Jay explained that, 'to most people', the materialist conception of history meant the only human motives were for pleasure, self-interest or economic advantage but that: 'Reason and idealism are just as essential to the Socialist cause as propaganda and money'. He was prepared to concede that the injustice of an uncontrolled price system and unearned incomes was the economic strength of Marxist doctrine but its weakness was its faulty analysis of value and profits, and

---

[i] H. N. Brailsford reviewing Franz Mehring's *Karl Marx*, *Socialist*, No. 8, June 1936.

[ii] D. R. Davies reviewing *Christianity and Social Revolution*, ed. by Dr. J. Lewis, K. Polanyi, etc. *Socialist*, No. 3, December 1935.

[iii] B. Russell, *Power*, 1938, p.174.

[iv] G. Orwell, *The Road to Wigan Pier*, 1966 edn., p.201.

[v] E. F. M. Durbin, 'Democracy and Socialism in Britain', *Political Quarterly*, July–September 1935.

[vi] Ibid. There was a narrow doctrinal rigidity in the British Marxism of the 1930s.

[vii] W. Milne-Bailey, 'The Strategy of Victory', chapter 14, *New Trends in Socialism*, ed. G. E. G. Catlin, 1935.

[viii] G. B. Shaw letter to F. Brockway, qu. in *Inside the Left*, 1942, p.245.

assertion that capitalism was *inevitably doomed* for some fundamental economic reason.[i]

A further clash arose between the S.L. and Party officials because of the use of Marxist interpretations by the S.L. to expose the ineffectuality of Parliamentarianism. In a review of Attlee's *The Will and the Way to Socialism*, A. Austen (for the S.L.) described the book as a simple essay on 'idealist Socialism' in which mention of the materialist conception of history and the class struggle was as far as possible *avoided*; the distinction drawn between capitalist and socialist planning was *unclear*, and there was no realisation of the impossibility of capitalist planning without transformation of the state into a totalitarian dictatorship! Austen also queried Attlee's description of the Empire as 'imperialism in the process of development into a commonwealth'[ii], but Attlee was to be proved right. Despite the S.L.'s determination to remain in the Party, it presented a difference in outlook between itself and the rest of the Party, centring around the Marxist analysis of the State. S.L. speakers concentrated on the class character of the State and the need to construct a state machine to effect the Socialist transformation,[iii] and in the S.L.'s frame of reference, 'the State' did not mean the machinery of a Parliamentary majority, but an organisation corresponding to the interests of the dominant class: 'Are we to have the old machinery of government, saturated with routine and inertia, and connected by thousands of threads with the capitalist class, or should it be broken up and replaced be something altogether new?'[iv] Even unions were represented by the S.L. as bodies in a State-controlled, regulated, profit-producing, profit-orientated industry. The S.L. was also handicapped by its sinister visions of the 'Fascist' menace at home.[v] It did not develop its theory of Socialist change beyond socialisation and changes in power, status and privilege, did not analyse the possibility of a mixed economy, and underestimated the regenerative power of capitalism to overcome its own crises, as well as the economic influence of union action. Its veneration of Marxism and the industrial achievement of the Soviet Union had a peculiarly adverse effect on the S.L.'s potential converts; Marxists concentrated on letting economic cats out of ideological bags, Socialism bound up with the idea of machine production, a completely mechanised, organised, ordered and efficient world'.[vi]

Accentuating the difference and the 'pace' of proposed Socialist reform set the S.L. against the Party. The S.L. proposed emergency powers (which the Press and Labour leaders dubbed 'dictatorial measures'). As late as April 1936, a letter appeared in *The Socialist* demanding that the S.L. not relinquish efforts to win Socialism *by constitutional means, utilisation of Parliament as a weapon in the class struggle, rather than conform to the static interpretation of Marxism*, although the writer was aware that Marxism was an analysis in movement, the application of which had to vary with objective conditions. Rosa Luxemburg had written: 'Without General Elections, without unrestricted freedom of the Press and assembly, without a free struggle of opinion, life dies out in every public

---

[i] Douglas Jay, 'The Economic Strength and Weakness of Marxism', *New Trends in Socialism*.

[ii] A. Austen, review, *Socialist Leaguer*, No. 12, June 1935. The adoption of a materialist view undermined Labourism because it promoted a fuller class awareness. It showed that 'organisation at the point of production or election to Parliament was not the limit of working-class emancipation but only a first step to power,' cf. S. Macintyre, op. cit., 1980, p.126.

[iii] Nancy R. Gray, letter to *Socialist*, No. 5, March 1936.

[iv] 'Jacques', 'The State and Socialism', *Socialist*, No. 4, January–February 1936.

[v] H. Dalton, *The Fateful Years, Memoirs (1931–45)*, autobiography, Vol. 2, 1957, p.43.

[vi] G. Orwell, op. cit., 1966 edn., pp.164–66, 169, 176.

institution... the dictatorship of the proletariat... consists in the *manner* of applying democracy, not in the elimination'.[i] The S.L. as a pressure group remained 'Marxist' in tone. The new *Tribune* policy in 1937 with a board composed of many S.L. members, was uncompromisingly Socialist, based on the knowledge that 'true liberty' had to be founded on economic freedom and that, in countries where the capitalist system prevailed, the central fact in social life was the class struggle'.[ii] For S.L. policy-makers, that struggle arose from the exploitation that divided nations into classes, bred poverty and unemployment, and was the mainspring of war. However, their application of Marxism to the contemporary situation offered little as to *how*, through their political methods, Britain would move from Capitalism to Socialism, how to reconcile Socialist commitment with regular political practice. But allow a great American writer to explain what this experience signified in the 1930s. Here is Arthur Miller:

> Through Marxism you extended your affection to the human race. The emptiness of days filled with a maturing purpose – the deepening crisis of capitalism, bursting into the new age, the inexorable approach of nirvana. It was the last of the foregoing philosophies. The deeds of the present, the moment, had no intrinsic importance, but only counted insofar as they brought closer or held back the coming of the new. Man-as-sacrifice was its essence; heroism was what mattered. We were in the Last Days, all signs pointed to Apocalypse. Self was anathema, a throwback; individual people were dematerialized... wherever Marx's vision had taken root. Joy was coming – no matter what... in truth a religious sweep was central to everything one felt, an utter renewal of mankind, nothing less. The mystic element was usually elided... because to share Marx was to feel contempt for all irrationality. It was capitalism that was irrational, religious, obscure... and Hitler was its screaming archangel.[iii]

(B) The Russian Revolution, Leninism, Stalinism, and the Socialist League

The prospects of the Soviet Union weighed heavily on the S.L.'s ministrations and coloured its attitudes towards the political, economic and social world. Of 63 books reviewed in S.L. journals between July 1934 and July 1936, 46 dealt with aspects of the Soviet Union, Lenin and Marxism (the majority concentrated on economic achievements and plans). They were reviewed by J. T. Murphy and J. F. Horrabin with contributions from H. L. Elvin, L. A. Fenn and Reg Groves. The choice of books reviewed shows the S.L.'s preoccupations and how the Soviet Union had come to affect S.L. perceptions of problems in the 1930s. Lenin had (for the S.L.) introduced into theory and practice the order, method and authority hitherto the prerogative of Governments; the S.L. translated his thesis that without revolutionary theory there can be no revolutionary movement, and the prerequisite of political action was a compact

---

[i] R. Luxemburg, *The Russian Revolution*, 1940 edn., pp.47–54.

[ii] S.L. Notes, editorial, *Socialist*, No. 13, December 1936–January 1937.

[iii] Arthur Miller, *Echoes Down the Corridor*, 2000, pp.129–130 (original edn.1973); 'Marxists offered remedies, including cross-class alliances and an empowering solidarity across nations. Here was the uplifting sense that one could change what had seemed essential and escape from 'the ghettos'. This energised efforts to create a socialist culture within the shell of capitalism,' cf. Caren Irr, *The Suburb of Dissent: Cultural Politics in the US and Canada during the 1930s*, 1998, p.100.

core, a revolutionary élite. The educative, organising rôle of this élite appealed to S.L. leaders when 'gradualism' was paralysing European Socialism.

Turning to the experience of the Russian Revolution, the S.L. questioned the possibility of Socialism by peaceful and legal means in a hostile political environment: 'Lenin insisted that the aim of a Socialist Party was not to fight for a 'pure' social revolution... but to mobilise all sections of the workers and petty bourgeoisie, no matter how heterogeneous, discordant, motley and incohesive so long as they would attack Capitalism'.[i] This gave credence to the S.L.'s strategy to unite the Left and the Labour Party against the Government. 'Leninism' as an active doctrine of change inspired the S.L. with a mission to challenge the existing social order and liberal democracy. The Russian Revolution also inspired in the S.L. an ethical concern for *social justice*, because it seemed universal in its approach and appeal.[ii]

To counteract the 'bankruptcy' of capitalist society, inadequacies of reformist Labourism, the miseries of long-term unemployment, the S.L. saw in the revolutionary experimentation of the Soviet Union hope for the future in Britain. Although this vision proved illusory as the 1930s progressed, it sustained the S.L. in campaigns to radicalise the Labour Party; Lenin's insistence on doctrinal integrity, his refusal to compromise, his grasp of essentials, his revolutionary will[iii] evoked virtues for the individual Socialist. He had applied Marxism to the specific conditions of Russia. (Lansbury, political father figure to Cripps, thought Lenin's strength came because he was impersonal; in the pursuit of the cause of Socialism, he could not be thwarted; he was not the 'boss' of Russia but the inspiring spirit and had devoted his life to the destruction of Capitalism)[iv]. Leninist orthodoxy was relied upon as a substitute for debate. From the Soviet experience, the S.L. created a policy for the conversion of representative institutions; the importance of retaining and using legal democratic rights, to take the bourgeoisie at their word and utilise the apparatus they had set up. Hence, the S.L. was to champion (in the Labour Party), support for C.P. membership to the Party (Lenin had insisted that the C.P. join the Labour Party because British workers were imbued with faith in Parliament, and the only way the minority could secure leadership was by participation in the Parliamentary struggle[v]). Leninism became the application of Marxist theory and practice. In such ways, the S.L. justified its function in the confines of the Party.

S.L. literature established that issues of modern politics turned upon 'class power'; Socialism could not be achieved unless the working class secured power over the essential parts of the economic apparatus; the problem was one of securing maximum public assent and co-operation, so the S.L. put its faith in the use of a parliamentary majority backed by the industrial power of workers.[vi] 'A vanguard of determined Socialists working within the Constitutional Movement'[vii] was what the S.L. cultivated.

---

[i] John Lewis, 'Leninism and the Labour Party', *Socialist Leaguer*, November–December 1934.

[ii] Cf. G. Barraclough, 'The Ideological Challenge', *An Introduction to Contemporary History*, 1964. Winston Churchill warned in June 1919 of the dangers of an international "league of the failures, the criminals, the unfit, the mutinous, the morbid, the deranged and the distraught in every land." (qu. G. C. Lebzelter, *Political Anti-Semitism in England, 1918–1939*, 1978, p.17.)

[iii] G. Barraclough, op. cit., p.211.

[iv] Quoting R. Postgate, *The Life of G. Lansbury*, 1951, pp.205–206.

[v] Cf. John Lewis, 'Leninism and the Labour Party', in *Socialist Leaguer*, November–December 1934.

[vi] L. A. Fenn, review of R. Fox, *Communism*, in *Socialist*, No. 2, November 1935.

[vii] J. F. Horrabin, reviewing R. Postgate's *How to Make a Revolution*, in *Socialist Leaguer*, No. 7, December 1934.

The Russian Revolution meant to the S.L. a new way of analysing society, having brought 'modern civilisation' to 'backward' people, and self-government for agrarian people through the Soviet system of collective farms. The Revolution demonstrated that Socialism *could* work, even under the most unpromising conditions, and seemed to have suggested *one* solution of the conflict between economic planning and political liberty. That Russians had gone through horrific sacrifices to devote their productive energy at the expense of consuming *increased* the worth of their system in the eyes of the S.L.: 'We in this country should not have to take such steps and could therefore immediately increase our volume of consumable commodities and so raise the standard of living'.[i] To the S.L., the Soviet system 'proved' that private enterprise was incompatible with the demand of the average citizen for freedom from want and fear. National planning, full employment, and universal economic security demonstrated that the common people could take power and run the State effectively (or so the S.L. was prepared to believe). When hope was at its lowest in the British Labour Movement, the Russian Revolution symbolised a gigantically successful achievement for the poor and oppressed.[ii] Its immediate relevance to the conditions of the 1930s *seemed to be* freedom from unemployment and exploitation, opportunity for all, State care for children, education and health, and disappearance of false money values and parasitism.[iii]

Another potent characteristic which the S.L. endorsed was that 'Soviet democracy' was economic in character, a new angle on 'freedom'. Here was an apparent efficiency of organisation which reached Socialism through proletarian discipline without passing through all the stages of capitalism[iv] (so it was claimed). S.L. leaders thought that a new principle of order had been instigated. Bold solutions, a willingness to cut through tangles, a dynamic belief in itself, raised the Soviet C.P. above the cautious pragmatism and crippling respect for entrenched interests in the West. Was it unrealistic to believe that something similar was possible here? The S.L.'s judgement concentrated on the beneficial effects of the amalgamation of political and economic power,[v] and a vision of a Socialist society. Thus, the S.L. stood for economic orderliness, achieved in the Soviet fusion of the ideals of 'modern democracy' and modern 'scientific intelligence' – as it appeared to the S.L., captivated by Russian culture: 'True equality bring with it opportunity for the full development of character and culture ... the most distinctive feature of Russian civilisation today is the astounding progress in culture amongst the mass of the people.'[vi] The Soviet Union was exemplar and guide. In direct cognisance of the Bolsheviks, Tawney spoke of a majority Labour Government of the future supported by 'a body at once dynamic and antiseptic, the energumens, the zealots, the Puritans, the religious orders, the C.P., whichever possesses, not merely opinions but convictions, and acts as it believes.'[vii] Disturbing implications from Tawney.

Following the 1931 débâcle, the Labour Party was advised to uphold 'class war', because 'one of the most populous and potentially wealthy countries has put into

---

[i] Cripps, letter, December 11th, 1934, Cripps Papers.

[ii] C. Hill, *Lenin and the Russian Revolution*, 1947 (1965 edn.), pp.236–38.

[iii] Cf. John Lewis, *The Left Book Club*, p.109.

[iv] Cf. E. H. Carr, *The Bolshevik Revolution*, p.36.

[v] B. Russell, *Power*, 1938, p.80.

[vi] Cripps in letter to Mr. Campbell, December 14th, 1934, Cripps Papers.

[vii] R. H. Tawney, 'The Choice Before the Labour Party', *Political Quarterly*, July–September 1932.

practice the Socialist theory ... Soviet Russia is with astonishing rapidity transforming itself according to Socialist principles'.[i] Wishful thinking, but for the S.L., one of the great achievements seemed the elimination of division between 'worker' and 'intellectual',[ii] so illusory in the British Movement. At root, the appeal of the new Soviet State was its attack on capitalism. The S.L. expressed this in exposure of 'sham liberties', 'spurious freedoms' of the free market economy. In contrast to the philosophy of acquisition through competition, inevitable social strife, economic crises, and war for new markets, Soviet Russia seemed the harbinger of the Left's long-frustrated hopes; it had weathered foreign intervention by capitalist countries; the inexorable laws of capitalist economics seemed to have been broken. Perversely, the S.L. idealised Soviet achievement *because* Britain had been saturated with accounts of the Bolshevik nightmare of unbridled anarchy, Comintern plots and allegations of C.P.G.B. plots to incite mutinies in the services and strikes in the ranks of labour.[iii]

Had the S.L. existed until 1940, it would probably have formulated a neo-Trotskyist position with regard to the Soviet Union. As it was, there *were* criticisms of the Soviet single party system which seemed 'un-Socialist', but no other reservations. There was never any discussion in S.L. journals about the reality of proletarian dictatorship, Soviet democracy or workers' control of industry. Information did not seem to be available, and it seemed quibbling when there were crucial issues of unemployment and the prospect of war. By the time S.L. members began questioning Soviet 'successes', unity was uppermost in the British Left, and uncertainties remained unresolved. Instead, the Five Year Plans provided evidence for the economically-minded S.L. that Soviet society was in a *healthier* state than Britain. It impressed far less militant Party members such as Hugh Dalton: 'The main objects of planning in the Soviet Union are to avoid the economic crises and trade fluctuations of Capitalism, to keep the whole working population in continuous employment and to raise their standard of living without permitting the growth of large inequalities, to a level higher than that of the workers in Capitalist countries, to achieve a large measure of economic self-sufficiency and to stimulate to the utmost the industrialisation of the country.[iv] Soviet Russia was the utopia for the S.L. on grounds of economic efficiency. The 'Workers' State' had become the model of a 'planned economy'.[v]

No one was more 'friendly to the Soviet Union'[vi] than D. N. Pritt (a member of the S.L. until 1936). It had for him a wealth of spirit and hope and gave a marvellous contrast to the flat pessimism of slump-ridden Western Europe.[vii] After visiting Russia, he returned to Britain with a newly-found political consciousness, a conviction that the private ownership of the means of production of unearned wealth and the ruling-class had to be radically changed, optimistic that Britain could build a Socialist State with its material wealth, its industrial basis and great number of skilled workers.[viii] This

---

[i] G. Lowes Dickinson, 'The Essential Issue', *Political Quarterly*, October–December 1931.

[ii] H. L. Elvin, review of Professor A. Pinkevitch, *Science and Education in the U.S.S.R.*, *Socialist Leaguer*, July–August 1935.

[iii] Lord Templewood, *Nine Troubled Years*, 1954, p.35. An Act banning Soviet imports was passed on April 19th 1933.

[iv] H. Dalton, *Twelve Studies in Soviet Russia*, 1933, p.31.

[v] A. J. P. Taylor, 'Confusion on the Left', *The Baldwin Age*, 1960.

[vi] D. N. Pritt, *From Right to Left*, autobiography, Vol. 1, 1965, p.28.

[vii] Ibid., op. cit., p.37. cf. H. Johnson 'The Socialist Sixth of the World', 1939, Left Book Club.

[viii] Ibid., op. cit., p.39.

growing regard for the Soviet Union's industrial planning achievements became a central part of the S.L. outlook, a framework from which to criticise British 'stagnation'. S.L.'ers found the apotheosis of all values in 'planning', application of science and reason to the reconstruction of society, and what was perceived as the 'moral dynamism' of Soviet leaders. Every progressive was interested in Soviet Russia; with an army of permanent unemployed at home and no prospect of a Government with a constructive policy, the Soviet claim to have 'cured unemployment' and to have a national plan of development, could not be ignored: 'Here was no industrial depression, no inescapable 'trade cycle', no limp surrender to the law of supply and demand. Here there was an unceasing industrial upsurge based on a planned Socialist economy... People in Russia were paying a tremendous price for industrialisation. But in Durham they were paying a tremendous price for nothing at all except unemployment.'[i] S.L.'ers agreed with Dalton's analysis, conscious that there might not be political freedom, but there never had been under the Czars, and perhaps, this 'freedom' had been over-valued relative to economic freedoms? Nothing more galvanised the S.L. than to witness efforts of the Soviet élite to modernise a vast, superstitious and conservative peasantry.

Largely through the S.L., Soviet Russia entered into the consciousness of the non-Communist Left in Britain. To the S.L., Soviet Russia was moved by a moral purpose and spiritual power which capitalism was unable to generate, exemplified in an S.L. assessment in May 1935: 'The Soviet Union, alone in the world, is building the new city of economic justice, firm in the knowledge that they build on a basis of economic planning... Russia today stands, bidding us... grapple with our own Capitalism'.[ii] Books reviewed in the S.L. journals described the conditions of Soviet workers, education, housing, technical training, standards of living, agriculture, electrification and the first Five Year Plan,[iii] workers' control, new towns, transformation of village life, the coming of a classless society, the liberation of women, Socialist democracy in practice,[iv] the new Moscow, collective farming, Soviet justice,[v] and how the U.S.S.R. had become 'a highly integrated social organisation in which over a vast area, each individual man, woman and youth is expected to participate in three separate capacities, as a citizen, as a producer, and as a consumer'.[vi] The S.L. had swallowed the Soviet myth whole.

In Britain the new consciousness of 'planning' was partially a result of the impact of Soviet practice and achievement. Just as production statistics became the thought and life of Soviet society, so the S.L. became galvanised by economics and 'planning'. For this reason, the S.L. was blind to the fact that for the sake of production, some fundamental tenets of Bolshevism had been sacrificed. Instead, the S.L. lauded the

---

[i] H. Dalton, *The Fateful Years, Memoirs (1931–45)*, 1957, p.43.

[ii] S.L. statement, 'Everywhere in Europe Is Naked Class War', *Socialist Leaguer*, No. 11, May 1935.

[iii] M. McCarthy, reviewing W. P. & Z. Coates, 'The Second Five Year Plan', *Socialist Leaguer*, No. 7, December 1934.

[iv] J. T. Murphy, reviewing Sir C. Trevelyan, *Soviet Russia*, in *Socialist*, No. 3, December 1935.

[v] T. C., reviewing M. R. Masani, *Social Sidelights*, in *Socialist*, No. 9, July–August 1936. On August 25th after a five-day 'show trial', 16 Bolsheviks were executed, including Zinoviev and Kamenev.

[vi] M. F., reviewing S. & B. Webb, *Soviet Communism: Dictatorship or Democracy?*, in *Socialist*, No. 12, November 1936.

trebling of Soviet industrial output, an economic growth rate of 9%, and the majority of the S.L. leaders regarded the industrialising perspectives of the Stalinist leadership as 'economically revolutionary'. Stalin's interpretation of Marxism-Leninism had seemingly been applied to productive planning, military strategy and management. However, contrary to the S.L.'s expectations, it was in the fields of social policy and education, not wealth and productivity, where the Soviet Union was to offer a lead.

Officially the S.L. believed that the Soviet Union had accomplished a political revolution hardly less momentous than that which it had achieved in the economic field. Thus the S.L. endeavoured to expose 'one of the most odious of recent capitalist sophistries... the attempt to put Nazi Germany and Soviet Russia under precisely the same ban'.[i] Unofficially, many S.L. members voiced the contradictions between a potentially egalitarian economic structure and dictatorial political system (which had never been an expression of workers' democracy). This outlook[ii] was not voiced in S.L. journals, though it was implied by the S.L.'s General Secretary, J. T. Murphy, in a review of Trotsky's *History of the Russian Revolution*.[iii] Murphy assessed Trotsky's controversies with the bureaucracy of the Soviet C.P. of which there were foreshadowings even in 1917. He quoted Trotsky: 'The conditions of war and revolution would not allow the Party a long period for fulfilling its mission,' and added 'this fragment has a moral much nearer home'.[iv] In June 1936, this Trotskyist position was echoed in the *Socialist*: 'To the Right we are 'revolutionaries gone mad', to the one-time Left 'betrayers of the Soviet Union...' through it all the S.L. has maintained its propaganda and increased its influence'[v] and in the last monthly issued by the S.L., there was an advertisement for the inaugural meeting of the 'Marxist Group (Trotskyist) for December 16th, 1936 at Memorial Hall'!'[vi] On December 8th, 1923, Trotsky had written his open letter stating democracy inside the Bolshevik Party would never come through the efforts of the Party machine until the bureaucrats stifling criticism had less power.[vii] By 1937, the S.L.'s approach to the Soviet Union was to give general but critical support. A legislative change might be misleading unless the actual administrative tendencies were constantly and critically watched',[viii] was the S.L.'s final position.

The response to Stalinism was one of the factors splitting the Labour Movement and the S.L. was inextricably implicated. The British Press was able to present the uncertainty of the Labour Movement on this issue; cult of the individual, crude privilege, anti-egalitarianism, and omnipotence of the police, could hardly be accepted by the S.L. as the results of Stalin's ascendancy. The S.L. had become accustomed to the denigration of the Soviet system in Britain but faith in the vision of a collective Party 'will' prevented most S.L. leaders from arguing that the will of the Party was becoming the personal whim of one man. If the 'proletarian State' proved to be a 'bureaucratic despotism', the S.L. saw no hope and no vision. While Soviet bureaucracy, Party hierarchy, and military personnel were coming to dominate, the

[i] M. F., ibid., November 1936.
[ii] F. Brockway, *Inside the Left*, 1942, p.262.
[iii] J. T. Murphy, *Socialist Leaguer*, No. 5, October–November 1934.
[iv] Ibid.
[v] Editor, 'Matters of Moment', *Socialist*, No. 8, June 1936.
[vi] *Socialist*, No. 13, December 1936–January 1937.
[vii] Quoting L. Schapiro, *The Communist Party of the Soviet Union*, 1960, p.280.
[viii] K. Martin, *New Statesman and Nation*, November 6th, 1937.

S.L. emphasised public ownership, laws against accumulating wealth, and abolition of inherited wealth.[i]

So, the S.L. as a Socialist pressure group classified disquieting features in Russia as 'errors' or 'temporary difficulties' which would disappear when the economic basis of society was 'fully socialised'. No part of the super-structure of society, no political, ethical or moral feature could conflict with the ultimate aims of the Revolution. In this, the S.L. became a victim of its vision, which it had projected onto the Soviet system. O.G.P.U.'s war against the peasantry, arrests, deportations, confiscations and trials (1933–34) to find scapegoats for industrial and agricultural shortcomings,[ii] depictions of Trotsky, Kamenev, Zinoviev and Bukharin as 'bourgeois agents' – none of these appear in any S.L. writings. There was no recognition that the 'working class' in the Soviet Union was fragmented and unable to find a social-political identity. The S.L. was blinded by public social services, collective not individualistic activities, educational not escapist forms of culture, the accent on social distribution rather than private acquisition.

Meanwhile, British Labour and union leaders were concerned about presenting a responsible alternative to the National Government. Soviet 'Socialism' was denigrated as extreme and impractical for a Parliamentary democracy, and presented as fanatical élitism, conjuring up 'Bolshevik commissars (half-gangster, half gramophone), shock-headed Marxists chewing polysyllables and machine-worship'.[iii] The doctrinaire elements in the S.L. were blamed for Press claims that the Labour Party condoned Soviet methods. In fact, the absence of 'workers' democracy' in Soviet Russia did create dissensions, but the S.L.'s National Council needed allies to bolster them, leading to uncritical acceptance of support offered by the C.P. after 1935. Moreover, a possible alliance with the Soviet Union (which the National Government treated as a pariah) seemed to offer the only hope of defeating Hitler. Typical of this was E. F. Wise's statement in 1933 that a section of the Tory Party had deliberately used the Moscow trial (of Vickers' engineers accused of 'spying') as a means to break with Soviet Russia, reckless of the effect on commercial interests, the accused engineers or the peace of the world.[iv]

At a time of crucial international issues, Soviet foreign policy caused the greatest friction in the Labour Movement. It was the final disillusionment. Soviet Russia, with reliance on the League of Nations by September 1934 and pacts with 'capitalist' Governments rather than reliance on unity with working class forces, had a deleterious effect on the S.L. It was mainly because of its appreciation of past Soviet international policies that the S.L. had built its opposition to the 'Imperialist' League of Nations, Instead, Stalin was using foreign conflicts as a cudgel to beat domestic resistance, focusing interest on 'the enemy' outside (Trotsky, Germany, Japan) to divert attention from domestic discontent, economic hardships and industrial shortcomings. The S.L. could never fathom why a 'Socialist country' could strive to find a modus vivendi with Capitalist powers, although some S.L. members were conscious that the Comintern

[i] Popular British attitudes to Russia in the 1930s show ill-informed confusion; opinions swayed quite arbitrarily from 'the purge-ridden dictatorship' to 'the workers' state', from 'the giants with the feet of clay' to the 'steam roller', G.S. Jones, 'History in One Dimension', *N.L.R.*, No. 36, 1966, reviewing A. J. P. Taylor's *English History 1914–45*.

[ii] L. Schapiro, op. cit., pp.394–397.

[iii] G. Orwell, op. cit., 1966 edn., p.190.

[iv] E. F. Wise, 'The Foreign Office and Soviet Russia', *New Clarion*, April 22nd, 1933.

had become an auxiliary of Stalin's diplomacy, and the C.P.G.B. had been transformed from the vanguard of the Revolution to the frontier guard of the Soviet Union. (The Nazi-Soviet Pact (August, 1939) eventually destroyed the myth that Russia was somehow morally superior and aloof from that world of realpolitik.)

During the 1930s, the S.L. lived through a stalemate in the class struggle, which enabled diplomacy to secure the peaceful co-existence of opposed social systems. The 'example of the Soviet Union', far from stimulating the Labour Movement, (as the S.L. thought inevitable), deterred it from pursuing Socialist aspirations: 'If the working-class public is confronted with the choice between capitalist democracy with all its nauseous insincerities, and undemocratic Socialism, it will choose the former every time',[i] wrote Tawney perceptively in 1938. The S.L. membership had viewed, in the Russian Revolution, the first major twentieth century test of Socialism. It was not prepared to dwell on the handicaps with which the Soviet Union was burdened – that a free, classless society could not come into being in a poverty-stricken, primarily illiterate land. S.L. members hoped for an English way,[ii] and S.L. branches, through the study of the Soviet Union, were led to the other fundamental aspect of the S.L.: its attempt to apply 'Marxism' and alter Labour Party policies through a Marxist frame of reference. As it was, the conclusions of Jurgen Kuczynski in 1939 were believed: 'In the Soviet Union the worker has gained within a few years more freedom than the workers in other countries have gained in a century.'[iii] Even in cultural Paris in 1950, *Les Temps Modernes* could state: 'In no country in the world is the dignity of work more respected than in the Soviet Union. Forced labour does not exist because the exploitation of man by man no longer exists.'[iv] Semantics!

There was the "cult of the naif" at the core of Thirties' Marxism: 'the image of the sun-bronzed young man bringing the radiant candour of his gaze to bear on the mess the fathers have made of the world... the appeal of fresh-faced young comrades marching together to smash the bastions of privilege, the bank and barracks of the old men.'[v] For the S.L., it was much easier to suppose that Stalin had been slandered by 'bourgeois propagandists', 'Right-wing manipulators' and 'Trotskyist wreckers'.[vi]

---

[i] R. H. Tawney, *Equality*, 1938 revised edition, p.201.

[ii] A. J. P. Taylor, *English History 1914–45*, 1965, p.348.

[iii] J. Kuczynski, 'The Condition of the Workers in Gt. Britain, Germany, and the Soviet Union 1932–38', 1939, p.92.

[iv] *Les Temps Modernes*, January 1950, quoted in Paul Webster and Nicholas Powell, *Saint-Germain-des-Prés: French post-war culture from Sartre to Bardot*, 1984, p.147.

[v] Martin Green, 'Children of the Sun', *A Narrative of Decadence in England after 1918*, 2001, pp.28, 287, 301.

[vi] F. Wheen, op. cit., 2004, p.296.

Chapter Three

The Membership and Function of the Socialist League

Nothing is as visionary and as blinding as moral indignation. Adolescence is a kind of aching that only time can cure, a molten state without settled form, but when at the same time the order of society has also melted and the old authority has shown its incompetence and hollowness, the way to maturity is radicalism. All that is ... is falsehood and waste, and the ground is cleared for the symmetrical new structure, the benign release of reason's shackled powers which is what Marxism claimed to offer ... having met other like-minded writers in an attempt to advance the idea of socialism, or more especially human brotherhood, however muddled and profoundly unexamined the means ... it had been far less a political than a moral act of solidarity with all those who had failed in life, an abnegation of power in a redemption from the self.

Arthur Miller, *Timebends*, 1987, pp.115, 395

G. D. H. Cole and H. Laski sought to find an intellectual standpoint some way to the Left of the official Labour Party position, which they mistrusted but far short of the position of the Communists, totally alien to their way of thought ... Cole's political creed was liberal in form, socialist in content. He accepted without qualms or reservations the orthodox aims of socialism: they seemed to him the unquestionable ultimate goal of that progress through rational persuasion ... Cole's final testimony was 'I am neither a Communist nor a Social Democrat, because I regard both as creeds of centralization and bureaucracy, whereas I feel that a Socialist society, that is, to be true to its equalitarian principles of human brotherhood must rest on the widest possible diffusion of power and responsibility, so as to enlist the active participation of as many as possible of its citizens in the tasks of democratic self-government.

E. H. Carr, *From Napoleon to Stalin and Other Essays*, 1960, pp.223–24

According to the S.L. leaflet following the October 1932 S.L. Constitution, the organisation was composed of Labour Party members who believed Socialism to be the only remedy for economic and social ills, and were prepared to work to secure the Party as Socialist in policy, and to apply Socialism in practice. The S.L. had to be engaged in working out details and implications of Party policies. It was to be the 'mind' of the Labour Movement, hammering out policy statements and resolutions on specific topics, to maintain pressure in favour of bold use of power for Socialist measures and administration, and preparation of Socialist knowledge in readiness for an appeal to the nation. Thus it began as a Socialist propaganda organisation to apply a Marxist analysis to working class experience, to learn from the mistakes of the two Labour Governments, and by discussion and study of the history of the Movement to find an alternative to Parliamentary gradualism.

Although the S.L. represented a quest for an intellectual revival,[i] it also epitomised its complex origins, the clash of intellect, empiricism, and working class experience, and brought to the surface resentments between middle-class leaders and working-class unionists, although its own leadership was not exclusively middle-class in origin. It would be a caricature to represent the S.L. as 'intellectual and nothing else', or 'all leaders and no followers',[ii] but its programme of ideas was of vital importance. There was no dichotomy in the fact that, although it claimed to be thinking *for the Party*, much of its thinking met with Labour's disapproval. The S.L. was compelled to act within a framework only partly of its own choosing. Its very existence as a propaganda body inside a mass Movement prevented the attainment of many of the ends which its leaders set themselves. (When the S.L. was disbanding, Cripps explained that organisations such as the S.L. were implements to be used to attain specific objectives, and that immediately their use became inappropriate, they should be replaced by another 'fresh implement' which could be used more effectively.)[iii]

In 1932 there was a vital need for a restatement of policies and a new approach to Party requirements: 'The Socialist League brought together the most Left-wing of the Party intelligentsia, a galaxy of intellectual talent (Christian Socialists, pacifists, Marxists, ex-Communists and ex-I.L.P. members').[iv] The S.L. National Council was a heterogeneous committee containing every nuance of the Left. They were in agreement against the centralising pattern of British policies, but more specifically, they challenged the governing ideology (or lack of ideology) of Party leaders and attachment to reformist policies and methods. The S.L. represented writers, political thinkers, militants (and some careerists) in the Labour Party, who based their beliefs on a moral critique of capitalism. They criticised both the Party's attachment to Fabianism, and the C.P.'s dogmatism, and wanted flexibility in thought and a clear delineation of alternatives in Socialist tactics.

S.L. leaders defined the economic crisis and proposed Socialist solutions. They did not *create* a new political perspective based on an interpretation of the class struggle, but stressed the wider context of Socialism and a militancy for the Labour Party, in which they were more alive to the human misery produced by unemployment, and were possessed with a sense of urgency, and the need for a theory of social change. Their Achilles heel was inability to create enough support to change Party policies.[v] The S.L. was accused of talking in generalities without practical experience, criticising without knowledge, proposing action without responsibility for the consequences, yet it was prolific in denunciations of the effects of the market economy upon working people; Socialism meant affirmation of a community in which *moral values* would take pride of place over the pressures of economics.[vi] There was a tension because the S.L. combined moral ideals with an awareness of the necessity for expediency, and S.L. 'thinking' was mainly on economics and unemployment.

To Party officials, practical politics was the lifeblood of the Opposition and S.L.

---

[i] D. Mirsky, op. cit., p.221 Margaret Cole thought *The Intelligentsia of Great Britain* was 'a screaming and biting book' which avoided facing the fact that Communist propaganda 'has just not come off', review in *Socialist Leaguer*, No. 11, May 1935.

[ii] A. J. P. Taylor, *English History 1914–45*, p.349.

[iii] Cripps, 'Unity Is Now the Issue', *Tribune*, May 21st, 1937.

[iv] E. Estorick, op. cit., pp.116–117.

[v] M. Foot, *Aneurin Bevan*, biography, Vol. 1, 1962, p.143.

[vi] M. Foot, 'Credo of the Labour Left', *New Left Review*, May–June 1968, p.34.

'causes' and 'missions' were a liability. Therefore, the rôle of the S.L. was precariously balanced, because it was held strictly to account for the leaders it presented: 'They were the people who wished to change the world, to reform it. They had at least to be people to be respected.[i] The S.L. gradually gathered support in local Labour Parties, Trades Councils, the A.E.U. and the Miners' Federation.

(A) The Leading Members of the Socialist League

Some characteristics were common to leading figures in the S.L. The 'militancy' in the S.L.'s public image was reflected in the dogmatic, moralistic tone in its leaders, a rectitude which exuded from S.L. lectures, combined with sincerity and awesome social conscience. S.L. speakers were controversial and eloquent, addressing a great many meetings throughout the country. The impatient tone of their speeches (particularly on the Means Test, the Unemployment Bill, Fascism, and the cause of Unity) was principled and idealistic in proposing solutions. An earnestness, a simplicity of expression, a Messianic quality (in the style of S.L. lectures and public speeches) reflected the S.L.'s belief that there would be a collapse of the Government if unemployment rose and the economy was not revitalised. Most of the energy and vitality in S.L. leaders was spent expounding the vision of a Socialist society, for economic planning, efficiency in Government, and criticisms of every aspect of capitalist society, liberally couched in Marxist terminology. S.L. leaders were programme-makers and resolution-formulators, somewhat doctrinaire and aloof as individuals. As a propaganda organisation, the S.L. viewed the Party machine as an encumbrance, while the 'protest' nature of the S.L. remained uppermost.

To the general public, **Sir Stafford Cripps** personified the S.L. and was recognised as 'the leading figure among those in the Labour and Socialist Movement who are striving for rapid and decisive action for Socialism'.[ii] Nephew of Beatrice Webb, son of Lord Parmoor, and a respected lawyer, Cripps was a religious man: he considered the Labour Party the centre of a moral crusade, his mission to educate everyone else in the Party. He joined the Party in 1929 because it seemed a Party of 'ideals and earnestness'[iii] and accepted the principles of the Party on the terms of a Christian philosophy of politics. A representative of the liberal Christian conscience, he wanted to prove himself a leader who had a contribution to the shaping of Party policies. From expounding high principles of brotherhood in international affairs and the application of Christian ethics in social relations, he began (in the same moral tone) to proclaim the class struggle.[iv] Cripps has been described as 'forming part of that humanistic trend of social and political life exemplified by Shaftesbury, Kingsley, Toynbee, Farrar, Arch and Temple'.[v] Although the staid, formal, clever legal man, shy with his colleagues, distant in manner, a technician rather than a politician, he was soon known in the Commons as the Party's best mouthpiece.[vi] Yet his life was given

---

[i] Amber Blanco White, *The New Propaganda*, 1939, pp.300–302.

[ii] S.L. Notes, *New Clarion*, December 9th, 1933.

[iii] C. Cooke, op. cit., p.93.

[iv] Cf. E. Estorick, op. cit., pp.24, 90, cf. P. Strauss, op. cit., p.11.

[v] C. Cooke, op. cit., p.188.

[vi] P. Strauss, op. cit., pp.47, 55.

not so much to politics as high moral purpose conceived in religion and executed in political action. No one did more than Cripps between 1932 and 1939 to revive the militant spirit of the Labour Party, and at a time when every Party member was re-thinking policy, he became one of the most controversial national political figures in Britain.

The notoriety seemed surprising because in the Government of 1929–1931 he had seemed just an able, orthodox advocate of Party policy, a doctrinaire, academic Christian Socialist: 'His arguments were theoretical and Christian Socialism was to him the same thing as Christianity.'[i] He was catapulted to the forefront because of the 1931 débâcle, after which he, Lansbury and Attlee, were the leading figures in the P.L.P. Reacting against the compromises of the 1929–1931 Labour Government, Cripps worked to commit the Party to a bold policy of social change, to state that policy to the electorate in unequivocal terms, and, if elected, proceed to carry out its programme rapidly. In this he owed more to George Lansbury than any other person.[ii] They saw in each other the same sincerity and purpose, and shared the same distrust of expediency at the expense of principle. Cripps mirrored Lansbury's refusal to compromise his Christian Socialist principles, forthright speech and action, and simple faith in Socialism; he modelled himself on Lansbury's earnestness and 'incorruptibility'; Lansbury's public image of honesty, humility and simple blunt language[iii] inspired the S.L. leader, while Lansbury viewed Cripps as a potentially great servant of the people. He admired the clarity of his mind, but worried about Cripps' tendency to follow his own reasoning and not listen to the arguments of others.[iv] The central factor was: Cripps and Lansbury were led to a Socialist outlook by the Christian principles of social justice and dignity of the individual.[v]

What made Cripps the most magnetic figure in the Party was not his family connections, but circumstances after the Party's defeat in 1931, and his individual characteristics which seemed attuned to the times. A man of intellectual ability, immense energy, delight in hard work, and a stamp of confidence,[vi] he played the rôle of a man with a mission, of integrity, devotion to the cause, so essential for a Party in the doldrums. He carried his skill and reputation from the Courts to the Commons.[vii] After the peculiar conspiratorial fall of the Labour Government, his public critique appeared refreshing, and his candour and outspokenness against 'National' Government policies and determination to stand by his beliefs against Party officials appealed to Socialists. To the Labour Left his incisive mind concentrated on essentials, his conclusions were stated with simplicity, authority, and persuasiveness. It is no coincidence that he and Lansbury became the most popular speakers, for they were the opposite of the smooth, verbose PM, Ramsay MacDonald, exhibiting none of his readiness to compromise, aptitude for expediency, or reverence for Parliamentary sophistications.

Cripps could be trusted in a time of Party uncertainty. What strongly recommended him to the Labour Left were his moral principles, his independence,

---

[i] Kingsley Martin, *The Editor*, p.51.

[ii] R. Postgate, *Life of George Lansbury*, 1951, pp.280–81.

[iii] Harry Short, 'The Days of "G.L.": A Picture from Labour's Past', *Plebs*, May 1965.

[iv] R. Postgate, op. cit., pp.280–81.

[v] *The Times*, obituary of Cripps entitled 'Selfless Devotion to Public Duty', April 22nd, 1952.

[vi] M. Foot, *Aneurin Bevan*, biography, Vol. 1, p.155.

[vii] Ibid., p.156.

and blunt Socialist statements. He brought to the S.L. potent debating powers, wide sympathies and idealism.[i] Churchill thought his intellectual and moral passions so strong they not only inspired, but dominated his actions,[ii] and part of the animosity expressed by other Labour leaders towards Cripps was caused by his faculty of stirring his audience through his speeches.

From May 1933, when he was elected Chairman, Cripps became synonymous with the S.L. Although he had reservations, J. T. Murphy saw Cripps as 'a very able Chairman – a very likeable person.[iii] He put his full energy and enthusiasm into the S.L. and attended weekly meetings of the Executive Committee, his legal mind invaluable in keeping discussion to the point, his urbanity useful in curbing more impetuous members; his courtesy and detached, impartial demeanour made him the stabilising figure. His campaigns for the S.L. also made him the most popular Party leader, who angered, not only the Government, but also many Party and union leaders (to such a degree that H. Dalton (in 1957) could still rebuke the S.L. as little more than *a rich man's toy*,[iv] a reference to Cripps' payment of S.L. deficits). As Party leaders grew increasingly concerned by the S.L.'s political activities and call for democratic representation within the Party, Cripps was accused of privately financing the S.L. for his own personal advancement.[v] Yet the easiest way to gain a place in the Party hierarchy had been by *not* causing any trouble to the leadership. Popularity increased for Cripps when he was publicly associated with more 'radical' proposals (attacks on Parliamentary institutions, the monarchy, abolition of the House of Lords). His 'indiscretion' boosted numbers at his meetings, as expressed by Sir Charles Trevelyan: 'Cripps has mastered the simple fact more completely that a new mentality had to be created out of the seething dissatisfactions which underlie our society'.[vi] The first essential for a crowd-puller is the ability to dramatise or personalise issues, and the moral, upright, austere-looking Cripps achieved this. He did not subordinate his own beliefs to considerations of Party or personal position, and never made personal attacks on individual politicians or imputed motives. His fervour gave his audiences a tonic. (By 1934 he was elected to the N.E.C. of the Party.) One of the major factors which pushed A. Bevan towards the S.L. was his appreciation of Cripps' character. In Bevan's estimate, he was a cleaner, more wholesome influence in the Party than anyone; Cripps' approach to Socialism might be crude, but was not a crude vitality preferable to cynicism and lassitude?[vii] Cripps and Bevan were in politics for a high purpose and each saw in each other qualities of political honour and intelligence. Cripps' public speeches inspired, as did his outstanding ability in the 1931–35 Parliament and his disagreements with Party leaders were on political *tactics*, and political *principles*.

Cripps gained more popularity and received more virulent abuse than any other Party member between 1932 and 1939. Outside the Labour Movement his 'dictatorial' speeches were lambasted in the Press, reviewers criticising him for naïve impatience at restrictions implicit in political action, and a tendency to overlook the human factor:

---

[i] Attlee on Cripps, *The Times*, April 22nd, 1952.
[ii] W. Churchill in House of Commons, April 21st, 1952.
[iii] J. T. Murphy, *New Horizons*, 1941, p.312.
[iv] H. Dalton, *The Fateful Years*, p.130.
[v] One of the accusations levelled at Cripps in 1939, *Labour Party Annual Conference Report*, May–June 1939.
[vi] C. Trevelyan, 'Political Parties and the Next Election: The Outlook of the Socialist League', *Political Quarterly*, April–June 1935.
[vii] M. Foot, op. cit., p.155.

'Having formed his own ideas it seemed to him a rather burdensome necessity that they should have then to be submitted to the test of facts and await the decision of minds less competent, less farseeing than his own'.[i] He conveyed responses in a dry, articulate voice, and his impatience to secure results (and intolerance of delaying tactics) prevented him assuming leadership of the Party. Typically sour resentment of Cripps was expressed by J. R. Clynes: 'Cripps served little, if any, apprenticeship in the building of the Party. His place seemed ready for him. He won an easy election victory at a time when Labour was popular, and walked almost immediately to the Front Bench... to fill one of the highest paid posts in the Government. He lifted on his way the title of 'Sir'.[ii]

This lack of a practical acquaintance with the Labour Movement was a constant source of criticism.[iii] Cripps suffered from two other limitations; he had no experience of the working class and no real knowledge of Socialist theory: 'He is not at home among the working class, and workers do not feel at their ease with him. When his voice is raised on their behalf, it is as a humanitarian outside their circles. As for Socialist theory, I doubt whether he had ever read Marx or any book of fundamental Socialist economics.'[iv] (That knowledge was provided by other S.L. leaders.) Resentment directed at Cripps flowed over into a deep suspicion of the S.L. and it is not surprising that Cripps' conviction that Party leaders had neither the inspiration nor policies to lead workers to Socialism was viewed with immense annoyance by that hierarchy. They had some justification for cursing his indiscretions and envying his notoriety. He appeared wayward, incalculable, the crier in the market-place of strange disquieting and uncomfortable words, user of undigested Marxist slogans. He declared the class war without ever having studied the contours of the battlefield,[v] yet his political innocence and naivety were an advantage in 1932.

Like many who become 'Socialists' because they grow impatient with the abuses of capitalism, but have no serious political education, Cripps was an individualist, (and became a "safe" Chancellor of the Exchequer in the third Labour Government[vi]). Although he had gained understanding of the Movement from Beatrice Webb, she described him as oddly immature in intellect and unbalanced in judgement, ignorant and reckless in his statements and proposals.[vii] Labour leaders could not abide Cripps' provocative utterances on Party platforms, yet his charisma attracted many more people into the Party than he deterred. It was condemnation of other Labour politicians to suggest that Labour voters were unable to distinguish between Cripps' Socialist messages and melodramatic accounts in the Press, but he was cautioned against making too much of that dependence on high-sounding phrases of little practical content, which formed the small change of political argument.

Although labelled an intellectual doctrinaire, Cripps was in fact weak on doctrine,[viii] but his reputation as the bête noire of the Labour Party stayed with him in 1935: 'To the Tories he is the bogey-man who proves the coming of a revolution. To the Labour

[i] *The Times*, obituary of Cripps, April 22nd, 1952.
[ii] J. R. Clynes, *Memoirs*, 1937.
[iii] C. R. Attlee, *As It Happened*, 1954, p.76.
[iv] F. Brockway, *Inside the Left*, 1942, pp.264–65.
[v] M. Foot, op. cit., p.156.
[vi] D. N. Pritt, op. cit., p.98.
[vii] B. Webb, *Diaries (1924–32)*, p.304.
[viii] R. Miliband, op. cit., p.206.

pundits he is the 'enfant terrible' who spoils their game of getting into power, owing to a fit of absent-minded indignation in the mass of the people at the feebleness and iniquities of the National Government'.[i] Yet Cripps, with very little political experience, was not a natural politician. He did not possess, like other leaders, the political judgement which waited for favourable tides of opinion, and yielded to opposition for the moment in order to return to the argument later. He was unaware how much he jeopardised Party electoral chances. For Clynes he became a liability to the Party: 'His speeches made for us very grave difficulties.'[ii] This lack of political sensitivity was partly created by his aloofness; a lone wolf, too conscious of his superiority to those around him, incapable of making contacts with the rank and file.[iii] Ideas did seem to matter to him more than people. Party leaders and union officials, instead of having to answer the formidable case which the S.L. presented, concentrated on Cripps' misdemeanours and the handicap of an irresponsible pressure group. Through this criticism of Cripps' personal characteristics, the S.L. was reprimanded, an evasion of the important issues which were up for debate.

Dalton was able to give credence to his label of Cripps as a new upstart Robespierre and a dangerous political lunatic,[iv] but justifiably showed how Cripps simplified everything into capitalists and workers: 'An adolescent Marxian miasma. He seems to be unaware of nationalist passions as a factor in politics'.[v] The Press pictured Cripps as this embryo-dictator, an image which Labour leaders seized upon to denounce the S.L. Contrary to many observers, Ernest Bevin held Cripps in high esteem, never suspected his motives, and recognised as little self-interest in his public forays as he convinced himself there was in his own, yet Bevin thought Cripps far too theoretical in his approach, too uncompromising on practical issues, too aloof from the real life of the mass of the Labour Party. Self-opinionated and sometimes fanatical, Cripps was not a good judge of men, and was always reminded that he had little experience with which to temper his enthusiasm.[vi]

In the S.L., only one other leading personality, J. T. Murphy, wrote about his experiences in the S.L. (other than G. D. H. Cole who left the S.L. in 1933). Murphy felt that Cripps was a trifle conscious of his old school tie. He did not regard Cripps as any kind of political theorist, but an orator who lost power by 'reading his brief'. It was a constant amazement for local S.L. members that a man known for his wide intellectual abilities always read his speeches, and often gave them to the Press before a meeting.[vii] He was more conscious of his lack of a basic knowledge of Labour history and Socialist literature than people realised. He was not politically passionate but had the eloquence of a very able lawyer. J. T. Murphy, who had lived through over thirty years of Socialist debate, expressed the chief characteristic of Cripps: 'an opportunist learning from experience and frequently burning his fingers'.[viii]

---

[i] C. Trevelyan, *Political Quarterly*, April–June 1935.

[ii] J. R. Clynes, op. cit., p.256.

[iii] K. Martin, op. cit., p.51.

[iv] Quoted M. Foot, op. cit., p.156.

[v] H. Dalton, *The Fateful Years*, May 4th, 1933, p.41.

[vi] C. R. Attlee, op. cit., p.76.

[vii] Most of Cripps' written speeches are in his Papers and do not include much that could not have been improvised on the political platform. It seems he had to write down provocative (and glib) statements before uttering them in a public speech.

[viii] J. T. Murphy, *New Horizons*, 1942, p.312.

Although not a member of the S.L., **Harold J. Laski**, the professor of Political Theory at the L.S.E., had a strong influence upon Left-wing thought.[i] From being the outstanding person on the Fabian Executive in 1930, he epitomised the Leftward move of political philosophers and combined Marxist analysis with Social Democratic sympathies – a preoccupation of the S.L. Laski embodied that contradictory position which Socialists exhibited as a reaction to Labourism; he articulated these difficulties and complexities. Just as the S.L. held a middle position between Labour policies and the I.L.P. and C.P., so Laski held a balancing position through his writings (some became S.L. pamphlets[ii] and standard political texts for the S.L) and, from the standpoint of Socialist thought in the 1930s, he was the most influential person with the exception of John Strachey. Laski's books on politics became increasingly propagandist and subject to Marxist influences, although there always remained in them a streak of utilitarianism.[iii] This mirrored the dichotomy in the S.L., which had to face the difficulties of a pressure group in an environment of pragmatic politics. Nevertheless, Laski stamped the whole decade with his political views. Moved by moral indignation at the injustices he saw, as a politically committed intellectual, few had such a profound, original knowledge of democratic thought and institutions'.[iv] The issues which he explored in *The State in Theory and Practice* (1935) were fundamental in moulding the S.L.'s ideas and challenging the Party's assumptions about Parliamentary 'democracy'.

Commentators have seen in Laski a follower of William Morris, but he was regarded in the S.L. as 'marxisant', characterising the Socialism of Marx as essentially humanist. The S.L. (and Laski as an independent thinker) tried to make the discussion about the methods and tactics of Socialism less doctrinaire than the C.P., and more militant than the official Labour leaders. Laski's prestige as a cogent writer to the Left of the Party boosted the S.L.; he worked to become the *'eminence grise'* of the Labour Party, and was the major academic figure to gain a prominent position in the Party. He criticised those intellectuals who analysed the decadence of capitalist society, yet encouraged their generation to seek ways of personal escape, and thought it the duty of the intellectual to ally himself with working-class people, who could not defend themselves against unemployment or Means Test humiliations. After contributing to S.L. pamphlets, and having left the Fabian Executive in 1936, Laski became a leading sponsor and selector in the Left Book Club, and was nominated as a representative of Divisional Labour Parties on the N.E.C. His involvement increased for a united Popular Front, although he was a critic of C.P. tactics in the Unity campaigns. Laski has been criticised for having too many irons in the fire;[v] he could not accomplish by his books, articles, lectures, memoranda and conversations the feat of re-channelling the policies of the Labour Party, because to redirect the Party's policy it was necessary to act as a politician and to change the balance of power within the Party'.[vi] Laski failed as a politician. He could not combine the rôle of popular leader with that of *'eminence grise'*. a lesson for S.L. leaders. Their epitaph and his was written by John Strachey: 'He who supposes that an Englishman of the present day can find his way either to

---

[i] M. Cole, *The Story of Fabian Socialism*, 1961, p.220.

[ii] Cf. *The Labour Party and the Constitution* and *The Roosevelt Experiment*.

[iii] G. D. H. Cole, 'Socialism and Fascism', *The History of Socialist Thought (1931–39)*, p.84.

[iv] Leon Blum, quoted by K. Martin, *H. Laski*, pp.270–271.

[v] M. Cole, op. cit., p.221.

[vi] K. Martin, *Harold Laski*, 1953, p.262.

intellectual certainty or political consistency without doubts, hesitations, and errors, shows little appreciation of the gravity or the complexity of the present situation.'[i]

In the formulation of the S.L.'s programme and function in the National Council of the S.L., **William Mellor** was the dominating personality. He also exercised more influence than anyone else upon Cripps.[ii] There were significant reasons which prevented Mellor from having *more* influence; he had been a founder member of the C.P.G.B. (after years as a Guild Socialist), and this resulted in suspicion in Labour and union circles in the 1930s. Like many S.L. leaders, he lacked the ability to fit in with others in the Labour Movement as a whole; he was a political puritan, hating compromise, refusing to make with the Party machine the accommodations of lesser (and more successful) men.[iii] Michael Foot presents an imaginative description of Mellor's character: 'All who might be suspected of betraying the Cause were in peril of being consumed by Mellor's private supply of hell-fire. A wonderful gentleness and generosity mingled with these ferocities... Working with Mellor was like living on the foothills of Vesuvius.'[iv] The most significant aspect of Mellor's character was his ability to transfer the instincts of his own raw Puritan upbringing from the field of personal morals to political action, and the shock he felt with Bevan's intellectual richness and laxity.

Mellor had a great deal of experience in journalism and the Socialist Movement. He was editor of the *Daily Herald* (1926–31), editor of *Town and Country Councillor* (1936–40), the first editor of *Tribune* (1937–38); unsuccessfully he contested Enfield (1931 and 1935 Elections), and became prospective Stockport Labour candidate in 1937.[v] He was Chairman of the S.L. (1936–37) and on the National Council of the S.L. throughout. Even those whom he displeased by his political intransigence honoured him for his sincerity and integrity and for the single-mindedness with which he devoted his abilities to Labour journalism.[vi] Mellor had a coherent Socialist philosophy, and, as a powerful speaker, expressed it in strong, direct terms. He lectured and wrote some of the best pamphlets for the S.L. *The Claim of the Unemployed*, dealing with the most crucial subject facing the Movement and the world,[vii] was written from a practical and uncompromisingly Socialist angle, as was *The Co-operative Movement and the Fight for Socialism*. Mellor had a much better grasp of economic realities than most Labour politicians in the 1930s. His tendency had always been to the Left of the Labour Party, but he never put himself outside the Party after leaving the C.P.G.B. in 1924.

Mellor was one of the few politicians/journalists of whom it was felt that he put principle *and* self-interest first every time! This prevented him from gaining the position among the leaders of the Party which his talents and integrity deserved. With his North Country accent, earthy language and evangelical oratory, he was one of the few intellectuals who took advantage of working-class antagonism to middle-class Socialists, turning it to his own benefit.[viii] The *Stockport Express* stated what most

---

[i] J. Strachey, *Left News*, quoted John Lewis, *The Left Book Club*, 1970, p.136.

[ii] J. T. Murphy, *New Horizons*, 1942, p.312.

[iii] Mellor's Papers (belonging to W. Mellor Jr.).

[iv] M. Foot, op. cit., p.245.

[v] *Stockport Advertiser*, Mellor's obituary, June 12th, 1942.

[vi] Cf. *Manchester Guardian*, obituary, June 10th, 1942.

[vii] S.L. News, *New Clarion*, August 5th, 1933.

[viii] Cf. N. Wood, op. cit., p.29.

Labour supporters in the 1930s thought of Mellor: 'One of the foremost Socialists of his day, and generation, forceful, learned and sincere ... a brilliant writer and a still more brilliant speaker'.[i] He exhibited the shrewdest mind in the S.L., and wrote many of the perspicacious Annual Reports. As the granite-like Socialist conscience of the S.L.,[ii] he characterised the group's rigorous and persistent nature, its moral tone, doctrinaire rectitude, and mélange of Marxist and Utilitarian phraseology. He possessed the intellect, passion and force of leadership which guided the S.L., in its difficult course and made its small reputation as a pressure group. In 1937, his knowledge and distrust of C.P. tactics made his participation in any United Front impossible. He was the most decisive personality to set against Harry Pollitt[iii] and he opposed Cripps over this final confrontation in the S.L.'s history.

H. N. Brailsford was a prominent member of the S.L.'s National Council throughout. As an editor, he achieved an even greater reputation than Mellor. He had played an important rôle in the formulation of I.L.P. policies in the 1920s (especially 'Socialism in Our Time') which were reflected in S.L. policy reports. As editor of the I.L.P.'s New Leader, he was more responsible than anyone for creating Socialists than any other person in the 1920s. Under his direction the New Leader became a journalist prototype; with its wood-cuts, literary contributions, and authoritative articles on philosophy, science, and politics, it was a magnificent experiment.[iv] Brailsford was one of the most influential Socialist intellectuals in the 20th century. With E. F. Wise, he helped to form the S.L. and his tolerance and wide knowledge of affairs and Socialist history were real assets[v] to the organisation. Yet, although he was an immensely respected writer, pamphleteer and veteran of the Labour Movement, and the most eloquent and incisive Socialist journalist of the age,[vi] Brailsford typified characteristics of other leading members of the S.L., aloofness and personal reserve. Although one must be wary of a C.P. member's judgement on him, (he was a critic of C.P. activities), there was a recognition of his character by W. Gallacher: 'When Brailsford jumps, no one knows where he is going to land...'[vii]

In the final analysis, Brailsford brought his morality, political experience and literary gifts to the S.L.'s counsels. His reputation in the Movement as an authority on international affairs was very high[viii] and he wrote most of the S.L. pamphlets on foreign affairs; The Nazi Terror: A Record,[ix] A Socialist Foreign Policy (an S.L. lecture in 1933), India in Chains[x] and Spain's Challenge to Labour (November 1936). He was an uncompromising fighter in the struggle against Nazism, a champion of the Republican cause in Spain, and the Independence movement in India.[xi] He, Strachey and Laski were the prophets of the young during those years.[xii]

---

[i] Stockport Express, June 10th, 1042.

[ii] M. Foot, op. cit., p.155.

[iii] F. Brockway, op. cit., p.266.

[iv] A. Marwick, Clifford Allen: The Open Conspirator, p.79.

[v] J. T. Murphy, New Horizons, 1942, p.312.

[vi] M. Foot, New Left Review, May–June 1968, p.20 and M. Foot, A. Bevan, op. cit., p.102.

[vii] W. Gallacher, The Rolling of the Thunder, 1947, p.162.

[viii] New Clarion, November 25th, 1933.

[ix] Ibid., April 22nd, 1933.

[x] Ibid., February 10th, 1935.

[xi] K. Martin, The Editor, pp.133–34.

[xii] Cf. New Statesman and Nation, February 9th, 1933, London Diary, August 22nd, 1936.

As the chief I.L.P. affiliationists in 1932, Brailsford and E. F. Wise were initiators in the S.L.'s foundation. **E. F. Wise** had also been responsible for constructing the I.L.P.'s *'Socialism in Our Time'* policy document, the outstanding contribution to Labour thought in the 1920s. The S.L.'s concentration on economic issues was a response to the conditions of the times, and the result of having E. F. Wise as the first Chairman (from October 1932 to May 1933).[i] Since 1918, Wise had been primarily interested in the formulation of plans for the economic reorganisation of society on Socialist lines. As one of the chief formulators of the I.L.P.'s economic policy, he became an expert on Russian economic affairs.[ii] He was one of the I.L.P. economic gurus who challenged the Treasury, and exposed 'the debility at the heart of capitalist society'. Before Keynes and Beveridge, he helped to diagnose the causes of mass unemployment (lack of effective demand induced by the system of production, subservience to balanced budgets and the Gold standard). Wise offered a critique on which opposition to the deflationary policies dictated by the Bank of England could be based. His two S.L. pamphlets: *Control of Finance and Financiers* and *The Socialisation of Banking* gave the S.L. its firm direction, and formed the backbone of the S.L.'s economic viewpoints and outlook towards banks and the rôle of finance in the transition to Socialism.

Wise helped present the S.L.'s first programme for creating the Socialist State within the lifetime of the next Labour Government, 'the subject of so much controversy' (as *The Times* blandly explained).[iii] He was also appreciated for his knowledge and long-view constructive mind. In the 1929–1931 Parliament, his reputation on economic subjects was enhanced, while he became a fearless exponent of Left-wing Socialism in a Parliament dominated by gradualism. His boundless energy played on immense part in the building of the S.L.[iv] Like Cripps, Mellor and Brailsford, Wise exhibited that trait of aloofness and detachment which presented Party leaders with accusations of 'middle class superiority'. Fenner Brockway explained how Wise 'lectured us at length from Olympian heights, showing his contempt for the contribution of less educated and more emotionally elementary colleagues, forgetting that the working-class experience of comrades around him might be as valuable as his civil service training and his mastery of economic facts.'[v] Nevertheless, Wise's economic ideas stand the test of scrutiny better than most other political prescriptions of that period.

No one in the S.L. was more conversant with the world of trade union activity than **J. T. Murphy**, who already had twenty years' experience in the Labour Movement, and had been (with Mellor of the S.L.) a founder member of the C.P.G.B. A trade unionist who had taken a leading part in the Shop Stewards' Movement during the First World War, he had resigned from the C.P.G.B. (and subsequently was officially expelled for opposing C.P. policies). Cripps claimed that Murphy's reasons for joining the S.L. in 1933 were an awareness that in the light of his own review of the historical development of Socialism in this country, he had abandoned his belief in the inevitability of violent revolution with a conviction that the change could be

---

[i] E. F. Wise was vice-chairman of the S.L., May–November 1933.

[ii] J. Lee, *This Great Journey*, 1942, p.154.

[iii] *The Times*, obituary of E. F. Wise, November 6th, 1933.

[iv] S.L. Notes, *New Clarion*, November 11th, 1933.

[v] F. Brockway, op. cit., p.239.

accomplished by political and industrial action.[i]

J. T. Murphy was the only S.L. member to write at length about his personal reasons for joining the S.L. (in the *New Clarion* April 15th, 1933), and later was the only S.L. member (other than Cripps and G. D. H. Cole) to discuss some of his experiences in the S.L. As he saw it, both Attlee and Lansbury had been outspoken in their denunciation of gradualism and insisted the next Labour Government should be 'really Socialist'. This reflected the mood of the Leicester Party Conference (October 1932): 'I felt a natural sympathy with this mood and thought that by joining the S.L. I should be able to help in its development'.[ii] He was convinced that, in the course of the 'conflict of the classes', the working class would, learning from defeats and disillusionments, eventually break through its old forms of organisations and leadership, and produce from its ranks, new leaders who would lead to power and Socialism: 'I felt that I should join with those who would consciously assist this process of differentiation. It was with this in view that I joined the S.L.'[iii]

Appointed S.L. General Secretary in 1934, he held the post for two years, issuing annual reports and descriptions of the S.L.'s progress in activities and meetings, nationally and locally, and writing regularly in the S.L.'s monthly journal. This brought him into close contact with Cripps and a number of his old comrades in the Labour Movement. As an official he had no vote on the National Council, but was able to participate in the discussions. He opposed the S.L. policy over Abyssinia, and left the S.L. before its disbandment to form his own Propaganda Peace Committee. Among other pamphlets and articles, he wrote *Trade Unions and Socialism* (in 1936) and *Fascism: the Socialist Answer* – both for the S.L.

With Reg Groves and Harold Clay, Murphy wrote about the importance of unions and Trades Councils for S.L. membership. **Reg Groves** wrote *Arms and the Unions: Trades Councils in the Fight for Socialism*[iv] and *Fascism, Socialism and the Jews in the East End*. **Harold Clay** with Murphy and later, Groves, on the National Council of the S.L., lectured on *Workers' Control* (March 19th, 1933) described as "clear, well-considered and persuasive", by the man who had electrified the last Party Conference in his duel with Herbert Morrison'.[v] Clay also wrote *Trade Unionism: Some Problems and Proposals* (given as a lecture on January 28th, 1934) after which he was depicted as one of those rare men who are willing to state a policy and see problems constructively, and base proposals on the closest study of experience and history.[vi] In 1934 he was Chairman of the London Labour Party.

J. F. Horrabin, an S.L. National Council member (1932–37), was a brilliant cartographer and illustrator of children's educational books. He had been a Guild Socialist and renowned I.L.P. member in the 1920s. A voluminous cartoonist with a poignant Socialist message, he contributed weekly and monthly cartoons to the *New Leader*, and all S.L. monthly journals, which he edited. He was by far the most genial and approachable of S.L. leaders, wrote *The Class Struggle*, and illustrated *Is Woman's Place the Home?* and *Socialism in Pictures and Figures*. Horrabin lectured on aspects of

[i] Cripps' introduction to Murphy's *Preparing for Power*, 1934. See p.13 above for Alison Macleod re. J. T. Murphy.

[ii] J. T. Murphy, *New Horizons*, 1942, p.308.

[iii] J. T. Murphy, ibid., p.309.

[iv] September 1935.

[v] *New Clarion*, July 29th, 1933.

[vi] S.L. Notes, 'Trade Unionism Tomorrow', *New Clarion*, February 3rd, 1934.

colonial and Imperialist rule, wrote *The Break with Imperialism*, and devoted a great part of his political life to waking up the Labour Movement on the question of the colonial Empire and what was to become of it.[i] With Mellor and Murphy, he reviewed the majority of books in S.L. journals.

Throughout the 1930s (and afterwards) **G. D. H. Cole** contributed much to the ideology of the moderate Left. Though he was suspicious of the formation of the S.L. and its possible rôle, he became a member of its National Council during its first year, and had considerable influence in the growing Socialist Movement in universities. He wrote a number of basic S.L. pamphlets in its first year, including the useful *Study Guide on Socialist Policy* (published August 1933), which carefully analysed the Derby S.L. resolutions, explained the principles behind them, and indicated the important points for discussion.[ii] This illustrated the thoroughness with which the National Council took its work, and was very popular as a resumé of S.L. ideas. Cole also composed a pamphlet on the S.L.'s function *The Need for a Socialist Programme* (with G. R. Mitchison),[iii] which supplied concrete suggestions set out for the Labour Movement to discuss.

G. D. H. Cole's lecture *The Working-Class Movement and the Transition to Socialism* (January 21st, 1934) was a provocative talk on the duty and place of unions, and the Co-operative Movement and the S.L., and his pamphlet *The Socialist Control of Industry* (February 26th, 1933 lecture) asked how a Socialist Government could set about its job in the first few months, how it could bring about control of industry, and which industries it would nationalise. He answered these queries and discussed planning, compensation and workers' control.[iv] Ostensibly, Cole resigned from the S.L. National Council due to pressure of other work, and in no way due to divergence over policy (as the S.L. was keen to emphasise),[v] yet Cole had always opposed any effort in the S.L. to play any other rôle than *a research and educational* organisation, especially any immediate political rôle. In 1947, he explained that he resigned because the S.L. was heading for disaster, very like that which had befallen the I.L.P., by putting forward a programme of its own in opposition to that of the Labour Party, instead of trying to work for improving the official Labour programme.[vi] G. D. H. Cole had been much appreciated in the S.L.: 'The emotional thread on which all Cole's work is strung is the feeling of social compunction because most people have a much worse time than himself, and the sense of being in love with Socialism.'[vii]

G. R. Mitchison, the S.L. Treasurer and, for a while, a member of the S.L.'s National Council, was a wealthy barrister, a Labour MP, and spokesman on housing. Like E. F. Wise, he helped to give an economic orientation to the S.L.'s ministrations, and wrote a long pamphlet on *Banking* in the S.L.'s Socialist Programme Series, as well as joining G. D. H. Cole in writing *The Need for a Socialist Programme*. His main contribution was his book, *The First Workers' Government* which was interpreted as a Socialist League version of the tasks of a future Socialist Government in office; he also wrote numerous articles on economics in Socialist League journals during these five years.

---

[i] S.L. Notes, 'A Socialist Programme', *New Clarion*, January 21st, 1933.

[ii] S.L. Notes, *New Clarion*, July 29th, 1933.

[iii] December 1932.

[iv] S.L. Notes, *New Clarion*, August 1933.

[v] S.L. News, *New Clarion*, June 17th, 1933.

[vi] G. D. H. Cole, *The History of the Labour Party Since 1914*, 1947, p.284.

[vii] L. A. Fenn, reviewing G. D. H. Cole, *The Simple Case for Socialism, Socialist*, No. 3, 1935.

The ex-Education Minister of the 1929–1931 Labour Government, **Sir Charles Trevelyan**, was also on the S.L. National Council. He gave the first S.L. public lecture on *The Challenge to Capitalism* (January 22nd, 1933), and another lecture *Mass Resistance to War* (December 3rd, 1933), although he wrote little of significance for the S.L. after this. His major disagreement with the S.L. was over the group's policy against the use of League of Nations' sanctions in the Abyssinia crisis of 1935. Like other S.L. leading figures, he spoke a great deal at public meetings, and was particularly popular in his constituency area of Newcastle and Gateshead, the major S.L. stronghold outside London.

D. N. Pritt, a legal colleague of Cripps, and also a K.C., joined the S.L. for the same reasons as Wise and Brailsford, because the S.L. aimed to take the place of the I.L.P. as the driving force in the Labour Party. Although Pritt said he was active in the Socialist League until the summer of 1936,[i] he wrote rarely and did not figure significantly in the S.L. National Council's activities. Pritt was a member of the National Executive of the Labour Party for three years and throughout the S.L.'s existence (and afterwards) he was the most consistent admirer of the Soviet Union, and later joined the C.P.

Of other influential people, **R. H. Tawney**, not an S.L. member, was similar in outlook and highly regarded by the S.L. His article *The Choice before the Labour Party* had a huge effect on S.L. attitudes, and was more widely read in the organisation than any other pamphlet. The S.L. saw him as one of the sanest and most level-headed of Socialists, with a lifetime of experience in and of the Labour Party.[ii] **C. R. Attlee**, who became the Party Leader (1935–1955) and **Dr. C. Addison**, both contributed one pamphlet each for the S.L. readership. **Louis Fenn**, also on the National Council, wrote articles in the S.L. paper about the functions of the professional classes and reviewed some of the books. **Glyn Evans** did an inordinate amount of work as the S.L. National Organiser, linking the activities of local S.L. branches and acting as a liaison officer for the National Council to its members. As Agent and Secretary of the Greenwich Labour Party, he became well known in the Co-operative and Socialist Movement as one of the most active, able and eloquent Labour officers in the country.[iii]

At a time when few women played a prominent rôle in politics, a large number of women played an important part in the S.L., which it was anxious to explain: 'One of the most attractive aspects of the Socialist Movement had been the insistence on women's rights... Every Socialist woman demands equality in the economic field ... the S.L. cares not of which sex are its officers and secretaries – a fair proportion of the branch secretaries are women'.[iv] The women's contingent in the S.L. included **Winifred Horrabin**, who wrote *Is Woman's Place the Home?*, **Constance Borrett** (The Organising Secretary and a National Council Member), **Storm Jameson** (who wrote articles and reviews), and four members of the National Council, **Jean Thompson** (of Sheffield S.L.), **Margaret McCarthy** (the General Secretary 1936–37), **Ruth Dodds** (the Regional Secretary for Durham and the North East), and **Barbara Betts** (later Barbara Castle) who wrote regularly on foreign affairs.

[i] D. N. Pritt, *From Right to Left*, autobiography, No. 1, 1965, p.99.
[ii] S.L. News, *New Clarion*, September 23rd, 1933.
[iii] S.L. News, *New Clarion*, December 31st, 1932.
[iv] S.L. News, *New Clarion*, May 20th, 1933, cf. Ruth Dodds' diaries, Chapter 6, pp.193–200

Other S.L. leaders were **F. C. Henry** (General Secretary January 1933 to July 1934) Financial Secretary of the Rochdale Trades Council, and editor of the Rochdale *Labour News*; **H. L. Elvin**, leader of the S.L. tour to U.S.S.R. in 1935 and writer of many S.L. book reviews and articles, **Donald Barber** (provisional General Secretary (July – November 1934), and **Ithel Davies** – all four were on the National Council of the S.L. and contributed to the formulation of S.L. resolutions for the Labour's Annual Conferences, and kept the National S.L. organisation aware of local problems.

(B) The S.L. as a National Organisation – Its Function and Outlook Through Pamphlets and Lectures

Weaknesses in Labour Party ideology, personnel and cohesion were exposed when MacDonald removed himself from the Party, which had become too reliant upon personalities and a small coterie for its programme. After 1932 the 'movement to the Left', a direct consequence of the impact of financial and political crisis, resided in the S.L.'s search for a new kind of opposition. S.L. propaganda claimed to represent the aspirations of rank and file workers, with the inherent 'contradictions of capitalism', its social inequality, uppermost. From the events of 1931, the S.L. concluded that the future required adherence to Socialist principles, an end to the compromise into which the Labour Government had been drawn. The S.L. explicitly urged the right to criticise Party policies, because the appeal in the Labour Government to 'Party unity' had been an excuse to control debate, and the Left-wing activist element had been a force with which Labour leaders had always had to reckon: 'the Left within the Party had at least reduced the leaders' freedom of action'.[i]

The S.L. sought to commit the Party to 'Socialist solutions' for foreign and domestic issues, although support for 'unity' as a Party goal would have involved approval of the status quo in terms of Party power and policy. Specific for the S.L. were Socialist principles, democratic debate, divergent political opinions, and the utility of 'ginger groups' in the Party.[ii] Yet, S.L. activities *in practice* exemplified that many disputes on the Left were *tactical*, not 'fundamental' differences. The S.L. functioned as a pressure group opposition to Government decrees, essentially a protest movement, for, although it inherited the outlook of the Fabians through the S.S.I.P., it soon incorporated the class-oriented philosophy of former I.L.P. members. The S.L.'s purpose was mapped out from 1931. C. Trevelyan wrote to Lansbury: 'I hope you and Cripps ... will take a strong line in uncompromising Socialism',[iii] while Mellor feared that the principle of national ownership might be lost sight of, especially the emphasis on 'control', which could divert Socialist propaganda and thought into 'dictatorial' paths, but he hoped (as he explained to Cripps) that pressure would be on the Party to recognise S.L. methods of propaganda and to do some hard thinking 'so that the application of our principles will not be allowed to go phut'.[iv]

So profound were the 1931 crisis conditions, so defined were the class issues in the measures proposed to deal with the crisis, that the P.L.P. did begin to speak the

---

[i] R. Miliband, op. cit., pp.14–15.
[ii] E. G. Janosik, *The Constituency Labour Parties in Britain*, 1968, p.93.
[iii] Lansbury Papers, October 29th, 1931.
[iv] Cripps Papers, November 14th, 1931.

language of 'class war', in full knowledge that the Party had to revise its programme. Sidney Webb unconsciously justified the S.L.'s importance in the Party when he boldly looked to the future: 'The Party has now the opportunity, during the next five years, of applying itself continuously to the ubiquitous educational propaganda by which alone it can double the number of its adherents.'[i] It had to work out in greater detail its constructive programme without prematurely committing itself to any but general principles. Webb regarded it as essential to accustom the public to one item after another in that programme by the publication of pamphlets, lectures and articles, developing within the Party 'friendly social intercourse among fellow-workers in a common cause'.[ii] This was exactly the rôle of the S.L.

At their Bradford Conference (July 1932), I.L.P. affiliationists expressed such sentiments. E. F. Wise made no attempt to defend the actions of the Labour Government, but, optimistically, saw nothing in the Labour Party's Standing Orders which prevented members stating their views in and outside the P.L.P.: 'The new I.L.P. Manifesto is full of revolutionary phrases, but there is no difference in policy between it and the new policies of the Labour Party and the resolutions from the Divisional Parties to be discussed at the Leicester Party Conference'.[iii] He hoped the I.L.P. would build the Left wing of the Labour Party, the onus being on the I.L.P., whether it wished to work for Socialism through Parliamentary action, through a revolutionary Movement, or through industrial action. David Kirkwood confirmed that the I.L.P. could only help workers by being attached to the Labour Party: 'It is Tory tactics to divide and conquer'; while Jean Thompson concluded that educational work was essential *inside* the Labour Party. Wise and Thompson soon joined the S.L.

Such hopes expressed by affiliationists were reflected in Wise's resignation letter to the I.L.P. (August 6th, 1932): 'Secession from the L.P. when it is more Socialist in outlook, intention and opportunity than at any time in its history, seems an act of treachery to the Labour Movement and suicide for the I.L.P.' Echoing the S.L.'s future rôle, he preferred to be 'an active Socialist' than a 'disgruntled disruptionist', because the Labour Party was the only organisation which, despite its imperfections, had any chance of achieving Socialism. (Maxton retorted that Wise had to produce *evidence* that the Labour Party was now 'more Socialist', and he rebuked H. N. Brailsford for his statement (in August 1931) that 'Socialist honour' required the I.L.P. leave the Labour Party,[iv] and Brailsford's subsequent volte-face.)

In such inauspicious circumstances, the S.L. held its first London Conference. F. Horrabin (presiding) reiterated that S.L. members would not be 'loyalists' to the Labour Party, a particular group or a Party machine, or official Party ideas: *'We will be loyal to the working-class movement'*. Brailsford appealed for personal discipline as in a monastic order, to renounce personal ambition for the sake of the Movement; G. E. G. Catlin recognised this personal discipline as the only way to challenge the Maxton section while the I.L.P.'s *New Leader* gloated that there were already divisions among S.L. members, (some supporting Ben Greene and Isobel Goddard who wanted S.L. members as local Labour Party members, but not affiliated officially to the Party

---

[i] S. Webb, 'What Happened in 1931: A Record', *Political Quarterly*, January–March 1932.
[ii] Ibid.
[iii] *New Leader*, August 5th, 1932.
[iv] *New Leader*, August 12th, 1932.

because it would duplicate machinery and follow in the old I.L.P. footsteps.)[i]

In the highly popular article *The Choice Before the Labour Party*, R. H. Tawney foretold what was to become the S.L. position: 'Until the void in the mind of the Labour Party is filled – till interests are hammered by principles into a serviceable tool, and a steady will for a new social order takes the place of mild yearnings to make somewhat more comfortable terms with the social order of today – mere repairs to the engines will produce little but disillusionment.' He outlined the most effective development for Socialism. The Party programme had been miscellanies rather than plans of campaign; it had no ordered conception of its task, possessed nothing analogous to 'a Scheme of Priorities'; had no stable standard of political values which could teach it to discriminate between the relative urgencies of different objectives, and lacked the ability to subordinate claims of different sections of the Movement to the progress of the whole (frittering away morale in inconclusive skirmishes). The S.L. stood to mobilise behind the Party a body of resolute convictions, because the dynamic of any Socialist movement was to be found in principles which united people.

The work of the S.L. was one of national and local engagement in clarifying details and implications of the accepted policy of the Party, and to assist in education of the rank and file and the general electorate (by lectures, meetings and local research projects). During 1933, it reiterated its function and purpose through its column in the *New Clarion*. It was proud of its unique basis for a Socialist organisation, and there would be no duplication of Party functions: 'In the past such societies have been either entirely separate from the Party or have had a purely formal affiliation to it. The S.L. rules contain a clause declaring that its branches shall not have power to put forward Parliamentary or municipal candidates.'[ii] Its work was to bring together all who realised that Socialism could only come through the Party, unions and the Co-operative Movement, and recognised the need for working out *in precise detail* what Socialism meant, and what part ought to be played by the three sections of the Movement, as well as changes in form and structure.

From its inception, therefore, the S.L. set its limits. It was not to be a rival political party, nor would it build a further elaborate, complicated organisation doing political and organisational work (which was the responsibility of the mass Party). Individual Party workers were invited to unite in the S.L., to exchange ideas and pool experiences, because 'it is an application of that co-operative principle we advocate for society generally.'[iii] Aiming to increase the effectiveness of the Movement by working out detailed solutions to problems, the S.L. espoused no dogmatism; the policies of the Labour Movement could only be settled by frank and open discussion: 'Our proposals are an attempt to face the problems involved in implementing Party Conference decisions and should be regarded as a contribution to the general pool of ideas.'[iv]

S.L. leaders denied they had any intention of 'imposing' policies upon the Movement. (There was little possibility of this happening). From October 1932 to October 1934, it concentrated on formulating lines of policy. It would not attempt to create a large membership or even build any organised body of opinion.[v] Membership

---

[i] *New Leader*, September 23rd, 1932.

[ii] S.L. News, 'Question and Answer', *New Clarion*, July 1st, 1933.

[iii] S.L. Notes, *New Clarion*, August 19th, 1933.

[iv] S.L. News, *New Clarion*, July 8th, 1933.

[v] Cf. Cripps, 'The Fight Goes On', *Socialist Leaguer*, No. 5, October–November 1934.

was presented as a privilege, a responsibility, in which the acid test would be a willingness to work for the Socialist cause. G. D. H. Cole explained to the S.L.: 'Facts form the basis upon which a realistic Socialist policy has to be built up. If we ignore facts we shall fail… the moral is not that we should be moderate, but that we should be sensibly extreme, looking facts in the face in order not to sacrifice our faith.'[i] Sensibly extreme was an apposite formulation.

The 'irresponsible' and 'impractical' Left was enhanced in official Party circles, and haunted the S.L. but Laski clarified intellectual discipline and the creation of an educational department in the Movement: 'If our triumph is not built upon the possession of solid knowledge by the rank and file, it is not going to be a triumph at all'.[ii] Confined within the Party's straitjacket, the S.L. could suggest alternatives. Sir Charles Trevelyan was anxious to present the S.L. as a constructive Party adjunct. In the first S.L. public lecture, he acknowledged the Party as the only instrument available for economic salvation: 'If deliberately, courageously and expertly used, it could become the greatest instrument ever created for the purpose of fundamental change.'[iii] Mixed with this idealism, Trevelyan added that the Party had to decide which industries to nationalise and how to limit the power of the House of Lords, to cease working for palliatives and become a Party for fundamental change: 'The next Socialist Government must be animated by a ruthless determination to carry through Socialist measures.'[iv] And 12 years later it was.

These fervent phrases typified S.L. leaders in its first year. The call for 'fundamental Socialist measures' attracted J. T. Murphy,[v] as Wise was calling for a 'Socialist Revolutionary Policy' which would lead the younger generation to challenge the 'mess and muddle' which democracy under capitalism had bequeathed. To Wise, the only way of rendering the young immune from Fascism was to offer 'adventure, aggression and action', to make plans for replacing capitalist control by that of the workers, to substitute a National Economic Plan for the waste of private enterprise, to safeguard peace by refusing to assist in capitalist or Imperialist war.'[vi] This appeal was stirring, rhetorical – and, to Party leaders, alienating. G. D. H. Cole had been claiming that the S.L. wanted to end 'mere vague talk' and offer 'concrete proposals' because a sharp break with the past was the only way forward.[vii] Cripps was equally adamant that if the Party 'worked hard' it would be able to create a sufficiently large body of convinced Socialists to bring about a Socialist Government, whereas if the Party formed another minority Government, it would be the finish of the Party, and he would 'have no further use for it' if it did not intend to bring 'an active programme of immediate Socialism.'[viii] He continued to fantasise about the transition period before the Socialist millennium, and there remained a perversity in his appeal for 'an instructed public opinion, knowing what we are seeking to do, and backing us up in

---

[i] G. D. H. Cole, 'The Working-class Movement and the Transition to Socialism', *Problems of the Socialist Transition*, No. 5, 1934.

[ii] H. Laski, *New Clarion*, March 4th, 1933.

[iii] Trevelyan, *The Challenge to Capitalism*, January 1933, S.L. pamphlet

[iv] Ibid.

[v] Cf. J. T. Murphy, *New Clarion*, April 15th, 1933.

[vi] *New Clarion*, May 13th, 1933.

[vii] G. D. H. Cole, *The Socialist Control of Industry*, February 26th, 1933.

[viii] Quoted in *News Chronicle*, November 21st, 1932.

detail[i], especially when the chronic state of the Party in 1932 precluded any such activities from having anything other than minimal appeal. This message continued. The fate of the German Democrats fostered more proof of the failure of gradualism, and the need for a practical, worked-out programme: 'The S.L. working within the Party would be a force which could save Britain from the fate of the German Social Democrats. Definite informative propaganda on steps to be taken by a Socialist Government was the best method of obtaining support in the country.[ii] The S.L. reiterated its tasks as convincing a majority of the electorate that Socialism provided a practical alternative to Capitalism, achieved by a programme which demonstrated practical means of applying the basic doctrine of Socialism to 'present-day circumstances'.

At first, Roosevelt's 'revolution by consent' was heralded by the S.L. because he seemed to have discovered a new social equation in which an irrational economic process could be transformed to serve social purposes. This appealed to the S.L.'s corporate imagination. The Roosevelt experiment justified the view; once a progressive Government won power, there would be immediate 'planning' in all fields, and the results of Roosevelt's moderate policies made S.L. leaders question hopes of any co-operation from British business, if the Labour Party began to follow Socialist resolutions. This was circumspection. Laski concluded that, since Congress had given Roosevelt large powers, the S.L.'s prescription of 'emergency powers' for a future Labour Government was the only rational response.[iii]

Incorporated into the S.L.'s central thinking was that the Party could not afford any success to be jeopardised by newspaper magnates: *'Free speech and a free Press are no more part of the eternal verities than Free Trade'.*[iv] The aim to debate issues publicly was not just an attempt to lay down policies for a Labour Government, but to prepare for *every* eventuality. Proposals to establish in advance the Party's answer to every form of opposition (from Parliamentary obstruction to a military coup d'état) was propaganda in a vacuum, ventilation of S.L. frustrations upon fictitious events. Cripps typified this, with his talk of working-class mobilisation, and its 'crystallisation' upon the essential points of the S.L. programme. He knew that vague phrases and wordy reasoning in the MacDonald tradition were futile, but his main concern was that, by wrapping up real intentions in vague, general terms (to avoid frightening nervous electors), the keenness of convinced Socialists would be lost, and no clear mandate would emerge.[v] By September 1933, Cripps was writing to the Durham S.L. organiser that *a clear presentation of the Socialist case* was essential, and it was no good holding out to workers the hope of permanent amelioration under the existing economic system.[vi] Cripps was not deterred by the misgivings of other S.L. leaders at his 'indiscretions'.

G. D. H. Cole expressed the prevalent view in S.L. groups that 'for Socialists, political honesty pays, for we cannot achieve Socialism without the real and intelligent backing of a big and determined opinion'.[vii] Summing up the S.L.'s first year, Cripps concluded that the organisation had contributed to the elucidation of problems which the Movement

---

[i] Quoted in *Hampstead Citizen*, December 2nd, 1932.
[ii] Cripps at Bristol S.L. meeting, reported in S.L. Notes, *New Clarion*, April 29th, 1933.
[iii] Laski, 'The Roosevelt Experiment', *Capitalism in Crisis*, Forum Series, No. 1, November 1933.
[iv] E. F. Wise, *New Clarion*, May 13th, 1933.
[v] Cripps, 'Democracy: Real or Sham?', *Problems of the Socialist Transition*, 1934.
[vi] Cripps to Charles Wilson, September 26th, 1933, Cripps Papers.
[vii] G. D. H. Cole, 'What a Socialist Government Must Do', *New Clarion*, April 22nd, 1933.

had to face; he denied that the S.L. had *confused* the rank and file: 'In these days of crisis, stocktaking, formulation of policy and preparation... our educational and propaganda activities within the wider Movement have been welcomed by constituent bodies and have caused fresh and vigorous discussion once again to flow through the ranks'.[i]

The presentation of the S.L.'s purpose as the honest, fearless facing of policy, strategy and tactics was the function of lectures and pamphlets. By March 1934, the S.L. editorial estimated that the S.L. had made a marked impression and that 'of all our methods, that of the pamphlet and the spoken word have proved themselves.'[ii] S.L. achievements were listed; a fair share of publicity in the general Press (despite inaccurate reporting), widespread interest in S.L. activities, an awareness of the S.L.'s methods of propaganda, discussion and persuasion: 'The S.L. has sought, within the terms of its Party affiliation, to arouse a lively sense of the need for an active and challenging Socialist outlook and policy'.[iii] It stood by its policy of making democracy effective by *using* the machinery of democracy, whether Parliamentary, union, co-operative or municipal. In fact, the content of pamphlets and lectures shows far more interest in opposition to Government policies and Acts (and even Labour policies) than in putting forward 'detailed alternatives', other than generalised Socialist aspirations. The most useful function was focusing opposition, for although the S.L.'s professed ideological leanings were expressed in pamphlets, periodicals, conferences, and national and local meetings, the overriding theme was *deficiencies* in the existing structure of social organisation and the S.L.'s elaborate schemes for economic and social reforms. (This represented wishful thinking; J. T. Murphy was conscious of this: 'The workers demand bread and we give them a propaganda speech'.)[iv]

S.L. educational activities in its first two years were for '*Socialism and Peace*', and to relate its projected legislation to long-term developments towards a 'classless society'. The most important element of the S.L. in the Movement was this adoption of a long-term view of progress, although the 'impracticality and outspoken irresponsibility' of the S.L. was contrasted with union leaders' pragmatism; the S.L. provided the bulk of the propaganda for a Socialist philosophy, and the insularity of the Movement was lessened by this 'intellectual ferment'. S.L. pamphlets were assertive in representing a political creed. In *The Need for a Socialist Programme*,[v] G. D. H. Cole and G. R. Mitchison stated that a practical policy had to be understood through all sections of the Movement and 'felt as something which the Movement had made'. This was a crucial point, since the main implications drawn from S.L. pamphlets were that 'Socialism' implied a personal attitude *and* a collective effort, which involved agreement as to the kind of society desired, the resistance to be overcome, the technique, methods and machinery required. These three aspects represented then the S.L.'s contribution to the Labour Movement's thought, for a reorientation in Party policy made in a language which could be applauded by Social-Democrat and Marxist. Gathered into a Forum Series entitled *Capitalism in Crisis*, the pamphlets irked Ernest Bevin, who had attacked the habit of adopting slogans at the annual meeting of the S.S.I.P.: 'To say that "Capitalism" was breaking down

---

[i] Cripps, *New Clarion*, October 1933.

[ii] S.L. Notes, 'The Will to Power', *New Clarion*, March 10th, 1934.

[iii] Ibid.

[iv] J. T. Murphy, *New Horizons*, pp.300–302.

[v] Published February 11th, 1933.

might be a comforting thought, but it was not true. Capitalism was adjusting itself far more rapidly than many people in the Labour Movement imagined. The view that its breakdown was inevitable was the product of intellectual inertia.[i] He was right but the S.L. remained unconvinced. The pamphlets presented a relentless barrage of facts showing that the existing economic and social system had a degrading effect. At no other time had so much been written on every aspect of political questions, yet the failure of the S.L. to build a large following after 1934 was due to its propaganda.

The total membership of the S.L. never exceeded 3,500, and the main appeal was the elaborate ideological discussions for those starved of political thought; the pamphlets offered a forum for viewpoints, rather than a presentation of a coherent policy. S.L. lectures at Transport House carried on the tradition inaugurated by the S.S.I.P.[ii] Cole and Mitchison's 1933 pamphlet[iii] dealt with the S.L.'s programme (where the points of resistance were likely to arise, what the key positions were, where the S.L. had to be prepared to fight, and by what means). It was a reasoned analysis of matters with which an incoming Socialist Government would have to deal, because the object of the S.L.'s series of memoranda on Party resolutions was to select proposals of outstanding importance, to relate them as part of a coherent plan of action, to anticipate difficulties in their application, and lay before the Party as clear an outline as possible of the steps by which *the first real Socialist Government*[iv] was likely. The memoranda were not statements of detailed policy; S.L. leaders were offering suggestions to spread a clearer knowledge of what the S.L. *meant* by 'Socialist' policy.

The S.L. assumed (from no historical precedent) that a Socialist programme would command strong public support if it had been *thoroughly explained in advance*, and objections answered, in order to dispel unreasonable fears and prevent panics due to deliberate misrepresentation by Press, radio and Parliament. This was the S.L.'s reaction to the 1931 crisis. It was a premise that the *limits* of improving conditions under capitalism had almost been reached. Although an incoming Socialist Government might devise ameliorative measures, the S.L. did not want these in a Party programme or for appeal to the electorate; S.L. memoranda would have served their purpose if they were criticised and replaced by other measures more carefully and more far-sightedly elaborated, while S.L. pamphlets defended Socialist values, taught practical lessons, enlarged S.L. members' experience by analysing human motives and interaction of circumstances and conditions upon individual and social fortunes. In March 1933, the S.L. announced that its 'Four Year Plan' as set out in the Forum lectures and pamphlets had been commended in 'quarters not usually too generous with their praise of Socialist ideas.'[v] It did not specify, but the Four Year Plan had not been put forward as a programme, but as the basis for discussion and further plans: 'They conquer who believe they can' was now translated into 'they conquer who think'. The S.L. had been in existence for only 5 months when it reported: 'The lectures have been one of the best answers to the people who ask *What is the Socialist League for?*'[vi] Every S.L. member was asked to *read these policy-building pamphlets*,[vii] to

i May 28th, 1932 reported in *Record*, June 1932, qu. A. Bullock, op. cit., p.329.
ii *New Clarion*, S.L. Notes, December 24th, 1932.
iii 'The Need for a Socialist Programme', February 1933.
iv *New Clarion*, S.L. Notes, February 11th, 1933. (My italics.)
v *New Clarion*, S.L. Notes, March 18th, 1933.
vi March 25th, 1933, *New Clarion*, S.L. Notes, 'Five Months Old'.
vii April 8th, 1933, *New Clarion*, S.L. Notes.

find out the S.L. National Council's views on Finance, Fascism, Workers' Control, Agriculture, Local Government, Unemployment and the Constitution.[i] In September 1933 was stated the need for intensive propaganda by pamphlets and speakers available to union branches and local Labour Parties.

Incorporating many of the S.L. lectures, the first S.L. book, *Problems of a Socialist Government* (August 1933) was indispensable to those who endeavoured to be in touch with developments in a Socialist outlook.[ii] It caused a negative stir in the Press, especially in the *Morning Post* with its contemptuous review and depiction of S.L. writers as a 'Rogues Gallery'. The headlines exemplified the *Morning Post*'s position: 'Socialist Scheme for a Clean Sweep... Complete Russianising of Great Britain... Remarkable Confession by Ten Leaders... Wholesale Confiscation – by Force (if necessary)... No Guarantee of a Peaceful Change'. It showed pictures of 'the Brains Trust of the Socialist Revolution', and judged the symposium as a call to comrades to believe the 'Socialist Party' meant business: 'It has proposals for rigging the Constitution to suit the Socialist book.'[iii] (What Constitution?) 15 years later, in the middle of the third Labour Government, David Stelling crudely reviewed the book as *'Cripps' Kampf: the bedside book of the Socialist Ministers'*. He saw Cripps as the instigator: 'It is to his keen mind and concentrated resolution that the book owes its importance as a political document. The colour of his thought suffuses every chapter and gives a unity and coherence to the whole.'[iv] Cripps was demonised as the first Socialist politician to discover that, if Socialism was to be translated from a doctrine into a political instrument, a revolution had to be engineered, and that it was not sufficient to discuss revolution in Bloomsbury bed-sitting rooms. Stelling outrageously approximated the Socialist mentality to the *'National Socialist'*, and claimed the book remained the Bible of the Labour Government: 'None of its authors has ever recanted a single word ... they have translated into action as many as possible of the items of the programme outlined in the book ... the gentlemanly revolutionaries laid their careful plans 15 years ago, and have been sedulously putting them into execution.' Such an impact would have been most welcome to the struggling S.L. in the early 1930s!

In the second Forum Series of 9 lectures (from November 1933 to March 1944) the first four were devoted to the challenge presented by the 'crisis in Western capitalism', and concentrated on the broad economic and social consequences of Roosevelt, Fascism in Germany, and the need for 'War Resistance'. The other five lectures dealt with clarifying opinion on the tactics of trade unionism, the Co-operative Movement, and professional workers. In the S.L., these lectures merited the closest attention from Socialists and trade unionists, because they were 'provocative of thought and debate, closely reasoned, clearly stated.'[v] Positing a Socialist David confronting a Capitalist Goliath, the S.L. visualised its new lecture series as indicating the weak spots in 'Giant Capital's armour' and slinging many a shrewd pebble at his troubled brow in the process.'[vi]

One of the pamphlets was G. D. H. Cole's *The Working Class and the Transition to Socialism*, a challenging affirmation of belief, a critical examination of the position of the

---

i June 24th, 1933, *New Clarion*, S.L. Notes.
ii August 26th, 1933, *New Clarion*.
iii *Morning Post*, August 28th, 1933.
iv February 1948, *New English Review* (in J. F. Horrabin's Papers).
v December 23rd, 1933, *New Clarion*, Views to Note (S.L. Notes).
vi January 13th, 1934, *New Clarion*, S.L. Notes on 'Forum Pamphlets'.

working class movement as a preliminary to proposals;[i] Cole sought to bring the unemployed back into the Labour Movement, to band unions together, and initiate a Socialist campaign in the Co-operative Movement. These proposals were accepted by the S.L. because Cole justified the S.L. as an organised body of thorough-going conscious Socialists.[ii] Laski reviewed the second S.L. book, *Problems of the Socialist Transition* (1934); its significance lay in the choice which confronted the Labour Party between a direct attack on capitalism and a policy of social reform with the minimum of disturbance. He recognised that the first might not result in an immediate electoral victory because it required arduous propaganda; the second provided the prospect of office in the next five years, and would mean considerable social reforms and amelioration of working conditions, but would leave untouched the possibilities of a Socialist Britain. For the S.L., it insisted that they were dealing with the foundations of *capitalist decay* and it was futile to deal with minor symptoms, whereas Party leaders were influenced by the psychology of the *market economy*. Laski was aware that the obstacles in the way of S.L. policy (even if accepted by the Party) were immense, and there was a tendency in the S.L. to underestimate them, but he believed that for the first time in a generation, Labour militants had begun to create a coherent Socialist philosophy, to counteract the dominant mood of Party leaders, entrenched in Liberal principles and presenting an omnium gatherum of disparate ideas.[iii] Distrust of the Party's Parliamentary methods was also reflected in pamphlets, although this was expressed in managerial terms. Here, the S.L. represented an extension of the idea of efficient administration based on accumulated knowledge, yet alienated the majority of the Movement because of its undigested use of Marxist phraseology ('bourgeois ideology', 'class consciousness', 'proletarian solidarity', 'expropriation of the expropriators') and S.L. leaders spent an inordinate time on a 'heresy hunt' against Labour and union 'reformists'.

The two most influential books in the S.L. were G. R. Mitchison's *The First Workers' Government* (1934) and John Strachey's *The Coming Struggle for Power* (1932). Mitchison's semi-official S.L. tract assumed a spontaneous Socialist conversion in the Labour Party (some assumption!) evading the problem of how to win over the Party Executive. Events worked against Mitchison's arguments when he had to assume the Party leadership fell to younger militants on the deaths of all the older leaders! The C.P.'s Palme Dutt pointed out that the book appeared with commendations from Labour leaders, and had left class war out of the picture.[iv] S.L. reviewer, H. L. Elvin saw in the book a picture of Socialism in England by 1980 (Thatcherism had just begun!) and thought the whole temper of the book to be uncongenial to the Party leaders. Mitchison's Labour leaders knew the difference between Socialism and the Corporate State: 'There is hard thinking in this book... If we are to get where Mitchison has imagined us to be in 1980, we must have a Labour Party that is 'Socialist', knows what that means, and is capable of starting resolutely on the road...'[v] Strachey's *The Coming Struggle for Power* also had an influence on the S.L.'s task of linking Social democracy and Marxism and the idea of a struggle for power was

---

i *New Clarion*, January 27th, 1934, S.L. Notes: 'Transition to Socialism'.
ii Ibid.
iii H. Laski, 'Direct Attack or Progressivism?', *The Socialist Leaguer* No.4, Sept/Oct 1934.
iv R. P. Dutt, 'The United Front and the Labour Party' in *Labour Monthly*, Vol. 16, No. 11 (November 1934).
v H. L. Elvin, review November–December 1934, *Socialist Leaguer*, No. 6.

congenial to S.L. policy-makers, since their approach was in opposition to gradualism: 'Strachey's lucid blend of Marxism and humanism had the force of a vision.'[i] The book helped to create a climate of opinion, while it expressed an S.L. assumption that there was some inherent virtue in the working class, and intentions of the Soviet Union were selfless and morally inspired! Strachey's book was a ready-made guide to a philosophy of action with its adherence to collective action, but he echoed the 1930s dilemma which gripped the S.L.: 'Verbal socialism, like religion, can become the opium of the people.'[ii]

The S.L.'s major source of strength was that it was establishing its credentials with a Movement whose political universe had been coterminous with the Party. Campaigns in the Party were essential for a viable S.L., but the price of admission to the political universe of Labourism was to leave the S.L. fragmented. Until the outcome of the Southport Conference in 1934, the S.L. was content to operate as a pressure group on Party leaders but its strategic failure was its inability or refusal to recognise the character and source of its weak position. The issues behind which the S.L. rallied were rarely argued or fought for in a way that related them to 'working-class consciousness', because the focus of its debate and agitation was largely directed upwards to pressurising Party leaders rather than outwards to unions or the wider electorate. S.L. attempts at independent political action failed or were localised, although in reaction to National Government policies, progressive opinion was shaped by the S.L.'s well-publicised denunciations, and its outlook was reflected in the oppositional political approach of the Labour Party, which was subjected to the pressures of the S.L. to adopt a radical programme.

All S.L. hopes rested on an assumption that the Party would commit to a radical programme; the S.L. had no elaborate plan to 'capture the centre of the Party', but was on solid ground when expressing dissatisfactions of the politically conscious to a situation with which established Parties were incapable of dealing. The difficulty for the S.L. was that as long as the shadow of Nazi and Fascist aggression hung over Britain, there was no chance of embarking upon a major experiment of social and economic reform, because the salvation of democracy was a stronger bind than any appeals of 'Socialism' for the majority of the electorate. And although the S.L. kept the Left 'as a significant group', it was no more successful in achieving its objectives than the I.L.P. The interests and priorities of the S.L. were different from those of the official leaders, and the 1934 Southport Party Conference altered the S.L.'s perspectives. C.P.'er Palme Dutt assessed the S.L.'s history and dilemma fairly accurately: 'The S.L. was intended to provide a model of an *auxiliary propagandist Socialist organisation* within the Labour Party, which should not repeat the errors of the I.L.P. The S.L. was at first to make no attempt to put forward an alternative policy to the Party Executive. Its leaders confined themselves to abstract propaganda for a legislative Socialist programme to be accomplished by the next Labour Government. The S.L. consists mainly of a group of leading writers in the Labour Party, with little working-class membership. Every precaution had thus been taken to create a 'safe' Socialist organisation… Within two years, the S.L. has found itself putting forward a complete alternative programme to the official Party programme and overwhelmingly voted down at the Party Conference, and already beginning to be faced with the same

i Julian Symons, *The Thirties*, 1960, p.44.
ii J. Strachey, *The Coming Struggle for Power* (1932), p.297

problems as the I.L.P.[i] So long as the S.L. confined itself to general propaganda of Socialist promises on behalf of a future Labour Government, it was tolerated as a useful *'rallying department'* by the Party Executive. However, I.L.P.'er Clifford Allen was disappointed that the slogan *'Socialism in Our Time'*, expressed in a carefully constructed, bold political technique, had been 'wrecked by those who had made a battle-cry of what should have been a spiritual and intellectual endeavour.'[ii]

For S.L. leaders, there seemed no alternatives. Outside the Labour Party it was impossible to influence the course of British politics. As Aneurin Bevan wrote to Jennie Lee: 'It is the Labour Party or nothing... I know all its faults, all its dangers, but it is the Party that we have taught millions of working people to look to and regard as their own.'[iii] Sir Charles Trevelyan (speaking for the S.L. in 1935) optimistically demanded, from the Party, propaganda throughout the country in support of Socialist measures: 'No Labour Government could exist in Parliament for a fortnight unless in the King's Speech it had announced the instant introduction of great Socialist measures for nationalising the banks, the land, and the major industries.'[iv] Likewise, G. D. H. Cole described the S.L. as 'a special society devoted to the propaganda of Socialism'; he was cognisant of the danger that the S.L. could become too wrapped up in itself, and so degenerate into a clique, and pained that the S.L. might become a home for straying intellectuals (like the Fabian Society) or for elderly and disillusioned union officials (like the S.D.F.); it might become a mutual admiration society or grow so conscious of its own superior virtue that it would be 'content as a Sectarian Party'[v] (in fact, the S.L. was too small, too isolated from the mass Movement to afford these kinds of self-doubts).

It was a generally accepted union view that the difference between the S.L. and Party leaders was temperamental: 'The S.L. leaders are romantic to the core. The achievement of their sort of Socialism involves not merely a 'revolution' but a 'Revelation'. There is something apocalyptic about the writings of W. Mellor and J. T. Murphy. They continue to give us an impression of the imminence of fiery wonders about to descend from the heavens with the Chairman of the Socialist League in the rôle of the Holy Ghost.'[vi] Union leaders thought it was futile to chase any 'Socialist Millennium' (why not?), and the S.L.'s resolution (refusing to take office with a Parliamentary minority) was pointless when the Party had to exert the maximum influence upon the National Government. Milne-Bailey dubbed the S.L.'s work *'a crude sentimental appeal'*, caused by the electoral avalanche of 1931, which had 'made some people lose their heads and fly to eccentric expedients.' And the S.L.'s propaganda was used by non-Socialists to evoke Labour's disarray. Cripps was presented as the best card in the hand of the Government because he was pledged to 'the destruction of the industrial system'.[vii] It irritated Labour leaders, the jibe that perorations by the Socialist League put obstacles in the way of the Party's practical policy; H. B. Lees-Smith[viii] betrayed the Party's annoyance that the limelight was

---

i R. Palme Dutt, 'The United Front and the Labour Party', *Labour Monthly*, Vol. 16, No. 11, November 1934. (My italics.)
ii C. Allen, *Britain's Political Future*, 1934, quoted p.129, Marwick, *C. Allen*, op. cit.
iii Quoted J. Lee, *Tomorrow Is a New Day*, 1939, p.151
iv Sir C. Trevelyan, *The Outlook of the Socialist League*, April–June 1935, *Political Quarterly*
v G. D. H. Cole, *The Working Class Movement and the Transition to Socialism*, No. 5, Forum Series 1934.
vi W. Milne-Bailey, 'The Strategy of Victory' in *New Trends in Socialism*, 1935.
vii F. Kingsley Griffith, 'The Liberal Appeal' in *Political Quarterly*, April–June 1935.
viii Rt. Hon. H. B. Lees-Smith 'Prospects for the Labour Party' in *Political Quarterly*, January–March 1935.

thrown on the war waged against Party policy by the S.L., which he incriminated for its lack of help in working out *detailed* programmes. He judged S.L. policies and outlook as similar to the I.L.P., commenting that the S.L. delighted in debating the confiscation of property, and sabotage of a Labour Government by financiers, armed forces and the Press. His conclusion was that the Party should expose the S.L.'s *'rhetorical appeals'* and *'irresponsible declamation'*.[i] It was not denied that there was opportunity for an independent Socialist organisation to arm the Party with intellectual penetration; research and education were essential needs, but the S.L. had wasted its opportunity 'by preparing *contrary programmes*... [which could be] sunk with intellectual criticism.'[ii] Little of the latter was forthcoming.

After the Party's Southport Conference, the S.L. decided to alter its direction. It conceived the same task of ensuring a core of convinced Socialists (a phrase borrowed from G. D. H. Cole) to create a temper and a spirit which would be proof against any kind of capitalist opposition, but there was much stronger S.L. criticism of reformist Party leanings: 'You can't fool the Capitalist: the idea that you can buy off capitalist opposition by anything short of a complete surrender of Socialism is a delusion. The smallest inroad on Profit and Privilege will be contested as implacably as a frontal attack on the whole foundations... Capitalism will make no more concessions.'[iii] S.L. policies after October 1934 were concerned with the 'tone' of the Movement, rather than the political programme of a future Government. This was an S.L. attempt to salvage, after the Southport Party decisions, some future as an activist organisation, to press the case for the *'class struggle'* as the only basis on which a Socialist Movement could be built. Mellor explained the altered rôle: 'Our methods must be broadened and enlarged... Our theoretical approach must be given immediate practical content... That involves our taking part in initiating and leading activities on daily questions confronting the workers – issues the solution of which is to be found in the application of our fundamental policy. The will to power cannot be created on a diet of theory or kept alive by telling the workers to wait until the General Election comes. It must be created and kept alive by constant agitation within capitalism.'[iv]

The S.L. National Council decided to organise conferences and demonstrations through the Party, Trades Councils and S.L. branches, on the *Unemployment Act* and its administration, the Means Test and scales of relief, 'Rents and Housing', union problems, and effects of rationalisation on industries. By activities on working-class rights, freedom of speech, the menace of Fascism, and the danger of war, the S.L. could become a rallying ground in the Labour Movement. While it was pressing for action on these, it initiated its own programme, and offered to aid Labour Youth in finding outlets for their energies more appealing than the formal activities of a local Labour Party.

Donald Barber (the new S.L. General Secretary) supplemented these methods by urging that the S.L. become not only an umbrella for 'loyal grousers' but an instrument for co-ordinating Marxist opinion and action in the Movement. Ellen Wilkinson summarised this need for a different approach in the Left wing of the Party in 1935: 'The new wave of Socialist thought must arise out of the experience of the

---

i Ibid.

ii E. F. M. Durbin, 'Democracy and Socialism in Britain' in *Political Quarterly*, July–September 1935.

iii Editorial in *Socialist Leaguer*, no. 5, October–November 1934.

iv W. Mellor, 'Southport and After: The Task for Socialists', *Socialist Leaguer*, October–November 1934, No. 5.

workers, manual, technical and administrative, deliberately and carefully encouraged to meet and discuss problems on the basis of coming to power, and on the lines of 'taking over'... Only by a revolution in its methods and approach, only by tackling the problems in terms of real power, can the Socialist Movement survive.'[i] What this revolution in methods and approach meant was not clear, but St. John Ervine was fulminating against *'the tin Trotskys of the Socialist League'*[ii], not that the S.L. possessed the union connections of Trotskyists. They were more interested in the aims of Socialism, to release creative forces frustrated by the institutions of a market economy, to abolish poverty, social inequality and fear of war, and to make a classless, prosperous society. Such slogans were Cripps' forte. In February 1936, he was highlighting the S.L.'s stand for the common ownership of the means of production, upon which could be based the planning of abundance, and the propaganda for the simple principles of Socialism.[iii]

Despite the alleged reformation in the S.L.'s approach, it remained central to the S.L. to work towards a clearer *theoretical* understanding of Socialism. While the responsibilities of His Majesty's Opposition curtailed Labour leaders, outspoken comment came from S.L. leaders who, as a result, emerged as national figures. S.L. members' differences from Party leaders grew with the advocacy of a programme which was a collective expression of the discontent of Socialist intellectuals with Party gradualism. In January 1935, a third lecture series began. It dealt with new capitalist attacks on workers': J. T. Murphy on *'The Attack on Workers' Rights'*, Cripps on *'The Beginnings of the Corporate State'*, H. N. Brailsford on *'The New Forms of Imperialism in India'*. Cripps retained the sentiments of 1932: 'I do not want to see the Party go back on the swing of the pendulum. I would rather wait until a firm foundation has been laid in the brains of the people for a true Socialist programme.'[iv] (Political writing was apt to consist of prefabricated phrases bolted together like the pieces of a child's Meccano set.') The S.L.'s theoretical work continued, and justified on the grounds that the more complex a society, the greater the need for *theory*. This was clarified in September 1935: 'Many workers take for granted the use of the theoretician in the spheres of everyday life, but show contempt for theory and its uses in the overthrow of the social order... There are many good, active Socialists who, simply because they have no basic principles, no standards of values by which to test and examine all propositions, fall victim to the emotional appeal or the catchphrase.'[vi] Could you ever trust the media?

On the practical level, S.L. leaders were aware of the Party's need to overcome the appearance of being dominated by the unions at Labour Conferences, and in the choice of Party candidates the S.L. concentrated on making Labour leaders aware of the choice between a 'Socialist' Party and a 'Social Reform' Party. This was the fundamental issue before the Party after the 1935 Election defeat. In S.L. terminology, the Labour Party had to become a Party which adapted the substance of Marxist philosophy to the historical conditions of British politics. Laski stated: 'The Labour Party has looked at formal political democracy as a system of principles and institutions abstracted from the capitalist foundations upon which it rests... The Party is always

---

i E. Wilkinson, 'Socialism and the Problem of the Middle Classes' in *New Trends in Socialism*, 1935.
ii St. John Ervine, 'Time and Tide', November 1934.
iii Cripps in letter, February 20th, 1936 (Cripps Papers).
iv Cripps quoted in *Manchester Guardian*, March 16th, 1935.
v G. Orwell in *Collected Writings*, 'The Prevention of Literature', p.318.
vi 'Jacques', 'Science, NOT Rule of Thumb', *Socialist*, No.1 September 1935.

tempted to minimise the significance of Socialist principles in order to prove that it is practical,[i] and Storm Jameson signified the perils which a Socialist Government would face if it had not worked out plans to the last detail.[ii] Reviewing four years of S.L. work, an editorial noted the lack of an analysis of events and their causes, upon which to base policy. The S.L. had worked to give the necessary analysis and to gather round it those within the Movement who realised that 'the capture of power' was the real issue. In national and international affairs, the S.L. had sought to expose the illusions and mirages of liberal belief in the purposes of 'democratic' capitalism: 'The watchwords are "No truce with Capitalism", "No acceptance of Capitalist promises", "No trust in any other unity but that of the working class"'.[iii] It was going to be a long haul.

Thus, when *Tribune* was launched as the new independent Socialist weekly (edited by Mellor), its purpose was to provide a platform for the challenging expression of Left opinion. It was to unite all those prepared to present a real challenge to the 'upholders of this system of exploitation', to be untiring in the fight for 'freedom', a 'champion of the workers' in their struggle, a fearless advocate of Socialism.'[iv] *Tribune*'s policy would have far-reaching effect throughout the working-class Movement. To its credit, the S.L. gave (in the Labour Party) a coherent analysis of capitalist power, significant for Socialist education, research and propaganda, and an authentic *'ideology of social change'*, while Party and union leaders subordinated everything to the management of a popular electoral machine: 'From 1932 to 1937 was an era of uncommon Party regularity with an iron resistance to the erratic, the different and the dynamic.'[v] The S.L. operated as a safety valve for Socialist sentiment within the Party and its historical relevance would not emerge for generations, not until a Labour Government jettisoned most of its Socialist baggage in the late 1990s. And the reason may relate to the 1930s: that 'Capitalism may be wicked, it may be oppressive, it may be exploitative, it may be commercializing and vulgarizing culture and destroying moral values, but there is more freedom in it, more variety, more self-expression.'[vi] That was not the Socialist League's perception, which was that freedom from poverty, hunger, inequality, exploitation, seemed more fundamental than civil liberties, more important than the free play of the market, which was interpreted in the 1930s as freedom of the few to exploit the many.

[i] H. Laski: 'The General Election of 1935' in *Political Quarterly* (January–March 1936).

[ii] S. Jameson, *Socialist*, No. 4, January–February 1936.

[iii] The Editorial, 'Matters of Moment', *Socialist*, No. 8, June 1936.

[iv] *Socialist*, No. 13, December–January 1936–37.

[v] M. George, *The Hollow Men*, 1965.

[vi] Isaiah Berlin, quoted by R. Jahanbegloo, *Conversations with Isaiah Berlin*, 1993, p.128.

Chapter Four

The Socialist League's Annual Conferences and Policy Resolutions

Socialist parties in European democracies have been misguided when they ground their moral appeals in the ideal of equality rather than justice ... The implicit moral appeal of 'Das Kapital' is to the in-built unfairness of the distribution of property under capitalism, which ensures ... that the labourer can never receive the just rewards of his labour which will be skimmed off as surplus value and distributed to the owners and controllers of the means of production. That is the core of the moral argument ... It links all who depend on the will of others for their survival ... If they achieve no access to fair consideration of their claims, and if they have a reasonable chance of success through violence, they will fight for justice ... This has always been the justifiable way of the dispossessed who have come to feel ... the injustice of which they are the victims and who have been denied the minimum decencies of procedural justice.

> Stuart Hampshire, 'Morality and Machiavelli',
> in *Innocence and Experience*, 1992 edn., p.185

The puzzle is this: how did the optimistic and progressive spirit of 18th century Europe give way to the dark and terrifying world of the 19th and 20th centuries? How did the Europe that produced Goethe and Kant, Voltaire and Rousseau, Tolstoy and Chekhov, also produce the Lager and the Gulag?

> Mark Lilla, 'Wolves and Lambs', *The Legacy of Isaiah Berlin*, 2001, p.33

One unfailing source of disagreement in the Labour Party has been ideological, stemming from the Socialist politics which pervaded the early years of the Party. This was written into the Party Constitution and continued to influence the Left of the Party. Controversy over Party policy took place between broadly-based moderate and narrowly-based Left attitudes and this schism between doctrinaire Socialism and pragmatic reform has not narrowed.[i] The S.L. expressed in its own Conferences and resolutions the essential *issue*, the Party's attempt to create a more efficient and humane administration of a capitalist society.

The policies adopted under MacDonald left an ideological vacuum for the Party in 1932. For the S.L. the task of those who believed in Socialism was to convince a majority of the electorate that it provided a practical alternative to capitalism: 'What is required is a programme which demonstrates beyond doubt that there are practical

---

[i] Edward G. Janosik, op. cit.,1968, p.88.

means of applying the basic doctrines of Socialism to present-day circumstances.'[i] In 1925 Clifford Allen had argued the electorate was concerned with constructive details of practical politics: 'It is impossible to introduce Socialism piecemeal... You can only commence Socialism by means of a co-ordinated plan. One should not refrain from action just because one is in a minority. By acting along bold constructive scientific lines one will quickly gain the support of the majority.'[ii] However, while the Labour Party was re-thinking long-term programme-making and Socialist analysis, S.L. policy resolutions would grow in soil denuded of a full measure of political manure. The Labour Party was divided, bickering and condemned to opposition and Party leaders' frustrations were released in hostility towards the S.L. version of Socialist philosophy, strategy and economics, yet the period from 1932 to 1934 was also marked by a reframing of Party policy and 'a healthy stir of ideas.'[iii] The predominant cause of the dissensions within the Party was its weakness in Parliament from 1931 to 1935, and a stronger P.L.P. would have lessened divisions and tensions concerning the formulation of future Party programmes.

The S.L. proposed a future Labour Government embark on a far more extensive programme of nationalisation than the Party had put forward; the S.L. also warned that a Government intent upon carrying through such a programme had to expect fierce, *possibly unconstitutional*, resistance by Conservative financial and business interests. The unreality of these S.L. proposals has been recorded: 'The question confronting the Labour Movement in 1932 was not what a Socialist Government would do after it had won a General Election. It was rather what kind of challenge a Labour Opposition would offer to the National Government – and on this question the Labour Left was rather weak.'[iv] The S.L. aspired to create more opportunities for the unemployed, to end inequality based on birth rather than service, to open education to all, to eliminate discriminatory practices based on class, religion, race or sex, to regulate the economy for the benefit of all, provide adequate social security, and rebuild society on the foundation of co-operation instead of competition and profit.[v] It included reform of Parliamentary procedure and of local government, the House of Lords to be abolished. There were five tenets in the S.L. as formulated in its Conferences: appropriation of property incomes; state ownership; workers' control of industry; social welfare through a Welfare State; and full employment.[vi] These were the only elaborated expression of the views of the Left of which the mass Movement took note, yet, the S.L. was a heterogeneous group following Fabian and I.L.P. traditions (while making concessions to Marxism). For the next Labour Government, the S.L. promoted an Emergency Powers Act, nationalisation of the credit system and land, increased unemployment benefits, the 40-hour week, a National Investment Board and a National Planning Commission (with employee participation in management).

In analysing S.L. Conference resolutions and policies, one notices many later incorporated into Party programmes. In the sympathetic environment of the Leicester Party Conference (1932), the S.L. was able to mount a successful critique of what it

[i] Cripps, preface to *The Problems of a Socialist Government*, op. cit.

[ii] C. Allen, *The I.L.P. and Revolution*, 1925.

[iii] H. Dalton, *Practical Socialism for Britain*, 1935, p.viii.

[iv] R. Miliband, op. cit., 1961, p.200.

[v] Cf. W. Ebenstein, op. cit., p.218.

[vi] Cf. *Labour and the New Social Order*, 1918, *Socialism in Our Time*, 1928, I.L.P., *Labour's Immediate Programme*, 1937.

regarded as the Party's unsevered attachment to gradualist ideas. It gained a swift success. The Executive was defeated on currency and banking proposals and nationalisation of joint stock banks, but the S.L. could never again hope for such a favourable position from which to launch an independent challenge to the leadership. Before its Conference at Derby in 1933, the S.L. had been preparing its resolutions for a Party for 'fundamental change';[i] G. D. H. Cole envisaged the rapid devolution of control over working conditions and of industry to councils with large union representation;[ii] while Harold Clay proclaimed the commodity status of labour could not be accepted. The Final Agenda was 42 pages of closely-reasoned resolutions to promote vigorous discussion on plans by which Socialism could be established, with resolutions on problems facing a Socialist Government's first days in office, the Programme of Action and Emergency Resolutions. E. F. Wise expressed the atmosphere of the Conference: 'Public opinion is looking for action. It is prepared for deep changes in the industrial and social life of the nation.'[iii] Hence the 16 policy resolutions to formulate the policy and programme of a Socialist Government.[iv] The 'Programme of Action' was for adoption of resolutions as immediate Party policy, including an Emergency Powers Act; abolition of the Lords; self-government in industries; elimination of compensation charges for nationalised property; an Anti-War Pledge 'never to take part in a Capitalist war'[v]; and a General Strike in the event of the threat or outbreak of an 'Imperialist' war. There was an emergency resolution on the 'Work or Maintenance' principle and T.U.C. minimum scale of maintenance; protests against the Government's Russian embargo, the persecutions in Germany and the negative attitude of the British Government at the Disarmament Conference.[vi]

There was some dissension to these resolutions, an augury of future internal divisions. E. A. Radice moved to refer back all policy resolutions because they dealt with the situation by piecemeal methods, and gave no proper lead, but E. F. Wise promised to specify the details, and delegates voted 82 to 29 to accept the resolutions in principle.[vii] The S.L. decided against any attempt to be a parallel organisation and committed itself to expressing Socialist opinions and policies as an integral part of the Party. So this first S.L. programme was limited to the work before the next Labour Government (apart from declarations against Fascism and war): 'This question of the tasks of the next Labour Government represents the form in which *the revolt against gradualism* has expressed itself in the Labour Movement as a whole up to the time of the "Fascist" Revolution in Germany,'[viii] assessed J. T. Murphy.

Criticism of the Derby S.L. Conference decisions came from the I.L.P., which assessed the S.L. had concerned itself with plans on the attainment of office, rather than participating in day-to-day struggles. (18 months later the S.L. followed the I.L.P.'s outlook.) The I.L.P.'s *New Leader* also criticised the S.L. for putting its faith in Parliament as the instrument of social change, 'not recognising the developments which were likely 'to create a revolutionary crisis before a Parliamentary majority of

---

[i] C. Trevelyan, *The Challenge to Capitalism*, S.L. pamphlet, January 1933.

[ii] G. D. H. Cole, *The Socialist Control of Industry*, S.L. pamphlet, February 1933.

[iii] *Derby Evening Telegraph* and *Derby Daily Express*, June 6th, 1933.

[iv] *New Clarion*, July 29th, 1933, S.L. Notes, 'National Council at Work'.

[v] *New Clarion*, June 17th, 1933.

[vi] The Government had refused to consent to the abolition of aerial bombing.

[vii] *Report of the Derby Annual Conference of the S.L.*, June 1933.

[viii] J. T. Murphy, *Preparing for Power*, pp.272–273, 1934. (My italics.)

resolute Socialists is attainable,'[i] yet, the *New Leader* acknowledged the S.L. had broken from gradualism in its awareness that Parliamentary democracy was meaningless without economic democracy. Reviewing this Conference 18 months later, Constance Borrett (of the S.L. National Council) commented that the S.L. resolved to concentrate on policy-making and policy propaganda, and that, only with adverse Party Conference decisions was that phase suspended.[ii] In one of Cripps' speeches in 1933 he summed up the S.L.'s juxtaposition of *pragmatism and idealism*; there were three ways to acquire economic power; 'Reformism and Gradualism' (which left economic power with the capitalists in the hope of depriving them of it in unnoticed ways); Violent Revolution (impractical); and Socialism by democracy through Parliament (which involved informing and educating people): 'It is necessary to come out into the open, state objects, desires and methods, and rally the workers to a standard of clear and honest intentions.'[iii] No vested interests would be allowed to stand in the way, and once 'Land and Finance' were in the hands of the community a start could be made to solve distribution problems, while industry would have to be taken out of private ownership.

By the time of the Annual Conference at Leeds in 1934, the S.L. had cemented its reputation as the rallying ground for dissidents and most persistent scorner of Conference decisions. Instead of being content to work in the Labour Party, the S.L. would put forward its own programme in opposition to it.[iv] Even leader of the Party, George Lansbury, was writing that Socialists could never rest content with *'the make-believe of gradualism'*.[v] Reiterating the Derby Conference resolutions, Cripps argued that alternatives to Socialism had failed, so the Labour Party had to go into the next election as 'the Party of Socialist Action.'[vi] At the Leeds S.L. Conference (May 1934), the S.L. drew up an elaborate programme, pledging itself to secure acceptance by the Party of measures which the S.L. considered the next Labour Government should introduce. The main business of the Conference was discussion of this policy statement, which became the backbone of the S.L. Entitled *Forward to Socialism*, it was presented in the form of an election manifesto, with a statement of 'ambulance proposals' to be applied immediately by the next Labour Government.[vii] One of the crucial results of this policy statement was that it was as an advocate of this programme that Cripps became the most popular speaker in the Labour Movement.[viii] J. F. Horrabin moved the resolution to accept *Forward to Socialism* as an alternative to gradualism, involving '**the first 5-year plan for a Socialist Government**'.[ix] S.L. proposals were largely an elaboration of the decisions at its Derby Conference, although they included specific recommendations for a national scheme for slum clearance; abolition of the Unemployment Anomalies Act; repeal of the Trade Disputes Act of 1927; and a comprehensive free State educational system (because 'class divisions are nowhere

---

[i] *New Leader*, June 9th, 1933.

[ii] C. Borrett, 'New Beginnings', *Socialist Leaguer*, December 1934, No. 7.

[iii] Cripps Papers, 1933.

[iv] F. Williams, op. cit., p.177.

[v] G. Lansbury, *My England*, 1934, p.72.

[vi] Cripps, 'The Message of Our Time', *Leeds Weekly Citizen*, May 11th, 1934.

[vii] *Leeds Weekly Citizen*, May 18th, 1934.

[viii] P. Strauss, op. cit. p.65.

[ix] Quoted in the *Daily Herald* and *The Times*, May 21st, 1934, under the heading 'The Objective of Socialism'.

more evident than in our present educational system').[i] 70 years on, a Labour government is working on this! Apart from these practical resolutions, the S.L. indulged in philosophical speculations, in which 'Socialism' appeared as crucial to increase communal wealth by enabling full use of the productive capacity of industries; to facilitate each person having a fair, equal opportunity of making a full contribution to society and to obtain fair share of wealth; to enable all to work reasonable hours under the best possible conditions; to provide an opportunity for everyone to render useful service, and to end exploitation of workers by the property-owning class and financiers by controlling the means of production and financial institutions.[ii]

Nothing had developed during the past year to justify any optimism about the Party's change from 'reformism to militancy', and yet the editorial in the *Socialist Leaguer* was ecstatic about *Forward to Socialism* in which (it was stated) was embodied all the S.L. represented, the purpose of its existence! Translate principles into practice; challenge the causes of evils, recognise democratic rights can be maintained only if they are used to end privilege and economic domination: 'that is the spirit which inspires the Socialist League.'[iii] This the S.L. regarded as 'realism in politics', but the candour of its appeal could not hide the apocalyptic overtones of its message,[iv] the temulence of its mood. The *Leeds Mercury* described the programme as the first step preparing the way to a larger plan for rapid socialisation of the means of production[v] while W. Hodgkiss saw it indicating *the most practical Socialist approach* the Party had constructed: 'It is brief, but it expresses the right temper.'[vi] The objective of the S.L. remained to make as large a contribution to constructive thought in the Party, and hoped the Party would adopt S.L. policies, and draw Socialist conclusions from current events. In 1934, it envisaged its function as concentrating on the general direction and 'tempo' of Party policy rather than *detailed* procedures necessary for its achievement; it trusted the Party would create the temper for action and make electors 'appreciate our objective, the most important steps that must be taken, the powers needed to deal with the Opposition and the speed with which the Socialist Government would have to act.'[vii]

There were wider divisions over *Forward to Socialism* than there had been at Derby. Jean Thompson (S.L. National Council member from Sheffield) complained that S.L. branches had expected a more detailed statement of policy with *less rhetoric*; the programme should be referred back 'on grounds of ambiguity';[viii] it failed to create the basis of 'the Will to Power', which could only arise from a confidence there was a programme and a knowledge of *how* it could be carried out. The Welwyn Garden City S.L. branch thought the programme not substantially distinguishable from existing public declarations of Party policy,[ix] while P. Arnold (of the Hendon S.L. branch)

---

[i] C. Trevelyan, moving this resolution, quoted in *Leeds Mercury*, May 21st, 1934.

[ii] Cf. *Forward to Socialism*, S.L. pamphlet, June 1934.

[iii] Editorial, 'Socialist Democracy – Forward to Socialism', *Socialist Leaguer*, June–July 1934, No. 1.

[iv] Cf. The final words of the editorial: 'Action must not be sickled o'er with the pale cast of political expediencies. War, Unemployment and Poverty are the children of Capitalism. Let us plan to end the parents' rule.'

[v] *Leeds Mercury*, May 21st, 1934.

[vi] W. Hodgkiss, *Socialist Leaguer*, July–August 1934, No. 2.

[vii] Cripps' opening address to the S.L. Conference at Leeds, May 20th, 1934.

[viii] *New Leader*, May 25th, 1934.

[ix] *Leeds Weekly Citizen*, May 18th, 1934.

concluded the document inspired no enthusiasm, was disappointing, vague and loose.[i] Even the *New Statesman and Nation* reported the 'intelligentsia' were critical of it because it outlined a far-reaching programme without adequate definition or clear thought; the S.L. was accused of having terminated the pioneering work of planning and research begun under G. D. H. Cole and E. F. Wise. The reply that this was now done by the N.F.R.B. did not mollify critics. There was a prevalent feeling that the emotional urge towards 'the Will to Power' must not be allowed to swamp intelligent planning,[ii] yet this journal did add that the document was written with a heartening vigour in a popular style and this had satisfied the unionist contingent in the S.L.

While there were other criticisms that the programme was an old-fashioned document,[iii] a mere propagandist broadsheet which said nothing not in Party policy reports; T. Howard of Rochdale defended the S.L. National Council's decision to write a popular leaflet rather than a detailed plan, because Party leaders lacked the moral courage to give effect to their opinions, and it was the duty of the S.L. to see they got support of the organised Movement for carrying out (by the Party) the Socialist programme.[iv] Socialists had to build up a well-informed membership to make impossible repetition of the last Labour Government's débâcle, to compel the Movement to face issues involved in 'the final overthrow of the Capitalist system.' Mellor added that theories were useless, unless one could create in the Movement a belief that people could achieve a Socialist society; the Labour Movement had to face the difficulties inherent in 'capitalist democracy'.[v]

Although one-fifth of the delegates disapproved of the programme,[vi] it had the majority support of the S.L. National Council, and the opposition had to give way on many points to William 'Steamroller' Mellor's cajolings. He delivered 'a sledgehammer speech,[vii] and the programme was passed by 51 to 13 votes. Press criticisms were predictable. The *New Statesman and Nation*'s[viii] London Diary commented (erroneously) that the Conference was so nearly unanimous that it lacked the spice of argumentative discord; the *Daily Herald*[ix] headlined the Conference: 'Bolder Policy Urged by Cripps... S.L. Adopts a 5-Year Plan... A Snatched Victory... No Use to Labour – Gradualism Condemned'; and, in the *New Leader*,[x] Percy Williams for the I.L.P. criticised the S.L. for staging its Conference in the surroundings of one of Leeds' most expensive and comfortable hotels, adding that members who could afford it could attend the Conference and influence its decisions without reference to or control by branch members. (The *Socialist Leaguer* retorted the C.P. had used the same hotel.)[xi] The *Manchester Guardian* enthused over the S.L.'s promise of 'a 'peaceful Socialist revolution', but remarked the S.L. was more certain of its ability to persuade electors of the wisdom of its policy than convincing the Labour Party that adoption of its

---

[i] *Morning Post*, May 21st, 1934.

[ii] *New Statesman and Nation*, May 26th, 1934.

[iii] Sheffield S.L. branch, quoted in *New Leader*, May 18th, 1934.

[iv] *Manchester Guardian*, May 21st, 1934.

[v] Cf. Mellor quoted in *Daily Herald*, May 21st, 1934.

[vi] *Leeds Mercury*, May 21st, 1934.

[vii] *Socialist Leaguer*, June–July 1934, No.1.

[viii] *New Statesman and Nation*, May 26th, 1934.

[ix] *Daily Herald*, May 21st, 1934.

[x] *New Leader*, May 25th, 1934.

[xi] *Socialist Leaguer*, June–July 1934, No. 1 in S.L. Notes.

programme would not be an invitation to suicide;[i] while the *Morning Post*'s reaction can be gleaned from its headline, 'Socialism in No Time – New Version by Cripps – All Power to the Proletariat', and *The Times* predictably recognised sinister motives: 'The S.L. plan would be as heavy as a millstone when the Labour Party is cast into the electoral sea. It is 'frantic socialism', an 'all-or-nothing policy'; alliance of Parliamentary and physical-force Socialism was impossible: '"Humbug" and "sham" described the S.L.'s plan and policy; humbug and sham to pretend that "emergency powers" in the S.L. was consistent with democracy... S.L. leaders were neither political innocents nor simpletons; they mingled the language of revolution and democracy of set purpose, but their aim was swift revolution and swiftly disastrous ... *the S.L. was developing the same recklessness, inordinate haste, itch for programme-making, which was the undoing of the I.L.P.*'[ii]

The dominant note of the Leeds S.L. Conference was that *Forward to Socialism* was haunted by fears of 'Fascism and Anarchy', spectacle of a world of armed powers, and the only choice – 'Poverty or Plenty'. In January 1935, an S.L. editorial commented on 'Politicus',[iii] who had opposed a merely insurrectionist policy, and had dubbed the S.L.'s 5-Year Plan 'a real danger to capitalism', because (as the S.L. editorial translated) it was a practical working scheme to establish Socialism. This had accounted for the sedulous belittling of Cripps by Tory-Liberal newspapers and many Labour speakers and writers.[iv]

Foreign affairs immersed the Bristol S.L. Conference (June 1935 and the Stoke S.L. Conference (June 1936), and therefore contributed to the alteration of the focus of S.L. objectives for the Party. At the Bristol Conference, the most important debate was the five hours on '*International Affairs*', although resolutions were passed on unionism, co-operatives, the Jubilee, and local authorities. Practical proposals were made for strengthening local units of the Movement as the foci of the S.L.'s work; Trades Councils and Labour-controlled boroughs were to secure advances for workers and demonstrate rank and file power. The remainder of the Conference was absorbed in foreign affairs. Never losing an opportunity to criticise the S.L. and the Labour Party, the I.L.P. commented that the S.L. was being crippled because it wanted to take Socialist action but the Party forbade it: 'The policy expressed in the S.L.'s resolutions was often correct, but rarely went far enough. The attachment of the S.L. to the Labour Party made these resolutions 'dead letters'.[v] On any issue where there was a possibility that something might be said undesirable to Party leaders, discussions were held in private. (This was so with resolutions on India, war and peace, the Co-operative Movement, and United Front proposals.) For a Conservative reaction, the *Morning Post*[vi] carried a cartoon by Wyndham Robinson, of S.L. leaders led by Cripps, hurling bricks and chairs at the 'Capitalist system', a 'Guy Fawkes' stuffed scarecrow. A newspaper headline, inserted into the cartoon, reports that 'the Glow Worm yields its secret: Light without heat!' Robinson's caption is: 'And Heat without Light in the Socialist League'. By now, as noted in that cartoon, the S.L. had become personalised in Cripps, the report by the *Bristol Evening Post* simply headed: 'Sir Stafford Cripps calls

[i] *Manchester Guardian*, 'A Programme for Labour – S.L. and a Bold but Peaceful Policy', May 21st, 1934.

[ii] *The Times*, May 22nd, 1934. (My italics.)

[iii] 'Politicus', *Adelphi*, January 1935.

[iv] S.L. Notes and Comments, *Socialist Leaguer*, February 15th, 1935, No. 9.

[v] *New Leader*, June 14th, 1935.

[vi] *Morning Post*, June 12th, 1935.

for Militant Socialism'.[i] How much less was the coverage of the S.L.'s Annual Conference in the press compared with those of 1933 and 1934!

In June 1936, the fourth S.L. Annual Conference at Stoke was dominated by foreign affairs, and in the politics of the possible united front of Left-wing groups against the Government. In its journal, the position confronting the S.L. was reviewed under the heading: '*The S.L.'s rôle in the Labour Movement widens*'.[ii] Before the 1935 Election, the S.L. had proclaimed a direct challenge to the 'Capitalist system' and had prepared S.L. resolutions as part of Party policy. Since then, the S.L. had continued to propagate principles by organising Conferences with a view to challenge every tendency of Labour and union leaders to policies of '*adapting the market economy*', and the consequent loss of the Movement's independence of action. The S.L., as a component part of the Movement shaping national and local policies, sought to induce the Party to initiate, and organise demonstrations, conferences and other agitational and educational efforts designed to deepen Socialist consciousness in the Labour membership. At Stoke, the S.L. sought to increase the 'class consciousness of workers',[iii] by winning support among technical and professional ranks, and would work for 'the elimination of reformism' from the Movement. The Stoke Conference was reported even less than the Bristol Conference in the national Press!

Had the S.L. been attacked for presenting realistic views of issues facing a Labour Government? Even in local Labour parties, S.L. criticisms had been stifled. By 1936, there were alternatives; the S.L. could break away and unite with the I.L.P. and C.P. in a United Front, or attempt to increase its own membership with the object of securing control in divisional Labour Parties and unions. All the S.L.'s work had brought it back to the initial choice in 1932. Through its conferences and resolutions, the S.L. had conceived its task of revitalising the Labour Party to an awareness of a new approach to Parliamentary politics but the impossibility of the S.L.'s objective to transform Party *policies* led to the S.L.'s marginalisation. Gradually S.L. leaders became aware that there was no place in the Labour Party for any organisation running a private programme of its own.[iv] As an organisation it had dug its own trap by formulating and promoting policies in opposition to, or at variance with, official Party policies. The S.L.'s ideological framework and its policy resolutions proved of less value in the formulation of a new Party programme than rationalising and focussing public indignation, a function which Party leaders were incapable of achieving themselves. Here the S.L.'s Socialism, instinctive and idealistic, founded upon the 1918 Party Constitution, discovered its relevance.

In inspiring *agitations*, the approach of the S.L. could be more significant than developing concrete programmes. After 1934, disillusioned with gradual reformism, its resolutions could give little guidance to a Party which had reformism as the central text of its programme. The S.L. could not front the development of a practical political strategy, because it was more interested in strengthening the Labour Movement than appealing to electors. Although there had been no evidence that the electorate favoured moderation in the Party, the S.L. failed to persuade sufficient Party and union members in its analysis of the Government's 'Fascist tendencies'. The 1930s were a

---

[i] *Bristol Evening Post*, June 10th, 1935.

[ii] *Socialist*, July–August 1936.

[iii] *Report of the Stoke Annual S.L. Conference*, June 1936.

[iv] Cf. M. Cole, *The Story of Fabian Socialism*, 1961, p.233.

retreat for the Socialist Movement: It produced no significant new ideas beyond the tactic of the Popular Front.[i] It failed to cope with problems set by the capitalist crisis and the advance of Fascism. Nevertheless, S.L. leaders were able to write *some* radical measures into the Party programme, which would bear fruit in 1945. In the long term, however, the Party could win an election only by stressing its moderation, and the S.L. was broken over the wheel of the United Front campaign, its last frantic attempt to breathe solidarity and militancy into the Party.

(A) S.L. Policy: The Constitutional Issue, the Monarchy and Parliament

The S.L. intended Labour's policy to reflect the new post-1931 situation by being prepared to combat obstruction, sabotage or a political coup if *Socialist policies* were attempted and blocked in the next Labour Government. This implied prior preparation and drastic changes in the outlook of the Party. To the S.L. there were two main issues: how to achieve a mandate for 'revolutionary change' in a profoundly un-revolutionary society, and how to make the cumbersome processes of Parliamentary democracy into effective instruments for carrying out that change. Linking these, the S.L. characterised the Labour Party as a *social movement*, not just a political party.[ii] Moderate Party leaders might be devoted to Parliamentary methods and established canons of political propriety, but the S.L. planned to escape from this confined rôle (without losing sight of Parliamentary democracy). The problem was not solved, but in their efforts, S.L. leaders opened up other possibilities for the Labour opposition.

Through its recommendations, the S.L. reflected the apprehensions of the time. It was the mercury in the Party's political thermometer in its anticipation of *resistance* to a future Socialist government. To the extent that politics was about 'means', Socialism was a method of changing society, and the S.L., in its ambivalent attitude to Parliamentarianism, followed traditions in the Labour Movement which accepted that a Socialist society *could* be established through Parliament and yet applied a Socialist critique of 'capitalist-dominated Parliaments'. The S.L. searched for a path to a 'revolution by consent' and questioned 'political democratic action' as the best method for radical reform, now advocating a programme which questioned the whole basis of parliamentary politics.

S.L. leaders were convinced that the methods through which a Socialist programme could be achieved had to be discussed *thoroughly* and the electorate had to be informed of the Party's objectives and the means necessary to fulfil them. For the S.L., this seemed a way the Party could regain lost votes. In September 1932, Cripps presaged this perspective: 'More and more people are showing their doubts as to the possibility of so fundamental a change as that from Capitalism to Socialism being accomplished by *constitutional means*. With a bold policy which faces the realities and difficulties of the opposition that will have to be met from vested interests, the Party may yet achieve power and accomplish its object of a *peaceful revolution*.'[iii] Laski inquired whether evolutionary Socialism had deceived itself in believing it could establish itself

[i] N. MacKenzie, *Socialism – A Short History*, revised edition 1966, p.166.
[ii] Cf. R. Lyman, op. cit., *Journal of British Studies*, November 1965, Vol. 5, No. 1, pp.147–151.
[iii] Cripps, 'The Future of the Labour Party', *New Statesman and Nation*, September 3rd, 1932. (My italics.)

by peaceful means within the ambit of the capitalist system, and developed a theme which became the backbone of the S.L.'s programme; the *inadequacy* of the constitutional system for a Socialist Party; an Emergency Powers Act (to prevent financial interference with the operation of a Labour Government's programme) and revision of the Constitution to prevent delay or defeat of Socialist measures (the creation of peers, abolition of the Lords, or delegated legislation in the House of Commons).[i]

For the S.L., the principles and main details of Socialist schemes should be firmly outlined *before* the Party took office again, because the Civil Service was geared towards the prevention of mistakes rather than encouragement of initiatives. The theory behind this was that the Constitution was about to be tested more profoundly than any since the 17th century. In its *Draft Constitution*[ii] the S.L. supported the use of existing Parliamentary institutions, not for their intrinsic value, but for the purpose of organising workers in the struggle to obtain control. In this context, the S.L. was aware that a Socialist government would have to be prepared to overcome every form of resistance that the privileged class might adopt.[iii] A plan to deal with the crisis that a future Labour Government might arouse was a feature of the Leicester Party Conference of 1932.[iv] The power of Parliament was not underestimated. It represented the mass mind of the people, with control over the main lines of policy; it allowed ample opportunity for discussion and criticism of a Government's defects; it retained control over ministerial and governmental decrees, and was the final arbiter between consumer and producer.[v] Where the S.L. diverged in its analysis of Parliament from the official Party position was in the concepts of '*democracy*' and '*Socialism*': 'It is no use having a Socialist Party which is more concerned with the preservation of democracy than the bringing in of Socialism.'[vi] This position became the stumbling block of the S.L.'s whole approach to Parliament.

The initial controversy arose over the S.L.'s idea about '*Emergency Powers*'. Here, the S.L. had the belligerent attitude that since an Emergency Powers Act *was* on the Statute book, the Party must use it; it might find before it had won office again that the Constitution had been refashioned as a bulwark against Socialism.[vii] Fear of financial panic or a 'counter-revolutionary Movement' obsessed S.L. leaders so much that one can appreciate Party suspicions that there seemed an attempt to attack Party leaders first, and challenge National Government majority decisions as a secondary consideration. S.L. demands inevitably became the pretext for Conservative/Press fulminations against the S.L. in particular and the Labour Movement in general. Nor were Labour leaders convinced of the S.L.'s platform, and in *For Socialism and Peace* (1934) the Party upheld its faith in political democracy. If an emergency situation arose, the Party, as a new Government, would seek necessary powers from Parliament: 'In this and other ways, the Party and the Socialist League seemed almost worlds

---

[i] Laski, 'The Labour Party and the Constitution', *Socialist Programme*, Series No. 2, S.L. pamphlets.

[ii] October 1st, 1932.

[iii] S.L. Draft Constitution, October 1st, 1932.

[iv] Cf. C. Attlee, in Leicester Labour Party Annual Report, 1932, p.205.

[v] Cripps' speech in Sutton, reported in the *Sutton Times*, December 11th, 1932.

[vi] Cf. Cripps', *Sutton Times*, Dec. 11th 1932. G. D. H. Cole, *The History of the Labour Party from 1914*, 1948, p.287.

[vii] 'The possessing class (might) invoke armed force as a means of resistance', G. D. H. Cole in *The Working Class Movement and the Transition to Socialism*, 1934.

apart.'[i] S.L. policy was that if the Party was serious in its determination to change capitalist society, it had to show *in advance*, and in a militant style, a readiness to act intrepidly during the first weeks after attaining office, but Party leaders were not interested in such theoretical possibilities, and the S.L.'s insistence that the Party plan for what *might* happen contradicted the edifice of compromise which His Majesty's Opposition upheld.

With a solution of the unemployment problem uppermost, S.L. leaders were searching for a Party which could combine strength of vision and ideology with individual freedoms to suggest alternative policies. Therefore, the S.L.'s questioning of Parliamentary assumptions was to suggest different methods of tackling Parliamentary politics. To envisage that a future Labour Government would have to overcome *opposition* from the Press, Whitehall, the Law Courts, the police etc, was all part of the S.L.'s endeavour,[ii] and the dominant theoretical question (for the S.L.) remained: whether it was possible to implement a Socialist transformation in society without the violence of a Communist revolution. Such a query was fantasy but basing criticisms on 'class struggle' principles, the S.L. could rationalise the situation in accordance with the logic of its analysis.

The S.L. found its identity by the advocacy of drastic constitutional changes. One of the most popular pamphlets issued by the S.L. was Cripps' *Can Socialism Come by Constitutional Methods?*[iii] in which he claimed the ruling class would go to any length to defeat Parliamentary action if the issue was continuance of their financial and political control: 'The possibility of finding a constitutional way... will largely determine whether Socialism comes peacefully or by violence. The decisive blow at capitalism can be delivered constitutionally.'[iv] Unwittingly, Attlee fanned these flames in his own S.L. lecture when he stated the issue was not to do things with the most scrupulous regard to theories of democracy or exact constitutional propriety but to 'get on with the job'.[v]

Reacting to the mysteries cloaking the Labour Government (1929–1931) it was a conscious S.L. choice to explain its methods and outline its objections, and this created vehement responses. While Kingsley Martin thought that the S.L. was discussing 'the gentlemanly ways of having a revolution',[vi] the *Daily Herald* was convinced warnings of a future Labour Government being *sabotaged* were 'just silly';[vii] the S.L.'s tone was taken to be the sum total of its thinking, yet it was the basis to S.L. argument that the reaction by Labour's opponents would determine the course adopted by a future Labour Government. This was not emphasised in the Press, and Lord Salisbury, who had criticised S.L. thinking, appeared in the S.L. as a man 'anxious to cover up his own designs by erecting a fearsome bogey'.[viii] The Labour Party's Executive emasculated the S.L.'s message and concentrated on the effect of irresponsible, exaggerated statements, although the argument that a Labour Government, which seriously attacked property

---

[i] C. L. Mowat, *Britain Between the Wars*, 1955, p.550.

[ii] J. T. Murphy, *Fascism: The Socialist Answer*, 1933, S.L. pamphlet, p.14.

[iii] S.L. lecture at Transport House, January 29th, 1933, *New Clarion*, June 3rd, 1933. The other most influential S.L. pamphlet was R. H. Tawney's *The Choice Before the Labour Party*.

[iv] *Problems of a Socialist Government*, 1933, pp.35–66.

[v] C. Attlee, *Local Government and the Socialist Plan*, February 1933.

[vi] K. Martin, 'A Gentlemanly Revolution', *New Statesman and Nation*, February 25th, 1933.

[vii] *Daily Herald*, November 5th, 1933.

[viii] *New Clarion*, S.L. Notes, December 30th, 1933.

rights, would be confronted with an opposition that would not yield to normal constitutional means, remained relevant. (In the 1964–1970 Labour Governments, international finance stultified any promise of a Socialist orientation in policy.)

S.L. policies were coloured by a belief in the State machine and the assumption of Socialist 'integrity'. A social transformation did not exclude innovations in the Constitution or such coercive use of the resources of the State as any Government must in the last resort be prepared to make in order to enforce its will.[i] The corollary was S.L. caution and suspicion that, though in control of the legislature, a Labour Government might have to face opposition from other sources of State power – civil service and judiciary. The S.L.'s veneration of State planning made it conscious of the impact made on forms of government by existing uncoordinated, unplanned expansion of the productive and distributive processes, so the S.L. questioned the meaning and practice of 'democracy': 'A vote for cheap beer (which allows the brewers to make a bigger profit) or extra facilities for betting (which provides another way of depriving the worker of some of his means of life) is claimed as an act of benevolence to the working class, and so the game of deception proceeds,'[ii] remarked Cripps.

Party leaders were alienated by S.L. pronouncements that a transition to national ownership of the means of production had to be 'carried through in the shortest possible time'.[iii] S.L. leaders could not envisage the Party coming to power *without* a financial crisis,[iv] so asked: What is democracy? Have we got it in this country? Can we get Socialism by democratic means? Is the House of Lords sacred? Is Parliament an efficient instrument for economic revolution? The S.L. maintained that ameliorative measures (proposed by the Party) could not even be implemented without the socialisation of finance, control of foreign trade, and adoption of large scale Socialist plans: '*Is the Party saying that it is possible to satisfy the wants of the workers within the Capitalist system? That position we challenge.*'[v] There was no valid reason for the Party's hesitation in demanding such measures[vi] and admitting the necessity of altering the *machinery* of government to relate it to economic needs, because *fundamental* economic changes could not be achieved without corresponding alterations in the legal and constitutional framework. This S.L. approach was its response to a disillusioning political situation. Concentrating on the S.L.'s means rather than ends, the Press built up an image of 'dictatorship and irresponsibility', obscuring any relevance of S.L. resolutions. Had the S.L.'s purpose been to capture public attention by questioning Constitutional mechanics, it might have succeeded, but the issues were confused, the S.L. became isolated.

One reason for this confusion was caused by events in Germany. Although the Nazi victory in January 1933 provided additional grounds for pessimism as to the viability of democracy in an age of crisis, and cast doubts as to the possibility of 'a peaceful, Parliamentary transition to Socialism',[vii] Labour leaders began to think more about defending *traditional values* than ways to achieve a Socialist society. S.L. protests against the destruction of working-class organisations in Germany accentuated the

[i] L. A. Fenn in *Problems of Socialist Transition*, No. 8.

[ii] Cripps, 'Democracy: Real or Sham?', *Problems of the Socialist Transition*, 1934.

[iii] Cripps at the Bristol Labour Party Rally, *Western Daily Press*, September 11th, 1933.

[iv] *Manchester Guardian*, November 5th, 1933.

[v] *New Clarion*, 'Bread and Butter Questions', S.L. Notes, October 21st, 1933.

[vi] *New Clarion*, 'Our Fight for Democracy', S.L. Notes, January 20th, 1934.

[vii] R. Miliband, op. cit., p.205.

resurgence of democratic electioneering by the Party. J. T. Murphy queried: 'Is the situation such that the Labour Movement can complacently proceed merely with election plans on the assumption that such an easy journey lies before it? Such an attitude would be fatal.'[i] As the danger to British democratic assumptions (from Fascism) increased, the S.L.'s mélange of class slogans and criticisms of the Government's 'democracy' floundered. On this issue, the S.L. began its decline in influencing Party policy, and its change from a group working to *alter* Party resolutions to *agitating on immediate issues*, which it had become by 1935. The advantages of a democratic regime outweighed any other, because the Labour Party and union Movement had not been made illegal, as they had in Germany and Italy, and this assessment of democracy was the central issue between the S.L. and Party leaders. Thus, the dilemma in which the S.L. was placed concerning its interpretation of 'democracy' was revealed in its *Forward to Socialism* policy statement. Here the S.L. called (nebulously) for 'true' and 'real' democracy, the House of Lords was 'a menace to democracy', and the Commons 'not yet an effective instrument of democracy,' yet the question was not whether the process of Socialism should be 'slow' or 'rapid', because the rate of change could not be greater than the strength of the forces demanding it, and 'democracy' *had* to be defended against totalitarianism.

Meanwhile, the C.P.'s criticism of the S.L.'s constitutional suggestions was that they could only strengthen the executive powers within the State machine and sharpen a knife to be used against workers.[ii] Labour and union leaders' concern was that anything which might convey the impression that the Party was prepared to resort to extra-constitutional methods would be electorally disastrous and totally unjustifiable,[iii] to which the S.L. retort was that decisive action had to be taken during the first year to *avoid* unconstitutional action.[iv] This ambiguity in the S.L.'s position was exemplified in Cripps' speeches, used against him in the 1935 Election campaign with a leaflet entitled *Crumbs from Cripps' Table*. In one speech he seemed to be counselling Republicanism, the next upholding constitutional monarchy,[v] supporting and opposing the League of Nations,[vi] suggesting an imminent constitutional crisis and later a financial crisis with a Labour Government,[vii] and for and against democracy.[viii]

A further cause of friction between Party leaders and the S.L. occurred with the results of the General Election of 1935. The S.L. held that this Election was a struggle between 'Socialism and Capitalism' (which no British election has ever been allowed to become): 'A large part of the rank and file of the Labour Party and all the leaders of the Conservative Party are going to take good care that the election shall be about Socialism.'[ix] This was an S.L. fantasy, another prognostication proved wrong. The Election hardly touched domestic issues; the record of the Government was not 'exposed'; election results revealed the nation state was more relevant than class war. In analysing the reasons for Labour's defeat, the S.L. concluded the Party had failed to

---

[i] J. T. Murphy, *Preparing for Power*, 1934, pp.274–77.
[ii] R. Palme Dutt, 'Notes of the Month', *Labour Monthly*, Vol. 15, No. 10, October 1933.
[iii] Citrine letter to Cripps, February 19th, 1935, Cripps Papers.
[iv] Cripps to Citrine, February 21st, 1935, Cripps Papers.
[v] *Daily Herald*, January 9th–10th, 1934.
[vi] *Hansard*, March 11th, 1935 versus letter to Bristol constituents, Sepbember 11th, 1935.
[vii] *Daily Telegraph*, May 27th, 1934 versus *Morning Post*, November 3rd, 1934.
[viii] *Yorkshire Post*, September 27th, 1934 (at Leigh) versus *The Times*, February 2nd, 1935 (London speech).
[ix] Cripps, 'Democracy and Dictatorship', *Political Quarterly*, October–December 1933.

convince the working class because there was an absence (in Party propaganda) of a clear challenge to the capitalist system; the Party had presented doubt, hesitancy, lack of confidence and lacked the burning conviction of the rightness of the Socialist cause;[i] for Party leaders, the cause of defeat lay in the Government's adoption of Labour policies, confusion of increased profits with national prosperity, and the impractical approach of Labour militants, such as the S.L., pursuing the path of a 'constitutional revolution', vaguely temporising with the 'Emergency Powers Act', covering indecision and ideological shapelessness with a thin veneer of Marxist terminology, and creating an esoteric, idealistic group which had little connection with electoral issues.

Another factor which accentuated divisions between the S.L. and Party leaders arose over **the monarchy**. It had always been recognised that the monarchy could not be a part of a Socialist State, although the Party had long since compromised on this. After 1931, the problem arose because of the veiled rôle of King George V during the crisis and formation of the 'National' Government. In *The Labour Party and the Constitution*,[ii] Laski made references to the position of the Crown, while Party leaders were happy to 'prove' the neutrality of the monarchy during the crisis. Laski expressed the S.L.'s position – a reduction of the royal prerogative to its narrowest limits: 'The right of the Crown to refuse its assent to legislation and to exercise a personal discretion in the choice of a Prime Minister must go…' Safeguards seemed essential to the S.L. against the right of the Crown to dismiss a ministry and the possibility of the monarch entering the Parliamentary battle as a 'patriotic act'. S.L. leaders also considered that the fewer Socialists bothered with the decorative ceremonial functions of royalty the greater would be the impulse to democratise society. 70 years on the same debate ensues.

On January 6th, 1934, Cripps made a speech at Nottingham University's Labour Federation Conference, translated (or skewed) by the Press as an attack on the constitutional monarchy, rather than one of Cripps' obiter dicta. In the Labour Movement as a whole, Cripps' popularity increased enormously, but as His Majesty's Opposition, the P.L.P. had to denounce him. Cripps believed in constitutional monarchy, but was convinced there *could* be opposition to a Socialist government from Court circles and financial interests attracted around Buckingham Palace.[iii] The *Manchester Guardian* commented 18 months later that, in 1931, 'Lombard Street' determined it was time to finish the life of the Labour Government; it was finished not by the traditional method of a hostile vote in the Commons, but by what Cripps dared to mention in Nottingham (and caused a considerable uproar in the Press): the Buckingham Palace influence.[iv] However, although the monarchy was regarded as incompatible with Socialism, some S.L. members realised that it was futile to centre any campaign on this.[v] Cripps could not picture the ultimate Socialist State under a constitutional monarchy, and believed it was a problem which had to be discussed when a Socialist Government had obtained economic control,[vi] but he had made the

---

[i] Cripps, *Borderer*, November 1935 and Cripps, 'Election Lessons that Must Be Learned', *Socialist*, December 1935, No. 3.

[ii] S.L. pamphlet, 1933.

[iii] Cripps Papers, January 10th, 1934.

[iv] July 8th, 1935.

[v] Cripps Papers, Catlin to Cripps, January 24th, 1934.

[vi] Cripps Papers, Cripps to Catlin, January 26th, 1934.

Nottingham speech for three interrelated reasons: to be provocative and controversial, to cement the S.L. opposition, and to express resentment at the almost impossible situation for a Labour rump to influence Government policies.

The issue of the monarchy re-emerged with the 25-Year Jubilee in June 1935, and again Cripps caused uproar in the Press. He saw 'the Jubilee ballyhoo' being succeeded by a wave of militarist nationalism, excused by the attitude of Hitler. The *Bristol Evening News* reported the S.L. Conference: 'Jubilee Celebrations Described as "Ballyhoo"',[i] while the S.L. noted the Government openly boasted that the Jubilee would be valuable propaganda in the coming Election.[ii] (Government publications were adorned with the pictures of the King and Queen.) What the S.L. resented was that the Conservative Party used loyalty to the Crown, country and flag as if these emblems of national sovereignty had been their exclusive property: '*These flag-waving-save-the-nation tactics have been used often in the past with tragic consequences for the workers.*'[iii] They are now the Weltanschauung.

Part of the S.L.'s ideological viewpoint presumed the Government would attempt any propaganda to redirect electors from its failure to offer working people a reasonable standard of life. The S.L. tried to expose this 'cynicism' by making sure the Labour Movement was uninfluenced by '*the nationalist wiles of Jubileeism or militarism*'.[iv] Unfortunately, Party leaders argued that S.L. opposition to Jubilee celebrations only revealed the unpopularity of political radicalism, although this was one attempt to isolate the S.L. which did not succeed, since the rank and file had more yearnings towards rational government to deal with unemployment, than interest in the royal family. Yet, the S.L. took the matter more seriously. At its Bristol Conference a resolution *was* passed regretting the attitude of Labour's Executive Committee to the Jubilee celebrations, and affirming that a hereditary monarchy and social distinctions inseparable from it were *incompatible* with the Socialist conception of society[v] (seventy years ahead of its time as well!).

The reactions in the Conservative Press suggested the S.L. had touched an extremely sensitive nerve. The *Morning Post* quoted Cripps' comments on 'the cry of false patriotism'[vi], the *Western Daily Press and Bristol Mirror* exclaimed that Labour councils who had refused to participate in the celebrations were *congratulated* at the S.L. Conference,[vii] and *The Times* was furious about these 'opposition manoeuvres', reporting that the S.L. had been rebuked by Labour leaders, which resented Cripps' conference speeches that celebrations were manufactured for political purposes. *The Times* saw in the S.L.'s attitude an example of 'more offences against taste and truth';[viii] St. John Ervine denounced the S.L. as mainly populated by '*disgruntled dons and ill-tempered members of the middle class*'! The paper's indignation did not subside. Another of Cripps' speeches was reported including reference to 'political capital being made out

---

[i] June 10th, 1935.

[ii] *Daily Herald*, June 10th, 1935.

[iii] *Socialist Leaguer*, June 1935, No. 12.

[iv] Ibid. The S.L. was not as anti-monarchy as the C.P., which regarded the monarchy in the 1930s as "a device used to sanctify the capitalist order and its imperial activities", cf. S. Macintyre, '*Little Moscows*' (1980), p.187.

[v] *Morning Post* and *Daily Herald*, June 11th, 1935 and *Socialist Leaguer*, July–August 1935, No. 13.

[vi] June 10th, 1935.

[vii] June 11th, 1935.

[viii] *The Times*, June 13th, 1935.

of a demonstration of national loyalty which had become the means for capitalist exploitation and assistance in an electoral campaign'.[i] Ormsby-Gore (Commissioner of Works) denounced Cripps as an 'intellectual snob above the ordinary considerations that moved ordinary people'; and Sir Thomas Inskip pronounced that until Cripps mentioned 'ballyhoo', no one had attempted to make political capital out of 'the national and worldwide rejoicings'.[ii] Politicians get jittery around monarchy.

The place of the monarchy and the attitude to it in the Labour Movement had accentuated the rift between the S.L. and Party leaders. On the death of King George V, and accession of Edward VIII, the S.L. reiterated its views: 'Is there any reason why the official Labour Movement should vie with society in its perfervid expressions of sorrow and loyalty. The masses of workers for Socialism feel deeply disturbed at the increased subservience in those who are supposed to lead the Movement in the war on poverty, injustice and oppression. First the Jubilee, then the funeral, next the Coronation!'[iii] An unrepentant S.L. member commented in the S.L. journal: 'I write to protest against the *Daily Herald*'s orgy of snobbery and sycophancy. The Jubilee outburst was bad enough, but nothing compared to the floods that followed the death of King George,'[iv] a viewpoint exemplifying the different aspirations of the S.L. and Party leaders! Labour leader Attlee, supporting PM Baldwin on the abdication crisis, smugly commented: "the intelligentsia can be trusted to take the wrong view on any subject!"[v] The latter adhered to Parliamentary action because the British Constitution was flexible and seemed the only practical way to power. Party leaders and the S.L. wanted the abolition of an undemocratic House of Lords, and there were mutual misgivings about the effectiveness of the Commons, where 'those who want to get things done will; those who want to get things said, luxuriate; and those who want neither are not uncomfortable,'[vi] yet the S.L.'s doubts as to the possibility of Socialism via Parliamentary machinery was a unique contribution to Labour politics: 'Evolutionary Socialism deceived itself in believing that it could establish itself by peaceful means within the ambit of the Capitalist system.'[vii] For the S.L., the 1931 crisis had been the first break since 1689 in the tradition of compromise, and proved institutions were *dependent* on the class structure. Not only was the introduction of Socialism by Parliamentary procedure impossible; the attempt disabled Party leaders; the Commons was inefficient as an instrument of regulative and organising government,[viii] and S.L. leaders pressed on the Party the need through Parliamentary democracy of 'a revolutionary change in the same sense as one speaks of a "revolutionary" change in fiscal policy.'[ix]

S.L. leaders were optimistic that a transition to Socialism could be achieved by a full use by workers of constitutional powers, although Socialists were not concerned to preserve all the details of Parliamentarianism but 'to develop a new and more efficient Parliamentary government suitable to a Socialist democracy'.[x] The constitutional

[i] Cripps at Caxton Hall, Westminster, June 24th, 1935.

[ii] *The Times*, June 24th, 1935.

[iii] The Editor, 'Matters of Moment', *Socialist*, No. 5, March 1936.

[iv] *Socialist*, No. 6, April 1936.

[v] 'Attlee', *Brief Lives*, 1999 edn., p.23.

[vi] H. Dalton, 'Practical Socialism in Britain', quoted by Dean McHenry, op. cit. pp.260–277.

[vii] H. Laski, *The Crisis and the Constitution*, 1932.

[viii] Cf. F. Brockway, *Inside the Left*, 1942, p.245.

[ix] Cripps Papers, Cripps to Attorney-General, March 23rd, 1932.

[x] Cripps, introduction to J. T. Murphy's *Preparing for Power*, 1934, p.14.

system might be inadequate for the purposes of a Socialist Party, because Commons' procedures had been devised for an atmosphere in which Government and Opposition were agreed upon the main objectives of the State; the character of legislation had to be transformed, so that Bills affirmed the taking of general powers.[i] There was a greater need for delegated legislation and conferment of powers on local authorities, more use of standing committees, regrouping of government departments on a functional basis, with less Prime Ministerial government, and the S.L. was dubious about the number of fait accompli decisions: 'The free use of orders in council has converted Parliament into an institution to register the decisions of the cabinet or of the ministers.'[ii]

These S.L. concerns suggested the pressure group had little faith in the routines of Parliament, and foresaw either a rupture or period of prorogued Parliaments with the Cabinet governing as a virtual dictatorship by means of orders in council with special tribunals and commissions to supersede recalcitrant courts and departments of the civil service. Essentially, the S.L. wanted to utilise Parliament because it could mobilise universal suffrage against the minority power of property ownership. J. T. Murphy concluded that the Labour Party should 'aim at securing a revolutionary Socialist majority in Parliament' because the old theoretical position of the Party, its hopes of gradual attainments 'through the prosperous evolution of capitalism', had proved impractical.[iii] And hadn't Lenin anticipated that in Britain the way towards Socialism might be through a Parliamentary crisis? The S.L. recognised that the stage reached was the struggle for Parliamentary power: 'To manifest one's "revolution" solely by dint of swearing at Parliamentary opportunism, by rejecting participation in Parliament, is very easy, but it is not the solution of a difficulty.'[iv]

Through questioning whether or not Parliament's authority had been undermined after the Election of 1931, the S.L. opened up further queries about 'political democracy'. Equality of voting power seemed less important in a battle in which economic control rested in the hands of a privileged few,[v] but Party leaders judged the S.L.'s queries about Parliamentary government and the democratic constitution as moves to destroy the foundations of Social Democracy;[vi] this brought the retort from E. F. Wise that democracy and Parliament *should* become the instruments for effecting the Socialist purpose: 'What use is it to talk of the beauties of Parliamentary government to the unemployed miner or the cotton operative?'[vii] At its Annual Conference at Derby, delegates agreed on the importance of giving democratic ideas and wishes 'an efficient modern machine'; the view was not that 'Parliament was played out', but if democracy was to survive, Parliament had to be 'spring cleaned'.[viii] The S.L. stood for a policy of 'Democratic Dictatorship',[ix] though Cripps invited

[i] Laski, *The Labour Party and the Constitution*, S.L. pamphlet, 1933.
[ii] Cripps' lecture at Kingsway Hall, London, October 27th, 1932.
[iii] J. T. Murphy, *New Clarion*, April 15th, 1933.
[iv] John Lewis, 'Leninism and the Labour Party', *Socialist Leaguer*, No. 6, November–December 1934.
[v] *New Clarion*, S.L. Notes, April 22nd, 1933.
[vi] A. Henderson, 'Your United Front', *New Clarion*, May 6th, 1933.
[vii] E. F. Wise, *New Clarion*, May 13th, 1933.
[viii] *New Clarion*, June 17th, 1933. 'Parliamentary democracy is government by oligarchs for the people and with the people's occasional advice,' commented Aldous Huxley, in N. Murray *Aldous Huxley: An English 'Intellectual'*, 2003, p.13.
[ix] *Manchester Guardian*, headline, June 6th, 1933.

misrepresentation by open-ended statements such as: 'Our policy is to bring about Socialism in the first instance and, if possible, by democratic means. We must invent some new and better way of getting the democratic opinion of the country expressed and transformed into legislative enactments.'[i] Given a 'Socialist' majority in the Commons, the S.L. would question whether it was possible to counteract the economic power of the 'profit-earning class': 'Unless the Parliamentary machine was adapted to meet changing needs, was there any hope of "Socialism" without resort to force? What was the answer to the menace of Fascism?'[ii] But a Socialist majority in the Commons was not an issue in the 1930s.

The S.L. investigation into Parliamentary democracy was not insignificant. It contained a traditional Socialist inquiry into economic institutions and their bearing on political and social controls. No one disagreed that the existing method of government could not create rapid or fundamental change, but the S.L. remained alone in its pessimistic view that the 'City of London', financiers and industrialists, would *prevent* Socialist measures by bringing to bear such economic pressure on a Labour Government that it could not continue in power constitutionally[iii]: '*Why should an old-fashioned political machine be the best for producing the legislation which Socialists want?*'[iv] The only conclusion which the S.L. could conceive was that the people who wished to see the existing distribution of wealth perpetuated, were the same as those who wanted to retain the inefficient political machine unaltered. The S.L. was not alone in this critique of Parliamentary procedure, the waste of time or lack of delegated legislation. Constitutional historian Ivor Jennings complained: 'Parliament used to be a gentleman's elegant pastime, and it has never taken its coat off.'[v] The maintenance of forms which had become 'obsolete and dangerous'[vi] and which could not give efficient service to people brought democratic government to a position of ineffectuality by its own growing futility in an increasingly plan-conscious European environment. That sounded like early 21st century debates.

(B) S.L. Policy: Democracy, the Press and Free Speech

'To tell a man he is a free citizen and can go where he chooses, when he hasn't a penny in his pocket; to tell him he can vote for whom he likes, when he knows nothing about politics; to tell him he can work for whom he likes when through his forced poverty he hasn't the power to demand his price – is sheer political hypocrisy.'[vii] This questioning of democratic advantages and the realities of free speech was a constant theme in the S.L., whose leaders were democratic Socialists by conviction and aspired to reshape democratic ideas to fit a new era, and they had little respect for the traditional trappings of democracy: 'As to Democracy let us recognise that as a tree is judged by its fruit, so democratic institutions must be judged, not by reference to history or philosophy, but by

---

[i] Cripps, 'Making Parliament Work', *Bulletin of the Marple Labour Party*, July 1933.

[ii] *New Clarion*, S.L. News, September 9th, 1933.

[iii] Cripps, 'Democracy and Dictatorship', *Political Quarterly*, October–December 1933.

[iv] Cripps, *Bulletin of the Marple Labour Party*, January 1934.

[v] Dr. Ivor Jennings, 'Parliamentary Reform', *Socialist Leaguer*, No. 8, January 15th, 1935.

[vi] Cripps, *Democracy Up-to-Date*, 1939, p.105.

[vii] Review of Phasa's *The Rights of Man*, *Tribune*, January 29th, 1937.

the results they can produce in satisfying the demands of our people.'[i] Democracy was suspect, and equality could not be obtained through Fabian tactics when there was a danger of suppression of working-class opinions and organisations, but the S.L. sought association with those who wanted to create a Socialist society by democratic means: 'We must use the present democratic machinery to achieve power, and when that is achieved, we must rapidly adapt the machinery of democracy to the needs of our changing society.'[ii] To the S.L., existing democracy had a bias towards conservatism; its machinery had to be reorganised and rationalised before the people could be persuaded to discard it in the belief that it could no longer serve their purpose. The failure of the *machinery* of democracy was no reason for abandoning the *principles* of democracy: 'The workers have everything to gain by democracy if it is made a reality, and everything to lose by following a political creed of violence.'[iii]

The S.L. was conscious that it might find itself driven by unconstitutional action by the opposition (if there was a Socialist government), to support a programme which was not 'constitutional' under the existing system, in order to safeguard its principles. Realising the necessity for democratic action and government, the S.L. Conference at Derby affirmed that this was not synonymous with 19th century Parliamentarianism.[iv] The S.L. believed Britain was entering the final stage of the struggle *for* democracy and, addressing the Leeds Conference, Cripps stated that frank debate was essential if democracy was to survive as an effective instrument of decision-making: 'The power that the workers have now through the ballot box will be of value to them only so far as they use it to accomplish the economic ends that they desire.'[v] This presented the choice of gaining economic freedom and economic democracy or finding the Labour Movement with the prospect of a 'capitalist leadership' which could resort to suppressive methods: 'Great difficulties must be encountered if we are to use this Capitalist democratic system to bring about the destruction of the very class privilege which it is designed to perpetuate.'[vi] In another *Morning Post* Wyndham Robinson cartoon, Mosley and Cripps are in a tug of war with the body of democracy, which is saying, 'Oh dear, I wish they'd stop defending me from each other.'[vii]

All Socialist organisations held that widespread communication, education and propaganda were biased in favour of the status quo; 'freedom of the Press' amounted to little if one lacked the necessary funds to start a newspaper; to anybody who had studied the news disseminated, emphasis was on that news likely to appeal to the bulk of the News Agencies' customers.[viii] E. F. Wise could see neither free speech nor a free press, but only 'panic-mongering'.[ix] After Cripps' 'Buckingham Palace' speech, Lady Cripps wrote to George Lansbury: 'The Press now come wherever Stafford goes, and it behaves like vultures, not caring for the substance of anything he says, but waiting

---

[i] E. F. Wise, *New Clarion*, July 15th, 1933.

[ii] Cripps, 'The Choice for Britain', *Capitalism in Crisis Forum Series*, No. 4.

[iii] Cripps, 'Democracy: Real or Sham?', *Problems of the Socialist Transition*, 1934.

[iv] *New Clarion*, June 10th, 1933.

[v] *Socialist Leaguer*, No. 1, June–July 1934.

[vi] *Socialist Leaguer*, No. 1, June–July 1934

[vii] *Morning Post*, May 23rd, 1934.

[viii] *Hansard 1826*, March 2nd, 1933.

[ix] *New Clarion*, July 15th, 1933. The BBC offered traditional middle-class culture, self-improvement tempered by triviality and Establishment views, cf. N. Branson, M. Heinemann, op. cit., 1973 edn., p.274.

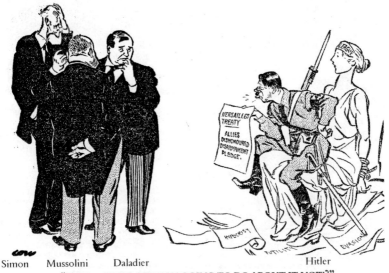

Simon Mussolini Daladier   Hitler

"WELL—WHAT ARE YOU GOING TO DO ABOUT IT NOW?"

October 2, 1933

The Hitler policy logically involved the destruction of all existing institutions upholding international law and order. He attacked the League of Nations on the favourable ground of the failure of disarmament. Because the rest of Europe had failed to disarm, Hitler denounced the disarmament clauses of the Versailles Treaty.

Hitler   Mussolini   Daladier Simon

IT WORKED AT THE REICHSTAG—WHY NOT HERE?

October 18, 1933

Hitler withdrew Germany from the League of Nations, with warmth of expression designed to set fire (metaphorically) to the whole Geneva edifice. "Germany went marching … to the suppression of Communism," said Hitler.

ISS DOT MUSSOLINI ?... YAH ?... PLEASSE TELL DER LEAGUE GERMANY MUST HAVE ARMS FOR DEFENCE AGAINST LITVINOV ARTILLERY... CIVILIZATION MUST STICK TOGETHER BEFORE BOLSHEVIK THREAT TO PATRIOTIC POLICIES OF HEROIC BLOODSHED ! ....

Göbbels Hitler Göring   Litvinov

ALL MUST NOT BE QUIET ON THE EASTERN FRONT

June 20, 1934

In Soviet Russia, the theory of World Revolution had long been abandoned. The Soviet Government had enjoyed normal relations with Germany and Italy, despite, latterly, their anti-Communist front. It now offered to make a German-Soviet pact of non-aggression. Hitler declined. He needed the "Peril of Bolshevism" as an excuse for increasing armaments.

"Voila! If monsieur will give his support to this side security will be assured   But if not—!"

Mussolini Hitler   Barthou   Litvinov   Simon

PLAYTIME IN THE EUROPEAN NURSERY

July 20, 1934

After signing a League pact of mutual assistance with Soviet Russia and Czechoslovakia, France now aimed at signing up in a bloc all those Eastern European nations willing to resist aggression. Germany was invited, but Hitler declined to sign anything with Soviet Russia.

for any word that… can be misused, to fall into their mouths.'[i] True, but Sir Stafford invited the response he got. For example, in February 1934, Cripps questioned 'What is this Freedom?'[ii] This was not one of preserving freedoms but attaining freedoms; it was not the possession of money and material satisfactions that was inimical to freedom, but the use of money and property to exercise economic power over others: 'Where the claim for liberty of action or expression has "come up against" the economic system, any sort of excuse was valid for its suppression (cf. Tolpuddle Martyrs and Tom Mann's imprisonment)'. 'Liberty' depended on the economic structure, and only in a community of economic equals could liberty be born again.[iii] Cripps had become a born-again Socialist.

Likewise, the Government's *'Incitement to Disaffection Bill'* (1934) justified S.L. suspicions of the dubiety of democratic freedoms. There seemed a large element in the Government oblivious to democratic sentiments, prepared to override rights (to keep the status quo) and the deepest suspicions were aroused that the Bill sought to obtain (during a period of comparative apathy) a weapon which could be used later to hamper and punish the expression of any political views, except its own.[iv] (The Bill made it criminal to possess documents which, if distributed to His Majesty's forces, might suggest to them some breach of their duty; and it attacked the freedom of writing and opinion. The Act was passed.) However, liberal democracy had, in 1934, to be preserved in the face of the Nazi threat to Europe.

At the Bristol S.L. Conference (1935) there was a resolution that expressed alarm at the powers of the police to attend meetings against the wishes of its convenors. It deplored the threat to liberties of free speech and criticism: 'The *"Incitement to Disaffection Act"* shows a growing tendency to suppress all opposition to a Government which regards itself as "national".'[v] There was an emergency resolution protesting against the militarisation of the police. It was a major issue and viewed as such by the *Manchester Guardian*: 'Power of the Police – S.L. Alarmed – Threat to Free Speech'[vi]. The resolutions against these extra-legal police powers and the *Sedition Bill* implied there was no effective resistance to preparatory Fascist processes, while the P.L.P. accepted the central clause of the *Sedition Bill*:[vii] 'If the police had reasonable grounds for believing that there might be a breach of the peace at a public meeting, they had the right and the duty to attend it. They had the same right and duty if the meeting was held in a private house or an S.L. branch.'[viii] This 'proved' the S.L.'s fear of the growth of Fascist tendencies under the 'National' Government, and the accentuation of class distinctions to preserve and strengthen the governing class.

G. R. Mitchison referred to how vital it was to Socialists that freedom of opinion, of speech, of assembly, should be seen in practice: 'We must have the right to simpler means of persuasion in the cheap pamphlet, the public meeting or the plain speech.'[ix]

[i] Lady Isobel Cripps to Lansbury, *Lansbury Papers*, January 10th, 1934.

[ii] *New Clarion*, February 17th, 1934.

[iii] Cripps, *Fabian News*, Vol. XLVI, No. 1, January 1935.

[iv] Cf. D. N. Pritt, K. C., 'Keeping the Army Pure', *Socialist Leaguer*, No. 1, June–July 1934; cf. R. Monk, *Bertrand Russell, The Ghost of Madness*, 2000, p.179.

[v] *Socialist Leaguer*, No. 13, July–August 1935.

[vi] Cf. *Daily Herald*, June 10th, 1935 and *Manchester Guardian*, June 10th, 1935.

[vii] *New Leader*, June 14th, 1935.

[viii] G. R. Mitchison, 'The Police', *Socialist Leaguer*, No. 13, July–August 1935.

[ix] G. R. Mitchison, *Socialist*, April 1936.

He questioned whether the police were impartial in political cases since there appeared a tendency to suppress pacifist demonstrations that were regarded as possible incitements to violence. Meanwhile, the National Council of Civil Liberties (endorsed by Attlee, Lansbury, Cole, Pritt and Tawney) was supported by the S.L., because it was active and vigilant in the cause of freedom of speech and opinion.

By the 1936 S.L. Conference, the S.L. had made it part of its agitational programme to promote and defend basic democratic freedoms. R. St. John Reade (of Bristol S.L.) urged the Labour Movement to keep in close touch with 'black-coated workers', and wanted to make it a criminal offence for any employer to interfere with the political opinions of his employees. In its final year, the S.L. commented on political consequences of the *Sedition Act* and the Cabinet's Bill to ban political uniforms: 'The government may give to the police the power to ban marches at any time they deem desirable, and this contains a real menace to the whole Labour Movement.'[i] However, in its interpretation of 'incipient Fascism' in the Government, the S.L. underestimated the strength of democratic sentiments which counteracted any authoritarian Government decrees.

(C) S.L. Policy: Fascism and Dictatorship

Socialists were galvanised by international events in the 1930s. British capitalism became equated with German Fascism because, *in the last analysis,* it was believed the ruling class would rally to the defence of its privileges in both countries. This totalitarian phenomenon was seen in the S.L. as the result of the falterings of Social Democratic parties. The S.L. even hinted that a 'Fascist putsch' in Britain could result from the combined decay of capitalist society and the official Labour leadership! The 'menace' was at home and the S.L. deduced that Britain was faced by many of the conditions of Fascism – breakdown of the party system, three million unemployed, anti-socialist decrees against free speech and a free press, and a vociferous and violent, if small, Fascist Party; Fascism seemed to hold a fatal attraction to Conservative governments, which found it impossible to defeat a challenge to their privileges within the framework of representative governments.[ii] The signs were clear: overt sympathy for Mussolini and Hitler, harsh treatment of unemployed demonstrations, anti-Soviet attitudes, and tough 'law and order' policies in a time of acute Depression/economic crisis.[iii] The S.L.'s prognosis or Weltschmerz proved relevant for the times.

While representative governments appeared paralysed, Fascism found concrescence. To the S.L., Fascism had gained the support of those who had no particular class interest in it, because democratic governments provided no hope of economic prosperity. It may have been the wiser course for the S.L. to focus on Fascism and its *threat to democracy*, not on its threat to Socialism, but it took the opposite course, advancing the Socialist alternative above the dangers to democracy. Naturally, this attitude to Fascism caused more friction with Party leaders. To the S.L., 'British Fascism' was born during the wave of intense nationalism in 1931 and the lesson to

---

[i] The Editor, 'Matters of Moment', *Socialist*, No. 12, November 1936.

[ii] Cf. Miliband, op. cit., p.205.

[iii] Cripps, *Why This Socialism*, 1934, p.13; "...xenophobia emerges as a form of sublimation of pervasive fear arising from unemployment, inflation, demoralization," G. C. Lebzelter, 1978, op. cit., p.45.

learn from events in Germany was that once a Labour Government returned to power, financiers and industrialists could not be left with the economic power in the State,[i] and it was a prevalent S.L. conviction that, if businessmen and economic advisers thought the Labour Party might win the next Election, they would try to *transform* the Conservative government into a Fascist regime.[ii] E. F. Wise, in his presidential address at the first S.L. conference, alluded to influences that had produced Fascist dictatorships, which might be successful in Britain,[iii] based on the fact that the call to 'national' solidarity and decrying of Party politics had occurred in 1931, and had been devices which led to the formation of Fascist governments in Germany and Italy.

To the S.L., *'Fascism was the apotheosis of Capitalism'*[iv] and used the weapons of violence and repression in its attempt to reverse social evolution: 'It is the black defender of private property, of rent, interest and profit, in the age when private property and the system of human exploitation are incompatible with the progressive development of society.'[v] It appeared as a counter-revolution, using the State to fetter the exploited to their exploitation, to rivet class divisions but the Labour Movement was aware that Fascist methods of government necessitated the forcible destruction of independent working-class parties and unions. To J. T. Murphy, Fascist foreign policy was a development of Imperialism, in which Fascism and war were inseparable; Government plans for centralising industry, increasing rationalisation, implementing protectionist economic policies were the *demonstration* of the growth of Fascist ideas in British politics, but Labour leaders believed this to be a rash assumption, which would create a backlash if the Party won office on a policy for 'planning'!

Cripps was swept along on the anti-Fascist crusade and wrote to George Catlin that he had received some rather disturbing confidential information that the Conservative Party was to take over the Fascist Movement: 'This greatly aggravates the criticalness of the situation.'[vi] The S.L.'s stance stemmed from the menace of Fascism; the coming Election for the S.L. was a confrontation between Fascism and Socialism, Cripps informed Lord Brougham.[vii] At the Leeds S.L. Conference (1934), the Barnsley S.L. branch urged the S.L. leadership not to ignore the possibility that the Government could be transformed into a Fascist administration without appealing to the electorate at the end of its 5-year term of office, and asked the S.L. to work out details for use of the General Strike in such circumstances.[viii] The *New Leader* put it thus: 'If there is no next election – a problem for the S.L.', while the I.L.P. criticised the S.L.'s ostrich-like stubbornness for refusing to consider the possibility of a suspension of Parliament by a Fascist dictatorship, under the heading: 'S.L. Evades Fascist Suppression of Parliament'![ix]

In its *Forward to Socialism* policy statement, the S.L. noted: 'the growth of Fascism in all Capitalist countries is Capitalism grown desperate.' It believed Fascism was a forcible attempt to stabilise the system of class relationships; much of the 'reactionary

---

[i] Cf. Cripps at Bristol May Day Demonstration quoted in *The Times*, May 8th, 1933.
[ii] Cripps, *Western Daily Press*, May 8th, 1933.
[iii] E. F. Wise, S.L. Derby Conference, June 2nd, 1933.
[iv] H. N. Brailsford, 'On Fascism', *New Clarion*, December 2nd, 1933, S.L. Notes.
[v] J. T. Murphy, *Fascism: The Socialist Answer*, S.L. pamphlet, 1933.
[vi] Cripps to Catlin, January 26th, 1934.
[vii] Cripps to Lord Brougham, February 4th, 1934, Cripps Papers.
[viii] *The Times*, May 22nd, 1934 and *New Leader*, May 18th, 1934.
[ix] *New Leader*, May 25th, 1934.

Press' had become propaganda sheets for Fascism; police forces were being militarised, the Air Force was a 'class proof' military arm, and a new defence force was being organised. The S.L.'s resolution demonstrated its determination: 'This Conference is at one with the whole British Labour Movement in calling for resistance to the danger of Fascism in this country. The 'National' government has forged in the *Sedition Bill* an instrument that can be used to suppress any frank discussion of Militarism or Imperialism.'[i] To Labour supporters who had not understood the message, Cripps spelt it out: 'Mosley and his Fascism may disappear, but the "capitalists" of this country are as ready to use methods of repression as other capitalists',[ii] and 'the "National" government is bending towards the ideology of the Fascist State.'[iii] What evidence there was seemed hidden from the public.

By January 1935, the S.L. was complaining that *The Times*' correspondents in Europe used 'the language of Fascism'; they discussed events in Spain as 'the struggle with chaos hidden beneath the cloak of Marxism';[iv] a resumé of events in Vienna, spoke of the necessity for 'cleaning up Marxism', and in the Baltic States a coup d'état had established 'a mild non-Socialist dictatorship, Parliamentary government now being in abeyance'. In Cripps' *National Fascism in Britain* (1935) the S.L.'s stance on Fascism emerged fully: attempts to subjugate workers' organisations; the appeal of 'Save the Nation' techniques against enemies abroad, and call for the sacrifice for the common good: 'Military training is to provide the type of worker required in a system which demands discipline, the co-ordination of all forces, and deeply felt sense of duty and sacrifice, with unquestioning obedience.'[v] The Defence Force, Territorials, Special Constables, and Women's Reserves were to be instilled with the habit of organised obedience; the Emergency Powers Act was a potential weapon for the Government; the *Trade Disputes Act* attacked the political power of Labour; a policy of economic nationalism was enhanced, and the Ottawa Conference was to reinvigorate Imperialist sentiment, and tighten the bonds of Empire. There had been closures of industrial plants; corporations controlled output, and there were imports with subsidies for owners without any conditions attached as to wages, hours or conditions of workers. Some national issues had been removed from the control of Parliament (the *Import Duties Act* (1932), the *Housing Act* (1933) and the *Unemployment Act* (1934)), while rumours of 'subversive propaganda' were fostered by the Government as an excuse for further repression. Cripps concluded: 'We have moved along the path towards the Corporate State in actual legislation and methods of Government, and in the psychology and ideology of our rulers, by *country gentleman's Fascism.*'[vi]

In combining 'National' with 'Fascism', Cripps had brought the twin labels of reaction and exposed the unobtrusive march towards the repressive Corporate State; 'the struggle for naked power' was applied to the Government, which had become 'a deceptive sham'. (S.L. member, R. George, talked of the Government's 'subtle innuendoes of suggestive propaganda', 'democratic camouflage', 'the guise of

---

[i] S.L. Conference at Leeds, May 20th–22nd, 1934.

[ii] *The Times*, June 11th, 1934, Cripps' speech at Newton Abbot.

[iii] Cripps, 'The Choice for Britain', *Problems of the Socialist Transition*, No. 4.

[iv] *Socialist Leaguer*, No. 7, January 1935.

[v] Ibid.

[vi] Cripps, *National Fascism in Britain*, 1935. (My italics.) His views were not far from the C.P.G.B.'s 1935 *Manifesto for Soviet Britain*, which analysed Britain under the thrall of capitalist fascism, see Clive Bloom, *Violent London*, 2003, pp.298–99.

benevolence with the slogan of impartiality and justice', the 'cotton wool façade of a benevolent capitalism', and 'the masquerading virtues of an outworn and decaying system of society'.[i]) At the Stoke S.L. Conference, the *Manchester Guardian* reiterated Cripps' phrase: 'Conscription Kites – Cripps and the Dangers of a Form of Country Gentleman's Fascism'.[ii] In his presidential address, Cripps claimed he did not expect a 'spectacular Fascist coup', but a drive for national unity in defence of God, King and Country (which meant a defence of 'Capitalists, Property and Profits')![iii] The S.L. retained its interpretation of the Fascist potential in the Government and despite pressure from the Party Executive to temper its tone, the S.L. stubbornly held that 'under the threat to their property, the owning class would turn to weapons of the lock-out, financial panic, Fascist provocation, police forces, armed forces and law courts'.[iv] Those S.L. prognostications seemed relevant years later.

The most important single element in Socialist thought and policies in the 1930s was the attempt to link 'democracy' with 'Socialism'. In Europe, successful Socialist Movements had grown in nations with healthy democratic traditions and the goal of the S.L.'s democratic Socialism was to make democracy more relevant by broadening the application of democratic principles from the political to economic and social dimensions. All political parties in Britain hailed themselves as 'democratic', their opponents as 'dictatorial' in approach. Allegations/counter-allegations were part of the political currency, but the S.L. never escaped from being labelled 'in favour of dictatorship' by Conservatives, Labour leaders and the non-political.

The S.L.'s view was that Britain was not a democracy but a dictatorship; a dictatorship of the bourgeoisie. The question was not '*Dictatorship or Democracy*' but dictatorship of the bourgeoisie or dictatorship of the proletariat.[v] The basis of liberal democracy, that the minority acquiesce in the rule of the majority, meant less and less in practice; the history of post-war Italy and Germany had shown that dictatorship had been snatched by the best-organised political force and all opposition had been suppressed.[vi] S.L. leaders believed this degeneration of politics into a naked struggle for power could not be ignored. However, by its open discussion of the pros and cons of a 'dictatorship', the S.L. got into difficulties. The main political parties opposed 'dictatorship' and used the word to expose a 'ruthless, repressive regime'. Too late Cripps explained it was desirable to avoid dictatorship because no person was fit to be entrusted with uncontrolled power, and dictatorships (as a permanent method of government) were bound to fail.[vii] But had he not already expressed the view that the 19th century form of democratic government had shown itself incapable of adaptation to the economic and social conditions of the 1930s, and the growth of dictatorship had taken place, as the result of a demand for a more efficient form of government?[viii]

'Dictatorships' could be regarded as good or bad depending upon how, or against whom, they were directed. The S.L. concluded that if their purpose was to prevent an exploited class from obtaining its rights, they were denounced; if, as in the Soviet

[i] R. George, 'Counter Revolution', *Socialist Leaguer*, No. 12, June 1935.
[ii] *Manchester Guardian*, June 1st, 1936.
[iii] *New Leader*, June 5th, 1936.
[iv] Jacques, 'The State and Socialism', *Socialist*, No. 4, January–February 1936.
[v] Cf. James Howell letter in *Socialist*, No. 8, June 1936.
[vi] Cripps' preface to *Problems of a Socialist Government*, 1933, p.10.
[vii] Cripps, 'Democracy and Dictatorship', *Political Quarterly*, October–December 1933.
[viii] Cripps' preface to *Problems of a Socialist Government*, 1933, p.10.

Union after 1917, a dictatorship was 'preventing exploitation', the S.L. claimed suppression of 'anti-social activities' was a worthy achievement! Unfortunately, such a rationale did not bargain for Press denunciations of the S.L.'s equivocal outlook. Press reports of such S.L. views contained a good deal of misunderstandings, misquotation, obfuscation, and exaggeration, and to denounce S.L. inquiries as 'undemocratic' was ironical, since it was S.L. policy to *explain* all reasons for every part of its programme to the Labour Conference. This misinterpretation of the S.L.'s position on Emergency Powers or constitutional changes were evident even within the S.L. G. Catlin was distrustful of the policy (begun by E. F. Wise) and did not share the apparent pessimism concerning the inevitability of a violent showdown; he reinterpreted S.L. proposals when claiming 'there is the sharpest difference between a government endowed with a duly recorded and renewed mandate by the majority exercising resolute force against insurrection by men of property, and any group endeavouring to carry through reform without that formal mandate.'[i]

Discussion on this issue rested on fear expressed by the S.L. that a coup d'état might occur before a future Socialist Government arrived. In setting up new machinery of Socialist control, a future Government would have to establish 'a system that could be relied upon to work quickly *and dictatorially*'.[ii] This statement brought the wrath of Labour leader Herbert Morrison: 'The trouble with the S.L. is that they have assumed there is going to be a mess-up when a Socialist government takes office. Having assumed this, they have indicated the necessity for dictatorial powers,'[iii] a caricature of the S.L. maybe, but it had its effect on Party members. This hypothetical situation continued, with Laski answering Morrison, stating a Labour Government which embarked on socialisation would have to act quickly and thoroughly to make its plans workable: 'Parliament can be made the effective vehicle of great changes if its machinery is adapted to that purpose.'[iv] Behind this backstabbing was a genuine division of opinion about the rôle of the Party and what 'Parliamentary Socialism' signified. The controversy, expressed in this veiled form, hindered the development of both groups. Six years later Morrison reiterated this suppositional argument: 'Will British democracy stand the strain of the transformation from Capitalism to Socialism? …If we resort to violence and dictatorship and do not succeed, then, in company with millions of innocent people, we may become the victims of that very Fascist violence which we shall have precipitated, and provided with an excuse for its terror.'[v] Here was Labour's warning.

On this issue of dictatorship the S.L. made a political blunder which coloured most of its Press notices. Accused of 'desiring a dictatorship' by Conservatives (and their newspapers), chided by Labour leaders for 'embarrassing' the Labour Movement, denounced by the Communist Party and the I.L.P. for 'betraying the workers', the S.L., meekly defended its misunderstood policy: 'What we are concerned with is to make the Labour Movement alive to the urgency of the situation.'[vi] Arthur Marwick deduced that the S.L. was 'an undemocratic brand of British Socialism',[vii] adding that

---

[i] Catlin to Cripps, January 9th, 1934, Cripps Papers.
[ii] G. D. H. Cole, *The Socialist Control of Industry*, February 1933, S.L. pamphlet.
[iii] H. Morrison, *New Clarion*, September 30th, 1933.
[iv] Laski, *New Clarion*, October 7th, 1933.
[v] H. Morrison, 'Social Change – Peaceful or Violent?', *Political Quarterly*, January–March 1939.
[vi] 'The Will to Power', *New Clarion*, March 10th, 1934, S.L. Notes.
[vii] A. Marwick, *Clifford Allen – The Open Conspirator*, pp.126 & 129.

132

Clifford Allen was irritated by the 'undemocratic challenge to democracy, particularly from the extremists of the S.L., who were still labouring under the shadow of "1931",' and a typical Party reaction came from George Hicks (Labour MP for East Woolwich) who 'definitely dissociated himself from the *dictatorship policy* of Sir Stafford Cripps.'[i]

S.L. leaders were aware of the attraction of bold challenges to working people in the mass Movement. It was a reason for the immense popularity of S.L. speakers. Summing up 'the Real Issue', Laski believed Labour's opponents aimed to convince the electorate the Labour Party had ceased to believe in democracy, by misquoting Cripps, yet 'British Capitalism is just as anxious as any other capitalism to preserve its privileges... Cripps has made more people alive to these realities in two years than all his critics in the Labour Party have done since they first entered it,'[ii] although Cripps' speeches and articles gave the Press a chance to misrepresent the Left wing of the Labour Party as 'a revolutionary movement aiming at a Jacobin, if not a Communist dictatorship, with Cripps assuming the rôle of Robespierre.'[iii] If only! The S.L. regarded the Press' attitude to Cripps with annoyance at its ignorance *and* pleasure at the provocation of the S.L.: '*Tory and Liberal journalists short of copy and tired of splits in their own parties accuse the S.L. of being composed of "would-be dictators". Even the Labour Party gets in a pother, and there is unofficial talk of a "clean-up".*'[iv] It was all based, as the S.L. saw it, on the old habit of commenting on policies from newspaper reports of speeches. Later, the S.L. noted more sinister motives; politicians and the Press wanted to panic the electorate before the next Election with screams of 'dictatorship' and attacks on the S.L., accused of trying to impose 'new and dangerous doctrines on the Labour Movement'.[v]

The Conservative Party conducted its own assessment into the meaning of the S.L.'s 'dictatorship' pronouncements. It believed the S.L. was attempting to make the Labour Party adopt a policy that could establish 'despotism' in the name of 'democracy', and Keith Feiling thought the S.L. wanted to acquire legislative machinery that would act rapidly and efficiently: 'Does Cripps propose to substitute for Parliamentary Government the Hitlerite, the Russian or the Star Chamber model?'[vi] The *Morning Post* carried yet another cartoon by Wyndham Robinson showing Cripps attempting to muscle into the same photograph with Stalin, Hitler and Mussolini, while Cripps' mother (the Socialist League) looks on appreciatively. The caption is: 'Sorry Ma'am, but your little Stafford doesn't fit the group.'[vii] None too subtle! At the Constitutional Club in November 1933, Lord Hailsham put it bluntly – Cripps had claimed the Labour Party was going to establish a dictatorship.[viii] While Conservative speakers denounced highly coloured travesties of S.L. proposals, there was a splendid advertisement for the S.L., made by Baldwin. The S.L. was delighted to agree with his comments that in the Labour Movement 'the gospel of gradualism has

---

[i] *Kentish Independent & Kentish Mail*, January 12th, 1934.

[ii] *New Clarion*, February 3rd, 1934. (My italics.)

[iii] A. Bullock, op. cit., p.529, although "the Robespierres always win out over the Dantons", E. Hobsbawm, 'Revolutionaries', 1999 edn., p.259. See Thomas Carlyle quoted above, p.15.

[iv] 'Critics, Take Note', *New Clarion*, June 24th, 1933, S.L. Notes.

[v] *New Clarion*, September 2nd, 1933, S.L. News.

[vi] *The Times*, June 7th, 1933.

[vii] *Morning Post*, June 7th, 1933.

[viii] *The Times*, November 22nd, 1933.

been contemptuously swept aside',[i] although Laski rebuked Baldwin for misleading the public that the S.L. sought to persuade the Labour Party to adopt 'dictatorial' methods.[ii] The S.L.'s proposals were to work out a technique for the rapid attainment of Socialism *by democratic means*, but this was lost in the drama of mutual recriminations about 'dictatorship'. In October 1934, the *London Mercury* included a portrait of Cripps by Wyndham Lewis, which the *Socialist Leaguer* denounced as a cheap confusion of ideas assiduously promulgated by the baser sort of anti-Socialist scribe.[iii] Lewis bracketed Cripps with Mosley under the heading 'Two Dictators'. The following year, Lewis wrote to Cripps about an article Lewis had written for the BBC. He expressed what Labour leaders surmised: 'I wrote of the danger of Cripps decreeing the sort of books that should be written, music composed or pictures painted. This is a form of reformist political fanaticism (whatever *that* meant!)… how can you in one breath recoil so violently from the word "despotism" or "oligarch" and in the next act in a fashion that would be more appropriate to the mind of a dictator?'[iv] Lewis later apologised to Cripps, describing him as 'a much-criticised man; a man of great and unusual sincerity'![v]

Cripps was (occasionally) surprised at the notoriety he gained from his speeches: 'People, fantastically enough, in order to misrepresent me, accuse me of desiring dictatorship… yet [can one regard] wage cuts, unemployment benefit cuts and the Means Test as prosperity?'[vi], but the initial S.L. blunder on the issue of 'dictatorship' was never allowed to rest by Government supporters. One described the choice as between the Government and dictatorship and the following dovetailing: 'The S.L. and the Fascists wish to abolish democracy and Parliament and hit everyone who disagrees with you on the head or put him into a concentration camp… I thank God as an Englishman that if either the S.L. or the Fascists start that game here the traditions and the spirit of our people will rise up and destroy them. In this country we know the difference between the strong man and the bully.'[vii] When the level of political debate could reach *such* a low ebb, one realises the mistake the S.L. had initially conceived in its open discussion forum.

All this allowed *The Times* to muster its high-minded, self-righteous indignation in denunciation of what, otherwise, were important public matters: 'The ways of the S.L. are those of compulsion – dictation in the dress of a sham democracy, and freedom would go out when this Socialism came in.'[viii] The S.L.'s 'strong measures' was linked in the Conservative Party with support for 'dictatorship', a stick to beat the Labour Party into Parliamentary compromise. Thus, Sir Henry Betterton (Minister of Labour) could get away with claiming the policy Cripps advocated 'was hardly to be distinguished from the policy of Hitler or, in some shape, Lenin; both in policy and technique, the Cripps policy bore striking resemblance to what was happening in Russia, the same attack on personal liberty and personal and private property, the same determination to rush through revolution in the shortest possible time in order that

---

[i] *New Clarion*, August 5th, 1933, S.L. Notes.
[ii] Laski, 'Mr. Baldwin Seeks to Mislead', *New Clarion*, August 12th, 1933.
[iii] *Socialist Leaguer*, No. 5, October–November 1934.
[iv] June 28th, 1935.
[v] Cripps Papers, July 24th, 1935.
[vi] *Bristol Evening Post*, January 20th, 1934.
[vii] *The Times*, April 27th, 1934.
[viii] *The Times*, May 22nd, 1934.

the people should not have the opportunity to protest: 'This country at the next election would have to decide whether it wishes our system of constitutional government to remain.'[i] This travesty of the S.L.'s exegesis on 'dictatorship' supplied another reason for Labour leaders' by-passing S.L. resolutions; any link the Press could make between the Party and 'dictatorial' policies would be utilised in an Election campaign: 'If the S.L. point of view were approved by the Party it would drive us to defend ourselves for the greater part of our time against Tory allegations of Bolshevism and dictatorship.'[ii] Disastrous PR.

(D) S.L. Policy: Economics, Capitalist Planning, and Public Ownership

The most significant factor in Britain in the 1930s was the malfunctioning of the economy. For the S.L. the 1931 economic crisis proved the Socialist case *against* the market economy of private enterprise, which could not cure the trade cycle, deal with poverty and inequality, or use idle factories and unsold food crops. The crisis made recruits for the Labour Movement, but the S.L. failed to anticipate the enormous potential demand created by the advance of technology in production: 'The National Minimum of Civilised Life continuously rose and more and more goods and services were produced or invented, and were demanded by the mass of people. Luxuries turned into necessities.'[iii] The story of the Twentieth Century. The S.L.'s egalitarian ideals might make economic and moral sense, but a Socialist economic environment would not necessarily remove the inequalities of capitalist distribution.

For the S.L., the principal issue was that tariffs, inflation, embargoes, debts, quotas, shorter hours and wage rates were by-products of the private ownership of the means of production.[iv] This was the S.L.'s most pervasive illusion, because it led to the S.L.'s conception of political aims in narrowly economic terms and veneration of the Soviet Union's economic 'achievements' divorced from their political and social environments. This concentration on economics was one of the main weaknesses of the Labour Left in the 1930s,[v] for the kernel of the S.L. economic argument was that the capitalist mode of production could *never* adapt itself to a new age of plenty,[vi] a conviction which reached its apotheosis in a review of Keynes' *The General Theory of Employment, Wages and Prices*, described as an eloquent confession of the bankruptcy of capitalist economic theory![vii] The S.L. assumed that 'finance-capital' could *never* accept the alteration in the distribution of wealth because the system of private property was not in harmony with modern techniques of production and had become an obstacle to

---

[i] *The Times*, June 11th, 1934.

[ii] H. Morrison, *New Clarion*, September 30th, 1933.

[iii] M. Cole, *The Bulletin of the Society for the Study of Labour History*, No. 22, Spring 1971, "The 1930s saw the demise of the traditional British economy", Francois Bédarida, *A Social History of England 1851–1975* (1979 edn.), p.176.

[iv] Cf. J. T. Murphy, *Preparing for Power*, p.266.

[v] M. Foot, 'Credo of the Labour Left', *New Left Review*, May–June 1968.

[vi] G. D. H. Cole, 'The Gospel of Scarcity', *New Clarion*, April 8th, 1933. In 1933, material expectations were low and most Britons utilised income spent chiefly on the modest necessities of life, E. Hobsbawm, *Interesting Times: A 20th-Century Life*, 2002, p.88.

[vii] D. R. Davies, *Socialist*, No. 7, May 1936.

the further development of social wealth and consumption.

Some S.L. ideas were gleaned from Strachey's *The Coming Struggle for Power* (1932), which analysed the growth of national planning monopolies, economic nationalism, instability of the free market (waste figured as the overwhelming characteristic), recurrence of crises inherent because production was planless, and lower wages increasing British competitive power. Cripps' judgement in *Why This Socialism?* (1934), was that discontent was caused by waste of resources (in terms of people and materials in a system designed to produce profits and not articles for use); the S.L. saw workers at the mercy of 'money power' in a system which could not allow the unemployed access to the means of production for fear of flooding the market with commodities which could not be sold. In this analysis, the S.L. envisaged a system in which there had been advances in the techniques of manufacture without changes in the economic structure of industry (which controlled distribution and production); prices had been forced up to create an 'artificial scarcity'; and the existing system of production could not deal with a possible abundance of goods. The S.L. was motivated by the prospect of recurrent booms for financiers and industrialists, gained by inflicting low standards on workers,[i] so the essence of the S.L.'s '*Forward to Socialism*' policy was to challenge an economic system which could not distribute the goods it could produce: 'Millions of people suffer from unemployment because there is insufficient effective demand for the goods at the price at which they are offered on the market.'[ii]

This obsession with productive processes was based on the S.L.'s belief in social control instead of profit as the regulating motive of the economy. There were two pillars of indefensible disparities of income and opportunity; inherited wealth and the class system of education.[iii] To the S.L., these inequalities caused inefficiency and confusion, and it was part of the S.L.'s educative rôle to clarify that England was economically and socially a class-differentiated society. Tariffs, industrial subsidies, marketing boards, these helped producers' monopolies, but the Government refused to locate new factories in 'distressed areas'. S.L. leaders exposed not only false political and democratic liberties, but the (false) assumption of 'economic freedom of the individual': 'The freedom of shareholders to do what they liked with their own, of property-owners to hold up public developments or exact exorbitant prices and so destroy wage levels, are examples of the false liberties with which we must deal.'[iv] The existing structure could not transcend a negative conception of 'freedom' (and this has not lost its relevance). The S.L.'s moral critique of people who gave 'no useful service' to the community, who could acquire vast wealth by owning a share in the means of production,[v] remained. Even under a prosperous capitalist system, the S.L. argued, the same class would continue to suffer, and 'the same people could exert an extra-Parliamentary control on the national life'[vi] unless the main controlling points of the economy, finance and land property could be 'supervised'. For Party leaders the dominating factor was the struggle for a Parliamentary majority; for the S.L. it was the clash of economic interests, to be resolved by 'communal ownership of economic power' and establishment of a classless society: 'We have got to decide on which side of

[i] Cripps, *Democracy: Real or Sham?*, S.L. pamphlet, 1934.

[ii] S.L. National Council, *Forward to Socialism*, June 1934.

[iii] R. H. Tawney, *Equality*, 1964 edn., p.34.

[iv] Cripps, *Democracy Up-to-Date*, 1939, p.48.

[v] *Tribune*, January 29th, 1937, Cripps on 'Private Ownership for the Few Means Scarcity for the Many'.

[vi] Cripps, Preface to *Problems of a Socialist Government*, 1933.

the economic conflict we belong, and having decided, face up to the implications of that conflict.'[i] S.L. leaders assumed a priori that the stage had been reached when the economic system could only continue if wages were reduced.[ii] In such a situation, when neither work, opportunities or security could be offered the working population, it was understandable to concentrate criticism on the extravagance, inefficiency and nepotism[iii] of a capitalist economic environment.

As stated, the S.L. developed a policy to anticipate unconstitutional opposition to a future Labour Government from private business interests. A theory of sabotage, from a flight of capital abroad to a strike of capital at home, was constructed. This resulted in a policy on banking procedures to prevent the City from being able to hinder Socialist economic measures. At the Leicester Party Conference, E. F. Wise's resolution to nationalise the Joint Stock Banks was passed, anticipating possible difficulties from obstruction or sabotage by private banks, with resentment (in the S.L.) of bankers who could run their business divorced from the general economic benefit of society: 'The difference was between the management of "money" and credit in the interests of a class and of private interests, and its management for the general benefit of a planned State.'[iv] The S.L.'s formulation would make the banks more accountable to the electorate by placing ultimate control in the House of Commons. It also saw distribution of incomes, wage cuts, unemployment and social service cuts designed to save the direct taxpayer at the expense of the wage earner, while every tariff increase was a block in the channel of international commerce: 'Tariffs are going to make very little difference to unemployment, while the economies have caused a whole lot more unemployment.'[v] The S.L. campaigned for a 'managed' currency, stabilisation of prices, maximum stability of foreign exchange rates, nationalisation of the Bank of England and Joint Stock Banks, and a National Investment Board (to prevent the waste and misdirection of long-term capital).[vi] Ultimate executive authority on economic matters would rest with a Cabinet Committee, responsible for reorganising the banking system and formulating and administering policy determined by a National Planning Authority. The Minister of Finance would embrace the functions of the existing Treasury; nationalisation would be achieved by the State take-over of ordinary share capital of banks, and limits of compensation would be defined, a Joint Stock Banking Board (composed of the Chairman and representatives from each bank) to co-ordinate banking policy. The banks would assist industries in Socialist reorganisation with cheap credit for socialised industries and services; deposit banking under public ownership would render unnecessary much of London's Money Market procedures, while the National Investment Board would secure the available sum was allocated in accordance with the National Plan.

The theory behind this scheme was that banks occupied the crucial position in the control of industry, and could defeat any Socialist planning if left in private hands; money had to be made the servant and not the master of society, while the consuming power of working people had to correspond to the power of the community to supply goods and services. Full employment could only be ensured if the supply of credit was

---

[i] B. A. Betts, 'Youth and Peace', *Socialist Leaguer*, No. 5, October–November 1934.

[ii] Cripps, *Cornish Labour News*, November 1932.

[iii] Cripps, *Labour News*, December 1st, 1934.

[iv] Cripps to Stephen Burge, November 4th, 1932, Cripps Papers.

[v] Cripps' speech at Redfield, Bristol, *Western Daily Press,* January 4th, 1933.

[vi] E. F. Wise, *The Socialisation of Banking*, S.L. Pamphlet, 1933.

regulated and distributed by a wages and prices policy: 'Socialists are neither Free Traders nor Protectionists; they aim at the planned control of international and internal trade.'[i] The socialisation of capital would involve changes in taxation, because, as property passed into private hands, the public services would have to be financed less by taxation of incomes and more out of the revenue of State services: 'The banking system could be used to end unemployment.'[ii] There would be sufficient capital for financing industrial reorganisation provided the waste of capital in socially useless enterprises was ended.[iii] By February 1935, the S.L. could claim that the public was beginning to understand banking, and intended that such an important power should reside in the community.[iv]

The issue of capitalist plans for economic planning was viewed warily by the S.L. At its Leeds Conference, alarm was felt at tendencies in the Labour Party leading to presentation of schemes of capitalist nationalisation as "Socialism".[v] It was no function of the working-class movement to assist in the stabilisation of capitalism. *Forward to Socialism* stated the Government was openly pursuing the reorganisation of agriculture on a 'Corporate State' basis, guaranteeing interest and profit to private owners at the expense of farm workers and consumers. In the iron and steel industries, cotton and mining industries and transport was the same tendency. Government plans for 'ownership' and 'planning' were not only 'useless' but 'positively dangerous'[vi]: 'The socialisation of the means of production could not be a reality unless accompanied by workers' control of industry.'[vii] Discussing the N.F.R.B. pamphlet, *An International Monetary Agreement*, D. R. Davies inquired, 'What business has an alleged Socialist organisation to mess about with policies of stabilising capitalism?'[viii] Socialists ever since have had to answer this.

The S.L.'s gloomy view by 1934 was that the Government was being driven from an unregulated, individualist capitalism via trusts and employers' associations, to a system of producers' corporations 'on Fascist lines'. These corporations raised the price of produce without regard to interests of consumers or workers. Politically, the S.L. diagnosed a risk in setting up bodies which could be run by a bureaucracy or directors, and over which Parliament and the Cabinet had no effective control. Under provisions for compensation, it was conceivable that such corporations would have to pay the income and capital to a class of secured rentiers, whose claims would come before those of workers for increased wages or cheaper goods or services. G. R. Mitchison exclaimed there was a danger from a Socialist point of view that a new class of rentier would be established.[ix]

Of other schemes in the 1930s, the S.L. devoted critical interest to Roosevelt's *New Plan*, the *Douglas Credit Scheme* and the *Next Five Years' Group*. Roosevelt's policies had helped absorb the unemployed into work, and reorganisation techniques in the United

---

[i] G. D. H. Cole, *A Study Guide on Socialist Policy*, S.L. Pamphlet, August 1933, p.7.

[ii] G. R. Mitchison, *Banking*, S.L. Pamphlet, Socialist Programme Series, No. 3, 1933.

[iii] E. F. Wise, *Control of Finance and the Financiers*, S.L. Pamphlet, February 5th, 1933.

[iv] *Socialist Leaguer*, editorial, No. 9, February 15th, 1935.

[v] Leeds S.L. Conference, May 22nd, 1934.

[vi] S. Cripps, *Socialist*, No. 5, March 1936.

[vii] *Forward to Socialism*, S.L. policy, May 1934.

[viii] *Socialist Leaguer*, No. 11, May 1935.

[ix] G. R. Mitchison, 'The Corporate State or Socialist Plan', *Socialist Leaguer*, No. 6, November–December 1934.

States made possible increased production, when each nation-state was seeking tariffs, quotas, embargoes and currency restrictions. The S.L.'s surmise as to whether Roosevelt's policies were leading towards 'Fascism' or 'Socialism',[i] concluded he was acting as the agent of the industrial sector of capitalism rather than financial groups. It did not believe his policy would make any real changes in the conditions of U.S. workers. This was the message of Laski's S.L. pamphlet, *The Roosevelt Experiment*, which analysed the experiment that might have been sprung on the U.K..[ii] Roosevelt was not regarded by S.L. leaders as a radical: '…he is rather a liberal-minded gentleman of great courage and honesty of purpose, but really devoid of any serious knowledge of finance or economics'.[iii] He was bringing U.S. labour conditions to the level attained 15 or 20 years before, though the S.L. saw him as a Liberal with a conscience. 18 months later, Cripps at the S.L. Bristol Conference concluded Roosevelt had failed to cure the inconsistencies of 'capitalism' by his reformist methods: 'This showed conclusively that in that direction the workers could not have any hope.'[iv] In Roosevelt's policies, the S.L. noted a move to 'planned capitalism', and they reacted to it in the same way as they responded to any mixed economy: '*To plan without any transference of economic power belied the fundamental Socialist urge towards a classless society, and cloaked a wave of reaction.*'[v] The S.L.'s response was a resistance to 'planners' whose desire was to maintain or recover profits for shareholders and win over the economy-minded unions. As to capitalist redistribution' of wealth or incomes, the S.L. argued there were limits to the possibilities of redistribution of wealth based on high taxation, G. R. Mitchison concluding there had been no change in the distribution of capital in the previous 25 years, such was the inefficiency of taxation and social services to remedy that particular injustice.[vi]

The *Douglas Credit Scheme* was dubbed 'Moral Capitalism'. Douglas' proposals involved an expansion of credit to keep pace with expanding productive capacity; if wealth increased, everyone must gradually be better off financially.[vii] He wanted to aid the deficiency of purchasing power which permitted gluts of commodities on the market by issuing steadily increased amounts of currency in national dividends.[viii] The S.L. deduced that Douglas was leaving the ownership of the productive process in private hands, and permitting *further* inequalities of income,[ix] although Cripps concluded that Douglas agreed that nothing could be done until economic power was transferred from private hands to the State.[x] Cripps read a great deal about National Credit as a scheme and discussed it with Douglas, and accepted that as a means of the distribution of purchasing power in a Socialist State during the transition period, 'something of this sort would be possible', yet he believed it could not be achieved

[i] *Spotlight on Roosevelt*, S.L. Notes, November 18th, 1933.
[ii] *New Clarion*, S.L. Notes, January 13th, 1934.
[iii] *New Clarion*, S.L. Notes, November 25th, 1933.
[iv] *Daily Herald*, quoting Cripps, June 10th, 1935.
[v] *New Clarion*, S.L. Notes, February 17th, 1934.
[vi] G. R. Mitchison reviewing *The Distribution of National Capital* by Daniels and Campion, *Socialist*, No. 9, July–August 1936.
[vii] Cf. M. Muggeridge, *The Thirties*, 1967 edn., p.44.
[viii] Cf. Douglas, *The Monopoly of Credit*.
[ix] *Tribune*, January 15th, 1937.
[x] Cripps in letter, July 11th, 1934, Cripps Papers.

until the banking system was under State ownership.[i] The majority opinion in the S.L. was that the Social Credit scheme was an escape mechanism, avoiding confrontation between 'Capitalism' and 'Socialism': 'It gives mental relief without economic anxiety. Douglas and his followers seek to maintain the profit system without tears.'[ii]

The Depression gave confirmation to more substantial economic theories, especially analyses of unemployment and investment by J. M. Keynes, who gave economists a new method of classifying forces determining the level of output as a whole.[iii] He constructed a new general theory, a new set of tools to diagnose economic problems, in which nations could deal with the accepted view of the automatic workings of economic laws. These ideas led to questions of planning. In 1931, *Political and Economic Planning* had been formed as a group of civil servants, businessmen, academics and professionals interested in the problems of industry. By 1935, a wider organisation, the *Next Five Years' Group*, was formed.[iv] Its recommended plans for Britain had (according to the *Daily Herald*) 'about five times as much Socialism as the United Front proposals were creating'.[v] It was in favour of State intervention, socialisation, varying degrees of public control over industries, and had a faith in public works as a means of coping with unemployment. To the S.L. it was an attempt at a Liberal revival detached from the class war and the S.L. held to its dogma that one could not uphold the capitalist system *and* redistribute wealth, whereas the *Next Five Years' Group* stood for evolutionary changes through some State control and a gradual diminution of economic inequality. G. D. H. Cole proposed the Labour Party might get the chance of acting in the spirit of the *Next Five Years' Group* and calling its action 'Practical Socialism',[vi] while Dalton felt that, although the Group carried little electoral weight, it could teach and learn in the Labour Party.[vii] Neither the S.L. nor the Labour Party could envisage the *Next Five Years' Group* as an augury for a new approach to economic reconstruction.

S.L. plans for nationalisation and State ownership reflected the principled, efficient and functional society proclaimed by R. H. Tawney in *The Acquisitive Society*.[viii] This construed that working people had to see that the solution lay in a planned, co-ordinated control of production. The S.L.'s declaration of the need to allot social and economic functions in accordance with people's capacity to put them to good use in the common interest ranked the S.L. with traditional Socialist belief in technological developments and large-scale industry as foundations of a Socialist society. The Labour Government of 1929–1931 had been unable to alter the inequalities of wealth, income or opportunity, so the S.L. offered, to a pragmatic Party, a working ideology and a set of principles to guide the Party's complex and sometimes conflicting economic initiatives.[ix] 'Freedom' was inextricably linked to the diffusion of power. In

---

[i] Cripps in letter, January 20th, 1935, Cripps Papers.

[ii] W. Mellor, *Socialist Leaguer*, No. 10, March–April 1935, review of *Social Credits or Socialism* by H. R. Hiskett and *Douglas Fallacies* by John Lewis.

[iii] R. F. Harrod, *Keynes*, p.465.

[iv] N.F.Y.G. included trade unionists, MPs, professors, churchmen, businessmen and members of all the main political parties.

[v] *Daily Herald*, July 26th, 1935.

[vi] G. D. H. Cole, 'Chants of Progress', *Political Quarterly*, October–December 1935.

[vii] Halton, 'The Popular Front', *Political Quarterly*, October–December 1935.

[viii] R. H. Tawney, *The Acquisitive Society*, pp.31, 48–9, 80, 139, 160–61, 178.

[ix] Cf. John Grieve-Smith, *Matters of Principle: Labour's Last Chance*, 1968, pp.14–15.

the economic realm too, there could be no freedom unless there *was* a redistribution of economic power. The S.L.'s concept of nationalisation implied diffusion of publicly-owned property, a planned economy to maintain a steady rate of economic growth, and avoidance of periodic waste of idle resources, underproduction and slumps.[i] If the Labour Party intended to embark upon such an immediate, far-reaching programme when it gained office, this had to be presented to the electorate. G. D. H. Cole believed the basis of industry could be changed through public ownership, while S.L. policy included socialisation of the banking system, nationalised industries, control of prices, minimum wage rates, compensation to previous owners of industries, a National Economic Council, Regional Development Councils, a National Planning Commission with a National Investment Board.[ii] If industry was to be managed by Boards, the S.L. wanted union representatives with a controlling place on them, because such Boards would play their part in a single Socialist Plan.[iii]

At a time when production was said to be growing rapidly only in the Soviet Union, the S.L. looked to Russian economic achievements with awe and justification for its own remedies. There was a simplistic rationale behind such S.L. assessments: 'The world could easily double its output of coal, iron, steel or cotton… Why not join together to use the huge productive resources at our command for the common benefit of all?'[iv] The S.L. believed it would be indispensable for a Socialist government 'to create a National Economic Plan of reconstruction', but it was 'no good promising people immediate tangible benefits if it was impossible to give them. That had been the mistake of the Labour Party before 1929.'[v] In *Why This Socialism?* Cripps analysed the waste, misdirection of effort, non-production, long-term unemployment, and sketched the S.L.'s vision of a Socialist economy. Rationalisation had failed to increase the standard of living, and economic scarcity was the form in which economic privileges were being maintained: '*Tariffs, Free Trade, Quotas, Restrictions, Inflation, Deflation, Subsidies and Marketing Boards have failed to distribute the commodities fairly or abundantly*',[vi] and Public Utilities Corporations would not in themselves provide any solution.[vii] 'We Can Plan Production and Distribution for Use',[viii] was an S.L. aspiration, to transform trade and industry from the chaos of competition to the efficiency of service.[ix] Its economic arguments rested on the premise that it was impossible to plan for abundance unless control of the means of production was in State public ownership. Hence the Five Year Plan in *Forward to Socialism*. By 1935, J. T. Murphy, reviewing S.L. achievements, considered it had played a considerable part for a planned advance to Socialism,[x] later reflected in the *Labour's Immediate Programme* (1937) and the nationalisation programme of the 1945–51 Governments. Even the 1939–45 War administration was compelled to acknowledge some S.L. proposals for planning, full employment, redistributive taxation and new social services, measures

---

[i] Cf. Schumpeter, *Capitalism, Socialism and Democracy*, 1942, p.195.

[ii] G. D. H. Cole, *The Socialist Control of Industry*, S.L. Pamphlet, February 26th, 1933.

[iii] G. R. Mitchison, *Socialist Leaguer*, No. 6, November–December 1934.

[iv] F. Horrabin and G. D. H. Cole, *Socialism in Figures and Pictures*, April 20th, 1933.

[v] Cripps in a letter, September 20th, 1934.

[vi] Cripps, *Why This Socialism?*, p.74. (My italics.)

[vii] Ibid., p.80.

[viii] Ibid., p.125.

[ix] G. Lansbury, *My England*, 1934, p.48.

[x] J. T. Murphy reviewing *Economic Planning in Soviet Russia* by Boris Brutzkus, *Socialist Leaguer*, January 1935.

deemed essential in a World War, and no longer the utopian dream of Left-wing idealists.[i]

There was never any uncertainty concerning the aims of productivity expressed in S.L. journals. The S.L. did not as a group develop its ideas further than thinking in terms of keeping productive efficiency at a maximum by expanding the volume of effective demand through control of production and remuneration. It did not debate whether industries were producing things people needed; rather, they wanted everyone to have access to anything which industries were capable of producing. The only uncertainty was an unformulated aspiration that there were some circumstances in which the Socialist would prefer *less* production of wealth provided he could achieve a *fairer distribution* of it.[ii] A child of the 1930s, the S.L. was an organisation which dreamt of a fully mechanised world of material well being. It was too theoretical and idealistic in its outlook to give constructive help in the electoral struggle ahead, but it was Cripps who would successfully by 1948 complete the transition from a war economy by marrying Keynesian techniques of budgetary manipulation to the system of rationing and controls. The relative recovery of the economy between 1934 and 1937, however uneven its distribution nationally, had a neutralising effect on Socialist critics,[iii] with the imposition of tariffs, new industries (assuaging the failures of old staple industries), a housing boom, cheap money, low interest rates (freeing investment potential), a shift in entrepreneurial expectations raising the marginal efficiency of capital, and (after 1935) the gradual establishment of the economy on a war footing (one-third of employment growth in the iron and steel industry in 1935–37, was caused by rearmament). Ironically, the major advantage of rearmament was its strong linkages to staple industries and the depressed regions. New techniques of economic management made a break with the past.[iv]

---

[i] Cf. Crosland, *The Future of Socialism*, p.52.

[ii] Suggested by A. L. Rowse, 'Mr Keynes on Socialism', *Political Quarterly*, July–September 1932. (My italics.)

[iii] Cf. John Coombes, 'British Intellectuals and the Popular Front', in *Class, Culture and Social Change: A New View of the 1930s*, ed. F Gloversmith, 1980.

[iv] Mark Thomas, 'Rearmament and Economic Recovery in the Late 1930s', *EHR*, November 1983.

Chapter Five

Unemployment, Professionals and Class Struggle

All I know is that my happiness is built on the misery of other people, that I eat because others go hungry, that I am clothed when other people go almost naked through the frozen cities in winter; and that fact poisons me, disturbs my serenity, makes me write propaganda when I would rather play.

John Reed, qu. R. Rosenstone, *Romantic Revolutionary:*
A Biography of John Reed, 1982 edn., p.277

Economic changes impel changes in social relationships, in relations between real men and women; and these are apprehended, felt, reveal themselves in feelings of injustice, frustration, aspirations for social changes; all is fought out in the human consciousness, including the moral consciousness... men make their own history: they are part agents, part victims.

E. P. Thompson, 'Socialist Humanism: An Epistle to the Philistines',
New Reasoner, 1957, p.122

If Marx is right, then it is a Party (which alone grasps the demands of the rational goals of history), which must shape and guide me, whichever way my poor empirical self may wish to go, and the Party itself must be guided by its far-seeing leaders, and in the end by the greatest and wisest leader of all... the 'engineer of human souls' to use Stalin's phrase, knows best; he does what he does not simply in order to do his best for his nation but in the name of the nation itself, in the name of what the nation would be doing itself if only it had attained to this level of historical understanding. That is the great perversion, which the positive notion of liberty has been liable to; whether the tyranny issues from a Marxist leader, a king, a fascist dictator, the masters of an authoritarian Church or class or State, it seeks for the imprisoned, 'real' self within men, and 'liberates' it, so that this self can attain to the level of those who give the orders.

Isaiah Berlin, *The First and the Last*, 1999, pp.64–65

(A) The S.L. and Unemployment

Before the United Front campaign of 1936–37, the main activities of S.L. members centred on the effects of unemployment and the Government's Means Test. Persistence of unemployment, with one to three million unemployed, made it more difficult to accept Labour's gradualist policies.[i] The Unemployed Movement was the

---

[i] The movements of resistance to the emergency legislation, outside the range of the official labour

only section of Labour which overtly challenged the State. It was an integral part of S.L. belief that a revolutionary crisis would probably be the result of mass unemployment and lowered standards of living. The tragedy was that Labour leaders believed there was little the Party could do to force the Government from its Means Test, while unemployment insurance was never claimed to be an end to unemployment: 'To relieve the unemployed as economically as possible was the great preoccupation.'[i] It was against this that the S.L. rallied its members during the first three years of its existence. The unemployment problem was the emotional, political and economic fulcrum for the S.L. (S.L. book reviewer, Walter Greenwood (the novelist), put into the mouths of his characters: 'There hangs over us that dread threat of unemployment – that is the price we are paying for this system's continuance...'[ii] He was a living corpse; a unit of the spectral army of three million lost men...'[iii] Wages controlled their lives, wages were their masters, they its slaves.'[iv]) J. T. Murphy, reviewing May 1934 to May 1935, deduced that opposition to the *Unemployment Act* was the most important campaign conducted by the S.L.[v] because it demonstrated what could be done through the Party when Socialists acted in an organised way.

Initially, the S.L.'s agitation began through pamphlets and lectures. In December 1932, was exclaimed: 'We are in the middle of the very worst crisis of unemployment; wages have been falling; social services have been restricted; prices have been forced up. Within [this system] there is no remedy for unemployment.'[vi] It was always a supposition in the S.L. that unemployment could *never* be cured by spending money; long-unemployed could not be brought back into employment because the system could not withstand such expenditure without collapse; a capitalist market economy could not provide the services required for the whole population. This doctrinaire class outlook remained the S.L.'s stance. To William Mellor, excessive unemployment represented the failure of the system of 'wealth production';[vii] a solution lay in a 25% increase in maintenance payment; abolition of transitional benefits, a 4-year Slum Clearance Scheme; the means to maintain the unemployed had to come from production and unionist demands for shorter hours was a weapon, but not a method of solving unemployment. Even emergency schemes were temporary palliatives, not cures, but the S.L. campaigned to translate 'Work or Maintenance' into effective action.

The S.L.'s argument was succinct and logical. With 30 million unemployed workers in the world,[viii] and huge stocks of unsold goods stored for want of buyers, the capitalist system was inefficient, irrational, wasteful. In England and Wales 1 in 10 people were living in over-crowded conditions, but there were 250,000 unemployed

---

movement, revealed a pattern which dominated the 1930s, cf. N. Branson, M. Heinemann, op. cit., 1973 edn., p.29.

[i] C. L. Mowat, op. cit., p.470.

[ii] W. Greenwood, *Love on the Dole*, 1933, p.89.

[iii] Ibid. p.169.

[iv] Ibid. p.125. A. L. Horner commented: "We were not ashamed, because we were being made outcasts by those who owned the means which could have given us a livelihood," *Incorrigible Rebel*, 1960, p.97.

[v] J. T. Murphy, 'The Year in Review', *Socialist Leaguer*, No. 11, May 1935.

[vi] *Sutton Times*, December 11th, 1932.

[vii] W. Mellor, *The Claim of the Unemployed*, S.L. lecture/pamphlet, February 19th, 1933.

[viii] International Labour Office Estimates, December 1932.

builders in 1933.[i] The Socialist argument, that unemployment was inevitable under the capitalist system, was irrefutable; the S.L.'s campaign was for provisions for maintenance of the unemployed on a uniform national scale,[ii] and by June 1933 the S.L. was at the head of the Party's protest against the Means Test.[iii] Opposing the Government's *Unemployment Insurance Bill* (with provision for two classes of unemployed, differentiated in treatment, benefits, and adhesion to the Means Test), the S.L. expounded the alternatives.[iv] S.L. leaders saw through the Bill, whose main object seemed to them to be to remove Parliamentary criticism against the U.A.B.: 'It is one more milestone in the direction of Tory Dictatorship.'[v] In the first year of hunger marches, 1934 brought to the surface the S.L.'s frustrations; the *Unemployment Bill* sought to stabilise unemployment benefits at their spurious 'crisis level', and was to re-enact the Means Test on a family basis. The unemployed were treated as if they were responsible for their own unemployment, with the indignities experienced under the Means Test: 'Even in times of acute depression, the profit-earner on the average does not do badly,'[vi] remarked Cripps.

The S.L.'s constructive alternative to the Government's policy was based on security for the worker through continuity of employment, or full maintenance (for reasons of changing industrial circumstances, ill health or old age). At the S.L.'s Leeds Conference (1934), a resolution was passed expressing hostility to the new Bill with its provisions for placing the unemployed under an 'extra-Parliamentary dictatorship', conscripting them into "training camps", perpetuating the Means Test, dividing the unemployed into two grades, and undermining union conditions.[vii] The S.L. judged the partial concession of promised restoration of cuts in unemployment benefit as an attempt to deflect public attention from the worst features of the Bill. As a precursor of the rôle which it was to adopt from 1935, it challenged the Movement to ignore the administration of the Bill if it became law, and urged the N.E.C. and T.U.C. General Council to undertake organisation of the unemployed, and use mass demonstrations 'to focus public attention upon the failure of capitalism, and the vital necessity for Socialism as the only cure for unemployment'.[viii] – the essence of the S.L.'s message.

By now, the S.L. was in an awkward situation. It rejected the opportunity to join Tom Mann and Alex Gossip at a National Congress to organise a united struggle against the Bill and the 'Conscript Labour Schemes' of the Government, because the Labour Party was not associating with this. Cripps expressed the dilemma: 'I must be loyal to their attitude.'[ix] Appeals from the C.P. and I.L.P. for unity were ignored by the N.E.C. and General Council, yet when the *Black Circular* was enforced (March 1935), the struggle against the *Unemployment Bill* became the clearest demonstration since 1920 that a united working-class defence could defeat a Government attack,[x] despite an enormous Parliamentary majority. To the S.L., Unemployment Assistance Boards

[i] J. F. Horrabin & G. D. H. Cole, *Socialism in Pictures and Figures*, S.L. pamphlet, April 20th, 1933.

[ii] G. D. H. Cole, *A Study Guide on Socialist Policy*, S.L. pamphlet.

[iii] G. D. H. Cole, 'On Agitation', *New Clarion*, June 10th, 1933.

[iv] *New Clarion*, S.L. Notes, November 18th, 1933.

[v] Tom Williams, MP, 'Workless – Touchables and Untouchables', *New Clarion*, December 23rd, 1933.

[vi] Cripps, *Democracy: Real or Sham?*, S.L. pamphlet, 1934, p.11.

[vii] S.L. Leeds Conference, 'Resolution on Unemployment', May 22nd, 1934.

[viii] Ibid.

[ix] Cripps letter, Cripps papers, January 23rd, 1934.

[x] A. Hutt, *British Trade Unionism*, 1962 revised edition, p.131.

(U.A.B.s) attempted to destroy ways of controlling the administration of relief, by dividing working people, and from January 1935, the S.L.'s task was to find means of helping the unemployed obtain maximum relief.[i] On February 3rd, 1935, the S.L. redoubled efforts to force the whole Movement in protest against the *Unemployment Act*. It appealed to the Party's Executive and the National Council of Labour to extend the protests by mass demonstrations, and meetings of the Movement and encouraged the National Council of Labour to organise a mass march to Hyde Park.[ii]

This agitation on behalf of the unemployed gave the S.L. an uplift when its initial fervour had waned. Now there was a cause, a new outlet. Judging the *Unemployment Act* as 'Fascism in its English dress', the S.L. reiterated its duty to unite 'Socialist agitators'.[iii] Calls for unity in the Movement against the *Unemployment Act*, its effects, its administration, was the forerunner to the broader call for a united front. The Act, designed to take the issue of unemployment *out* of politics had, by its very operation, brought it *into* the streets. The S.L. became involved in calls for rank and file unity as it exposed the divisive nature of the Act,[iv] and it agitated to make unemployment a matter of national responsibility, because the Government was determined to prevent political party influence in the relief of the unemployed by placing administrative authority outside Parliament: 'The Government has set up a new body with the avowed intention of taking unemployment out of politics ... and regarding the unemployed as evil.'[v] The S.L. was determined to keep the problem in the forefront as a political issue and was particularly encouraged by later withdrawal of U.A.B. regulations, as Cripps announced: 'Never before has a Government had to withdraw so important a measure so rapidly because of the outspoken criticism throughout the whole of the country.'[vi] C. Trevelyan concurred.[vii]

What emerged from the reaction of the S.L. against the *Unemployment Act* was antagonism towards the T.U.C. General Council, which the S.L. was convinced had not marshalled the Movement dynamically, but was 'clinging to the stereotyped, old-fashioned method of sedate indoor protest'[viii] when the route to make demands and voice opinion was through national agitation. J. T. Murphy wanted the S.L. to help the unemployed acknowledge the economic causes of their problems, although conscious it was difficult to maintain political keenness during prolonged unemployment. It was the Means Test itself which was the bête noire of the S.L., with 'its impertinent, contemptible searching into the earnings of those living with an unemployed person, its assumption that disability pensions were legitimate plunder by which ratepayers' money could be saved, and its attempt to put responsibility for unemployed members of a family on to those who are working, making the unemployed a person of pity and contempt.'[ix] In March 1936, the S.L. was clinging to the hope that Party leaders would

---

[i] *Socialist Leaguer*, No. 8, January 15th, 1935.

[ii] S.L. Minutes, Reg. Groves Papers, February 3rd, 1935.

[iii] Editorial Notes and Comments, *Socialist Leaguer*, No. 9, February 15th, 1935.

[iv] The Act split the unemployed into those who maintained the number of stamps on Unemployment Insurance Cards (and those who became entitled to Unemployment Insurance Benefit for 26 weeks in 1 year) versus those who had exhausted their benefit, with no recourse, except the Poor Law.

[v] W. H. Mainwaring, *Socialist Leaguer*, No. 9, February 1935.

[vi] Cripps, *Western Daily Press*, February 11th, 1935.

[vii] Sir C. Trevelyan, 'The Outlook of the S.L.', *Political Quarterly*, April–June 1935.

[viii] *Socialist Leaguer*, No. 10, March–April 1935.

[ix] Margaret McCarthy (S.L. Secretary), *Socialist Leaguer*, No. 11, May 1935.

cogently denounce the principles on which the *Unemployment Act* was based.[i] Rent allowances might be fixed in the new regulations, but landlords had priority claims on the income of the unemployed, and the machinery of appeal was impossibly bureaucratic. The S.L. invited Trades Councils and local Labour Parties to consider the new regulations, take action, and renew the campaign and G. R. Mitchison had moved the resolution opposing the *Unemployment Act* at the S.L. Bristol Conference (1935); this called on the Movement to pledge itself to remove the measure from the Statute Book and establish a system of non-contributory maintenance: 'The Unemployment Assistance Boards are as far removed from the workers as they could possibly be.'[ii]

The S.L. contended that the issue of unemployment was 'the greatest social issue of our times upon which to fight'. It held out bait for Party leaders to join in mass demonstrations as a policy in order 'to ensure a Labour triumph at the polls'! It welcomed the T.U.C. declaration against the Act, while noting the pragmatic response to each issue which prevented an analysis of cause and effect: 'The Labour Movement needs faith in its own fundamental remedies, faith in Socialism and faith in the workers' power.'[iii] Awaiting such faith, the S.L.'s Stoke Conference (1936), concentrated on the delay with the new regulations governing the granting of benefit, and the T.U.C.'s silence. In its third Conference resolution on unemployment, the S.L. pledged its local branches to active opposition to any resolutions which included any Means Test.[iv] By 1936, the S.L.'s opposition to the *Unemployment Act* had merged into the call for a united front: 'Here is a Popular Front (Smash the Unemployment Regulations – and the Act) – End any Means Test',[v] exclaimed S.L. Chairman, W. Mellor. Again, the aim was to mobilise the Movement on the issue of the regulations: 'The Act is a necessary part of the machinery of British Capitalism for the depression of wages. The National Government is unable to make the maintenance of the unemployed a national responsibility because, to them, the cost is too great.'[vi]

In September 1936, the S.L. congratulated the P.L.P. on its protest against the regulations and the Means Test, and issued its own call to S.L. branches and Area Committees outlining a campaign to explain the full significance of the regulations, as part of a movement leading to demonstrations throughout Britain before the regulations came into operation.[vii] Another S.L. demand was for a lead from the N.C.L., since union leaders appeared disconcerted, confused and indeterminate; the T.U.C. ought to give a lead if unionists wanted to prevent the unemployed being used to depress their own standard of living.[viii] After the T.U.C. Conference of 1936, S.L. leaders were disappointed in the decision to reject proposals for action against the new U.A.B. regulations, and augured 'a heavy price for their refusal to prepare any serious action on behalf of the unemployed'.[ix] As B. B. Gilbert concludes, the 1930s' sufferings

[i] Editorial, *Socialist*, No. 5, March 1935.

[ii] 'Notes and Comments', *Socialist Leaguer*, No. 13, July–August 1935.

[iii] *Socialist*, No. 1, September 1935.

[iv] *Manchester Guardian & Daily Herald*, June 2nd, 1936.

[v] Mellor, *Socialist*, No. 9, July–August 1936.

[vi] Mellor, ibid.

[vii] *Socialist*, No. 10, September 1936.

[viii] Jim Griffiths, MP, 'The Fight Against the Means Test' (A Plea for United Action), *Socialist*, No. 10, September 1936.

[ix] 'Militant', 'The T.U.C. Sits', *Socialist*, No. 11, October 1936.

constituted a fixture of folklore and made *worker security* the central tenet of socialists.[i]

The final phase in the S.L.'s policy on unemployment was to link the Means Test to the growth in armament manufacture. The new regulations, deduced the S.L., were part of the structure through which the Government would carry through reductions in expenditures, and provide the means for making use of the unemployed in war preparations. Reduced payments to young workers was part of the recruiting campaign. Trades Councils were asked to begin an *Unemployed Association*, so that every trade unionist was compelled to realise how valuable was the existence of an organised unemployed movement in contact with unions during a widespread strike movement.[ii] In the final months before the S.L.'s disbandment a new plan on unemployed agitations was being evolved. It was accepted that only a Socialist Government working with a national plan (and overriding private capitalism) could hope to save the Distressed Areas, but it was also acknowledged that an urgent requirement was the creation of one national unemployed movement, which could become an integral part of the Labour Movement. Unemployed agitations were too spasmodic, its organisations constantly changing in personnel, too much at the mercy of booms and slumps, while unemployed workers were too ill-nourished to continue a long-sustained fight, and hold gains over any period of time. The S.L., nationally and locally, had been the one organisation within the Labour Party to contribute *consistently* to unemployed agitations. By actively campaigning in this way, the S.L. increasingly distanced itself from the Party Executive. It was only a matter of time before Party discipline would play its part in 'uniting' the Party but throughout this campaign, the S.L. had accused Party and union leaders of neglecting the requirements of the unemployed, and, therefore, allowing the Government scope to use a potential weapon against union conditions.[iii] The irony was that the agitations of the S.L., I.L.P. and C.P. were to be the excuse for the Government to attack the Labour Party in 1937. The United Front issue would split the Labour Movement, and resulted in the S.L.'s irrevocable decision to dissolve itself.

(B) The S.L. and the Professional Worker

In its political courtship of the middle-class professional worker, the S.L. exhibited an inherent ambiguity. This dichotomy was a result of the middle-class background of most leading S.L. figures and their awareness of the non-Socialist aspirations or nature of most professionals. Admittedly, the wooing of the professional technician and administrator was a subsidiary activity of the S.L.: 'Socialism must be built by the working class itself, and professional support would be dearly purchased by any recrudescence of the diluted liberalism of the MacDonald regime.'[iv] However, the need for professional help in the struggle for a Socialist planned society was reiterated in S.L. circles, for it was recognised that the emerging middle class of technicians and administrators in the 1930s, although small in numbers, was highly trained and

---

[i] B. B. Gilbert, *Britain 1914–1945: The Aftermath of Power*, 1996, p.84. (My italics.)

[ii] 'Militant', 'The Means Test and War', *Socialist*, No. 12, November 1936.

[iii] *Socialist*, No. 13, December 1936–January 1937. 40% of miners were unemployed in 1932, 19% were still unemployed in 1937, N. Branson, M. Heinemann, op. cit., 1973, p.117.

[iv] L. A. Fenn, *What of the Professional Classes?*, S.L. lecture/pamphlet, February 11th, 1934.

potentially immensely powerful. They gave the immediate orders and undertook essential administration, which set industry on a planned basis or brought it to a standstill. Therefore, it was an S.L. policy 'to cultivate the expert in the hope of securing his help'.[i] So what did the professional worker want?

Professional advice and support was attached to the S.L.'s platform of constitutional revolution – the non-violent accomplishment of a Socialist economic system, which would involve the acquiescence of these very people. The professional classes had to, somehow, be well disposed to the Socialist project. The problem was not how to do without the professional, but what to do with him (mainly him) so the S.L. aim was to induce these specially-favoured workers to enter the Socialist Movement on a basis of similar interests with working-class people. It was accepted that these professionals were largely unreached by Labour propaganda, and the S.L. could act as a *recruiting agent* performing an invaluable service. Ellen Wilkinson concluded that the real problem for the Socialist was how to detach that section of the middle class who would be required in the transition to Socialism'.[ii] It was for this reason that S.L. contributors, such as W. Mellor, G. D. H. Cole and H. Laski, campaigned for a University Labour Federation. It was essential that support should be won among those holding administrative, technical and academic posts. The U.L.F. would promote Socialist activities among students, and act as a link between them and the Labour Party.[iii] The S.L. also showed how conscious it was of this middle-class approach by passing a resolution at Stoke (1936) that the Movement was being 'increasingly deprived of the services of the ablest children born into working-class houses',[iv] i.e. professionals most welcome.

The problems of capturing the professionals' vote were made more difficult by the nature of the latter's work. A profession was viewed as a vocation whose members often worked directly for the individual consumer without the intervention of a capitalist employer; they possessed collective control over the ethics of their calling and conditions of entry. To the S.L., the professional individual was disciplined, not by an employer but by the nature of his work. As a highly skilled craftsman, he worked under conditions of exceptional freedom: 'There is to be found among professional workers a real enthusiasm for their work and a real desire to be free from external and irrelevant considerations.'[v] In this, the S.L. recognised the clash in temperament, purpose and interests between the middle-class professional and the working-class Movement. An example was Jacques' description of the '*Class Struggle and Fabianism*'.[vi] He noted the influence in Labour ranks of the strata of technical and professional workers, who, divorced from the direct ownership of the means of production, were able to assume a critical attitude to the capitalist system, yet there was resentment in the Party towards this kind of professional: 'Standing between the proletariat and the capitalists this group is especially prone to "produce schemes" whereby the contending classes can reach satisfactory agreement. This "third class", however, has neither the

---

[i] L. A. Fenn, 'Those Intelligentsia', *Socialist Leaguer*, No. 2, July–August 1934.

[ii] E. Wilkinson, *New Trends in Socialism*, edited by Catlin, 1935, reviewed by H. L. Elvin, *Socialist*, No. 4, January–February 1936.

[iii] *Socialist*, No. 2, November 1935.

[iv] Quoted in the *Daily Herald*, June 1st, 1936.

[v] L. A. Fenn, *What of the Professional Classes?*, p.3.

[vi] *Socialist*, No. 2, November 1935.

State power of the capitalists nor the numbers and organisation of the workers.[i] Yet the professional was deemed worth capturing, or at least enticing.

Such suspicions and resentment of the 'classless' professional hindered hopes in the S.L. to attract this kind of supporter. A profession maintained standards which the S.L labelled 'governing-class standards'. It seemed therefore very difficult for the professional man to realise that, as a worker, he should be campaigning on the basis of 'the class struggle'. In his training he revered processes of thought which were characteristic of a tiny minority; he believed in freedom of thought and the importance of rational discussion in a world where, as the S.L. saw it (because of class stratification) rational processes played a much smaller part in public life than the sheltered existence of the professional allowed him to perceive. The S.L. sought to question the 'freedoms' which the professional believed existed in capitalist society, and challenged the professional's concern that, in any fundamental social change, he was likely to lose a favoured economic position and 'intellectual freedom'. An awareness of this problem was expressed in typical S.L. terminology: 'Even where an interested sympathiser is convinced of the general economic and social arguments in favour of a change, he is apt to hold back from any definite decision or action in favour of that change for fear that he himself may suffer unduly during the transaction. The temptation then arises to hold on to what little comfort or security he possesses... He joins himself to the forces of reaction and vested interests. In his dilemma, he falls an easy prey to the ever-ready advances of the Capitalists.'[ii] But still the professional was worth pursuing.

In his review of Lawrence Benjamin's *The Position of the Middle-class Worker in the Transition to Socialism*, J. T. Murphy acknowledged that some propaganda had scared middle-class workers, who, as a result, envisaged a Socialist economy offering them only a reduction of income. He was convinced the middle class could be reached with Socialist propaganda 'if they were properly approached'.[iii] The ambivalent position towards the middle-class professional was part of the wider S.L. struggle in the Labour Party. The editor of the *Socialist* exemplified this clash of opinions in January 1936 concerning proposed C.P. affiliation to the Labour Party: *'Fear of the effect on middle-class voters should not be allowed to determine action'*.[iv] This approach exhibited itself in attacks on the 'motives' of some S.L. members: a typical view published in the S.L.'s journal inquired on what foundations would be built the S.L.'s 'Will to Power', if the aim was to 'destroy the power of Capitalism and to overthrow the domination of money in the land: 'Are there a dozen men and women in our Socialist League who will band together to free their own lives, as far as possible, from the domination of money? ... As an organisation we shall accomplish nothing as long as we talk bravely and live comfortably.'[v] Not many could survive that level of moral scrutiny! Did not the professional man merely ask for 'the promise of security'? Did he not 'cuddle up' to the capitalist class for the sake of trade and stability?[vi] That's why he was a professional! The S.L.'s ambivalence remained.

Despite these queries, the S.L. appealed to the middle-class sympathiser in its

---

[i] Ibid.

[ii] Cripps, 'Democracy: Real or Sham?' in *Problems of a Socialist Transition*, 1934.

[iii] *Socialist Leaguer*, No. 11, May 1935.

[iv] 'Matters of Moment', *Socialist*, No. 4, January–February 1936.

[v] *Socialist Leaguer*, No. 7, December 1934.

[vi] L. A. Fenn review of *New Trends in Socialism*, in *Socialist*, No. 4, January–February 1936.

campaign for a constitutional revolution. S.L. propaganda assumed if Socialists were resolute, persuasive, and well-advised, the transition from a capitalist to a socialist society could be carried out by the will of the electorate 'in an orderly way', without the great human cost which would be involved in the forcible establishment of a new regime. This was part of G. D. H. Cole's conception of Socialism in *The Simple Case for Socialism*; if there was to be a transformation through constitutional means, 'we must enlist considerable support from the "better-to-do" middle classes and especially the professionals'.[i] With this concern went anxiety about a middle-class acceptance of Fascism as an answer to economic and industrial problems, because S.L. leaders were certain there was, for many professional people who had never had to think about the processes of human society, a considerable Fascist tendency. L. A. Fenn analysed the interest exercised by the idea of a corporative State on the professional classes: 'Fascism promises to get things done without apparently endangering the cultural standards of educated people'.[ii] Cripps was asked whether in the struggle against Fascist influence, he would consider the formation of 'a respectable middle-class Movement called "The Imperial British Democracy Defence League"'. Instead of answering that this League was an oxymoron, he replied that he did not think there was any 'halfway house' under existing economic conditions: 'We have got to convince the middle class of the necessity of going the whole hog'.[iii] The S.L. position was that the lower middle class also had to align itself with one of the two classes in the conflict. The proof was to be found in an examination of Fascist and Nazi development in Europe.

In the kind of transition the S.L. envisaged, the professional classes had a position of strategic importance and the S.L. used two arguments to attract this middle-class support; the erratic nature of the economic system (with the danger of loss of one's job, and security) and the need for a planned society. Lansbury clarified this when he proclaimed it essential the Movement revise its propaganda to appeal intelligibly to all those harassed and desperate members of society: 'Producers in every grade, the clerk, the artisan, the book-keeper and the navvy are all liable to replacement'.[iv] To the S.L., the middle-class worker could be made to realise that the existing economic environment could only provide him/her with insecurity as well.

The peculiar concern in S.L. circles in this particular appeal was shown in a curious way in the formulation of S.L. policy at its Leeds Conference. The Chelsea S.L. branch preferred a clause: 'Large sections of the middle classes are being pressed down to poverty level' rather than 'being driven into the ranks of the poverty-stricken workers'![v] At the previous Conference at Derby, Sir C. Trevelyan had put the same point in class terms, as only a 'Sir' could: 'Capitalism is not only at the end of all it can give, but it is going to get back if possible something of what it has given. In the next ten years, it will be the turn of the salaried and lower-middle classes. They are beginning to "get it in the neck".'[vi] The difference between these two attitudes epitomised the sensitivity about middle-class support. Sybil Wingate claimed the young technicians, administrators and scientists were, in economic fact, proletarians. To encourage the S.L. further, she added: '...much of the unscrupulous propaganda

[i] Reviewed in *Socialist*, No. 3, December 1935.

[ii] L. A. Fenn, *What of the Professional Classes?*, p. 5 in S.L. Notes, *New Clarion*, February 17th, 1934.

[iii] Cripps letter, January 22nd, 1934, Cripps Papers.

[iv] G. Lansbury, *My England*, 1934, p.203.

[v] Reported by Percy Williams, *New Leader*, May 25th, 1934.

[vi] *Manchester Guardian*, Trevelyan on 'Next 10 Years', June 5th, 1933.

directed against Sir Stafford Cripps and the S.L. by the Yellow Press, far from injuring us with these young men, is an asset in appealing to them"[i] To cement this financial appeal to the professional worker, it was elucidated that the general manager of a railway was just as much in the class of salary and wage earners as the telegraphist or porter; although the existing exaggerated differences in reward masked this similarity,[ii] both were servants liable to dismissal at the whim of directors. The determining factor was whether any individual had a share of economic power or was dependent upon money for his livelihood. A worker who had saved a little money or managed to purchase his house had acquired no economic power: 'The real question which every elector must determine… is whether he prefers security and certainty under Socialism, or the chance of his savings preserving him from destitution under Capitalism.'[iii] The latter remained a huge issue.

This strategy in the S.L. to explain that all people with insecure incomes were fighting the same battle was a less-emphasised argument for the support of S.L. policies compared with the need for a planned, efficient society. The editorial in the first issue of the *Socialist* clarified: 'Our job as Socialists is to find an appeal which will prevent the first clerical workers, independent producers, merchants and manufacturers falling into despair, with a replacement by machinery, by showing them that Socialism is their economic salvation… We must persuade experts that they can only prevent their talents being used for war by a Socialist policy of peace and nationalisation.'[iv] The S.L. could do the Party a great service by pioneer work in this field. The professional workers were to be approached with plans which offered them freedom in work and greater responsibility. The expert was afraid of being ordered about by committees, but the S.L. was not proposing to 'level down' the professional man to the standard of the dock labourer (perish the thought), but looked forward to a near future in which professional standards of life would be possible for everyone: 'We are most likely to rope in the expert … by convincing him that Socialism comes not to destroy but to fulfil.'[v] Some task in the 1930s.

There was always a danger that the S.L.'s urge towards the 'Will to Power' in its *'Forward to Socialism'* policy would swamp intelligent planning: 'Without that planning there is no hope that the technicians and the younger professional men will rally to the Labour Party, and without their help it cannot carry out an economic transformation'.[vi] Therefore the S.L. had to make an appeal to the professional person's vocation with the Socialist's promised 'mastery of economic forces'. In its endeavour to do this, some of the S.L.'s propaganda was geared towards stimulating and attracting the middle class. For example, the Cole's *Guide to Modern Politics* was described by J. F. Horrabin as the right kind of propagandist material to convert a larger number of technicians and skilled workers to Socialism;[vii] and Cripps' *Why This Socialism?* (a short account of the economic theory behind Socialism), it was hoped would be read by technicians and middle-class people.[viii] The S.L.'s policy was to induce the rising classes of

---

[i] Ibid.

[ii] Cripps, *Are You a Worker?*, L.P. pamphlet, 1933.

[iii] Ibid.

[iv] 'Matters of Moment', *Socialist*, September 1935.

[v] L. A. Fenn, 'These Intelligentsia', *Socialist Leaguer*, No. 2, July–August 1934.

[vi] 'A London Diary', *New Statesman and Nation*, May 26th, 1934.

[vii] J. F. Horrabin review, *Socialist Leaguer*, No. 5, October–November 1934.

[viii] *Socialist Leaguer*, No. 6, November–December 1934.

technicians and administrative workers to acknowledge that only under a Socialist reconstruction of society could their professional ability be given full scope. Economic planning was essential, and coloured the S.L.'s view towards this socially valuable section which Socialists had to attract, because the inventors and administrators were regarded as indispensable to any future planning.

The S.L.'s interpretation of the professional man's dilemma was based on an economic and class premise: 'Scientific men are professionally employed to improve our fisheries, while entrepreneurs in pursuit of profit cast back into the ocean a miraculous draft of fishes... This kind of thing has for many professional people a shattering effect on their *vocational self-respect*'.[i] That was the S.L.'s hope. The S.L. argument was that such people were driven by the insufficiencies of the economic system to doubt whether they were serving worthy human purposes. In this way, the professional man did not differ from the manual worker, who experienced the *same* kind of resentment at a system which made nonsense of his working life. Thus, the S.L. argument was to attempt to prove that a professional occupation involved the code of capitalist society in which *considerations of profit* played the crucial rôle: 'The scientist in industry, though he rules his own professional life by the maxim that "the truth shall make us free" finds his labour ultimately prostituted to the service of a world whose motto is caveat emptor – "let the buyer look out for himself".'[ii] In the S.L.'s analysis, 'Socialism' aimed at the fullest cultural and intellectual development for every individual,[iii] and interpretations of the 'class struggle' extended to its perspective of the professional man; class divisions had no necessary relationship to birth or even to wealth, and professionals were worth recruiting for the cause. Labour's 1997 Election landslide provided the elixir, professionals and Labour in harness.

(C) The S.L. and Class Struggle

Three aspects are peculiar to the study of history: concern with events, with change, and with the particular. Incorporating these in its analysis of '*class struggle*', the S.L. exhibited a specific feature in its affiliation to the Labour Party. S.L. leaders acknowledged a deeper sense of class, a more obvious social stratification, and stronger class resentments than in any other country in the 1930s; because it permeated all attitudes and conditions in society, the 1930s' class system, for the S.L., was taken for granted. In the Socialist tradition, the S.L. defined 'class' by its place in production i.e. capitalists owned the means of production. In the manifesto of the original S.L., (written in 1885), William Morris had stated that 'the possessing class, or non-producers, can only live as a class on the unpaid labour of the producers... The profit system is maintained by competition... the workers, although they produce all the wealth of society, have no control over its production or distribution: the people who are the only real organic part of society are treated as a mere appendage to capital – as a part of its machinery.'[iv] The S.L. of 1932–37 inherited Morris's prognosis and, in tribute to him, replaced the I.L.P. as the forcing ground of socialism; *class struggle* was

---

[i] L. A. Fenn, *What of the Professional Classes?*, S.L. pamphlet, 1934, pp.7–10. (My italics.)
[ii] Ibid.
[iii] Cripps, 'There Is No Middle Way', *New Clarion*, October 28th, 1933.
[iv] W. Morris, S.L. Manifesto, 1885.

seen as the central issue, because the idea that wielders of economic power would co-operate with a Labour Government was unrealistic to the S.L. Socialism could come by constitutional means *only* if private economic interests were controlled by a Labour government; the authority of Parliament could only survive healthily if it was exerted to the full *against* private economic and industrial interests. For the S.L., the slightest wavering in the face of such economic interests would mean the inevitable 'bondage of Parliament' and even 30 years later the S.L. case had not been eroded: 'Had Capitalism become less powerful, more subservient to the whims of Parliament than in the 1930s? Were the great corporations of the 1960s more democratic and more easily controlled than the demoralised industries of the 1930s? Had the conflict between economic interests and Socialist aims diminished?'[i] Had the class struggle vanished? Not really.

To the S.L., it was axiomatic that 'class' was the determining factor in politics;[ii] workers faced capitalists in an era of capitalist decay; no balance could be struck to satisfy both sides. After the 1931 Labour defeat, the Socialist case was put with more force and simplicity. Labour Party members questioned whether there should be the enrichment of life (under Socialism), or purely materialistic monetary gains.[iii] S.L. leaders judged that the Socialist method, approach, and cure had not been attempted by Party leaders; there had been no endeavour in the Labour Government to challenge the capitalist system. The situation prompted new Party leader, George Lansbury, to observe that Britain was rapidly becoming filled with a new property-less class of workers: the educated classes, who now found themselves faced with the problem of unemployment.[iv] The conclusion arrived at, through the S.L.'s analysis, was promulgation of the class struggle. A synopsis of Cripps' *The Choice for Britain*, exemplifies this: Capitalist economics was increasingly having to face fundamental difficulties; more countries in their desperation were turning to economic nationalism as a last refuge, while workers were the pawns; the World Economic Conference collapsed because the capitalist countries wished to preserve their economic weapons, and the Disarmament Conference ended inconclusively. The lowering of workers' standard of life, protection of the home market, and depreciation of currency, brought a "National" Government tending towards a Fascist conception of industry. Parliamentary democracy was not, as yet, a useful means for Socialist change.

Within this analysis were hostages to fortune. However, for the S.L., political activity which failed to question the legitimacy of capitalist society could not hope to change the system. The very rules of the economic, political and social game had to undergo alterations; 'Socialism by instalments' served to warn the capitalist enemy; failure to acknowledge this weakened Party leaders at critical moments.[v] Visionary aspirations lay behind the apparent realism of the S.L.'s class approach. Prior to the inaugural S.L. Conference, J. F. Horrabin had aspirations that in its new programme the Labour Party would take an unflinching class stand: 'it is the business of Socialists

---

[i] Paul Foot, 'Harold Wilson and the Labour Left', *International Socialism*, No. 33, Summer 1968.

[ii] This understanding of 'class' did not encompass significant changes in class structure that occurred in the 1930s. The S.L. simplistically regarded *every organ of the state* as a tool of the 'capitalist ruling class' (Parliament, civil service, Press etc.). This propensity to regard political phenomena as expressions of the economic struggle was pervasive, S. Macintyre, op. cit. *A Proletarian Science*, 1980, p.187.

[iii] Cf. Lord Ponsonby, 'The Future of the Labour Party', *Political Quarterly*, January–March 1932.

[iv] G. Lansbury, *My England*, 1934, p.202.

[v] Cf. R. Lyman, *Journal of British Studies*, November 1965, Vol. 5, No. 1, p.143.

to see that it does.'[i] In the Draft S.L. Constitution, democratic self-government could be realised only within a classless community because the forms which professed to embody 'democracy' were nullified by a system based on the extraction of rent, profit and interest from workers. Realising the dangers that a violent conflict would bring, the S.L. sought to avoid the occurrence by building the Socialist Movement: 'To promote within its ranks a spirit that subordinates personal aims and ambitions to the common creative purpose and to spread this spirit throughout the working-class Movement.'[ii]

J. Strachey's *The Coming Struggle for Power* underpinned the S.L.'s class analysis, convincing Socialists. of the classic interpretation of history (Feudalism had given way to capitalism, to Imperialism, to Fascism which would give way to a social revolution of the dictatorship of the proletariat). The logic of history! The S.L. position echoed Strachey's words: 'The capitalist system had outlived its usefulness, and Social Democracy was intent upon functioning within the degenerating capitalist system to implement mediocre liberalism.'[iii] The S.L. also mirrored his analysis that 'organisations of working-class revolt,' which workers had created over 50 years, had now passed over to the side of existing State authorities. It was the S.L.'s task to help build new ones.

During 1933, S.L. leaders formulated their class approach through lectures, speeches and pamphlets. In January 1933, Cripps exclaimed with apocalyptic panache the imminent time when electors would have to decide between the 'prolongation of the present basis of the organisation of society, finance and industry, and a clear-cut departure from that basis along a new line; the necessity for a full appreciation of the implications of the Socialist policy becomes 'more and more necessary', presented in a 'logical and clear manner.'[iv] Sir Charles Trevelyan added why S.L. policies would be a 'root and branch challenge' to the existing system', the only choice was the Socialist alternative or a prolongation of the existing Capitalist regime.[v] The S.L.'s heuristic exegesis was that the era of Liberal Democracy had ended, and when capitalist organisations began to contract, the struggle for power would become too acute to be accommodated within the democratic system; political parties would become more totalitarian, and democratic government would become incapable of adapting to the economic and social conditions of the 1930s.

Active Socialists needed an organisation, like the S.L., in which they could meet to devise long-term and immediate policies, work out their general strategy of class conflict, and discuss and reinforce their political views. However, the class structure had become more complex: 'The petty bourgeoisie does not peacefully endure the threat of submergence in the proletariat; it resorts to Fascism. The great capitalists do not "swallow up" the small; they dominate and use them. The workers are not driven into a homogeneous mass of the increasingly miserable; they are more and more differentiated with a submerged tenth of unemployed at one end, and an aristocracy of semi-technicians at the other.'[vi] S.L. leaders reiterated that poverty continued and

---

[i] *New Statesman and Nation*, September 10th, 1932.

[ii] Draft Constitution of the S.L., October 1st, 1932.

[iii] J. Strachey, *The Coming Struggle for Power*, 1932, p.301.

[iv] S. Cripps, *The West Fulham Labour Magazine*, January 1933.

[v] Sir C. Trevelyan, *The Challenge to Capitalism*, S.L. pamphlet, January 1933.

[vi] G. D. H. Cole, 'The Working-class Movement and the Transition to Socialism', *Problems of the Socialist Transition*, No. 5, 1934.

increased *because* a social system was tolerated which made not social wealth but profits the aim and purpose of production. Employers would only employ people if they could make a profit out of their labour, and capitalists would not allow the State to compete with capitalist industry.[i] So, quo vadis from this stalemate?

The S.L. analysed the struggle as one for economic power (one class to succeed in placing in the State the economic power that rested in those who constituted the other class). The aim had to be a classless society, to challenge the existing Government's 'class supremacy'. So long as profits were accepted as the motive power of industry, the profit-earner had to retain the economic power which enabled him to control the lives of his employees: '*This insistence upon class distinction, which is the root basis of the National Government's ideology, forces upon the country the class struggle.*'[ii] This was the S.L.'s diagnosis; employer and employee were mutually interdependent slaves of the economic system; the fundamental impetus towards social change could only come through the working class organised as a Movement to defend or advance its own interests. J. F. Horrabin puts the S.L. case: 'The class struggle provides us with a simple and adequate test of every measure in a Socialist government's programme. Does it in some way, to some extent, raise the status and conditions of the workers as a class, and correspondingly weaken the power of the owning class?'[iii] The class struggle was a call to battle and an inspiration. This interpretation was all-consuming, based upon a belief that class exploitation infected every part of society, poisoning its art, literature, science, social and sexual relationships, as well as economic elements. A class society could not evoke the enthusiastic, conscientious co-operation of underprivileged classes: 'The British ruling class regards as its guiding principles, Capitalism, Christianity and Democracy, giving to the two latter terms the embodiment that will best secure the continuance of capitalism with its attributes of power, privilege and wealth for that class.'[iv]

The S.L. identified some common delusions; that prosperity was 'coming soon', (without planning or drastic change); that capitalist organisation of society would, with increasing benevolence, turn into Socialism; that there existed a short cut to prosperity through monetary and credit alterations and a 'get-rich-quick' mentality. The S.L.'s belief that capitalist society was breaking down had always been part of Socialist thought (or myth), especially with World economic depression. E. F. Wise concluded that existing difficulties had arisen because the market economy had become uncontrolled, although he did not expect a complete collapse because adjustments were taking place all the time: 'Society is hesitating between Socialism and a reorganised Capitalism and the way to get power is to transfer the 40% Labour vote to 55%.'[v] Cripps had inquired in October 1933 '*Which Side Are You On?*'; the S.L. should be clear '*as to the existence of the class struggle*': there could be no intermediate class because there could be no intermediate policy.[vi] This conviction, that a prosperous industrialist resulted in an exploited worker and a world of comparative scarcity, was an attempt to reinvigorate the Movement, since workers in general had worn the badge of inferiority without serious protest: 'The stage is set for a decisive battle

---

[i] G. D. H. Cole & J. F. Horrabin, *Socialism in Pictures and Figures*, 1933.

[ii] Cripps, *Are You a Worker?*, L.P. pamphlet, 1933.

[iii] J. F. Horrabin, *The Class Struggle*, S.L. pamphlet, 1934.

[iv] Cripps, *Democracy Up-to-Date*, 1939, pp.22–23.

[v] E. F. Wise at I.L.P. Summer School, August 19th, 1932.

[vi] *New Clarion*, October 21st, 1933.

between those who desire the full use of our productive resources, and those who aim, through artificial scarcity, to maintain the profit system and the dictatorship of the owning class: that is the class struggle,[i] concluded L. A. Fenn.

For the S.L. there was no alternative scenario – profits could only be increased by reducing the costs of production; wages formed an important part of these, so there was an inevitable economic struggle: '...the fundamental power in every capitalist "democratic" country is Money Power. It was that power which in 1931 brought down the Labour Government by organising a financial panic and raising the cry of "the country is in danger".'[ii] The S.L.'s Marxist leanings, its Marxiana placita, deduced that the *innate contradictions* of capitalism were producing the forces necessary for its own reform; the mission of capitalism was one of preparation: the mission of Socialism was one of fulfilment.[iii] Such was the implacable rhetoric.

Within the Labour Party, the S.L.'s plain speaking on class struggle included an awkward declaration that Parliamentary forms were neither an absolute nor the best for democracy; the machinery of Parliament was not an end in itself but a means, although the S.L.'s equation of the National Government with Fascism created more problems. The class struggle issue revealed differing responses to the deepening economic depression and a desire for a more effective Party policy to counteract 'Fascist' techniques; it intensified frictions within the Labour Party, because S.L. leaders were convinced that, with the rise of the Nazis and reactions of the National Government to that, and the Government's profound suspicion of the Soviet Union, the world was moving towards war, and British political parties would become polarised. For the S.L., the only force to counteract this was a united working-class Movement conscious of the class structure of society. Headlines such as 'The Revolutionary Situation Is Here' and 'We Must Meet the Fascist Challenge' were symptomatic of this polarisation of political viewpoints by the S.L, under which the Government came into the category of a 'thinly disguised dictatorship,'[iv] deduced A. L. Rowse.

The S.L.'s explanation for the rise of Fascism was a class analysis: Fascism was characterised as an inevitable attempt by capitalist Government interests to beat back any working-class advance. The lesson from the failure of German Social Democracy was that the British Labour Movement could avoid that fate if it adopted the S.L.'s tactic of 'a rapid transition to Socialism', and an active struggle for increased wages and better conditions in industry,[v] but the moment workers asserted their right to just and equitable distribution of the products of their industry, the economic system would be plunged into a deeper crisis: 'When this moment comes, the forces of capitalism will more definitely and decisively turn towards Fascism'[vi] – that was the S.L.'s credo. Its resolve was for the ultimate conflict, Socialism versus Fascism,[vii] in *Forward to Socialism*: 'Desperate in the face of the inability to solve the vast economic and social problems created by private enterprise, the Capitalist forces have gathered in a universal effort to save themselves – Fascism and war threaten the workers.' This S.L. perspective

---

[i] L. A. Fenn, 'Science Versus Snobbery', *Leeds Weekly Citizen*, June 29th, 1934.

[ii] J. F. Horrabin, *The Class Struggle*. op. cit.

[iii] Cf. Paul Sweezy, *Socialism*, 1949, p.258. Marxist teachings.

[iv] A. L. Rowse, *New Clarion*, March 11th, 1933.

[v] S.L. News, 'What Breeds Fascism?', *New Clarion*, September 23rd, 1933.

[vi] Cripps, *The Choice for Britain*, S.L. pamphlet, p.4.

[vii] *The Times*, April 24th, 1934.

brought its own difficulties. In Italy, Germany and Spain, Labour leaders thought class propaganda had resulted in the isolation of the 'advance guard' from the mass Movement: 'The minatory proletarianism definitely excites the capitalist will to dictatorship... In the form of *S.L. Marxism*, the cry to the workers to rally is heard by "capitalism" as a demand for them also to combine... If political violence does break out on issues created by Marxist propaganda, the workers will be defeated.'[i] The S.L. incorporated one question for the Labour Movement: 'Socialism or Fascism? Which is it to be?'[ii]

In Europe, the S.L. perceived 'Naked Class War' in action – in Germany and Italy 'May Day' had ended; Poland, Hungary, Spain and Yugoslavia had reactionary governments; Austria was resisting through its Labour Movement, but only in France had the will to working-class unity any chance. By 1935, the task for the S.L. was 'to give direction to the instinctive class feeling on which the Labour Movement rests'[iii] by mobilising the Movement in an active contest against the Government's decrees: '*Our May Day message is of class antagonism and class conflict.*' In the S.L.'s blunt declaration on the subsequent brutal suppression of democracy and freedom in Austria, it reaffirmed its belief that 'only on the basis of the class struggle can the forces of the working class achieve victory over Reaction, Fascism and Exploitation'.[iv] The question of peace or war was, to the S.L., a class issue, because no British Government had utilised armaments under its control for the liberation or freedom of workers *in any country*. The S.L.'s frustration with official Party policy on this was illustrated in the S.L.'s last major conference at Stoke (in 1936): 'It is because we have forgotten the reality of the *class struggle* that the Labour Party has been led into the offer to co-operate with an Imperialist Government in its foreign policy.'[v]

As far as the class struggle was proclaimed in the Labour Party, the S.L. appealed to the Party Constitution of 1918, and it was Richard Crossman who observed that the Labour Party of 1918 required militants, politically-conscious socialists, to do the work of organising the constituencies, but since these militants tended to be 'extremists', a Constitution was needed which maintained their enthusiasm by apparently creating a party democracy which excluded them from effective power![vi] For the S.L. the party was committed to uniting workers and producers against owners and non-producers, an acknowledgement of the basic struggle: 'The Class Struggle is a fact which must affect all our Socialist thinking and planning ... the old habit of thinking about Trade Union policy or the activities of the Co-op Movement as things entirely different and distinct from the Socialist aims of the political wing of the Movement is fatal to any real success.'[vii] There was to be no question of collaboration with other sections of Capitalist society. Making the system work more smoothly was not Socialism, for the S.L. perceived Socialist aims in the Party to be declared, not concealed, regardless of the loss of '2 seats and 20,000 votes': 'It is exceedingly doubtful if the party would lose any working-class votes by straight Socialist pleading. Party voters would be much more likely to be disheartened by timidity in Labour leaders than frightened away by

[i] Robert Fraser, 'The Front Against Fascism', *New Trends in Socialism*, 1935.
[ii] Walter Greenwood reviewing N. Mitchison's 'We Have Been Warned', *Socialist Leaguer*, No. 12, June 1935.
[iii] *Socialist Leaguer*, No. 11, May 1935.
[iv] 'Austria and Its Lessons', *New Clarion*, February 24th, 1934.
[v] Speech by Cripps, *Daily Herald*, June 1st, 1936.
[vi] D. Powell, *What's Left? Labour Britain and the Socialist Tradition*, 1998, p.129.
[vii] J. F. Horrabin, *The Class Struggle*, S.L. pamphlet.

plain speaking; and a majority which was not a conscious majority for Socialism would be of no use if real social changes were to be made.'[i] Unionists had to be shown that only by political changes could they win economic security. This was the gist of the S.L.'s effort to attract the official Movement to its class outlook.

The S.L. aimed to make the Labour Party face its destiny as a class Party, although Cripps' rhetoric irritated Party leaders, who found it difficult to be persuaded by his presidential address: 'We must obtain a mandate for the use of every power that exists under the Constitution with which to arm a working-class government in the final round of the struggle for economic power.'[ii] It was even more difficult to convince them that the economic system was moving inexorably to an ever-deepening crisis, and it was extremely unlikely to succeed in explaining why 'War and Poverty' would overwhelm Britain. The Party refused to fight the 1935 Election on the basis of 'Socialism versus Fascism', while the S.L. continued to believe that on 'class struggle' the policy and tactics of the Labour Movement had to be based. To hide from this was a betrayal; to shirk its consequences was political ineptitude: 'The class struggle' was to teach the lesson that a direct and unmistakable challenge had to be made on the whole basis of society, politically and industrially: 'The S.L. works to ensure that the Labour Movement's actions are based on the firm knowledge that it is a Class Movement.'[iii]

Party leaders were not enamoured by the S.L.'s concentration on State ownership of land, the factories and financial institutions *before* fundamental 'liberties'. Even after the 1935 Election, the S.L. continued its class theme, suggesting only two options; a reformist programme or a 'Socialist' policy based on the class struggle. That was the lesson evinced by the S.L. from the Election;[iv] to relate the needs and demands of working people for Socialism. It was not wages that were on trial, but the wage system; what was needed was the linking of working-class struggle, for wages, better conditions, unemployment maintenance, abolition of the Means Test, with political freedom and economic justice into one class struggle. This new S.L. campaign was designed to agitate on day-to-day issues.[v]

The Liberal democratic state was being eviscerated in the conflict between capitalist forces and workers,[vi] yet Labour leaders remained sceptical of the S.L.'s accentuation on 'class issues'. To the Party, one emergency followed on another in politics; there was no practicable bridge between the class struggle thesis and the Party's social democracy. Labour leaders changed political terminology, or what it meant by it, until it reached a position expressed by Jennie Lee: 'I don't use abstract words such as 'capitalist', 'socialist', 'fascist' or 'democratic' any more often than I can help. I am profoundly distrustful of them. For each of us, according to our background and political leanings, it means something different when we use such terms. I wish politicians would stop using them altogether. If, instead, they would use concrete and particular language, we might at least begin to understand what our problems are.'[vii] And what were these 'problems'? How were they to be delineated?

S.L. leaders were unrepentant after the S.L.'s demise. With the S.L.'s dissolution,

---

[i] S.L. News, *New Clarion*, August 26th, 1933.

[ii] Cripps' presidential address to the Leeds S.L. Conference, May 20th, 1934.

[iii] S.L. Notes, *New Clarion*, February 24th, 1934.

[iv] S. Cripps, 'Election Lessons that Must Be Learned', *Socialist*, No. 3, December 1935.

[v] The editorial, 'Some Matters of Moment', *Socialist*, No. 4, January–February 1936.

[vi] S. Spender, *Forward from Liberalism*, 1936–7, reviewed by B. Betts, *Tribune*, January 20th, 1937.

[vii] Jennie Lee, *This Great Journey*, 1963 edn., p.128.

Cripps reiterated the S.L.'s outlook in the pages of *Tribune*: 'Class collaboration or class struggle? Which is it to be? In the next few months we must decide in the Labour Movement whether we are to adopt the attitude of complacent servitors of capitalism in its difficulties or whether we are to challenge its right to continue in its domination of our lives.'[i] This was the epitaph for the S.L.'s approach to politics. Never again in the British Labour Movement would an organisation, affiliated to the Labour Party, be able to base its attitudes so clearly upon an analysis of the class struggle. It was the final illusion in Labour's hierarchy, the ultimate reality for the Socialist Movement. As William Morris had put it: 'The real business of Socialists is to impress on the workers the fact that they are a class, whereas they ought to be society; if we mix ourselves up with parliament we shall confuse and dull this fact in people's minds...'[ii] There lay the dilemma for the S.L. in the 1930s, and the Labour Party ever since. As Francis Wheen deduced, by 1997, Britain was governed by a Labour PM who regarded 'comradeship and collective association' as anachronisms that should be excluded from the political lexicon: 'What was the Third Way? ... Somewhere between the Second Coming and the Fourth Dimension.'[iii]

---

[i] S. Cripps, *Tribune*, May 21st, 1937.

[ii] D. Powell, op. cit., 1998, p.48.

[iii] F. Wheen, op. cit., 2004, pp.208, 224.

Chapter Six

Socialist League Local Branches

As contumacious and contradictory as the constituencies they professed to represent, Marxists and anarchists, trade unionists and Christian Socialists, latter-day Owenites and Nonconformists of every persuasion peddled their political nostrums, each as jealous of their prescriptions as they were confident that, once accepted, their ambitions would be realized.

David Powell, *What's Left? Labour Britain and the Socialist Tradition,* 1998, p.39

What my father detested were not the good things of life but a system in which they were appropriated by people who didn't deserve them. Equally, he despised leaders of the Labour or Socialist movement who fought the workers' cause as a profession but lived high on the hog with padded expense accounts while they did so. He exhorted Party members to perform their daily work with diligence and quality, whether this be in factory, mine, office, school or university. For him, there was a practical as well as an ethical streak in this because the lazy, incompetent or dishonest worker, student or professional could never win the respect and still less lead his fellows... one of the more corrosive forces gnawing at popular morale were 'the revolutionaries' who preached popular sacrifice while being indolent or corrupt.

Brian Pollitt on his father, C.P. General Secretary Harry Pollitt, in ed. Phil Cohen, *Children of the Revolution: Communist Childhood in Cold War Britain* 1997, p.121

The subordination of the moral and imaginative faculties to political and administrative authority is wrong; the elimination of moral criteria from political judgement is wrong; the fear of independent thought, the deliberate encouragement of anti-intellectual trends amongst the people is wrong; the mechanical personification of unconscious class forces, the belittling of the conscious process of intellectual and spiritual conflict, all this is wrong.

E. P. Thompson, 'Through the Smoke of Budapest', *New Reasoner,* 1965, No. 3, p.313

(A) Local Government and the Labour Party

The Socialist League was a protest movement grounded in local party organisations, and to a lesser extent in local union branches. During its five years, the S.L.

concentrated more on influencing activities and attitudes of local groups, as its importance at Party Conferences was gradually sidelined. In the Party's Constitution, local parties had been reorganised, so people could join the Party as individual members. Ward, constituency and borough parties continued the basic work of the Party,[i] local parties were preoccupied with local electioneering, council affairs, raising money, social activities, canvassing. Although given the task of training a future leadership, the Labour Movement had scarcely begun to think about local government, and the Labour Government (1929–1931) had opposed the Bill granting powers to larger municipalities to conduct trading enterprises.

In terms of influence in Party Conferences and policy statements, the S.L. was almost as powerless and under-represented as local party organisations; after 1934, the S.L. harnessed constituency parties in the struggle for greater 'Party democracy' against the overriding control of the unions. This theme can be traced in the work of local S.L. branches, commencing with surveys, forums, study groups, research and propaganda in local areas; continuing (from 1934) with agitations against the *Unemployment Act* and the effects of the Means Test; culminating with support for the Labour League of Youth, the Constituency Party Association, and the Unity Campaign in 1936–37. Each of these developments led to increased speculation about the relation of the S.L. to official Party directives, and to a dissipation of the S.L.'s significance in the Movement until it reached its 'death-wish' zenith in the Unity Campaign.

Because local Party organisations felt under-valued for their contribution in the 1930s, S.L. criticisms of Party structure found favour, and local parties chose more of their officials and candidates from among the Left-wing of the Party. Policies were being furthered by those responsible for shaping local opinion, but the most the S.L. could achieve in local parties was a change in the composition of their representation on the N.E.C., while making individual membership sections 'more Socialist' in outlook. The hopes of the S.L. that 'changes which are necessary will come from within the Labour Movement as the conflict of interests between the workers and the capitalists explode the theories of the leaders,'[ii] did not fructify because S.L. local influence did not extend much outside the old militant areas, which it had inherited from the I.L.P. (especially in the North East, South Wales, and London areas like Holborn, Stepney and Battersea).

Interest in local affairs increased after the Labour Government failure in 1931 and Lansbury's acceptance of the Party leadership. He had contributed so much in local administration in the previous 40 years, and had built up a personal connection with more of his fellow-citizens than any other man of his generation except Keir Hardie.[iii] He had been a Guardian, working to alter the system of poor relief, had opposed the 1911–12 *Insurance Acts* (as a way of financing reforms), had behaved as if Party discipline did not exist[iv] (very S.L.), and in Poplar, he had resisted the Government policy of lowering the standard of living. Cripps was Lansbury's acolyte: 'Local Government is the means of providing for the people these very essential services... At every turn the common people contact with duties and powers of the local authority ... it is the needs of the majority, the ordinary, working-class people that must be the

[i] Dean McHenry, *His Majesty's Opposition 1931–38*, 1938.
[ii] J. T. Murphy, *New Horizons*, 1941, p.311.
[iii] R. Postgate, *The Life of George Lansbury*, 1951, p.42.
[iv] Ibid., pp.113–115.

true criterion of purpose and action… and not the fears or desires for economy of the property-owner.'[i]

C. R. Attlee expressed the S.L.'s thoughts on local government reform in one of the S.L.'s main lectures.[ii] He envisaged the period of the first *Socialist* Government in power (he was PM 12 years later) as one of crisis, so each locality would have an administrative machine controlled by the Government, England and Wales being divided into 10 regions, each with its own Commissioner, the latter as more than a public servant: 'He is the local energiser, and interpreter of the will of the Government. He is not impartial. He is a Socialist, and therefore in touch with the Socialists in the region, who are his colleagues in his campaign… rather like the Russian plan of Commissars and Communist Party members.'[iii] An intriguing analogy from a future Labour PM! Attlee explained the S.L.'s belief in the formation of regional planning committees to work out the application of the national plan, to counteract any passive resistance of anti-Socialist councils.

The clearest exemplification of S.L. policies in local government was provided in *Socialism for the Small Town*, published in February 1934.[iv] The civic centres are characterised as 'intensifications of ugliness in vast areas of desolation', the outward symbol of economic mismanagement and inefficient, uncontrolled urbanism. Remedies form the S.L.'s local outlook; Attlee's regional planning is extended to the use of the factory as a centre for cultural and social life and removal of schools from town centres. Local construction was carried out half-heartedly because of tangled vested interests (the building society, the bank, ground landlord, house owner, all had to be coaxed, outvoted or bought out); what was needed was an *Enabling Bill*, because local authorities' powers were limited, their areas too small, revenues inadequate and inflexible. National reconstruction needed sympathetic municipal effort in larger towns (small towns were inefficient as units of administration). A municipal income tax should be instituted in 10–12 Regional Authorities adaptable to Socialist change.

What was highlighted was a central feature of S.L. local branch work – insistence on research projects into local conditions. The greatest defect of the local Labour programme and Labour work locally was that too much was left to the Councillor. What was required was a local *municipal research group*, examining the needs of the town, reporting activities of other municipalities, giving the Councillor local details and statistics, revealing financial results of public utilities, and the cost of social services. It was axiomatic in S.L. branches that *'objective Socialist research'* meant realistic detail with detached analysis of cause and remedy while the S.L.'s Socialist principles implied phasing out the private contractor and middleman, support for local authorities' insurance societies rather than for commercial companies, and it assumed S.L. local branch research into housing, health and educational facilities. Underlining the S.L.'s plans was the conviction that 'the small Northern and Midland towns … are the hotbeds of English Socialism, the real springs and driving force of social reconstruction.'[v] Idealism resided in the S.L., Mellor commenting in November 1931, 'I do hope that the pressure is now on to get the Party to reorganise its methods of

---

[i] S. Cripps, *A Toast to Ald. Frank Sheppard*, Bristol, n.d., Cripps Papers.
[ii] C. R. Attlee, *Local Government and the Socialist Plan*, March 5th, 1933, S.L. pamphlet.
[iii] Ibid.
[iv] *Socialism for the Small Town* by F.B. (from Bradford), February 10th, 1934, S.L. pamphlet.
[v] Ibid.

propaganda and to get some really hard thinking done';[i] and Cripps added that Party reorganisation was vital:[ii] 'We must all spend the next year or two consolidating our position in the constituencies, not only by explaining the full details and implications of Labour Party policy, but also by reviving the true spirit of Socialism.'[iii] This meant consolidating Labour membership in a revivalist campaign: 'The longer we try to patch up this system, the greater will be our difficulty in effecting the changeover to Socialism.'[iv] The message of the S.L. to local members was a plea for knowledge of Party aims (and difficulties), and of policies which the Party intended to implement in a future Socialist government, to bring back *that old fiery zeal of the Pioneers, something of their evangelism.*[v] A tall order.

When the S.L. was formed in October 1932, the Press were quick to censure; the S.L called itself a 'Socialist organisation', which the I.L.P. had always declined to do for tactical reasons;[vi] here were merely 'Bloomsbury Socialists',[vii] an 'uneasy mixture' of S.S.I.P. intelligentsia and I.L.P. affiliationists who did not mix temperamentally, differed in policy,[viii] and were suspicious of each other; they were archetypal 'Reluctant Allies'.[ix] The Press did not refer to the S.L.'s views on local affairs, except for the *Daily Herald*'s '300 Branches by Christmas' headline.[x] From its inception the S.L. recognised that local organisations could provide the Socialist side of the Movement with fresh enthusiasm, and were excellent for *research and propaganda*. The main difficulty was that activities of the local parties were too frequently limited to the whist drive and the weekly "social"! Their membership was, as a rule, pitifully small and largely made up of persons who could not afford more than a penny per week, or unemployed who could not even afford that, so that money-making was their first concern.[xi]

In the inaugural S.L. Conference, Rule 7 stated the S.L. was to direct and encourage Socialist investigations and propaganda *by branches*. As organisations affiliated to local Labour Parties, all S.L. branches would have the right to nominate candidates for adoption by divisional parties, and adopted candidates would be required to accept the Constitution of the Labour Party and the Standing Orders of the P.L.P., although the S.L. would have no financial responsibilities for them. In the Draft Constitution of the S.L., members had to acknowledge the strategy, daily tactics, and outlook of the Labour Movement, in the political Party, unions, and Co-operative Societies. The S.L. was formed for Labour Party members who were prepared to work actively 'to secure a wider and more firmly appreciated understanding of what was involved in the attaining of Socialism',[xii] through the instrumentality of democratic political power and industrial organisation, people who were convinced that it was

---

[i] W. Mellor to Cripps, November 14th, 1931.

[ii] Cripps to Mellor, November 16th, 1931.

[iii] Cripps to Edge Hill Divisional L.P., January 1932, Cripps Papers.

[iv] Cripps in January 1932, *Labour Magazine*.

[v] Cripps' opening speech of Leicester Conference, October 1932.

[vi] *Morning Post*, October 3rd, 1932.

[vii] *Morning Post*, October 6th, 1932.

[viii] *New Leader*, October 7th, 1932.

[ix] *Manchester Guardian*, October 3rd, 1932.

[x] *Daily Herald*, October 3rd, 1932, (in fact, there were 70 branches by January 7th, 1933, cf. *New Clarion*).

[xi] *New Statesman and Nation*, August 27th, 1932.

[xii] S.L. Notes, *New Clarion*, December 23rd, 1933.

'right and sound to have Socialistic control of the vital services of the country'.[i] All very positive and optimistic.

Much of the advertisement for the S.L. involved references to youth and bold and energetic thoughts. Local party opinion would have to become more vocal, and there would have to be structural alterations in the Labour Party. The Leicester Conference was the sign of a new militancy. Sir Charles Trevelyan posited in *'Act Now (Youth Must Remake the World)'*: 'We intend to become a Party constantly forming opinion from below'.[ii] Below what, though? In 1932, all that liberalistic doctrine, belief in the Committee, talking shop, machinery of democracy, 'faith in the human personality', had hardly filtered into local party work. G. B. Shaw captured the mood when he wrote that most people had no intelligent interest in politics, nor knowledge of social conditions outside their own social circles, but they could be roused to *'intolerant fury or gushing idolatry'* by any appeal that played skilfully on their ignorance and 'their cinema-nourished enthusiasms'. Could one do that in 2005? Probably: 'It is useless … to face this peril with no better equipment than a handful of worn-out negative Liberal platitudes about liberty. Nothing can fortify us against such facile bulldozing and political chicaning, but a positive faith stronger and more resolute in resistance than the drunken crazes excited by mob oratory and sensational journalism.'[iii] Local S.L.s would have to work hard.

In the attempt to instil local organisations of the Labour Party with that 'faith', the S.L. was safeguarding its own rôle as a viable contributor to official Party policies. It diagnosed that insufficient attention had been placed on local government, and Labour activities in municipal politics were uncoordinated and lacked a common policy (even on the Means Test). Could not the S.L. clarify a Socialist local government policy which could be followed by all Labour groups on local government bodies? The S.L. saw that a municipal policy related to the task of achieving Socialism was a possible means of mobilising working-class support through utilisation of the relationship between local councillor and working-class elector. So that use could be made of Labour's strength on local councils, the S.L. encouraged the N.C.L. to form a national Federation of Labour-controlled local authorities (for joint action and a common national policy). Such a Federation could assist in the application of Socialist policies in the event of a Labour majority in Parliament. Local Labour parties in control in county boroughs were urged to use their powers to refuse Government directions which were not in the interests of the working class:[iv] 'if the numerous Labour local authorities had refused to co-operate with the Government in the application of the Air Raid Precautions, it would do much to show up the farcical nature of so-called "Precautions".'[v]

Recognition of the rôle which local parties could play in the Labour Movement was a main feature of the S.L.'s struggle to get its own voice in Party counsels. It was also used as a criticism of the system of voting at Party Conferences and resolutions from affiliated organisations. These characteristics exasperated groups which sought to change the Party line through Constituency Parties (in which delegates were chosen

[i] Cripps, *Manchester Guardian*, October 3rd, 1932.
[ii] *New Clarion*, November 26th, 1932.
[iii] G. B. Shaw letter to F. Brockway, *Inside the Left*, 1942, p.247.
[iv] *Western Daily Press & Bristol Mirror*, June 11th, 1935.
[v] A. L. Williams, 'Powers that Should Be Used', *Socialist*, No. 2, November 1935.

after discussion in Ward Parties and Management Committees), and essential work without which the Party's local government could not be maintained. S.L.'ers criticised the 'vast feather bed of inflated block votes' that 'descended on almost every kind of criticism, and suffocated genuine attempts at innovation'.[i] Socialists who wanted their theories translated into action had to get them understood by local Party members; S.L. councillors were urged to turn to good account the exasperation of Labour colleagues at the way the opposition could ignore any constructive proposal: 'If the morals are quietly pointed out, there will be few Labour Councillors left with any illusions about Britain being democratically governed.'[ii] As J. T. Murphy had explained, the first phase of the S.L.'s local activity was crystallising the determination of the Labour Movement not to repeat the experiences of 1929–1931. To this end, the S.L. conducted a great deal of propaganda in the localities and 'undoubtedly influenced the whole of the Labour Party in deciding its attitude to capitalist obstruction to the Socialist measures of the next Labour government.'[iii] The S.L.'s first year was one of feverish growth, which created many organisational problems. It was faced with the additional necessity of declaring a policy and securing publicity by pamphlets. The organisation was only overhauled after the Special S.L. Conference in November 1934.[iv]

(B) Local Activities

What was the S.L.'s modus operandi in the localities? What did S.L. branch members do? The S.L.'er saw his function as one of working out Party policy and 'making himself a nuisance' to further this end. The member was to prepare within the S.L. for problems to be met in the wider Movement, how to make Labour organisations 'more militant' and highlight the problems of the unemployed, how best to use local authorities: 'The keynote of their thinking is not how they can make the S.L. more powerful, but how they can make the working-class Movement more effective.'[v] S.L. branches began *research* into local problems – municipal government, housing, local industries, on which propaganda for local elections could be based; they trained and provided speakers on Socialist policy. Similar work was done by S.L. members active in their unions or members of the Co-operative Movement: 'This combined with the inquiries into national problems which are to be undertaken by the S.L. as a whole should result in a great stimulus to propaganda throughout the Movement.'[vi]

In S.L. local branches workers exchanged ideas and pooled experiences. Their responsibility was to help make organisations of the working class 'more Socialist', by the fullest participation in those organisations, 'to face the situation clearly and honestly'.[vii] In March 1934, the S.L. reviewed its local work, concluding it had aroused a lively sense of a challenging Socialist outlook in unions and unemployed

---

[i] L. A. Fenn, 'Democracy Within the Party', *Socialist*, No. December 1935.
[ii] Barbara Pearse (S.L.'er), 'Local Governing', *Socialist Leaguer*, No. 7, December 1934.
[iii] J. T. Murphy, *New Horizons*, 1941, p.312.
[iv] Cf. C. Borrett, 'New Beginnings', *Socialist Leaguer*, No. 7, December 1934.
[v] S.L. Notes, 'Making Himself a Nuisance', *New Clarion*, July 22nd, 1933.
[vi] Inaugural S.L. Conference, October 1st, 1932, quoted in *New Clarion*, October 8th, 1932.
[vii] S.L. News, 'Who Said Archangels?', *New Clarion*, August 26th, 1933.

demonstrations: 'Our methods are those of propaganda, discussion and persuasion… the pamphlet and the spoken word have proved themselves.'[i] Previously there had been a relative neglect of the educational element in local groups, while in 1932 it was H. G. Wells who envisaged 'local groups of between 6 and 200 members, each planned primarily as a society for self-education, research and propaganda.'[ii] This was what S.L. intellectuals brought from the S.S.I.P., a spirit of disinterested social inquiry. However, parochial anti-intellectualism and suspicion that the Party was being taken over by the middle class, worked against London S.L. intellectuals on their propaganda tours to effect a closer liaison between central and local organisations. Nevertheless, the S.L. campaigned against the 'stunts and panic-mongering' of 1931: 'The real significance of the Leicester Conference lay in the general conviction that the overriding need of the times was for decisive and concrete Socialist plans capable of immediate application by a Labour Government in power.'[iii] George Latham, S.L. Chairman, spoke of the sustained effort *to educate and instruct the public* on the new Labour programme: 'If we concentrate on this work of converting and reforming the electors before the next election is upon us, we shall be more likely to blunt the teeth of misrepresentation.'[iv] Some hopes, but it meant a policy of *'back to the soap-box, on to the lecture room, and the study circle'*.[v]

Collating and comparing ideas and facts was the forte of the S.L. branch. The temper of the Movement was such as to bring forward local inquirers to research into social and economic problems. If the 'bold programme' adopted by the Leicester Conference was to have any chance of success, it had to be understood as widely as possible. S.L. branches had to spend less time on internal affairs, and more on preparing factual material for speakers. Facts concerning bad housing and the social and economic effects of the Means Test had to be collated. *'The Right Research'* meant a topic thoroughly investigated by each S.L. member,[vi] and facts made available to the whole Movement; S.L. members were to find out how the Means Test worked in their locality, and bring the unemployed into touch with local Labour organisations, and the best method to achieve this was through door-to-door inquiries which S.L.'ers made in homes, factories and Labour Exchanges. No national scheme for public works could prosper unless it was linked with local needs, so S.L. branches were asked to work out *in detail* the kind of schemes which could be implemented in their areas. This meant finding out (at the local town hall) which schemes had been postponed for 'reasons of economy', and putting forward their own 'practical schemes'.[vii] S.L. members also inquired into the organisation of local industries, extent of union organisation, financial status of individual firms, and wages and conditions of employment, all such facts useful in local elections. By November, some S.L. branches had begun investigations into housing conditions which the S.L. hoped would provide 'a veritable *Doomsday Book*; the doom of slums',[viii] 'to find out all there is to be known

---

[i] S.L. Notes, 'The Will to Power', *New Clarion*, March 10th, 1934.

[ii] H. G. Wells, 'Project of a World Society', *New Statesman and Nation*, August 20th, 1932.

[iii] G. Latham (Chairman of Leicester Conference), quoted in *New Clarion*, October 15th, 1932.

[iv] Ibid.

[v] J. Simmons (former MP for Erdington, Birmingham), ibid.

[vi] One question was 'What proportion of their income do rich and poor pay towards the maintenance of local government services?'

[vii] S.L. Notes, 'Facts on the Doorstep', *New Clarion*, November 5th, 1932.

[viii] S.L. Notes, 'Winter Harvest', *New Clarion*, November 26th, 1932.

about the area in which their branch operates'.[i] For example, Holborn S.L. branch set up an enquiry into improvement of methods of Socialist propaganda, wanting to discover how far pamphlets were effective, the value of street-corner speaking, forum discussion meetings, and public demonstrations.

Head Office asked all branches to confront the *class nature of the law* by sending in cases of prosecutions of unemployed demonstrators or others arrested 'for acting in the interests of the proletariat',[ii] and of action by authorities which proved an anti-working-class bias. By January 1933, the S.L. had over 70 branches, a network of *Research Groups, Discussion Circles* and *Study Groups*, monthly conferences and new pamphlets. What were they doing? Yorkshire branches were using local papers, syndicating articles on aspects of Socialist planning; the Mold S.L. was engaged in a housing survey; Bristol S.L. was involved in an enquiry into local conditions, and made use of novel forms of propaganda (floodlights and films on local housing); Leicester S.L. was writing on the effects of a financial or House of Lords sabotage of a Socialist Government; Birmingham S.L. was organising lectures on 'the problems of a Socialist Government', while 20 London S.L. branches were working on the 'Doomsday Book'.[iii] Head Office asked for full particulars on research work, so there were full records.

Why all this frenetic research work? It was the effect of '1931', in which the lack of Government 'concentration upon facts' resulted in the Left-wing assertion of the gullibility of Labour politicians, and a desire to clarify the Party's principles. '*Research work*' was also a unifying medium for disillusioned supporters who felt the need to do something constructive, to make sense of the bewildering problems of mass unemployment. The S.L. could thus justify its existence satisfactorily; research work was questioning existing conditions, which suited a new organisation in the process of building; involvement in observing, compiling, synthesising facts was a therapy, for 'to attempt the best survey possible of each constituency would not only enable election propaganda to be carried out with far more economy and intelligence, but in its various phases would provide a most valuable training for many types of members of the party'.[iv] The S.L. was aware of the difficulty of maintaining optimism and discipline in Party ranks. Creating 'shock troops for Socialism'[v] performing a 'vigorous service' was vital to those presenting 'Socialism as a faith'. Work on 'propaganda' was an encouragement, a stimulant, not only on local social and economic details, but also on Socialist ideas, through weekend schools, lectures, theatre, socials and study groups; one of the objects in research was to find out facts and figures needed, nationally and locally, 'to make possible real Socialist administrations'[vi] and to awaken a desire for a Socialist society; the S.L. thought the answer lay in propaganda by local parties: 'If you know what is really needed in your own locality, you are in a much better position for making Socialist converts and getting a real Socialist programme and policy.'[vii] If a Labour government was to put through a Socialist programme, Socialists had to be made *in the localities* because 'half the Labour vote was not a

---

[i] S.L. Notes, *New Clarion*, December 10th, 1932.

[ii] S.L. Notes, 'Class Struggle and the Law', *New Clarion*, December 24th, 1932.

[iii] S.L. Notes, '3 Months Old', *New Clarion*, January 7th, 1933.

[iv] Amber Blanco White, *The New Propaganda*, 1939, p.355.

[v] Gex, 'The Nobodies Will Rally to a Blazing Socialist Faith', *New Clarion*, November 5th, 1932.

[vi] S.L. Notes, *New Clarion*, December 10th, 1932.

[vii] Ibid.

Socialist vote'.[i] The research group would channel interests of Party supporters into seeking a thorough understanding of Socialist policies.

Research work was a symbol of the 1930s, with enquiries into depressed areas, the *Political and Economic Planning Group*, *Next Five Years' Group*, and *Mass Observation* with its voluntary and professional observers, experts, public opinion sampling techniques, to discover the mass-life of mass-man; *Mass Observation* and the *Labour Research Department* were two manifestations of the value to progressive movements of accumulating facts.[ii] The S.L.'s branch work between 1932 and 1935 fell into this mould, and S.L. pamphlets analysed in detail the practical steps which a future Socialist government would have to take. The S.L.'s *'Socialist Programme Series'*[iii] gave concrete suggestions for the Movement to discuss, and S.L. research was like an intensified study group where branch members met to discuss a Socialist approach to a problem and its enforcement, what they would like to see done, how they thought it could be enacted, precisely how the Movement could be brought to see and demand it. To report local conditions *accurately* was to condemn them: 'The era of uncertainty, of guesswork, when one opinion was as good as another since none could be verified, is over, and an epoch of genuine investigation, in which facts and deductions can be tested and established, has opened.'[iv] Herein lay the research lesson.

Most S.L. branch work and policy ideas disseminated in the localities had originated in the I.L.P.,[v] but the S.L. did extend that. Lending libraries of Socialist books and pamphlets, weekend schools (first suggested by George Catlin[vi]), a photographic circle, speakers' classes, and the anti-war conferences, were S.L. initiatives. Glyn Evans, the S.L. National Organiser, toured England and Wales, helping to form branches and convene conferences, especially in the first 6 months of the S.L.'s existence, while other S.L. national figures toured the country on speaking engagements. The S.L.'s lecture series at Transport House was repeated in the provinces. All sounded apocalyptic: *'The S.L. is setting out to create advance guards of the Revolution.'*[vii] On February 5th, 1933, the S.L. brought its local branches on the Hyde Park Unemployed Rally, and took an organising rôle in the agitation against the *Unemployment Act* and Means Test. The official S.L. point of view was diplomatic: 'Like most infants, the S.L. grows in somewhat startling directions, and many activities not originally contemplated, but all exceedingly useful, have developed.'[viii]

One of the more significant reports to S.L. inquiry groups was the Leicester S.L.'s research into the *'First Steps in a Socialist Government'*.[ix] The questions formulated were later to represent the S.L.'s position. Would there by any danger of Capitalist forces using unorthodox methods of opposition? Did this mean financial or constitutional sabotage? How could a Socialist Government ensure efficient control of nationalised industries and social services? Would a system of rationing foodstuffs be necessary? What would be the attitude regarding trade with existing Capitalist countries,

---

[i] 'Educating the Electors', S.L. Notes, *New Clarion*, November 19th, 1932.

[ii] D. E. S. Maxwell, *Poets of the 1930s*, 1969, p.33.

[iii] Under the editorship of G. D. H. Cole and G. R. Mitchison.

[iv] John Strachey, *What Are We To Do?*, 1938, p.258.

[v] Cf. R. E. Dowse, op. cit, pp.90–91.

[vi] G. Catlin, 'We Need a New Morale!', *New Clarion*, December 31st, 1932.

[vii] 'Advance Guard of the Revolution', S.L. Notes, *New Clarion*, January 14th, 1933.

[viii] '3 Months Old', S.L. Notes, *New Clarion*, January 7th, 1933.

[ix] February 4th, 1933.

including the British Dominions? Must a Socialist Government prepare for a boycott? What would be the nature of immediate financial control taken under these emergency measures? This kind of questioning led Cripps and Laski to challenge the *entire* basis of the Party's gradualist agenda: 'Iconoclasts, as cavalier with political reputations as they were careless of the sensitivity of the unions, their full-frontal assault on the conservatism of the Labour establishment was to provoke an equally vituperative response from its apologists.'[i]

By March 25th, 1933, the popularity of S.L. *pamphlets* had 'surpassed the most sanguine expectations', and the demand for pamphlets on immediate issues was so high that a second forum series of lectures (transformed into pamphlets) was inaugurated in November 1933, the duty of every branch secretary to secure copies and create discussions on the theories presented: 'S.L. branches have a special responsibility for the distribution of these pamphlets.'[ii] In spite of the claims of new propaganda techniques, S.L. branches' pamphlet-selling predominated. At the S.L.'s second Conference at Leeds, Cripps explained that the S.L. had, in the previous 18 months, published numerous pamphlets with the object of providing material for self-education, *to meet all the arguments of opponents*.[iii] In the reorganisation of the S.L. after November 1934, new methods of accounting for 'literature secretaries' were introduced 'to improve branch affairs in pamphlet selling'[iv] and in May 1935, the appeal was to every branch to make a special effort to ensure a large sale for two new pamphlets.[v] Reviewing the year (to May 1935), J. T. Murphy noted sales of publications had increased threefold, and in launching a national campaign of propaganda and recruiting for 1936, he repeated the essential requirement – 'intensive sales of S.L. publications'[vi] to unions, trades councils, Co-operative Guilds and local Labour Parties.

Two S.L. pamphlets were specifically aimed at local organisations.[vii] *A Countryman Talks About Socialism* by H. B. Pointing (March 1933) traced the history of individual capitalist farming and industrial growth, and pleaded for local Socialists to be 'true through life to the vision they have seen... to believe in a cause and work for it'. He explained that merely 'patching up' the existing system by keeping prices steady, 'getting control' of the banks and adding bits to the workers' wage was not enough. Positing the need for public ownership of basic industries and services, he exclaimed: 'then we will not work for someone's private good, but... will take part in a great public service'. What kept people jealously guarding their possessions and sacrificing their social creativity were fears which Socialists had to surmount. *Is Woman's Place the Home?* by Winifred Horrabin (1933) was written to interest working women in the aims of the Labour Movement, in common ownership of the means of production and communal distribution for the benefit of all. She clarified *how* household duties were the beginning of politics, how outside forces controlled a housewife's life; even if women wanted to keep their homes separate, there was no stability on which they could build, because the home was not immune from social, economic and political

---

[i] D. Powell, op. cit., 1998, p.185

[ii] *Forum Pamphlets*, January 13th, 1934.

[iii] Cripps, 'The Message of Our Time', *Leeds Weekly Citizen*, May 11th, 1934. (My italics.)

[iv] J. T. Murphy, *Socialist Leaguer*, No. 9, February 1935.

[v] *India in Chains* by H. N. Brailsford and *National Fascism in Britain* by Cripps.

[vi] J. T. Murphy, 'Our Challenge to Gradualism', *Socialist*, No. 4, January–February 1936.

[vii] Excluding 2 pamphlets discussed, i.e. C. R. Attlee, *Local Government and the Socialist Plan* & F. B., *Socialism for the Small Town*.

pressures: 'Is it sensible for women to ignore these facts and leave to others the conduct of the life of the community?' The effect of political action was constantly entering the lives of everyone, so it would be more purposeful to try to find out what was alterable for the benefit of all people: 'If women work for Socialism and a planned system they will be protecting the welfare of their children and home.'

It would be easy to sneer at the naivety of locally-orientated pamphlets and their simplistic messages, but in a time of mass unemployment and fears for the future, they provided an optimistic, constructive alternative outlook: 'From a psychological angle, it is really important that the party should offer points of social attachment for new adherents.'[i] Yet, from the point of view of 'practical politics' it was not difficult to remind the Labour Movement that the Government had an overwhelming majority, and the control of Labour policies was more distant from the Left wing. This did not deter the S.L., but it made its efforts seem meagre in the tough reality of the 1930s.

The work of the S.L. for its membership remained absorbing throughout 1933. In the first Weekend School in London[ii] the subject was *'The Alternative to Gradualism'*, with talks by G. R. Mitchison on *'The State and the Constitution'*, E. F. Wise on *'The Problem of Finance'*, J. F. Horrabin on *'A Word on Leadership'*, and the ever-present questions as to how and by what methods and organisation S.L. members should act, and what a Socialist council could be expected to do. In March, research was into banking, price levels, broadcasting, 'obsolete' laws, Empire problems, the Party's 'gradualism', and co-ordination of research. S.L. Head Office thanked S.L. members for their 'persistency, courage and intense devotion'.[iii] By April, propaganda meetings for the unemployed were attracting attention, as were social events, hiking, cycling and photography. S.L. branches were co-operating with local Labour groups in a recruitment drive in rural areas, aiding them with speakers, canvassers, literature and distributors.[iv] In the May Day Demonstrations ('against Fascism') S.L. branches were represented in force, and were at a similar demonstration at Kingsway Hall ('against war and Fascism'). Given the later clash between the S.L. and the official Party leadership it is noticeable that this information was presented under the headline *'Chains or Change?'*)[v] After eight months' effort, the S.L. General Secretary claimed the most satisfying method of work had been *'Research to find out the facts, Education to appreciate and apply the facts, and informed Propaganda to bring the facts home to the people.'*[vi] At a Bristol S.L. meeting, Cripps reiterated the importance of having an active organisation for the propaganda work of Socialism: 'Such an organisation as the S.L. can do a great deal towards the preparation (for a Socialist government) and at the same time will banish the apathy overrunning all political parties.'[vii] Banishing apathy was no small feat.

Preparations of resolutions for the first S.L. Conference at Derby in June (1933) involved local branches. That Conference was characterised by the youth of its participants, the majority of delegates under 35; the members agreed that what was required in the Party was the initiation of 'open discussion', policy-making and policy

[i] Amber Blanco White, op. cit., p.350.
[ii] February 26th–27th, 1933.
[iii] S.L. Notes, *New Clarion*, March 25th, 1933.
[iv] 'Those Rural Areas', S.L. News, *New Clarion*, July 15th, 1933.
[v] S.L. Notes, *New Clarion*, May 7th, 1933.
[vi] 'Eight Months Harvest', S.L. Notes, *New Clarion*, May 27th, 1933.
[vii] *Bristol Evening World*, April 10th, 1933.

propaganda,[i] which meant in practice, to work out details of a practical Party programme within a framework of loyalty to Party Conference decisions. As in all pressure groups, finances figured high on the list of priorities and branches were asked to send a steady subscription[ii] to Head Office, 'to facilitate the S.L.'s work', and in July, a pamphlet and propaganda fund of one guinea per annum for all S.L. publications was begun. (It was this latter method of financing local activities which predominated until the Unity Campaign). After the Special S.L. Conference in November 1934, the new campaign for increased membership would bring financial difficulties, so a larger proportion of S.L. expenditure would have to be devoted to organisation; the S.L. made its first appeal for a '*Special Effort*' to raise funds for initial expenses: 'Send donations before Christmas ... every reader could send a list of likely subscribers.'[iii] Throughout the first two months of 1935, there were branch membership campaigns: 'the big question before the S.L. National Council and S.L. branches is funds.'[iv]

By the Special Conference decision, contributions to the S.L. Head Office had been reduced from 4d to 2d per member per month, to make it easier to recruit a mass membership. This was endorsed by every branch. Finances were essential for new publications, administration, and launching the national membership campaign; local finances could be supplemented by donations, increased membership, burgeoning sales of literature. The S.L. in February 1935 sent out another appeal for donations. There were now monthly appeals for money. On March 31st 1935 branches were urged to have a 'settling day' with every member concerning branch contributions and to square accounts with Head Office. As the *Socialist Leaguer* monthly inquired: 'Has your branch organised a special fund to help the finances of the S.L.?'[v] Each branch was asked to send a donation to the Special Appeal Fund. In August 1935, a Head Office circular to branches asked them to organise a 'Conference Fund' of ½d per week, per member, so that every branch could, by Conference time, send its full quota of delegates.[vi] In the first issue of the *Socialist* (September 1935), the S.L. inserted an advertisement pleading: 'You believe in the S.L.'s policy. You want to see the Labour Movement virile, active and challenging... Help us to increase our propaganda, to carry on the war against War and Capitalism.' J. T. Murphy urged a 50% increase in sales of the paper during the month and the need to foster literature sales. The National Council was warned about the S.L.'s financial position, and decided a scheme should be prepared for 'Socialist competition' (horror!) between the branches for recruiting members, raising finances, and selling literature. In November 1935, Murphy was complaining that many branches were in arrears in the payment of contributions; another ingenious scheme, a new 'Half-Crown Fund' was implemented. The important part of financial organisation was revealed at the Branch Officials' Conference in December 1935, in which there were discussions on registration, payment of dues, sales and literature, and branch accounts to make local organisations more efficient. Double the S.L. was the task for January 1936, and a minimum quota of two copies of the *Socialist* for every employed S.L. member and one

---

[i] C. Borrett, 'New Beginnings', *Socialist Leaguer*, No. 7, December 1934.

[ii] S.L. Notes, *New Clarion*, June 24th, 1933.

[iii] C. Borrett, 'New Beginnings', *Socialist Leaguer*, No. 7, December 1934.

[iv] J. T. Murphy, S.L. Notes, *Socialist Leaguer*, No. 9, February 1935.

[v] 'What the S.L. Is Doing', *Socialist Leaguer*, No. 10, March–April 1935.

[vi] Ruth Dodds' Papers (Dodds was Regional Secretary for the S.L. in the North East and a National Council member in 1935).

for every unemployed S.L. member. In May 1936, a reversion to the old 4d rate of contribution was put forward by the National Council, evading the implications of failure to increase membership by stating that 'the growth of membership depends far more upon the development of political conviction than upon the size of the contribution'! The culmination was when members were asked to give *a day's earnings* for the struggle in Spain,[i] and the brief existence of the Unity Campaign revolved around pleas for finances.

After the S.L. Conference at Derby, there was little mention made in official S.L. papers of local branch activities and researches. An S.L. committee was making films as the nucleus of a Socialist film service, available to local Labour groups, including documentaries, housing surveys and newsreels.[ii] A series of area conferences were held in September 1933, attended by National Council members, for discussions on policy and the election of area secretaries[iii] (to advise on ways of increasing the S.L.'s effectiveness) and attempts were made to further the activity of individual members and secure continuous study on policy questions. At the Hastings Conference, S.L. proposals consisted of a series of amendments to draft policy reports, to clear up 'obscurities'. Arthur Henderson surveyed the previous two years with satisfaction for the official Party (which had re-marshalled its forces, strengthened its organisation, intensified its propaganda and educational efforts, and drawn up plans for action): 'No two years have been more fruitful for the Party either in the range and results of its general activities, or in the preparation of constructive plans than those which are covered by the Leicester and Hastings Conferences.'[iv] The S.L. was delighted, seeing its branch work welcomed by constituent Party groups because it had brought 'healthy, free and vigorous discussion once again to flow through the ranks'.[v] In boosting the morale of local parties, the S.L. could be proud of the part it had played in the Conference in aiding Party policy.[vi] S.L. members were to remind local Labour groups to carry out the Hastings decisions for a campaign against 'Fascism and War', and to continue the work on the 'Constitutional Issues' (Emergency Powers, abolition of the Lords, reform of the House of Commons). A circular was sent to branches in January 1934. In calling S.L. members to keep to the forefront of local activities, the S.L. Council was trying to debate the problem of 'democracy' in a capitalist environment: 'Most significant is the growing appreciation of the 'constitutional issue' as a necessary concomitant to securing bread and butter for employed and unemployed' Office invited branches to take the Hastings resolutions on war, Fascism and disarmament to every local party meeting, to discuss their implications and answer the following questions: Were the important decisions taken at the Party Conference understood and supported by the rank and file? In the event of war, or threat of war, would local Labour organisations know what they were pledged to do? Would S.L. members be prepared to join in a strike against war? This was where the S.L. could assist the local Labour Movement – 'to secure unity of action in the struggle against

[i] *Socialist*, No. 10, September 1936.

[ii] Daisy Lansbury quoted in June 6th, 1933, *Daily Herald*.

[iii] J. B. Ashworth, H. Clay, R. Dodds, L. A. Fenn, J. Hirst, Gwyn Hopkins & M. Wigglesworth.

[iv] A. Henderson, 'From Hastings to Victory', *New Clarion*, September 30th, 1933.

[v] S.L. News, 'The Work Goes On', *New Clarion*, October 7th, 1933.

[vi] S. Cripps, S.L. Notes, 'Our Part', *New Clarion*, October 14th, 1933.

[vii] S.L. Notes, *New Clarion*, February 17th, 1934.

reaction and Fascism at home and abroad'.[i] There is a distinct change in Head Office's plans for local S.L. branches from January 1934. The branches were now invited to help local Trades and Labour Councils, to make surveys of local resources, contact other local organisations, and have plans prepared for speaking and canvassing. This exemplified the S.L.'s increased involvement in such immediate issues as unemployed agitations.

On March 4th, 1934, the National Council issued a draft Statement of Policy to give a lead to branches at the Leeds Conference. A press and publicity section was established, and local branches were to appoint press and publicity secretaries. At the Leeds Conference (1934), Cripps (the Chairman) claimed the S.L.'s contribution was to the stock of constructive thinking on the direction and tempo of Party policy,[ii] and S.L. branches were directed to give attention to finance (budgetary, compensation, investment, and price level); socialisation and workers' control; foreign policy, and overseas trade, branches to send in statements of their conclusions, to be collated in draft reports. This was to present to the Labour Party conclusions on details of policy. The Leeds Conference was mainly a gathering of youth, and the *New Statesman and Nation* reporter seemed surprised to see so many manual workers and unionists there![iii] The accent and purpose of the S.L. had changed since 1932. Under Cripps' direction, the main emphasis had been placed upon 'the will to power', determination to capture economic power by a Parliamentary majority, and to use it for an ambitious Five Year Plan, Soviet-style. By 1934, for S.L. branches, the tone of the Conference was less euphoric. Branches overtly aired their grievances by expressing their dissatisfaction with the agenda. Four S.L. branches urged a less ambiguous, more practical programme; Welwyn Garden City S.L. wanted a more detailed policy;[iv] Burnley S.L. and Holborn S.L. supported a United Front;[v] P. Arnold (Hendon S.L.) observed: 'The document inspired no enthusiasm, was disappointing, unfair, vague and loose';[vi] Watson (Southend S.L.) called *Forward to Socialism* a 'mere propagandist broadsheet, saying nothing not in Labour Party policy reports'.[vii] Only Howard (Rochdale S.L.) regarded it as a popular leaflet (rather than a detailed plan which would have been impracticable).[viii] Another irritation was that 'visitors' were allowed to take part in the Conference proceedings, so that Susan Lawrence, who was not a delegate, was allowed to reopen the question *against* a United Front. Members who could afford to attend the Conference and influence its decisions could do just that without reference to or control by branch members. It did not augur well for the S.L.'s Conference struggles to loosen the bias of block voting at the forthcoming Southport Conference.

In June 1934, the S.L.'s London Area Committee issued two circulars to branches: (a) that every S.L. member should get his union branch, Co-operative Guild, Council or party ward to pass resolutions against the *Sedition Bill* and send them to the Government and MPs, and call upon the Executive of the Party and T.U.C. General Council for a national day of protest; (b) ask branches to get the local Labour Party and

---

[i] S.L. Notes, 'Austria and Its Lessons', *New Clarion*, February 24th, 1934.

[ii] Address by Cripps, Leeds Conference, May 20th, 1934.

[iii] 'A London Diary', *New Statesman and Nation*, May 26th, 1934.

[iv] *Leeds Mercury*, May 21st, 1934 & *New Leader*, May 18th, 1934.

[v] *The Times*, May 22nd, 1934.

[vi] *New Leader*, May 25th, 1934.

[vii] *Daily Herald*, May 21st, 1934.

[viii] *Manchester Guardian*, May 21st, 1934.

union branch to contact the Party Executive to organise demonstrations against 'War and Fascism'. The area committees held meetings in September to explain the policies which the S.L. would put forward at the Labour Conference at Southport, and amendments on education, housing and the Party's *'For Socialism and Peace'* policy, were circulated to branches.

The Southport Conference was a deflating experience for S.L. members. By registering definitive decisions against S.L amendments, it nullified much of the work achieved in S.L. branches in the preceding two years. The Conference marked the end of the first chapter of the S.L.'s history, in which S.L. branches had concentrated their efforts on the *discussion of policy and propaganda work* (written and spoken). At Southport, William Mellor explained that the Party Executive evaded the really controversial issues; the block vote worked against the S.L.; no arguments could affect the vote; and S.L. members could only speak for ten minutes each. The Conference made it impossible for the S.L. to launch that side of its work further. It had to reconsider its functions and activities. In solace, the S.L. concluded: *'It is the first business of practical Socialists as distinct from dogmatists and theoreticians, to keep as closely as possible in touch with the great organised masses of the workers' movement.'*[i] The task of S.L. members would be to construct what methods and changes in organisation and what immediate issues could revitalise the S.L. in the Labour Movement.

The Special S.L. National Conference (November 25th, 1934) decided on changes in the S.L.'s methods,[ii] to make it a prime aim to increase membership and widen the basis and nature of its appeal. Propaganda and educational work would be extended, the theoretical approach would be given an immediate practical content, activities on daily issues would be initiated. Locally, the S.L. would organise conferences and demonstrations (either through Labour parties, trades councils, or by itself) on the *Unemployment Act* and its administration, on scales of relief, on rents, housing, effects of rationalisation, consequences of state capitalism, on freedom of speech, menace of Fascism, and the danger of war. A defined theoretical approach would not be jettisoned, while the National Council, area committees, and branches would need to act consistently on a planned basis. This was the essence of W. Mellor's conclusions.[iii]

In this, there was much anger at Labour leaders' timidity, and at the bureaucratic success in overriding rank and file opinion and suppressing discontent. The S.L. Special Conference did express the apathy and discouragement rendered by official Party policies. Future activities of the S.L. had to *attract and inspire* those who needed incentives: 'The Movement must recapture the old "tub-thumping" spirit of the pre-respectable days ... Our job is to help build up a real "Will to Power" in the working-class movement ... The times are ripe for a crusade.'[iv] This was in contradistinction to the official party's 'muffling respectability'. The S.L.'s Conference fired up its members to apply their Socialist attitudes to conditions in their own towns, 'rousing discussion, making suggestions for proper action, and acting.'[v] However, for all the talk of 'individual responsibility' of S.L. members, it primarily meant selling more pamphlets and papers in Labour Party wards and union branches.[vi]

---

[i] 'The S.L.'s Next Step', *Socialist Leaguer*, No. 5, October–November 1934.

[ii] Donald Barber (provisional National Secretary).

[iii] W. Mellor, 'Southport & After: The Task for Socialists', *Socialist Leaguer*, No. 5, October–November 1934.

[iv] Editorial, *Socialist Leaguer*, No. 6, November–December 1934.

[v] Storm Jameson, 'On Our Way', *Socialist Leaguer*, No. 7, December 1934.

[vi] Cf. Editorial on S.L. National Conference, November 24th–25th, 1934, ibid.

Although the S.L. National Council decided that it was changing its organisation, methods and policy because of the urgency of the time, the urgencies had long existed. The S.L. plumped for 'immediate activities' to shield its untenable political stance vis-à-vis the rest of the Movement. Boldly it announced: *'We have passed out of the realm of programme-making into the realm of action'*. Quietly, there was a recognition of the inadequacy of any rôle it might like to play. Sadly, jargon came to its defence with references to 'a new disciplined plan of advance', 'a Call to Action', 'a new course … in the day-to-day life of the working-class movement'. Ironically, Constance Borrett proudly announced: 'An organisation which can change its functions and its methods three times in less than three years and still survive must have an uncommon tenacity of life.'[i] Equally such an organisation does not *know* what rôle to play.

The S.L.'s failure at Southport resulted in reaffirmation of local activities as a solution. The November 1934 Special Conference declared that the Southport decisions made the S.L. 'more than ever necessary'. Via *Forward to Socialism*, the S.L. was now committed to propaganda-by-action as the most effective method of challenging the theoretical fallacies held by Party and union leaders. J. T. Murphy described the Special Conference as 'the most important event of the S.L.'s year… It sharpened the process of transforming S.L. branches *from research groups into active political units'.*[ii] (Murphy became the National Secretary of the S.L.). Cripps launched the S.L.'s Membership Campaign at Caxton Hall, Westminster (December 21st, 1934). One feature was the use of business reply cards, the first time a political organisation had used this form of publicity.[iii] By February 1935, there were six new S.L. branches, membership had increased, sales of the *Socialist Leaguer* were rising: 'At no time since its formation had the S.L. shown more signs of rapid advance.'[iv] The S.L. tried to refocus its activities by propagating ideas and principles to rank and filers, rather than to the Party Conference. S.L. branches inquired into the newly channelled function of the S.L. at the London Weekend School (February 23rd and 24th, 1935). D. M. Fraser spoke on the question, *'Can the S.L. win the Labour Party for its policy?'* while in March, W. Mellor talked on *'The Function of the S.L.'* at the S.L. St. Pancras Branch. The S.L. had set itself the task of rousing 'a Socialist consciousness',[v] incorporated more trade unionists into S.L. ranks, and augmented the number of S.L. branches by 30% by May 1935.

(C) Local Agitation Against the Unemployment Act, and the 'Mass Resistance Against War' Conferences

The S.L.'s main local agitation was centred on the Government's *Unemployment Act*. On February 3rd, 1935, the S.L.'s National Council called for local S.L. protests against the Act's administration. London S.L. branches stirred local Labour parties to protest against the Unemployment Assistance Boards (U.A.B.s), and S.L.'ers were informed it was 'the primary duty of Socialists to be "agitators"… against the callous brutalities of

---

[i] C. Borrett, 'New Beginnings', *Socialist Leaguer*, No. 7, December 1934.

[ii] J. T. Murphy, 'The Year in Review', *Socialist Leaguer*, No. 11, May 1935. (My italics.)

[iii] Suggested by the Gateshead S.L., July 26th, 1934.

[iv] J. T. Murphy, S.L. Notes, *Socialist Leaguer*, No. 9, February 1935.

[v] A. Austen, letter in May 1935, *Socialist Leaguer*, No. 11.

the *Unemployment Act*', which was cutting maintenance, invading family rights, dividing working people. In March and April 1935, S.L. branches were active in their local Labour parties for repealing the Act, and putting forward the Socialist alternative of work or adequate maintenance. It was deemed 'the most important campaign conducted by the S.L.'[i] On April 6th, there was a meeting for all London S.L.'ers to discuss 'the culmination of the fight against the *Unemployment Assistance Act*', and S.L.'ers were urged to awaken 'class feeling' against the Means Test. By June, this had become the dominant issue in S.L. branches.[ii]

At the S.L.'s Bristol Conference (1935), a resolution was passed popularising trades councils as the local unifying centres of the Movement, and to get unorganised workers into the Movement through unemployed organisations. By December 1935, the S.L. was linking its *Anti-War Conferences* with struggles for higher wages, unemployment maintenance and abolition of the Means Test. The S.L. claimed the Labour Party had abandoned the attempt to regard unemployment as an 'insurable proposition'; Party and T.U.C. leaders were less involved in unemployed agitation, demonstrations, marches, battles with police, yet, more than at any time since the 1880s, the condition of the working class had become the centre of theoretical and practical inquiry, with social surveys and mass observation in all large industrial centres: '*The social surveys... revealed the degree of want existing among large masses of the working population.*'[iii] The T.U.C. ignored the N.U.W.M. because of its Communist leadership, and recommended to trades councils the formation of *Unemployed Associations*, which were not intended as instruments of unemployed agitation! The 1932 Leicester Party Conference had recorded its 'emphatic protest' at the Means Test, and reaffirmed support for work or maintenance for the unemployed, but the Executive's admission of near impotence went unremarked.[iv]

In May 1934, the *Unemployment Act* reshaped unemployment relief, centralised its administration under Unemployment Assistance Boards (U.A.B.s), a U.A. Fund, an Unemployment Insurance Statutory Committee, widening eligibility for relief, and bringing a modified Means Test. These new U.A.B. regulations brought losses of relief, resulting in protest meetings, marches and deputations from local Public Assistance Committees. Labour leaders meekly followed up with its '*Appeal to the Public Conscience*' on February 1st, 1935, but S.L.'ers had joined in demonstrations previously condemned or ignored by Party leaders, and now the success of the Movement rested on protest, agitation and efforts of local supporters. When the Government suspended new U.A.B. scales it was lauded as one of the most decisive victories of the working class during the whole of the inter-war period.[v] The politics of discontent could not be kept in strict channels, and the agitational temperature had been raised; the Government had been confronted with the biggest explosion of popular anger since the 1926 'General Strike': 'Much the biggest single Labour victory of the 1930s ... was the defeat of the U.A.B.'s regulations ... by Parliamentary manoeuvre and the mobilisation of a united working class, marching and demonstrating.'[vi] The S.L. played its part.

---

[i] J. T. Murphy, 'The Year in Review', *Socialist Leaguer*, No. 11, May 1935.
[ii] *Socialist Leaguer*, No. 12, June 1935.
[iii] A. Hutt, *Postwar History of the British Working Class*, 1937, p.246.
[iv] The N.U.W.M. was the National Unemployed Workers' Movement.
[v] A. Hutt, op. cit., 1937, p.265.
[vi] M. Foot, *Aneurin Bevan – A Biography*, Vol. 1, 1962, p.205.

By August 1936, W. Mellor was alluding to a Popular Front which would create a united Movement attacking new Unemployment Regulations and the existing Means Test.[i] On September 12th, 1936, S.L. branches organised a demonstration against U.A.B. regulations and the S.L. alerted all branches and Area Committees, outlining a campaign to clarify the significance of regulations to come into operation in November. S.L. branches were asked to reiterate 'work or maintenance' and expose the maintenance scales, governed by the Means Test, which constituted a reduction of wages for large sections of workers: 'The Means Test compels them to contribute heavily out of their wages to the maintenance of those families unemployed.'[ii] There were protests by the South Wales S.L. Area Committee and the Tyneside S.L. Area Committee, Cripps as speaker against the U.A.B. regulations. On November 8th, 1936, S.L. branches joined trades councils, union branches, I.L.P. and C.P. branches, headed by the South Wales Miners' Federation, in the organisation of a Hunger March. S.L. representatives were appointed to the London Reception Committee, S.L.'ers to be present at the Hyde Park Demonstration, while local S.L. branches appointed representatives to committees, aided them in securing accommodation, collecting funds, organising support. This was the largest Hunger March of the 1930s, and it stimulated official Party and union support,[iii] but the humiliation for the unemployed was that Labour leaders believed there was little they could do to compel the Government.[iv] For the S.L., there seemed one answer to the 'loneliness of helplessness surrounded by indifference ... the mass demonstration will have to be resorted to if the conspiracy of silence of Capitalist society is to be broken by the insurgent voice of Labour.'[v] That was Aneurin Bevan's mellifluous, impassioned message.

From 1935, foreign affairs and threats of war dominated S.L. enactments for local branches. In June 1935 an editorial looked back on a year of increased membership, expanding influence, growing activity. The Bristol Conference would extend the S.L., deepen its theoretical grasp of Socialist policy, strengthen its organisation and discuss resolutions on the Unemployment Act, India, Unions, Co-ops, and the International Situation and War: 'A Socialist Conference should be a battleground of ideas and a source of inspiration.'[vi] Before the Conference took place, the first conference of branch chairmen, secretaries and treasurers occurred, and their conclusions on leadership and organisation were incorporated into a Branch Handbook, published in June.

At the Bristol S.L. Conference (June 1935),[vii] practical proposals were made for strengthening the local units as the foci of agitations, and the Conference was more united than at the Leeds Conference. Instead of an S.L. magazine, it was hoped to produce a more popular newspaper. The title of the Conference was *'Fight Now Against War, A Call to Action'*, and a new technique was adopted by the Standing Orders Committee to ensure the fullest discussion; Trades Councils were envisaged as

---

[i] W. Mellor, *Socialist*, No. 9, July–August.

[ii] S.L. Executive, *Socialist*, No. 10, September 1936.

[iii] Cf. M. Foot, op. cit., p.237.

[iv] R. Miliband, op. cit., p.216.

[v] A. Bevan, 'Challenge of the Hunger March', *Socialist*, No. 12, November 1936.

[vi] 'What the S.L. Is Doing', *Socialist Leaguer*, No. 12, June 1935.

[vii] Cf. *Bristol Evening World*, June 11th, 1935 & *Daily Herald*, June 11th, 1935: R. George, D. N. Pritt & R. Dodds were elected to the National Council of S.L., replacing H. N. Brailsford, Sir C. Trevelyan & John Lewis.

potential defences against 'Fascist violence', organising people through sports activities, Tenants' Leagues, campaigns in shops and factories, harnessing S.L. members among union members. There was a split over a 'United Front' before the majority of the 200 delegates voted *against* it, and although the I.L.P. gained an impression of 'a leadership without followers', the significance was the organising of *'Mass Resistance to War'* *Conferences* with representatives of the Labour, co-operative and union Movement, to discuss ways and means of opposing war. These conferences would constitute a 'magnificent political demonstration', a further means of increasing the S.L.'s influence.

Preparing the *'Anti-War' Conferences* absorbed local branches, so that at the 17 conferences between September 14th and 21st, 1935, there were delegates from unions, local Labour parties, Co-operative Societies, S.L. branches, Trades Councils, Women's Groups, Ward Associations and the Labour League of Youth.[i] The S.L. proposed 'workers and their organisations' resist war preparations, and war propaganda by agitation in factories, councils, branches and public meetings. Hopes for an increased S.L. membership were underlined when, in November 1935, S.L. Area Committees were to convene special 'organisation conferences' of branch officials to examine their methods of work and put into practice methods outlined in the Branch Organisation handbook. In fact, the incongruous nature of the S.L.'s *Anti-War Conferences*[ii] was made explicit by its own internal divisions over the question of sanctions imposed by 'Imperialist' powers in the League of Nations, and the fact that the S.L. decided *not* to conduct an oppositional campaign in the constituencies against the Labour Party decision to support those sanctions.

Because of the General Election of 1935, the S.L.'s plan to hold conferences in each area was postponed. A lesson was learnt in the Election. S.L. canvassers often found a significant ignorance of simple economic and political facts in many working-class houses (so what's new?), and expressed surprise that electors knew so little about elementary facts and analyses which S.L.'ers took for granted. (Blame it on the elementary education offered.) A suggestion was made that S.L. propaganda work should be of the simplest kind: 'We are not yet beyond the age of the soap box.'[iii] Branch executives were scolded for not using the handbook and applying its principles on organisation and methods of work. Emphasis was again on doubling membership by the next S.L. Conference and launching a nationwide campaign for sales of *The Socialist* and pamphlets, especially on lessons of the General Election and problem of relating S.L. views to struggling workers in industries.[iv] Couched in terms of 'getting closer to the day-to-day issues before trade unions and the masses'[v] was the S.L.'s objective.

So, the rejuvenating force which the S.L. hoped to convey was its advance along more independent lines within the Movement. J. T. Murphy was right; the S.L. had

---

[i] There were 1400 delegates at the London Conference; 311 at Leeds; 300 at Newcastle; 285 at Cardiff; 205 at Manchester; 200 at Hull; 182 at Birmingham; 133 at Swansea; 120 at Brighton; 130 at Bristol; 108 at Durham; and 90 at Nottingham.

[ii] The format of mass agitation with a public meeting, speeches and resolutions preceding a mass march reproduced a style of popular protest dating back to the Chartists, cf. S. Macintyre, *'Little Moscows'*, 1980, p.107.

[iii] Joseph Arch letter to *Socialist*, No. 3, December 1935.

[iv] J. T. Murphy, 'Organise, Educate, Agitate!', *Socialist*, No. 3, December 1935.

[v] W. Mellor, London Area Committee Meeting, November 23rd, 1935.

been more of a *'Socialist propaganda appendage'* to the Party than an independent organisation, so it had to function in 1936 more as an affiliated organisation of the Party than as an organisation of individuals diffusing S.L. ideas in the Party. There would have to be more meetings, more activities in the name of the S.L.: 'The workers must see the S.L. as an organised body of Socialist opinion within the Labour Party operating definitely and in an organised manner to win the Party to its point of view.'[i] To this end, predictably, 50 conferences were organised, appeals were sent to every S.L. branch to become active in this campaign to recruit members, to increase the sale of S.L. publications, and raise funds.

The message in these conferences[ii] would be to support the struggle for wages and working conditions, build up a fighting fund for workers, expose schemes for the 'reconstruction of capitalism', to explain that economic struggle for higher wages and better conditions was a political struggle, and prepare plans for greater power to the constituency parties. The S.L. was showing signs of frustration. Borne of desperation was an idea to revise the rule which made individual membership of the Labour Party a condition for membership of the S.L. (which meant extra fees): 'Why shouldn't membership of the S.L. carry with it membership of the Labour Party through affiliation as in the case of the old I.L.P., Fabian Society or S.D.F.?'[iii] With the S.L.'s revitalisation as an active organisation in all areas, 'ready to educate the electorate in the bedrock principles of a real Socialist Policy',[iv] the campaign of conferences and meetings might have the effect of stimulating 'Socialism' in the Labour Movement.[v] In February and March 1936, the S.L.'s campaign was in full swing, membership increasing (a little), but some branches dissented from participation, arguing that a mass membership was unnecessary. The official S.L. view was that the organisation could not be built without independent S.L. meetings and without bringing the S.L. 'more openly before workers'.[vi] A 'speakers' class' at Head Office devoted half its time to *how* to speak, half to Socialist theory, an indication of the importance attached to conferences, while the S.L. decision to support the C.P.'s reapplication for affiliation to the Labour Party (March 16th, 1936) mirrored the attempt to manufacture an independent S.L. line vis-à-vis Party leaders.[vii]

To accentuate the S.L.'s new rôle its National Council drew up a *'7-Point Resistance Plan to Rearmament and the National Government'* in April 1936. This extended ideas embodied in the *Anti-War Conferences* of 1935, with suggestions for protests against military and industrial conscription; mass demonstrations in opposition to the Government, and agitational and organisational committees in every locality (by Trades Councils, local Labour parties and Co-operative Societies). The campaign conferences and meetings, organised by the S.L., were devoted to opposing the *Government's White Paper on Rearmament*, and its annual 'May Day Message to the Workers'[viii] had the exhortation: 'Win Your Way to Security and Peace by Winning Class Power – Unity Is Strength'.[ix]

---

[i] J. T. Murphy, S.L. Notes, 'Our Challenge to Gradualism', *Socialist*, No. 4, January–February 1936.

[ii] Resolution of the 50 conferences, January 1936.

[iii] Letter from J. Stephens, *Socialist*, No. 4, January–February.

[iv] Cyril Jones (Wrexham S.L.) to Cripps, December 3rd, 1935, Cripps Papers.

[v] Cripps to Hector L. Roberge, February 11th, 1936, Cripps Papers.

[vi] *Socialist*, No. 5, March 1936.

[vii] Cf. Editorial, *Socialist*, No. 6, April 1936, which threatened the Labour leaders with a possible C.P./S.L. collaboration 'against Capitalism' – a provocation not forgotten.

[viii] *Socialist*, No. 7, May 1936.

[ix] ibid.

The *Anti-War Conferences* had 'profoundly stirred' the Labour Movement and the 3000 delegates who attended, although it was regretted that not sufficient advantage had been taken to recruit new S.L. members: 'The S.L. has not yet passed from the stage of diffusing influence to organising it.'[i] A contributory factor to the development of the S.L. during 1935 and 1936 was attention to theoretical study through day and weekend schools and study circles, with the *Socialist* as a political weapon to provide self-education and recruit more members.[ii] The *Anti-War* campaign had been the first effort to develop independent S.L. activity; the second was the campaign of conferences and mass meetings between January and March 1936, which focussed on gradualism and democracy in the Labour Movement. The conferences were useful, but only a few public meetings were well attended: 'Until now, the S.L. work and its Area Committees' activities have been far more intensive than extensive.'[iii]

At the Stoke Conference 1936, the dominating note was the issue of *unity*: 'There has never been a time since the S.L. was formed when the opportunity for growth and expansion was so golden.'[iv] The Conference concluded that the S.L.'s rôle had *widened*, with the mass conferences, demonstrations, and educational efforts to 'eliminate' the Movement's 'reformism', whatever *that* might entail! One resolution (which was passed) stated the S.L. had now to take the initiative in organising mass agitation and propaganda for the Socialist policies of the S.L.[v] Other resolutions were for free expression for the Labour League of Youth, equal pay for equal work for women (a Labour Government was working on that 68 years later) and a State Medical Service. The S.L. also distanced itself: 'It proclaims its continued loyalty to the Labour Party in *the rôle of candid friend*,'[vi] so it critiqued the selection of Parliamentary candidates, confined more to men who could put down a substantial sum of money.'[vii] One amendment (which *was* defeated) hoped to reorganise the S.L. as 'an independent revolutionary leadership within the Labour Movement in opposition to the reformist bureaucracy'!'[viii] Cripps reminded delegates that it was more important to capture the Party than to go outside it and set up a rival concern,[ix] while in an article entitled '*Socialists in the Labour Party (Should They Leave It?)*', the I.L.P.'s *New Leader* commented that the S.L.'s Conference left 'a rather tragic impression', because, although there was a militant spirit among delegates and little evidence of careerist elements, there was a feeling of 'a small group of intellectual leaders without followers', which would inevitably imply exclusion from the Labour Party if S.L. resolutions were implemented. A suitable retort might have been: 'Where was the I.L.P?' And how many members did the I.L.P. have?

In the summer of 1936, the challenge of the rank and file to various Executive Committees was prevalent in conferences of engineers, railwaymen and miners, and reflected the S.L. challenge to the 'bureaucratic authority' of Party and union leaders. The S.L. kept 'Distressed Areas' in the foreground with Demonstration against U.A.B.

---

[i] J. T. Murphy, 'From 3rd to 4th Conference', *Socialist*, No. 8, June 1936.

[ii] J. T. Murphy, ibid.

[iii] A.C., 'Area Notes', *Socialist*, No. 8, June 1936.

[iv] Editorial, 'Matters of Moment', *Socialist*, No. 9, July–August.

[v] Quoted in *Daily Herald*, June 2nd, 1936.

[vi] *New Statesman and Nation*, June 6th, 1936.

[vii] Cf. Trevor Pugh at Stoke Conference.

[viii] J. E. Winecour (London), quoted in *Manchester Guardian*, June 2nd, 1936.

[ix] Cripps, June 9th, 1936, Cripps Papers.

regulations and S.L. branches found a new lease of life in support for a 'Popular Front', especially collections for Spanish workers. The S.L. asked branch members to agitate for freedom of working-class action to aid Spanish workers and prevent supplies for Franco leaving Britain, and S.L. branches were invited to conduct propaganda to explain the issues of the Spanish Civil War, refute Press bias, collect one day's pay levy from members,[i] support union action to prevent aid to 'rebels', and urge the National Council of Labour to abandon 'neutrality'. The S.L. had a reasonable case for extra-parliamentary action, at last!

(D) The S.L. and the Labour League of Youth

Momentous issues were fought out at the Edinburgh Party Conference in 1936 which involved local S.L. branches. Apart from the crucial issues of Communist Party affiliation, the Spanish Civil War, and Labour's position on rearmament, two themes emerged for S.L. local branches; the rôle of the Labour League of Youth and the rôle of the Constituency Parties. The S.L. recognised in the League of Youth a potential ally against the heavy voting odds massed against minorities, and a potential militant organisation supporting S.L. branches. The League of Youth was conceived as 'a team of vigorous and enthusiastic workers'[ii] who would offer a steady influx of members aware of the implications of Socialist policy, and provide revitalisation that progressive movements required.

However, the S.L. soon perceived, in the Party's treatment of the League of Youth, the same intolerance and obfuscation which was shown towards the S.L.[iii] As a result, the S.L. would support it in any confrontation with the National Executive, which was 'muzzling' the League of Youth. At a Special Conference of the London League of Youth on Labour leaders and the 'War question', it demanded a General Strike if there was a possibility of war, but measures had been taken to prevent the LL of Y from entering any 'United Front' agreements. In order to sidetrack its growing insistence on representation at the Party Conference and the N.E.C., and the right to discuss Party policy, Party leaders recommended amendments to the Constitution to allow two representatives to attend the Party Conference, one seat on the N.E.C., in both cases 'ex-officio' (minus voting rights).[iv] The S.L. took up the banner on behalf of the League of Youth.

During the 1935 S.L. membership campaign, all branches were requested to get League of Youth members to link up with the S.L. The S.L.'s thinking was succinctly penned by B. Betts (later Barbara Castle): 'The Labour League of Youth has a distinctive political contribution to make ... Youth's job is to keep the Party flexible by demanding *the restatement of objectives and the reconsideration of tactics.*'[v] Quite so. The S.L. was attracted to the LL of Y since the latter had grown critical of Party leaders' lack of drive, and the N.E.C. would not allow the LL of Y to register opinions on Party policy.

---

[i] The response to this request was not encouraging (cf. M. McCarthy, S.L. Notes, 'What the S.L. Is Doing', *Socialist*, No. 11, October 1936.

[ii] *Labour Magazine*, March 1932.

[iii] Cf. A. Austen, 'Which Way Youth?', *Socialist Leaguer*, No. 2, July–August 1932.

[iv] Cf. John Gollan, 'Muzzling the League of Youth', *Labour Monthly*, No. 12, Vol. 16, December 1934.

[v] B. Betts, 'Socialist Youth Day', *Socialist Leaguer*, No. 9, February 1935.

By 1935, there was awareness that the League of Youth had to be diverted from the S.L.'s influence! H. B. Lees-Smith[i] pleaded that the Party's new *'Socialism and Peace'* policy called upon youth for 'far higher qualities than are required by merely rhetorical appeals'; it asked them to combine their idealism with 'the drudgery of realistic policies' (what youth yearned for drudgery?), and he claimed the victories of the official party in recent local elections offered more scope to youth than years of 'irresponsible declamation', presumably by the S.L.

Not surprisingly, at its Bristol Conference (1935) the S.L. passed a resolution opposing attempts of the Labour Movement 'to stifle Youth'.[ii] The S.L. stated Socialist Youth organisations had an important part to play in preparing the working class in the fight against capitalism and in the transition to Socialism, so the S.L. would 'render all assistance in its power to the Youth organisations',[iii] and was determined the latter would have the right to discuss matters of policy and reach decisions. This was not developed any further until March 1936, when the S.L. devoted more attention to Youth organisations. At succeeding conferences of the League of Youth, resolutions had been passed for organisational independence, the right to discuss policy, and more representation on the N.E.C.; all had been refused. The S.L. was keen to intervene because 'the League of Youth is far in advance of the other sections of the Labour Party… it can be transformed into a really powerful and effective Socialist Youth Movement.'[iv] Not only that. The Labour League of Youth had protested against class collaboration, argued for the lowering of the salaries of Party officials (!), and criticised the *Daily Herald*; now the N.E.C. was planning to reduce the age-limit for League of Youth members from 25 to 21. Hence, it was 'at the crossroads'[v] and searched for S.L., local Labour and union support in its protest against the N.E.C. decision. S.L. branches had to 'throw all their weight' into this struggle.[vi]

The S.L.'s hope of mass membership was to be adversely affected by the N.E.C.'s statement to keep the League of Youth as a 'junior' section of the Party, instead of allowing and encouraging its development into a Socialist Youth Movement. As long as the Party Executive avoided the challenging, urgent political issues, the majority of working-class youth perceived the S.L. would not become interested in the cause of socialism. (The majority of working-class youth has *never* been interested in socialism). However: 'Youth needs revolutionary theory to guide its instinctively militant feelings and responses… the battle between the Left and Right in the Labour Movement for the Youth is truly one of life and death.'[vii] In the 1936 Stoke S.L. Conference there was another resolution on the League of Youth to co-ordinate their activities; all S.L. branches to devote more time to political guidance of their League of Youth branches. The conference welcomed establishment of Socialist Youth Committees, and the S.L. would give every assistance to S.L. members working on these committees. W. Mellor averred: 'The Labour Party tried to turn the League of Youth into a nursery school

---

[i] .Rt. Hon. H. B. Lees-Smith, 'Prospects for the Labour Party', *Political Quarterly*, January–March 1935.

[ii] Bristol Conference resolution, June 1935.

[iii] Ibid.

[iv] A. G. Bennett in a letter to *Socialist*, No. 5, March 1936. A.G. Bennett was Secretary of the Socialist Youth Committee.

[v] Ted Willis (National Council of Labour League of Youth) on 'League of Youth at the Crossroads', *Socialist*, No. 6, April 1936.

[vi] Cf. A. G. Bennett, 'Youth Battles for Its Socialist Rights', *Socialist*, No. 7, May 1936.

[vii] Reg Groves, 'The Labour Party and the Young Workers', *Socialist*, No. 8, June 1936.

whose teachers had passed an examination set by Transport House. That is a very dangerous attitude.'[i] As for reducing the LL of Y age limit to 21, the I.L.P. noted: 'It is doubtful if the Leagues of Youth can successfully resist such a decree by the senior Party. They will be faced with the alternative of losing themselves in the Labour Party or turning to the I.L.P. Guild of Youth and the Y.C.L. in an extra-Party Youth organisation.'[ii] Cripps deduced that the League of Youth was being used as a cheap source of labour; its members had to learn to see Socialism, not as some 'abstruse theological doctrine' but as a way of life; the common desire inspiring all youth members had to be the wish to get rid of (or at least reduce) suffering and exploitation of workers, and this keenness must not be smothered under a deadweight of instruction and education in economics: 'Let no one who has the desire for romantic self-sacrifice and service be deterred by too strong a dose of economic education.'[iii] Wise advice from a future Chancellor of the Exchequer.

Recognising its own dilemma, the S.L. knew that the League of Youth could not grow while denied freedom of expression, freedom to discuss Party policy, to control its own journal, to have a full-time organiser, and concentrate on enrolling young workers. This was to avoid being clamped within the limits of the Party machine, for, as the S.L. judged it, so long as *"reformist ideology"* dominated the Movement, youth would remain indifferent: 'The fight to win Youth to the banner of Socialism is the fight for the adoption of militant policies by the working-class movement as a whole.'[iv] However, at the Edinburgh Conference, the N.E.C. criticised the conduct of the League of Youth, suspended publication of its journal,[v] and decided not to convene the Youth's Annual Conference in 1937. It was not to meddle in policy, and should confine itself to *recreational, education and electoral work*.[vi] The N.E.C. had dismantled the League of Youth as an active political organisation.

The reaction of the S.L. to this was aggressive – to demand a National Youth Movement in alliance with militant workers of the rank and file. Youth branches were called to reverse the memorandum, intensify propaganda among working-class youth, affiliate to the Socialist Youth Committee and support its paper, *Socialist Youth*. The S.Y.C. *was* a radical alternative; it opposed coalitions with non-working-class parties and organisations, believed in preparations against industrial and military conscription, and forcefully stated capitalism offered no future to young workers. The S.L. editorial uttered: 'No decision at Edinburgh so openly illustrated the dictatorial powers of the Executive as the action taken to stifle the League of Youth.'[vii] The block vote was mobilised to reduce the age to 21; the N.E.C. stood fast by its nursery school. There had been a Left-wing swing in the Youth Movement, and it had acquired 20,000 members by 1936, but through Party leaders' decrees that the main activity should be social and recreational, and the age limit lowered, membership diminished to 4,000 by April 1937. This showed that the aim of Party leaders had been to build a children's social club: 'Of all the stupidities of the Labour Party in recent years, the attempt to prohibit the Labour League of Youth from taking any part in the formulation of Party

---

[i] Quoted in *Daily Herald*, June 2nd, 1936.

[ii] *New Leader*, June 5th, 1936.

[iii] Cripps in *Young Politician* (League of Youth's paper), July–August 1936.

[iv] Editorial, *Socialist*, No. 11, October 1936.

[v] *Labour Party Annual Conference Report*, October 1936, p.247.

[vi] Quoting G. D. H. Cole, *History of the Labour Party Since 1914*, p.343.

[vii] 'Matters of Moment' by the Editor, *Socialist*, No. 12, November 1936.

policy is the most stupid and self-destructive.'[i] As for the S.L., the Unity Campaign now brought new hope to the Youth Movement. There was hardly a branch of the League of Youth that was not in favour of unity and did not realise that the Unity Campaign represented an effective move to rouse the fighting traditions of Labour: 'The fight of the League of Youth for self-government is the same fight as that of the Unity Campaign'.[ii] The main support for youth demands came from Labour workers in the Unity campaign, and 'the only solution was a national campaign on the basis of a reorganised self-governing League of Youth',[iii] a United Socialist Youth League. S.L. aspirations for the League of Youth came in Cripps' Stockport speech: 'Youth is more Left-wing and class conscious than the older generation', but the problem of the Youth organisation for Party leaders was an omen for the S.L.'s own confrontation after the Edinburgh Conference.

(E) Local S.L.s, Constituency Labour Parties, and The Left Book Club

The other factor of crucial importance to local S.L. branches was the *constituency Labour party*. Although the politics in constituency parties covered the spectrum of Labour politics,[iv] there were reactions from constituency party activists in the context of a consistent Left-wing response to policies of the Party Executive.[v] Oswald Mosley was one of the first to foresee that cleavage between constituency parties (led by Left-wing enthusiasts) and unions (generally led by moderate officials), although a more typical Labour view was delicately expressed by Sydney Webb: 'The constituency parties were frequently unrepresented groups of nonentities dominated by fanatics, cranks and extremists.'! As D. Powell remarks, the Webbs' idea of a discreetly regulated freedom had to be in accordance with the 'three b's' – benevolent, bourgeois and bureaucratic.[vi] But 'fanatics, cranks and extremists' deserved to be heard!

Local Labour parties began to play a rôle urging unions 'left', but were enjoying little success because they lacked influence, despite selecting Parliamentary candidates and conducting election campaigns.[vii] Labour councils tended to give more public assistance benefits, more educational and health facilities; some even refused to administer the Means Test, but the Labour Party lacked a *comprehensive municipal programme*. Even though the Party was successful in the L.C.C. elections of 1934 and Attlee, Morrison and Lansbury were committed to major local government initiatives, local Labour parties were subjected to centralised control, which had not been exerted to such an extent before the fall of the 1929–1931 Government.[viii]

---

[i] G. D. H. Cole, *The People's Front*, 1937, p.46.

[ii] Under 25, 'Youth's Crisis and Need', *Tribune*, April 30th, 1937.

[iii] Ted Willis, 'Labour Youth Calls for Unity in Action in Fight for Socialism', *Broadsheet*, No. 2, April 1937.

[iv] An argument extended by E. G. Janosik, op. cit., 1968, cf. p.58.

[v] Cf. R. Miliband, op. cit., pp.105, 107, 110, 173, 252, & 319.

[vi] Quoting B. Webb, *Diaries*, May 19th, 1930, folios 53–4 (quoting R. T. McKenzie, *British Political Parties*, p.505), D. Powell, op. cit., 1998, p.125.

[vii] Cf. D. McHenry, op. cit, pp.85–106. (In 1931, local Labour parties sponsored 320 candidates; unions 129 and the Co-op 15. In 1935, local Labour parties sponsored 400 candidates: unions 128, the Co-op 21 and Scottish Socialist Party 4.)

[viii] J. Jupp, *The Left in Britain in the 1930s*, p.99 (1956 thesis).

Local Labour parties, expressing the political opinions of local unionists and political activists, had little effective influence in Party Conference decisions. Their representatives were elected, not by their own delegates, but by block votes of the entire Conference. Since membership of the S.L. was confined to Party members, constituency Party members joined because it was a link through which the local Labour parties were able to present joint resolutions to the Annual Conference,[i] and the question of representing local opinion against the centralised opinion of union and Party machines was the issue propelling the demand that the Party be made 'more democratic', and the Constitution revised, through decentralisation of union political funds to allow adequate resources for local parties' representation at Party conferences.[ii] Between 1932 and 1937, 90% of the resolutions and amendments tabled at Party Conferences originated with the Divisional Labour Parties. Of these, 10% reached the floor of the Conference, only 3% adopted. Most of the other proposals had been sponsored by unions of which 33% were debated, and most of them were adopted.[iii] This was the reason, (as the S.L. deduced), for the comparatively passive, ill-informed local constituency membership. The S.L. judged that it was the rôle of its branch members to recreate the confidence, self-sacrifice and comradeship which had marked earlier phases of the Movement. Had the Party turned too rapidly from a mainly propagandist to a practical political Movement?[iv] The S.L. perceived that it had.

As in the case of the Labour League of Youth, the S.L. colluded with constituency parties, and found it easy to do so, for its strength lay in the large cities where communications were good and S.L. speakers were far more likely to visit, and because the initiative for offering *amendments* to the Party Constitution came largely from the S.L., since it complained that the distribution of power in the Party worked to the advantage of Labour's Right or moderate factions. The first occasion (other than in S.L. pamphlets) in which the S.L. specifically stated its support for strengthening Constituency Labour Parties was on August 5th, 1933,[v] in a denial to Conservative leader Stanley Baldwin that it intended to supersede recalcitrant local authorities by district commissioners, if a Socialist Government came to fruition. However, by 1934, Labour's more creative work had been in local government administration, in recognition that municipalities provided '*a laboratory for experimentation with socialised services*',[vi] and at the Southport Conference of that year there was a proposal to give constituency parties the right to elect their own members to the N.E.C. Mellor put it bluntly: '*The Party lies in the constituencies and recognition of this fact is overdue.*'[vii] It is no coincidence that the S.L. had just suffered a debilitating defeat of *its* amendments to the Party programme; the elevation of constituency parties offered a renewed lease of life.

After Labour's local election victories in London, Glasgow and Leeds in 1934, an S.L. appeal was made to the newly-elected Labour councils to use their powers for 'a

[i] P. Strauss, *Cripps: Advocate and Rebel*, 1943, p.64.

[ii] G. D. H. Cole, *The People's Front*, 1937, pp.301–302.

[iii] D. McHenry, op. cit., pp.30–31.

[iv] Amber Blanco White, op. cit., p.380.

[v] S.L. News, 'Mr. Baldwin and Other Critics', *New Clarion*.

[vi] D. McHenry, op. cit., pp.202–228. (My italics.)

[vii] W. Mellor, 'Southport and After: The Task for Socialists', *Socialist Leaguer*, No. 5, October–November 1934.

real battle on the Socialist front[i] against the Means Test. As well as education and local housing, Public Assistance was a central issue for working people: 'Its levels of payment should not be allowed to be depressed by any failure on the part of industries to pay a living wage.'[ii] The S.L. reminded local parties that borough councils were circumscribed in their powers because local government finance was based on rates (which were based on property). Here was an attempt to link more combative constituency parties to the S.L.'s outlook, the beginning of a distinct S.L. tactic which extended to its demise and dissolution in 1937. Meanwhile, the Brighton Conference of 1935 called for renewed attention to the nature of democracy *within* the Party; the S.L. proclaimed that constituency parties were the *'living core of the Labour Party'*,[iii] and the *Birmingham Town Crier* opened its columns to rank and file contributors under the heading: *'What Is Wrong With the Labour Party?'* Some answers were; it should 'abandon heresy-hunting'; 'apathy comes from the top'; 'apathy is due to lack of leadership and to vagueness'; and membership 'had little opportunity for voicing opinions on policy'.[iv] The Labour establishment, by demonising *'the enemy within',* had undermined the confidence of large sections of the Labour movement in its own political integrity, as David Powell construed in 1998.[v] 70 years on, similar issues.

At the Edinburgh Conference of 1936, frustration for the constituency parties came to a head when, on resolutions on Spain, the League of Youth and 'Unity', union votes drowned the voices of local parties. Over 200 delegates had wished to speak on matters affecting the Party Constitution but only on the last day of the Conference was 'constitutional reform' raised, and there were protests when it was announced that this would be referred to the Executive. A delegate exclaimed:[vi] 'I am voicing the opinion of every Divisional Labour Party when I say we do not get a fair deal from the Executive. I hope they realise our dissatisfaction.' He had to make do with a memorandum dealing with the selection of candidates for local elections, and organisation of Party groups on local councils. At spes non fracta.[vii]

The constituency parties exhibited their revolt against the official line when 250 delegates met under the chairmanship of Cripps, and decided to appoint a committee to collect evidence and further their claim for a reform of Labour's Constitution, to give local organisations an equitable voice in Party counsels. The S.L. linked itself (personally and politically) with the constituency parties' struggle, instanced by H. N. Brailsford, who categorised the movement as one of 'revolt', breaking Party conventions and discipline, seeking vocal expression and permanent organisation: 'The vitality that the Labour Party has lost can be supplied only by those sections of the Labour Movement which *wage the class struggle relentlessly...* the Labour Party is a devitalised, incoherent group today. It can rally its own natural adherents and hope to attract others only when it had recovered its faith and its self-respect.'[viii] So, like the S.L, the constituency parties were critical of Party leaders' vacillation and were keenly alive to the danger of a split in the Party: 'Divisional parties have been treated by

[i] R. George, 'Local Government: Use Your Power', *Socialist Leaguer*, No. 6, November–December 1934.
[ii] Ibid.
[iii] *Socialist*, No. 2, November 1935.
[iv] Quoting A. Hutt, op. cit., pp.282–83.
[v] D. Powell, op. cit., 1998, p.13.
[vi] Quoting A. Hutt, ibid., pp.299–300.
[vii] Cf. G. D. H. Cole, *History of the Labour Party Since 1914*, p.344. 'Hope is not yet crushed.'
[viii] H. N. Brailsford, 'What Next After Edinburgh?', *Labour Monthly*, Vol. 18, No. 12, December 1936.

Headquarters with a contempt and neglect which had virtually killed the spirit inside the Movement. I am simply appalled at the break-up of our local Party organisations. There are divisional parties that have returned Labour MPs that have not had a meeting since the last General Election,'[i] complained C.P.A. secretary, Ben Greene.

While the Constituency Party Association was attempting to secure a larger, more direct representation of local parties on the N.E.C., the **Left Book Club**, begun in the Summer of 1936, was providing a high standard of political literature from a Socialist viewpoint. It supplemented the S.L.'s activities and *Tribune* (begun on January 1st, 1937),[ii] its importance signified by the warning given from the Labour National Agent to local Labour parties *not* to join it! The object of the Left Book Club was to enlighten, educate, and supply information and theoretical analysis of immediate problems. The times called for the kind of enlightenment that only the dissemination of literature could provide. Later the Left Book Club took over the rôle of defunct S.L. branches, giving Summer Schools, club meetings, discussions on political and social issues, drama productions, debates, films, and joint meetings with the local Co-operative Society, the I.L.P. and C.P.[iii] Dormant constituency parties, with declining numbers and activities, were galvanised into action.[iv] The Left Book Club became a powerful voice and moulder of Left-wing opinion and the intellectual reorientation of the L.B.C. (and eventual organisational changes effected by constituency agitation) had the most far-reaching consequences of any of the work done by the Left in the late 1930s.[v] Indeed, the S.L. was quick to harness its own agitation in the Unity Campaign to these developments whereby local organisations were given some sense of common identity and purpose.

The Edinburgh Conference 1936 made the constituency parties conscious of their rôle as the cornerstone of the whole political Movement, and they recognised they had been neglected, especially since they paid £1,000 towards the central Party Fund; they now wanted regional conferences, control over finances, more representation on the N.E.C., to make the constituency parties the most influential section in the Party. The S.L. did not find it easy to unite them. Ben Greene (for the C.P.A) was convinced the time for affiliated Socialist Societies had ended, and the only place for Socialists was in local Labour parties, raising *their* intellectual life, and making divisional Labour parties respected: 'We Constituency Party members are bound to have a deep suspicion and resentment of any organisation that tends to take away members from active constituency work.'[vi] This brought a retort from the S.L. that not only had the S.L. never tried to *detach* members from their local party organisations, but the S.L. had weakened itself numerically and financially by its insistence on the need for every Socialist worker to be actively involved in the local party: 'The job of S.L. members in the campaign is to see that its aims are not confined solely to matters of 'machinery'. The differences at Edinburgh which emphasised the gulf between the constituency party delegates and the trade union bureaucracy were differences of *policy* ... the

[i] Ben Greene (Secretary of C.P.A.) at Manchester Conference of Local Associations, Cripps Papers.
[ii] *Tribune* was conceived at the Edinburgh Conference by Cripps, Mellor, Bevan, Strauss and Laski (M. Foot, op. cit., p.235).
[iii] John Lewis, *The Left Book Club*, 1970, pp.67–68, 94.
[iv] John Lewis, ibid., p.94.
[v] J. Jupp, op. cit., p.190.
[vi] B. Greene, 'The Constituency Parties', *Socialist*, No. 13, December–January 1936–37.

constituency parties must formulate new policies.'[i]

The N.E.C. side-stepped the issue of democracy inside the Party. At Edinburgh it offered no discussion on the Party Constitution (except every three years) and the suggested Area Consultative Conferences were a mystification and diversion. Ben Greene explained: 'If the N.E.C. is really desirous of Party unity it should cease to look upon the very modest request for democracy in the Party as a sign of sinister and disruptive activity.'[ii] George Lansbury underlined this – the solution to the Party's Constitution was a new federation to comprise representatives of unions, co-operative societies, and constituency parties.[iii] Ben Greene then wrote to Cripps to complain that the United Front campaign had complicated the work of the C.P.A. and confused the issues when local parties were dissatisfied with official Party leaders: 'I have had to make it clear that this Committee has no connection whatever with the Unity Campaign.'[iv] The S.L. wanted to keep the Unity Campaign and Constituency Parties movement working 'in loose double harness',[v] and this had been the overall message made at the Birmingham Conference of the Constituency Parties: 'To leave Cripps in the lurch now would be not only a breach of faith but really bad policy: it was very important that they should make the N.E.C. understand that the policy urged by Sir Stafford Cripps was desired by the great majority of the rank and file.'[vi]

In March 1937, the Constituency Party Conference agreed its Committee should approach the N.E.C. to secure alterations in the Party Constitution to ensure greater influence for constituency parties in regard to Party policy, organisation and finance. They required schemes for the organisation of constituency parties into regional associations (each with direct representation on the National Committee) to co-ordinate the views of local parties. They exhibited the division between industrial and political sides of the Movement (manifest at Edinburgh) as ruinous to Labour solidarity, and 'only by the development of democracy within the trade unions and Labour parties can the threat of working-class disunity be defeated'.[vii] The Unity Campaign Committee declared support for further democratisation of the Party Conference,[viii] and saw a great source of strength in local Labour parties, which had grown by 400,000 members. (The local parties had consistently urged a more active line on Spain). To be fully recognised, Constituency Associations needed a programme to help in the formulation of policy, and needed recognition as the spearhead of a new section in the Party demanding greater political activity: 'They stood for the beginning of a new phase when Labour parties shall no longer be mere electoral machines, but shall be charged with whole-time political work,'[ix] pronounced Patrick Gordon Walker.

After the S.L.'s dissolution, branch members claimed the movement for associations of divisional parties were the Party's salvation. Over 270 divisional parties had sent delegates to the March Conferences, and there had been almost unanimous

[i] Editorial on Ben Greene, 'Matters of Moment', *Socialist*, No. 13, December 1936–January 1937.
[ii] B. Greene, 'Constituency Parties', *Tribune*, January 1st, 1937.
[iii] *Tribune*, January 22nd, 1937.
[iv] February 11th, 1937, Cripps Papers.
[v] St. John Reade (Bristol S.L.) to Cripps, February 14th, 1937, Cripps Papers.
[vi] *Birmingham Town Crier*, February 5th, 1937.
[vii] Constituency Party Conference, March 6th, 1937.
[viii] *Tribune*, March 19th, 1937.
[ix] P. Gordon Walker, *Tribune*, April 23rd, 1937.

approval of resolutions demanding constituency party election of their own *five* representatives on the N.E.C., and increase of those representatives to *nine* (i.e. one N.E.C. member responsible to divisional parties in each area). In this, ex-S.L. members visualised another move towards *'democratisation* of the Movement', which would also imply the canalisation of union political activity into the constituency parties. R. St. John Reade suggested[i] unions should pay 50% political levy to divisional parties (to provide divisional parties with a steady income between elections, essential for adequate organisation and propaganda); and the divisional parties should be placed in an independent financial position, able to choose the best qualified candidate. Meanwhile, *Constituency Party Associations* monopolised the S.L.'s thoughts, suggesting ways and means of forging the Party machine into a more fitting vehicle for rank and file opinion. Building constituency parties into financially independent bodies would prevent the policy of 'divide and rule' which had dominated the N.E.C., although Ben Greene noted frictions between ex-S.L. members and the C.P.A.[ii] He was disturbed by S.L. activities in furthering the United Front, claiming that in certain constituencies, efforts were being made to remove (from positions of influence) those opposed to United Front proposals. In the C.P.A.s he wanted all variety of Socialist opinions to be discussed and debated by democratic methods, on a wider basis than was afforded by the Party. He accused ex-S.L. members of trying to make the Associations serve their own purpose[iii] and asked Cripps: 'Can I have your assurance that no concerted efforts are being made by the Unity Committees to change the complexion of local parties... for the purpose of furthering the Unity proposals?'[iv] Cripps stated cryptically that the views on policy held by an individual was a test as to whether or not he was fit for the job as an official of the Party,[v] and hoped for more Left-wing representation on the N.E.C. at the Bournemouth Conference: 'The rank and file of thinking Labour people is largely with us ... in the next year we have got to try and crystallise this opinion, and it may be that we can do it in the Constituency Party Associations.'[vi]

On September 21st, 1937, in a speech at Garston, Cripps warned that the Labour Party might become *'a lifeless machine' controlled by the opinions of a few people who had influential positions*! It would be a 'sad day for the workers', politically, if ever membership and office in the Party was only allowed by permission of union leaders. This would mean the virtual abandonment of 'Socialism' and the devitalisation of the constituency parties.[vii] He thought the focal points during the coming months should be *Tribune* and the C.P.A.: 'We must test out the feeling of the Constituency parties at Bournemouth... If the Constitutional amendments are turned down, we may get some vitality into the Constituency Party organisation and be able to use that as a progressive block.'[viii]

Despite the fears of Labour's Right wing that to give constituency parties' powers would strengthen the Left within the Party, the revision of the Constitution took place at the Bournemouth Conference (1937). The Executive allayed discontent in the

---

[i] R. St. John Reade, 'Democracy for Labour', *Tribune*, May 21st, 1937.
[ii] Ben Greene to S. Cripps, July 22nd, 1937, Cripps Papers & Greene to Cripps, September 30th, 1937.
[iii] Ibid.
[iv] Ben Greene to S. Cripps, July 30th, 1937, Cripps Papers.
[v] S. Cripps to Ben Greene, July 26th, 1937, Cripps Papers.
[vi] S. Cripps to Herbert Rogers (his election agent), July 26th, 1937, Cripps Papers.
[vii] Cripps Papers, September 21st, 1937. Cripps' warning was prophetic.
[viii] Cripps, September 23rd, 1937, Cripps Papers.

constituency parties in the hope of making them more amenable to Party discipline. Increased representation of constituency parties from 5 to 7 members was carried, as was the right of these parties to elect their representatives separately.[i] For the first time since 1918, the Party Constitution was changed in a progressive direction, and this concession had been won by the activities of the rank and file during the year to October 1937.[ii] Constituency parties were now perceived as the chief instrument of Socialist propaganda. From now on they would be able to influence the leadership by the direct election of part of the N.E.C., and because the chosen constituency representatives were 'first-class politicians', and union representatives knew that those elected by the constituencies were nominees of the active political movement[iii]: 'It is this new channel of agitation and pressure that we ask all those who desire to see a more militant fighting policy to use to the utmost,'[iv] exclaimed Cripps.

Although the 'unity front' was defeated, and the Party did not have a policy 'against armaments', the Bournemouth Conference brought a new spirit of hope. The frustrations of rank and file and constituency parties was alleviated; C.P.A., S.L. activities, and the Unity Campaign had made their contribution to the change that had been effected and to the new spirit of vitality within the Party.[v] Had the Party overcome the disillusionment, apathy and confusion after the desertions of 1931? Authority bends in obeisance to its source, like a proud king momentarily humbling himself before an ancestral shrine, then straightens and continues as before,[vi] and such occurred to N.E.C. and T.U.C. leaders. Extraordinary swings of local opinion (aided by newspaper and radio 'hypnosis') favoured the Party leadership while Jennie Lee summed up the attitude of local Party members: 'Why were all the finest people I knew in the grip of a kind of spiritual paralysis? Where was all the vigour, the belligerency, the robust certainties that had characterised the Labour Movement?... Those people had grown jaded with so many emotional ups and downs. Now they seemed to be settling down to a grey twilight of indifference. They could no longer be searingly disappointed. For they no longer hoped for much.[vii] ... The Labour Party, which working people did so much to build, left them stranded, became the prey of piddling little career politicians, measured up so inadequately to events, was so dangerously timid, so depressingly orthodox, so unsure of its distinctive purposes.'[viii] Yet, for Labour pragmatists there could be no alternative but compromise and neither section could compromise with the other: 'Thus the vendettas and bloodlettings, the witch hunts and purges that have bedevilled Labour.'[ix]

In the last few months of the S.L.'s existence in 1937 the local S.L. branches concentrated on the Unity Campaign and the Spanish People's Front, especially in South Wales, the North East, and the East End of London. In the latter, S.L. branches carried out an anti-Fascist recruiting campaign. Delegates at the October 31st, 1936 Whitechapel Conference agreed that 'the Mosley menace could only be effectively met

[i] Quoting G. D. H. Cole, *History of the Labour Party from 1914*, pp.350–51.

[ii] D. N. Pritt, op. cit., p.97.

[iii] G. R. Strauss, 'Bournemouth and After', *Labour Monthly*, Vol. 19, No. 11, November 1937.

[iv] Cripps quoted in *Manchester Guardian*, October 6th, 1937.

[v] Cripps, Speech in Birmingham, October 10th, 1937, Cripps Papers.

[vi] M. Muggeridge, *The Thirties*, p.146.

[vii] J. Lee, *This Great Journey*, p.169.

[viii] J. Lee, ibid., p.186.

[ix] D. Powell, op. cit., 1998, p.15.

by the unity of the workers of the East End'.[i] The conference declared the riots in East London had been due to attempts of Fascist organisations to divide working people by spreading racist and religious antagonisms. An *East End Socialist Front Committee* arranged meetings, there were loud-speaker tours 'against Fascism', a union recruiting drive was instigated, but the main campaign was to create working-class unity against the Government and war (plus establish a 40-hour week, abolish the Means Test, and have national maintenance of the unemployed). In January 1937 W. Mellor expounded: 'In every locality, let the S.L. raise the banner of working-class unity, of democracy within the movement, of insistent opposition to the rearmament plans of the National Government, and of justice for the unemployed.'[ii] On the issue of Spain, the S.L. appealed for money for its campaign on behalf of Spanish workers, and the campaign should be organised by the Labour Party (for the removal of the embargo on armaments, resistance to the Government's 'neutrality' policy, and active vigilance committees at docks). The S.L. was inundated with requests for speakers on Spain.[iii]

The S.L.'s reaction to the N.E.C.'s statement on loyalty and the threats of discipline (against S.L. involvement in the Unity Campaign) was one of defiance at first. For Socialists, a period of crisis was a time for firm and uncompromising decisions:[iv] 'We must accept the S.L. Conference's decision on the Unity Campaign … the "anti-Unity" Socialist Leaguers' opposition now would be disastrous in strengthening the reactionary forces in our Movement'[v] and 3,700 Unity pledge cards had been signed in January. In the Party's decision to disaffiliate the S.L. was suspicion that the N.E.C. was contemplating a 'heresy-hunt'.[vi] S.L. branch members were still being asked to send in their union news (if there was talk of a strike, members should name the firm, the profits it was making, politicise the workers involved).[vii] By the middle of February, the National Committee of the Unity Campaign had held 11 mass demonstrations (with 12,000 people), 8,000 pledge cards had been filled, £600 collected; by March 19th, 18,000 pledge cards had been forwarded; 66 local committees and 32 demonstrations had been held.[viii] Disappointments of S.L. branch members were re-channelled into frenzied activities, while the disaffiliation of the S.L. from the Labour Party was followed by expulsion of individuals from union district committees: 'By its decisions the Party Executive is challenging the whole trend of events and is acting upon the assumption that the rank and file of the Movement are unmindful of the real purpose of the Unity Campaign, and incapable of seeing that the disciplinary action taken against a propaganda organisation, such as the S.L., will, unless challenged, be used in other directions.'[ix]

In April 1937, the S.L. put on a brave face: *never in the S.L.'s history had so many new*

---

[i] Quoted in *Socialist*, No. 12, November 1936.

[ii] W. Mellor, 'Get Together, Comrades, Working-class Unity on Workers' Issues', *Socialist*, No. 13, December–January 1936–37.

[iii] M. McCarthy, 'What the S.L. Is Doing', *Socialist*, No. 13, December–January 1936–7.

[iv] 'Our Unity', *Tribune*, January 15th, 1937.

[v] A. Austen, 'The Die Is Cast', *Tribune*, January 22nd, 1937.

[vi] Cf. 'Labour Party Executive's Attitude to Unity', *Tribune*, January 27th, 1937.

[vii] *Socialist Broadsheet*, No. 1, February 1937. This new periodical replaced *Socialist*. Edited by J. F. Horrabin, it was the official organ of the S.L., and issued 'as the political situation demands'. The greater flexibility of publication was supposed to be of great advantage to the National S.L. Council and S.L. branches. In fact, it exemplified the diminishing rôle of the S.L.

[viii] *Tribune*, March 19th, 1937.

[ix] W. M. Thomson, letter to *Tribune*, April 9th, 1937.

members been enrolled in so short a time![i] S.L. members now held key positions in many local Labour parties and trades councils, and the S.L announced continued work in the Party for the Unity Campaign. There had been 28 resolutions from local Labour parties protesting against the S.L.'s disaffiliation, 2 from the Labour League of Youth, 4 from Co-operative Guilds,[ii] and, at its Easter Leicester Conference, the S.L. voted 56 votes to 0 to go forward with the Unity Campaign, *even at the price of the sacrifice of its own organisation!* By June 11th, 1937, 36,000 pledge cards had been signed (60% of the Labour Movement's membership), but for the S.L. local branch members, their obituary had been written two months before: 'The S.L. has recently played an important and central rôle in the battle for working-class unity … By its actions it has brought that vital matter to the forefront … Had it accomplished nothing else than to make the struggle for unity a reality, it would have justified itself … It has in its four years of activity done much more – and its work has profoundly and beneficially influenced the attitude of the rank and file of the Labour Movement, not the least of youth.'[iii]

(F) A Socialist League Branch in Action[iv]

The Gateshead S.L. branch was a paradigm of an active local branch, the largest in the North East, and one of the busiest in the country. Since it originated in an energetic I.L.P. area in a North East renowned for its local commitments, it is the most fully documented branch and represented all aspects of local work throughout the S.L.'s existence. On October 6th, 1932, the S.L. Gateshead branch elected an Executive Committee of 6 (a chairman, vice chairman, secretary, financial secretary, assistant secretary and a literature secretary). Membership altered from **75** members (November 17th, 1932) to **77** (including 18 unemployed, December 8th, 1932); from **85** members (January 21st, 1933) to **89** members (March 2nd, 1933); from **98** members (June 8th, 1933) to **104** (August 5th, 1933, of whom 20 were 6 months in arrears for subscriptions); **113** members (March 8th, 1934, of whom 30 owed subscriptions), down to **87** members (July 26th, 1934, 26 on full subscription of 4d and 43 unemployed at ½d), **69** members (February 20th, 1935) but **80** members (40 owing subscriptions) on July 23rd, 1936.[v] During the same time, the I.L.P. lost 75% of its membership.

The main activities organised by the Gateshead branch were attempts to remain solvent through affiliation fees, union contributions, football pools, social events (bazaars, dances, fairs, jumble sales) and individual contributions. Finances were bound to figure significantly in this region of high unemployment, but it was agreed to lessen the financial business to a minimum and have a lecture or discussion at *every* branch meeting on Thursdays.[vi] Literature from the S.L. Head Office was sold in large

---

[i] *Socialist Broadsheet*, No. 2, April 1937.

[ii] B. A. Betts, 'The Progress of the Unity Campaign', ibid.

[iii] Editorial, *Socialist Broadsheet*, No. 2, April 1937.

[iv] The information for this section has been gathered from Ruth Dodds' *Executive Committee Minutes* (November 1932–July 23rd, 1936), *Gateshead Herald*, S.L. journals, and interviews with R. Dodds (September 1970).

[v] R. Dodds' Executive Committee Minutes.

[vi] Ibid., December 8th, 1932.

quantities; old age pensioners were made honorary members (½d per week was paid for them out of branch funds);[i] 2/6 was sent to the *Meerut Prisoners' Fund*; but S.L. subscriptions dwindled from April 1933 as unemployed members increased. In September 1933, two concerts were arranged to aid Head Office funds, and a register of members began. Whist drives provided most of the funds for the upkeep of Westfield Hall: 'When the I.L.P. split off from the Labour Party, the branch was nearly equally divided, and as most of the Trustees of the Hall – an I.L.P. Hall – refused to leave the Party, some of those responsible for the purchase and running of the Hall formed themselves into an S.L. branch, the Hall being treated as the joint property of the I.L.P. and S.L. The I.L.P. claimed the property, but took no legal action, so the Hall was run by a joint committee of management… surprisingly the arrangement worked fairly well!'[ii]

At the April 1934 Cripps' meeting, there was a 6d delegation fee, but unemployed S.L. members acted as stewards and were supplied with free tickets. 14/6d went to the *Austrian Workers' Fund* (at the Labour Party Conference 1934, the N.E.C. proscribed *the Relief Committee for Victims of German and Austrian Fascism* as a C.P. front organisation and proposed to expel any party members who had connection with it). To improve the financial position it was agreed that 'either a Social Evening or a Concert should be held on a Thursday evening once a month'.[iii] Special efforts were made to raise money to send two delegates to the Leeds S.L. Conference. The difficulty was that, by May 1934, the *majority* of S.L. members were unemployed.[iv] The branch made a great effort to sell pamphlets (especially *Forward to Socialism* and *The Choice for Britain*) and the *Socialist Leaguer* at the Northumberland and Durham Miners' Galas in July.[v] It was the Gateshead S.L. branch which suggested a membership application form on a business paid postcard to be attached to the back cover of S.L. pamphlets on July 26th, 1934.[vi] 21/- was sent to Head Office's Pamphlet Fund in October 1934 and 21/- to the Election Fund; 7/4d was made on pamphlet selling at the Durham Gala, and 9/5d at Mellor's Conference. But, by December 1934, sales of the *Socialist Leaguer* were decreasing,[vii] and the S.L.'s band had to sell some of its instruments for £13,[viii] although the proposed sale of the billiard table, agreed by the Management Committee, was turned down by the I.L.P.!

Meanwhile, in February, a circular from Head Office requested subscriptions to the Special Effort Fund, and a campaign for mass membership – at a time when the Gateshead funds were diminishing, as was its membership. Head Office considerations took priority. In March 1935, there was some friction between the I.L.P. and the S.L. Some I.L.P. members objected to posters (other than those dealing with I.L.P. or S.L. matters) being displayed in the windows of Westfield Hall. They also asked for £5 from Hall Funds to send delegates to an Easter I.L.P. Conference,

---

[i] Ibid., April 20th, 1932.

[ii] R. Dodds' letter to the writer, July 18th, 1970.

[iii] R. Dodds' Executive Committee Minutes, March 8th, 1934; D. Powell, op. cit., 1998, p.191

[iv] 'A London Diary', *New Statesman and Nation*, May 26th, 1934.

[v] *Socialist Leaguer*, No. 2, July–August 1934.

[vi] Implemented by the S.L. National Council, December 21st, 1934, Caxton Hall, Westminster.

[vii] Copies of the *Socialist Leaguer* were costing 4/6 per month, but regular sales were only 3/2d. (February 20th, 1935, Dodds E.C.M.)

[viii] Proceeds were divided between the I.L.P. and the S.L. – it had been an I.L.P. band.

and another row arose over closing the billiard room.[i] The I.L.P. was a smaller group at this time, held its own meetings at Westfield, and was less involved locally than the S.L. branch, but they joined together in drama productions. In May 1935, a £1 donation was sent to Head Office and 5/- to the E. F. Wise Fund (for better relations with Russia). The financial report in July 1935 stated the balance on May 9th as £8.6s.6d. and with subscriptions, total income was £11.6s.10d. Expenditure consisted of the £1 donation to Head Office, the 5/- donation to the E. F. Wise Fund, £2.18s.6d. for a delegate to the Bristol S.L. Conference, municipal elections (£1.16s.0d.), advertisements in the *Gateshead Herald* (11/-), a donation to the local Party (10/-) and affiliation fees for the N.C.L.C. (5/-). Ways and means of raising funds were discussed, and it was agreed to set aside 2/- out of every £1 to send an extra delegate to the Annual S.L. Conference.[ii] At the Stoke Conference (June 1936), expenses for two Gateshead S.L. delegates were £5.18s.6d. When the conference decided to raise Head Office dues to 4d per member per month, two proposals were put forward to the branch. Either all members should pay 2d per week (except unemployed and League of Youth members, who paid 1d per month) or men should pay 6d per month and women 3d per month. It was agreed to recommend the branch to accept the Head Office scheme.[iii]

When the Gateshead I.L.P. branch decided to split itself in half, the funds were divided equally between the affiliationist and disaffiliationist members of the branch. Prominent I.L.P. members had always been in the forefront of Party activities in the borough, and it was an indication of the trend of thought in the branch that 4 out of 5 members on the Town Council group decided to remain with the Labour Party through the S.L.[iv] A research group soon began work on finances, housing and the health services in Gateshead, and a Study Circle (meeting on Thursdays fortnightly) was formed. At the North East Area Conference, with Sir C. Trevelyan and E. F. Wise as main speakers (December 10th, 1932), 'all came away from the conference firmly convinced of the great part that the S.L. is going to play in Labour politics'.[v] Two circulars were received on general organisation and on a Labour Doomsday (local surveys of industrial and social conditions) in January 1933. The Secretary of the branch wrote to Head Office and to the local Labour party asking what could be done in local propaganda by the S.L. Newcastle and Gateshead S.L. branches decided to have joint forum meetings. The object was to keep people interested and 'stir their minds', while the S.L. branch worked closely with the local party and trades council (4 S.L. members were on the local Party executive committee). Head Office exaggerated the 'programme of activities' achieved by the Gateshead branch,[vi] but social service work was begun, constituting child welfare and school clinics, rents, pension rights, legal cases, debts, and putting people in touch with councillors and local MPs.

The operation of the Means Test had 'saved' £15 million per year at the expense of the unemployed, and public works and housing schemes of £75 million had been abandoned.[vii] The S.L. had issued its first 6 lecture series of pamphlets for Study Circles by March 1933, and the Gateshead branch inaugurated a new method of

---

[i] R. Dodds' Executive Committee Minutes, March 28th, 1935.
[ii] R. Dodds, ibid., December 5th, 1935.
[iii] Ibid., July 23rd, 1936.
[iv] S.L. Notes, *New Clarion*, October 15th, 1932.
[v] S.L. Notes, *New Clarion*, December 17th, 1932.
[vi] S.L. Notes, *New Clarion*, January 28th, 1933.
[vii] Cf. 'The Doctors', *Gateshead Herald*, January 1933.

propaganda to be repeated – a play on a local theme, with reference to local conditions.[i] Another feature of the branch's activities was an illustrated lecture by a specialist. (In 1933, Krishna Menon lectured on oppressions in India.) Discussion meetings were held fortnightly and provided 'keenly argued verbal encounters'.[ii] The first of such debates on March 23rd, 1933 had the intriguingly ambiguous title: 'A Dictatorship Is Necessary in the Event of Socialists Obtaining Power, but it Must Be a Democratic Socialist Dictatorship'![iii] Discuss?

In March 1933, the branch was working on G. D. H. Cole's *'Plan for Britain'* in which he explained that a planned economy under capitalism was a contradiction in terms: 'It is fantastic to suppose that such a balance between consuming power and productive capacity could possibly be secured except under a completely Socialist system'.[iv] Glyn Evans gave a talk on *'The Challenge of the S.L.'* Rural propaganda was organised, there was a large collection of film slides for Winter lectures, a propagandist play and a Debating Team Contest.[v] In the May Day Demonstration, the Gateshead S.L. presented a tableau of the 'Sick World' lying in bed, dosed by the nostrums of 'Dr. Capitalism', and refusing the cure offered by 'Socialism' and 'Enough for All'![vi] The two S.L. pamphlets, *Is Woman's Place in the Home?* and *Local Government and the Socialist Plan*, were relevant to the branch, and sales of them were substantial.[vii] The S.L. winter propaganda in Gateshead was kept as varied as possible by Forum Lectures, Debates, Addresses, illustrated by dramatic shows and lantern slides.[viii] In June 1933 there was an open meeting on 'Our Challenge to Capitalism'; in July an open debate on 'Can Gateshead Afford More Homes?', and an address by R. Butchart on 'Shorter Hours in the Distributive Trades'. At the August Durham Miners' Gala, Cripps criticised the Government, which had decided to inquire from every man under the Means Test whether he was paying less than 5/- per week rent, and if he was, to deduct the difference from his transitional benefits! Yet the Government was giving £5½ million to certain bond holders, and this was hailed in the City as 'a splendid gesture, indicative of Britain's determination to maintain the spirit of its obligations to investors at whatever cost'.[ix] Shameful.

In the local branch was instituted a circulating library of pamphlets and books among members. R. H. Tawney's *The Choice Before the Labour Party*, republished in September 1933, had a particular message for an area like Gateshead, with its exposure of disparities of wealth, opportunity, social position and economic power. On September 24th, 1933, J. F. Horrabin opened the first forum meeting at Westfield Hall for national and local speakers to put forward various aspects of a Socialist policy for Britain. Each of these Sunday evening meetings was preceded by half an hour of gramophone records, and this cultural emphasis was extended when the S.L. branch took 34 adults and some children for an outing to the home of Sir Charles Trevelyan

---

[i] *Gateshead Herald*, March 1933.

[ii] Ibid.

[iii] Ibid.

[iv] *Gateshead Herald*, April 1933.

[v] *New Clarion*, April 29th, 1933.

[vi] *Gateshead Herald*, May 1933.

[vii] Ibid.

[viii] R. Dodds' Executive Committee Minutes, June 8th, 1933.

[ix] Quoted in 'Durham Miners' Gala', *Gateshead Herald*, August 1933.

'to get away from streets and factories, pits and offices, and the toil of domestic life.'[i] What was thought of Sir Charles' home was not recorded in the Minutes! In the October local elections, the S.L. branch combined with the local Labour party and trades council to denounce the fact that 800 Gateshead families were on Public Assistance owing to unemployment benefit stoppages, when there could be full-time work on the clearance of Gateshead slums. There were lectures on 'Pensions at Sixty', 'The Evolution of Public Cleansing' and 'Town Planning' in January 1934, and the S.L. began organising the unemployed in trade and local clubs. In March there were further lectures by Donald Barber on 'The Co-operative Movement's Opportunity', Sir C. Trevelyan on 'The Work of Socialists in Austria Against Fascism', Constance Borrett on 'The Rise of Fascism' and J. F. Horrabin on 'The Class Struggle'[ii] – all at Westfield Hall.

A Speakers' Class was begun in March 1934. The branch brought forward a group of young Socialists to speak and chair at meetings, and to conduct a piece of detailed research into the condition of Gateshead. During the urban and county council elections, S.L. members were busy assisting, and were successful in securing the election of a number of its members. S.L. speakers were addressing Labour parties, unions and Co-operative Guild meetings, and 'placing before them the need for a strong Socialist policy'.[iii] There were inter-branch demonstrations to strengthen the S.L.'s influence in the Northeast, and Gateshead S.L. organised a representative conference of delegates and members from unions, Co-operative Societies and local parties addressed by Cripps.[iv] By July 1934, the local Labour League of Youth had increased its membership by 50%, and the S.L. branch took a close interest in its activities and supplied speakers for its meetings (cf. Mr. Barron on 'The Socialists' Position in the Event of a War', and Councillor F. Campbell on 'Arguments for and against Socialism').[v]

During the Summer of 1934, the S.L. membership in Gateshead diminished from 113 members to 87, despite the fact that the S.L. had published Forward to Socialism and had begun a regional forum lecture series again. S.L. membership fell to 69 members by February 1935, which suggests that disappointments of local branches expressed at the Leeds S.L. Conference were not transitory, and that initial fervour had diminished. The only significant lecture between June and December 1934 was a visit by W. Mellor to speak on 'An Economic Policy for a Socialist Government' and an inquiry by him (at the same all-day conference on September 23rd) on 'Must There Be Revolution by Force?'[vi] although in October there were locally relevant debates at Westfield Hall on 'Labour's Job in Local Government', 'Some Impressions of a Short Holiday in Soviet Russia' and 'Education and the Child'. The S.L. branch invited the League of Youth to a social with the object of promoting friendly intercourse between members of the two organisations.[vii] The S.L.'s national conference (November 25th, 1934) which decided the time for research and policy reports had to be made subsidiary to 'day-to-day struggles' was only a reflection of the activities of S.L. branches since their inception. Nevertheless, there were signs of increased activity, expressed in the Gateshead Herald's headline: 'What Does the S.L. Stand For? – Helping the Workers – Strengthening the

---

[i] Mrs. Barrass, Gateshead Herald, September 1933.

[ii] Gateshead Herald, March 1934.

[iii] Socialist Leaguer, No. 1, June–July 1934.

[iv] Ibid.

[v] Ibid.

[vi] Socialist Leaguer, No.2, August 1934. See p.193 for membership fluctuations.

[vii] Socialist Leaguer, No. 7, December 1934.

Labour Party!'[i] and an appeal by F. Campbell (a local S.L.'er) to 'rouse the conscience of the masses at street corners' because the task of Labour's election machine would be eased if there was an 'intensive outdoor campaign'.[ii]

In practice, there were no dramatic changes in policy or activities. At the 3rd Annual Aggregate Tyneside Conference (January 26th, 1935) G. R. Mitchison addressed the members on the purposes of the S.L. and 'its work in the advancement of Socialism',[iii] and the next day he spoke at Westfield Hall on 'The First Few Months of a Socialist Government', a subject dear to the heart of the S.L. In February, the S.L. joined in the huge Gateshead demonstration for the repeal of the Unemployment Act and Cripps came to Newcastle (February 17th) to talk about the profit motive restricting production and raising prices.[iv] Throughout March, the S.L. branch in Gateshead was heavily involved in demonstrations and lectures on unemployment and U.A.B. regulations. A vigilance committee was set up to investigate cases of hardship and to help applicants who had no other organisations to assist them;[v] there were discussion meetings at Westfield Hall in favour of industrial unions and schemes to keep the unemployed inside unions. The other major fear – war – filtered through to the Gateshead branch, but it remained a secondary consideration to the practical problem of large-scale unemployment. Head Office sent a circular urging the local branch to secure three books which incorporated S.L. policies: Problems of a Socialist Government, Problems of the Socialist Transition and Cripps' Why This Socialism? Two copies were ordered by the Literature Secretary.[vi]

The S.L.'s 'Mass Resistance to War' Conference at the Co-operative Hall, Gateshead, was duly attended by S.L. members, but it was seen as merely one of a number of important and immediate issues. The miners' wage campaign, Fascism in Germany; Abyssinia; Unification of the Labour Movement on Tyneside; the Soviet Union's achievements, and the problem of dictatorship – all were debated at Westfield Hall between September and December 1935, although there were no executive committee meetings to discuss tactics during the municipal and general elections during this time. Perhaps the first three months of 1936 show the hopes which the S.L. Conference of November 25th, 1934 had expressed. There were more discussions on local affairs than ever before, ranging from 'Gateshead's Open Spaces' to 'Our Health Services', and 'Gateshead's Rates', and the production of four short plays on local problems. A series of S.L. Conferences in the Northeast (with C. Borrett, W. Mellor, R. Butchart, W. Monslow and L. A. Fenn as speakers) did result in the formation of new S.L. branches and an increase in membership, even in the Gateshead branch,[vii] and the sales of the Socialist substantially increased by May 1936[viii] in Gateshead.

At a Gateshead Labour Party and Trades Council demonstration on June 28th, 1936, W. Mellor linked the themes of unemployment and war, which dominated S.L. branch activities in 1936. He analysed the causes of war and poverty as basically the same; no Government 'based on exploitation' could bring 'peace', there could only be

---

[i] Socialist Leaguer, No.8, January 1935.
[ii] Ibid.
[iii] Socialist Leaguer, No. 9, February 1935.
[iv] S.L. Notes, Gateshead Herald, March 1935.
[v] Ibid., April 1935.
[vi] R. Dodds' Executive Committee Minutes, July 25th, 1935.
[vii] Up to 80 members by July 23rd, 1936, Jarrow: The Glory of Private Enterprise.
[viii] Socialist, No. 7, May 1936.

collective insecurity caused by 'greedy nationalism': 'The biggest thing we could do for 'peace' is to reverse the motive of industry, uphold the doctrine of service instead of personal profit, and bring in co-operative development instead of competitive exploitation, to spend more on the needs of the people: 'When Britain and the British Empire establish a system of economic justice… as the peoples of Russia are doing, in their own way, …[he believed] then the world could get rid of the fear of war.'[i] The Gateshead S.L. believed Jarrow was being sacrificed 'to the greed and narrow-mindedness of iron and steel employers'.[ii] Hence it demanded further agitation to abolish the Means Test and the march on August 31st in the Mass Demonstration to Newcastle. This was linked to the 'People's Front' and the need to join local unions, the N.U.W.M., local sections of the Labour Party or the S.L.[iii]

By October, the North East had become the main centre of S.L. activity on the unemployment issue, and Spain.[iv] The Means Test was seen as the visible sign of the inability to distribute the wealth that could be produced, and the local S.L. had another battle with the Ratepayers' Association; the call for unity in the Labour Movement strengthened locally when the local Labour Party narrowly held its majority on the Council. Unity would 'defeat reaction locally, would bring into politics a new energy that is so sadly lacking.'[v] 'On the greatest issues of our age, the Labour Movement … is giving no lead to the masses … the Movement is faced, during a year which should be one of active campaigning, with a resolution on war and armaments which was ambiguous,[vi] commented an S.L. member, A. Austen.

It was fairly easy for the S.L. to join with the I.L.P. and Communist Party in the Unity Campaign in Gateshead. The tradition of unity in unemployment battles helped; there were soon joint meetings at Westfield Hall showing films on 'Russia' (January 24th, 1937) and 'Spain' (February 7th, 1937) and a play on 'The United Front' (January 17th). On March 11th there was a full-scale Unity meeting of 60 delegates from union branches, local Labour parties, the Labour League of Youth, the Co-operative Party, the S.L., I.L.P. and C.P.S. at Westfield Hall; on March 21st a mass Unity meeting in Newcastle with G. R. Strauss, W. Gallagher and J. Maxton speaking on the *same* platform! The S.L.'s head office continued to publish exaggerated reports of the Gateshead S.L.'s 'extension of S.L. propaganda' and 'fast recruiting campaign',[vii] when the S.L. had become engulfed in Unity demonstrations and would not be allowed to emerge again. Instead, attention focussed on the constituency parties: 'The day of large-scale political bodies affiliated to the Labour Party had gone.'[viii] There was still room and need for local S.L. research, education and publishing activities, but these tasks could now be fulfilled, it was believed, by local parties who could cement the political and industrial sides of the Movement and nurture the interest of union branches in political decisions more successfully than the isolated attempts of S.L. branches. Unfortunately, it did not work out like that. The overworked local party officers had neither the time nor the commitment to political agitation on national matters. S.L. local branches *had* served a

[i] Quoted in *Gateshead Herald*, July 1936.

[ii] Ibid.

[iii] Allan Henderson, 'The Need for a People's Front', *Gateshead Herald*, August 1936.

[iv] S.L. Notes, *Socialist*, No. 12, November 1936.

[v] *Gateshead Herald*, November 1936.

[vi] A. Austen, ibid., 'A Lead for Democracy', December 1936.

[vii] *Socialist Broadsheet*, No. 2, April 1937.

[viii] A. Austen, *New Life in the Constituency Parties*, June 1937.

particular function, which could never quite be duplicated, because of their uniquely independent position which they held for this short while in the 1930s.

What was that particular mood in the S.L. local branch in those years? Ruth Dodds described the feelings in an article called *Heartbreak Hall: A Farewell*[i] which expressed the fervours and disillusionments at Westfield Hall during the S.L.'s existence. She typifies the passionate commitment of a Socialist League branch member: 'I was walking the city streets in a mystical rapture, my heart whispering: "You are a Socialist; all men are your brothers." My badge gave me a strange secret joy; it marked me out as one of the chosen people who were going to banish poverty from this world. It was childish, but it was immense… selling literature to indifferent and hard-fisted passers-by, canvassing in an agony of shyness, and bursting with convincing arguments that would not turn into coherent speech … "Heartbreak Hall" was the place where people let you down, and you let other people down, where you were accused of officiousness if you tried to be helpful, and of slackness if you tactfully stood aside. Brutality was called frankness, uncontrolled temper passed as positive proof of honesty… gentleness was weakness, common politeness flattery, and a tendency to be kind an attempt to corrupt the stark manliness of higher natures. Sentiment was, however, freely resorted to, in the tiresome form of boasting of past service and reproaching other people for not doing so much … this whirl of accusation and counter-accusation was largely a matter of convention. Hard words were very often mere jargon. People who were really doing work of importance together were bound to reach a degree of mutual trust. As unemployment or the fear of losing a precious job more and more corroded the bodies and minds of the members, so the atmosphere at Heartbreak Hall became increasingly bitter. For the Hall stood in a dying industrial area, and all hopes were fixed on the good days that never came back. To look forward to a Socialist future became harder as that future seemed to become more and more distant. It was in good times that workers were most militant, and in bad that their dissensions became most distressing, because a man embittered by suffering turns and hits someone near… Only the most determined could persevere. Our main troubles were simply abominable bad temper and bad manners, and a love of a row for its own sake… It was politics under the most severe conditions, and under the most depressing circumstances. Did any good come of it, of all those years of effort, exaltation, exasperation and dogged "sticking-in"? We did not achieve what we set out for, a more just social order, but we helped to bring new sanitation, new schools, new libraries, new clinics, new playing-fields, several thousands of new houses built and a number of unsavoury slums abolished… Our aspirations soared to the stars, but our problems were of dustbins and refuse disposal. Our methods might provoke despair or laughter, but a great deal of good of a simple, homely, solid kind has come from all the tribulations of Heartbreak Hall.' This energy and commitment contrasted with a Labour establishment which compromised its socialist principles:[ii]

> People tend to see the stubble fields of transitoriness but overlook and forget the full granaries of the past into which they have brought the harvest of their lives: the deeds done, the loves loved, and… the sufferings they have gone through with courage and dignity.[iii]

---

[i] Article given to the writer, September 1970.

[ii] D. Powell, op. cit., 1998, p.13.

[iii] Victor E. Frankl, *Man's Search For Meaning*, 2004, p.151.

Chapter Seven

The Socialist League and the Labour Party

The mixture of 'minor public school morality', Methodist unction and technocratic busy-bodying served as the well-springs of Labour activism.

Isaiah Berlin, qu. in *A Life of Isaiah Berlin,* Michael Ignatieff, 1998, p.196.

Politicians belong to that special class of liar who seem to be genuinely unable to discriminate between special pleading, the suppression of material evidence and outright falsification of the record... Habituated by decades of party conferences and parliamentary party jockeyings to take decisions, not in terms of any fixity of principle, but upon an estimation of block votes to be garnered, of the balance upon the right and the left of the party and the proper quantum of ambiguity which may propel a compromise through the centre...

E. P. Thompson, *Writing By Candlelight,* 1980, p.56
qu. in *New Society* 29/07/1971

Robert Michels in *'Political Parties'* states there is always a rather small number of persons in the organisation who actually make decisions and the leader becomes less concerned with the interests of the rank and file or the ideology of the party and more concerned with staying in office. Leaders become conservative, they want to preserve their organisation and not jeopardise it on risky ventures, even if the party's ideals call for it... they have the legitimacy of being the existing leadership, whereas any opponents are labelled 'factions' and 'splitters' who represent only themselves, and who aid the Party's enemies by creating internal dissension. The united leadership can wield power out of all proportion to its numbers because it controls the material and ideological resources of the organisation... the dispersion of power away from the membership, and into the hands of the leaders who control the administrative apparatus occurs in many formally democratic organizations.

R. Collins and M. Makowsky, eds, *The Discovery of Society,* 1993, pp.222–24.

Working through established institutions and modifying them to meet social needs (when clearly proven) was exhibited by the Labour Movement in the 1930s, but it is one of the peculiarities of inter-war history that the Movement suffered from the loss of buoyancy and self-confidence which followed from Britain's decline as a world power, results of the First World War, and the twin phenomena of economic growth and crisis which ran parallel. The resultant urge to 'play safe' favoured the Conservatives, as did decline in idealistic and religious beliefs: '...periods of religious vigour are likely to be periods of political radicalism, periods of religious quiescence of political conservatism'.[i] However, the emergence of Bolshevism as a world force challenged the Labour Movement fundamentally.

---

[i] T. Wilson, *The Downfall of the Liberal Party,* 1966, pp.388–89.

It was difficult to work in a Parliamentary system which a 'Socialist' Soviet Union denounced as 'corrupt', and yet maintain the Labour Movement's objective 'to transform this Capitalist system of exploitation into one of co-operation'.[i] The statement sounded hollow, yet the strength of the Movement's argument was based on a moral critique of an inegalitarian society. At the level of local organisation, the working-class movement had been nourished by religious nonconformity, self-reliance and endurance – essential qualities to survive in the 1930s. Lansbury, Party leader (1931–35), thought in a Christian moral vein about politics: 'Multitudes of people do not understand the foulness of the present system of competitive strife for security and food...[ii] 'We spend many millions (of pounds) providing prisons, mental institutions, hospitals, and health services for dealing with preventable crime, sickness and insanity ... we should take the necessary measures to ensure that everything is done to prevent such evils arising.'[iii] Such 'evils' *were* rising, however.

In the 1930s, the Labour Party was working towards integration of a competitive capitalist system with State ownership and regulation, an economy comprising, with a variety of degree and method, direct State control, public and semi-public concerns, and private enterprise. However, the Labour Movement was also comprised of local councillors, union officials, Co-operative Society members, with no unified political perspective except recognising the conventions of constitutional government. The S.L. held the conviction that Socialism could only be established by 'united action of the entire working-class movement', the Labour Party and unions being 'necessary rallying points' in the political and industrial fields. So the S.L. urged (in its Constitution) all its members to take an active part in the work of the Party and unions with a view to the adoption by both of 'a definitely Socialist attitude and policy'.[iv] The Party's Annual Conference was supposed to give the rank and file a chance to initiate policy; in practice, it was largely restricted to ratification of resolutions approved by the Party Executive, supported by union block votes.[v] The Executive directed the Party organisations between Conferences, and exerted an influence on every subject before the Conference;[vi] it interpreted the Party Constitution, the Standing Orders and the Rules, conferred with the Parliamentary Labour Party (P.L.P.), proposed resolutions, endorsed Party candidates, supervised Party machinery, and made recommendations on organisation, policy and Party objectives. The National Council of Labour (composed of the T.U.C. General Council, Party Executive, and the P.L.P. Executive Committee) agreed on a common policy on international issues and home affairs. To maintain 'internal harmony', declarations made by the N.C.L. had to be followed,[vii] and unions increased their external control over the P.L.P. through the N.C.L.,[viii] where an increasing number of important decisions were made.[ix]

In 1928, H. Dalton had sensed the caution and anti-Leftism in the P.L.P. which mirrored the General Council's inclination towards industrial peace and agreements

---

[i] G. Lansbury, *My England*, 1934, p.11.

[ii] Ibid., p.15.

[iii] Ibid., p.55.

[iv] S.L. Constitution (October 1st, 1932) quoting G. D. H. Cole, *A Study Guide on Socialist Policy*, August 1933.

[v] D. McHenry, op. cit., p.30.

[vi] Ibid., p.36.

[vii] Ibid., p.43.

[viii] Ibid., pp.162–180.

[ix] Ibid., pp.280–297.

with employers: 'There is a distinct danger of courage evaporating'.[i] The Mond-Turner talks were just one feature which implied, to Labour militants, 'vote-fodder for the projection of Mondism'[ii] on to politics. Labour policy was not determined by individual members who carried out the Party's work, nor by divisional parties (which included union branches), but by block vote of large unions: 'In an organisation without democracy, minorities feel frustrated, cannot adjust themselves, and always tend to be driven out'.[iii] Together, Parliamentary leaders, professional organisation and union official had control over the policy and activity of the Party, maintained by the appeal to 'loyalty', and the natural inertia of the mass Movement: 'Neither the working classes nor their leaders deserted their pragmatic and conservative traditions'.[iv]

What did *'democracy'* entail to leaders of the Labour Movement? 'Democracy' meant, on the practical level, free elections, a free Press, freedom of political association, freedom of thought and speech; equality before the law, the right to oppose the government, to move freely within one's country, to develop one's mental and moral faculties to the fullest.[v] Labour leaders adhered to Parliamentary practice, rational empiricism, emphasis on the individual, an instrumental theory of the State interfering when voluntary efforts failed; voluntary association in political parties, unions and employers' associations, the law behind the State, emphasis on means (not ends), discussion and consent, a basic equality of opportunity.[vi] In this 'Socialism' would be the outcome of the fruition of democracy, through the inevitability of gradualness. A.N. Whitehead summarised this in 1935: 'The essence of freedom is the practicability of purpose'.[vii] Labour leaders, influenced by the Webbs, believed in democratic institutions and tended to neglect the rôle of the *working class* in the contest for political power.[viii] However, the S.L.'s stance was that 'freedom' was the prerogative of the property-owning classes, and what use was 'freedom from coercion' to a starving man? What use were 'democratic values' when the organisation through which you were working seemed undemocratic or unrepresentative? (A. Bevan put it: 'If you get selection from above you always get the Yes-men'.)[ix] The fact was that leaders of the Movement saw Socialism as any *device* whose aim was to save individuals from the difficulties or hardships of the struggle for existence by the intervention of the State, a concept of *welfare economics without an ideology*. This was thrashed out by C. R. Attlee, H. Morrison, H. Dalton and E. Bevin, in an identification of interest between organised industrial labour and pragmatic Labourism by the mid-1930s.

The rank and file of the Movement were the losers; the moral tradition of the working-class Movement, with emphasis on local democracy, local participation, setting of human above economic standards,[x] this tradition found its main political instrument, a weak Labour Party, dominated by economic pragmatists and Parliamentarians. Hence, most Labour leaders were as outraged by Cripps' provocative

---

[i] H. Dalton, *Call Back Yesterday*, 1953, p.171.

[ii] A. Hutt, *British Trade Unionism*, revised edition 1962, p.122.

[iii] F. Brockway, op. cit., pp.345–346.

[iv] A. Marwick, *Britain in the Age of Total War*, p.143.

[v] W. Ebenstein, op. cit., pp.139–140.

[vi] Ibid., pp.142–150.

[vii] A. N. Whitehead, *Adventures of Ideas, 1935, p.84*.

[viii] D. Powell, op. cit., 1998, p.53.

[ix] Quoting M. Foot, *A. Bevan*, January 31st, 1937, Vol. 1, p.247.

[x] R. Williams, 'The British Left', p.24, *New Left Review*, March–April 1965.

speeches as were Liberals and Conservatives.[i] From the S.L.'s viewpoint, the apparatus of 'social democracy' and the huge union machine were in danger of becoming part of the machinery of capitalism.[ii] Defeat of the 1929–1931 Labour Government highlighted, in the Party, conflicts of personality and ideology. It began a debate which involved a series of disputes and dissensions in the Party conducted against a background of international crisis and political frustrations. There were three stages to this struggle: the period of programme-making, controversy about Labour's attitude to international aggression (which brought a re-examination of its pacifist tradition), and internal struggle over policy (the Party's relationship to the C.P. and the problem of affiliated organisations). Michael Foot addressed the immensity of this confrontation; there has been nothing comparable to the agony that the Labour Movement had to endure after 1931.'[iii] It was five years of agony and angst for the S.L.

The Labour Movement was in a confused state including the Labour intellectual who 'had a not-quite paralysing capacity for seeing seven sides to every question and foreseeing all the dangers of any course of action'.[iv] There was a distaste for any prolonged theoretical discussions in the Party, but the S.L. was prepared to work within the Party, however unpalatable were official policies, because influence in one section of the Movement implied influence in another and the 1930s called for 'moral courage and intellectual honesty'[v] (a great deal of the propagandist activity in the Labour Party was in the hands of radicals who had to bear the brunt of criticism about 'morality' and 'intellectual honesty'. It has been estimated that one third of the 'active' members in the 1930s were favourable to 'radical policies',[vi] whatever that implied). S.L. influence was there, but remained in traditionally militant areas, for the amount of new recruits was negligible. The S.L. was simply unacceptable to the average Party and union member, and it did not matter how well organised it was, it could not control *any* section of the Movement, even though it was an educational driving force. It was always a 3,000 minority, so that whenever there was a clash between this minority and Party leaders, the minority always lost *in the end* and became more fragmented. By 1940, no separate group remained in the Party with its own machinery, leaders or policies, and any experiment in inner-Party democracy had been abandoned.

Yet, as seen in relations between the Party and the S.L., the Movement was unable to continue campaigns, widen its support or maintain its strength *without* Labour Left members, and S.L. activities exposed the failure of the collective leadership of the Movement, which was unsuited to the type of *protest campaign* required in the 1930s. In this activity the S.L. excelled. However, in the whole country, if the Labour Party had espoused a Socialist society, on S.L. lines, the country would have rallied to the defence of the Government because 'the majority of people had no wish for "extreme" political doctrines to be put into practice'.[vii] The S.L. discovered this aspect of British society for themselves. (Lansbury bluntly added: 'People who desire Capitalism to prosper do not employ Socialists to carry on their policy'.)[viii]

---

[i] E. Estorick, op. cit., p.126.
[ii] J. Strachey, *The Coming Struggle for Power*, 1932, p.333.
[iii] M. Foot, 'Credo of the Labour Left', p.20, *New Left Review*, May–June 1968.
[iv] K. Martin, *The Editor (1931–45)*, pp. 4–6, 1968.
[v] Robert Briffault, *Breakdown (The Collapse of Traditional Civilisation)*, 1935, p.288.
[vi] J. Jupp, op. cit., p.562.
[vii] H. W. J. Edwards, op. cit., p.72.
[viii] G. Lansbury, *My England*, 1934, p.146.

The message from the S.L. was that the Labour Movement had to learn the lesson from German and Austrian events; compromise and subordination of Socialist purpose and practice to electoral and tactical calculations would end in defeat, because Fascism fed on the caution and respectability of the Labour and Trade Union Movement. Hence the S.L.'s frustrations, directed against the dilution of Socialist purposes, so the refrain was: 'Are the Labour Party and Trade Union Movements wedded to mere reformism, to mere craving for office?'[i] Was social justice and economic growth compatible? Was it true that 'critics on the Right felt themselves too practical for Socialism, critics on the Left too Socialist for practicality'?[ii] The Labour Left believed fear of expressing unorthodox views crippled Labour leaders: 'A mighty tide of emotion and anger and exhilaration was swelling in the distressed areas, on the hunger marches, at the Unity demonstrations, at the universities, in the Left Book Clubs, in literature and in the very spirit of the age... to lap in vain against the locked doors of Transport House... A great gulf seemed to be fixed between the politics of the streets and the politics of the Westminster committee rooms.'[iii] The gulf was epitomised between Labour and S.L. leaders.

(A) S.L. Leaders and Labour Party Leaders

In 1918, the Labour Party proclaimed four demands: a minimum standard of living; socialisation of the means of production; the capital levy and taxation on ability to pay; and surplus wealth for the common good. What mattered were principles as the basis of social organisation, economic activity to be treated as functional, tested by its relation to social purpose.[iv] The Party's *Labour and the Nation* (1928) was an amorphous expression of Socialist ideals, but the Election manifesto of 1929 contained an unqualified pledge that Labour would deal with the major problem – unemployment. J. T. Murphy deemed that *Labour and the Nation* contained no analysis of the 'crisis of capitalism', but merely claimed trade would improve through increased spending power and the scientific organisation of industry.[v] Both *Labour and the New Social Order* (1918) and *Labour and the Nation* (1928) had been statements of objectives which did not commit a Government to anything precise, in the S.L.'s assessment.

To Labour leaders in 1931, opposition meant a presentation of their case in the Commons, and a practical programme to be offered at the next Election. The main criticism by S.L. leaders (of the 1929–1931 Government) was that the crisis failed to propel Labour's leaders into offering an audacious solution.[vi] Instead, the Party was to be the principal agent of the absorption of the working-class movement into the liberal, democratic order, *its institutionalisation into the status quo*. Here was a Party of disparate groups weakened by mutual suspicions which governed the relationship between political and industrial wings, unionists, Parliamentarians, propagandist crusaders, and intellectuals. The Party credo included Socialism, reformism, Utopian

---

[i] Editorial, 'Socialist Democracy – Forward to Socialism', *Socialist Leaguer*, No. 1, June–July 1934.
[ii] R. W. Lyman, *The First Labour Government*, op. cit.
[iii] M. Foot, *Biography of A. Bevan*, op. cit. p.248.
[iv] Cf. The main theme of R. H. Tawney, *The Acquisitive Society*, 1921.
[v] J. T. Murphy, *Preparing for Power*, 1934, p.247.
[vi] Fenner Brockway, op. cit., pp.222–239.

idealism, and 'sound financial orthodoxy' but solving the economic difficulties was unoriginal and ineffective. Instead of a rallying of the ranks and a major campaign uniting the Movement, the Labour Party retreated. Not surprisingly, faced with a choice between the sectional interests of Labour and the interests of 'Government and the economy', they were unable to opt for the former; the philosophy of Labour leaders remained a defence of the status quo, yet '…the slump meant the moment of truth for social democracy, presenting a choice of revolution or reform'.[i] Labour leaders in 1929–1931 held to orthodox economics. The crisis of 1931 was a question of priorities, and the Party's hopes of distributing some of the surplus economic growth could not function in a slump (when cuts had to be made). At such a time, the capitalist system needed *'confidence'* (that irrational ingredient of every capitalist economy) and Labour was vulnerable to the accusation that it commanded less confidence by the businessman 'than his own businessman's Government'.[ii] The irony was that economies which MacDonald went to such efforts to institute (to persuade New York bankers that Britain was 'credit-worthy') would scarcely have financed for a single day the War from 1939 (and continued for over five years without reducing the country to bankruptcy)!

In December 1930[iii], Cripps announced Labour's refusal to countenance cheeseparing economies in social services or unemployment grants, and praised Government achievements in making useful public works with a sympathetic treatment of the unemployed, and minimising 'hardship and suffering', although progress was slow (because of the Lords' veto and the Party's minority position in Parliament.)[iv] The gist of his argument was that the world could not exchange the goods produced, nor give to those whom it could not employ enough money on which to live; capitalism had 'broken down'; somehow the Labour Party would have to 'eliminate' the 'privileged classes' and industry for private profit; the next Labour Government would have to control 'sources of finance and trade'; the crisis was a struggle between workers and capitalists.[v] However, the Government had gone so far that it had become an instrument for doing disagreeable work for the Conservative Party, and Labour remained a constitutional, reformist party, choosing leaders of the same empirical, constitutional mind, final proof of MacDonald's influence in the Movement.[vi] Tom Mann asserted that MacDonald had long ago exchanged his socialist principles for membership of the finest club in Europe[vii] and the description of MacDonald, as expressed by G. Lansbury, suited the Labour Left's mood in 1932: 'J. R. M. is a terrible mixture of vanity, cowardice and utter lack of principle. He is like a rudderless vessel, just drifts … He never could have believed in civil liberty and Socialism. His whole mind is one web of tortuous conservatism; he has no solid rock of conviction anywhere except perhaps a lingering kind of Protestant faith as expounded by

[i] E. Hobsbawm discussing Marquand's *The Dilemma of Gradualism 1929–1931*, Bulletin 21, Society for the Study of Labour History.

[ii] S. Pollard, *The Great Disillusion*, a review of R. Skidelsky's *Politicians and the Slump*, Bulletin 16, Spring 1968, Society for the Study of Labour History.

[iii] S. Cripps to East Bristol Labour Party, December 6th, 1930, Cripps Papers.

[iv] S. Cripps, Speech at Birmingham, July 18th, 1931, Cripps Papers.

[v] *Bristol Times*, September 5th, 1931, Cripps Papers. Also *Bristol Times*, October 1st and October 12th, 1931 & *Western Daily Press*, October 13th, 1931.

[vi] C. L. Mowat, Bulletin 4, Spring 1967, Society for the Study of Labour History.

[vii] D. Powell, op. cit, 1998, p.15.

John Knox.[i] The perfect Labour leader for the twenty-first century? Equally damaging for the S.L.'s relations with Party leaders were MacDonald's 'betrayal', the 'bankers ramp'[ii] and the 'National' Government's attempt to destroy the Labour Party, 'an attack of unprecedented magnitude and unparalleled intensity, a campaign of calumny, misrepresentation, intimidation and appeal to fear and prejudice... their hope was to smash the Labour Party... Never was a political knockout blow more carefully planned or more violently delivered.'[iii]

Labour Party problems were a product of the international situation, and the Government's supine action (in handling unemployment). In a period of financial stringency, a Labour Government was at a disadvantage, and could not expect to recover from the heavy electoral defeat without consequences. The Party faced the Election, unable to shape the issues on which the contest was fought. Once defeated, within the Party was a questioning of its structure, criticisms of 'vague Party programmes'[iv] which 'touched on everything but committed Ministers to nothing';[v] the Party treating votes as equivalent to convictions 'without the painful necessity of clarifying its mind, disciplining its appetites and training for a tough wrestle with established power and property', [vi] as R. H. Tawney concluded. MacDonald, Henderson, Thomas and Snowden had roots in the union movement and local parties and had led the programmes of the Party. Post-1931 leaders, Lansbury, Attlee and Cripps, aided by their mutual hopes for a 'Christian revolution of heart and mind',[vii] were the happiest collaboration that Labour had known at the top.[viii] Lansbury was one of the most engaging figures, eloquent in debate, sentimental, enthusiastic, and subordinated his personal Left-wing convictions to express the Party's moderate opinions: 'his chief work was marshalling Labour's small group in the Commons into an effective Opposition.[ix] He did not play any important part in the revival of Socialist militancy in the Movement, but was by nature an evangelist rather than a Parliamentary tactician,[x] and became the mentor for Cripps' crusading spirit. Lansbury and Cripps were the most garrulous members in the Commons between November 1931 and June 1932. While H. Morrison enthused about Cripps' personal honesty and sincerity,[xi] H. Laski surmised that the next five years would win for Cripps a political reputation 'not less high than that which he has already won in the legal realm';[xii] he appeared 'the rising hope of the Socialist intelligentsia'.[xiii] Cripps was not only outstanding in presenting Labour's case, but was soon depicted as the 'eminence grise', while Lansbury kept within the bounds of Party policy as determined by the P.L.P., the N.E.C., and the N.C.L.

---

[i] G. Lansbury, December 31st, 1932, Lansbury Papers.

[ii] Cf. Cripps, 'The Ramp Against British Banking', *Bristol Times*, October 14th, 1931.

[iii] *Leicester Party Conference Report*, October 1932, p.157. The 'National' Government commanded 554 of 615 MPs, the largest majority ever; Martin Green, op. cit., 2001, p.302.

[iv] Cripps, *Western Daily Press*, November 31st, 1931 (at Redfield, Bristol).

[v] R. H. Tawney, 'The Choice Before the Labour Party', op. cit.

[vi] Ibid.

[vii] E. Estorick, op. cit., p.119.

[viii] M. Foot, *A. Bevan*, op. cit., p.165.

[ix] D. McHenry, op. cit., p.139–160.

[x] C. R. Attlee, *As It Happened*, p.76.

[xi] *Kentish Independent*, February 14th, 1930.

[xii] *Daily Herald*, January 17th, 1931.

[xiii] *Bristol Times*, October 22nd, 1931.

Groping towards new foreign and domestic policies and training a new leadership were the new tasks of the Party: the S.L.'s views were later delineated: 'The trouble in the Party was in the structure and the programme, not in any so-called betrayal of the Party by trusted leaders and the erroneous strategy of taking office without having secured Parliamentary power'.[i] Because the elements composing the Party were miscellaneous, cohesion was indispensable. What a future Labour Government could do depended on what an Opposition could educate its supporters to believe could be achieved. For Cripps, the lesson was to re-state nationalisation proposals but in more detail,[ii] and have political power sufficient to override vested interests in the financial and industrial framework;[iii] 'attempts to patch up the worn-out methods' would be futile,[iv] because neither Free Trade nor Protection policies could accomplish much, when a fundamental reorganisation of the social, political and industrial aspects of society was required.[v] The case for a Socialist society was unanswerable on economic grounds; 'Until we can as a community determine and plan production for the benefit of our consumers, and regulate our finances for the benefit of the State, we shall never be able to bring about stable conditions in our country'.[vi] Dangers in a 'social democracy' had to be explained, to overcome delays in Parliamentary practice; 'with our little band of believers we will do more – because we will keep our faith'.[vii] 'Keep the faith' became the S.L.'s mantra, while Lansbury sought to restore the Party's confidence and turn Labour's Opposition 'into a propaganda meeting', because, 'the Party did not want another Olympian autocrat or a Parliamentarian who could slur over difficulties by wordy formulas'.[viii] The S.L. was a reaction to MacDonaldism.

When the I.L.P. disaffiliated from the Labour Party in 1932, the clash between the Left and Party leaders was in the open. I.L.P. leaders had criticised the Labour Party for denying Socialist members the opportunity to express radical policies without censure;[ix] as Jennie Lee averred: 'The right to speak, vote and agitate for Socialist alternatives is vital ... I shall carry on with Socialist propaganda from platforms where I am free to promise to vote and act in strict accordance with the policy I advocate'.[x] Loyalty was required from any propaganda body inside the Party. This the I.L.P. would not accept, but the S.L. would; the leaders were not as important as the whole Movement, therefore 'there must be an intense idea of *loyalty to the Party* and its ideals':[xi] 'It has always been with the greatest regret that I have observed the tactics of the I.L.P., especially their attacks upon the Labour Party in the House of Commons, and throughout the country which have done a great deal of harm to working-class solidarity,'[xii] espoused Cripps. This comment would backfire later, when used to expel

---

[i] Cf. Cripps at Upminster, March 15th, 1935, Cripps Papers.

[ii] S. Cripps at Edinburgh (opening L.P. drive for 1 million new members), January 18th, 1932, *Daily Herald* (Scottish edition).

[iii] *Bristol Labour Weekly*, September 10th, 1932.

[iv] Cripps, *What Will 1932 Bring Forth?*, January 1932, Cripps Papers.

[v] Cripps, 'The Alternative to Capitalism', *Bristol Labour Weekly*, Februay 13th, 1932 & July 30th, 1932.

[vi] 'Socialism the Only Way', *Bristol Labour Weekly*, Cripps, June 25th, 1932.

[vii] Cripps to Lansbury, January 13th, 1932, Lansbury Papers.

[viii] R. Postgate, op. cit., p.277.

[ix] F. Brockway, 'Why the I.L.P. Has Left the Labour Party', *New Leader*, August 5th, 1932.

[x] Jennie Lee, 'Why Socialists Must Leave the Labour Party', *New Leader*, September 2nd, 1932.

[xi] Cripps at Hampstead, November 26th, 1932, Cripps Papers (a comment subsequently used to expel Cripps from the Party).

[xii] Cripps to Kate Spurrell, November 26th, 1935, Cripps Papers.

him from the party, but for the S.L., there would be less room for misunderstanding and less difference of opinion if the Party was more certain of its own policies. A beginning had been made with the loss of MacDonald and Snowden, and a Government which had been the abject servant of the City.[i] Was there not hope that, with discussions inside the Party about the Conference programme, dominating N.E.C. personalities would for the first time not be Parliamentary leaders? Maybe there could be a declaration of principles, a comprehensive programme, a new inspiration? There was certainly an optimism in Cripps: 'Many people regard the Party's aims as organised State charity rather than a fundamental change of the whole economic system ... Insistence upon the importance of the amount of administration of unemployment benefit, old-age pensions and workmen's compensation... has tended to mask the far more important features of the party programme, its economic programme of co-operation, planning and control, the spirit of the Movement and the intense desire for *social justice* which alone can counteract the essentially dulling effect of "organisation"'.[ii] The Leicester Conference could create that new spirit.

The moral which delegates at the Leicester Conference drew was that the right course should compel the Party to construct a definite programme. E. F. Wise stated that S.L. members were forming this new organisation to strengthen and assist the Labour Party in the tasks which lay ahead.[iii] From its beginning, the S.L. would attract public and Party attention by the use of Conference resolutions, urging Party members to state their convictions *unburdened by office, unhindered by distracting loyalties.* Resolutions were passed; the main objective of the Party was 'Socialism'; the common ownership of the means of production and distribution the only means by which producers could secure 'the full fruits of their industry';[iv] on assuming office next time, Socialist legislation would be immediately promulgated,[v] and the Party would nationalise key industries. Lansbury and Cripps could unite on that platform. This was not to be an otiose opposition.

(B) Socialist League Successes (1932–1933)

The S.L. scored an immediate success by carrying Wise's resolution for nationalisation of the joint stock banks since it was impossible to carry through Socialist policies so long as joint stock banks remained under private control.[vi] Wise maintained that control over short-term credit, as well as long-term capital, would be essential to frustrate deflationary monetary policies. The vote in favour of this nationalisation was a symbol of the contest between the S.L. and Party and union leaders.[vii] On 'workers' control', H. Clay advocated the direct representation of labour on national industries' boards, while Morrison sought a combination of public ownership, public accountability and business management, which Clay dubbed as 'a plan for an efficient

[i] H. N. Brailsford, quoted in *New Leader*, August 19th, 1932; cf Cripps Papers, October, 1932.
[ii] Ibid. (My italics.)
[iii] Quoted in *Daily Herald*, October 3rd, 1932.
[iv] *Labour Party Annual Conference Report*, October 1932, p.202.
[v] Ibid., p.204.
[vi] Quoted in *Daily Herald*, October 5th, 1932.
[vii] Joint Stock Banks nationalisation resolution was omitted in 1935, 1937 and in 1945 – without explanation by Party leaders.

bureaucracy with workers left powerless!" The place of workers in socialised industries was unresolved, and the reports on the socialisation of transport and electricity did not mention 'workers' control', but C. Trevelyan noted the confidence of the Party at Leicester in putting the leaders under a mandate to introduce Socialist measures on attaining office, however far in the future that might be. There was a peculiar optimism that by passing resolutions it could achieve its ends."

In effect, the Conference failed to evolve new tactics or produce new leaders; the approach to power was solely through Parliament, the leaders were old faces Lansbury, Clynes, Dalton and Morrison, and the block vote rendered the Conference impervious to argument. Party leaders remained gradualist, as was the new programme. Resolutions on joint stock banks and 'definite Socialist legislation' were Pyrrhic victories." Because proposed legislation in the 1929–1931 Labour Government had been hindered, the Party now stood for propaganda and education in the Movement," but the Executive would only tolerate divergent opinions so long as they were unimportant: '...education and propaganda was, in fact, a new form of "attentisme"." Previous election programmes were criticised as being uncommitted to a specific course of action, but A. Henderson expressed the predominant view of Party leaders, that nothing had happened to the Party or electoral opinion to warrant any radical change in programme, policy or methods of the Party. Drawing a veil over the Labour Government, A. Greenwood construed there was little to be gained by holding a coroner's inquest on the corpse." (The rôle of the S.L. would be to force the pace in political education. Hence, as H. Dalton noted, there was suspicion of the S.L. in orthodox circles at Transport House and on the National Executive and Dalton would soon be busy recruiting a new generation of young Labour intellectuals (such as Hugh Gaitskell and Douglas Jay) to oppose the 'melodramatics of the S.L.'") The Party itself was still largely led outside Parliament by those closely connected with the fallen Government. Having made the decision in 1932 to obey Standing Orders and regard continued membership of the Party as the first necessity, the S.L. found the initiative always lay with the official leadership. For the C.P., of course, the Leicester decisions produced the same old box of pills (banking, electricity, transport and agriculture) behind even the 1918 'Labour and the New Social Order' in challenging capitalism." Would the Labour Party be allowed to rationalise capitalism when the mainspring of production was the individual investor? When the latter was apprehensive about the fate of a possible investment, would he not hold tight to his liquid capital? The S.L. was not going to be applauded for querying whether the Party could become an instrument for promoting a planned economy without Party reorganisation!

The S.L. had initial problems of identity: an educational or a political propaganda organisation? Should it concentrate on the national Movement or local parties? Should it unite around a single theme? The New Clarion reported the Leicester Conference

---

[i] Quoting C. Brand, op. cit., p.169.

[ii] E. Shinwell, op. cit., p.144.

[iii] C. A. Smith, 'Men Versus the Machine', New Leader, October 7th, 1932.

[iv] Labour Party Annual Conference Report, October 1932, p.4.

[v] R. Miliband, op. cit., p.194.

[vi] Daily Herald, August 23rd, 1932.

[vii] H. Dalton, The Fateful Years, p.24; D. Powell, op. cit., 1998, p.185. (My italics.)

[viii] R. P. Dutt, 'Notes of the Month', Labour Monthly, Vol. 14, No. 10, October 1932.

under 'Socialism Wins the Day':[i] "Half-hearted" measures have been abandoned... for the first time our problems and institutions are challenged forthrightly'. The S.L. found a partial identity in reflecting and regurgitating the aims of the old I.L.P., in its promotion of communal ownership of Land and Capital, dissemination of Socialist principles, and emphasis on the processes of production, distribution and exchange as social functions. While P.L.P. leaders judged the Party's efficiency in electoral terms, the S.L. saw a new rôle for the Party as an educational body, an agency for creating Socialists. This remained the essential difference in approach in the Party from 1932 onwards, and the implication made (by the S.L.) was that the Party was incapable of changing society because of its susceptibility to the *conventions of Parliamentarianism*. To Party officials, the S.L. was thus a provocation in its attempts to force a Socialist programme on the Party and the incessant questioning of 'the position of the Socialist in the Party', which added insult to criticism.

The S.L. had little influence in the policy-making P.L.P., or in the choice of Party officials. Although the Party Conferences of 1932–34 debated many proposals (which came from the S.L.) on the future of the Party, the fact that these culminated in a Party Conference suggests that verbal victories of the S.L. had little influence on the Party's praxis, but were important in bolstering the morale of activists. When the Party accepted a few S.L. resolutions, the autonomy of the S.L. seemed justified. With its equivocal position in the Labour Party, the S.L. was in a mid-position between C.P. perspectives and empirical Labourism. Internally, S.L. dissensions were generated by the usual conflicts of a propagandist organisation focussing its attention on a Parliamentary Labour Party. Attacked by the Left outside the Party, the Right inside the Party, and the press throughout, by November 1934, it still pictured itself (as Socialist organisations in the Labour Party always did) as *a ginger group, a spearhead*, a tug pulling the great ship 'Labour' to the harbour of Socialism, *an intellectual storehouse of ideas and research*,[ii] but inside the Party, the sense of 'capitalism in crisis' led the S.L. to posit a theory of Socialist tactics to counteract what it considered to be the Party's weakness – its lack of a philosophy of action. Another breach between the S.L. and the Party was the former's reiteration that the next Labour Government would need to deal with opposition from *entrenched interests* (a choice between winning floating voters or holding to inflexible principles). Both sides believed they were talking about 'practical policies', but the S.L. represented frustrated idealists, not disillusioned realists. Could the Party afford to be a middle Party, moderate in its advocacy and out of date in its ideology? Or would the inevitable controversies and differences be the lubricant of a democratic movement?[iii] The Thirties would unravel both questions.

In the first two years of the S.L.'s life, annoyances at S.L. leaders' public remarks were directed by Party officials at Cripps. What could be said in private discussion within the S.L. could not be said in a public speech by a Labour leader without repercussions. S.L. statements on the implementation of Socialist policies through constitutional changes were bound to bring out the labels 'revolutionary', 'dictatorial', 'violent' and 'conspiratorial' to characterise the S.L. To a disillusioned, possibly unemployed local Party worker, nothing in 1932 could capture the imagination so

---

[i] The front page showed a picture of the Labour Party's House being window-cleaned to let in 'the light' from 'the Socialist Sun', *New Clarion*, October 15th, 1932. Such idealism 73 years ago.

[ii] Cf. I.L.P. Annual Conference Report 1926, p.28.

[iii] E. Shinwell, *The Labour Story*, pp.214–216.

fully as a provocative Cripps' speech: 'If we are to witness a change in the economic and social structure of our country ... such a change can never be brought about under the existing Parliamentary forms... Those who at present hold the economic power will refuse their support to any Labour Government. The idea that if the Labour Party is gentle and well behaved it will persuade the capitalists to hand over their economic power to the Government is quite fantastic. It will be necessary... to carry through drastic changes within a short period of time, to have at their disposal machinery of Government... which is capable of rapid action').[i] Cripps' popularity was unnerving for Labour leaders.

On January 6th, 1934 in Nottingham, Cripps commented that a future Labour Government would have to overcome opposition from 'Buckingham Palace'. This, so foreign to the political temper of Britain, provoked immediate disclaimers from Party leaders, and Cripps had to state publicly that he would vastly prefer a constitutional monarch to a political president![ii] Inadvertently, when he criticised the Government's expenditure on the Jubilee of George V and the Coronation of George VI, using the word 'revolutionary' when he meant 'active', and 'Socialist' when he meant 'Labour Party', he revealed the Party's adherence to the unwritten canons of political behaviour and accepted traditions of 'politically responsible' leadership. He achieved another thing which infuriated Party officials; he made a name for himself in the public eye. People wanted to hear him speak in case he transgressed against the Party's official view! Local S.L. members were enthralled. Here is S.L. Executive member Ruth Dodds: 'Cripps was one of the few men who can fill any hall in Britain with people listening to a purely political speech. What was the secret of his appeal? [...] There was no tension in the hall... yet there was a very definite emotional atmosphere ... a good presence. Cripps had a round, rather jolly countenance (so unlike the Press photographs), a very pleasant voice, bearing and expression which conveyed an impression of great candour. Retaining decent reserve, he would say quite naturally in a public speech what he would say in a private conversation... [enough to horrify a Labour leader!] he utterly believed that what he was saying was true and of deep importance... Was he listened to because of the strange contrast between what he really is and his reputation? To find such an 'ogre' in the shape of a very quiet, well-behaved person, very clear in exposition, might have the charm of the unexpected... His replies to questions were courteous, direct and sensible, and he made you feel friendly, whether you agreed with him or not.'[iii]

Mainly due to Cripps' public persona the S.L. was treated in a hostile manner by Party officials. All his 'embarrassing' public displays were seen as possible only through his position on the S.L. National Council. When he spoke at the Hastings Conference (October 1933) in favour of any future Labour Government taking immediate emergency powers, Party leaders criticised such proposals as ill-judged (when Hitler was adopting 'similar measures'), and were irate when Cripps received more publicity than the Party's denunciation of his speeches: 'The Capitalist Press, knowing full well the suspicions of the workers against wealthy people, see an opportunity to exploit this suspicion against Sir Stafford Cripps. So they spread the story that Cripps has been

[i] Quoted in *Daily Herald*, April 12th, 1933.

[ii] *The Times*, January 15th, 1934.

[iii] R. Dodds, *Metropolitan Sunday Night*, February 1935, R. Dodds' Papers.

"brought to book" by the Party Executive for his socialist speeches'.[i] Because the S.L. stood for 'more democracy inside the Party', and because people began to think that Conservative attacks might be a measure of Cripps' honesty, when a Party member was a nuisance the best way to make him behave properly was to burden him with responsibility.[ii] Cripps was elected to the N.E.C.! Meanwhile C.P. and I.L.P. criticisms of the S.L. focussed on the possibility the S.L. was serving to create the illusion there could be a radical position *in* the Labour Party: 'The surest way of breeding cynical contempt for democratic government is for men and women, once elected, to be willing to vote contrary to their convictions or even to become neutral, in obedience to the instructions of a Party whip'.[iii] This was not quite the S.L.'s future rôle, because ideological, structural and power-control factors contributed to factionalism within the Party, which allowed the S.L. to challenge the leaders' policies at various points in the organisation, so long as the S.L. appealed to and organised at the local level. The Party leadership was the object of the S.L.'s rancour, because it acknowledged (and symbolised) the power asserted by moderates, while the N.E.C. (enforcing the Party Constitution and endorsing Parliamentary candidates) was accused by the S.L. of discriminating against the Left wing, in its control of the agenda of the Annual Conference on topics debated and content of resolutions submitted.[iv]

Until 1935, the S.L. put its energies into winning paper victories at Annual Conferences. Its tendency was to translate political issues into questions of leadership, an obsession which sprang from the Party's Parliamentary conception of political power. J. T. Murphy's reaction exemplified this: 'All the weight of tradition, of vested interest, of inertia, of administrative habit and ineffective challenge from within the Movement, have retarded and stifled the development of revolutionary leadership… to make the necessary changes in the leadership of the Labour Movement from bottom to top is the all-important issue in the race between Socialism and Fascism'.[v] Not that "a revolutionary leadership" was possible. By focussing its attacks on 'the leadership', the S.L. deluded itself into a belief that Labour's reformism was dependent on the *personal predilections* of a few individuals, when the S.L.'s mode of activity within the party carried the seeds of its own failure by accepting 'activism within the Party' on terms laid down by that reformist leadership: 'The Movement may have the finest programme imaginable, but without a leadership *inspired* with the will to dare to operate it … there can be no victory for Socialism,'[vi] was the S.L.'s preferred reading.

As an organisation, the S.L. did not comprehend that politics was a question, not of being right but of exercising power. Party leaders regarded the S.L.'ers as a nuisance, because they only criticised, were neither loyal nor grateful, would not give the Party a moment's peace, tended to fragment into little groups and make Party action difficult by their continuing objections. Yet Party loyalty was not enough. In the 1930s too many forgot.[vii] Party leaders categorised the conflict as between the so-called S.L. 'extremists' and the solid, loyal supporters, took advantage of the S.L.'s tactical errors, and created a sense that the S.L. was damning the Party's electoral chances in the eyes

[i] *Bristol Labour Weekly*, December 30th, 1933.
[ii] *Manchester Guardian*, quoting P. Strauss, op. cit., p.72.
[iii] J. Lee, *This Great Journey*, op. cit., p.221.
[iv] E. G. Janosik, op. cit., p.95.
[v] J. T. Murphy, *Preparing for Power*, p.285.
[vi] Ibid. (My italics.)
[vii] F. Williams, *A Pattern of Rulers*, p.260.

of moderates. The powers of Party officials were interpreted so freely that eventually any manifestation of opposition could be construed as flouting 'reasonable Party discipline' as Aneurin Bevan commented in 1937: 'If every organised effort to change Party policy is to be described as an organised attack on the Party itself, then the rigidity imposed by Party discipline will soon change into "rigor mortis". The Labour Party should take special care not to transform itself into an intellectual concentration camp'.[i] Not that the Party ever went *that* far.

S.L. leaders reacted in a provocative way because they were isolated, always eventually defeated, their demands for more independent decisions met by an increasingly autonomous rôle claimed for the N.E.C. To the huge union section in the Party, the S.L.'s frustrations seemed incomprehensibly exaggerated because the Party asserted the authority and exacted the discipline *appropriate* to an orthodox mass Party. The S.L. acted on its own initiative because a common policy had not been properly discussed before the 'loyalty and discipline' features were implemented. Had not the Party failed to define an economic programme, been excessively concerned to appear respectable, did it not vacillate over rearmament and unemployment, had not '1931' led to a re-examination of the Party's fundamental political position? These questions could not be evaded as the peculiar bent of the S.L., which was given neither a positive rôle nor independence by the N.E.C. Meanwhile, S.L. writers looked to 'State Socialism' as 'taking over industry by a worker-controlled State', which Party leaders had pruned to mean a form of 'centrally-directed industry' with a profit basis: 'the reformist regards the State as standing above the class struggle, unaffected by the economic interests which dominate society. Whenever the Labour Party has been in office the State has continued to function in exactly the same fashion – for the employers against the workers... *the present Party leadership is not the kind likely to challenge the employers' interests even if they had a majority*'.[ii] That S.L. position led to despair and inertia, and was the S.L.'s conundrum. An remains so.

The S.L.'s conclusions might be unrealistic, but the organisation did develop its understanding of 'Socialism'; it was educating some new (and old) Party members into clarifying the implications of democratic Socialism by denunciation of compromises, to evolve a principled Socialist viewpoint, and campaign for a more representative Party machine. Little could be done concerning the issues which brought disciplinary action, considering the S.L.'s affiliation to Standing Orders. To paraphrase official Party criticism: what was in question was not the right of minority groups to continue to work in the Party to change its views, but the claim to set aside *majority* decisions and act apart from and in conflict with the organisation to which they had declared their allegiance.[iii]

In 1933, a clash between the S.L. and the Party erupted during the first S.L. Conference at Derby; Transport House had wanted a 'clean-up' of the Party to end the 'dictatorial' attitudes percolating from the S.L.! This was seen by S.L. leaders as a fundamental (possibly intentional) misunderstanding of their policies, and an early attempt to dragoon the S.L. E. F. Wise interpreted that the Party had only reached a convalescent stage: 'It has not yet built up its strength or laid its plans for a new fight... Some Labour leaders seem to be thinking too much in terms of the struggles and

[i] Quoting M. Foot, *Biography of A. Bevan*, op. cit. pp.290–92.
[ii] 'Jacques', 'The State and Socialism', *Socialist*, No. 4, January–February 1936. (My italics.)
[iii] F. Williams, *Ernest Bevin*, p.213.

issues of the past'.[i] The S.L. was guilty of that also, but Sir C. Trevelyan told Party members: 'If the Labour Party had been an out and out Socialist Party in 1930–31, it would have insisted on its leaders turning to Socialism instead of capitalism'.[ii] He concluded that the Labour Movement was beginning to realise that the existing economic system could not bring secure lives for workers. But whose system could?

Events in June 1933 revealed the conflict of ideas reaching a critical stage. Party leaders were convinced that to accept the S.L.'s emergency powers' proposals would *postpone* a return to power. Yet, it was not in itself "undemocratic" to ask for special powers on the ground that without them the policy the nation had voted for could not be carried out.[iii] The S.L. placed its trust in the Labour Party, but underestimated the bureaucratic machine and the weight of its Conference procedures and electoral machine, and was beginning to be treated by Transport House as the I.L.P. had been: 'On the whole the S.L. Conference was dull and kept well within the limits prescribed for it by the parent body',[iv] commented the I.L.P. What the latter ignored was that one of the features was insistence by delegates and the S.L. platform on working within the Party: 'The policy agreed upon at the Annual Party Conference must be our guide, and our aim must be to persuade that Conference to adopt certain views which we consider the best policy for the working-class movement',[v] E. F. Wise put it succinctly.

Throughout 1933, columns of S.L. publications discussed relations between the S.L. and the Party. Was there a danger of overlapping, duplication and ultimate friction? Was the Party's central work for *electoral purposes*, a function which the S.L. never held for itself? While such queries were being assessed, the S.L. was becoming the target of frantic newspaper articles which accused the S.L. of fomenting dissensions in the Movement, plotting to saddle it with a policy of 'dictatorship'.[vi] Commenting on such accusations that it sought to *impose* policies upon the Party, the S.L. replied that its organisation exercised the right of affiliated sections to put forward policies and plans for *consideration and discussion* by the Party Conference.[vii] The S.L. was working out the practical implications of Conference decisions on Socialist policy and bringing them forward for discussion by the Movement: 'We are fulfilling the positive duty of all members of the Movement if policy is to be democratically decided … the S.L. will take the opportunity to raise questions with which pamphlets, books and S.L. policy have been concerned at the Party Conference'.[viii] The S.L. sought a radical reorganisation of the machinery of Party and Government, but not without thorough debate.

Confrontation between the S.L. and the official Party was exhibited in a public argument between H. Morrison and H. Laski. The former was convinced S.L. views would spread uncertainty in the Labour Movement, and the effect of S.L. colleagues' public and private activities would embarrass the Party, confuse the public as to Labour policy, and worst of all, the Emergency Powers' proposal 'would drive us to defend ourselves for the greater part of our time against Tory allegations of

---

[i] *Derby Evening Telegraph* and *Derby Daily Express*, June 5th, 1933.

[ii] Ibid.

[iii] *New Stateman and Nation*, June 10th, 1933.

[iv] *New Leader*, June 9th, 1933.

[v] E. F. Wise, quoting *New Clarion*, S.L. News, June 10th, 1933.

[vi] Cf. 'Free Speech for Labour', *New Clarion*, S.L. News, July 8th, 1933.

[vii] 'Mr. Baldwin and Other Critics', *New Clarion*, S.L. News, August 5th, 1933. (My italics.)

[viii] 'Ourselves and the Party', *New Clarion*, S.L. News, September 2nd, 1933.

Bolshevism and dictatorship'.[i] Laski responded to allegations as to S.L. discussions 'embarrassing the Party'; 'I do not think the sober confrontation of reality is ever embarrassing in the long run, but it is certainly the only honourable thing to do'.[ii] Uncertainty or honour? These two viewpoints express the major difference between the S.L. and the Party, not only in 1933, but to the end, in 1937. But Conservative allegations of 'Bolshevism and dictatorship' stuck.

For the Hastings Party Conference (1933), S.L. proposals were a series of amendments to draft Policy Reports to clear up obscurities. In the section 'Labour Goal – Socialism', the S.L. amendment was that it include proposals for abolition of the House of Lords, an Emergency Powers Act (to regulate financial machinery), revision of Commons' procedure (to facilitate rapid constitutional changes), and an economic plan for industry, finance and foreign trade.[iii] The section 'International Economic Co-operation' would include economic co-operation with Russia and other Socialist Governments; and in 'Banking', the S.L. asked for 'complete control' of financial institutions not just 'a considerable measure'; there was 'no room for financial middlemen... because it is not possible to maintain a National Financial Organisation with private financiers.'[iv] The N.E.C. accepted S.L. proposals for "consideration" rather than opposing them completely. Confrontation between the S.L. and N.E.C. was thus postponed, and, discussion went into debates on Party policy, without the bitterness of debates on party discipline, C.P. affiliation and the United Front, which characterised later Conferences: 'The 1933 Conference was in the main marking time in respect of the controversy between the Right and Left wings. There were echoes of the temper of the Leicester Conference but there were also signs that the Executive, though unwilling to challenge the Left wing outright, was disinclined to accept its proposals and was playing for time'.[v] (Between 1932 and 1937, the Executive was defeated in Conference only 10 times; 7 were in 1933 and 1934.)[vi] The S.L. sought a place somewhere between submission to the N.E.C. and a repetition of the I.L.P.'s challenge.

Reactions to the S.L.'s rôle in the Conference were significant for the future. Lord Ponsonby delighted in the vitality of the S.L. which referred to the 'steam roller' of the Executive "smashing up revolution" – the machine "smashing the soul of our Movement", domination of unions and the vote of active workers "relegated to the limbo of Executive consideration".[vii] The New Clarion claimed the S.L. had every reason to be satisfied with its reception by floor and platform, while Cripps thought the Conference marked a step forward: 'A number of our amendments were designed to cross the "t's" and dot the "i's" of the Socialist policy set out in the policy reports'.[viii] There were signs of a steady progress since the policy report on 'Housing and Slums' was withdrawn by the N.E.C. following S.L. objections, and workers' control of industry as a statutory right was accepted as Party policy, after S.L. pressure. Even The Times thought 'Cripps and the S.L. had won *a moral victory for their policy of political direct*

---

[i] 'H. Morrison replies to H. Laski', New Clarion, September 30th, 1933.

[ii] H. Laski, 'H. Morrison's Challenge', New Clarion, October 7th, 1933.

[iii] C. Brand, op. cit., p.170.

[iv] New Clarion, S.L. News, September 30th, 1933.

[v] G. D. H. Cole, History of the Labour Party Since 1914, p.288.

[vi] D. McHenry, op. cit., pp.29–30.

[vii] F. L. Stevens, 'The Debate on Policy', New Clarion, October 7th, 1933.

[viii] S. Cripps, 'Our Part', S.L. Notes, October 14th, 1933.

action,[i] Cripps depicted as the dominating figure of the Conference, 'the pivotal point of Labour policy. Far from having disrupted the Party by his pronouncements, he has given a lead which has rallied the whole of the younger generation of Socialists to his side'.[ii] The Press could afford to be generous.

However, there were signs that this Conference was the Indian Summer of the S.L.'s influence at national Party level. Personalities intruded; this Conference saw the first of many encounters in which E. Bevin and Cripps found themselves on opposite sides during the next few years.[iii] Bevin thought S.L. proposals were *too theoretical* and devoid of political sense: he supported the Morrisonian concept of nationalisation; 'Socialism' (for Bevin) was a matter of emancipating workers from the stigma of inferiority in a class-ridden society – that's how Bevin operated. H. B. Lees-Smith, meanwhile, thought S.L. policies were 'extravagant and irresponsible', deplored the tendency to label as 'Right wingers' those (like himself) who had the job of analysing and fulfilling some of the amplifications of 'S.L. propaganda', and A. M. Thompson, acknowledging the S.L.'s contention that gradualness and constitutional Parliamentary procedure were slow to keep pace with modern social needs, was convinced that the difference between the S.L. and the Old Guard appeared on close examination to be 'one only of *methods*'[iv] – as if that did not represent a gulf!

(C) 'Forward to Socialism' or 'For Socialism and Peace' (1934)?

Until 1934, the Labour Party was shaken in its political philosophy, suffering from lack of solidarity and self-confidence, faced with the need for a policy and programme offering a distinctive alternative to 'National' Government attempts to rescue the economy by reduction of living standards. The Party, condemned to Parliamentary opposition, watched mounting international crisis, economic distress, aggression in Europe and Asia, and rapid disintegration of the Left in Europe.[v] The Right-wing majority in the Party controlled Conferences, union leaders were in a cabal in alliance with that leadership, while the P.L.P. was failing to retain the prestige and authority it had held in the Movement in the 1920s:[vi] 'We have known Labour politicians reduced to political bankruptcy by the discovery when they reach the House of Commons and meet the rich man face to face that they are most of them individually quite without malice and as anxious to set the world to rights ... *such Labour leaders have no solid intellectual foundation for their Socialism*'.[vii] The S.L. exposed the Party's lack of a common ideology.

Not only had the Party shown little sympathy towards short-term protest movements; it had 'deliberately adopted the method of constitutional action and rejected the tactics of revolution;[viii] it wisely in its view inhibited and discouraged unconventional methods of protest and opposed unemployed demonstrations as

---

[i] Quoting S.L. Notes, November 11th, 1933.

[ii] *Bristol Labour Weekly*, October 5th, 1933. (My italics.)

[iii] R. Miliband, op. cit., p.205.

[iv] Alexander M. Thompson, 'United for Socialism', *New Clarion*, October 7th, 1933.

[v] F. Williams, *Ernest Bevin*, p.175.

[vi] H. Pelling, *A Short History of the Labour Party*, 1968 edn., p.74.

[vii] 'A Christmas Sermon', *New Statesman and Nation*, December 24th, 1932. (My italics.)

[viii] C. R. Attlee, *The Labour Party in Perspective*, p.113. (My italics.)

irresponsible; it considerably modified its economic philosophy, satisfying itself (in 1934) with a programme consisting of welfare state legislation and socialisation of a few industries: social reform was the goal of the Right wing of the Party; Left-wing Labour in the S.L. wanted constitutional revolution and rapid socialisation.[i] The P.L.P. was settling down to compromises by 1934, which the Parliamentary system of Government necessitated, and accused the S.L. of scaring away the marginal voter, of not accepting Parliamentary government, of opposing Party policies. (*Scaring away the "marginal voter"* should do the trick.)

At Party Conferences, the official leadership was fortified by block votes. It was government of the officials, by the officials, for the officials. It concentrated on *education and organisation*, but did little to further it by any militant organisation or protest outside Parliament in defence of working-class interests. The Party managed to become more respectable and acceptable to the middle classes, and some distinguished Party members were offered (and found themselves able to accept!) knighthoods and other honours.[ii] Conflicts in the Party might confuse the electorate, but compromises would have the same effect. The S.L.'s potential militancy was mediated by a Party whose reformist ideology, parliamentary mode of activity, and bureaucratised organisational structure made it peculiarly resistant to Socialist theory or practice. Added to this, the differences among sections forming the Movement led to compromise in the selection of a Party leader: 'The safe and reliable Chairman was more capable of ironing out obstacles and effecting compromise than the extremist, whether on the Right or Left, whose purpose was to exercise authority rather than to be a representative spokesman'.[iii] Gradually, techniques of mass communication enhanced the rôle of the Party leader and reduced that of particular interest groups in the Party.

1934 opened with a declaration from the N.E.C.: the Party stood for Parliamentary democracy and opposed individual or 'group dictatorship' whether from the Right or from the Left. The only tolerable Government would be one with a free electoral system, and an active, efficient Parliamentary machine for reaching effective decisions after reasonable opportunities for discussion and criticism.[iv] This statement was directed against an S.L. calling for 'drastic reform' of Parliamentary procedure to make possible a rapid enactment of Socialist measures. Cripps, unrepentant, repeated the need for emergency legislation, abolition of the Lords, reform of Commons' procedures, etc.[v] Lansbury wrote to him: 'It is the economic situation which determines the politicians who govern; it makes statesmen into cheats and liars – and I put myself in with these because of the make-believe I had to agree with in our late Cabinet … I shall be quite satisfied if the Party stands by its resolutions'.[vi] As it was, after 1933 the S.L. never came near to winning a single Conference decision, and the idea of 'transforming Party policy' faded, though there had been little reasoned debate about S.L. proposals. 1934 was a year of tentative economic recovery and diminishing economic and political tension – cuts in social benefits were restored, the Labour Party won a majority on the L.C.C. and the S.L.'s theme at its Conference at Leeds was for the Party to show its decisiveness: 'Where the Labour Government failed last time was in

---

[i] D. McHenry, op. cit., pp.260–277.

[ii] Peter Teed, *Britain 1906–51: A Welfare State*, p.181.

[iii] E. Shinwell, op. cit., p.209.

[iv] 'Democracy and Dictatorship', *Labour Party Annual Conference Report*, October 1934, p.9.

[v] 'Organise for Action', *New Clarion*, S.L. Notes, January 6th, 1934.

[vi] G. Lansbury to S. Cripps, Lansbury Papers, January 1st, 1934.

action ... the creed of Socialism ... was left entirely on one side'.[i] The S.L. launched its appeal and determination to capture economic power by a Parliamentary majority, to use it for a Five Year Plan; the Party to retain flexibility to adapt policy to changing conditions.

In his opening Conference address, Cripps propounded the view that the spirit of comradeship would prevent disagreements degenerating into schism. He warned that S.L. convictions would allow no compromise, but this was better than hiding differences of views. There were, of course, conflicts over means: 'We must be quite clear that it is *Socialism and not State Capitalism*, or some amorphous and indeterminate collection of ideas parading as a policy'.[ii] Why not the latter – if it kept one in power? For the Labour Movement, he continued, there was a need for political stimulants, not soporifics; bold policies would have greater appeal than cautious policies of slow reform: 'The assumption that we must moderate our demands because of the effect upon the electorate is to misread the lesson of post-war Europe and misunderstand the psychology of the people'. Discuss? Not yet. The test would be 'the readiness of the Party at its next Conference to adopt the S.L.'s proposals for emergency powers, speeding up parliamentary procedure, and a head-on collision with the Lords'.[iii]

When the S.L. was equipped with a detailed policy ('*Forward to Socialism*'), its difficulties with Party leaders intensified. The N.E.C., wary of the tone of speeches, writings and policy suggestions by S.L. leaders, confirmed the Party's devotion to Parliamentary democracy.[iv] The Party's programme '*For Socialism and Peace*' was designed to replace '*Labour and the Nation*' as the authoritative exposition of Party policy. It was also an N.E.C. move to challenge the S.L.'s claim that Socialism could not be brought about by methods of 'Parliamentarism'. The Party's programme contained little which was not in its predecessors of 1918 and 1928,[v] but served to neutralise the S.L.'s '*Forward to Socialism*' programme and lessened the S.L.'s appeal to the rank and file. In the Party's '*For Socialism and Peace*' there was no specific reference to the S.L.'s views, but the official Party programme was to be taken as the reply to the S.L. and, with encouraging local election results, the party was in a stronger position as a potential alternative Government. Even so, the Party's programmatic statement was its most radical in the 1930s.

'*For Socialism and Peace*' was a considerable advance on its predecessor as a statement of Socialist objectives. It committed the Party to seek peace by removing the causes of international disputes by consultation and arbitration; to secure for every person a satisfactory standard of life, (with equal opportunity for all); to convert industry from a struggle for private gain to a planned national economy, for democratic expansion of education, health and social services; and to adjust taxation to make provision for maintenance and improvement of the national apparatus of industry and the surplus to be applied for the good of all.[vi] *The Times* considered that the S.L. would not find much fault with this programme although 'it will miss the time-table and the touch of *dictatorship* which are included in its own methods'.[vii] The differences were limited (*The*

---

[i] Sir C. Trevelyan, 'A Party of Socialist Action', *Leeds Weekly Citizen*, May 11th, 1934.

[ii] S. Cripps, Opening Address at Leeds S.L. Conference, May 20th, 1934, *Socialist Leaguer*, No. 1, June–July 1934. Labour for the first time had a clear majority on the LCC, March 8th 1934.

[iii] 'A London Diary', *New Statesman and Nation*, May 26th, 1934.

[iv] Cf. *Labour Party Annual Conference Report*, 1934, p.9

[v] C. L. Mowat, op. cit., p.549.

[vi] *Labour Party Annual Conference Report*, 1934.

[vii] *The Times*, July 25th, 1934. (My italics.)

Times continued) to the S.L.'s demand for Socialism within the lifetime of a single Parliament; the emergency powers' resolution; the Party's decision to leave the selection of policies to the P.L.P.; and the S.L.'s hope that the Party would only accept office with an overwhelming majority in contrast to the Party's avoidance of any 'revolutionary' phraseology. When *The Times* suggested the Party's programme might prove an anti-climax, because it had less of a programme of action than a *complete catalogue or window display of all the measures*, here was the kind of critique the S.L. would make.

Apart from public ownership of industries and services and reform of the machinery of government,[i] the S.L. could see no proposals which had not been long-standing for political and administrative reform, although the entire Statement had been conceived in terms of long-term objectives rather than a programme for a Government in power. S.L. leaders challenged the principles as not sufficiently explicit to constitute any precise commitments for an incoming Government, a response which Labour leaders had anticipated. Typically, Cripps reacted in his dogmatic mien: 'The Right wing take the view that even at the risk of delaying Socialism it is necessary to get a Parliamentary majority at the earliest possible moment. They are therefore prepared to modify the programme in the direction of gradualism... The Left wing insist upon telling the people frankly that certain definite things must be done immediately if it is to be possible to bring about the economic change democratically. They are prepared to take the risk of waiting, if necessary, until a sufficient body of the electors can be convinced of the necessity for a Socialist programme'.[ii]

Labour's edifice of gradualism was carefully constructed.[iii] The Party was drawing out the sting of the S.L. arguments and S.L. leaders were exasperated by the Party's references to 'Socialist reconstruction by persuasion', 'fair compensation to existing owners' and 'reasonable' wages and prices. William Meilor recorded his antipathy: 'The phrases used by the Executive would be acceptable on every political platform. It is not a plan for Socialism, but a repetition of the 1929 attempt to work within *declining capitalism*'.[iv] *'For Socialism and Peace'* was the culmination of battles between the S.L. and constituency parties on the Left and the majority of union and Parliamentary leaders on the Right. To the S.L., the Party's programme was uninspiring, unimaginative, offering palliatives that had the added disadvantage that the opposition could offer similar measures dressed up in similar guise: 'Search this "Programme of Action", you will not find any real sign that the Party's purpose and intent is the planning of the economic life of this country by a *Socialist* Government ... only the reorganisation of industry on the lines of the London Passenger Transport Board'.[v] The S.L. also criticised the Executive's plan for the transfer of property from private ownership to public administration, because existing owners were going to receive compensatory annual payments, and a return of their capital holdings. The result would be abandonment of any pretence of 'socialisation' even of primary industries. The S.L. wanted to know what the 'Programme of Action' actually was, and what it would produce.

[i] *Labour Party Annual Conference Report*, 1934, pp.261–63.
[ii] S. Cripps, 'The Alternatives Before British Labour', *Foreign Affairs*, September 1934, p.128.
[iii] D. Powell, op. cit., 1998, p.186.
[iv] Quoting A. Hutt, op. cit., p.261. (My italics.)
[v] S.L. Editorial, 'Socialism or Liberalism – Which?' (The Issue Before the Labour Party), *Socialist Leaguer*, No. 3, August–September 1934.

(D) The Southport Conference and the S.L.'s 75 Amendments

It was to be expected that the S.L. would now ask whether the Party would uphold Socialist principles irrespective of electoral chances, whether it aimed at cautious social reforms or the principle of State intervention in the whole economy;[i] it was not surprising the S.L. saw a fundamental fallacy that any socialistic changes could be allowed to be made within the capitalist system when 'the whole history of the Social Democratic Movement negatives any such idea'.[ii] Least of all shocks was the S.L. National Council's decision to mount a major critique of *'For Socialism and Peace'* with 75 amendments, including deletion of the draft statement of aims and substitution of a *Five Point Programme of Action*. Challenging the whole programme practically ensured that the S.L. would not succeed in amending the draft programme on *any* particular point. Objecting to the absence of an immediate programme, the S.L. sought a decisive change, so Party leaders now juxtaposed the views of the S.L. and those of the official Party: 'The S.L. represented an intense reaction to the disaster of 1931, not sufficient to drive it out of the Party with the I.L.P., but strong enough to range it in sharp opposition to the *constitutionalism* of the Party leadership',[iii] concluded G. D. H. Cole.

The Party, prodded by the T.U.C., was by October 1934 determined to protect itself from mutinous groups within the Party and among those who, though disaffiliated, were synonymous with Labour 'in the public mind'. The N.E.C.'s request to the Southport Conference was to give it powers to discipline individual members who took part in United Front activities, while more time would be allotted for resolutions and amendments arising from Policy Reports (less time to general resolutions). This gave the N.E.C. control over the agenda and reduced the power of affiliated bodies; the Labour Left was suspicious of this: 'The powers for which the Executive asked were designed to cover up its own inertia, lack of enterprise and insipidity ... by launching a heresy-hunt'.[iv] Yet *'For Socialism and Peace'* had been influenced by constructive proposals advocated by the S.L. since 1932. K. Zilliacus had criticised[v] the S.L. proposals in *'Forward to Socialism'* as fragmentary and contradictory, especially since Soviet Union entry into the League of Nations had transformed the international situation and made the S.L.'s amendments inapplicable and impossible to defend in the Southport Conference; the indefensible S.L. amendments questioned the *principles* of Party policy without substituting any clear alternatives: 'the Conference, feeling thoroughly pugnacious and heated, would vote by huge majorities for the existing texts'. Cripps could only reply lamely that S.L. amendments should lead to an 'interesting discussion':[vi] he did not imagine they would be accepted by the Conference, but thought there would be 'no harm in that, if the Conference faces up to the issues.' As for the possibility of a split on foreign policy, Cripps dismissed this as most unlikely since the Executive and everybody else, including many members of the

---

[i] Cf. W. Hodgkiss, 'What Is the Lead To Be?', *Socialist Leaguer*, No. 2, July–August 1934.

[ii] S. Cripps, *New Nation*, September 1934.

[iii] G. D. H. Cole, 'History of Socialist Thought', *Socialism and Fascism 1931–1940*, pp.74–75.

[iv] A. Bevan, quoted by A. Bullock, op. cit., p.553, from *Labour Party Annual Conference Report*, 1934, p.139.

[v] K. Zilliacus to S. Cripps, Cripps Papers, August 29th, 1934.

[vi] S. Cripps to K. Zilliacus, Cripps Papers, September 4th, 1934.

S.L. are 'far too vague in their ideas.'[i] (Who was to blame for that?)

The S.L. prepared to debate the question of ends and means at the Southport Conference in yet another *'landmark in the history of Social democracy in England'*.[ii] The electoral programme for the Party would be substantially decided – hence the urgency of the S.L.'s presentation of rapid socialisation and emergency powers for a Labour Government: 'The capitalists, if left with a large measure of economic power for any considerable time, will inevitably bring about the defeat of a Socialist democratic Government... The actual machinery of our democracy is essentially capitalist in its form, and so long as that form survives nothing but capitalist legislation will ever emerge from it'.[iii] So far, so defeatist. At the Conference, the S.L. was forced into an almost impossible position, challenging the Executive while remaining loyal to its discipline. All major policy questions were to be covered by Executive-sponsored resolutions, to which alternatives would have to be presented in amendments, because on such important questions the initiative could not be left to the floor.[iv] In the interests of 'as wide a discussion as possible', all other speeches were limited to 10 minutes each.

The sting was extracted from the S.L.'s 75 amendments because they were not presented piecemeal, but compressed into composite resolutions by the operation of the 3-year rule (another problem for the S.L.): 'that rule is becoming an instrument by which the Executive is all-powerful, for under it, debate on principles can be forbidden',[v] observed Mellor. S.L. proposals appeared vague, and Dalton and Morrison jibed at the S.L.'s 'skeleton statement'[vi] and promoted 'unity' behind *'For Socialism and Peace'*. The S.L. failed to persuade the Conference even to make vague promises to take 'necessary powers' to push through root and branch measures, and the S.L.'s amendment to delete the Party's Aims and substitute a *Five Point Programme of Action* was defeated.[vii] The 11 to 1 majority proved conclusively that the 'Leftward surge' from the immediate post-1931 period had subsided, to the extent that one could not initiate any proposals without acquiring permission from the National Executive.

Dissociating the Party officially from the constitutional ideas of the S.L. and ignoring S.L. proposals from the Hastings Conference,[viii] the N.E.C. proclaimed that the Party saw no reason why 'a people who first in the world achieved through Parliamentary institutions their political and religious freedoms should not by the same means achieve their own economic emancipation'. Why not, indeed, but the Southport Conference put an end to S.L. advocacy of constitutional changes as an inseparable part of a Socialist programme, and compelled the S.L. programme to concentrate henceforth on ends not means. The S.L., which had seized the initiative at Leicester, suffered one defeat after another at Southport, on foreign policy, Party programme and United Front, and, since the S.L. had come out in opposition to the

---

[i] Ibid.

[ii] S. Cripps, 'Putting First Things First' (The Facts at Southport), *Socialist Leaguer*, No. 4, September–October 1934.

[iii] Ibid.

[iv] Cf. H. Dalton, *The Fateful Years*, p.45.

[v] W. Mellor, 'Southport and After: The Task for Socialists', *Socialist Leaguer*, No. 5, October–November 1934.

[vi] *Labour Party Annual Conference Report*, 1934, pp.160–164.

[vii] Ibid, 1934, p.165.

[viii] Ibid, 1934, pp.148–151.

Executive on every major issue, the Executive uttered a warning, which E. Bevin triumphantly corroborated: 'Nothing annoyed him more than the freedom claimed by the Left to snipe and jibe at the Party leadership and to go on criticising decisions with which they disagreed. [It was] … the irresponsibility, the scorn for organisation and discipline which Bevin most disliked in the intellectual rebels of the Left… the freedom claimed by the S.L. confused great issues and threatened to split the Party'.[i] That was one interpretation – and it helped Bevin's career.

E. Bevin's plea was for loyalty to the Party's policies. For two years the S.L. had produced 'too detailed' a plan of action, and the Executive had criticised the S.L. then for attempting to commit the Party too closely to a plan of action (which might be invalidated by later events). This exposed the crux of the matter: the Executive was going to control the whole Movement, in whatever way it could. Any alternative proposals could be ignored in that ultimate purpose, so the S.L. performed one negative function – of clarifying the true 'arguments', and reinforcing the structure of power in the Party. This gives a hollow note to Morrison's appeal to the S.L. 'not to fritter away their own energies, not to cause these troubles, but loyally behind the decisions of the Conference to devote all their time to the maximum possible extent to the building up and development of the Labour Party',[ii] and it augments Lansbury's comments to Attlee: 'Our poor old Movement is in a rather reactionary mood – at least those on top – only because they really think they can get some things done which are worthwhile even out of capitalism. Of course, experience will prove how wrong this is'.[iii] Or how right?

Despite the fact there were S.L. group meetings daily to discuss the best line of action during the Conference, the procedure made effective criticism of the platform almost impossible. Internal Party democracy was sidetracked, but Mellor saw some S.L. comfort. In the '*Education*' amendment, the S.L. secured recognition that 'equality' meant bringing universities and public schools into the free education system of the State; and on the House of Lords and 'Emergency Powers', the S.L. secured valuable concessions.[iv] Mellor noted that the Executive had evaded controversial issues such as the Party's approach to Parliament, Socialism, the class structure of capitalism, but the S.L. had failed to juxtapose Socialism and Gradualism and could not break through the web of procedure. In the debate on the S.L.'s '*Five Year Plan*', the S.L. relied on the Executive allowing free expression, so S.L.'ers were put on the defensive and the Plan was debated on an amendment. The experience of these debates affected S.L. strategy, for it decided in November 1934 to widen its activities: 'Southport should strengthen our resolution to go forward with our work. To be outvoted is not to be disheartened.'[v] But it brings doubts.

The Southport Conference initiated debates on the function of the S.L. The first reaction was one of disappointment: 'Our task has been made more difficult by the Southport Conference'.[vi] Yet, the S.L. had been the protagonist in the most important debates; being outvoted had not implied its debates on policy were any the less valid.

---

[i] A. Bullock, op. cit., p.553.

[ii] *Labour Party Annual Conference Report*, 1934, p.142.

[iii] G. Lansbury to C. R. Attlee, Lansbury Papers, September 5th, 1934.

[iv] W. Mellor, 'Southport and After: The Task for Socialists', *Socialist Leaguer*, No. 5, October–November 1934.

[v] W. Mellor, ibid.

[vi] S. Cripps, 'The Fight Goes On', *Socialist Leaguer*, No. 5, October–November 1934.

In the *Socialist Leaguer*, the urge to overhaul Party machinery became a priority, since S.L. members suspected leaders of timidity, a bureaucratic desire to override rank and file opinion and suppress discontent. (Labour leaders likewise suspected the S.L. of lack of judgement and rash refusal to face up to practical difficulties.) The second S.L. reaction was one of anger at the contempt shown by Labour leaders for the enthusiasm of people for a political idea with a series of categorical negatives: 'The Socialist who finds his passionate desire to express his Socialism *in deeds* balked at every turn by 'thou shalt not's' is more than likely to transfer his allegiance to some party or group less intent on demonstrating the virtues of Olympian calm'.[i] Party leaders were more concerned to curb militant responses by prohibitions (and excommunications if necessary) than devise means of harnessing the active members for a cause over which they might cede control. H. B. Lees-Smith dubbed the S.L. Conference proposals 'hot air' and the S.L. 'ephemeral' and 'amateurish', but this brought a stinging reply from the S.L.: 'What one would expect from the kind of desiccated mentality which sees political salvation in the multiplication of Yellow, Blue and Pink books carefully designed to prove that Socialism is safe – for capitalists'.[ii] The painful truth was that while the Left was dominated by small groups, it was easy for Party leaders to ignore the implications of S.L. activities. Now S.L. leaders began to acknowledge what the I.L.P. and Communist Party accepted; a Party Conference was not to decide policy but to *project the public image*; the P.L.P. could disregard Conference decisions (since Parliament was responsible not to a Party but to an electorate); and the Party leadership could disregard advice even from its N.E.C. or P.L.P. since it was in possession of 'secret information' and it was its business 'to govern'.

Criticisms of the S.L. and Labour Party from the C.P. angle throw another perspective on the S.L. Dutt thought publication of *'For Socialism and Peace'* polarised issues between the S.L. and Labour leaders, because the S.L. could not passively accept this explicit programme of the corporate state and of imperialist war [sic] *without committing political suicide*.[iii] (Not yet!) Cripps' election to the N.E.C. (with a mandate to take responsibility for and carry out a programme condemned by the S.L. as gradualism and reformism) merely underlined the defeat and rejection of S.L. policy. To Dutt, Southport represented the offensive of the ruling Right wing in the Labour Party to consolidate control and policy. William Rust was also critical of the S.L for its 'running away tactics'[iv] and avoidance of questions of immediate struggle when it had been so lavish with Socialist propaganda; he thought the Conference represented a turning point for the S.L., because no change in its policy and tactics would be 'an open admission of futility'. He quoted a Liberal newspaper which dubbed the S.L.'s attack as a 'fizzle' because all talk of a Labour Government arming itself with emergency powers and taking dictatorial measures in the interests of workers, disappeared,[v] and saw the S.L. in the debate on 'Compensation' trapped by its own inconsistencies and contradictory statements. (Cripps justified partial compensation as 'the price of a peaceful transition to a new economic state', conceding the principle which the Executive was defending in relation to full compensation). Labour leaders

---

[i] S.L. editorial, *Socialist Leaguer*, No. 6, November–December 1934.
[ii] S.L. editorial, ibid.
[iii] R. P. Dutt, 'The United Front and the Labour Party', *Labour Monthly*, Vol. 16, No. 11, November 1934.
[iv] W. Rust, 'The S.L.: What Next?', *Labour Monthly*, Vol. 16, No. 11, November 1934.
[v] Rust quoting *Manchester Guardian* in his article.

were basing the strategy of the Movement on preparations for the next Election: 'Every question was weighed in the election balance'.[i] And ever more would be so.

For local party delegates, a vote for the S.L. was a vote for a policy of action, yet the S.L. at Southport had been an officially-approved opposition in agreement with Party leaders. The S.L. had not acted according to conclusions stated in *'Forward to Socialism'*, so all it was doing was helping official leaders by canalising discontent into harmless channels. The effects of mass unemployment and international events began to sideline debate about the Party's programme and intentions on achieving office, but the signs in October and November 1934 were that the S.L. would be unable to participate. J. Strachey asked Cripps if he would support the *Memorandum on Anti-Fascism*, but Cripps replied he had done all he could to urge the Party to take a more militant position in demonstrations, but he supported the Party against 'disruptive tactics of outside Left-wing organisations'; he was convinced of a growing Left wing in the Party and the only realistic policy was 'to try to stir up the Party from inside'.[ii] Likewise, Cripps refused to answer questions on the *Youth Front Against Fascism and War* organised by the *British Anti-War Movement*. His secretary replied: 'In view of the decision of the Labour Party at Southport with regard to the Party and ancillary bodies, he cannot reply to the questionnaire'.[iii] *The British Anti-War Movement* responded: 'We think it strange indeed that people are not even allowed to express their political position in relation to War because they happen to be members of the Labour Party ... you could put forward the views which we heard you express at the Southport Conference'.[iv] Cripps' rejoinder was terse: 'Any publicity that I wish for my views against War will be through the Labour Movement ... and not through the *British Anti-War Movement'*.[v] He also declined the offer to become an Associate Member of *'The Democratic Front'* because 'the proper attacking force is the Labour Party, and I do not wish to dissipate my energies outside'.[vi] Eight months on he was opposing S.L. co-operation with the *British Section of Women's World Committee Against War and Fascism* for official reasons – proscription by the N.E.C!*[vii]

S.L. members were now sufficiently cautious of committing any misdemeanours: 'A Labour MP was entitled to have a conscience, so long as he revealed it only in isolated abstentions ... the sin against the Party machine was the "organised conscience"'.[viii] And Party officials' successes against the S.L. at Southport made it impossible to question the legitimacy of the system itself. Party members (Left, Centre and Right) participated in the devices of self-protection, whereby a network of structures, agreements and controls developed, a consensus style of resolving issues evolving. Attlee explained the mind of Party leaders; the Party based its propaganda on ethical principles, had done much to humanise and modify the capitalist system, and upheld the value of every individual; this had to be expressed through social institutions.[ix] At the same time, the official leadership was redefining itself, to fit into a

[i] W. Rust, ibid.
[ii] S. Cripps to J. Strachey, Cripps Papers, October 16th, 1934.
[iii] Miss G. Hill, Cripps Papers, November 5th, 1934.
[iv] Cripps Papers, November 6th, 1936.
[v] Cripps Papers, November 9th, 1934.
[vi] Cripps Papers, November 5th, 1934.
[vii] Cripps Papers, July 11th, 1935.
[viii] M. Foot, op. cit., p.149.
[ix] C. R. Attlee, *As It Happened*, pp.106–110.

mixed economy, a voting machine, an effective bureaucracy and an administration, which claimed no more than to run the existing system more efficiently. The S.L. had to face it: the Party had become absorbed, at the level of government and political decisions, into the structures of capitalist politics; the Party *was* a compromise, between working-class objectives and the traditional power structure, and seventy years on there would be a conscious effort to exorcise the Party's past ideological commitments.[i]

(E) The General Election (1935)

For Labour's leaders, the 1930s was 'a time of retreat',[ii] despite its four campaigns: the '*Call to Action*' (1932–33), the '*Victory for Socialism*' (1934–35), '*For the League of Nations*' (1935–36) and '*Labour's Immediate Programme*' (1937). Party leaders did not think through too closely what they meant by 'Socialism' and whether it was willing for Britain to lose its status as a world power and accept that of a Scandinavian state. The S.L. might want an agitation; Labour leaders wanted a careful investigation.[iii] By 1935 there was widespread awareness in Party ranks that the Party's organisation needed revision; the method of selecting candidates was limited; financing candidates and organisational work was inefficient; essential were attempts to raise the political consciousness of Party members.[iv] In internal Party dissensions and personality clashes, division between Party and union leaders, and S.L. leaders was about *policy*. The S.L., I.L.P. and C.P. were convinced that 'crisis in Europe' was moving to its zenith and the choice was Socialism or Fascism, but Labour leaders 'always had some fresh reason for not acting.'[v] The Party still would not commit itself to unemployed demonstrations, let alone a Socialist society introducing a new creative impulse into social life, while J. F. Horrabin's comment on J. T. Murphy's *Preparing for Power* was apposite: 'His book will cause annoyance to those politicians whose one fear seems to be lest any straightforward statement of Socialist aims should lose us two constituencies and 20,000 votes'.[vi]

Party Conferences had become the battleground of these two lines of thought, ending with the victory of union leaders at Brighton in 1935. Had there been a stronger representation of Labour in the Commons from 1931 to 1935 the division between political and industrial wings of the Party might have been reconciled; but the two men who had linked both sides (A. Henderson and H. Morrison) were no longer in Parliament. The battle for the Party leadership took place while the dissensions of the S.L. and development of a Party programme were being displayed; H. Dalton was correct to summarise the years 1931 to 1934 as years of *recovery* for the Labour Party: 'We have re-examined our faith, restated our purposes, and regained our drive'.[vii] And there was always an influential section in the Party leadership who deprecated the existence of such bodies as the S.L. Cripps was not supported for statements like: 'Nothing could be more fatal to the

---

[i] D. Powell, op. cit., 1998, p.275.
[ii] A. Marwick, *Britain in the Age of Total War*, p.222.
[iii] J. Jupp, op. cit., p.610.
[iv] Cf. Allan Young, 'The Political Problem of Transition', *New Trends in Socialism*, ed. G. E. G. Catlin, 1935.
[v] M. Foot, op. cit. p.235.
[vi] S.L. Notes, *New Clarion*, March 3rd, 1934.
[vii] H. Dalton, *Practical Socialism*, 1935, p.18.

| Simon | Laval | Mussolini | Stalin | Eden | Hitler |

ALL QUIET ON THE EASTERN FRONT

April 5, 1935

Hitler was still refusing to join any peace pact to which Soviet Russia was a party.

LAST POST OR REVEILLE?

September 13, 1935

Nazi Germany had taken advantage of the League of Nations' attention to the Italo-Abyssinian war to break the Versailles Treaty and to reintroduce conscription. It sounded bad for the League of Nations.

Hitler   Hoare

"GERMANY MUST IMPORT RAW MATERIALS, YA!—
BUT SHE MUST ALSO EXPORT MANUFACTURES!"

September 18, 1935

Hitler asked for the return of the German ex-colonies. Britain proposed an "Open Door" arrangement with a fair share-out of raw materials to all needful states. But Hitler wanted not the mere fruits of colonies, but the colonies themselves as springboards for his proclaimed "world crusade against Bolshevism".

PEACE GESTURE

March 4, 1936

Hitler explained that his towering armaments were necessary as defence from the armaments of others. Nazi leaders pointed out the tremendous menace of Soviet Russia.

workers of this country than a Lib-Lab combination'[i] and in the Executive's *'Unity: True or Sham?'* he was denounced for his statement at Preston in 1934: 'There must be no compromise over Socialism, no coalitions or arrangements with others who were not Socialists. That way lay suicide'[ii], and for his belief that a body of Socialists (such as the S.L.) should make clear to the electorate the dangers involved in 'Socialist democracy' through Labourism, and for his denunciation of Party policy of preserving 'democracy' at all costs, clinging to the League of Nations as the one hope of peace: 'The Labour Party as a whole... has shown itself quite prepared to relegate Socialism to the background for the sake of preserving the forms of democracy'.[iii] A battle of words between the *Daily Herald* and the S.L., with accusations of misreporting and denigration on both sides, transpired.[iv]

These confrontations resulted in Party efforts to close ranks and define principles and methods, which Dalton thought to be the Party's central concern in its Policy Reports. The Left's main criticism did not alter; its argument was that the Party had *'a policy for calm weather'*;[v] but no policy for crisis in a world that was now in a state of crisis: 'The Party still looks at the world obliquely through a 19th century mirror'.[vi] It had not accepted the new challenge, because there was hope in a Labour Government being allowed to carry through one piece of social reform after another: 'the belief that the ruling class will allow itself to be legislated out of existence... it sounds incredible after its 1931 experience and all that has happened in Europe since, that any vestige of that early faith should remain'.[vii] This was one of the major anxieties; Labour leaders had learnt *never again* to propose collaboration with Labour's opponents. By 1935, Attlee, Dalton, Morrison, Greenwood, Bevin and Citrine had formed a respectable, assured, professional official Opposition in Parliament and unions. To preserve the Party's Parliamentary strategy, political action was narrowed to Parliamentary activities and conciliatory union negotiations.

In this environment of Labour politics, the S.L. could not successfully offer Socialist crusades without appearing extremist: 'The Party's 'Gradualism' assumed that the development of Socialism could take place within the context of the ordinary political struggle of the Ins and Outs, the traditional parliamentary game, and 'socialism by instalments'.[viii] Although it proclaimed itself a mass movement, Labour had rejected any programme of mass activity (by 1935) in favour of that exclusively parliamentary mode of politics, so the S.L.'s extra-parliamentary activities opposed the whole trend of Party development. Political and industrial actions were becoming more rigidly defined and separated because a fragmentation in these areas of potential militancy in localities would strengthen the 'unifying' agency of Parliamentary leadership, and in Parliament itself: Left-wing MPs might urge the leadership towards more Socialist policies but were dependent for their seats on the Party label and subject to the discipline of a party leadership backed up by loyalists and office holders.[ix]

By 1935, Party leaders concluded that the Party could only obtain a majority with a

---

[i] Cripps at St. George's Bristol, 'No Lib-Lab Alliance', *Bristol Evening Post*, March 12th, 1934.

[ii] Cripps at Stanhope, Co. Durham, July 28th, 1935, quoted in *Daily Herald*, March 20th, 1934.

[iii] Quoted in *Daily Herald*, December 22nd, 1934.

[iv] Cf. Cripps Papers, November 8th–12th, 1934, Cripps wrangled with the editor of the *Daily Herald*.

[v] J. Lee, *This Great Journey*, pp.109–110

[vi] Ibid.

[vii] Ibid.

[viii] R. Lyman, 'The Conflict Between Socialist Ideals and Practical Politics Between the Wars', *Journal of British Studies*, November 1965, Vol. 5 No. 1, p.142.

[ix] R. Looker, 'Future of the Left in Britain', *Studies on the Left*, Vol. 7, No. 2, pp.49–69, March–April 1967.

practical programme by constitutional means and the imposition of internal loyalty and self-discipline: *'Reliability* was a quality which during the 1930s became increasingly rare and highly prized in the Party'.[i] Here, the Party's Fabian tradition was updated to incorporate Keynes and pragmatism, exemplified in the studies of E. Durbin, H. Gaitskell, D. Jay and H. Dalton (whose book *Practical Socialism for Britain* (1935) expressed the Party's new path and campaign against the S.L.'s melodramatics). Dalton confidently asserted years later: 'What we accomplished in 1945 to 1950 was most surprisingly close to what we planned in 1931–4, and what I urged in *Practical Socialism for Britain*'.[ii] In the latter, Dalton announced Labour's list of required social reforms; Parliamentary procedure was 'unbusinesslike', 'time-wasting', inefficient, and debates had a 'disjointed discursiveness'.[iii] Wanted was a 'systematic plan for the allocation of parliamentary time',[iv] 'liberation from excessive detail',[v] abolition of the Lords (with its powers of obstruction and delay); the Party had to guard against its fondness for committees ('a habit-forming drug'),[vi] more rank and file participation in Party decisions, more consultation etc. Who in the Movement could disagree? Dalton's interests were finance and the economy and he expressed Labour tenets (fixed payments to private investors, private profit eliminated, rising standards of service to consumers, socialisation of financial institutions, social purpose (as distinct from profit-seeking) into financial operations,[vii] responsibility of financiers to public authority, Government control over banks):[viii] 'British finance is not a planned system ... it provides better facilities for the investment of capital abroad than at home ... it is wasteful ... and honey-combed with nepotism and patronage ... too many soft jobs for influential people, too many multiple directorships ... carrying fat fees without real functions.'[ix] The Labour Party had an alternative to the Gold standard in a commodity standard so monetary policy would aim at stabilising wholesale prices, preventing profiteering by middlemen; the needs of industry (not financial salesmanship) would be the primary consideration. Dalton also formulated the Party's proposal for a National Investment Board (to license and direct investments and mobilise financial resources, control public issues on the capital market, and the Stock Exchange) and the N.I.B. would become an instrument of social control; the Party proposed amalgamation of the 'Big Five' into a single Banking Corporation;[x] and a new credit institution created under public ownership.[xi] These financial suggestions did not imply abolition of private property, only 'excessive' inequalities. Labour upheld equality of opportunity; industrial legislation to soften inequalities; State pension schemes and a State medical service. The chief causes of inequality of incomes (inherited wealth and distribution of property) would remain. Daltonism would triunph in the late 1940s.

---

[i] K. Martin, *Harold Laski*, p.77. (My italics.)

[ii] H. Dalton, *The Fateful Years*, p.59.

[iii] H. Dalton, *Practical Socialism for Britain*, pp.44–46.

[iv] Ibid., pp.48–50. What the Liberal Party fought against in the 1935 General Election, was a "reckless subversive Socialism", qu. from T. Wilson *'The Downfall of the Liberal Party'*, 1966, p.377.

[v] Ibid., p.60.

[vi] Ibid., pp.82–86.

[vii] Ibid., p.185.

[viii] Ibid., pp.202–205.

[ix] Ibid., p.191.

[x] Ibid., pp.213–232.

[xi] Ibid., p.236.

However, to many of the politically unattached and particularly young people, the Party appeared uninspiring. It seemed to lack courage, or urgency: 'If your leaders said to us "Go and demonstrate for Socialism", that would be something. They don't. They say: "Sit at home, draw the curtains, keep calm, don't get excited, enthusiasm is unnecessary"'.[i] The S.L.'s new message was formulated at its *Special Conference* (November 1934). Hitherto the S.L. had concentrated in the Party on a programme for a Socialist Government and winning over the Party Conference. This tactic would not be abandoned. Attention would remain directed to what a Labour Government should do to be 'Socialist' (abandon gradualist policies, secure public ownership of key economic positions etc.), but the S.L. would urge 'immediate day-to-day activities' to provide challenges at the local level, and not merely at intervals at the ballot box.

The S.L. analysed the mid-1930s as a time of repression, potential Fascism, indeed, possible destruction of the Labour Movement: 'there are new Government forms of oppression. Democracy is being swept aside. Fascism holds down internal revolt, and faced with its failure to solve its own economic riddle, Capitalism moves steadily towards War ... In Britain ... liberties are restrained, the economics of nationalism and of protected units become dominant, the race in armaments is accelerated ... the *Trade Disputes Act* is succeeded by the *Disaffection Act*, the *Unemployment Act* establishes non-responsible Government and unconcealed threats to sabotage a Labour Government's policy are made by Government representatives of Big Business and Finance'.[ii] Here began the mounting ferocity of the S.L.'s attack on a circle of power – legislative, Crown and capital – that (the S.L. maintained) colluded to promote the *illusion* of a liberal democracy to perpetuate its own hegemony, what Tawney had named '*our religion of inequality in the interests of the power elite.*'[iii] After its great disappointments at Southport, the S.L. had returned to its original theme – 'the crisis of capitalism/dangers of a corporate state – the vagueness of which accentuated its grasp on the imagination of disillusioned Left-wing members. S.L. leaders propounded 'fanatics for a cause'[iv] (or anything which suggested action sufficient to bolster up the S.L.'s flagging hopes).

In basing its agitation on the dangers of Fascism, war and unemployment to working-class interests, the S.L.'s policy of quotidian practical activities would impinge on the C.P.'s local influence, especially in heavily unemployed areas. Either the S.L. would have to link with these local organisations and relinquish Labour membership, or agitate in the Party (as ineffectively as it had done in the previous two years). The Party Executive began manifesting its proscription powers against any affiliated members' connection with I.L.P. or C.P., just when the S.L. began to widen its objectives.

Despite the S.L.'s analysis of capitalism in crisis, economic recovery in many areas was obvious. By the autumn of 1934, employment had recovered to its 1929 level in spite of an increase in population,[v] production by 1937 was 20% above the level of 1929, and although exports made only a slight recovery after initial fall of 32% in

[i] Storm Jameson, 'To a Labour Party Official', *Left Review*, No. 2, pp.32–33, November 1934.

[ii] S.L. editorial, 'On the Basis of a Policy of Class Struggle – the S.L.'s New Task', *Socialist Leaguer*, No. 6, November–December 1934.

[iii] D. Powell, op. cit.,1998, p.186. (My italics.)

[iv] W. Mellor.

[v] The number of insured persons unemployed in the U.K. was just under 3 million (August 1931 to January 1933), 2.5 million (August 1933), 2 million (July 1935) and 1.6 million after July 1936. C. L. Mowat, op. cit., p.432.

volume and 50% in value, imports had returned to the old level in volume (though 32% less in value). Government policies of tariffs, import quotas, marketing schemes, devaluation, exchange control and cheap money made little difference *in comparison with* the fall in the cost of living which provided the margin for increased investment, the housing boom, growth of consumer industries, and the beginnings of rearmament.[i] The S.L.'s simplistic economic analysis appeared blunt when contrasted with the Government's 'smoothing over' of underlying structural problems: 'The National Government's financial policies made the best of both worlds: they seemed sufficiently deflationary to restore confidence, and sufficiently inflationary to assist recovery by maintaining the purchasing power of the people'.[ii]

By 1935, three years of Labour's search 'for the cause' in which the Party had been elaborating policy (with regard to banking, investment, electricity, transport, agriculture, iron and steel, parliamentary procedure and foreign affairs) had occurred. The public mind was turning to ideas of large-scale *social reconstruction* because the Government's programme seemed exhausted, and the numbers of unemployed proved the bankruptcy of national policies; the word "Socialism" no longer terrified the middle class, thousands of whom had lost their job'.[iii] Dalton's *Practical Socialism for Britain*, epitomising Party leaders' central beliefs, was praised by E. F. M. Durbin for containing a careful, sober, persuasive defence of the broad principles of policy in *For Socialism and Peace*'. The proposals were limited but practicable, offering a solution to transfer economic power to the State by democratic methods: 'It is not a spectacular programme ... the experience of 1929–1931 discouraged Utopian expectations in the Labour Party ... *and the S.L. is an historical failure*'.[iv] Or so it appeared. Careful, sober, persuasive – Labour's way in the 1930s.

These two examples of official Party views suggest the issue between so-called Party 'realists' and S.L. 'doctrinaires' had been settled at Southport. The S.L. perceived the confrontation was merely suspended, although efforts were made in the coming months to reassure Party leaders that the S.L. would remain 'loyal'. This dual reaction appeared in February 1935, when the S.L. denied it had 'pigeon-holed its 5 year plan', or swallowed any of its convictions: 'The S.L. is convinced that any Labour Government which pursues a gradualist policy is doomed to failure... and it is remaining in the place where alone the propaganda of its convictions can have any practical results, i.e. in the Labour Party'.[v] However, the S.L. *was* rechannelling its energies into areas which might bring it into eventual conflict with the Party's gradualist policies. S.L. criticism of Party leaders became more serious when critics were supported by a large independent outside organisation, when the agitation became continuous and organised, and was no longer concerned with details of Party policy but specific assumptions pertaining to that policy. Caught in an impossible political position, the S.L. could continue to worry about 'world peace' and steps which a Labour Movement *ought* to take. Describing the S.L.'s new outlook, Trevelyan denied there would be any changes because the Party had evolved workable plans for Socialist reconstruction.[vi] In fact, S.L. leaders were convinced that the Party's inaction

---

[i] Cf. C. L. Mowat, op. cit., p.434.

[ii] Ibid., p.455.

[iii] Rt. Hon. H. B. Lees-Smith, 'Prospects for the Labour Party', *Political Quarterly*, January–March 1935.

[iv] E. F. M. Durbin, 'Democracy and Socialism in Britain', *Political Quarterly*, July–September 1935.

[v] S.L. editorial, *Socialist Leaguer*, No. 9, February 15th, 1935.

[vi] 'The Outlook of the S.L.', *Political Quarterly*, April–June 1935.

forced people to become more involved in political activism, but it was the unassailability of the Executive's position which stymied opposition.

Reviewing S.L. activities from May 1934 to May 1935, J. T. Murphy reassessed the S.L.'s position: 'We cannot have it both ways – be in the Party and act as if we were out of it'.[i] The S.L. had taken its stand on loyalty to the Party and Cripps endorsed these sentiments at Bristol: 'The S.L. is an integral part of the Party… we must not allow ourselves to be diverted into activities definitely condemned by the Party which will jeopardise our affiliation to and influence within it.'[ii] The S.L.'s only choice was to convert more unionists and Party members to 'Left-wing thinking', because outside the Party the S.L. would be 'destined to complete futility'.[iii] The S.L.'s position was expressed in an article entitled *'Everywhere in Europe is Naked Class War'*: 'The S.L. has never sought to minimise difficulties nor to paint rosy pictures of any easy path to Socialism. It believes that the first decisive steps to victory can be taken by the Labour Party, backed by a Trade Unionism that knows that Capitalism cannot and will not surrender without combat'.[iv] Yet the S.L. acknowledged there was in the political and industrial wings of the Movement a willingness to accept and act on the belief that 'there was no real class struggle and no class conflict.'[v]

At the Bristol Conference, Cripps admitted that the programme on which the Party was to fight the next Election was not the one the S.L. had hoped for, but 'we have done our best to contribute to its reality and effectiveness'.[vi] He was convinced that, except for the issue of peace, S.L. leaders could not alter the Party's programme. As expected, the I.L.P. was quick to highlight the S.L.'s difficulties, pointing out that S.L. leaders knew their limitations were due to Party affiliation and the impossibility of changing the internal policy of the Party. The I.L.P. was also conscious that the S.L. had the unenviable task of maintaining belief in the Labour Party as a 'radical change' agent. Unlike the I.L.P.: 'S.L. members are putting loyalty to a Party machine and belief in "big battalions" before their revolutionary socialist principles and practice'.[vii] *The Times* diagnosed infantile psychological motives behind the S.L: 'The S.L. Conference gave some idea of the character of the opposition's only armoury. It has been officially snubbed by the Labour Party, and is annoyed at the refusal of the Party to accept all its doctrines.'[viii]

What was happening at the S.L. Conference was an acknowledgement that, despite its change of tactics since November 1934, debate, organisation, propaganda and action were only possible on the Executive's terms. If S.L. members wanted to express disagreement with Party policies and act contrary to Party dictates, they were welcome to do so – outside Party ranks. It is no exaggeration to state that any opposition to the Executive was ascribed to the crudest personal motives, an ego trip by wealthy members for personal prestige. This was intensified when Cripps resigned from the N.E.C. (September 1935), H. Dalton, remained punitive: 'As to Stafford, he *is* naïve,

---

[i] J. T. Murphy, 'The Year in Review', *Socialist Leaguer*, No. 11, May 1935.

[ii] *Daily Herald*, June 10th, 1935.

[iii] Cripps (in letter), Cripps Papers, March 4th, 1935.

[iv] *Socialist Leaguer*, No. 11, May 1935.

[v] Ibid.

[vi] *Morning Post*, June 10th, 1935; New Leader, June 14th 1935.

[vii] Ibid.

[viii] These 'doctrines' were defined; a Labour Government would face a 'first-class financial crisis' and an 'undisguised party dictatorship' would be implemented', 'Opposition Manoeuvres', *The Times*, June 13th, 1935.

often to the point of sheer imbecility ... many of us have bridled our tongues in public with an iron control these last four years, thinking that public squabbling was undesirable, even in the face of great provocation and damage to the prospects of our candidates'.[i] By the Brighton Conference, Dalton and Bevin were formulating alterations in Labour policies sufficient to mark the end of one phase of temporary radicalism in the Party and its return to moderation, under great provocation!

At Brighton, the Party continued its work of policy-making by dealing with a mixed collection of reports from the Executive, with plans for socialisation of fuel, power and industries (W. Mellor received assurances that provisions relating to workers' control would be brought in line with general policy laid down by the Party and T.U.C.), and reports on 'Socialism and Social Credit' and 'Local Government and the Depressed Areas'. There was a more significant contretemps among factions within the Party; the protagonists Lansbury, Cripps and Bevin, representing respectively the political and moderate side of the Party; the intellectual and semi-revolutionary wing; and the solidarity and 'common sense' of unions.[ii] Cripps explained the S.L. would have to show, at Brighton, the daily struggle against capitalist injustices. He hoped, when the problem of the depressed areas and unemployment was debated, it would be on the basis of fundamental remedies, not palliatives. He reiterated the S.L. stance (foreign to Party leaders about to face an Election): 'If we make the touchstone of our propaganda and our decisions the stark fact that within Capitalism there always is ... a class struggle, we shall not go far wrong in assessing the necessities of the political situation'.[iii] Perish the thought!

Debates at Brighton determined the future of the Party leadership and possible future for the S.L. The Executive presented a choice of submission to its pronouncements or expulsion for militant opposition. Criticisms of Party leaders were projected as attacks upon the whole Movement; the 'responsible' and 'reasonable' approach was revealed by G. R. Shepherd: 'We always allow latitude for differences on particular points, but we do not believe that the doors of the Party should be open to persons who want to come in merely for the purpose of changing policy'.[iv] Promote that man! Changing policy *was* the S.L.'s aim, and its leaders brought renewed attention to 'Party democracy' because of evident signs that the 'big stick' was again being used as a weapon for inducing conformity: 'The Party Executive might do worse than survey the possibilities of a reorganisation of the Party which will give greater weight in its counsels to those without whose constant toil the Party would atrophy.'[v] Think on it!

The S.L., at their fourth Party Conference, knew that Party policies were based on conciliation and arbitration, and class-less socialism dominated the Party's approach. The Labour Movement had met three trials of strength with the philosophy and outlook of Fabianism dominant in the minds of leaders (i.e. 'Black Friday', General Strike 1926, and the 1931 Crisis) – on each occasion the Movement suffered a defeat and the ruling class was able to emerge with increased prestige.[vi] So deduced the S.L. The Brighton Conference and results of the General Election in 1935 heralded the

---

[i] H. Dalton to K. Martin, quoted in *The Editor*, p.173, September 24th, 1935.

[ii] C. L. Mowat, op. cit., p.551.

[iii] S. Cripps, 'What We Must Do at the Party Conference', *Socialist*, No. 1, September 1935.

[iv] *Labour Party Annual Conference Report*, October 1935, p.140.

[v] *Socialist*, No. 2, November 1935.

[vi] 'Jacques', 'Class Struggle and 'Fabianism', *Socialist*, November 1935.

beginning of a new period of Party disunity prompted by local party radicalism, united unemployment demonstrations, and a United Front campaign. At the Election, commitment of Party members was dissipated by disillusionment, political victimisation, an apathy provoked by a leadership which 'only wanted votes'. The Election campaign relied less on personal activity, more on effective use of newspapers and wireless; Left-wing Party members were experiencing a learning process, a consciousness that power lay in the Executive's leadership, and this could in the 1930s only aid the Conservative Party: 'An organisation designed primarily for winning elections is out of date. It may be good enough for parties of the Right. They possess elaborate, expensive propaganda machines directed automatically from the centre which can work up last-minute stunts, sudden scares and similar appeals to primitive instinctive urges at election times'.[i] Labour's election learning curve took a decade.

There were other reasons for the Conservative victory in 1935. After a major economic crisis, the electorate was more likely to prefer stability and wish to extend the life of a 'National' Government; the Conservatives used Labour policies (support for League of Nations' sanctions against Italy, and peace and disarmament talks); George V's Jubilee favoured upholders of the status quo; economic conditions had stabilised with the housing boom, improved export trade, increased home markets, floating voters frightened by candidates' warning that a Labour victory might bring further financial crises and reduce unemployment benefit. Conservatives scaremongering implied 'Socialist policy would mean war', heavy expenditure for propaganda and advertising by Conservative Central office; Baldwin 'the man you can trust', and the international situation, gave the Government a winning formula; BBC broadcasts, by their national and paternal tone, tended to favour the Conservatives, and the fact that Lansbury did not broadcast exacerbated Labour's squabbles over the traditional pacifist nature of the Party.[ii]

The Labour Movement's sections reacted differently to the results of the Election.[iii] Dalton was optimistic because so sensitive was the electoral system to small shifts in voting strength that less than **15%** of a vote swing would put the Labour Party in power,[iv] so the result of the Election was a *justification* for Party leaders' policies.[v] An unfortunate feature of the Election was that, although most leaders defeated in 1931 recovered their seats, few younger Party candidates were elected (only 2 Labour MPs were under 30, only 8 under 40, after the Election), yet Party leaders had kept dissensions to a minimum, and there was an agreed programme in both domestic and foreign affairs. For the S.L., the result exposed Labour's refusal to take risks: 'Both in strategy and in propaganda, defeatism, passivity and scepticism did their work only too well'.[vi] Gradualism had weakened Labour's appeal by removing its distinctiveness, and any Socialist message was allegedly blurred by compromise and Parliamentary 'good manners'. Even E. Shinwell stated that a Party with ideals and vision had a better prospect of long-term progress than the Party which catered for electoral support on a

[i] A. B. White, op. cit., p.377. The election resulted in 432 Cons., 154 Lab., and 20 Libs. (Labour had trebled its MPs since 1931).
[ii] Cf. D. McHenry, op. cit., pp.181–200.
[iii] 387 Conservatives, 33 National Liberals, 8 National Labour, 154 Labour MPs, 21 Liberals.
[iv] H. Dalton, 'The Popular Front', *Political Quarterly*, October–December 1936.
[v] Lord Samuel's broadcast address, November 6th, 1935, quoted by T. Wilson, op. cit., p.377.
[vi] A. Hutt, op. cit., pp.273–274.

popular but superficial policy'.[i] S.L. leaders noted that the Party Executive did not want mass demonstrations, nor strikes, which might involve the Movement in non-electoral pursuits, while Cripps blamed the Executive's strategy for the defeat: 'The Party suffered because they largely failed to make clear by their group leadership or by their mass propaganda that they really were wholeheartedly anti-capitalist and pro-Socialist. Their policy and propaganda was sufficiently "vaguely Socialist" to give their opponents a basis for "scare" politics,'[ii] adding provocatively: 'Nothing will make people doubt the capacity of the Labour Party to govern more than the impression, which is widespread today, that they are *frightened of the logic of their own proposals*'.[iii] Yet he knew that, for the S.L., the best place for fighting the Party leadership (as long as one was allowed) remained within the Labour Party.

There were more practical and constructive comments on the Party's Election performance from Laski, who considered there had been no coherent or unified philosophy in the Party's appeal (on unemployment, housing, slum clearance, or naval/military policy), so the elector did not feel certain of what a Labour Government would do. The Party had remained formally a Socialist party, but relied on measures of social reform and had devoted most energy to attacking the Government's record rather than promulgating its own proposals: 'The voter was never sure for what policy the Labour Party stood. Did it mean social reform? Did it mean socialism? What were its fundamental objectives; what was the scheme of priorities the Party has adopted in relation to them?'[iv] The Party had given no decisive lead, and another four years would be necessary before the Party could hope to recapture the mood of 1929. It had to maintain a leadership with sufficient continuity to make its impact on the electorate; it needed to offer to younger members seats that could be won: it had to improve local organisation and use wireless and cinema more consciously; the Left maintained the official Party was 'sluggish, wary, and bureaucratically pedantic in providing leadership for the protest against poverty and industrial decay'.[v]

From Left and Right in the Movement, the problems facing the Party were met with hope, more than analysis indicating prospects. There was no significant Socialist movement, so different sections turned to local issues, dealt with limited problems, continued in an anti-ideological Movement (and yet believed in a future strategy of social change), while the majority of union leaders viewed the Party as a representative of working-class interests campaigning for limited protective and welfare legislation. This situation made it difficult for the Executive to accept S.L. criticisms and it was not forgotten that Cripps had commented, after the Election, that the Government had made considerable achievements in the volume and quality of its legislation: 'There is really very little case at all for an alternative Government within the Capitalist system'.[vi] He had exposed the Party's wooing of ex-Liberals and the middle class vote, of having 'presented Socialism as the distant Utopia'; he had ridiculed the Party's propaganda which could never inspire the enthusiasm to get an anti-Capitalist Government into office; to suggest the Party 'in its existing structure' was *an improbable instrument of Socialist change* was to invite recriminations; to intimate the Party was formally

[i] E. Shinwell, op. cit., p.214.

[ii] Cripps, 'Election Lessons that Must be Learned', *Socialist*, No. 3, December 1935.

[iii] Cripps to Kate Spurrell, Cripps Papers, November 26th, 1935.

[iv] H. Laski, 'The General Election of 1935', *Political Quarterly*, January–March 1936.

[v] A. Bevan, quoted by M. Foot, op. cit., p.151.

[vi] *Oxford Mail*, November 30th, 1935, used in *Unity: True or Sham?*, February 1937.

committed to Socialism but in practice functioning as *the inheritor of a reforming Liberal Party* could only lead to further limitations on freedom of action in the Party's confines.

Another conflict was played out following the Party's tentative decision to turn away from planning for the future to the immediate task of safeguarding existing social services. The controversy between Parliamentary Socialism and economic socialism remained a factor embodied in moderates, Morrison and Bevin, whose viewpoints coloured discussions and helped isolate the S.L. Shadow-boxing was indulged in by Bevin and Morrison over nationalisation proposals, which the latter regarded as founded primarily on a concept of efficiency and the public interest, and the former presumed were to elevate the industrial worker; both viewpoints followed a policy of 'not rocking the boat' by further measures of socialisation.[i] Another characteristic which emerged from Morrison's and Bevin's 'differences' was the new force of local politics. As Secretary of the London Labour Party and organiser of its L.C.C. victories, Morrison commanded an organisation comparable in its influence in the Party to that of unions.[ii] Bevin reacted to this, believing that power rested at the point of production (a factor S.L. leaders had reiterated) whereas Morrison represented the official Party's preoccupation with the 'face' presented by the Party to the electorate, *the search for the middle class vote*, and attempts to heal controversies (which might harm the Party); Bevin's contribution was to transpose organisational loyalty from the union to the Party world. From both Morrison and Bevin, S.L. leaders insinuated their oppositional position against electoral and loyalty considerations.

(F) Ambiguities at the Edinburgh Conference (1936)

By 1936, three aspects in the Party the S.L. challenged; the leadership lacked popular appeal or a public figure (Transport House repudiated its most popular orator, Cripps); the Party needed a shorter, less complicated programme; the Party was too exclusive and looked like a faction trying to catch votes, not a *broad-based* democratic movement. There were signs in the first months of 1936 that the S.L. was becoming less tolerant of official attitudes; J. T. Murphy announced that the S.L. had to function more as an affiliated organisation than an organisation of individuals *diffusing* S.L. ideas in the Party: 'Up to the present, our speakers have spoken for the Party, in the name of the Party and without the slightest reference to the S.L.'[iii] A resolution from the 55 Conferences organised by the S.L. in February asked the Party Executive to prepare plans for giving greater weight to constituency parties (on which fell the daily work) and to explore ways by which the bond with the union movement could find expression through these local units.

Reviewing *New Trends in Socialism*[iv] Lionel Elvin for the S.L. could not refrain from inquiring if new trends in the Labour Party were due to the discovery that it was to fulfil the historic mission of the Liberal Party! Cripps also made scathing comments about the party leadership (in February 1936) as 'hesitant and weak' with 'no clear idea

---

[i] Cf. P. Sweezy, *Socialism*, pp.50–60. The middle-class vote was Labour's in 1997 and 2001.
[ii] F. Williams, *Ernest Bevin*, pp.184–87.
[iii] J. T. Murphy, 'Our Challenge to Gradualism', *Socialist*, No. 4, January–February 1936.
[iv] *Socialist*, No. 4, January–February 1936.

of its objectives or strategy': 'We are moving towards a capitalist concentration of power in this country which is likely to draw trade union and Labour elements with it ... it is essential within Democracy to have a parliamentary form of Government with a clear-cut *distinction* between Party policies'.[i] In March, he accused the *Daily Herald* of 'boycotting him', so the *Daily Herald* editor, W.H. Stevenson, asked him to forward press advances of his proposed speeches.[ii]

At the S.L.'s Stoke Conference (1936) disappointments emerged; the opportunism of Labour and union leaders had created a feeling of defeatism and indifference on political issues. For the S.L., the Party had made little or no attempt to activate the mass of working people: 'The Labour Party... seemed dowdy, more concerned with respectability than action'.[iii] (Labour leaders would have agreed: *respectability* was the aim). S.L. leaders noticed the Party's concern to interest local members in the election machine: 'Underneath this "sticking to routine" lies the memory of past treacheries and failures of the leaders, and a present lack of belief.'[iv] Reg Groves for the S.L. exhorted that challenging calls to political endeavour, urgency in response to possible war, or pressures of hardships by the unemployed, were avoided by the Party Executive *because* the Party was led by 'politicians of pre-war days' when the Party was under the influence of Liberal policies. These leaders substituted direct challenge and struggle for manoeuvres and combinations aimed at preserving their own political existence: 'The effect of this control by the dead hand of the past could be seen in local parties, where the old 'unending progress' conception of politics was regarded as 'a series of elections'.[v]

A resolution moved by Mellor at Stoke (in June 1936) was passed, stating the S.L. Conference was 'opposed to all forms of collaboration with capitalist parties and organisations.[vi] The capture of parliamentary power would remain an essential part of the struggle, although another resolution stated defiantly that the Conference regarded developments in the larger Movement as 'menacing to Socialism and inimical to the independence of the Movement and its aims';[vii] the S.L. had to take the initiative in organising agitation and propaganda for Socialist policies. Cripps talked of a Labour Party giving a lead in a policy of opposition because it was 'no time for any nice balancing of tactical expediency ... or for considering whether by moderation we can attract some Liberals or discontented Conservatives';[viii] he was adamant that the S.L. had to work in the Movement to convince Party members there was no hope for reformism. The S.L.'s proclamation would remain – loyalty to the Party in *'the rôle of candid friend'*.[ix] This was true of the S.L.'s anti-war conferences. Cripps had gravely uttered that there was a serious danger of co-operation of organised Labour with capitalists to carry through the rearmaments programme,[x] while J. T. Murphy was anxious to reassure the Party and unions that the Anti-War conferences were not 'a

[i] Quoting E. Estorick, op. cit., p.149.
[ii] Cripps Papers, March 9th, 1936.
[iii] D. E. S. Maxwell, *Poets of the 1930s*, 1969, p.2.
[iv] Reg Groves, 'The Labour Party and the Young Worker', *Socialist*, No. 8, June 1936.
[v] Ibid.
[vi] Stoke S.L. Conference at Hanley, June 1st, 1936.
[vii] Ibid.
[viii] Cripps' presidential address, quoted in *Stoke on Trent City Times*, June 6th, 1936.
[ix] *New Statesman and Nation*, June 6th, 1936.
[x] Cripps Papers, May 14th, 1936.

splitting movement' but 'a step towards better organisation of the S.L. within the Party'.[i] Opposing the rearmaments programme was a much more questionable S.L. strategy.

In June 1936, Cripps contacted Lansbury to ask if he would join a committee for organising a new paper to be called *Tribune*. Lansbury replied that he would prefer to help as a weekly contributor, and added, poignantly, words which had significance for the S.L.'s position: 'My work for the Party as a Party is finished. I see life ever so much broader than in days gone by ... The Party nearly chokes me. I want to shout out *against* them. Beatrice Webb is right when she says Democracy will not function until we are all more disciplined in our minds and bodies'.[ii] Party leaders, and not the S.L., could have organised the only effective resistance to the Government; through meetings, demonstrations, rallies, petitions, to unite all opinion to challenge Government policies, obstruct Parliamentary business, bring the unions on strike to pressure the Government, or create an anti-Government alliance. As it was, the rank and file of the Movement was subdued, because of uninspiring leadership and the lingering disappointment of the last Election. As long as the Party programme consisted of a long list of different kinds of measures with no indication as to when or how they could be implemented, the S.L. was sure electors would not be convinced. While Cripps urged a short-term policy programme,[iii] G. R. Strauss demanded 'nothing short of a dramatic reorientation of policy... the first step must be the formation of a united front.[iv] Momentous decisions would result from discussions at the Conference at Edinburgh, decisions affecting C.P. affiliation, the League of Youth, response to the Spanish Civil War, and rearmament.

The Edinburgh Conference was the last Conference held under union domination. Attlee's support for the Spanish Republican Government and Morrison upholding the increase in constituency representation on the N.E.C. indicated a new mood even among moderate leaders while the S.L.'s critique of Party and union leaders met 'the Conference steam-roller, which was in perfect working order; all deviations towards the Left suppressed with vigour and promptitude'.[v] The S.L. had fervently proposed abolition of the Lords, but the Executive decided at Edinburgh that 'pageantry' was not in itself objectionable! The S.L. had opposed knighthoods and honours for Labour members, but the Executive considered that so long as the Lords continued, the Labour case had to be presented there, and creation of peers (in large numbers) might prove to be the only possible way to abolish the House of Lords! Catch twenty-two. To the S.L., Edinburgh revealed a Party that had lost faith in itself, however momentarily. The leadership made ambiguous statements on policy, shrouded the issues, failed to stand forward as an alternative with a coherent political line; Dalton admitted the Party was disappointed by the small advance made at the 1935 Election, was unsure of itself, its leaders, programme, Constitution: 'unsure whether, fighting alone and by democratic methods, it could hope ever to win power...'[vi] He thought the malaise was curable, provided the N.E.C. and Transport House machine showed originality and initiative: 'The widespread complaints that we were all very slow and stodgy had some

---

[i] *Daily Herald*, June 2nd, 1936.
[ii] G. Lansbury to Cripps, Cripps Papers, June 20th, 1936.
[iii] S. Cripps, 'A Short Programme of Action', *Socialist*, No. 9, July–August 1936.
[iv] G. R. Strauss, 'Problems of a Labour Policy', *Labour Monthly*, Vol. 18, No. 8, August 1936.
[v] G. D. H. Cole, *The People's Front*, 1937, p.291.
[vi] H. Dalton, *The Fateful Years*, p.115.

justification … everybody was grumbling … we must give them all something new to do and think about'.[i] How about a new programme?

The Conference administered a severe shock to the Labour Movement: 'Nobody can leave this Conference … with any feeling of hope about the future of our Movement' (J. Howarth of the Railway Clerks); 'another Conference of the same kind would destroy the Party as an effective force for a long time to come' (Dr. Addison); 'If delegates and visitors came expecting inspiration, they went away empty' (J. R. Leslie of the Shop Assistants Union); 'The bold, imaginative leadership … is still to be found' (*Reynolds News*); 'This slouching leadership, this parasitic attitude towards the Government of the other class would attract no young man' (H. N. Brailsford); 'Wherever I have been since the Conference, I have heard dismay expressed at its temper and results' (Cripps).[ii] 'The leadership was 'fumbling and incompetent. There was no sense of direction … and no clarity of purpose'[iii] (Laski); 'it was the worst Conference ever staged by the Labour Party. Never had the block vote been used so ruthlessly and with such "evil" intent',[iv] (C.P.'er W. Gallacher). No recommendations there. In fact, no major transformation in the Party had taken place as a result of the 1931 crisis, mass unemployment or European Fascism; S.L. efforts to activate the Party had been resisted by Labour leaders with a resolve it *never* displayed against the Government! Mellor thought the Left was by 1936 more conscious of itself, more effective in its opposition to the Executive than at any Conference since 1931 (regardless of block vote defeats) but he saw negative effects: 'Party delegates were forced to disperse with a sense of frustration and disillusionment … the uncertainty of the rank and file deepened … A few inconsiderable organisational changes within the Party are to be granted as a sop to the constituency parties'.[v] The S.L. was made conscious at this, their last Labour Conference (as an affiliated organisation), that the Executive had no definite direction on *any* aspect of international affairs or internal politics. For Cripps, the tragedy was 'the tight-rope walking by the platform',[vi] yet he was quizzical because the platform seemed to have derived no inspiration from its achievements: 'They were far too worried by their own dissensions to get satisfaction from any apparent victory. This left the Conference more leaderless than ever, and created such a feeling of confusion and bewilderment'.[vii]

The National Council of Labour had refused to lead the Hunger March (to arrive in London at the beginning of November), so the March was 'adopted' by the South Wales Miners' Federation, the I.L.P. and C.P. This official reaction was deflating when a mass response could have been mobilised A. Bevan inquired: 'Why should so much of our strength be spent in overcoming the inertia of a moribund leadership?'[viii] No answer was forthcoming. This pervaded the mood of Cripps' Stockport speech[ix] for which he was admonished by the Party Executive. The S.L. leader stated the Conference (of 1936) had shaken the rank and file into realisation for immediate

---

[i] Ibid.

[ii] All quoted by A. Hutt, op. cit., pp.299–301.

[iii] H. Laski, *Labour Monthly*, Vol. 18, No. 11, November 1936.

[iv] W. Gallacher, *The Rolling of the Thunder*, pp.173–175.

[v] W. Mellor, 'Edinburgh Conference and After', *Socialist*, No. 12, November 1936.

[vi] 'The Elector', *New Statesman and Nation*, October 31st, 1936.

[vii] Cripps, *Controversy*, November 1936.

[viii] A. Bevan, 'Challenge of the Hunger March', *Socialist*, No. 12, November 1936.

[ix] November 15th, 1936.

action, 'to get down to bread and butter politics', and pointed to the fine example of the hunger marchers, the class struggle in Spain, the need to base Party policy on class consciousness: 'Can we trust the "National" Government with armaments?' Then he uttered a provocatively misleading conviction that '*it would not be a bad thing for the British working class if Germany did defeat us. It would be a disaster for the profit-makers and capitalists, but not necessarily for the working classes … Russia was defeated in the last war yet her working classes benefited most from the war*'.[i] Cripps' 'working classes' was a theoretical abstraction. His arguments appeared a counsel of despair; a pseudo-Marxist interpretation attempting to clarify that the British 'working class' would not necessarily suffer through the defeat of 'British Imperialism'. Cripps in his tortuous way was asking working people to realise the disparity of interests between *their* class and capitalists in foreign policy and armaments and thought he was unmasking the official Party view that defeat of British Imperialism would harm the British working class and would lead the Party to support the Government in its rearmament programme, its recruiting, its Imperialist policy, and possibly support of European Fascist powers against Soviet Russia! This analysis was nonsensical, unhistorical and irrelevant, and the general reaction (of the Left) to Cripps was 'warm affection and hope for leadership'.[ii] A resolution from the Bristol East Labour Party claimed the outbursts by the *Daily Herald*[iii] and the N.E.C. against Cripps were a calculated endeavour to discredit him in the eyes of workers, because of his growing influence among the rank and file, his outspoken utterances on socialism with its boomerang effect on the 'betrayers of the working class', and the lead he gave to the constituency parties in their endeavour to democratise the Party.[iv] (Most letters which Cripps received about his speech blamed the *Daily Herald* for misinterpreting him, and saw Cripps as having made 'a bold stand' against the apathy of Party leaders.)[v] However, the N.E.C. issued a statement on November 25th, 1936 'unanimously dissociating itself' from and 'categorically repudiating' Cripps' views regarding the position of the working classes in the event of a defeat in war: 'These opinions do not reflect the mind of the British Labour Movement'.[vi] J. S. Middleton (Party Secretary) invited Cripps to discuss his complaints, but Cripps refused because it was a 'somewhat curious proposal that having delivered their judgement, the Executive should now invite me to meet their officers'.[vii] Support for Cripps grew, and he was urged to defy the 'stuffy bigwigs who misrepresent the feelings of rank and file Socialists'[viii] and launch his own national anti-recruiting campaign; Ebbw Vale Labour Party denounced the *Daily Herald* for harming the Socialist cause by its victimisation;[ix] many local parties wrote to Cripps to compliment him: 'there is no other single individual in the whole Party who is doing the strenuous work that you are doing';[x] some local parties even sent

[i] *Stockport Express*, November 19th, 1936.
[ii] D. N. Pritt to Cripps, Cripps Papers, November 20th, 1936.
[iii] *Daily Herald* distorted Cripps' reply to a question on his speech, November 19th, 1936.
[iv] Cf. Resolution of Bristol East Labour Party, Cripps Papers, November 23rd, 1936.
[v] Letters to Cripps, Cripps Papers, November 21st–24th, 1936.
[vi] N.E.C., November 25th, 1936.
[vii] Cripps to J. S. Middleton, Cripps Papers, *Bristol Labour Weekly*, November 26th, 1936–December 5th, 1936.
[viii] J. F. Jackson to Cripps, Cripps Papers, December 4th, 1936.
[ix] Cripps Papers, December 5th, 1936.
[x] Letter to Cripps, December 9th, 1936.

resolutions of protest to the N.E.C. for its 'contemptible treatment',[i] and expressed complete confidence 'in Cripps' effort to establish working-class unity for the cause of socialism and peace'.[ii] Not that this answered the substance of the N.E.C.'s rebuke.

Although this issue subsided with a slapped wrist and Middleton's hope that Cripps would 'avoid similar unfortunate incidents in the future',[iii] plus Cripps' informal talk with the Party Chairman,[iv] the S.L. leader now acknowledged that the S.L. needed alignments with other Left groups if it was to function successfully. It might have to shed its pacifist section and recognise a class struggle basis. The Stockport speech symbolised the parting of the ways for the S.L., the parting from Party pronouncements. Exposing 'Imperialism and Nationalism' brought the S.L. leader much closer to the I.L.P. leader (J. Maxton) and the C.P. leader (H. Pollitt) in outlook and phraseology, and into the Unity Campaign.

Meanwhile, Party leaders had to adopt S.L. arguments to lead the opposition to the Government's economic policy. From a resolution at Edinburgh, *a Special Commission on the Distressed Areas* was at last set up, with Dalton as Chairman admitting, with almost Marxist ferocity, that 'the populations of the Distressed Areas ... are the innocent victims of an unplanned Capitalism ... mercilessly ground down by the operation of the Means Test and fobbed off with odds and ends of private charity'[v] (future Cabinet material), although C. R. Attlee reiterated that the Party opposed Government policy but 'it does not carry on a campaign of resistance, passive or active, to hinder the ordinary functions of Government'.[vi] While the circumstances of the 1930s had prompted many to adopt neo-Socialist views, a powerful Left popular movement could not be organised and led exclusively (or even primarily) from within the Party because the Right-wing leadership would use its power to thwart them.[vii]

(G) Labour's Immediate Programme or The Unity Campaign (1937)?

By January 1937, the S.L. had been driven (partly in reaction to Party leaders, partly of its own volition) to take a stand at the risk of expulsion. Bevan typified Left-wing anger at Labour leaders' refusal to fight on matters of principle: 'It refuses to arouse the electorate on the Means Test, the 40 hour week and Spain ... It is too respectable and too statesmanlike, *too frightened of offending the middle class*'.[viii] The S.L. had to recognise that the Labour Party by 1937 was assimilated into the orthodox structure of British politics, and the sword of Damocles hung over the S.L. while it grew frantic in the last months of its existence in reaction to what was labelled as yet another 'betrayal', by Party leaders. This mood reflected that of 1931 and brought an equally unrealistic response. To accuse Party leaders of having become 'part of the mechanism of

---

[i] Chester-le-Street Labour Party, Cripps Papers, December 8th, 1936.

[ii] H. E. Rogers for Bristol East Labour Party, December 20th, 1936.

[iii] J. S. Middleton to S. Cripps, Cripps Papers, December 10th, 1936.

[iv] S. Cripps to J. S. Middleton, Cripps Papers, December 11th, 1936.

[v] H. Dalton, *The Fateful Years*, p.121.

[vi] C. R. Attlee, *The Labour Party in Perspective*, 1937, p.219.

[vii] Cf. Arnold Kettle, 'The Failure of the Left', *Marxism Today*, January 1966, pp.5–9.

[viii] Quoted by M. Foot, op. cit., p.259. (My italics.) This 'fear' had been resolved 60 years on.

Capitalist democracy, to perpetuate more smoothly the domination of a ruling class of property-owners',[i] could not lengthen the S.L.'s affiliation! Mellor's vitriolic abuse levelled at Labour leaders was equally destined to lead the S.L. out of the Party: 'alignment with arch-imperialists, the criminal hesitancy to fight rearmament, callous and tragic supineness on the Spanish issue, the collaboration against Communism on the Public Order Bill … trade unionism shirking class issues, and prosperity built on armaments condoned'.[ii] Mellor had put it on the line!

In March 1937, the Executive published *Labour's Immediate Programme* and Dalton described it as an attempt to arouse interest, maintain self-confidence, and discredit the disloyalists.[iii] It certainly emasculated the S.L., with its programme of measures of social amelioration to keep the mind of the Movement busy with positive and constructive ideas. Ostensibly, it was to summarise debates from the previous five years, a brief and practical document for a programme of nationalisation (the Bank of England, public enterprises, transport, coal, gas, electricity, railways, transport services), to ease unemployment, provide adequate pensions, shorten the working week (to 40 hours), extend health services, raise the school leaving age, reinvigorate the League of Nations, and somehow to halt the Arms race.[iv] This promised enough to satisfy most Party followers, was adopted at the Bournemouth Conference,[v] and *was not far short* of what the Labour Government of 1945–50 put into effect. C. R. Attlee proudly proclaimed: 'In *Labour Party in Perspective* I set out the programme which I thought a Labour Government in power should carry out. In 1945, I had the pleasure of seeing that programme implemented'.[vi] G. D. H. Cole considered that this programme had the merit of precision,[vii] A. Bullock that it corresponded with Bevin's ideas on policy and on the 'right way' to approach the electorate: 'No one had played a greater part in defeating the doctrinaires in the struggle over the character and programme of the Party following the 1931 split'. Bevin judged that the Party had not been reformed on the pattern of the S.L. or the I.L.P., nor on Lansbury and pacifists, but by the centre group, to which he, Attlee, Dalton and Morrison belonged.[viii]

Would the Party have found its centre of gravity further to the Right had it not been for the S.L. and its activities? The S.L. remained critical of what it perceived as *the ideological bankruptcy* of the official Movement, but it was not true to say 'it accepted the new programme almost without criticism'.[ix] S.L. writers were fully aware that their Joint Stock Banks amendment had been bypassed, there was no mention of workers' control, land was not to be placed under State control, the document was a retreat from *'For Socialism and Peace'*, and had returned the Party to marginal collectivist ideas. S.L. leaders were also suspicious of the Programme because of the timing of its announcement, when the Executive had banned Party members from S.L. membership, 'the first time that proscription had been applied against a bona fide

[i] Cripps, *Socialist*, No. 13, December 1936–January 1937.
[ii] Mellor, 'Get Together Comrades – Working-class Unity on Workers' Issues', *Socialist*, No. 13, December 1936–January 1937.
[iii] H. Dalton, *The Fateful Years*, op. cit., p.125.
[iv] *Labour's Immediate Programme*, L.P. pamphlet, 1937.
[v] *Labour Party Annual Conference Report*, October 1937, p.186.
[vi] C. R. Attlee, *As It Happened*, 1954, p.87.
[vii] G. D. H. Cole, *The History of the Labour Party from 1914*, p.346.
[viii] A. Bullock, op. cit., pp.597–98.
[ix] J. Jupp, op. cit., p.296.

organisation of the Labour Left'.[i] The S.L. was advocating alternative policies at public meetings and in general propaganda, conscious of the greater emphasis on discipline and loyalty by the Executive. The Programme was part of this tactical move. The S.L. reaction was to ask the same questions it asked on Party policy: 'Would the Party repeal the *Trade Disputes Act* and the *Sedition Act*?[ii] Did it recognise Socialist measures would have to involve a change in the economic order?[iii] The struggle for a Labour Government had to be more than a propaganda campaign on *Labour's Immediate Programme*: 'It has got to be a conscious organised struggle, industrial and political, now for immediate objectives – shorter hours, higher wages, abolition of the Means Test and *Trade Disputes Act*, against capitalist rearmament, against non-intervention in Spain'.[iv] The first programme in 1918, *'Labour and the New Social Order'* had attached the Party to Socialism but the S.L. believed that as soon as the foot of Labour was on the ladder of government, the irreconcilable contradiction between the aims of Socialism and the 'practical politics' of Labour would begin to reassert itself.

Nevertheless, the issue of *Labour's Immediate Programme* was a step forward in one distinct aspect. It did clarify the Party's intentions and Cripps admitted it was an achievement to present an easily understood programme representing a challenge to capitalism (if carried through),[v] even if it was not as 'Socialist' as the S.L. had propounded. The programme was most notable for its rejection of more radical policies adopted by the S.L. in the aftermath of MacDonald's defection, and John Parker concluded that the rôle of a body affiliated to the Labour Party, but which is itself *primarily a propaganda body*, 'is at an end, as it is bound to get into serious conflict with the views of the Party as a whole'.[vi]

The keynote of all S.L. agitations in the Party had been a rejection of methods previously used, because the S.L. believed the Labour Party would not inspire the necessary enthusiasm to win a majority at a General Election, if it was regarded as an inefficient alternative capitalist Party. The S.L.'s short life opened up a questioning attitude in the Movement as to whether the value placed on 'loyalty and discipline' would not ultimately lose the diversity, idiosyncrasy and vitality of individual militants. Bevan's comment was prophetic: 'The Party Executive was using its giant strength to convert the Labour Party into a mass of sycophantic robots',[vii] which was what was feared about the majority of Labour MPs in 1997 and 2001. By the time of the Bournemouth Conference (October 1937), the Party was beginning to eliminate the 'sources of discontents'; 'increased integration' in the Party was perceived to be the answer to mutual suspicion and distrust between Transport House and the S.L. (which was claimed to have dissipated the energies of the Party in sectional struggle). All the S.L. feared was in A. L. Rowse's comments: 'If the Labour Party is ever to govern, it must get rid of this miserable inferiority complex of an oppressed class … it is so necessary to attract recruits from other classes … Lansbury's pacifism must have cost the Party a dozen seats at the last election; the Conservatives estimate Cripps' idiosyncrasies as worth 30 seats to them … the Party has failed to capture the patriotic

---

[i] R. Miliband, op. cit., p.251.

[ii] *Tribune*, March 12th, 1937.

[iii] *Tribune*, April 16th, 1937.

[iv] 'Today's Need', *Tribune*, May 14th, 1937.

[v] Cripps' speech in Garston, Cripps Papers, September 21st, 1937.

[vi] *Political Quarterly*, April–June 1939.

[vii] Bevan at Bournemouth Conference, October 1937, quoting M. Foot, op. cit., p.265.

cry, it has failed to identify the interests of the country with itself … The masses do not understand programmes or policies … What the people understand is a man'.[i] If ever the S.L. had needed a justification for their intellectual efforts, A. L. Rowse supplied it in his crude reductionism. From Attlee to Blair…

It would not have astounded S.L. members that Labour and Conservative parties in later years would bear similar traits, and endless battles of percentages between the scandalous mismanagement and the wise and steady efficiency of whoever was government and opposition should revolve around continuing the centralising policies of each Party; this was all part of the fact that the Labour Party had failed to solve the problem of incentives in a Socialist direction during the S.L. years. The blame cannot be placed at Labour's door, because in the 1930s it was sufficient to demand a living wage. Anyway, by 1939, the Labour Party had its objectives clarified, a programme developed,[ii] and the S.L.'s vision of the 'coming religion of Socialism' no longer evoked starry-eyed optimism; the political parties were becoming similar in practice, and the system of Parliamentary democracy, instead of seeming undemocratic (by the S.L.'s Socialist standards), was presenting one of the bulwarks against totalitarian governments and had itself become de rigueur and indispensable.

In some ways, the problems of the Labour Party in the 1950s mirrored those of the 1930s, and D. Marquand's description of the 1950s could apply to the earlier decade: 'For most of the ten years, the Labour Party behaved in a fashion perfectly calculated to destroy its chances of power. The arthritic rigidity of the Old Right alienated the idealists; the empty intransigence of the Old Left alienated the uncommitted voter; the most unbelievable personal virulence of both wings of the Party alienated those who dislike the use of character assassination as an instrument of politics'.[iii] The fact that the Labour Party was a coalition led to marginalisation of theory, and any attempt to go beyond general definitions led to strains in a complicated alliance. Parliamentary and electoral needs took priority over political principles; the S.L. in the 1930s had to struggle against Party leaders' proposals to detach class identification from unions and mollify the formal commitment to Socialism. This makes it easier to comprehend the relative unproductiveness of Labour's social thought in the 1930s compared with the detailed work of the *Next Five Years' Group* or *Political and Economic Planning*,[iv] although *Practical Socialism for Britain* (1935) impacted in 1945.

The important contribution made by the S.L. to debates in the Party was its belief that the traditional routine of Labour politics would not suffice, that S.L. declarations, manifestos, pamphlets, or programmes would alter nothing without *involvement in campaigns* (against the Means Test, on the Hunger Marches, in the localities, on immediate problems). The alternative was cynicism: 'The leaders of the P.L.P. advise the Party Conference as to what the Conference should advise the P.L.P. to do. When the leaders are in substantial agreement they can be reasonably sure that they can (with the aid of a majority of trade unions) get the Conference to advise them to do what they want to do anyway'![v] Or not to do. The greatest safeguard against S.L. members'

[i] A. L. Rowse, 'The Present and Immediate Future of the Labour Party', *Political Quarterly*, January–March 1938.

[ii] C. Brand, op. cit. p.194.

[iii] D. Marquand, 'The Liberal Revival', *Encounter*, July 1962, p.66.

[iv] A. Marwick, 'The Labour Party and the Welfare State in Britain (1900–1948)', *American Historical Review*, 73, 1967, pp.380–403.

[v] R. T. McKenzie, *British Political Parties*, p.426.

Socialist commitment was to make the Labour MP into just another 'character', who lacked a philosophy which would steer him passed the complex reasons for doing nothing advanced by the Civil Service, to become just one of a herd of MPs whose loyalty was essential for the Labour Party's electoral success. However, thanks partly to the S.L.'s contribution, Labour's 1945 manifesto stated "the Labour Party is a Socialist Party. Its ultimate aim is the establishment of the Socialist Commonwealth of Great Britain."[1] The S.L. had made an imprint, and had, in the process, analysed most avenues for Socialist influence in the society of 1930s' Britain.

---

[1] C. R. Attlee, *Brief Lives*, ed. Colin Matthew, 1999 edn., p.27.

Chapter Eight

The Socialist League and the Trade Union Movement

The State and Bureaucracy have been the Jekyll and Hyde of human civilisation. They have indeed represented the virtues and vices of human society and its historical development in a manner more concentrated, more intense, than any other institution. State and bureaucracy focus in themselves this characteristic duality of our civilisation: every progress achieved so far has been accompanied by retrogression; every advance that man made has been bought at the price of regress; every unfolding of human creative energy has been paid for with the crippling or stunting of some other creative energy.

Isaac Deutscher, *Marxism in Our Time*, 1972

On the continent, mass movements *could* develop on the basis of a political attitude which in Britain merely isolated a militant minority... The outlook of the working class was overwhelmingly liberal-radical rather than revolutionary... British Labour has traditionally shared the conservative outlook of the British middle class ... the Fabians were a body of professional men and women drawn from the middle class ... they were thus able to reformulate social doctrine in terms which appealed to the rising managerial stratum and to the educated class in general – moreover their ideology was anti-liberal as well as anti-Marxist.

Eric Hobsbawm in 'Hobsbawm's Choice', in *Encounter*, March 1965, pp.70–74

The experience of Labour Governments had made it increasingly evident that even the most comprehensive measures of fiscal and social reform can only succeed in masking the unacceptable and unpleasant face of capitalism and *cannot* achieve any fundamental changes in the power relationships which dominate our society.

N.E.C., Labour Party, 1973

A conflict between industrial and political interests was inherent in the Labour Movement's structure. Unions no longer had as their *primary* aim the elimination of private profit as the controlling motive of industry and the substitution of a system of common ownership; by the 1930s they had become *negotiating organisations* concerned to obtain the highest rates of pay, shortest hours, and the best conditions of work within the existing structure. Labour's Parliamentary leaders and professional organisation could not now function without the approval of the dominant figures in the union Movement, who ensured support for the Party, provided most funds, controlled Conference decisions and the National Council of Labour.

The background to this union rôle in the Movement was the defeat of the General Strike in 1926.[i] This ended an epoch in union history. To union leaders, belief in unions'

---

[i] The majority of T.U.C. leaders after the 1926 débâcle wanted to avoid any large-scale conflicts with

economic power through direct action had been disproved. Hope was subsequently placed in union activities through the Parliamentary machine, because unionists furnished the bulk of Party membership, stability and solidarity. This created a quandary for Socialists in the Party. Outnumbered within the Party, voted down when they protested, Left-wing Party members reacted equivocally: 'They have pledged themselves to working-class representation as part of the process of making the manual labourer conscious of his disinherited condition, and of arousing in the working class, faith in the class struggle. But, they are, by their adhesion to the present Parliamentary Party, bolstering up a fraud – pretending to the outside world that these respectable but reactionary trade union officials are the leaders of the Social Revolution'.[i] Beatrice Webb's observations a decade earlier had relevance.

Between unions and political groups, the struggle for influence was never absent. What made the attempt so keen was the emergence of union ambitions to utilise the Party's political machinery coinciding with changes confronting the nation and the individual. The Party was rooted in the bedrock of unions, which gradually reasserted their rôle in Party Conferences (and on the Executive), until any deviation to the Left led to heresy-hunting. From its inception, the S.L. was conscious of the conservatism and economism of unions and their leaders' insistence on searching for *economic concessions* rather than Socialist changes. To the S.L., unionism had been a creation of the capitalist system: 'The bread and butter of its existence is ... the negotiation of wages and conditions of employment between employers and employed'.[ii]

The lines of dispute between union leaders and the Labour Left were drawn in August 1931, when Lansbury took over the Party leadership. Although union leaders were satisfied that he would not be another autocrat, the two most influential union leaders, E. Bevin and Sir W. Citrine, were temperamentally hostile to Lansbury and his emotional, old-fashioned Christian Socialist style; after the Election defeat, they were determined to have more say in Party policy, because it was thanks to union solidarity that the Party had not split; the unions, far from relaxing their political effort, would be more ready to help the Party, especially in 'political education'.[iii] Proposals were put forward to reconstitute the National Joint Council; the P.L.P. and N.E.C. would each send its Chairman and two others to meet the Chairman and six members of the T.U.C. General Council once each month, because one lesson from 1931 was closer understanding between the Party and T.U.C. The National Council of Labour issued policy statements, and became the most authoritative body in the Labour Movement in formulating policy and was the main vehicle (besides the Annual Conference) through which Bevin was able to influence the Party's policy on foreign affairs and defence'.[iv] In this time of Party disillusionment and disarray, the T.U.C. General Council under Bevin and Citrine abandoned its rôle as the sheet-anchor of the Labour Party and took the helm.[v] For an organisation like the S.L. it was unfortunate that union leaders participated more in politics, because more influence within the Party could be the only outcome, and the central direction of the

employees; the Bevin-Citrine policy was to rely on cooperation through constitutional means with government and employers, cf. N. Branson, M. Heinemann, op. cit., 1973 edn., pp.99, 145.
[i] B. Webb Diaries (1919–1924), p.19.
[ii] C. Cooke, op. cit., p.131.
[iii] E. Bevin, 'The Election and the Trade Union Movement', *Labour Magazine*, December 1931.
[iv] A. Bullock, op. cit., pp.511–512.
[v] H. Pelling, 'Convalescence: The General Council's Party (1931–40)', *A Short History of the Labour Party*, 1968, ch. 5, p.77.

Movement would be in the hands of the General Council.[i]

The S.L.'s initial analysis of the economic crisis appeared foolhardy and impracticable for most union leaders, but no trade unionist disagreed with Cripps that the 'National' Government had reduced workers' standard of life and the final collapse of capitalism would depend on the vigour with which workers insisted on their right to a higher standard of life.[ii] S.L. leaders did, however, realise that cohesion could not occur automatically when the Movement was a loose federation of many groups, individual interests of which were frequently in conflict. To this end, the S.L. sought to alter the 'block vote' (the result of which would exacerbate tensions by infringing union rights), and campaign for nationalisation (E. F. Wise's successful amendment to nationalise the joint stock banks annoyed E. Bevin).[iii] The S.L. was convinced that the union movement could have immense power if it possessed a Socialist outlook. At the Leicester Conference there were hints of a new radical tendency among union representatives.[iv] Harold Clay's statement: 'I believe political democracy… can only be complete if you have industrial democracy. Our demand is for the application of the principle of industrial democracy to the government of industry'[v] was taken as the S.L.'s viewpoint.

Union leaders opposed the S.L.'s reiteration of 'workers' control' each year. The S.L. position took the via media between I.L.P. workers' councils and union leaders' 'enlightened bureaucracy of the public corporation'. The Leicester Conference resolved that schemes for socialisation would be carried out by the next Labour Government, so the S.L., particularly H. Clay and J. T. Murphy, formulated a Socialist position on the subject. The central argument, accepted as an S.L. position, was that development of science in the technical field had placed more people in a new relationship to production; the worker had no voice on industrial policy or rules relating to workshop administration (apart from negative control exercised by unions), and Socialists could not accept the permanence of the commodity status of labour: 'Workers in an industry are not an "interest" but an element in the industry whose knowledge, skill and experience have not been utilised or appreciated'.[vi] A worker should not be a cog in the wheel, but a conscious partner in a social service, a person who should have a right to share in the making of rules. The Party had put forward schemes for dealing with transport and electricity in public corporations (with control vested in a board appointed by a Minister, subject to an economic plan by a future Labour Government). The S.L.'s vision was of a new motive pervading industry; workers had to claim the right to representation on boards to gain a new purpose in industry: *'Workers' Control must be part of the Socialist claim … applied through the trade unions'*.[vii] Here were implicit criticisms of union leaders, who primarily saw unions as contestants for a greater share in the product of industry,[viii] pressing for increased responsibility for the conduct of industry. The S.L. view was not conducive to fraternal comraderie with union leaders, especially since union membership by 1933

---

[i] Cf. A. Hutt, *British Trade Unionism (1800–1961)*, p.125.
[ii] Cripps, *New Leader*, February 29th, 1932.
[iii] Cf. C. Cooke, op. cit., p.151.
[iv] *Manchester Guardian*, October 8th, 1932.
[v] *Daily Herald*, October 6th, 1932.
[vi] H. Clay, lecture 'Workers' Control' at Transport House, March 19th, 1933.
[vii] Ibid. (My italics.)
[viii] Ibid.

had sunk to less than 4 million (its lowest point between the wars and half it had in 1920). The S.L. had most influence when unions were weakest, but that situation did not last more than a year. Meanwhile, union officials were forced into a series of wage negotiations to mitigate the economic cuts, did not shoulder responsibilities for the unemployed, and were unsympathetic to the S.L.'s radical suggestions. J. T. Murphy commented: 'When collective bargaining is accepted as a permanent procedure and becomes the first principle of action for the working-class movement, then it involves the acceptance of Capitalism as a permanent form of society, and the unions will have to take just what the capitalists can afford to give them'.[i]

(A) E. Bevin and W. Citrine or G. Lansbury and S. Cripps?

In opposition to the S.L., J. R. Clynes applauded unions in their existing form for *preventing* the follies seen abroad, of proposing a strike or using threat of organised action for every injustice: 'There is a necessity of persuading angry men to resort to the ballot'.[ii] The difference between the S.L. and union leaders was that the latter took their stand on the ability of the economy to recover soon, and opposed the S.L. suggestion that the Party should consider 'Emergency Powers'. By 1935, 'the cash plus voting power ascendancy of the trade union junta, headed by Citrine and Bevin',[iii] arrived, Bevin with his courage, independence, obstinacy, directness, roughness of phrase, shortness of temper, and overbearing manner; W. Citrine with his clerkly, finicky character, a mind as clean, clear and precise as himself, speeches as models of passionless but convincing argument.[iv] They turned the T.U.C. from a not very effective open forum for debate into a positive instrument of policy and their distrust of S.L. 'intellectuals' and all non-official unionists was the result of the defection of MacDonald, Snowden and Mosley, labelled as betrayal by 'intellectuals'.[v] When describing S.L. leaders, 'irresponsible' and 'intellectual' were interconnected, as Bevin and Citrine intended to control the Party to avoid 'betrayal' again; Party Conferences witnessed the success with which they carried out their intention. Bevin resented S.L. leaders' elaboration of Party policies without consulting the T.U.C. (although only between 5% and 10% of union members ever had a say in votes recorded in *their* name). The chief interest of union leaders lay in reaching for their disciplinary daggers: 'Neither Bevin's bombast nor the card index mind of Citrine could awaken the national response which the times required',[vi] although Bevin endorsed the 'reality of power' as the main factor in human affairs, and became one of the most potent forces shaping the political thought of the Movement,[vii] someone who could say one thing and do another without any sense of inconsistency, because what he said was what seemed practical at that moment, a moralist who knew that absolute morality was

---

[i] J. T. Murphy, *Trade Unions and Socialism*, S.L. pamphlet, June 1936.

[ii] J. R. Clynes, *Memoirs (1924–37)*, p.280.

[iii] J. Lee, op. cit., p.136.

[iv] R. Postgate, op. cit., p.289. Yet Bevin said of Marxist miners' leader A. J. Cook: "He was abused probably more than any other man of this generation, and yet all the time he worked and fought, guided by the highest motives", qu. Paul Davies, "A. J. Cook", 1987, p.185.

[v] K. Martin, *The Editor*, p.50.

[vi] M. Foot, op. cit., p.178.

[vii] F. Williams, op. cit., p.147.

250

'an uncertain and even dangerous guide in industrial negotiation'.[i]

For the S.L., union policy was exclusively confined to this *bargain-making*; it was not directed to any *Socialist* aim of challenging the economic system which gave rise to the struggle between workers and employers. That was why wage struggles were uncoordinated and the T.U.C.'s commitment was to 'all kinds of plans for reconstructing Capitalism',[ii] as J. T. Murphy put it bluntly. The proof of this was (for the S.L.) union leaders' phlegmatic reaction to mass unemployment and European Fascism, yet Bevin had a more organised theory of the rôle of Labour than the S.L., and although his strategy had no effect on the Government, it insinuated itself upon Labour Party leaders. (His was the notion of institutionalised co-operation between unions, management and the State, supplemented by the Parliamentary pressure of the Labour Party for legislation beneficial to the working classes).[iii] The conflict between the S.L. and Bevin was continued through the *Daily Herald*, where the T.U.C. controlled the political and industrial reportage, and Bevin was the key figure among union directors of it! He secured his objective of making sure final authority in the interpretation of political policy followed by this official organ of the Party should reside in the hands of unions. Alan Bullock's comment on the *Daily Herald*'s effect was a litotes: 'It fell short of the militants' ideal of a propaganda broadsheet'![iv]

Bevin was never slow to admonish Lansbury, the Party leader, for his S.L. links. In March 1933 he wrote to Lansbury protesting against his speaking on an S.L. platform without acquiring prior permission from the National Council of Labour: 'Why ignore them and so create suspicion and disunity again'.[v] Bevin added that the N.C.L. had not turned down any suggestion of a Hyde Park Mayday meeting, and he looked to P.L.P. leaders to help preserve unity of action: 'I was very concerned about E. F. Wise's statement to me today that he thought that at a great public meeting you would all have greater freedom'. Lansbury apologised for appearing to have slighted Bevin and Citrine, but claimed he had suggested the S.L. ask the *Daily Herald* to run the meeting. He added that the S.L. had the right to carry on propaganda (like any other affiliated body) and the meeting was an opportunity for helping people understand Party policy: 'There was never any question of doing this behind the back of the National Council of Labour'.[vi] These divergences of two of the key Labour leaders was symptomatic of misapprehensions existing in the Movement at the highest level, and barely concealed resentments and suspicions between unionists and Left politicians.

In May and June 1933, suspicions came out into the open. Citrine, in an article *In Defence of Freedom* in the Labour magazine, objected to Cripps' and the S.L.'s constitutional proposals and 'Emergency Powers' suggestions: 'Phrases of this kind when used by prominent people may convey the impression that Labour is turning its back upon democracy'.[vii] For him they represented a grave *electoral* handicap on the Party, because the method of obtaining and exercising authority when in office was all-important, and the logical conclusion of the S.L.'s proposals would be to create the political climate 'which Mussolini and Hitler had exploited to establish their

---

[i] Ibid., p.91.

[ii] J. T. Murphy, *Trade Unions and Socialism*, June 1936.

[iii] R. Miliband, op. cit., p.206.

[iv] A. Bullock, op. cit., p.589.

[v] Bevin to Lansbury, Lansbury Papers, March 8th, 1933.

[vi] Lansbury to Bevin, Lansbury Papers, March 9th, 1933.

[vii] Cf. Citrine, *New Clarion*, June 24th, 1933.

dictatorships'. (This was the argument used to quell Left-wing demands!) Likewise, moderate Party leaders, like A. Henderson, expressed concern lest the active Party members move too fast for the economically-minded trade unionists;[i] and a Liberal newspaper stated that S.L. proposals had not been brought before the Party Conference or the T.U.C. and had received no endorsement from any of the 'organs of authority' in the Movement. The paper's headline clarified its attitude: 'The Labour Clean-Up – T.U.C. and Sir S. Cripps – The Dictatorship Issue'.[ii] Other newspapers' headlines were equally illuminating: 'Socialists Fall Out – Cripps on Dictators – Sharp Attack on Citrine',[iii] while *The Times* concentrated on 'Sir S. Cripps – Reply to Mr. Citrine'.[iv]

The S.L. campaign against what its leaders considered to be 'reactionary tendencies' in the unions and Bevin's power in the union hierarchy, pursued to the point of excluding more positive action, was a chief cause of the S.L.'s union position. In any reorganisation of the Party machine, the S.L. knew the union base had to be preserved 'for therein lies the Labour Party's class strength',[v] but the crucial factor was building the Party into an instrument of agitation 'for the down-and-outs as well as for the less poverty-stricken sections among the workers'.[vi] This was the reason for the S.L.'s anxiety about lack of democracy in unions, (the Party Conference Agenda was rarely circulated to the branches for discussion). The S.L. believed criticisms were not welcomed by union leaders because the latter's power might be threatened by any change in the Constitution; the change which the S.L. sought was that unionists should vote at Conference through their local Labour parties instead of nationally. Since, in the Labour parties locally, the agenda *was* often thoroughly discussed and the delegates mandated by the majority vote, this would mean decisions of the Conference would be decisions of the majority of Party members.

(B) The S.L. and Union Leaders (1932–1934)

In the summer of 1933, the S.L. decided to intensify Socialist propaganda in unions. What methods of organisation should be adopted for socialised industries? What changes in unionism would be needed to adapt it to new requirements of socialisation? Such questions were linked to a new status in industry for unions, especially as unionists experienced the waste and inefficiency in their own industry, and for which their own members had to pay. Unionism had to be built in new industries; perhaps there should be amalgamations between unions; possibly the use of the strike as a political weapon if war threatened? G. D. H. Cole and H. Clay considered *'workers' control'* to be linked to union structure; there was a need for an effective central authority for industrial labour with wider powers and duties than those exercised in

---

[i] E. Estorick, op. cit., p.119.

[ii] *Manchester Guardian*, June 8th, 1933.

[iii] *Morning Post*, June 6th, 1933.

[iv] *The Times*, June 6th, 1933. F. Raphael observes that while E. Bevin was the plain man's plain man and the best British bulldog Labour could breed, Sir Stafford Cripps was the Socialists' serious ascetic, principled enough to be blind to the horrors of Stalinism and eager for everyone to have an equal share of joylessness; F. Raphael, *The Necessity of Anti-Semitism*, 1997, p.176.

[v] *New Clarion*, S.L. News, August 5th, 1933.

[vi] G. D. H. Cole, 'Agitation', *New Clarion*, June 10th, 1933.

the T.U.C. Constitution. Cole in particular believed it would be necessary to set up a governing Council or commission for each socialised service, with union representation, and regional and local workers' control in the workshops to bring new motives of public service into play.[i] To S.L. leaders, the T.U.C. Conference in 1933 proved the need for sustained and organised propaganda in the union movement on S.L. lines. The T.U.C. was said to have 'lacked' leadership, had supported contradictory policies, had 'confessed its inability to challenge Capitalism',[ii] the T.U.C. General Council had prevented positive action by its resigned approach towards wage demands or shorter hours. What Bevin and Citrine thought about this S.L. analysis was soon to appear in print. Implicitly, the S.L.'s approach received short shrift, for it involved just the type of challenge that the T.U.C. had decided *not* to take. All S.L. ideas were blanketed, including recognition by statute of the right of workers to partnership in control of socialised industries. S.L. leaders could not have been surprised that its call for a 'class struggle' became subject of derision while union leaders opposed S.L. demands for *'industrial action to prevent war'*, and resolutions on *workers' control* and *Emergency Powers*.

This was Bevin's task at the Hastings Party Conference in 1933. S.L. proposals were "doctrinal nonsense", preparations against dangers that "might never come", and would alienate potential Labour supporters. As a regular attendee at Party Conferences, Bevin was one of the most consistently powerful influences on decisions[iii] and in discussions on a practical Socialist programme, he embodied (for the S.L.) the conservatism of unions. It was he who assaulted some of the most cherished traditions and prejudices of his audience,[iv] as he contrasted the S.L. with his union view (as one which had to deal every day with the masses). It was *pragmatism versus idealism*: 'Our work is eminently practical, and it is to deliver the goods to our members and we know, as leaders, the absolute folly of putting up programmes that are not likely to be realised'.[v] Cripps often moved S.L. resolutions at Conferences, so his views vis-à-vis Transport House leaders were apparent and the resolutions were unpopular for union leaders because the S.L. advocated greater local representation in unions and the Party Conference. Cripps commented: 'It is as difficult to make democracy effective *within a party* as within a State; in both cases, frank and fearless discussion is necessary if democracy is to survive'.[vi] Mutual resentments and suspicions of Cripps and Bevin for each other have been explained, but what differentiated their attitudes were the organisations they represented.

Opinions polarised at the Hastings Conference, on *'nationalisation'*. The commitment of the Party to 'common ownership of the means of production, distribution and exchange' (nowadays consigned to the dustbin of history) had not come near to being an operative goal of the Party. The S.L. wanted it to spell out a will to transform society, while Party leaders were vague about methods of controlling socialised industries,[vii] or of compensating former owners of industrial concerns. Nationalisation lent itself best to industries or services that were highly standardised,

---

[i] G. D. H. Cole, *A Study Guide on Socialist Policy*, August 1933, pp.9–10.
[ii] 'What Is the Goal?', *New Clarion*, S.L. News, September 16th, 1933.
[iii] F. Williams, *Ernest Bevin*, p.177.
[iv] A. Bullock, op. cit., p.534.
[v] *Labour Party Annual Conference Report*, October 1933, p.161.
[vi] Quoted by P. Strauss, op. cit., p.64.
[vii] D. McHenry, op. cit., pp.280–297.

where uniform rules could be applied, yet the traditional concern of Socialists was with *distribution* rather than production. For Party leaders, nationalisation was sentiment and symbol, a consolation and an evasion. (By the late 1940s, the Labour Government had built up the public sector alongside an intact private sector by creating new public enterprises in the science-based and growth industries, until a position was reached when industrial power rested with a managerial class responsible to no one. Then the form of ownership was irrelevant. State control over nationalised industries was as difficult as share-holder control over private firms.)[i] The S.L.'s 1933 resolution looked to a concept of socialisation in which new forms of industrial organisation were to be created on the basis of the wage-earners' share in the direction of socialised industries, while the Morrisonian concept was that nationalisation involved the administrative machinery to improve the performance of an industry or service to be organised by managers on business lines, controlled by a Minister. The Labour Party eventually moved away from nationalisation towards the welfare state, economic security and social justice (the limits of the welfare state set by ability to pay for benefits, not differences in ideology). In the 1930s, the S.L. formulated a resolution which viewed with alarm tendencies in the Party towards presentation of schemes of *'capitalist nationalisation'*.[ii] What the S.L. meant by socialisation of an industry was a Central Board with a Secretary for the industry and Regional Boards as the best form of control; *'workers' control'* would be through works councils, which would elect representatives to the regional boards; the Central Board and unions would lay down the basis of policy on works' conditions; the motto, 'production for use and not for profit'.[iii] It was foretold that socialisation of a service would not do much for economic equality, but it would end unlimited profits, divert future surpluses and windfall increments to social purposes, and facilitate a taxation programme to reduce inequalities: 'Of the measures for achieving social equality, for a Socialist, the most fundamental is the extension of the socialised sector'.[iv]

The S.L.'s nationalisation proposals were partly aimed against union leaders' policies (they had not placed themselves at the head of the agitation for the unemployed, nor used their influence to challenge Government economic policies by an aggressive industrial policy). Union leaders were (to S.L. leaders) holding back the rank and file from industrial action, because the former were tied by collective agreements: *'The trade union leaders want to patch up things with the employers and to play a waiting game till better times return'*.[v] New technical developments in industry were temporarily lessening unionism, because new industries were growing in areas remote from centres of union strength, so the S.L. saw the potential of a new union strategy (as unofficial strikes had shown), without the endorsement of union leaders. Under the auspices of Trades Councils,[vi] the S.L. supported local Unemployed Workers' organisations, and for workers' control in the workshops of the localities, while S.L. leaders expressed concern that the union vision was coloured by the changing hue of

---

[i] *New Leader*, August 17th, 1957.

[ii] Leeds Conference of the S.L., *Manchester Guardian*, May 22nd, 1934.

[iii] Ingot, *The Socialisation of Iron and Steel*, reviewed by *Socialist*, No. 7, May 1936.

[iv] H. Dalton, *Practical Socialism for Britain*, 1935, p.327.

[v] G. D. H. Cole, *The Working Class Movement and the Transition to Socialism*, S.L. pamphlet, 1934.

[vi] Trades Councils between 1926 and 1939 never had the membership and range of functions they had developed in the 20 previous years, cf. A. Clinton, "The trade union rank and file: Trades councils in Britain 1900–1940", 1977, p.171.

the economic situation: 'Not only trade union officials, but the upper strata of manual workers acquire the manners and expectations of the *petit bourgeoisie*'.[i] Who could blame them?

Another struggle between the S.L. and union leaders until October 1935 was the attempt by union leaders (Bevin, C. Dukes, and J. Marchbank) to remove Lansbury from the Party leadership, and, with him, the so-called woolly, humanitarian, 'sentimental Socialist' approach to politics. Lansbury expressed a Christian Socialist message (that workers who created the material wealth of the nation should live under better conditions';[ii] labour should be organised to supply needs, not make massive profits for the few; 'mountainous slag heaps piled up as monuments to the Capitalist society'[iii] represented unearned wealth made at the expense of ugliness). He believed in workers' control, workers' share in management to determine how goods should be distributed, all trades on which lives depended be nationalised: 'To work for the profit of another person is a disheartening business... all the energy you put in only goes to line some shareholders' pockets'.[iv] Bevin became Lansbury's Nemesis, while union leaders were under the critical gaze of the S.L.,[v] which questioned the influence of unions at Party Conferences, in view of lack of influence of rank and file unionists over political decisions in their own organisations (votes of the membership at conferences were decided by the union executive or the delegation to conferences). This resulted in the S.L. resolution in *'Forward to Socialism'* for the *'adoption of a class philosophy' by the union movement*, which should campaign for 'mass resistance in unions to Capitalism'.[vi] The new task envisaged by the S.L. was to make a survey of existing union membership to ascertain where workers were organised, study the structure and function of unions,[vii] caution proffered by T. Howard (of the Rochdale S.L.): 'If we are not very careful we may divorce ourselves from the ordinary membership of the trade union organisations by getting too far away from their outlook'.[viii]

Before the T.U.C. met at Weymouth (1934), the S.L. turned to Morrison's public utility corporations and boards. Instead of plans for the reorganisation of industry on Socialist principles, union leaders were accepting socialisation and workers' control *in theory* but discarded both in 'practical' policies. The mood of S.L. unionists was captured by Frank G. Jacques who asked *what* machinery had been evolved at Transport House for the transition from capitalism to socialism? What did union leaders mean by a *'socialised industry'*? Collaboration with directors upon capitalist boards would not be 'workers' control'; the union Movement had to cease regarding its function as negotiating within capitalism, and reclaim the unemployed for the Movement: 'A long experience of trade union administration under capitalism has bred a fatal *excess of caution* in the leaders of the Movement'.[ix] Caution *was* the proud watchword for union leaders, hence the General Council's reluctance to organise mass

---

[i] G. D. H. Cole, op. cit., S.L. pamphlet, 1934.

[ii] G. Lansbury, *My England*, 1934, p.65.

[iii] G. Lansbury, ibid., p.28.

[iv] G. Lansbury, ibid., p.211.

[v] Letter by Cripps, Cripps Papers, March 16th, 1934.

[vi] 'Forward to Socialism', May 20th and 21st, 1934.

[vii] Cf. H. Clay, 'Tolpuddle and Today', *Socialist Leaguer*, No. 1, June–July 1934.

[viii] *Morning Post*, May 21st, 1934.

[ix] F. G. Jacques (delegate to the T.U.C.), 'Will Congress Move Forward?', *Socialist Leaguer*, No. 1, June–July 1934.

demonstrations or strikes against the *Unemployment Act*, which it was believed would 'fragment the union movement'. J. T. Murphy criticised a 'drifting movement, of leaders in retreat, of phrase-mongering taking the place of organised action',[i] and for the S.L. the conclusions of the Weymouth T.U.C. presaged disappointments at the Southport Conference. The resolution for 'a General Strike in the event of war' was most unwelcome; 'struggle for shorter hours' was an issue relegated to secondary considerations; industrial 'reorganisation' was the subject for academic discussion; and the T.U.C. decided socialisation of industries would be attained by transforming private industry into more efficient, larger combines. For the S.L. other disillusioning features of the T.U.C. followed; co-ordination of wage movements was sidetracked (because the economic crisis would soon pass) and a rising standard of life would be granted workers without any fundamental change in the motive of industry or its structure. This epitomised the T.U.C.'s determination not to risk any 'irresponsible militancy' compared with the S.L. 'confident of support from the rank and file in the trade unions and in the constituencies, confident that it is giving expression to the deep convictions of the mass of conscious workers'.[ii] Confidence has its place, but not there.

After the Southport Conference, the S.L.'s W. Mellor reflected with misgivings on Party conclusions on workers' control, compensation and public utility corporations, because the N.E.C. had been motivated not to alarm 'the small man with savings'; union leaders were committed to public utility corporations without relating it to Socialist planning, but since the S.L.'s defeats at Southport, a new S.L. tactic was implemented: 'It is vital for us to get into direct touch with trade union branches and to increase our trade union membership'.[iii] From October 1934, the S.L. renewed analysis of the union movement. This continued until the Party Conference at Brighton (1935), after which the S.L. redirected energies to the miners and unemployed unionists. The dominant philosophy of union leaders was their claim for practical, immediate benefits (dependent on profits). Hence, the S.L. recognised a union policy of 'aiding capitalist revival' and disregarding Socialist analysis. Did union leaders believe that industry was made for man or existed for profits? (Posing this stark choice was a certain means of polarising the S.L. and union leaders!). Had not union leaders supported the Mond-Turner talks, flirted with Beaverbrook's 'Economic Empire'? Shouldn't the pursuit of higher wages, shorter hours, better conditions and security carry the trade union movement into the class struggle?: 'Only a Trade Unionism with a Socialist and class objective and purpose can aid effectively to achieve the raising of the status of the workers ... It will look upon 'agreements' as forced truces... It will consciously regard its industrial activities as a means, not merely of winning temporary advances or staving off attack, but of building up the Will and Power in the minds of the workers'.[iv] This was a mood, not a policy, and, as such widened the standpoints of union leaders and the S.L., the former unable to accept the latter's belief in direct action and mass strikes, which the S.L. could not implement.

By 1935, there was little possibility of a reconciliation between Bevin and Citrine (for the unions) and Cripps, Mellor and J. T. Murphy (for the S.L.), on questions of

---

[i] J. T. Murphy, 'What Will Congress Do About Fascism?', ibid.

[ii] *Socialist Leaguer*, No. 4, September–October 1934.

[iii] W. Mellor, 'Southport and After', *Socialist Leaguer*, No. 5, October–November 1934.

[iv] 'Judex', 'Who Said the Social Millennium?', *Socialist Leaguer*, No. 6, November–December 1934.

rank and file representation. Union leaders assumed every member had adequate opportunities for discussing policy, but the S.L. continued to question whether they had sufficient opportunity for *acquiring* the education in Socialism necessary for forming judgements when 'saturated with the conventional capitalist view of society'.[i] Union leaders knew a union was primarily a business organisation for collecting contributions, paying benefits, negotiating wage rates, and making responsible decisions; the S.L. sought the inculcation of Socialist education in promoting the candidature of competent and reliable Socialists for official positions. It deplored the decline in militancy, which union leaders depicted as a measure of unions' success. S.L. criticisms against union leaders' 'respectability and responsibility' missed the point that, with the eclipse of ginger groups (like the S.L.), the political consciousness of unions had become the critical factor in Labour's future: 'Failing a renaissance of a capable and responsible Left group, free from careerism and embittered jealousies, *the unions have the onus of fashioning Labour policy*',[ii] observed E. Shinwell. That was why the industrial leadership refused to consider the use of industrial action for political purposes and why union votes at Party Conferences were invariably cast against the S.L.; Bevin and Citrine avoided industrial clashes; they acted as heads of *centralised enterprises*, engaged in routinised bargaining and compromise.[iii] In this context S.L. demands for industrial militancy were absurd when *these union leaders* were proof of the higher status of labour within a capitalist system: 'They were not the men to press more militant political postures upon their Parliamentary friends'.[iv]

This contrast between union leaders and the S.L. pointed to the marginalisation of the S.L., which repeated 'workers' control of industry' as if a Socialist Government was imminent, and to justify their 'educational' rôle within the Movement. Reduced to uttering axioms about the positive functions which unions would assume in a Socialist society, omitted the cold fact that, in 1935, the Party was solidly based on unions giving it stability with their practical outlook and common sense,[v] as Dalton had observed.

(C) The S.L. and Union Leaders (1935–1937)

1935 witnessed S.L. attempts to involve themselves more directly with union activities, especially at the local level. J. T. Murphy addressed a Conference of Labour organisations in Leeds on the subject of *Socialism and the Trade Unions*.[vi] By May he thought that considerable headway had been made in extending S.L. influence into unions through local educational conferences. The S.L. would have to carry this a stage further stating the relationship of Socialism to unions and their policy.[vii] Since the S.L. had been formed, most of its activities had been devoted to working out a constructive policy for the political Movement; it had lacked a statement of its position

---

[i] Cf. J. H. L. (an active trade unionist), 'Towards Democracy', *Socialist Leaguer*, No. 7, December 1934.
[ii] E. Shinwell, op. cit., p.211.
[iii] R. Miliband, op. cit., p.236.
[iv] Ibid.
[v] H. Dalton, *Practical Socialism for Britain*, 1935, p.17.
[vi] *Leeds Mercury*, March 10th, 1935.
[vii] J. T. Murphy, 'The Year in Review', *Socialist Leaguer*, No. 11, Mary 1935.

vis-à-vis the union Movement; what was needed was a common policy which Socialist unionists could work out in their own unions, because there was a lack of ventilation of opinions in union journals. (As a result, one union branch secretary sent his proposals to the *Socialist Leaguer*,[i] here were the essentials; a policy linking wage struggles with ideas for a Socialist society; more Socialist education in unions; rationalisation of union organisation by adoption of the workplace as local unit; propaganda to incorporate unorganised workers; freedom of discussion and consultation between unionists with regard to union policy; decisions on major union matters and items on the T.U.C. agenda by democratic vote of the rank and file; working arrangements between the C.P. and official union internationals; alliance between manual and non-manual workers, and closer alliance with the Co-operative Movement.)[ii] Such ideas were considered at the S.L.'s Bristol Conference, along with controversies over unofficial strikes and the T.U.C.'s *Black Circular*. S.L. unionists took the view that unofficial strikes arose because unions involved had not listened to workers' needs, and behind the ban was an attitude deploring use of the strike weapon at all. *The Black Circular's* ban on militants was for S.L. unionists an attempt by the T.U.C. to impose political restrictions upon unionists: 'To ban certain members from office because of their politics is the most dangerous step trade unionists can take... To impose political qualifications on members as a condition of office is to transform the trade unions into political parties. That is a violation of their purpose and function'.[iii] Was the S.L. alone in this analysis, within the Labour Party?

At its Bristol Conference (1935) the S.L. announced that if another '1931'-type crisis occurred the Movement would depend on workers' organisations rather than Parliamentary representation. In the resolution on unions, (moved by J. T. Murphy), the S.L. sought to transform unions into 'industrial unions', while a 'British Roosevelt plan' was deemed a danger to unions: '"New Deals" in Capitalism ... are old deals writ large'.[iv] So there was no outlet there. Strengthening S.L. union activities could include recruiting members for unions, encouraging Trades Councils, intensifying organisation of the unemployed (through unions and Trades Councils), and organising workshop and factory committees. Another resolution for the repeal of the *Trade Disputes Act* was awarded the usual vociferous headline: 'Defence of an England Owned and Controlled by Workers'.[v] J. T. Murphy advocated development of Trades Councils' *Unemployed Associations*, but omitted to mention that in the constitution of these bodies, the T.U.C. had inserted clauses debarring members of so-called 'disruptive' organisations from *Unemployed Associations*.[vi] This nullified S.L. resolutions, and presented the S.L. with another problem; S.L. members claimed, as loyal Party members, they would not co-operate with political associations which the Party regarded as hostile, but the S.L. regarded unions and Trades Councils as industrial organisations, not political pressure groups.

Then, at a disillusioning period for the S.L., Trades Councils were presented as 'potential Soviets' which ought to be developed as the most practicable framework for working-class power. S.L. unionists suggested that if the S.L. wanted to win the

[i] T.U. Branch Secretary; 'Socialists and the Trade Unions,' *Socialist Leaguer*, No. 11, May 1935.

[ii] Bristol Conference resolution on trade unions, June 1935.

[iii] John Sheffield, 'Damping Down? A Word to Trade Unionists', *Socialist Leaguer*, No. 12, June 1935.

[iv] Bristol Conference resolution on trade unions, June 1935.

[v] *Bristol Evening Post*, June 11th, 1935.

[vi] *New Leader*, June 14th, 1935.

interest and support of unionists, Trades Councils could perform this function, relating basic issues to technological changes, and arranging local area conferences in which rank and file delegates clarified ideas before the Annual Conference.[i] In May 1935, a weekend school was held under the S.L. Area Committee's auspices to discuss *Trade Unions and the future of the Trades Councils*,[ii] and at the Bristol S.L. Conference, Reg Groves moved the resolution on Trades Councils. The Conference recognised the effective concentration of local forces within the Movement, and Trades Councils could accomplish this unifying function within the shortest time. The S.L. would popularise Trades Councils as 'the local unifying centres of the Movement, to be utilised for winning the unorganised to the cause of Socialism, and the basis for well-directed local defence against Fascist violence;[iii] Trades Councils could form the foundations of strike organisation (including a General Strike or any other emergency action), and be centres of agitation and propaganda on day-to-day issues. The S.L. was instructed to draft, with Trades Councils, a programme of development for combining union, Co-operative Society and Labour council work to bring unorganised workers into the Socialist Movement (through sports, Tenants' Leagues, unemployed organisations, and agitation on local grievances).

In the summer of 1935, R. Groves' pamphlet, *Trades Councils in the Fight for Socialism* was an extension of the S.L.'s effort to arouse interest in the part to be played by Trades Councils. Described as 'written on a matter of tremendous importance to the growth and expansion of the Labour Movement'[iv] (when the S.L. was trying to extend its influence into the union field, it changed its journal title from the *Socialist Leaguer* to the *Socialist*), the arguments forwarded by Groves needed elucidating: they represented a departure from the pre-November 1934 S.L. tactics.[v] Groves wrote that national and local Labour leaders should become, 'not merely administrative officials', but positive leaders of the Movement, to seize every discontent and grievance, and shake routinised and habit-formed thinking. (Not the best way to win support from the T.U.C.) What was being analysed by Groves was a growing Socialist spirit which had to be transmitted to union organisations, since it had failed to enervate Party Conferences. Unions in the old industries had been numerically and morally weakened by mass unemployment; newer industries (employing mainly unskilled youthful labour) were largely unorganised, as were 'black-coated' and distributive workers: 'Trade Unionism needs centralisation, amalgamation, the widening of its appeal and the extension of its organisation'.[vi] This was being prevented, he argued, by vested interest and craft antagonism, difficulties surmountable only by leaders with a grasp of the Movement's political needs. This intimation of a form of *class unionism* further pitted union leaders against the S.L. However, Groves was stating a plea for *local participation*; national campaigns depended on localities; without energetic local centres a continual agitation at the national level could not be maintained; Trades Councils seemed most suited to become co-ordinating bodies; they occupied a

---

[i] Cf. Letters to *Socialist Leaguer*, Nos.6 & 7, November–December 1934.

[ii] May 19th, 1935.

[iii] Resolution on Trades Councils, Bristol Conference of the S.L., June 1935.

[iv] *Socialist*, No. 1, September 1935.

[v] Trade union leaders were unwilling to push resistance to the point of national strike action and saw no hope but acquiescence in the rationalization of basic industries by employers, supported by the banks and Government, cf. N. Branson, M. Heinemann, op. cit., 1973 edn., p.150.

[vi] R. Groves, *Trades Councils in the Fight for Socialism*, S.L. pamphlet, 1935, p.3.

strategic local position in the Movement and could unite unionists in localities, although they needed to widen their constitutions to become Trades, Labour and Co-operative Councils: 'The future of the Trades Councils will be determined by the extent to which they become the *central co-ordinating bodies* for the whole movement and the extent to which they dominate the life of the workers in their district at every point'.[i] Trades Councils (T.C.s) would have to be all-inclusive, with no organised grouping of employees outside. By leading campaigns, publicity, agitation and petitions, T.C.s could bring unorganised workers directly into touch with the Movement.

These ideas confronted sectional interests, as well as union traditions, methods and policies. To propose that every Trades Council be a combination of local union branch, Co-operative organisation and Labour Party, was part of a broader strategy; Groves claimed that 'threat of war' made necessary active, widely-supported local leadership in the Trades Councils: 'Those trade union officials who protest at the trade unions having to bear the main burden of war resistance have the remedy to hand in the Councils which, given the encouragement and direction, can *assemble for anti-war action* all the workers in the localities'.[ii] This S.L. aspiration was for Trades Councils to unite existing working-class organisations, somehow extend the class conflict, and make conscious the polarised interests of Government and the Labour Movement. (S.L. unionists, in March 1936, opposed the London Trades Council scheme for union reorganisation in the capital because they thought it would separate union branches from political sections, weaken the democratic form of Trades Councils, and fragment workers' movement in the localities. They wanted Trades Councils to co-ordinate the work of union branches, create a London federation of local councils, while developing local Labour councils, uniting union and political wings of the Movement with the Co-operative Movement into 'Councils of Labour'.)[iii] The large vote against the General Council's *'Black Circular'*[iv] was an encouraging sign for the S.L., proof that the moment unions attempted to impose political restrictions there would be disruptions. An instance of the S.L.'s attitude appeared in J. T. Murphy's *Modern Trade Unionism* (September 1935). This was a study of the control of industry and position of unions in the stages of transition towards a Socialist society, Murphy hostile to the "collaborationist policy" of the T.U.C. General Council in promoting capitalist recovery. He was also critical of bureaucratic State Socialist policies and of gradualist Labour leaders, and stated the S.L.'s case for workers' control could be won mainly by 'fighting from below', through union works committees, which could take over managerial functions.

Labour's Brighton Conference brought the S.L.'s theories back to reality sharply. A decision had to be made in relation to Party leaders and policy; union leaders decided the fate of the Labour Party, and reasserted their influence. In the process, some of the most vital elements in the Party, Lansbury's idealism and the militancy Cripps could awaken, were 'heavily bruised'.[v] Bevin voiced the union declaration against Lansbury's pacifism, and accused Cripps of having 'stabbed us in the back' by resigning from the

---

[i] R. Groves, ibid., p.6.

[ii] R. Groves, ibid., p.9.

[iii] R. Groves, 'Maintain and Strengthen Local Unity', *Socialist*, No. 5, March 1936.

[iv] T.U.C., September 1935.

[v] M. Foot, op. cit., p.211.

N.E.C. and thus not following a collective decision when the Party needed unity to face an election: 'People have been on this platform today talking about the destruction of Capitalism. The middle classes are not doing too badly as a whole under Capitalism... lawyers and members of other professions have not done too badly... *The thing that is being wiped out is the Trade Union Movement*'.[i] When Bevin and Citrine took the lead in remodelling the policy and structure of the union movement, they set their compass towards collaboration with employers and the State. Bevin's speeches now were a warning that the policy they had formulated was about to dominate the Labour Party.

After the General Election of November 1935, S.L. leaders turned their attention on the union front to the miners' struggle and sought from the Movement a *'Fighting Fund for the Miners'*.[ii] While the coal owners were continuing their long war of attrition on miners' wages and conditions with threats of dismissal, subsistence wages and the Means Test, A. Bevan proposed a National Wages Board to form the basis of unity;[iii] 25% of the miners were unemployed, half those employed worked short time, and the miners (under six Governments) had reiterated demands for nationalisation. For the S.L., this had become a crucial Labour agitation, and in launching a national campaign through the union movement, thought Trades Councils could organise the unions. With signs of militancy focussed on the miners' cause, and union organisation at last emerging in the newer industries, S.L. leaders had some hopes: 'Now is the time for S.L. members to show the sincerity of their fight for the workers' cause by giving every assistance in their power wherever these struggles take place'.[iv]

In January 1936, the S.L. grew bolder. Resolutions for the *55 Conferences* of Labour, union and Co-operative organisations (held throughout the country under the S.L.'s auspices) demanded full support to workers in the mining, cotton and engineering industries striving to improve their wage conditions. It urged the T.U.C. to co-ordinate action in these wage struggles and build up a Fighting Fund, because *'every economic struggle of the workers for higher wages or better conditions is in reality part of the struggle for political power'*.[v] To the S.L. the miners' struggle offered just such an opportunity. The coal industry had witnessed changes taking place in capitalist organisation, with over-production and unrestricted profit-making leading to an increase in the price of coal. This explained a key feature of the S.L.'s unionist approach, that organised Labour would *always* lose on the political field the fruits which it won by industrial strength. The only answer was to call Trades Councils' meetings, organise mass demonstrations, the T.U.C. to have a National Fighting Fund: 'The crisis in the mining industry is an opportunity not only to mobilise assistance for our struggling comrades in the minefields, but also to educate the workers for the final conflict with capitalism'.[vi] Final? Well, yet *another* conflict with... What had to be recognised was the class character of issues raised in these wage struggles.

When the miners' strike ended, the S.L. blamed union leaders for not believing in the possibility of welding the miners (and other workers) into a co-ordinated strike movement. As a result, district settlements were firmly fixed, disparities in district

[i] E. Bevin, *Labour Party Annual Conference Report*, 1935. (My italics) Bevin knew a lot about 'back stabbing'!
[ii] *Socialist*, No. 2, November 1935.
[iii] Ibid, A. Bevan, 'The Miners Are Fighting for Plain Justice'.
[iv] A. Austen, 'On the Wages Front', *Socialist*, No. 2, November 1935.
[v] Editorial, *Socialist*, No. 4, January 1936.
[vi] 'The Real Menace of the Coal Crisis', *Socialist*, No. 4, January–February 1936.

wages set, miners more sectionalised; the tragedy was the gap between political and industrial sides. When unions advocated 'direct action', Party Parliamentarians distrusted them; when unionism had a setback, the Movement was rechannelled into politics. Two other aspects of the S.L. towards union issues emerged in March 1936. With the Government's measures for extending unemployment insurance to agricultural workers, S.L. unionists stated unemployment was not an insurable proposition (workers should not be levied because they were forced into unemployment through no fault of their own). The other aspect was the record number of *unofficial strikes*; there was something wrong between union leaders and workers if strikes caught them unawares or if they allowed employers to drag out negotiations to such inordinate lengths that patience was exhausted and workers had to act on their own: 'The only way to break through this ... is to breathe into the S.L. branches of the trade unions the spirit of Socialism and of the Class Struggle'.[i] Some breath! However, the S.L. point was the usual one, that there would be fewer unofficial strikes if union leaders were more intent on leading workers rather than conciliating employers.

By April 1936, the unions were facing the brunt of the challenge of the Government and its war programme, and S.L. unionists recognised the danger of union acquiescence in collaboration between State, employers and workers (a situation which had occurred in 1914–18, D.O.R.A., the Munitions Act, and Whitley Council Schemes). It was S.L. policy to aid unions to retain their independence in order to determine their own conditions; S.L. members proposed development of the Shop Stewards' Movement in every factory (to unite unions), and in the S.L.'s 7 *Point Resistance Plan to Rearmament and the National Government,*[ii] the T.U.C. was invited to extend to the industrial side consequences of political opposition expressed in the N.L.C.'s White Paper, and to resist proposals for the 'dilution' of labour or abolition of the right to strike (or any attacks on union customs). In this cause, Trades Councils would call Conferences of local Labour, union and co-operative organisation to protest against rearmament, especially industrial conscription.[iii] That was the theory.

The S.L.'s May Day Message to unionists was that they should refuse to co-operate with the Government's intention to regiment industry on war lines, and should retain freedom to strike.[iv] Provocatively, the S.L. asked, in view of the fact that C.P. members were excluded from Trades Councils, what was the T.U.C. going to do about those who were active 'Peace and Reconstructors in capitalist industry'?[v] J. T. Murphy applauded the A.E.U.'s resolution on the agenda of the Margate T.U.C., calling for co-ordination of wage struggles of workers to ensure no union entered into a struggle without the support of the whole union movement, while the General Council hid behind complex constitutions, multitudinous 'agreements', and different types of negotiating machinery. In *Arms and the Unions*, Groves analysed effects of the Government's armaments plans on workers, and their menace to union freedom, and the S.L. supported the A.E.U. programme of May 1936, for restoration of the 1931 cuts, a 40-hour week without loss of pay, withdrawal of the memorandum on

---

[i] Trade Unionist: 'It's the Class War', *Socialist*, No. 5, March 1936.
[ii] April 1936.
[iii] *Socialist*, No. 7, May 1936.
[iv] Ibid, 'Win Your Way to Security and Peace by Winning Class Power'.
[v] Ibid., 'Matters of Moment' by the Editor.

unofficial disputes, right of unions to negotiate for youths and apprentices, and recognition of Shop Stewards and unions to be enforced on all Government contracts.[i]

At the S.L. Stoke Conference (1936), Groves was vehement, the S.L. could bring discontented and militant elements in the rank and file and *'weld them into a weapon to turn against the trade union bureaucracy'.*[ii] The S.L. had reached a point when their antagonism towards union leaders was equivalent to their animosity towards Right-wing Labour Party leaders. Touring the country, A. Bevan espoused the militancy of the rank and file; for him the Party Constitution had enfranchised the bureaucracy and disfranchised the rank and file: 'Trade union officials now become "yes men" … bartering with each other at Party Conferences over the election of the Party Executive, which consists of elderly trade union officials and executive members of trade unions… it is unrepresentative, insulated from the rank and file's proposals, and takes its inspiration from the Head Offices of the trade unions'.[iii] He wanted to know why the rank and file could not determine policy when they supplied the finances; he deduced that 'a handful of trade union leaders bully the Conference every year by waving block votes that represent nothing but a conspiracy of the headquarters'. The S.L.'s position was set.

In J. T. Murphy's S.L. pamphlet *Trade Unions and Socialism*, (June 1936), the S.L. attitudes to unionism were presented; workers had to rely on their power to strike because they only possessed labour power: 'The ballot box needs to be supported by the economic power of the workers';[iv] when unionists fought employers on wage questions and labour conditions they were really fighting against the 'consequences of the private property system'.[v] It was the S.L. view that unionism represented an attempt to organise monopolies of labour power to break down the competition between workers (who in the labour market were 'commodities for sale') and establish monopoly prices for labour – the inevitable contradiction of a capitalist economy, the struggle between two classes. For Murphy unions should be weapons of the working class in that struggle against capitalist interests. Union members had to envisage their fight in the industrial field linked with a future Socialist Government; organisation of the workers 'at the point of production' in shop stewards and workshop committees was the S.L.'s outlook: 'The greater the crisis of Capitalism, the more desperate the Capitalists become, the more certainly will they take issue with the trade unions on every question'.[vi] Not necessarily! This was making an unjustified assumption that the conditions of labour which unions sought to maintain or establish would become increasingly inimical to 'the existence of Capitalism'. Nevertheless, the S.L. now advocated amalgamation of unions in each industry into one union, 'democratisation' of unions, executive positions subject to ballot vote, affiliation of all union branches to the industrial section of the local Labour council, a National Labour Council[vii] to co-ordinate economic and political struggles of workers, and local Councils of Labour corresponding to it (with workshop, factory, mill and pit committees represented on the Councils of Labour).[viii]

---

[i] 'Trade Unionist', 'Engineers Alert: No Collaboration', *Socialist*, No. 8, June 1936.

[ii] *Manchester Guardian*, June 2nd, 1936.

[iii] A. Bevan, *Labour Monthly*, Vol. 18, No. 6, June 1936.

[iv] J. T. Murphy, *Trade Unions and Socialism*, 1936, p.1.

[v] Ibid., p.3.

[vi] Ibid., p.7.

[vii] General Council of T.U.C., Labour Party Executive, P.L.P. Executive, and Executive of Cooperative Union.

[viii] J. T. Murphy, 'Trade Unions and Socialism', S.L. pamphlet, 1936, p.8.

In the summer of 1936, the S.L. lambasted the T.U.C. for having 'done nothing' except issue an apology for declining to co-ordinate wage struggles. There had been challenges by the rank and file to Executive Committees in conferences of engineers, railwaymen and miners, and the S.L.'s conviction was that the A.E.U. should lead the agitations, state the terms of employment for every section of workers, and launch a mass recruiting drive. The S.L. focussed on Jarrow, which symbolised *the complete inability of a society to plan its economic life with public interest as its guiding motive*;[i] B. Betts contrasted this situation with that of France, where Blum had met most of the strikers' demands (40-hour week, collective contracts, paid holidays, recognition of workers' rights, a minimum wage).[ii] Union leaders in Britain by comparison were confused and indeterminate, because the T.U.C. General Council and Party Executive reacted more against Communists (and S.L. members) than against employers: 'They fear to fight Capitalism as it might mean revolution while they shout about disruption from the Left'.[iii] The S.L. aimed its frustration at a T.U.C. 'marked by considerable lack of initiative and by too great a measure of self-complacency'.[iv] On the wages front there was little evidence of any co-ordination; the T.U.C. had become a largely political assembly which, meeting only a few weeks before the Labour Party Conference, could marshal union battalions behind official policy and re-register T.U.C. decisions at Party Conferences. At the Plymouth Conference, resolutions were carried for a 40-hour week and holidays with pay, but union leaders proposed no campaign to secure these; new U.A.B. regulations were condemned, but every proposal for action was rejected. There was overwhelming opposition to the 'United Front', Citrine objecting to a C.P. 'subsidised from Moscow' and the T.U.C. performed its annual function of legitimising its 'collaborationist' policy (according to S.L. unionists), but the Left in the unions had been weakened. For the S.L., 'the re-creation of the Left in the Trade Union Movement was one of the most urgent tasks'.[v] And one of the least likely to succeed.

Another disappointment for the S.L. was the T.U.C.'s silence concerning the Government's increased armaments, and plans and rumours that the T.U.C. was preparing to support this. ('Dilution' was operating, with unemployed 'trainees' brought in at 2d to 4d below the union rate, and there were proposals to extend unemployed training centres and run the apprenticeship system as a method of providing employers with cheap labour.) *Government war plans* included extension of strike-breaking machinery, surveyance in workshops and shipyards, dismissal of militant unionists. Hence Groves (for the S.L.) argued all work in connection with war plans should be treated as any other employer proposals, with no concessions to 'patriotic' appeals, no surrender of union rights, retention of unions' freedom of action, shop stewards' recognition in Shop Stewards' Movements (in all factories), intensive union recruiting in war industries, with workshop committees and stewards for protection of workers'.[vi] G. D. H. Cole commented: 'It suited the Labour Party managers well enough to have the trade union big stick brandished at the malcontents of the S.L., League of Youth and local Labour parties'.[vii] Citrine had condemned the Hunger Marchers for

---

[i] 'Matters of Moment' by the Editor, *Socialist*, No. 9, July–August 1936.

[ii] B. Betts, 'Leon Blum's First Days' *Socialist*, No. 9, ibid.

[iii] 'Trade Unionist', 'Will the T.U.C. Lead?', *Socialist*, No. 10, September 1936.

[iv] 'Matters of Moment' by the Editor, *Socialist*, No. 10, September 1936.

[v] Militant, 'The T.U.C. Sits', *Socialist*, No. 11, October 1936.

[vi] Reg Groves, 'Menace to Unions', *Socialist*, No. 11, October 1936.

[vii] G. D. H. Cole, *The People's Front*, 1937, p.293.

'unconstitutional protests', but this did not prevent the S.L. helping set up Solidarity Committees in Trades Councils to organise demonstrations, poster parades and Reception Committees for Marchers,[i] nor did it affect the Whitechapel S.L. Conference (October 1936) which campaigned for a union recruiting drive and a stewards' organisation from union and Party members, "to protect working-class demonstrations". Union leaders did not reach the same conclusion; the power of Labour had remained undeveloped because co-operation between middle-class leaders and union leaders had been poor,[ii] or as Bevin stated it: the difference between the unionism of the 1920s and that of the late 1930s was that *those were the days of advocacy. Ours is the day of administration'.*[iii] Touché.

In 1937 the arguments for co-ordinated union activity continued apace. The existence of competing unions in any industry created sectional demands and the S.L.'s conviction to support the interests of those whose property was their labour power stood, even though it proved impossible to harness unionists to the doctrine that wage movements should become methods of 'class advance'. When the S.L. was in the process of dissolution, schemes were being presented to make workers in war industries fit into Government emergency regulations, and Government rearmament schemes were attempting to supersede union rights.[iv] Shinwell remarked years later: 'The task of broadening the outlook of the trade unionist to induce the consideration of issues less parochial than the day-to-day conflicts within the capitalist system, has been ceaseless and complete success has yet to be achieved.'[v] The task is alive today.

Appendix: The S.L. and the Co-operative Movement

The Co-operative Party had 5 million members in 1935, and won 9 seats in Parliament. There was a monthly 4-page propaganda newsletter called *Co-operative Politics*, which defended co-operative trading interests. However, co-operative interests suffered from the Government's marketing schemes and D. McHenry painted this picture of the Co-operative Movement's quandary: 'The feet of the Co-operative giant slid into the pond of Labour politics, but the body remains sprawled on the bank... The giant is confused further by the angry barking of capitalist bulldogs on the bank and by the inviting croakings of Socialist bullfrogs in the pool'.[vi] The S.L. hoped the Co-operative Movement would play a decisive part in a future Socialist Government.

The S.L. held that full recognition and encouragement had to be given to the principles of Consumer Co-operation. It proposed the Co-operative Movement bring under centralised control private organisations engaged in retail trade, and acknowledged the value of giving Co-operative employees a share in the control of distributive services. The Co-operative Movement was to be recognised as forming part of the structure of socialised industry and would be included in the National Plan.[vii] Cripps was convinced

---

[i] Margaret McCarthy, S.L. Notes, 'For the Workless and Spain, *Socialist*, No. 12, November 1936.

[ii] H. Dalton, *The Fateful Years*, November 1936, p.110.

[iii] E. Bevin quoted by A. Bullock, op. cit., December 1936, p.600. (My italics.)

[iv] Jay See, 'The Workers' Front Line', *Socialist Broadsheet*, No. 2, April 1937.

[v] E. Shinwell, *The Labour Story*, 1963, p.209.

[vi] D. McHenry, op. cit., pp.108–134.

[vii] G. D. H. Cole, 'Retail Trade and the Co-operative Movement', *A Study-Guide on Socialist Policy*, August 1933.

that extension of the Co-operative Movement was a step towards a Socialist State, but he was also sure that if Socialists waited for that means of achieving Socialism, the Movement would be suppressed by Fascists long before the goal was reached: 'I believe that the workers have got to use their political power within the next few years or definitely resign themselves to a reactionary regime'.[i] Four days later he was stating that Socialists should become members of their Co-operative branches and try to direct their policy.[ii] Co-operative leaders tended to look upon Co-operation "as an end in itself" and not as a means to a Socialist State, and he hoped that one day Labour and Co-operative Parties would 'wake up' to a realisation of an active Socialist programme. His was the 'wake up' call.

Whatever differences between the Co-operative and the Labour Movements on wages policy relating to Socialist economic planning and Co-operative Parties' activities, they both fought against private interests. Mellor, in his S.L. lecture (and subsequent pamphlet) *The Co-operative Movement and the Fight for Socialism*, appealed to the Co-operative Movement to oppose wage reductions and to give its own employees a share in control; State control and regulation of external trade would marginalize laissez-faire views in the Co-operative Movement; he recommended that Co-operative political expression be through the Labour Party (not the Co-operative Party), as the Labour Party was the only political force capable of securing the change from Capitalism to Socialism rapidly, and the Co-operative Movement in a Socialist economy would become the distributive agency for the community.[iii]

An essential part of the distributive mechanism of a Socialist community was conceived by Mellor to be the distribution and production of consumable goods utilising the device of dividend on purchase. In this, the function of the Co-operative Movement would be to secure a fair price and good quality, and establish a *democratic organisation* for the supply of necessities which would 'give members control over their economic life'. Mellor was not happy with the existing Movement because there had been too much emphasis on the trading side (similar to the methods, ethics and practice of competitive firms).[iv] In wholesale and retail establishments the worker was still 'a hand', his claims to status not welcomed, his 'interference' in management and policy resented. The Co-operative Movement should oppose wage cutting *as a principle* which could not be sacrificed in the search for markets: '*The goal of superseding Capitalism forms the link between the Co-operator and the Socialist*',[v] and socialisation of foreign trade would involve for the Movement a sacrifice of methods and a philosophy which had been necessitated by its struggle to establish itself 'inside Capitalism'. There had to be a reassessment of the political relationship between the Co-operative Movement and the Labour Party.

In 1934, G. D. H. Cole proclaimed that unionists and Socialists needed to dominate local Co-operative Societies and bring the Co-operative Movement into Socialist politics.[vi] He was unconcerned whether 'workers' control' was achieved by State or by Co-operative ownership, so long as Consumers' Co-operation became a valuable social

---

[i] S. Cripps, Cripps Papers, January 26th, 1934.

[ii] S. Cripps, Cripps Papers, January 30th, 1934.

[iii] S.L. Notes, 'An Appeal to the Co-operatives', February 10th, 1934.

[iv] W. Mellor, *The Co-operative Movement and the Fight for Socialism*, S.L. lecture at Transport House, February 4th, 1934.

[v] Ibid. (My italics.)

[vi] G. D. H. Cole, *The Working Class Movement and the Transition to Socialism*, S.L. pamphlet, 1934.

movement. Mellor's pamphlet[i] had caused a feud in the Co-operative Movement, and Joseph Reeves (Secretary of the educational section of the R.A.C.S., and an active S.L. member) was prepared to argue the issue. He conceded that the Co-operative Movement would make a contribution towards the realisation of a 'Socialist State' in proportion to the use it made of trade, propaganda and education. He also admitted the Movement had grown within capitalist society and been conditioned by the ideology of the capitalist class and economically stultified by that, but he saw it as essentially a *voluntary* movement of consumers organised to provide its members with as complete a service of goods as possible on a non-profit-making basis and believed the Movement had become primarily a *retailer* of goods: 'It is because it has failed to develop its productive side that its contribution to Socialism will be less than it might have been'.[ii] However, the Co-operative Movement had been built to place *some* economic power into the hands of workers, to be used to mitigate the worst features of a class society. What was needed was a scheme of amalgamation in the Movement towards the realisation of a *national* society, incorporating the functions of retail, wholesale and productive societies, the Co-operative Union and the National Co-operative Press. Dividend would have to be used not just as a money-saving device but as an instrument of policy for economic co-operation: 'Until the Co-operative Movement becomes economically unified, it will remain a mere counterpart of laissez-faire'.[iii] Co-operation was the consumption aspect of Socialism, while S.L. members believed there would *never* be social distribution along egalitarian lines until there was social ownership and control of production.

At a weekend school held under the S.L. Area Committee's auspices, J. Reeves delivered a lecture *The Relation of the Co-operative Movement to Socialism*, and on the same day, May 18th, 1935, Mellor addressed a Conference of Labour organisations at Reading Town Hall on *Socialism and the Co-operative Movement*. It was Mellor who moved the resolution on the Co-operative Movement at the S.L.'s Bristol Conference (1935): 'The S.L. believes that the Co-operative Movement is a powerful weapon which may be used as a means of weakening the capitalist system … it should become the main distributive organisation of society, providing the workers with *the foundations of a planned system of distribution*'.[iv] The Conference proposed the S.L. use influence as Co-operators to direct the Movement along Socialist lines, and to ensure that the Socialist point of view be represented on the governing bodies of the Movement. The Co-operative Movement itself had to lessen its dependence on private manufacturers by utilising its surpluses for widening trading and productive scope. It had to amalgamate societies into regional units preparatory to establishment of a national society incorporating the Retail, Wholesale and Productive Societies of the Co-operative Union,[v] or as dramatically headlined: '*The Co-operative Movement should be a Working Class Army*'.[vi]

Reg Groves, later in 1935, considered Co-operatives could establish closer relations with unions, because the Co-operatives provided the most effective of all organising

---

[i] W. Mellor, *The Co-operative Movement and the Fight for Socialism*, S.L. lecture at Transport House, February 4th, 1934.

[ii] Joseph Reeves, 'Can Co-operation Bring Socialism?', *Socialist Leaguer*, No. 10, March–April 1935.

[iii] Ibid.

[iv] S.L. Bristol Conference, June 1935. My emphasis.

[v] Mellor on Co-operatives in *Bristol Observer*, June 15th, 1935.

[vi] June 11th, 1935.

mediums for bringing the housewives – 'the weakest link in the chain of working-class organisation' – (Debate?) – into the Labour Movement. Another reason was that 'both Trade Unionism and Co-operation are bring driven more and more into politics and into a unity with each other and with the political organisations'.[i] It had become imperative for S.L. members to concentrate every organisation for the Labour Movement as a whole. Trade Unionism and Co-operation – the two main recruiting and organising agencies of workers – could continue to function effectively as Labour groupings if they broke through the restrictions of capitalism. This was the S.L.'s message for Co-operatives.

In January 1937, Joseph Reeves summed up the history of the Co-operative Movement as one of subordination to the ideology of laissez-faire, although its function should be or could be *'one of the instruments of the economic emancipation of the dispossessed class'.*[ii] The Co-operative Movement as an economic organisation *was* enmeshed within the capitalist system. Its vast membership had been obtained because of immediate economic benefits it offered, not because the majority of members were conscious that by any associated effort they were contributing to any so-called 'emancipation of a class'. The Co-operative Movement could enable workers to gain experience in management of productive and distributive enterprises, could provide a foretaste of tasks which would have to be tackled if social ownership was to supersede private profit-making, but S.L. writers did not develop any further ideas on this.

---

[i] R. Groves, *Trades Councils in the Fight for Socialism*, S.L. pamphlet, September 1935.
[ii] Joseph Reevs, 'Co-operators and the Class War', *Tribune*, January 29th, 1937.

Chapter Nine

Labour and Communism

They wanted a church, they wanted a religion. It gave to them the sense of being part of something glorious, fulfilling, ideal and wonderful and international, within which their own lives and attitudes made sense. Specifically it was the anti-fascist movement ... and that huge contempt for the British ruling class and the way it handled fascism ... Our parents' generation had incredible historical luck to be young at a time when the issues of the world were very polarised. It was very dangerous but you could take a side ... and the prospect of your side winning was serious. And if your side won then something really glorious would happen to the whole world. They lived with that possibility. If you look historically that opportunity occurs incredibly infrequently, it is like being French in 1789. Most people don't have that, they don't have death or glory problems. As well as that, their generation had the war and they won, and that was an immense thing for them... they set a standard that was not repeatable and we just have to do the best we can with a different situation.

Martin Kettle on his father Professor Arnold Kettle,
in *Children of the Revolution: Communist Childhood in Cold War Britain*
ed. Phil Cohen, 1997, pp.179–185

While the C.P. had perforce publicly to pretend that it had no intention of sabotaging the war effort or of turning the war into civil war, our members could at the same time be discussing in their classes every conceivable detail of how best to achieve the defeat of one's own government in war.

Douglas Hyde,
"I Believed": the Autobiography of a former British Communist,
1951, p.75

I am fired with a new zeal ... what a difference it would make to have something in life to strive for ... that gives you strength and imagination and the courage...which gives a meaning to life where before there was nothing but a selfish search for pleasure, that helps you to feel in true relationship not only to present history, but to all history... help our great-grandchildren to live in a world where the dread of war will be a bad dream, where man is no longer exploited by man, where all mankind will collaborate in fighting against famine, drought and disease... instead of spending the greater part of their income on preparing us for a deep destruction.

Keith Woddis in the 1930s,
qu. in *Children of the Revolution: Communist Childhood in Cold War Britain*
op. cit. p.152

(A) The Labour Party, the C.P. and the S.L.

Anti-Communism was a lubrication for Right-wing Labour policies throughout the 1920s and 1930s. It aimed to prevent 'militant posturing' intervening in Party activities. An ideological war against Communists[i] was pursued and successfully kept the Labour Party out of that field of influence. By 1939, exclusion of Communists (and rejection of association with them) was one aspect of the consolidation of an amorphous Labour Movement into a 'united Labour Party'. J. R. Clynes represented the Labour view: 'The Communist Party's plan is the grasping of control of the Army, Law, Press, Schools, Banks, Land, Railways, Industries, Money, Goods and Property without compensation. The League of Nations is repudiated as a Capitalist Institution... Physical force operating through the armed forces is to be the chief method of converting British citizens into contented Reds. Labour's weapon is the ballot box, the Communists is the rifle'.[ii] No banns; only a ban, because Labour leaders viewed the C.P. as 'whoring after other gods'.

To some S.L. members, and S.L. leaders who had been members of the Communist Party in the 1920s, events at home and abroad rendered less defensible the treatment of C.P. members in the 1930s as pariahs. The S.L. supported (as part of its own policy and programme) C.P. attempts to affiliate with the Labour Party. Unless the Left saw the combating of anti-communism as one of its central functions, it could not fulfil its essential raison d'être, bringing progressive social change.[iii] Gradually, S.L. leaders began to evolve its position as the development of a mass struggle, which meant taking politics into the streets and factories, based on helping people recognise *their* power to change society. Only a later generation could gawp at the naivety and idolisation by 1930s Socialists of the Soviet Union. Transformation of economic life and social forms did not automatically entail fundamental changes; the same alienations could continue, the same murderous bureaucracy as well, often in a caricatured form, as in Stalinism.[iv]

Since the foundation of the C.P.G.B. in 1920, it had been its tactic and policy to *infiltrate* the Labour Movement and its organisations, and this was intensified when intellectuals left the C.P. (partly because the *Communist International* was becoming little more than an instrument of Soviet foreign policy). The increased tempo of the bureaucratisation of national Communist Parties, growing demands for ideological conformity, and cultivation of 'Soviet infallibility' contributed to Labour anxieties.[v] Despite their continued adherence to the labling of the 'Social Fascist' policies of the Labour Party, C.P. leaders were trying to establish contacts with the rest of the Labour Movement, and began to play the rôle of a Party pressure group. It was under the C.P. banner that most of the hunger marches in the 1930s were staged. From 1931, the

---

[i] 30th October 1931, *Cowdenbeath Advertiser* quoted a local priest who warned his congregation not to vote for C.P.'er William Gallacher, because "he represented a party that denied the existence of God, advocated absolute and unlimited free love and would destroy the work ethic by rewarding the lazy"! qu. S. Macintyre, "Little Moscows", 1980, p.162.

[ii] J. R. Clynes, *Memoirs 1924–1937*, 1937, p.102.

[iii] Arnold Kettle, *Marxism Today*, 10, January 1966, 'The Future of the Left', pp.5–7.

[iv] David Cooper, 'Beyond Words', *Dialectics of Liberation*, 1968 edn. by D. Cooper.

[v] N. Wood, *Communism and British Intellectuals*, 1959, p.21.

C.P.-led *National Unemployed Workers' Movement* captured the field as the leading champion of the unemployed, and large numbers of Labour Party S.L. members were caught up in demonstrations led by C.P. members (by November 1932, of 5,400 Communist Party members, 60% were unemployed).

Three professional groups, scientists, poets and writers, were dominated by Communist intellectuals[i] and the C.P. seemed to possess an élan and spirit appropriate to the times.[ii] [Edward Upward's protagonist in *The Thirties*, Alan Sebrill, a conscientious, sensitive, middle-class poet, chooses the C.P. as offering hope, sees Communism as the only force which is uncompromisingly on the side of the doomed and against those who wanted to keep them doomed: 'It aimed at the overthrow of a society which was dominated by poshocrats and public school snobs'.[iii] To Alan, the C.P. believed and demanded that its converts should have faith not in the supernatural nor in anti-scientific myths, but in man: 'There was only one way for him to live and to extricate himself from the effects of a daily drudgery into which economic need had forced him... and that was by giving himself more and more in his free time to the service of the working-class movement. His next goal must be to join the C.P.'][iv] That was the *Communist* Weltanschauung!

This kind of fervour was transmitted to the S.L., but Labour leader, Lansbury, had been handicapped in his influence in the Movement by his continued friendship with the C.P. in the 1920s; he had advocated their admission to the Labour Party, although by the early 1930s he possessed strong doubts as to the C.P.'s usefulness.[v] The first initiative for unified action with the C.P. came from the I.L.P., when the latter was still affiliated to the Labour Party. On September 29th, 1931, the N.U.W.M., the C.P. and I.L.P. joined forces for campaigns on unemployment, and for repeal of the *Trade Disputes Act*, but in January 1933, Hitler's accession to power dramatically affected the relationship between the Labour Party and the C.P., and Clynes declared: 'Any marked increase of Communism here would recruit the British Fascist ranks just as heavily ... the country does not want Communism, no matter how it is disguised ... the Socialist case and its strength lies in its constitutional appeal'.[vi] So why did the S.L. pursue C.P. affiliation to the Labour Party?

(B) The Labour Party's 'Democracy and Dictatorship' (1933)

On March 11th, 1933, the N.C.L. rejected C.P. advances. The destruction of the German union movement and Social Democratic organisations in Western Europe had jolted the Labour Movement, but Labour and union leaders reacted to the C.P.'s proposal for a 'United Front' by issuing a Manifesto on March 24th, 1933, *'Democracy and Dictatorship'*, which claimed its kerygmatic aversion to 'dictatorships of Left and Right'. It rejected 'the iron Dictatorship of Capitalism and Nationalism and the Dictatorship of the Working Class', reaffirmed its faith in 'Democracy and Socialism',

---

[i] Ibid, p.61.

[ii] R. Miliband, op. cit., p.220.

[iii] E. Upward, *The Thirties*, 1962, p.40.

[iv] E. Upward, ibid., p.107.

[v] Cf. R. Postgate, op. cit., pp.238, 294.

[vi] J. R. Clynes, op. cit., p.249.

and its central tenet that 'a united Working-class Movement founded and conducted on the broadest democratic principles can establish a Socialist Society as soon as the workers are sufficiently advanced in political wisdom as to place their own Movement in the seat of Government, armed with all the power of the Democratic State'.[i] The Manifesto also claimed that British Labour had led the world in industrial and political democracy, and its *historic task* was to uphold the principles of Social Democracy: 'If the British Working Class hesitate now between majority and minority rule and toy with the idea of Dictatorship, Fascist or Communist, they will go down to servitude such as they have never suffered.'[ii] Was that clear enough for the S.L.?

Labour leaders warned S.L. members against *any form of collaboration* with C.P. members in anti-Fascist organisations under C.P. control or influence.[iii] To the S.L., *'Democracy and Dictatorship'* had been formulated because no heed had been paid to the lessons of disunity, passivity and capitulation (the collapse of German Social Democracy)[iv] and the S.L. gleaned from the manifesto that the more, constitutional and 'democratically minded' the Labour Party showed itself, the less would be the danger of Conservative resistance to its purposes. Cripps had stated his views when he helped bring prominent European lawyers to a Legal Commission in London on the responsibility for the Reichstag Fire. The Commission deduced from the facts that it was not the Communists but the Nazis who had organised the burning for tactical political reasons.[v] (Sixty years later the Commission was proved right!) In April 1933, Cripps replied in the Commons when Sir John Simon suggested banning Russian imports; Cripps retorted that 'this sort of emergency action is to treat Russia in a way in which no country has ever been treated before'.[vi] A 'United Front' against War and Fascism, against a break with the Soviet Union, and for building resistance against 'attacks on workers' conditions' had been concluded between the C.P. and I.L.P. in 1933, and the S.L., at its first Annual Conference at Derby, listened to a proposal from one member which pointed out that if the C.P. was prepared to come into the Labour Party, the S.L. should be pleased to welcome it. This was endorsed.[vii] A confrontation was bound to occur between the S.L. and Transport House over the issue. And it arrived immediately. E. F. Wise had been invited to speak at a *German Relief Committee* meeting; W. Mellor and J. F. Horrabin supported the request, and Wise considered his association would not harm the S.L.: 'The opposition of Transport House to this effort seems to me to be unreasonable ... they regard this particular fund as a pernicious attempt on the part of the Communists to ruin the Labour Party. This seems to me to be utter nonsense.'[viii] Yet it was Labour policy, so it seemed churlish to pursue this to a dead end.

Cripps claimed that S.L. leaders should participate in any practical attempt to gain 'unity of action' which did not raise 'fundamental issues'. Equally important was to make Transport House understand that rank and file opinion in the Movement wanted to find a way round any proscriptions: 'It seems to me to be ridiculous to have

---

[i] *Labour Party Annual Conference Report*, 1933, pp.277–78.

[ii] *Labour Party Annual Conference Report*, 1933, p.219.

[iii] Cf. Labour Party pamphlet, *The Communist Solar System*, 1933.

[iv] A. Hutt, *British Trade Unionism*, revised edition 1962, p.128.

[v] Cf. E. Estorick, op. cit., p.127.

[vi] Cripps, Hansard, April 5th, 1933, Cripps Papers.

[vii] Derby S.L. Conference, June 1933.

[viii] E. F. Wise to Cripps, June 22nd, 1933, Cripps Papers.

people going about the country as official Labour Party speakers who are the chairman and treasurer of an officially banned body'.[i] K. Zilliacus debated with Cripps the issues of Fascism, Socialism and Communism; if 'nationalism and war' became the issue, Socialists had to oppose national sovereignty and private enterprise; Labour leaders might sink into impotence through dullness and timid opportunism but: 'Left-wing Socialism tends to become theoretical and crypto-Bolshevik in policy, to go in for alliances and understandings with communism, to embrace communist ideas and to adopt much of the communist tactics and phraseology ... the Left, in its fear of Fascism, is resorting to flirtations with Communist ideas'.[ii] Was the S.L. flirting with the C.P.?

Essential was for the S.L. to restate Socialist principles, rather than offer union leaders the opportunity to characterise the S.L. as a 'dictatorial' body mouthing neo-Marxist platitudes. The T.U.C. outlook was that the Movement should be thankful for democratic procedures in Britain: 'There are some who deny that freedom can exist in a capitalist society. They regard it as a bourgeois institution of no real value to the people... the State has not yet the authority to shoot citizens without trial. Nor do people disappear at the hands of the secret police, nor is criticism of the Government a crime'.[iii] H. Morrison added that the S.L.'s view was that the Party should loud pedal in condemning Fascist dictatorships and soft pedal on Communist dictatorships and he queried Laski: 'Would you like a "Communist dictatorship" in Great Britain?'[iv] Laski thought the analogy a red herring! There was a complete opposition between 'dictatorships' which had overthrown constitutional governments (as in Italy and Germany) in the interest of a capitalist class, and one which (as in Russia) was born of war and oppression in a period of widespread confusion and disaster and sought to realise the well-being of all citizens on the basis of equality[v] – a viewpoint asserted by S.L. leaders (with a few reservations about purges and 'state capitalism' in the Soviet Union!).

Throughout 1933 the C.P. sought to collaborate on a 'United Front' within Labour organisations, but the Hastings Labour Party Conference firmly opposed the C.P.'s request for unity, regarding it as just another manoeuvre to give the C.P. a chance of getting inside the Labour Party and unions, to discredit the leaders and disrupt the existing organisation. The Conference defeated the resolution calling for a United Front. In February 1934 there was a *National United Front Conference* in Bermondsey, including delegates from the C.P., I.L.P., N.U.W.M., and Labour and union members, but the Labour Party's N.E.C. rejected this as well because the C.P. did not believe in Parliamentary democracy: 'The C.P.'s real aim is to destroy the Labour Party's influence and to disrupt its membership... the C.P. wants to enter Parliament to destroy it "from within"'.[vi] Although C.P. leaders deserved the reaction they received from the Labour Party after their 'Social Fascist' labelling of Labour leaders' policies, the S.L. reminded Labour leaders of their *own* failures in suspicious circumstances in 1931.

Other factors helped to explain (to the S.L.) Labour leaders' attitude towards the

[i] S. Cripps to E. F. Wise, June 23rd, 1933, Cripps Papers.
[ii] Konni Zilliacus to S. Cripps, July 26th, 1933, Cripps Papers, Zilliacus Letters.
[iii] E. Bevin in T.U.C. Report, September 1933, Appendix C, p.434.
[iv] H. Morrison replies to H. Laski, *New Clarion*, September 30th, 1933.
[v] H. Laski, 'H. Morrison's Challenge', *New Clarion*, October 7th, 1933.
[vi] *Labour Party Annual Conference Report*, 1934, p.11.

C.P. 1934 witnessed Labour successes in local elections. In March, the London Labour Party won a majority on the L.C.C., there were provincial successes in County and District Councils, followed by large gains in municipal elections. The most encouraging by-election victories were at East Fulham (October 1933), North Hammersmith (April 1934) and the Upton Division of West Ham (May 1934).[i] To augment this, with Lansbury's illness in December 1933, Attlee took over the leadership and was less amenable to C.P. activities in connection with the Labour Party. Henderson extolled Labour's position: 'Real unity of common action by the workers has already been established through representative organisations of the Labour Party, T.U.C., and Co-operative Movement',[ii] and the Labour Party proscribed membership for all C.P. 'front' organisations (including the *League Against Imperialism*, *Workers' International Relief*, *International Labour Defence*, 'The British Anti-War Movement', the *European Workers' Anti-Fascist Congress*, and the *N.U.W. Committee Movement*)![iii] United action with the C.P. or ancillary organisations was incompatible with Labour Party membership; full disciplinary powers would be taken.

The S.L. was never blindly committed to C.P. affiliation to the Party. J. T. Murphy and W. Mellor (both founder members of the C.P.) were critical of the C.P. by now; both agreed with C.P. analysis that any 'unity' with capitalism split the working class, but these S.L. leaders deduced that C.P. leaders were not the custodians of infallibility. Murphy in particular thought the fundamental defect of all C.P.'ers efforts towards working-class unity lay in their attitude to the working-class movement itself: 'It neither allows for new differentiations to grow in the Labour Movement, nor will it consider the possibility of any Labour leader being honest or honestly changing his views'.[iv] He criticised the C.P. for seeking to detach people from the Labour Party instead of becoming Labour Party members and changing it from within and trying to win influence in the Labour Movement, while he regarded the *Communist International* as a sect which mouthed phrases 'instead of an international mass working-class party of Revolution'.[v]

Insulation from Communist influences was extended by the T.U.C.'s *'Black Circular'* of October 1934 which aimed to debar persons associated with 'disruptive organisations'[vi] from any official position, either in unions or Trades Councils.[vii] The Labour Party Youth Officer, Maurice Webb, claimed the C.P. 'wants to smash us',[viii] and relations with the C.P. warranted a full-scale debate at Southport. The Labour Executive issued a new edict for checking 'ad hoc' joint activities between Labour members, C.P.'ers and I.L.P.'ers. Bevin and Bevan clashed at Southport over this issue. Bevan took the S.L. position that extra-Parliamentary activities were being frowned upon because they were *exposing* the incapacity of Labour leaders and inability of the Executive to face up to workers' problems;[ix] Bevin took the union stance: 'A previous speaker said that the C.P. was an insignificant party. It would not have been if

---

[i] G. D. H. Cole, *History of the Labour Party from 1914*, p.294.
[ii] Quoted by *New Leader*, March 9th, 1934.
[iii] *Labour Party Annual Conference Report*, 1934, p.13.
[iv] J. T. Murphy reviewing R. Dutt's *Fascism and Social Revolution*, in *Socialist Leaguer*, No. 2, July–August 1934.
[v] Ibid.
[vi] *Labour Party Annual Conference Report*, 1934, p.13.
[vii] T.U.C. Annual Conference Report, 1935, pp.110 ff.
[viii] *New Nation*, August 1934.
[ix] Quoting M. Foot, op. cit., p.175.

you gentlemen had had your way; we would have been split like Germany ... if you do not keep down the Communists, you cannot keep down the Fascists ... Our friends on the Continent failed at the critical moment to maintain discipline ... With the voice of dictatorship on every side, I hope that there is sufficient self-discipline in this Party ... that everybody will stand against every attempt to divide us'.[i] Bevin again won the 'unity' argument.

In 1935, the C.P. approach was to continue applications for affiliation to the Labour Party and hope for co-operation against 'War and Fascism'. After the withdrawal of C.P. candidates in the November 1934 municipal elections, Harry Pollitt (of the C.P.) thought the C.P. had to develop a positive political line towards a future Labour Government,[ii] and, as a result, the C.P. withdrew its candidates (except 3). On November 25th, 1935, Pollitt submitted the C.P.'s application to affiliate to the Labour Party now that 'the failure in the General Election proved the futility of hope from a divided Labour Movement'.[iii] While Labour leaders remained hostile, the S.L. was becoming attracted to the prospect of ending feuds and boosting their own morale, although the C.P. viewed the S.L. as insignificant: 'Fortunately for the British working-class movement, such organisations (as I.L.P. and S.L.), with no mass connections or mass influence or record of mass struggles in any part of the country, are of little significance at the present time',[iv] claimed the Communist International in November 1935. So why would the C.P. seek 'unity' with them?

This did not deter the S.L. from asking the Labour Executive to take the C.P.'s application seriously and bury past recriminations. The S.L. urged the Executive to meet C.P. representatives for a discussion of all that would be involved, and if the Executive could not recommend affiliation, to state on what terms it *would* be prepared to accept.[v] Oliver Harris counselled for unity: 'The C.P. and Labour leaders have said a lot of harsh things about each other. There is no quarrel more bitter than a quarrel between brothers. But we hope that both Parties now see the folly of attacking each other as they have done for the last few years to the delight and profit of their common enemy'.[vi] Cripps added that it was wrong that he should be allowed to share platforms with Conservatives, Liberals or any political group of the Right and prohibited from doing the same with the I.L.P. or C.P. He put the S.L. view that the C.P., by applying for affiliation, was asking not for a coalition of forces, but for a real unity; he was prepared to admit that Communists had given the most devoted service to workers, and there was little risk entailed by accepting Communists as Party members compared with the danger from continued disunion: 'We in the S.L. have always insisted that the proper place for Socialists is within the working-class movement'.[vii] But did the C.P. support 'democracy'?

[i] E. Bevin, *Labour Party Annual Conference Report*, 1934, pp.140–141.
[ii] H. Pollitt, *Communist International*, January 20th, 1935.
[iii] C. Brand, op. cit., p.189.
[iv] *Communist International*, November 5th, 1935.
[v] 'Some Matters of Moment' by the Editor, *Socialist*, No. 4, January–February 1936.
[vi] Quoted by A. Horner, *Incorrigible Rebel*, 1960.
[vii] S. Cripps, 'Weld the Workers Together', *Socialist*, No. 5, March 1936.

(C) The Labour Party, the S.L. and the Unity Campaign

By March, small allegiances between the C.P. and sections of the Labour Party were in existence. In January 1936, the University Labour Federation accepted amalgamation with the C.P.'s Federation of Student Societies, and the separate Student Internationals joined in a United Students' International. The C.P.'s British Youth Peace Assembly was supported by the Labour League of Youth and University Labour Federation, and at its Easter Conference, the League of Youth narrowly voted for "working-class unity".[i] In April, the S.L. complained that any C.P./Labour Party joint activity was being met by N.E.C. threats of disciplinary action. This further angered the S.L. because 'these same Labour Party theologians either approve of, or silently acquiesce in joint activity with capitalist politicians and political groups... You may join up with Lloyd George, but not with Harry Pollitt'.[ii] This suggested that the Labour Executive should take action to investigate the 'solar system' of Lloyd George, and ask what Labour leaders were doing as his satellites! An S.L. warning was issued that, although the S.L. refrained from joint activities with the C.P. in obedience to Conference decisions, unless the N.E.C. took action against 'collaboration with capitalism', then it had neither the right nor authority to condemn joint activity against capitalism with Communists. The *Daily Herald* headline on the S.L.'s Stoke Conference (1936) 'Staying in the Labour Party: But Want the Communists in, too',[iii] quoted Mr. Davidson (of Battersea S.L.) who expressed the minority in the S.L. that 'the C.P. has no genuine desire for affiliation, and if admitted the result would be to undermine the usefulness of the Labour Party'; it was impossible to co-operate with a Party which did not have a policy based on the needs of workers of this country but based on the policy of a foreign country. (However, the majority of the S.L. saw C.P. affiliation in the interests of working-class unity,[iv] because the continuation of conflict in the Movement was 'a crime against Socialism and an encouragement to the forces of Reaction'.)[v] Mellor, moving the resolution, stated the S.L. and the C.P. had a fundamental singleness of purpose: 'We do not take H. Morrison's view that the C.P. is opposed to the principles and purpose of the Labour Party. His attitude is that the C.P. members are not to be trusted. You will never get working-class unity if you work on the basis of suspicion against those who, despite differences, had a good record in the fight for working-class emancipation and freedom'.[vi] He was convinced the C.P., for all its faults, was required to break down 'the complacency and bureaucracy of the Labour Movement', and to bring in 'a real virile power with the honesty of purpose and courage', although he admitted that the S.L.'s disagreements on policy with Pollitt and Gallacher were known to everyone.[vii]

At the Edinburgh Conference, the C.P.'s application for affiliation to the Labour Party was easily defeated on grounds that co-operation with the C.P. would repel Labour

---

[i] Majority of 82 votes to 75 votes.
[ii] 'Some Matters of Moment' by the Editor, *Socialist*, No. 6, April 1936.
[iii] *Daily Herald*, June 1st, 1936.
[iv] *New Statesman and Nation*, June 6th, 1936.
[v] Stoke Conference, June 1936, *Socialist*, No. 8.
[vi] Quoted by *Manchester Guardian*, June 1st, 1936.
[vii] W. Mellor, 'Here Is a Popular Front!', *Socialist*, No. 9, July–August 1936.

voters.[i] The N.C.L. put the official view in *British Labour and Communism*: 'The Labour Movement will not attempt to achieve spurious unity with those who hold principles so completely irreconcilable with Labour and who have no faith in democracy'. Augmenting this decision were efforts by the C.P. to exploit the Spanish Civil War situation which confirmed Labour leaders in resistance to all forms of united front activity at home. Labour Party leader, C. R. Attlee remembered: 'The Spanish struggle was the occasion for a very determined attempt by the C.P. to get into the Labour Movement by devious methods, but the majority of the Labour Party were too experienced to fall into the trap.'[ii]

Mellor typified the S.L.'s disappointment at the failure of the C.P.'s application for affiliation by stating that debate was guillotined,[iii] while Laski considered 'debate' to have been 'farcical'[iv] (the *Daily Herald* assessed the 592,000 votes for C.P. affiliation as 'a numerical and moral rout', whereas the Spanish non-intervention minority of 519,000 votes was 'impressive', the resolution having been adopted 'with misgivings and with a heavy mind').[v] Labour leaders firmly believed the difference was between the democratic policy and practice of the Labour Party and the '*policy of dictatorship*' which the C.P. promoted to utilise Labour facilities on the platform, in public conferences and the Labour press to displace their democratic and Socialist character.[vi] As it was, before the S.L.'s dissolution, C.P. membership had increased to 12,250 (May 29th, 1937), the *Daily Worker* had reached a 70,000-copy circulation, the Y.C.L. paper *Challenge* had increased to 20,000.[vii] (C.P. membership was to increase further in 1938 (15,570) and 1939 (18,000) to its peak of c.50.000 in 1943.)

The N.C.L. opposed the suggested 'United Front' because C.P. members were 'potential infiltrators', believers in 'violence, revolution and dictatorship', under the orders of and financed by the *Communist International*, and affiliation of the C.P. would lose Labour votes and cause dissension in the Movement. Rational arguments against Labour leaders' views missed the point. To suggest that the Russian C.P. was only faintly interested in promoting revolution in other countries, that the C.P. never had a belief in violent revolution or dictatorship was irrelevant to the issue of a power struggle in the Labour Party and union movement. In Cripps' hopes for a 'United Movement' were the same features of a power struggle in the Labour Party, a question of life or death for the S.L.: 'I do not see any difference fundamentally existing between the outlook of the I.L.P., the C.P. and the Labour Party on the basic question of replacing capitalism and imperialism by a different economic system... We must be prepared to sink our differences and combine together'.[viii] An arena was about to be built in which the S.L. was a pawn between the Labour Party and union leaders on one side and the C.P. and the I.L.P. on the other. Let's close on the Thirties' febrile radical, from the pen of Arthur Miller:

---

[i] *Labour Party Annual Conference Report*, 1936, p.50. C.P. application for affiliation was defeated by 1,728,000 to 592,000.
[ii] Attlee, *As It Happened*, 1954, p.95.
[iii] *Socialist*, No. 12, November 1936.
[iv] H. Laski, *Labour Monthly*, Vol. 18, No. 11, November 1936.
[v] R. P. Dutt, 'Notes of the Month: After Edinburgh', *Labour Monthly*, Vol 18, No. 11, November 1936.
[vi] J. Middleton (Secretary of Labour Party), *Labour Party Annual Conference Report*, 1936, p.51.
[vii] Report of the 14th C.P. Congress, May 1937.
[viii] S. Cripps, *Cripps Papers*, 1936.

Once nipped by Marx, the Thirties radical felt he was leading a conditional life... its real, its secret meaning... was that it taught the worker his strength and was a step toward taking state power away from the capitalist class... his life moved into a path of symbols, initially ways to locate himself in history... The Thirties radical soon settled into *living for the future*, and in this he shared the room of his mind with the bourgeoisie... Remember the radical of the Thirties came out of a system that had stopped, and the prime job was to organise new production relations that would start it up again. ...How often have I heard survivors of the Thirties astonished that they could have said the things they said, believed what they had believed. A faith had been running underneath that newfound pride in objective social analysis, that sense of merging with the long line into the inevitable, and a faith exploded is as unrecoverable to the heart in its original intensity as a lost love.[i]

---

[i] Arthur Miller, 'Miracles' (1973), quoted in *Echoes Down the Corridor*, 2000, p.131–133.

Chapter Ten

The Socialist League and Foreign Affairs

Leftists need to learn from liberals about the mixed, ambiguous nature of things, the charm of nuance and singularity, the difficulty of determinate judgements, the preciousness of the fleeting and fragile, the pathological shyness of truth. Liberals, for their part, need to learn that when it comes to the major political conflicts which rive our world, there is no standing judiciously in the middle. In each of these cases someone is roughly in the right of it and someone else in the wrong of it; and in clinging to this faith, non-liberals are in the right of it.

Terry Eagleton, *The Gatekeeper: A Memoir*, 2001, pp.36–37

Truth is one of the strongest weapons of those who have no power ... With regard to all basic questions of individual and social life, with regard to psychological, economic, political and moral problems, a great sector of our culture has just one function – to befog the issues.

Erich Fromm, *The Fear of Freedom*, 1960 edn., p.215

Disdain for history is symptomatic of the malaise of today's youth culture and of the larger society which nurtured it. Resenting death, we murdered time. Almost too late we see that what we have slain is not time but our sense of ourselves as humans. To reject the past is to deprive today of its meaning tomorrow. To evade the significance of time is to empty life of its significance. It is that meaninglessness which pervades the age of instant gratification and instant results and permanent dissatisfaction.

William V. Shannon

In its views on British foreign policy and the possibility of war, the S.L. was profoundly affected by 1914 to 1918, the first war to collect no romance or glamour around it. The S.L. made little contribution to the hesitant and confused development of Labour's foreign policy, and based its own position on a prevention of 1914–1918 occurrences such as the arms race, secret diplomacy and economic rivalry. If the S.L. had one particular stance, it was the conviction that the roots of war were economic in origin and 'Imperialist' in inspiration. For the S.L., the Government's approach to foreign policy was in its assumption that economic considerations were paramount because, true to the instincts of a trading nation, Britain stubbornly believed that trouble-making foreign governments would lay aside their political ideologies when opportunities for profitable business presented themselves.[1]

Labour's views on foreign affairs were derived from pacifism, neo-Marxism, and

---

[1] F. S. Northedge, *The Trouble Giant*, 1966, p.620.

historical criticism of British foreign policy which stemmed from Fox, Cobden and Bright. The 1914–18 war had challenged the principles on which Britain's foreign policy had been conducted and tested all institutions, while the Russian Revolution made 'democracy' a relative concept, especially to the Left. The War helped foster scepticism, irony and irreverence.[i] Labour leaders' answer to 'future wars' was to rely vaguely on 'international working-class action', but fundamentally on *disarmament, and war resistance*, with the League of Nations to enforce peace. These confusions were exacerbated after 1931 because the Party was the Opposition, and absence of responsibility resulted in a plethora of pacifist pronouncements.

This featured prominently in the Movement and had as its symbol, Labour leader George Lansbury with his Christian Socialist sentiments: 'I want neither armies, navies, nor air forces – no Imperialism'.[ii] He expressed the humanitarian feelings, an integral part of the Movement's psychology; he saw fear as the greatest enemy, fears of poverty and insecurity compelling people to join wars;[iii] it was insane for 'civilised' Governments to rely for security and peace on preparations for war;[iv] he linked this with the economic structure of British society: 'Neither nations nor individuals can possibly live at peace with each other if they rely on force to enable them to become wealthy and believe that ruthless competition for raw materials and markets is the only way of life'.[v] To find *a way of preventing war* became the raison d'être of the Labour Movement. Labour leaders regarded the French perspective, keeping Germany as a second-class power, as counter-productive, and a major factor determining Labour's attitude, particularly on the Left, was the pro-German, anti-French sentiment dating from the 1919 Versailles Treaty.[vi] This posed a conflict between those who believed war was primarily due to economics and those who argued it was a political problem; the Labour Party incorporated *all* opinions – collective security through the League of Nations, pacifism, hostility to the Nazis, opposition to capitalist exploitation of working people for 'Imperialist wars'. Implicit in all was that assumption: Socialists somehow had a responsibility for preventing war.[vii] This transpired into a mere gratis dictum, the S.L.'s idée fixe.

The Left-wing approach (inherited by the S.L.) stemmed from a conviction about the 1914–18 war: 'The group loyalty of a Socialist is due to the dispossessed, to the millions… doomed by Capitalism to exist in poverty, who are denied the good things of human life, who are driven to slaughter each other in war'.[viii] To the S.L., war was the result of rival imperialisms in search of colonies and markets; patriotic propaganda, defending 'national interests'; even the League of Nations was a product of this capitalist mentality; this suspicion by the Left was a response to 'an age of pretending',[ix] painfully emerging from the consequences of and from effects of the World War. The S.L. thus attempted to polarise working class and capitalist interests in foreign affairs: 'If our Socialism is sincere, our sense of identity with the exploited victims of

[i] A. Marwick, *Britain in the Age of Total War*, pp.112–114.
[ii] G. Lansbury, *My England*, 1934, p.176.
[iii] Ibid., p.183.
[iv] Ibid., pp.177–181.
[v] Ibid., p.184.
[vi] A. J. P. Taylor, *The Troublemakers*, quoting M. Foot, op. cit., p.197.
[vii] K. Martin, *The Editor (1931–45)*, 1968, p.1.
[viii] F. Brockway, *Inside the Left*, 1942, p.342, (an I.L.P. view).
[ix] F. Williams, *A Pattern of Rulers*, p.252.

Capitalism of all lands must be as absolute as the true patriot's for his nation'.[i] The S.L. aroused indignation against the Government's foreign policy *and* against Fascism and the key was the unity of Labour and Socialist organisations. For a short while, in 1937, these organisations were transformed from factions into a wider influence on public opinion, exposing ineffective Government foreign policy. This 'unity' could not last while diverse groups refused to lose their identity, even though the short success of this *Unity Campaign* revealed common beliefs and aspirations. A vital lesson *was* experienced; perhaps 'unity' had never been of much practical importance to Labour leaders except for a plea for 'loyalty' when dissensions threatened Executive authority. 'Unity' as a value within the Labour Party was useful for PR purposes.[ii]

In practice, the S.L. was as confused and incapable of giving a lead on foreign issues as was the Party N.E.C. Confusion in the Movement sprang from the conflict between Socialist preconceptions about *causes* of international confrontations, the *conduct* of international affairs, and the *immediate necessities* of a situation; both Left and Right exhibited idealistic/practical attitudes as foreign events unfolded. For the S.L. the issue was adapting a neo-Marxist approach to rapidly changing realities; in this it remained far more the protest sect than an organisation with a coherent policy, because its leaders accentuated their belief in economic motivation, an analysis too simplistic to apply to the myriad causes of international events in the 1930s. The S.L. was correct in envisaging that the future of society depended on an *international morality*, but believed this possible in a world of dictatorships. M. Muggeridge summed up the 1930s as 'lost in the darkness of change',[iii] and described the conflicts that were part of the S.L.'s world: 'Two rival heavens-on-earth have been put on the market whose protagonists hurl abuse at one another... a clash between nationalism and internationalism, Christianity and atheism, dictatorship and democracy, capitalism and communism, tyranny and freedom, bourgeoisie and proletariat... a deep discord between two expressions of the same spirit of romantic materialism – a Brave New World facing a Brave Old World and menacingly flourishing the same weapons... this conflict came to provide the underlying pattern of thought, whether in politics, literature or religion'.[iv] There are five areas on which the S.L. built its shaky reputation in international affairs – the British Empire; Nazi Germany; the League of Nations; the Spanish Civil War; and the 'Unity' of the Labour Movement.

(A) The S.L. and the Empire

The S.L. upheld the creed that interpreted Fascism as the incorporation of new methods of capitalism, with oppression of working-class organisations and national rivalries promoted as a method enabling an Empire to maintain itself. At a *Peace and Empire Conference* in July 1938, Cripps expressed what had been the S.L.'s position, that 'Peace' and 'Empire' were contradictory because justice had never entered into the methods of the Empire; people within the Empire were 'the victims of capitalism';

---

[i] F. Brockway, op. cit., p.343 (an I.L.P. attitude endorsed by S.L. pronouncements).

[ii] E. G. Janosik, op. cit., 1968, p.93.

[iii] M. Muggeridge, *The Thirties*, 1967 edn., p.20.

[iv] M. Muggeridge, ibid., pp.45–46.

Empire was built on the exploitation of a depressed class,[i] and Fascism was as old as the Empire in the colonial countries. For the S.L.: 'The touchstone is political, economic, and legal justice, and the principle of self-determination',[ii] the conditio sine qua non. J. F. Horrabin's *The Break with Imperialism*,[iii] enunciated the S.L.'s stance. Looking ahead to a possible Socialist Government (as the S.L. always did) he stated the British Empire offered no practical foundation for building a *Socialist Commonwealth*, because the former was based on the exploitation of one people by another: 'You can no more think of British capitalism as something apart from its Empire base than you can think of British Socialism as apart from its trade union basis'.[iv] A Socialist Government would, regarding overseas territories, as a trustee put the interests of native inhabitants first, because 'Socialists stand for the ending of white domination'. There could, in this policy, be no preferential Dominion treatment, since Socialism could not be built on the basis of one race or one language, but he conceded that a 'Workers' United States of Europe' was more likely than a 'socialist British Empire'! (The Empire was the City's most valued area of investment.) Horrabin then added a typical 1933 S.L. statement (which the *Morning Post* printed in dark type, to exaggerate its importance): 'As Socialists, for instance, we are much more concerned with linking ourselves to Russia economically than with making any bonds which would tie us to capitalists of the same race and language as our own present masters'.[v] Red rag to the capitalist bull!

The S.L.'s policy vis-à-vis the Empire was also diagnosed by G. D. H. Cole and H. N. Brailsford. Lecturing on *A Socialist Foreign Policy*, Brailsford analysed Liberal and Socialist notions of foreign policy when the economic aims of a capitalist Empire were considered. 'Diplomacy' appeared to Socialists (in this context) as a means of furthering the interests of the possessing class with permanent investment of capital abroad: 'Debt or investment is the real nexus of Empire'.[vi] Brailsford went to the heart of the issue: 'A Socialist Party ... [had to] reach the truth about the exploitation of native labour in the Empire'. G. D. H. Cole detailed the S.L.'s position in *A Study-Guide on Socialist Policy*. The aim was rapid advance to self-government in the Crown Colonies and Dependencies: 'The S.L. denies the right of Great Britain to insist on any people remaining within the Empire against its will'.[vii] It was a feature of the S.L.'s approach here that the Empire should remain in being as a *voluntary federation of self-governing communities*, and it should be a right of the Irish Free State or of any other Dominion to secede from the Empire. The S.L. stood by a policy of granting to India, Burma and Ceylon self-governing constitutions.[viii]

In an S.L. review of Leonard Barnes' *The Duty of Empire*[ix] the hypocrisy of British colonial policy was 'exposed', and a Socialist policy outlined. The reviewer commented it was Marx who pointed out that in the colonies the truth about production in the home country could be unveiled; the S.L.'s outlook was in reference to the colonial

---

[i] London Peace & Empire Conference, July 15th, 1938, Cripps Papers.

[ii] Lecture/pamphlet for the S.L., February 12th, 1933.

[iii] J. F. Horrabin, ibid.

[iv] Lecture/pamphlet for the S.L., February 12th, 1933.

[v] Quoted in *Morning Post*, August 28th, 1933. (The same quotation formed the basis of David Stelling's 'Cripps Kampf' – a vitriolic denunciation in the *New English Review*, February 1948 – 15 years later.)

[vi] H. N. Brailsford, 'A Socialist Foreign Policy', *Problems of a Socialist Government 1933*.

[vii] Published in August 1933.

[viii] G. D. H. Cole, ibid. (My italics.)

[ix] Review by John Gild, *Socialist*, No. 3, December 1935.

Empire as a field for the investment of British capital, and for a policy to control the export of capital, while the general apathy of Labour leaders in regard to Empire was noted: 'Socialists who are uneasily aware that they cannot establish a classless society at home while supporting exploitation abroad should read and discuss this courageous book'.[i] Another criticism of Party leaders' on the Empire was by Lionel Elvin, reviewing *New Trends in Socialism* in 1936.[ii] Elvin remarked that John Parker, in his contribution, had suggested the Party might have to build a 'Socialist Empire' policy. (Orwell's comments on the Left-wing attitude towards the Empire helps to set the balance: 'The same streak of soggy, half-baked insincerity runs through all "advanced" opinion ... Every Left-wing "intellectual" is ... an anti-Imperialist. He claims to be outside the empire racket as automatically and self-righteously as he claims to be outside the class racket'.[iii] This mirrored Party leaders' reaction against the glib formulations emitted from S.L. leaders on 'the Empire and the Labour Movement'.)

At its first conference, the S.L. considered the National Government's principal plea at the next election would be 'Imperial in nature'.[iv] In the S.L.'s document *Forward to Socialism* (1934), a new approach to the Dominions, India, and Colonial dependencies was anticipated. Here, the S.L. sought a policy based on recognition of Dominion and Indian nationhood (with the right of secession), and a future Labour Government to establish economic and political relations advantageous to workers.[v] The S.L.'s argument was for a new approach from Party leaders to colonies and dependencies. At the time of the S.L.'s Conference in 1935 Lansbury wrote *Labour's Way with the Commonwealth* to stimulate S.L. comment on the mutual interdependence of Socialist construction at home and social and economic revolution in the Colonies.[vi] This showed how the British Commonwealth could fit into a Socialist scheme; the argument that Labour had to think in terms of the unity of the Empire as a means for leading the world to an international federation, resulting from the necessary dependence of Britain's Imperial economic policy on agricultural policy at home. The S.L.'s case was elucidated at the Bristol Conference: 'Self-determination, which has been the keynote of Socialist policy in Imperial matters, must find a fuller and more real interpretation in our [Party] policy than has yet been the case'.[vii] In terms of the S.L.'s new colonial policy, three books reviewed in 1936, pointed the way; *The Future of the Colonies* by Leonard Barnes; *The Demand for Colonies* by Lionel Birch, and *Peace and the Colonial Problem* by Sir Arthur Salter. The S.L. reviewer noted that 'Peace supporters' had made the painful discovery that Britain no longer kept an open door in her colonial Empire! There was also a tendency among Labour leaders to believe that extending the mandate system would dissolve existing discontents,[viii] while British investors and manufacturers were drawing their profits from administration of the colonies.

The S.L. was the only group in the 1930s Labour Party to alert the Movement that the Government was holding overseas territory by *armed power*, and was using its sovereignty for economic ends. India was not only a market for British goods – it was a

[i] Ibid.

[ii] *Socialist*, No. 4, January –February 1936.

[iii] G. Orwell, *Road to Wigan Pier*, 1937 (1966 edn.), p.139. For a critique of Orwell, see p.380 below.

[iv] *Derby Evening Telegraph* & *Derby Daily Express*, June 5th, 1933.

[v] Leeds Conference of the S.L.: 'Forward to Socialism' (document on policy), May 1934.

[vi] *Socialist Leaguer*, No. 12, June 1935.

[vii] *Bristol Evening Post*, June 10th, 1935, quoting S. Cripps at Bristol S.L. Conference.

[viii] John Gild, *Socialist*, No. 6, April 1936.

closed field for British capital investment: 'Empire, said Joseph Chamberlain, is commerce. It would be more exact to say that Empire is debt'.[i] Here, H. N. Brailsford characterised the S.L.'s perspective; in Britain was the same association between the Empire, armaments and a structure of industry that accumulated capital for investment abroad: 'The owner, working for private profit, must regard wages simply as costs, and must keep these, like all costs, as low as possible'. National industries sought an escape by monopolising Imperial markets; this would lead to war unless there was a fundamental change in the structure of industry. When he wrote *India in Chains* in 1935, Brailsford had viewed the chains as those of Imperialism, fetters on the Indian people and on producers of goods and services in the ruling country;[ii] the S.L. saw the Empire as an essential element in capitalist survival and a potent shield *against* Socialist alternatives. This was the axioma medium from the S.L.

Rechannelling S.L. energies into Socialist postures after 1935 was in the S.L.'s *May Day 'Message to Workers'* in 1936: 'Let us turn our backs resolutely on all preparations for capitalist and imperialist war ... To the workers and peasants of India, to the natives of Africa, to the people of Egypt, to all those bent under the yoke of Imperialism, we may say again on May Day: "We fight with you against Imperialist tyranny".'[iii] This was hardly likely to appeal to Party and union leaders, but by then it mattered little if there was denunciation. Cripps wrote in 1936: 'The solution of the World's Imperialist problems has got to be tackled primarily from the economic point of view';[iv] this reflected the S.L.'s core belief. The May 1936 issue of *'No More War'* provided material for those S.L. members who wanted to convince people it was absurd celebrating 'Empire' in the nation's schools and H. R. G. Greaves' *Reactionary England* (July 1936) eschewed the class character of the Foreign Office, a glorified system of outdoor relief for 'ruling' families! Commenting on the Foreign Office, the reviewer added, 'As a close preserve of bourgeoisdom, it is no wonder that secret diplomacy is its life and soul'.[v]

By the summer of 1936, the S.L. was warning Labour leaders of the Movement's 'imminent collapse' unless it made opposition to British Imperialism the *central* feature of its foreign policy. F. A. Ridley in *Next Year's War?*[vi] prophesied correctly that *Britain would have to fight a second war against German Imperialism* and he spoke of the danger of preaching the crusade against Fascism while Labour leaders refused to stress the iniquities of British Imperialism. That month's S.L. editorial stated: 'Empire is sheer domination concealed by smooth words and phrases ... "Empire" and "War" are inseparable... we must make our protests effective by mobilising working-class power at the heart of the Empire to end the class domination at home on which race domination depends'.[vii] By the time of the Unity Campaign, the S.L. propounded even more their anti-Imperialist attitudes. S. Cripps asked *'Which Is the Enemy – British Imperialism or Foreign Aggression?'* Was he about to make another faux pas? He stated that 'Imperialism' attempted to solve rivalries by war, and this could only be opposed by international class struggle: 'No working class can come to power until its own

[i] H. N. Brailsford, 'The Root of War', *Socialist Leaguer*, No. 2, July–August 1934.

[ii] H. N. Brailsford, *India in Chains*, S.L. pamphlet, 1935.

[iii] 'Win Your Way to Security and Peace by Winning Class Power', *Socialist*, No. 7, May 1936.

[iv] Cripps to Captain Cookson, May 26th, 1936, letter in Cripps Papers.

[v] D. R. D., *Socialist*, No. 9, July–August 1936.

[vi] Reviewed by M. F. (Michael Foot?), *Socialist*, No. 9, July–August 1936.

[vii] 'Matters of Moment', by the editor, ibid.

national Capitalism or Imperialism has been defeated'.[i] This could apply in Spain and India, with the struggles of working people there. Cripps thought there was a danger the Government would repeat rallying workers to a war à la 1914–18: 'If the British working class lacks the initiative to save itself from the horrors of a fresh Armageddon by now bringing about the political and industrial defeat of British Capitalism, it must either resign itself to continued exploitation or else await the defeat by some other outside power of British Imperialism'.[ii] (In 1937, Reg Groves was writing about Karl Liebknecht, symbol of workers' struggle against capitalist war, who had become a battle-cry for anti-war forces in the First World War: 'Today we are faced with the need for an uncompromising struggle against Imperialist war'.)[iii]

Between 1932 and 1937, the S.L. had presented dangers that the Labour Party could become involved in an "Imperialist War" camouflaged in the nuance of the League of Nations. Its view was challenged when Bevin appealed at the Edinburgh Conference for a United Front *with* the Government to combat Fascism and Imperialist aggression, an appeal which baffled the S.L. and the rank and file alike: 'Has the Labour Movement forgotten that British Imperialism is the biggest aggressive fact in the world and that Britain was partly responsible for the Versailles Treaty?'[iv] S.L. leaders had always been convinced that the Government would not fight on the side of a 'Socialist' France or a Soviet Russia, because 'victory would mean the triumph of Socialism over Capitalism'. Unfortunately, the S.L.'s diagnosis fell short of an understanding of the complex issues involved in international affairs, and relied on the Labour Party to reconsider policies adopted at Southport and formulate an anti-Imperialist policy to expose the trusteeship of Empire.[v]

(B) The S.L. and India

J. T. Murphy yearned for every S.L. member to read *How Empires Grow* by J. F. Horrabin, to study the nature of Imperialism 'until he burns with a passionate hatred of all it means',[vi] to understand Indians, Africans and native populations of all empires against white rulers who for profit had robbed, persecuted and plundered the brown, black and yellow populations of the Earth. Cogent arguments for Indian self-government appeared in H. N. Brailsford's S.L. pamphlet *India in Chains* (in 1935). The S.L. explicitly associated itself with his proposals for a new approach to the 'India Question', stating the Indian people, unhampered by privilege and property, should decide freely how it would wish to conduct its own affairs, and a future Socialist Government would have to ensure *that* freedom of decision as a necessary step towards 'the liquidation of Imperialism'.[vii]

The main argument forwarded by Brailsford was that the dominant British attitude maintained Indians could not seriously desire self-government, yet after 150 years of

---

[i] *Socialist*, No. 13, December 1936–January 1937.

[ii] Ibid.

[iii] R. Groves, 'The Man Who Dared the War Lords', *Socialist Broadsheet*, No. 1, February 1937.

[iv] Wilfred Wellock, 'Labour's Foreign Policy', *Socialist Broadsheet*, No. 1, February 1937.

[v] Cf. 'Imperial Stewardship', *Socialist Broadsheet*, No. 2, April 1937.

[vi] Books and Reviews, *Socialist*, No. 1, September 1935.

[vii] H. N. Brailsford, introduction to *India in Chains*, 1935, p.1, Forum Lecture, February 10th, 1935.

British rule, the mass of the Indian population was poor, partly because it continued a costly white garrison, sent abroad an annual tribute of interest to the British investor, and 'had to live with its parasitic native usurers.'[i] At the Round Table Conference, Indian delegates had been chosen by the British Government and leaders of the largest Indian party (the National Congress) were, throughout most of the critical period, in prison! Every propertied interest was scrupulously represented, but the mass of peasants and rural labourers had *no* representation; the Constitution was an imposed settlement which the elected spokesmen of Indian opinion had rejected; control of the army remained entirely in the Viceroy's hands, (he alone controlled foreign policy) and the Constitution was undemocratic: 'The armed power and the money power of the Empire remain intact'.[ii]

H. N. Brailsford construed that the princes were autocrats who did not recognise civil or political rights: 'The Empire perpetuates the Conquest by taking into partnership the Indian propertied class'.[iii] The S.L. opposed the Constitution because it did not contain any means by which the promise of Dominion status could be realised; it was undemocratic because princes had majority representation and the scheme erected a fortress for propertied classes; the S.L. supported self-determination for Indians, the first duty to enable the Indian nation to create a political organisation capable of taking over the responsibilities the British Government possessed, and to have an army of its own. Indians should shape everything in their Constitution; it should rank as a Dominion with a Dominion's rights. Brailsford summarised the conflict: 'The "National" Government's Constitution ... places the Indian masses, without hope of peaceful liberation, under the heel of property and the princes. Our task is to enable the workers and peasants to take their share in the work of *self-determination*.'[iv] Writing in the *Socialist Leaguer* in May 1935, V. K. Krishna Menon understood what was at stake; Brailsford's analysis had revealed India as 'a vast continental slum', a land of hunger and pestilence, of illiteracy, squalor and misery, where movements of protest were suppressed by a Police State;[v] *India in Chains* was a provocative study, a challenge to Socialists which would justify its publication if it made a few people consider the *implications* of Imperialism. It was a challenge to Labour leaders, since Labour's policy was based on the acceptance of Attlee's amendment to the India Report, therefore Labour was colluding with 'National' Government proposals. This was in spite of the fact that, in 1933, the Labour Party stated: 'The objective of the Colonial policy of the Labour Party may be summed up in the two words – socialisation and self-government'.[vi] Also, a Labour pronouncement had been made that a Labour Government would seek to end economic Imperialism, and would look forward to the 'United States of India', with full equality of status, among the British Dominions.[vii]

So, the Labour Movement was pledged to grant self-determination to India, and to achieve this self-government; Lansbury spelt out requirements from Socialists: 'We

[i] Ibid., p.4.
[ii] Ibid., p.6.
[iii] H. N. Brailsford, ibid., p.7.
[iv] H. N. Brailsford, ibid., p.11. (My italics.)
[v] *Socialist Leaguer*, No. 11, May 1935.
[vi] *Labour Party Annual Conference Report*, 1933, Cripps regarded the National Government's attitude over India as 'most reactionary', *Western Daily Press*, December 14th, 1932.
[vii] Quoting H. Dalton, *Practical Socialism for Britain*, 1935, p.366.

should ask Indians themselves to summon a Constituent Assembly'.[i] From its inception, the S.L. had been aware of 'Imperialist hypocrisy' at the Round Table Conference (where safeguards that destroyed pretence at self-government were imposed). India had been made secure for British investors and remained a province of the City of London.[ii] In 1933, Krishna Menon, under the title, *Safeguards that Cripple Freedom*, critiqued the Government White Paper on the proposed All-India Federation. Although Labour leaders voted in the Commons against the resolution, the S.L.'s disappointment was that the Party conducted no campaign when the Indians rejected the Constitution. The Indian princes had entered into agreement after securing a definition of their rights and privileges, and it was not in the power of the British Parliament or Indian Legislature to impose on the princes a democratic franchise: 'This Constitution hands over India, tied and bound, to be ruled in perpetuity by property'.[iii] A gloomy prognosis from the S.L.

What the S.L. believed was that the Constitution was *not* the one promised at the Round Table; that is, a Constitution to be created by negotiations between equals. It was a system *imposed* by one Party upon the other, incapable of alteration; it established a dictatorship of property; there could be no legal opposition: 'The British ruling class ... is trying to bring about an alliance between the Indian and Imperial propertied classes ... India will be governed by the landlords and usurers',[iv] reiterated Brailsford. Labour leaders had to defeat the Constitution and prepare to grant to India a machinery of government which could reshape the whole system. The problem voiced by the S.L. was that the princes in the Federation would halt Indian democracy and dominate the Federation however the representatives of 'British India' were chosen: 'Indian people have the ear of the MacDonald Government; to the voice of the Indian people it is stone deaf'.[v]

In the S.L., V. K. Krishna Menon questioned the India Bill as designed to render India safe for Imperialist exploitation and to make Imperialism secure;[vi] the elaborate machinery of Assemblies and Councils, of 'non-political' banks, Statutory Corporations, emergency powers and special responsibilities of Governors and Viceroys were devices which secured the Imperialist power while cloaking it with 'representative institutions'. The majority of Indians would gain nothing since economic and fiscal policies were the preserve of British financial interests. The S.L. objected to Attlee's Labour proposals which accepted the Government's Bill; there was no demand from Labour for adult suffrage, and Labour's official policy subscribed to the creation of special constituencies for religious sections and vested interests. Krishna Menon concluded: 'The Labour Movement will never fully appreciate the situation until it treats this issue... as an essential element in the attainment of socialism... In the new "Federal" India, capitalism will seek new opportunities. The territories of the Indian Princes are the heaven of the capitalist who seeks cheap labour and no labour legislation'.[vii]

By 1935, the S.L. was delighted to announce that Indian Socialists were in favour of the anti-militarist banner: 'The Congress Socialist Party has, on the issue of War and

---

[i] G. Lansbury, *My England*, 1934, p.173, 'Yet neither Cripps nor Lansbury joined the Provisional Committee campaign for the early release of the Meerut prisoners, Cripps Papers, February 2nd, 1933.

[ii] H. N. Brailsford, *New Clarion*, January 21st, 1933.

[iii] H. N. Brailsford, 'The Labour Party and India', *Socialist Leaguer*, No. 8, January 15th, 1935.

[iv] H. N. Brailsford, ibid.

[v] H. N. Brailsford, 'International Notes', *Socialist Leaguer*, No. 10, March–April 1935.

[vi] V. K. Krisna Menon, 'Labour and India', *Socialist Leaguer*, No. 10, ibid.

[vii] V. K. Krisna Menon, op. cit., 1935.

Peace, adopted in all essentials the policy of the S.L., which stands firmly for the right of India to determine her own destiny'.[i] In October, M. R. Masani (joint secretary of the All India Congress Socialist Party) spoke at Caxton Hall on 'Socialist tendencies in India'; he discussed the war of aggression in which Britain was involved; the Press gagged, unions suppressed, indefinite imprisonment in concentration camps without trial (for over 2,000 Bengalis) and a form of martial law in several districts. India was denied her national independence, denied a voice at Geneva (except through Britain's nominee, the Aga Khan): 'The bulk of Indian opinion, both Nationalist and Socialist, will certainly be no party to India (herself a victim of Imperialism) being made a pawn in the diplomatic game'.[ii] In December 1935, Cripps celebrated the Golden Jubilee of the Indian National Congress with an article for the Bombay Chronicle. In it he spoke of Congress' great work in focussing sentiment for national self-government; considered the recent India Act 'typically imperialist in origin', seeking to rivet British financial control on India: 'Until the Indian people can have complete control of their own economic organisation, they cannot be politically free. Nor is it possible for a Constitution to be forged by the British Government which will suit the needs and requirements of the great people of India'.[iii] The S.L. was on the right track.

Jawarhal Nehru, President of the Indian Congress, made his contribution for the S.L. in April 1936. To him, solving 'the Indian problem' meant ending the Imperialist tradition and relinquishing Empire. Poverty, unemployment, repression, denial of civil liberties, could not be tackled by protecting the interests that flourished on them. Nehru viewed India as an essential part of the world crisis, India the most important symbol of world Imperialism.[iv] H. N. Brailsford spoke of Nehru as a rationalist with a Western scientific training, for whom the Mahatma's old-world asceticism and mysticism were often repugnant, an aristocrat (with 3.000 years of Brahmin tradition behind him!), a Socialist, a man who opposed Indian Liberals for wanting to change India's rulers while leaving the system of exploitation and enslavement intact: 'To become a rebel means to abandon career and wealth, and to face long and repeated intervals of gaol life'.[v] It was Nehru who was advocating opposition to the Government of India Act and closer collaboration with the workers and peasants: 'The Socialist Party is on the map in Congress as never before ... Under Nehru's leadership, the Socialist Party in India is going forward to greater influence and keener struggle.'[vi] Betts saw an equivalent analogy between the S.L.'s 'popular front' and the new Indian Communist line of collaboration with Socialist and Social-Democratic Parties.[vii] Clutching at straws?

At its Stoke Conference, an S.L. resolution was passed for the repeal of the Criminal Law Amendment Act which made permanent ordinances depriving Indians of civil liberty, freedom of speech, of movement, of association and of the Press. The S.L. declared its opposition to the India Act because it subjected Indians to the domination of their own propertied classes, the princes, and British Imperialism: 'It is neither a step towards independence nor towards Dominion status and denies to the Indian

---

[i] Editorial, 'Matters of Moment', Socialist, No. 1, September 1935.

[ii] M. R. Masani, 'India in Chains – Under the Union Jack', Socialist, No. 2, November 1935.

[iii] Bombay Chronicle, December 28th, 1935, Cripps Papers.

[iv] J. Nehru, 'Imperialism Must Go, Root and Branch, if India Is To Be Free', Socialist, No. 6, April 1936.

[v] H. N. Brailsford reviewing J. Nehru: An Autobiography, in Socialist, No. 13, December 1936–January 1937.

[vi] Barbara Betts, 'India', Socialist, No. 8, June 1936.

[vii] Barbara Betts, Socialist, No. 7, May 1936.

masses any possibility of progressive emancipation. This imposed constitution has met with universal condemnation from the Indian National Congress'.[1] The S.L. proposed a policy which would give self-determination through a freely-elected Indian Constituent Assembly, to annul the restrictive penal laws, release political prisoners, ensure free speech and assembly, encourage organisation of workers and peasants to take an effective part in the Constituent Assembly, take financial and economic measures to control Indian finances, withdraw all British troops, and implement a new Constitution.

The basic cause of India's poverty was perceived to be land tenure and revenue. Attempting to rationalise the apparatus of India's production was tinkering with the vast conundrum of that poverty, and British policy (alternating conciliation with suppression) was similar to tactics of installing conciliatory and repressive Viceroys.[2] For S.L. commentators, releasing peasants and workers from degradation and insecurity was essential. The Government was criticised for pursuing a policy of bans on meetings and processions, interfering with the election campaign, restricting liberty of movement, and arrests for sedition: 'The real problem of India remains; the Government continues to make preparations for its mock elections. The peasants and the workers continue to bear the brunt of the fiercest depression … and over 70% of the population (250 million) are dependent on the produce of agriculture'.[3]

In November 1936, the S.L. stated efforts were being made to stultify Congress' activity; a ban placed on Congress' political correspondence, measures taken to cripple the Socialist Party (with its leader, M.R. Masani, externed from the Punjab.)[4] R. Lobia complained about a police search of his office, all copies of foreign newsletters seized. By January 1937, the S.L. was reporting that the Indian Government had banned the 'Left Book News'. An editorial concluded heatedly: '*A war of Defence will be a war to defend an Empire in vast areas of which there is not, and never had been, any more pretence of Democracy than in Germany*'.[5] After the disaffiliation of the S.L, a resolution was incorporated into the *Unity Campaign* congratulating the Congress on its struggle against 'British autocracy' and against the imposed Constitution.[6] It hoped the British Labour Movement would secure the withdrawal of the 1935 Act so that a Constituent Assembly, freely elected by the Indian people, could determine the future of India, and declare its 'support for the struggle of the Indian and Colonial peoples against Imperialism'.

Throughout 1937 and 1938, individual ex-S.L. members continued to assess the struggle of the Indian people as an economic struggle: 'It will be of no great advantage to the Indian masses if they merely succeed in substituting for the domination of British Imperialism, the exploitation of the Indian Capitalists', concluded Cripps in the *Daily Pratap*'.[7] The *India Act* laid down a method by which Indian capitalists and State rulers could have a larger share in the Government, and warned that the Congress Party should not become so involved in its participation in the provincial

---

[1] Resolution of the S.L. Stoke Conference, June 2nd, 1936.

[2] R. M. Lobia (Secretary, Foreign Department, All-India Congress Committee), 'The New Indian Regime', *Socialist*, No. 10, September 1936.

[3] M. F., 'What India Really Needs', *Socialist*, No. 11, October 1936.

[4] Editor, 'Matters of Moment', *Socialist*, No. 12, November 1936.

[5] Editor, 'Matters of Moment', *Socialist*, No. 13, December 1936–January 1937.

[6] Cripps Papers, March 1937.

[7] *Daily Pratap*, August 7th, 1937, Cripps Papers.

Government of India as to constitute itself the upholder of the Imperialist regime. As expressed in a speech at Chapleton (in 1938): 'the India Act is to preserve British Capitalism with Indian capitalism as a junior partner while the Indian Congress wants the right of self-determination, abolition of Fascist Rule, and the fight against the exploitation of poverty and the masses'.[i] The S.L. had assumed the process of eroding tradition would be a rapid development once the oppressed had seen 'the light of Socialism', but the tortuous slowness was a bitter pill. Kingsley Martin summed up the disillusionment: 'The greatest disappointment of all was the discovery that peoples who had been held together under Imperialist rule would not co-operate with each other when they were free'.[ii] Fortunately for S.L. members, it was not necessary for them to rescind their enthusiasms for colonial self-determination; it remained a hopeful goal for the future.

(C) The S.L. and the League of Nations

In its policy towards the League of Nations, the S.L. veered from the official Labour position. Because of its ideological commitment to counteract 'Imperialist' wars fought for a capitalist class, the S.L. was wary of the 'national interest'. As a result it took an unrealistic attitude towards the question of rearmament (war resistance was all) and the League of Nations was viewed as *an anchor of British Imperialism*. This S.L. outlook contrasted with Labour's official support for the League of Nations; 'the Geneva spirit' upheld conscience against force, rule of law against power politics, international obligations against 'national interests', arbitration in place of war, disarmament not armaments: 'We were not gullible ninnies who expected the League of Nations to overcome sovereignty, but we thought it the only hope and fought for it long after it was betrayed. We, not the Tories, were the realists who saw that isolated defence was an out-of-date conception and that the collective idea alone made sense'.[iii] That was Labour's perspective, which the S.L. challenged.

Under cumulative effects of acts of international aggression, the Labour Party was driven to re-examine (in part to modify, in part to discard) its preconceptions. The S.L. argued about sanctions against Italy and questioned non-intervention, appeasement, rearmament, and conscription. Attlee's was the official Labour view: 'The setting up of the League of Nations was the expression of the desires for the establishment of moral principles in international relations',[iv] but, unfortunately, fervent nationalism had returned with the breakdown of the world economic system and failure to *act* on moral principles; the tragedy was that the League of Nations lost authority because nations were not prepared to make it work: 'From 1931 to 1933 Britain was prey to diplomatic bigamy which proved damaging to her moral pretensions. Those in control of her policies shilly-shallied between the League of Nations and power politics'.[v] Supporting economic boycotts through the League of Nations against any aggressor, Labour was not in favour of unilateral disarmament, but

---

[i] S. Cripps, Cripps Papers, February 5th, 1938.
[ii] Kingsley Martin, *The Editor*, p.326.
[iii] Ibid., p.323.
[iv] C. R. Attlee, *As It Happened*, pp.106–110.
[v] F. Williams, *A Pattern of Rulers*, p.157.

aspired to armament manufacture lowered to the Plimsoll line of safety, yet opposed Britain going 'naked' in an armed world (as Bevan famously claimed years later). Doubts about the powers of the League had emerged during the 1931 Manchurian crisis. The betrayal of the Chinese by Western powers when the Japanese invaded Manchuria roused the indignation of the Labour Left, destroying Socialist illusions about the League, and the crisis was a turning point of the League's powers, even more so the withdrawal of Japan and Germany from the League in 1933.

The S.L. view on the League of Nations was adumbrated by H. N. Brailsford in 'A Socialist Foreign Policy' written for the S.L.'s *Problems of a Socialist Government*. The argument was that the League of Nations could not cure economic maladjustments that drove nations to military activities; the Manchurian affair and failures at the Disarmament Conference had a deleterious effect on the League; now among seven major powers, two were Fascist, three were outside the League; a majority derided the idea of 'internationalism': The S.L.'s locus classicus was: *'This League of Nations can only legislate and administer in the capitalist interest'.*[i] To the S.L., foreign policy was either Socialist or Imperialist; the League of Nations was a dangerous delusion, 'an organ of imperialism': 'Collaboration in the international field with capitalist states is as dangerous as coalition at home with capitalist Parties'.[ii] The League of Nations remained an international *ideal*, and had achieved worthwhile non-political work, (standardisation of health services and economic investigations), but the S.L's Socialist or Imperialist perspective coloured its analysis of the League of Nations' purpose and raison d'être.

Behind the hard-line, S.L. policy towards the League was not hostile. It regarded the League's ambitions as limited; within constrictions it had consolidated procedure for the settlement of disputes, acted as some check on ultra-nationalist, imperialist powers, provided at Geneva a centre for meetings and publicity, embodied the ideal of 'conference', its rule of unanimity protected countries, it provided a new diplomatic technique. The S.L.'s ideological concern (and its differences with Party policy) was thus: 'We must utilise the League of Nations, but *it cannot be the vehicle of a Socialist foreign policy*, which aims at welding the working mass of humanity and wages, with constructive militancy, in an incessant struggle against Imperialism'.[iii] In August and September 1933 Brailsford wrote further articles for the *New Clarion* on 'Building a League on New Foundations'[iv], 'Labour and the League'[v] and 'The rôle of an international peace-keeping force'.

The S.L.'s International policy was elucidated by G. D. H. Cole in the summer of 1933. The S.L. envisaged the reorganisation of the world (big plan!) as a federation of autonomous, closely co-operating Socialist republics. (The U.S.S.R. had the same idea!) It still advocated continued membership of the League of Nations and the International Labour Office, subject to attempts to use the League of Nations for the 'preservation of world capitalism' (which would result in resignation from the League); any obligation to the League had to be subject to claims of loyalty to the international working-class movement![vi] At the Hastings Party Conference, Labour's

[i] H. N. Brailsford, 'A Socialist Foreign Policy', *Problems of a Socialist Government*, p.281.
[ii] Ibid., pp.282–84. Japan left the League of Nations on February 25, 1933.
[iii] Ibid., pp.285–86.
[iv] *New Clarion*, August 12th, 1933.
[v] *New Clarion*, September 23rd, 1933.
[vi] G. D. H. Cole, *A Study Guide on Socialist Policy*, August 1933.

policy was presented: organisation of peace through the League of Nations, ending secret alliances, abolition of private manufacture and sale of armaments, settlement of international disputes by pacific means. *'Removal of the causes of war'* was in there as well, but that was a very tall order! Sir Charles Trevelyan for the S.L. hoped to commit the Party to *'war resistance'* and a *'general strike in the event of war'*, while the S.L. damned the League as reflecting the economic conflicts of the capitalist system.[i] The Conference stated the primary aim was finding an alternative to war; the Left and Right looked in different directions for a road to peace, the majority leaning towards Geneva, peace through disarmament and collective security, a League of Nations with sanctions. In the European crisis, the S.L. agreed with Lansbury that Fascism and War, failure to disarm and the inherent weakness of the League of Nations, were part of 'Capitalism in decline', which would mean further degradation for workers, exacerbating national animosities, an appeal to force (at home and abroad): 'The answer of Socialists and of the working class to European and World Crisis must be the sharpening of the attack on the present system of Capitalism, and not dependence on the existing League of Nations'.[ii] Not of much practical use in the climate of 1933 and the year of Nazis in power, especially when Germany left the League.

1934 opened with a plea from Lansbury to Socialists to work for reconstitution of the League of Nations, to make it representative of all races: 'We should have faith in our ideals of universal brotherhood'.[iii] In May, the N.C.L. sent a deputation to the Prime Minister in support of strengthening the League, and Attlee spoke at the Geneva Institute of International Relations on 'the socialist view of peace', and to give authority to the League with an international police force.[iv] Brailsford inquired: 'Is the League of Nations an Illusion?'[v] and 'Must We Have a Force Behind Peace?'[vi] His conclusion – a collection of States (some Imperialistic, some Fascist) could not produce 'peace', could never remove 'the causes of war', and Russia and the United States would have to enter the League if it was to become the custodian of world peace.

At its Leeds Conference (1934), the S.L. carried a resolution on *'War and Peace'* castigating the League of Nations for its impotence and lack of international co-operation.[vii] The Conference concluded that 'competitive nationalism cannot organise world peace'; the time had come to abandon the illusion that pacts or covenants could effect a change; the S.L. envisaged no hope of 'peaceful co-existence' except in the transformation of the economic system. Despairingly it stated: 'This Conference renews its pledge of active resistance to Capitalist and Imperialist wars'. It could not perceive the League of Nations as the organisation through which a Socialist ideal of internationalism could be realised, and the S.L. stuck to its formula (i.e. war was inherent in the economic structure of capitalist society; it could not be banished by a League composed in part of Imperialist and Fascist States, fettered by the rule of

---

[i] *Labour Party Annual Conference Report*, October 1933.

[ii] S.L. Notes, *New Clarion*, October 28th, 1933. Germany left the Geneva Disarmament Conference and League of Nations on October 14, 1933, cf. Sebastian Haffner, 'Defying Hitler: A Memoir', 2003 edn., p.219.

[iii] G. Lansbury, *My England*, p.192.

[iv] C. R. Attlee, *As It Happened*, p.90.

[v] H. N. Brailsford, *New Clarion*, January 20th, 1934.

[vi] H. N. Brailsford, *New Clarion*, February 24th, 1934.

[vii] Leeds Conference Resolution on 'War and Peace', May 1934.

unanimity, based on retention of absolute national sovereignty.[i] A Socialist Government would have to look at those States in which workers were in control (which ones?); there should be a treaty with the Soviet Union to secure economic and political co-operation. These aspects were incorporated in the S.L.'s *Forward to Socialism*.

To the S.L. there was no via media between Labour's policy of 'improving' the League of Nations and the S.L. promoting a Russian alliance. Criticism levelled by L. A. Fenn at the N.F.R.B.'s pamphlet *The Prevention of War or Labour and the League of Nations*[ii] emerged: no technique of security could render war impossible so long as the economic basis of Imperialism remained. Therefore, the S.L.'s reaction to the *Birmingham National Peace Council Congress* and its discussion of 'collective security' was predictable. Brailsford remarked that collective security directed against Japan by Imperialist governments was 'sheer humbug'. G. R. Mitchison excoriated: 'I have often seen a wangle, but I have never before heard a wangle publicly announced'.[iii] Mellor rebuked the T.U.C. for believing the League of Nations could end war; the T.U.C. had not distinguished between the policy a Socialist Government should pursue, and policy the Movement had to implement under a capitalist government: 'The League of Nations, as events have proved, was incapable of dealing with the causes of war'.[iv] The S.L. had an answer: *'mass resistance to war'* through the General Strike. Not that support for this was close at hand.

While Labour was solemnly announcing that the next Labour Government would put an end to the arms race and danger of war (by submitting at Geneva proposals for disarmament), and while the S.L. urged the Party at the Southport Conference to declare against participation in capitalist or imperialist wars (some aspiration!) and to view the Soviet Union as its ally,[v] the Soviet Union *joined* the League of Nations (September 1934)! Now the S.L. had to reorientate its policy vis-à-vis the League to save face, (just as the C.P.G.B. had to do a volte-face with the Nazi-Soviet Pact of 1939). The S.L. had swallowed the policy advocated in Brailsford's *Property or Peace*, which believed the League had been an 'impotent talking-shop'; the S.L. had acclaimed political and economic relations with Socialist Governments, yet advocated economic and political agreements with *any* States, *and* supported a general strike against war, whether or not it was acting in conformity with its obligations under the Covenant. Documenting the S.L.'s ambivalence, K. Zilliacus asked the S.L. to make clear *what* its attitude to the League's collective defence system was.[vi] Not easy to answer.

The S.L. difficulty was that from 1934 there was a reversal of Labour's traditional position on the League of Nations, collective security and rearmament. The Executive's *'War and Peace'* report to the Southport Conference repeated the dedication to disarmament and attachment to collective security through the League of Nations, the Government to settle disputes by peaceful means and eschew force. However, responsibility for opposing war was not to be placed on the union movement; there was a proviso that the Movement would support the Government if the latter had to

[i] Leeds Conference Resolution on 'Foreign Policy', May 1934.

[ii] H. R. G. Greaves, *Socialist Leaguer*, No. 2, July–August 1934.

[iii] 'Ishmael', 'National Peace Council Prepares War', *Socialist Leaguer*, July–August 1934.

[iv] W. Mellor, 'The Menace Today', *Socialist Leaguer*, No. 2, July–August 1934.

[v] Editorial, 'Forward to Socialism', *Socialist Leaguer*, No. 4, September–October 1934.

[vi] K. Zilliacus to S. Cripps, Cripps Papers, September 10th, 1934.

use military and naval forces to restrain an aggressor nation.[i] The S.L. claimed the League of Nations was bound up with the Treaty of Versailles and *incapable of doing more than upholding the 'status quo'*, and its amendment reiterated relations with the Soviet Union and workers to resist war with a General Strike.[ii] Cripps and Brailsford thought Labour's foreign policy amounted to support for the Government (which could not be relied upon to defend democracy or peace). To these S.L. leaders, support for the League was anathema because the value of the League of Nations depended on the 'motives which underlay its actions' (which depended on Governments at Geneva), and the League of Nations seemed to be losing authority as an instrument of justice and peace, embroiled in the new balance of power.[iii] The S.L. was willing to support an anti-Fascist policy, but not prepared to see this obfuscated by support for the status quo.

The S.L.'s interpretation was that the Government had attempted to bargain with Germany during the Disarmament Conference, and followed Mussolini's lead towards a revision of treaties. The logic remained: war came from economic conflicts within a capitalist system; the League was the creation of this, a future Labour Government should not rely on the League, but seek peace by establishing close relations with the Soviet Union and countries where 'Socialist Governments were in control'; workers in capitalist countries should prepare *resistance to war* declared by their own Governments. At Southport the S.L.'s amendments were lost,[iv] so the Labour Movement pinned its hopes on the League (possibility that support for the League might involve war was no longer excluded). For the S.L., debates at Southport illuminated its approach; *'Socialist ends were not served by capitalist wars, whatever the slogan fought under: "Democracy", "Liberty" or "the League of Nations".*[v] This made apparent the Executive's tactics, because the debate had been preceded by a resolution on 'entry of Russia into the League of Nations', and a 60 minute speech from A. Henderson glorifying the League, the Collective Peace System, the International Police Force and the Peace Act![vi]

Reg Reynolds summarised the effect of Labour's *'collective security'* i.e. maintaining peace by placing armed forces at the disposal of the League of Nations. For the S.L., 'peace' imposed by capitalist states would be based on the very structure that Socialists were seeking to alter; security without Socialism meant security for the capitalist order, and insecurity for working people. The S.L. was, here, a counsel of despair: 'It is impossible for the Socialist to work for the overthrow of capitalism – particularly in its Fascist and Imperialist forms – where there is no shadow of "democracy" – if he at the same time guarantees the State against external aggression'.[vii] The S.L.'s answer was the distant ideal of dismantling the system of class and racial domination (Imperialism) and organising resistance against Fascist rulers of Italy, Germany and Austria. What did that mean? To support 'peace' by collective security was to support the existing order: 'Peace based upon the capitalist system, with "Law and Order" maintained by its "International Police", must be the greatest bulwark against the classless democracy of

---

[i] Cf. *Labour Party Annual Conference Report*, 1934, p.17.

[ii] Ibid., p.176.

[iii] Ibid., p.168. The U.S.A. established diplomatic/trade relations with the U.S.S.R. on November 17, 1934.

[iv] Ibid., p.178. Amendment lost by 1,519,000 to 673,000.

[v] B. A. Betts, 'Youth and Peace', *Socialist Leaguer*, No. 5, October–November 1934.

[vi] W. Mellor, 'Southport & After – The Task for Socialists', ibid.

[vii] R. Reynolds, 'Capitalism and Collective Security', *Socialist Leaguer*, No. 5, October–November 1934.

Socialism';[i] 'a League of Capitalist Nations' would remain an 'Alliance of Sovereign States'; there was only one idea which could challenge the capitalist doctrine of national sovereignty' – (Guess?) international working-class solidarity: '"Workers of the World, unite" ... is the essence of the only policy which will end War'.[ii] This S.L. aspiration of 'working-class internationalism' as the basis of Labour's anti-war policy was moonshine.

By 1935, Labour leaders had sidetracked Conference resolutions for a General Strike and 'mass resistance to war'. In the *Government's Defence White Paper* (March 1935) the S.L. faced abandonment of collective security as an effective instrument of national security. If everything else failed, the S.L. was ready to accept the arbitrament of arms if with other nations in defence of League principles; the basis of security had to be willingness to subordinate national wishes, or interests to international agreements, each nation to sacrifice some factor in its national armaments.[iii] What required resolution was the equation of arms and economic power; nations had to renounce the use of armaments to defend their economic power. The S.L. was convinced old peace treaties were the source of new wars and this could not be overcome by increases in armaments. (The S.L. was right.) The problem had to be tackled from the view of economic co-operation, and until some more equitable method was devised for sharing raw materials and markets of the world, it was futile to deal with the armaments problem in isolation.

In May 1935, H. N. Brailsford presented the S.L.'s position on the League of Nations and possibility of war; Hitler had suppressed unions in Germany, while the League's support consisted of British and French 'capitalist empires': 'This is not a war of classes or a battle of ideas. It will be, like the war of 1914, a battle for power'.[iv] Germany had withdrawn from the League, unable to obtain a recognition of her equality in rights; the Germans' offence against the League had been rearmament without their permission. The S.L. view was that two capitalist empires, determined to retain military supremacy, had used the League for their own purposes, and feared Germany: 'It is a Holy Alliance for the maintenance of an unchallengeable "status quo". It has no workable machinery for the revision of treaties. Its Courts, if they arbitrate a dispute, can only interpret and re-impose the series of treaties dictated in 1919'.[v] The police mechanism of collective security was perpetuating the 'dictatorship' of the Versailles victors. The League's ideal operated where it was in the interest of Britain, France or Italy – not in Manchuria or in Abyssinia, but within the area regulated at Versailles. The S.L. stood opposed to British Imperialism and the Locarno Treaty, which had tied Britain to the new European system: 'Our policy of mass resistance to any capitalist war is still the right one ... *let us struggle to save the Labour Movement from its idolatry of the League of Nations*'.[vi] A League of Nations 'war to prevent war' would terminate as cynically as the 1914–1918 War, that was supposed to end such confrontations for ever.

Pro-League of Nations sentiment in Britain had risen to its highest, symbolised in

---

[i] Ibid. On December 16, 1934, Mussolini rejected the League of Nations' arbitration in its dispute with Abyssinia.

[ii] F. Horrabin, 'Class Rule and War', *Socialist Leaguer*, No. 7, December 15th, 1934.

[iii] S. Cripps in House of Commons, March 11th, 1935, C. Cooke, op. cit. p.172.

[iv] H. N. Brailford, *Socialist Leaguer*, No. 11, May 1935.

[v] Ibid. The League of Nations denounced German reintroduction of conscription, 17 April, 1935.

[vi] H. N. Brailsford, 'Facing the Next War (The Problem for Socialists)', *Socialist Leaguer*, No. 11, May 1935.

the *Peace Ballot* in 1935. The N.C.L. and the League of Nations' Union co-operated in the Ballot, 'the greatest poll ever undertaken in Britain',[i] in an unprecedented effort to influence official policy. The results showed unanimity on membership of the League, support for reduction of armaments, abolition of national military and naval aircraft, prohibition of private traffic in armaments. The policy based on the League and sanctions *confirmed* the foreign policy of the Labour Party. In the *Ballot*, there was overwhelming support for economic and non-military measures against an aggressor: 'The force behind the Labour Movement in the country is great and growing, and the Peace Ballot showed it',[ii] crowed Dalton. At its Bristol Conference the S.L. was not deterred: 'the Government might claim to be fighting on behalf of the League system in conjunction with the Soviet Union, but would have led the country into war to preserve the interests of British Imperialism.'

Despite the Ballot and the intensive peace propaganda, the S.L.'s worry hinged on the *Government's Paper on Defence* and decision to treble the Air Force. Betts, for the S.L., criticised Henderson's confusion of collective security with the League when the problem that faced the Socialist was not whether s/he preferred impartial arbitration to the use of force for settlement of disputes or collective security to retention of national armaments, but what was the best way to achieve these objectives.[iii] The system of regional pacts was seen as, not a growth of the League's authority, but an attempt to substitute pre-war alliances for 'collective security'. The S.L. deduced that capitalist States would not yield national sovereignty, and Labour leaders were accused of ignoring the real motives of the Soviet decision in joining the League! (The S.L. was split in its reaction to Soviet twists in policy, some supporting Molotov's logic that the League *could* play a positive rôle guaranteeing peace.) However, the bias of the Covenant against dispossessed nations and inadequacy of its provisions for the peaceful 'revision of treaties' had driven out nations which did not benefit from the status quo.[iv] An alternative view in the S.L. came from Sir Charles Trevelyan in *Mass Resistance to War*: 'All real reliance on the League of Nations as a buttress in emergency against war has ceased… all hopes of substantial disarmament are at an end;'[v] the Movement could not rely on the League for peace; it was a League of Governments who had dishonoured their obligations to humanity, having led the world away from peace: 'We today deal with a League of Nations dominated by some militarist powers, despised by other militarist powers, and therefore useless to save us'.[vi] Neither S.L. position was adequate for the urgency of the times.

From the beginning of 1935, most S.L. members were convinced that re-thinking was required on foreign policy, but there were two currents of opinion in the S.L at its Bristol Conference and it was on the Socialist estimate of the international situation and the attitude to war and peace that the S.L. was divided.[vii] A considerable element of the S.L. was pacifist, the remainder took the view that the enemy was at home, that any war waged by the Government, (in support of the League of Nations or not) would be a 'capitalist war' etc. This latter group held that the coming war would find Britain and

---

[i] C. Brand, op. cit., 1964, p.180.

[ii] *Labour Party Annual Conference Report*, October 1935, p.156.

[iii] B. A. Betts, 'The Way to Peace', *Socialist Leaguer*, No. 12, June 1935.

[iv] B. A. Betts, ibid.

[v] Ibid.

[vi] C. Trevelyan, *Mass Resistance to War*, S.L. pamphlet.

[vii] J. T. Murphy, *New Horizons*, p.313.

Germany on the *same* side against the Soviet Union. (Mellor, G. R. Mitchison and Cripps supported the policy opposing a war led by a capitalist Government; the issue was simplified to one of 'War or Socialism'. Opponents of this view, such as J. T. Murphy, went the route of a pact of mutual assistance with the Soviet Union (even if such a pact was made by the National Government), believed the League *could* be used for strengthening pacts of mutual assistance against the aggressor, and supported *any* war against Nazi Germany. This shrewd, perspicacious position was in the minority. The majority view remained convinced a war would be directed against the Soviet Union. Mixed with traditional pacifism, a doctrinaire opposition to the Government and fear of a non-Socialist Government introducing military and industrial conscription, the Conference was won over. J. T. Murphy ruefully expressed the controversy: 'Nor was it other than natural that a Movement which had come into being out of a protest against the non-Socialist character and policy of the 1929–1931 Labour Government should so fiercely reject the idea of assisting anything which suggested the possibility of supporting a Government which was anti-Socialist'.[i] It was *natural* but misguided and flawed. In the resolution on *'the International Situation'*, passed by the S.L.: 'The League has provided neither a sense of security to the satisfied Powers, who have remained members, nor a sense of justice to the discontented ones';[ii] it had been unable to call on member States to modify their national sovereignty … 'The new armaments race is, therefore, only a political symptom of the economic system … countries are manoeuvring again for a strategic position… they are in fact substitutes for the security the League has failed to provide'.[iii] Suspicion remained that Covenants and treaties would be repudiated when economic interests of 'national capitalism' ran counter to those of collective security. (The S.L. majority pronounced that a future Socialist Government would *reconsider* treaty commitments.)[iv] The only constructive conclusion by the S.L. was that the League could be made a 'World forum'[v] for the propagation of the Socialist conception of society, adapting international machinery through adjustment of economic and territorial injustices.[vi] Another distant dream.

Confrontation inside the S.L. and in its relations with Labour policy also came over *the Abyssinian issue*. By February 1935, nothing decisive had come from Abyssinia's application to the League of Nations to intervene in her dispute with Italy; in March, Brailsford criticised the League for allowing Mussolini to apply military pressure while taking no steps to enforce the treaty that pledged him to arbitrate all disputes with Abyssinia.[vii] The S.L. position was that a formula had been found which left to Italy what Mussolini had wanted, no interference from France or Britain in his military preparations: *'Abyssinia is in the process of being sacrificed within the framework of the League of Nations* where … the manoeuvres of power politics go merrily forward.'[viii] S.L.

---

[i] Ibid., pp.316–17.

[ii] Bristol S.L. Conference resolution, embodied in the S.L.'s 'Fight Now Against War: A Call to Action', June 10th–11th, 1935.

[iii] Ibid., p.5.

[iv] Bristol S.L. Conference resolution, embodied in the S.L.'s 'Fight Now Against War: A Call to Action', June 10th–11th, 1935.

[v] 'Cripps' Peace Plan: League of Nations as World's Forum', *Daily Herald*, June 11th, 1935.

[vi] 'Fight Now Against War: A Call to Action' (S.L. policy), June 1935.

[vii] H. N. Brailsford, 'International Notes', *Socialist Leaguer*, No. 10, March–April 1935.

[viii] Notes and Comments: 'Power Politics', *Socialist Leaguer*, No. 12, June 1935.

frustration was directed against Stanley Baldwin, who was seen as a 'League man' hymning praises on internationalism yet knowing how useful the Geneva machine could be to 'an Imperialist Power', building the Air Force to make 'British Imperialism' strong in the system of alliances, calculating whether Government interests could be served by aligning it with France and Russia or with Germany. The S.L. wanted to know how the Movement proposed to combat consequences of power politics, although one S.L. member candidly admitted, 'to reiterate phrases and slogans from a policy which could only have a chance of succeeding if there were a Socialist Government in power, would seem to be rather more than futile'.[i] This was the S.L.'s misfortune.

The National Council of Labour hoped the Government would utilise the League of Nation's machinery (in July, 1935) when the T.U.C. supported League sanctions against Italy.[ii] Meanwhile, in the real world, the Italo-Abyssinia dispute was striking at the foundations of the League of Nations; Mussolini aiming at political and economic control over Abyssinia, France inclined to acquiesce in these colonial ambitions (being opposed to the Anglo-German Naval Agreement), but for the S.L., unscrupulous word-playing by major Powers revealed the sham of international law: 'In view of the Imperialist uses to which the Covenant is put by those who remain in the League, can the Labour Movement of this country seriously maintain that the submission of a 'bold and far-reaching plan' at Geneva would bring Europe back on to the track of collective security?'[iii] This S.L. member, B. Betts, concluded that the Government wanted to enforce the Covenant because its violation would threaten British imperialist interests in Africa; to pass Peace Acts and submit 'bold plans' at Geneva would be adding to existing confusions.

The war in Abyssinia threatened the efficiency of sanctions. In September 1935, the International Labour Movement upheld sanctions to halt Italy, although the major objection of pacifists was not to military action, but to action by Britain for *any* purpose other than defence of collective security under the League of Nations. The T.U.C. voted to support the League in restraining the Italian Government[iv], while the S.L. highlighted the Italo-Abyssinian question in its anti-war conferences with debates on military sanctions.[v] Differing Labour viewpoints were aired in the *Socialist*. One S.L. position was that discussion for partitioning the world's resources under the League was cynical; another corroborated the S.L.'s exposure of the Imperialist nature of member states of the League, but queried the S.L.'s contemplation of a Socialist Government remaining a member of that League. A third position opposed the S.L.'s 'No Sanctions' line, which seemed to be pro-War, pro-Fascist and pro-Government – pro-War because it repudiated stopping the existing war, pro-Fascist because it enabled Mussolini to carry out his aggression on Abyssinia, pro-Government because it enabled the Government to back out of any action against Mussolini.[vi] That analysis summed up the confusions in the S.L.

The S.L.'s 'agreed policy' appeared in the S.L.'s *Anti-War Conference* on September 14th, 1935. Cripps admitted there was confusion about war and armaments, because of

[i] Ibid., *Socialist Leaguer*, No. 12, June 1935.

[ii] *Bristol Evening Post*, quoting S. Cripps, June 10th, 1935.

[iii] B. A. Betts, 'International Notes', *Socialist Leaguer*, No. 13, July–August 1935.

[iv] *Survey of International Affairs II*, 1935, p.187.

[v] S. Cripps, 'What We Must Do at the Party Conference', *Socialist*, No. 1, September 1935.

[vi] *Socialist*, Nos. 1 and 2, September and November 1935.

association with League of Nations' activities' or evasions hiding behind 'collective action'. The immediate danger was the Italo-Abyssinian dispute.[i] British Imperialist interests were involved in Somaliland, the Sudan, the Mediterranean, and the Suez Canal. Neither Germany nor Japan were any longer in the League, Italy might leave.

So long as competitive capitalism survived as the central inspiration of foreign relations, tariffs, quotas, trade and shipping restrictions, colonial monopoly markets, spheres of influence and protectorates, all were devices used in this struggle.[ii] The S.L. had dug itself into a trench on this issue. Cripps quoted Baldwin, that a nation with its back to the wall would break any treaty to win economic victory and Cripps was convinced *the League of Nations represented 'Capitalist humanitarianism' placing a veneer of order over chaos and anarchy of Imperialist competition.* Substantially the League was used to maintain the order established in the 1919 Treaty: 'We cannot support the League in its policy of perpetuating Imperialism just because it prefers our own Imperialist nation to another';[iii] economic sanctions might entail military sanctions which could bring a European war; if Labour looked at the situation from the workers' point of view, they would make support of the League conditional (upon support for an international order which the Movement believed to be 'just'): 'We cannot support the Capitalist Government of this country in any action as regards the League, while we profoundly condemn their Capitalist and Imperialist foreign policy.'[iv] The S.L. had no new ideas to get out of this impasse.

Not all members on the S.L.'s National Council condoned Cripps' reading of the situation. Sir Charles Trevelyan wrote to Cripps that he was in favour of the League of Nations using sanctions if Mussolini began a war, provided all nations agreed (including France and the Soviet Union), and provided they would support each other if Mussolini attacked one. Trevelyan disagreed with the S.L's. majority position that imposing sanctions was 'simply imperialist policy'; 'if Russia supports sanctions that becomes a frankly ridiculous attitude'.[v] Cripps replied immediately; the S.L. had formulated its attitude at Bristol; the question of sanctions had been thoroughly considered: '*I have always taken the view that Russia's foreign policy at the present time was extremely dangerous to the working classes of other countries*'.[vi] (This was a private letter, not for public debate!) Sybil Wingate wrote to Cripps, supporting S.L. policy, but warning 'You will be very much alone, and very much attacked by nearly everyone, both inside and outside the Labour Movement … to some extent this applies to all the National Council of the S.L.'[vii] The abuse and outcry would be levelled at Cripps, but she anticipated that if a few Socialists could maintain the 'Socialist position', it would be a focus for the Movement: 'I am sick of the talk of strategy, and how to be in the majority. Let us be in the right. The majority will look after itself'.[viii] September 1935: Cripps resigned from the N.E.C.! Ostensibly it freed him to put his own views on foreign policy and armaments to Party Conference. He used a pacifist/anti-Imperialist argument: 'What's worth fighting for? Having decided this question in our minds, we

---

[i] Cripps Papers, S.L. Anti-War Conference, September 14th, 1935.

[ii] Ibid.

[iii] Ibid.

[iv] Ibid.

[v] Sir C. Trevelyan to S. Cripps, September 15th, 1935, Cripps Papers.

[vi] Sir S. Cripps to Sir C. Trevelyan, September 15th, 1935, Cripps Papers.

[vii] S. D. Wingate to S. Cripps, September 15th, 1935, Cripps Papers.

[viii] Ibid. Mussolini's forces invaded Abyssinia on October 3, 1935.

can (ask) whether it is the sort of war in which we are prepared to sacrifice our own lives… We cannot support wars, the objective of which is to perpetuate the system we not only dislike but which we believe to be the fundamental cause of war'.[i]

At the 1935 Labour Party Conference the gulf between pacifism, 'collective security' and the S.L.'s war resistance, emerged. The Party stood for collective security through the League (but sought security through eventual disarmament); the S.L. feared a bargain made with Mussolini, holding that the test of Government sincerity would be whether Ethiopian independence emerged; Lansbury's pacifism meant opposing military sanctions through the League. He used a pacifist/Marxist argument: 'I cannot rid my mind of the sordid history of capitalist deception. The empty hollow excuses of 1914 … "the War to end War", the need to fight to save democracy, the cry to crush the foul autocracy of Prussian militarism, a state of war automatically exists… We must fall back on the attempt to use working-class sanctions'.[ii] Pessimism ensued. However, the debate on sanctions was the longest in the history of Party Conferences. Sir C. Trevelyan acknowledged the League of Nations as the only hope in 'a world of political gangsters'; Lansbury convinced there was no difference between mass murder *organised* by the League and that conducted by nations individually; Cripps thought it mattered less what should be done than who controlled the action, and Mellor believed British workers could not at that moment be effective in the international political field.[iii] Those four perspectives represented the different positions expressed in the S.L., but the Conference resolved on sanctions; the S.L. suffered a resounding defeat.[iv] The League, an 'international burglars' union', had turned policeman.[v] The S.L. had no practical alternative to place before the Party.

Bevin now set out to defeat Lansbury's leadership, and achieved his goal by demanding that the Party leader should not accept responsibility incompatible with his conscience. He used the call for 'Party loyalty' against Lansbury and Cripps. Lansbury was reprimanded for remaining on the Party Executive when he disagreed with its policy; Cripps denounced for resigning from it for the same reason.[vi] Nevertheless, S.L. leaders continued to find the League of Nations defective; preservation of 'national sovereignty' by each member State made it impossible to have effective control; 'economic reorganisation' could not happen since the League was based on the territorial status quo.[vii] (The Communist Party supported sanctions in obedience to Soviet policy, and dubbed S.L. objections to the League as *'pseudo-Socialist negativism'*);[viii] the I.L.P. opposed sanctions on pacifist grounds and hoped for a working-class boycott; and the S.L. majority opposed the League's sanctions. The complexity of these positions developed because 'war' had previously implied rivalry between capitalist powers and intervention *against* the Soviet Union; now simplicity was challenged by conscription in Germany, invasion of Abyssinia, the Soviet Union as a League member, and soon the Spanish Civil War. Which should come first in a Socialist policy – checking Fascism in Europe, defeat of British capitalism? The S.L. was caught in a

---

[i] S. Cripps, 'Where I Stand', *Sunday Referee*, September 15th, 1935.
[ii] G. Lansbury Papers, quoted by E. Estorick, op. cit., pp.142–43.
[iii] *Labour Party Annual Conference Report*, October 1935, p.158.
[iv] *The Times*, Cripps' obituary, April 22nd, 1952.
[v] S. Cripps, *Manchester Guardian*, October 2nd, 1935.
[vi] A. J. P. Taylor, *English History (1914–45)*, p.382.
[vii] Cf. S. Cripps Letter, Cripps Papers, October 25th, 1935.
[viii] *Imprecorr*, October 12th, 1935.

dilemma, wishing to oppose Fascism, but not under this Government.

The Labour Movement had been compelled to re-examine fundamentals in its foreign outlook because of German rearmament and the Abyssinian crisis. No Labour leader could avoid taking a view on British rearmament or for Government to militarise to prevent Italian aggression, but Labour leaders had faith in economic sanctions: 'The issue of sanctions and the preservation of the League machinery were vital, the one policy that could prevent the World War'.[i] The P.L.P., while ready for Britain to make its contribution to collective security, was opposed to national armaments increases. (It had given little attention to defence problems; the idea that liberal democracy could be overturned by dictators (such as Hitler and Mussolini) would have seemed very far-fetched.[ii] And that's why, to the S.L., Labour's insistence on disarmament was inconsistent with rejuvenated support for the League of Nations. The ambiguity was in a policy which called for action against the aggressor while refusing to will the means in rearmament. The Party N.E.C.'s arguments was *for* sanctions and *against* rearmament; appealing for a strong League, urging support for the Disarmament Conference. It might have been possible to base a League of Nations policy on disarmament but by 1935 *only an armed system of pooled security* stood any chance of stopping dictators.[iii] Half-hearted sanctions could not succeed; the result would be to unify the nationalism of the country on whom they were imposed; League of Nations members considered their own interests; sanctions fizzled out, the end of League powers justifying the S.L.'s view of its 'deception': 'It marks the dividing line in the 1930s ... the one hope that England would stand for a constructive world policy came to an end ... the British Lion had once again threatened to bite with its false teeth'.[iv] Enter Churchill, but not yet.

The S.L.'s alternative strategy was disappointing. The debate at Brighton had been a battle of ideas, but the S.L. offered an artificial opposition typified by Mellor's argument: 'The positive action of fighting your enemy at home is greater in value than the negative disaster of defending your home enemy abroad'.[v] The logic of this was that incantation that only a Socialist Government could pursue constructive policies. This was a philosophy of paralysis.[vi] Declarations in favour of sanctions had not budged Mussolini from war preparations, so, for the S.L. the League of Nations had proved a slow-moving legalistic machine, which acted too late'.[vii] Cripps maintained the League of Nations was used as an instrument for stabilising Imperialism and the S.L. was not retracting its majority decisions: 'If the result of the League's action turns out to be the loss of Abyssinian independence ... then the hollowness of its claim to be an instrument of International Justice will be well proved'.[viii] The S.L. wanted to see that Abyssinia was not brought within the 'sphere of influence' of any major Power; there should be resistance to any increase of British armaments; the Movement had to expose the idea that

---

[i] K. Martin, op. cit., p.171.

[ii] C. R. Attlee, *As It Happened*, p.96.

[iii] Cf. G. D. H. Cole, *History of the Labour Party*, p.323.

[iv] K. Martin, *The Editor*, p.178.

[v] *Labour Party Annual Conference Report*, October 1935, p.172, Mellor added: 'Our enemy is at home'.

[vi] R. Miliband, op. cit., p.225, cf. A. J. P. Taylor, 'Confusion on the Left', *The Baldwin Age*, p.77, ed. J. Raymond. Economic sanctions were imposed on Italy by the League of Nations on November 18th, 1935.

[vii] B. Betts, 'Policies on the Anvil of War', *Socialist*, No. 2, November 1935.

[viii] S. Cripps, 'Your Enemy Is at Home!', *Socialist*, No. 2, November 1935. See Mellor's comment at L.P.A.C., Oct. 1935

Imperialist nations (sharing economic opportunities for raw materials or markets) could solve the contradictions of Capitalism or could bring any peace.

'Abyssinia' was the test case. The S.L. had prophesied a deal with the Italian Government within the framework of the League, enabling Mussolini to call off his armies to preserve the Franco-Italian alliance, encourage Hitler to look eastwards, leaving Britain the 'balancer of Europe'. This would create a world heading for war, realignments, a League of Nations pretending to be effective.[i] L. A. Fenn chided ex-S.L. member G. D. H. Cole for claiming there was no Socialist anti-war policy which could succeed, and considering Socialists should strengthen the League, even the risk of a 'sanctions' policy, to gain time.[ii] Cole had a better grasp of realpolitik than Fenn, because Abyssinia was invaded, Labour leaders condemned Italy's flouting of the League; the N.C.L. urged sanctions, and denounced the agreement as a betrayal of the Abyssinian people. Labour leaders hoped if the anti-Fascist powers rallied to the League, Germany and Italy might be curbed (without large-scale rearmament). However, confusions in Labour's foreign policy now arose from an awareness that support for 'rearmament' *meant* arming a Government which had just shown lack of faith in the League (and was as likely to use arms against India as against Germany, Italy or Japan).[iii]

The S.L.'s position was freshly presented by Cripps; people dealt with fear and suspicion between nations as if they were the causes rather than results of economic and political policies: 'An attempt has been made without any economic alterations to bring about political peace';[iv] the League of Nations had become a device to dampen the most dynamic forces for change; the S.L. was now in favour of a League and collective security (provided it was not to secure capitalism and Imperialism): 'A firm foundation for Peace, more sure than the shifting sands of Imperialist competition, exists in the united desires of the workers'; economic inequality was the environment that produced the disease. The S.L. was divided over Abyssinia and the League's reaction, and this was obvious at the Durham *Anti-War Conference*. The miners were dissatisfied because no speaker stated whether the S.L. was opposing or supporting a 'sanctions' policy, nor could give any advice as to *how* workers should act to prevent war.[v] For the S.L., the deception of Baldwin and Chamberlain was highlighted: 'they turned their propaganda away from the Imperialist point of view towards the Liberal humanitarian viewpoint',[vi] the Government's policy had not altered; the League was 'a means of regulating imperialist rivalries amongst imperialist powers'.[vii]

After 1935, 'collective security' became increasingly a mere slogan. The threat of war overshadowed other debates but Labour leader, Attlee, proclaimed 'we shall never agree to piling up armaments and following a policy either of imperialism or of alliances, but *only collective security through the League of Nations*'.[viii] With recognition by the Government that remilitarisation of the Rhineland had destroyed the League as an instrument of peace the N.C.L. issued its manifesto for collective security: *Labour and*

---

[i] Editor, 'Some Matters of Moment', *Socialist*, No. 3, December 1935.
[ii] L. A. Fenn reviewing G. D. H. Cole, *The Simple Case for Socialism*, in *Socialist*, No. 5, December 1935.
[iii] Cf. G. D. H. Cole's argument, *History of the Labour Party*, p.321.
[iv] Cripps' speech (at Norwood, Willesden, Brighton and Stratford) December 1935, Cripps Papers.
[v] Letter from M. Archer, *Socialist*, No. 3, December 1935.
[vi] S. Cripps, 'Fight Imperialism – the Enemy of Peace and Justice', *Socialist*, No. 4, January–February 1936.
[vii] Letter from M. Archer, *Socialist*, No. 3, December 1935.
[viii] C. R. Attlee, *As It Happened*, p.100.

the Defence of Peace (1936); the plan reflected a policy of collective League action. This was different from the S.L.'s approach, as Mellor wrote: 'A grave danger to real Peace today is the illusion of the League of Nations';[i] he was convinced that the most dangerous illusion was that workers should determine their policy towards war by a hatred of Fascism and a liberal belief in good intentions of 'democratic' Capitalism; and it was an S.L. hope that the Soviet Union was a League member for the possibility of alliances with anti-German, anti-Japanese forces: 'The Abyssinian war shows that the spark is near the powder barrel'.[ii] Mellor was right. Rearmament was occurring all over Europe even if the League of Nations was a cover under which leading Powers played the game of international obligations when it suited them. It could not preserve peace; the Abyssinian affair had shown that it could not end wars once they had begun; the basis for peace was economic, and Mellor concluded the League could only be a forum used for the expression of broad principles, not as an instrument for peace.[iii]

Cripps wrote to K. Zilliacus in April 1936 that Labour leaders could extricate themselves by stating they would have nothing to do with this Government as the League was being made to behave by its Imperialist controllers: 'The more that the Labour Party talks about "collective security" and the League, the more it plays into the hands of the Tories, who are able to 'cloak their actions behind the camouflage of these phrases'.[iv] In May 1936 the N.C.L. objected to Italy being allowed to succeed in its aggressive policies, while Leonard Woolf in *The League and Abyssinia* made three specific points against the S.L.'s position; that, although the S.L.'s analysis of Imperialism was 'sound', the League of Nations might postpone war; peace and war were determined not only by economic causes, but by ethical ideas; and a world of Socialist States would probably be nationalistic and *need* a League of Nations. Elvin, for the S.L., acknowledged that a federation of Socialist States would require federal machinery, but the existing Government was encouraging Mussolini, and any Government could use the pretext of League ideals to invoke the support of the Labour Movement for a war which was in defence of its own interests: 'We are not prepared to abandon socialist opposition to imperialism, merely because the imperialist government has given its old policy a coating of French polish or Geneva varnish'.[v]

Just before the S.L. Stoke Conference, Cripps pondered about the Italian victory over Abyssinia, and what it should teach the Movement; the '*League of Nations*', '*security pacts*', '*collective security*' and '*non-aggression*' deceived working people as to the aims of the Government;[vi] support of sanctions would tie the Labour Movement to Government. The S.L. considered the N.C.L.'s *Labour and the Defence of Peace* manifesto as correct in theory, but unrealistic in practice, because it was essential to eradicate problems arising from economic exploitation of colonial territories.[vii] At Stoke, a resolution was passed which reiterated the League of Nations under capitalist control was incapable of removing causes of war or preventing any major Power from engaging in aggression; to cherish the illusion that sanctions applied by the Government were applicable to a policy of collective security obscured the causes of war and paved the way to

---

[i] W. Mellor, *Socialist*, No. 5, March 1936.

[ii] Ibid.

[iii] C. R. Attlee, *As It Happened*, p.100.

[iv] S. Cripps to K. Zilliacus, April 18th, 1936, Cripps Papers.

[v] H. L. Elvin reviewing L. Woolf, *The League and Abyssinia*, in *Socialist*, No. 7, May 1936.

[vi] S. Cripps, 'National Unity a Delusion', *Socialist*, No. 8, June 1936.

[vii] Editor, 'Matters of Moment', *Socialist*, June 1936.

collaboration with the Government's rearmament programme and war preparations. The working-class movement should maintain its independence, resist every plan for rearmament and industrial mobilisation, and expose dangers of the League based on a capitalist philosophy.[i] That's where the S.L. had reached.

The I.L.P. welcomed the S.L. resolution on war policy and against League sanctions.[ii] S.L. principles had been reaffirmed at Stoke, not only that the League of Nations was a method of upholding British interests abroad but that the Labour Movement required 'a completely different basis for our foreign policy'.[iii] In July 1936, Cripps summed up where the S.L. stood – as anti-sanctionist, opposed to co-operation with a Government prepared to fight an imperialist war, and support for working people against being drawn into any war. Betts criticised the Mandates system because it perpetuated Imperialism in the modern guise of "trusteeship"; this system had been instituted to prevent Imperialist annexations, but was being used to suppress Arab people by the British Government. She considered that Labour support for the machinery of Geneva had led it to support the Mandates system: 'The uncritical belief in the Geneva institutions leads the Labour Movement to side with strange allies.'[iv] Likewise, Horrabin (reviewing *Towards a New League* by Brailsford), estimated the bankruptcy of capitalist statesmanship. Brailsford's suggestions – members pledged to mutual defence, pooling of economic and military resources, nationalisation of arms manufacture, revision of treaties,[v] were worthy but soon to be by-passed.

At the Edinburgh Conference, the Labour majority upheld League of Nations' action. While opposition was shown towards unilateral rearmament, there was 'qualified' support for increased armaments. The S.L. was in a dilemma, between its decision to organise opposition to 'Fascists' and conviction that armaments in the hands of the Government would be "used against working-class people". Party policy held that the armed strength of countries loyal to the League had to be conditioned by armed strength of the potential aggressor: 'The policy of the Labour Party is to maintain such defence forces as are consistent with our country's responsibility as a member of the League of Nations'.[vi] Meanwhile, Constituency Parties, following the S.L.'s majority assessment, submitted a resolution expressing loss of confidence in the League of Nations (because it was used by Powers for their own imperialist purposes), demanding a campaign against military and industrial conscription, and for working-class unity in resistance to 'capitalist and imperialist war'.[vii] The Party's N.E.C. had dissociated itself from the international policy of the Government, which was accused of having 'betrayed' the League and Abyssinia, and having broken pledges to electors to follow a League line, but Party leaders confirmed belief in the League, disarmament by international agreement, the principle of collective security. The Party resolution was carried. This illuminated the truth; the S.L. was impotent to influence Party decisions. For all the S.L.'s efforts to galvanise the Party into rethinking its perspective on the

---

[i] Quoted by *Manchester Guardian*, June 2nd, 1936.

[ii] *New Leader*, June 5th, 1936.

[iii] S. Cripps in letter, June 23rd, 1936, Cripps Papers. However, on July 3, 1936, a Viennese Jew, Stefan Lux, shot himself at the League of Nations in protest at the Nuremberg laws. A letter on him explained: 'I can find no other way to reach the hearts of men,' qu. Ian Thomson, *Primo Levi*, 2003, p.65.

[iv] B. A. Betts, 'Britain's Clapham Junction', *Socialist*, No. 9, July–August 1936.

[v] J. F. Horrabin reviewing *Towards a New League*, in *Socialist*, No. 10, September 1936.

[vi] *Labour Party Annual Conference Report*, October 1936, p.182.

[vii] Ibid., p.96.

League of Nations, the only result was confusion, indecision and self-contradiction within the S.L.,[i] and the S.L.'s decision to follow through its conviction (that a collective peace system was nonsensical so long as economic interests dominated the League of Nations), determined its relations with the I.L.P., the C.P. and Labour leaders in the final six months of the S.L.'s existence.

(D) The S.L. and German Politics

From January 1933, Nazi Germany became another huge issue in the S.L.'s battles vis-à-vis official Labour leaders. Fascism in Italy and Austria, Nazism in Germany, had a profound effect on the thinking of the S.L., because totalitarian ideologies confirmed Socialist policies and its uncompromising opposition to 'capitalist policies'. Nazism was different from any previous ideology in power and instead of the S.L.'s conviction that this new phenomenon would *reconcile* divergent elements in the Labour Movement and *unite* the Left, the truth gradually dawned that differences would be exacerbated, the Labour Movement more fragmented, in its varying responses. Nazism provoked hostility towards totalitarianism per se, pacifism, and even determination to challenge the British capitalist Government, which S.L. writers denounced for *its* 'Fascist tendencies'.

In the pages of the *New Clarion*, the first mention of Hitler's Government occurred in March 1933 when William Gillies (Secretary of the Labour Party's International Department) saluted the 7 million fighters for democracy in Germany, in an article headed '*Germany in Chains: The Triumph of Desperation*'.[ii] The following week, another S.L. writer declared Hitler had achieved a great deal: 'He has exposed the pretensions of capitalist Europe, and has shown with vivid sharpness the conflict that lies inherent in the capitalist structure'.[iii] At this stage not much had filtered through of Nazi intentions, although barbarous suppressions of democratic organisations in Germany were reported and the remorseless logic of competition in armaments heralded a renewed class war. Nazism, it seemed, could only be stemmed by common purpose of all workers' organisations while the conduct of Nazis towards Socialists in Germany converted the British Labour Movement from advocates of reconciliation with Germany to its firmest opponents. In April 1933, the Party's N.E.C. supported a mass meeting at the Albert Hall to protest against Nazi atrocities and anti-Semitism and the National Joint Council instituted a *boycott of German goods*. On the same day came Brailsford's pamphlet *The Nazi Terror: A Record*. This was the S.L.'s first response; Hitler's arrival and Governmental decrees were a '*Counter-Revolution*', '*an event so momentous for the future of Europe*';[iv] the Nazi Movement had grown from 810,000 in 1928 to 17,000,000 in March 1933; it had utilised resentment against the Versailles Treaty: 'The Nazi Movement represented a violent reaction against democracy,

---

[i] Cf. G. D. H. Cole, *History of the Labour Party*, pp.324–26.

[ii] *New Clarion*, March 11th, 1933. Hitler had declared 'war on parliamentary democracy' at a Nazi rally on February 10, 1933.

[iii] 'The Tyke' says 'Close the Ranks', *New Clarion*, March 18th, 1933.

[iv] H. N. Brailsford, *The Nazi Terror – A Record* (S.L. pamphlet), April 12th, 1933, p.1. In *Mein Kampf*, Hitler had blamed the defeat of Germany on 'the Marxist leaders', qu. M. Gilbert, '*Auschwitz and the Allies*' (2001 edn.), p.13.

pacifism and internationalism';[i] Nazism had succeeded primarily because of six million unemployed and economic chaos, but Hitler had suppressed freedom of expression in the Press and assembly, had instituted and encouraged raids, beatings, crude torment, the killing of unarmed civilians;[ii] German Labour, unionists, and Socialists were imprisoned; Socialists and Communists, and pacifists were under arrest'.[iii] The Enabling Act authorised Hitler to promulgate laws without the assent of the Reichstag: 'The German working class has lost in this counter-revolution all its legal means of political action'.[iv] Economic terror was enacted; the machinery of legal repression installed. All this was known publicly within months of the Nazi takeover.

By April 1933, the S.L. was not only witnessing dictatorship in Germany and Austria but (what its leaders conceived to be) 'veiled dictatorship by consent' in the U.S.A. and Britain.[v] The analogy was wide of the mark. J. Reeves, G. D. H. Cole and R. H. Tawney had seen the threat of Nazism immediately and appealed to all who supported the workers' cause to present a *united front to the twin dangers of War and Fascism'*.[vi] E. F. Wise put his signature to this in April 1933. In May, Brailsford warned that the Nazis could be preparing infiltration into Austria;[vii] in June he asked: 'How ought the civilised world, above all the Socialist world, react to the ruthless Nazi campaign and the menace to European peace that a rearmed Germany constitutes?'[viii] This was the question from the time of the first S.L. Conference, in which E. F. Wise saluted a United Front 'since small unattached parties were a source of weakness, as the German situation proved'.[ix] The civilised world was reacting very slowly.

The situation in Germany did not figure again directly in S.L. publications, resolutions or statements, *until* Hitler's Government had left the League and the Disarmament Conference. A. L. Rowse asked in November 1933, 'Are we playing Germany's game?'[x] Gradually, the S.L. formulated an international dimension on Nazism. It despised the reactionary repressions and anti-Soviet virulence expressed by the German Government, but some S.L. leaders were certain the British Government wanted to recognise Hitler's Government and trade. J. F. Horrabin yoked 'Hitlerism in 1933 as Kaiserism in 1914' – another aspect of twentieth century capitalism,[xi] just as Lansbury was convinced that Fascism and Nazism had one basic aim – to keep workers in subjection and defeat Socialist plans for national ownership of land and industry[xii] – a grave underestimation of Nazism.

In February 1934 there was an S.L. declaration on suppression of democracy and freedom in Austria; Mellor paid tribute, on behalf of the S.L., to resistance displayed by the Austrian Labour Movement; the Austrian Government was now masquerading

---

[i] *The Times*, March 23rd, 1933.

[ii] *The Times*, March 14th, 1933. It was reported that Jews were leaving Germany in great numbers.

[iii] *The Times*, March 23rd, 1933.

[iv] H. N. Brailsford, *The Nazi Terror – A Record*, p.6. On March 20th the Nazis opened the first concentration camp at Dachau.

[v] S.L. News, *New Clarion*, April 22nd, 1933.

[vi] *New Leader*, April 28th, 1933. The T.U.C. called for a boycott of German goods on May 24th.

[vii] H. N. Brailsford, 'Where the Storm May Break (The Nazis Threat to Austria)', *New Clarion*, May 6th, 1933.

[viii] H. N. Brailsford, 'Hitler versus Mankind', *New Clarion*, June 3rd, 1933.

[ix] Chairman's Opening Speech to S.L. Derby Conference, June 5th, 1933. 30,000 marched on Hyde Park to protest against Nazi anti-semitism on July 23rd.

[x] *New Clarion*, November 4th, 1933.

[xi] Letter to *New Clarion*, November 11th, 1933.

[xii] G. Lansbury, *My England*, 1934, p.197.

as a 'bulwark against Fascism', but was itself 'Fascist' in practice. The S.L. paid tribute to those who died fighting for Socialism and working-class liberty[i] in Austria and hoped working people would give financial assistance to relieve distress among Austrian Socialists. Would the Labour Movement learn the lesson of the events in Germany and Austria? – compromise and subordination of Socialist practice to electoral and tactical calculations ended in defeat. These were not the only 'lessons' but were a beginning; Fascism fed on the caution and respectability of Socialist and union Movements.[ii] In May 1934, the S.L. Leeds Conference protested at the unjust imprisonment and inhuman treatment of working-class leaders and the rank and file in Austria and Germany.

In this action, union leaders joined the S.L. and Walter Citrine wrote that voluntary institutions of trade unionism and political organisations had been destroyed in Italy, Germany and Austria'.[iii] He linked Fascist dictatorship and 'militarisation of politics', but J. T. Murphy (for the S.L.) was unhappy Citrine refused to consider a general strike against war: 'Is "industrial action" against Fascism also to be cut out of the policy of the T.U.C.?'[iv] He warned the course pursued by Labour leaders was equivalent to German Labour leaders prior to Hitler's regime. Would the T.U.C. allow the General Council to retreat from its decision concerning organised industrial action against Fascism?: 'The fight against Fascism … is the most tremendous action ever undertaken by the forces of the working-class movement'.[v] (Citrine was not drawn into sniping from the Labour Left.) Meanwhile S.L. readers could start understanding the German situation. Books on Germany were reviewed, such as *The Secret of Hitler's Victory* by Peter and Irma Petroff, and *Fascist Germany Explains* by C. Strachey and John Gustav Werner.[vi] By December 1934, the S.L. was reporting activity in the German armaments industry; 'purification' of officers in the army and navy was taking place; this was the culmination of the stabilising of 'German Fascism', which had begun with the 'Night of the Long Knives' on June 30th, 1933. What position should Socialists take on the struggle in the Saar? The united front in the Saar, supported by local Socialist organisations, was one of the opponents of the Nazis; the Saar had the largest population per square mile in Europe, its people were mainly proletarian, but the League of Nations had decided the fate of the Saar *in favour of* the German Government: 'A victory for the Saar's 'Freedom Front' on the issue of the status quo would be the first blow against the Fascist dictatorship in Germany'.[vii] Too late: the struggle of the 'Freedom Front' for the status quo in the Saar became part of the anti-Fascist struggle.

At the launch of the S.L. membership campaign in December, 1934, Cripps was pessimistic: 'In country after country, working-class democracy has gone down under the onslaught of brutal reaction – in Italy, Germany, Austria and Spain.[viii] H. L. Elvin explained that, behind the enthusiasm and national mysticism, the Nazi dictatorship had one main aim – consolidation of 'big interests' through monopoly capitalism, handing

---

[i] February 18th, 1934, in *New Clarion*, February 24th, 1934, S.L. Notes: 'Austria and its Lessons'.

[ii] S.L. Editorial, 'Socialist Democracy – Forward to Socialism', *Socialist Leaguer*, No. 1, July 1934.

[iii] W. Citrine, 'Trade Unionism and the Fascist Menace', *Socialist Leaguer*, No. 2, July–August 1934.

[iv] J. T. Murphy, 'What Will Congress Do About Fascism?', *Socialist Leaguer*, No. 3, August–September 1934.
[v] Ibid.

[vi] *Socialist Leaguer*, No. 4, September–October 1934.

[vii] 'The Saar Problem', by a Continental Socialist, in *Socialist Leaguer*, No. 7, December 1934.

[viii] S. Cripps at Caxton Hall, Westminster, December 21st, 1934, Cripps Papers. The peak of anti-Semitic agitation in England was 1934–37. This coincided with a period of increasing domestic stability and national consensus. By the time the B.U.F. instrumentalised anti-Semitism as an escape valve for socio-economic tensions, the economic tide had turned, G. C. Lebzelter, op. cit., 1978, p.45.

over industry to large industrialists like Thyssen, finance to bankers like Schacht, and repression by Storm Troops. (The S.L. was aware that the German Communists had not assisted the Socialist cause with its opposition to Social Democrats in Germany, thereby fragmenting the working class.[i]) With the 1935 agreement between French and British Governments, air forces were to assist the victim of any unprovoked attack from the air. But who was to determine what constituted 'provocation'? With prescience, H. N. Brailsford asked: 'What is to happen if the Germans decide to ignore the sections of the Versailles Treaty which turned their Rhineland territory into a demilitarised zone?'[ii] The Germans had been promised the nullification of Clause 5 of the Versailles Treaty, which had condemned them to military inequality.

The S.L. was very perturbed by events in Germany, and this affected S.L. relations with Labour leaders; for the S.L., every victory gained by the Germans was credited to the Nazis, brought a European war nearer, and strengthened Nazi control over German working people. Not only that: 'Every speech by Labour Party leaders attacking the Versailles Treaty is printed by the Nazi Press and is used as propaganda for Nazi policy'.[iii] The S.L. had, from its inception, disapproved of the injustices of the Versailles Treaty, but was not prepared to uphold an alteration of the Treaty as long as the German people supported the 'anti-democratic Nazi regime'. The S.L. now argued that *political and economic boycott of Germany* would be the only effective method of ending Nazi domination. But not all S.L. members believed the issue to be so simple: H.L. Elvin recognised that 'Hitlerism' had an immense sway over working-class Germans; Fascism was a method by which major capitalists (especially financiers) defeated working-class organisations to safeguard profits; when a capitalist society was denied the Imperialist outlet it turned to 'colonialising' its own people: 'Germany is now the exploited colony of German finance capital';[iv] war production the only method of solving the contradictions inherent in that environment. (By 1935 the real effect of a Nazi Germany in Europe was being understood.)

In its analysis of foreign events, the S.L. did not view the struggle between Nazis and Socialists in Germany as confined to that country, but saw similar conflicts in Czechoslovakia, Holland, Austria and France.[v] Reg Groves noted a growing readiness of French workers to oppose Fascism: 'Every hesitation, equivocation, substitution of parliamentary manoeuvres for working-class mobilisation by the Movement increases the support for Fascism'.[vi] There was growing opposition among the working class in Germany to Hitler's regime, but there was instigated a new Nazi repression; thousands of workers arrested and tortured.[vii] By December 1935, there were reports of Jew-baiting, pogroms, mass arrests, a new purge of the Nazi organisation: 'There had been a bureaucratisation and militarisation of the whole of German public life, the personal

[i] H. L. Elvin reviewing Roy Pascal, 'The Nazi Dictatorship', *Socialist Leaguer*, No. 8, January 15th, 1935.

[ii] H. N. Brailsford, 'The Coming War (Manoeuvring for Position)', *Socialist Leaguer*, No. 9, February 15th, 1935. On March 4, 1935, new expansion plans for U.K. Army, Navy and Air Force were announced.

[iii] F. L. Kerran letter to *Socialist Leaguer*, No. 11, May 1935.

[iv] H. L. Elvin reviewing *Fascism: Make or Break?*, *Socialist Leaguer*, No. 11, May 1935.

[v] Cf. 'H. V.', 'Socialism Abroad', *Socialist Leaguer*, No. 12, June 1935.

[vi] R. Groves, 'After the French Congress', *Socialist Leaguer*, No. 13, July–August 1935.

[vii] A. Austen, 'Activity Behind the Nazi Terror', *Socialist Leaguer*, No. 13, July–August 1935. Victor Klemperer wrote in his diary 26/06/1935: 'The enormous foreign policy success of the Naval Agreement with England consolidates Hitler's position very greatly … many otherwise well-meaning people, dulled to injustice and … not properly appreciating the misfortune of the Jews, have begun to halfway acquiesce to Hitler. Their opinion: if at the cost of going backwards internally he restores Germany's power externally then this cost is worthwhile.' V. Klemperer, *I Shall Bear Witness: The Diaries of Victor Klemperer 1933–1941*, 1998, p.121.

corruption of the new leaders, and the braggartism of promoted Nazi officials.[i] There appeared the most systematic terror, unrest, fear, betrayal, persecution, but 'this multitude of avenues in which grumblers give vent to their anger necessarily prevents their political concentration upon one aim for attack'.[ii] Being unorganised and not politically conscious, mass criticism was not a power which could affect the regime. For S.L. leaders, the parallel with their own, less dangerous, problems in the Labour Movement, was drawn. The answer to both was the same – working-class unity in the Labour Movement to counteract Fascism and War.

In March 1936, the Rhineland was remilitarised. The argument that Germany could not be treated as a second-class power, that reparation clauses at Versailles were unworkable, had proved true. The S.L. criticised the *Daily Herald*'s naiveté for accepting Hitler's manoeuvres as 'honest gestures of peace', and for ignoring the danger to the Soviet Union.[iii] It estimated Hitler's march into the Rhineland as the logical consequence of rearmament and the Anglo-German Naval Treaty.[iv] In reviewing *Germany's War Machine* by Albert Muller, Reg Groves characterised the escalation of German war plans; Muller concluded that the extent of armaments led to one conclusion: 'the Hitler Government is preparing an attack;[v] the Third Reich was being mobilised; productive capacity of militarily-important industries were being expanded at the sacrifice of every other consideration. The tragedy was that sections of the German Workers' Movement exalted war as something above politics and class division; but the interests of industrial workers would always remain irreconcilable with those of armament manufacturers: 'An insurmountable antagonism lives on in the consciousness of the German factory hand'.[vi] Optimism has its place.

At the Stoke Conference, the S.L. maintained that to suggest the forces of capitalism in democratic countries could be expected to be harnessed to an anti-Fascist crusade was to deceive workers: 'Fascist Germany is the most important enemy to peace and of the working class and must be checked at all costs'.[vii] But how? And what could be done about the following: 'The revival of a Jackboot Germany with modern improvements in the way of concentration camps and cosh-carriers'.[viii] And what were the achievements of a Fascist country? Elvin wrote that the Italian Government had saved the country from Bolshevism, ended strikes, made employers and workers co-operate 'in the public interest', improved social services, and superseded old-style capitalism and democracy by a 'corporative state'; Italian workers had lost 40% to 50% of their wages, agricultural labourers had lost 50% to 70% of theirs, both had their organisations destroyed, there was imprisonment for any protest, the only check on big business was the desire of army officers, civil service or party official for a bigger share

---

[i] James Norman, 'Hitler's Potential Peril', *Socialist Leaguer*, No. 3, December 1935.
[ii] Ibid.
[iii] Cf. Letter by 'Nunquam', *Socialist*, No. 6, April 1936.
[iv] 'Seven-Point Resistance Plan to Rearmament', *Socialist*, No. 6, April 1936.
[v] A. Muller, *Germany's War Machine*, reviewed by Reg Groves, *Socialist*, No. 9, July–August 1936.
[vi] Victor Klemperer in Berlin observed on 16/05/1936: 'The majority believe it is inopportune in terms of Realpolitik to be outraged at such details as the suppression of civil liberties, the persecution of the Jews, the falsification of all scholarly truths, the systematic destruction of all morality. And all are afraid for their livelihood, their life, all are such terrible cowards.' Op. cit., 1998, p.158.
[vii] Stoke S.L. Conference resolution, June 6th.
[viii] 'Gadfly', *Socialist*, No. 11, October 1936.

Hitler   Sarraut
"ACH! SO YOU WON'T BE PEACEFUL, HEY? YOU BIG BULLIES!"

March 11, 1936

France's excuse for keeping clear of the Italo-Abyssinian war was the uncertainty as to Hitler's next move. In March 1936, the Anglo-French coolness gave Hitler the cue to violate the treaty of Locarno and to re-occupy and fortify the Rhineland. At the same time, he produced a "Peace Plan".

Hitler Eden Litvinov Blum
WAITING FOR THE WINDFALLS

July 5, 1936

Hitler had already won the preliminaries of his policy by confusing, dividing and demoralising his opponents.

Stalin

"IT'S QUEER HOW YOU REMIND ME OF SOMEONE, JOSEPH…"

August 28, 1936

Stalin showed that by monopoly of political power and by successive purges of his opponents, he had noted the methods of his Fascist and Nazi rivals.

Hitler   Mussolini   Eden Stalin Blum

NON-INTERVENTION POKER

January 13, 1937

In Spain, civil war was in progress. General Franco led a military fascist revolt against the democratic government, and was openly supported by Hitler and Mussolini on the excuse that they were fighting Bolshevism… France and Britain pretended all was honourable.

of power.[i] By April 1937, J. F. Horrabin was analysing Czechoslovakia, which had been created by the Treaty of Versailles. 20% of its population was German, and had preserved forms of capitalist democracy. It had been the subject of the propaganda of violence from Goebbels who claimed the country was an outpost of Bolshevism;[ii] Hitler was looking to the Southeast for his next manoeuvre. The German situation was depressing. The S.L. looked for inspiration elsewhere.

Amidst the gloom, the S.L. saw a ray of joy in the *French 'Front Populaire'*, in which parties of the Left, the Communists, Socialists and Radicals, were united. This Popular Front was not a means of introducing Socialism, but seemed to offer one way to save democracy from Fascism, by pursuing a constructive peace policy, and economic, social and political reforms. There were unique features in the 'Front Populaire' which the S.L. knew could *not* be applied in Britain. The French C.P. was strong enough to enter the People's Front on equal terms with the Socialists, and unions endorsed the policy. Because the French electoral system provided for a second ballot, it was also possible for parties which ran rival candidates to gain support at that ballot: 'For French believers in democracy, the wholehearted support of the "Front Populaire" is the right policy today'.[iii] B. A. Betts commented that 'Front Populaire' hoped to win the coming election with reform of the Press, equality for political and social organisations, freedom of conscience in schools, action against the Fascist Leagues, a Committee of Inquiry into political, economic and moral conditions in French territories overseas, strengthening of collective security, progressive disarmament, and extension over Eastern and Central Europe of a system of pacts based on the Franco-Soviet pact.[iv] These plans greatly appealed to the S.L.

A few months later Betts was applauding the French Socialists and Communists for having denounced the devaluation of the franc.[v] Leon Blum had checked the heavy drain in gold and fall in the franc; the Popular Front's programme was to defeat the oligarchy behind the Bank of France, make the rich pay for social needs, nationalise the armaments industry – requirements which could apply to Britain. In July, Betts was lauding Blum's actions for French strikers, a Bill for a 40-hour week, paid holidays, a minimum wage, and a national unemployment fund.[vi] By September, the French C.P. tactic was for a broad popular front and to win middle classes to the side of working people.[vii] Blum's Government was worried that they might be internationally isolated,[viii] but the French Popular Front had a profound effect on the S.L. leadership's final dramatic involvement in a *Unity Campaign*[ix] at the end of 1936; it was stressed in the S.L.'s campaign that no political group would lose its identity if it involved itself in a Popular Front in Britain. Here was solace and consolation. But in Germany, the legacy was that authoritarian, 'revolutionary', or expansionist regimes had to be resisted by force if necessary, anywhere in the world.[x]

---

[i] H. L. Elvin reviewing G. Salvemini, 'Under the Axe of Fascism', ibid.

[ii] J. F. Horrabin, *Socialist Broadsheet*, No. 2, April 1937.

[iii] G. D. H. Cole, *The People's Front*, 1937, p.120.

[iv] B. A. Betts, 'French Face Both Ways', *Socialist*, No. 5, March 1936.

[v] B. A. Betts, 'What Next in France?', *Socialist*, No. 8, June 1936.

[vi] B. A. Betts, 'Leon Blum's First Days', *Socialist*, No. 9, July–August 1936.

[vii] B. A. Betts reviewing M. Thorez, *France Today*, *Socialist*, No. 10, September 1936.

[viii] B. A. Betts, 'Blum and the Franc', *Socialist*, No. 11, October 1936.

[ix] B. A. Betts, 'Leon Blum's Restive Friends', *Socialist*, No. 12, November 1936.

[x] B. B. Gilbert, op. cit, 1996, p.93.

(E) The S.L. and the Spanish Civil War

The Spanish Civil War was another field of conflict which questioned the application of Socialist principles to foreign policy; more than any other event in the 1930s it divided British opinion. Inside the Labour Movement it illustrated the dichotomy between the official Party upholding social progress and evolutionary development, and the S.L.'s cavalier acceptance of the class struggle and 'overhauling the existing social order'. Five major events before the Civil War had led to consolidation of these two positions in the Labour Movement; the First World War (for the Labour Right a struggle against German militarism, for the Left the outcome of capitalist imperialism); the Russian Revolution (for the Labour Right dictatorship without personal freedom, for the Left bringing the first Socialist country); the General Strike (which the Right saw as disastrous, the Left as part of the class struggle betrayed by Labour and union leaders); the World Economic Crisis (for the Labour Right ameliorating capitalism, the Left as the beginning of the collapse of capitalism); and Nazism and Fascism (the Labour Right regarded as arising from political and economic crisis, partly Communist pressures, the S.L. convinced exposed monopoly capitalism to be opposed by working-class Socialist unity.)[i]

For the S.L. the 1930s was a decade of frustration, *except* for the Spanish Civil War. Most S.L. members possessed a burning international social conscience which only an anti-Fascist policy could solve; they could relate economic struggles in Britain to the Spanish Civil War. This gave S.L. members a new lease of life; it inspired them; it was one of the oddities of the era that Left-wing movements gained few recruits when denouncing the effects of the Depression, much more when galvanised into action by a war in Spain, which was transformed into a battleground of rival ideologies,[ii] and provided for a generation, 'the emotional experience of their lifetime'.[iii] The Spanish Civil War widened divisions between the Government and the Opposition, brought class consciousness into foreign policy (to an extent hitherto unknown), and led to a reversal of 'peace' and 'war' Parties. The Left became war-minded (even union officials lost their pro-negotiation stance), while the Government proposed non-intervention: 'Non-intervention and pacifism crossed over from the opposition to the Government; "no war" became the slogan, not of the Left, but of the Right'.[iv] The intrusion of the spirit of class warfare became more obvious month by month, and the S.L. got involved from the start.

For the first time since the General Strike, the agitation (over Spain) represented and envisaged a campaign in which groups such as the S.L. could reassess the principles of freedom and democracy, and resist a threat of dictatorship, with working-class unity and a Socialist alternative: 'The Spanish Civil War ... provided a concentrated meat-extract of all the emotions which the Left had experienced in previous years. Resistance to Fascism, class war, the unity of the Left – difficult slogans

---

[i] K. W. Watkins, *Britain Divided: The Effect of the Spanish Civil War on British Opinion*, 1963, pp.141–44.
[ii] A. J. P. Taylor, *English History (1914–45)*, p.395.
[iii] Ibid.
[iv] C. L. Mowat, *Britain Between the Wars*, 1955, p.578.

at home, but easy to use in Spain'.[i] Spain became an alternative for the Utopia that had been Soviet Russia, the battlefield in which the Labour Party and the S.L. contested for the soul of the Movement. The Labour Movement supported the Republicans, but the first official Party policy was to preserve *neutrality* to prevent the war from spreading. Yet, in the final analysis, no foreign question since the French Revolution would divide intelligent British opinion or so excite it.[ii]

A few years later, George Orwell analysed the different attitudes and political positions which he had gleaned during the conflict. He had admired the generous feelings, shabby clothes and gaily coloured revolutionary posters, the universal 'comrade', and anti-Fascist ballads as emotionally enriching experiences,[iii] and viewed the central issue as the attempt of ordinary people to win the decent life against the Spanish bourgeoisie who took their chance to defeat the Labour Movement with aid from the Nazis. However, Orwell was profoundly disillusioned: 'The Left intelligentsia made their swing-over from "War is hell" to "War is glorious" not only with no sense of incongruity but almost without any intervening stage. Later the bulk of them were to make other transitions equally violent'.[iv] He could have been describing the S.L. intellectual. Orwell noted that atrocities in the war were believed or disbelieved solely on grounds of political predilection; he saw newspaper reports which bore no relation to facts; eager intellectuals building superstructures over events that never happened; history being written not in terms of what happened but of what ought to have occurred (according to 'Party lines'). While the outcome of the War was settled in London, Paris, Rome and Berlin, Orwell mused: 'The very concept of objective truth is fading out of the world... the chances are that those lies ... will pass into history'.[v] One aspect at least was *fact*. In March 1937, it was the conflict between the I.L.P. and the C.P. over supposed occurrences in Spain that helped to result in the dissolution of the S.L. and fractured the *Unity Campaign*.

The Spanish Civil War was the beginning of realpolitik for many intellectuals and S.L. members, who had always lauded 'unity in the Movement', without fully understanding how intangible that was. As early as November 1934, the division of the Spanish working class into Syndicalists, Socialists and Communists was, to the S.L., a "cause of defeat".[vi] D.N. Pritt interpreted the Spanish workers' struggle against Fascism then as requiring the united action of the working-class movement.[vii] By April 1936, the S.L. deduced that moderate solutions were no answer, unless democracy was utilised to give land to the peasants, dispossess landowners, and break the hold of industrialists, Fascism would rise to power.[viii] In the following months there was the success of the general strike (called by leaders of the Labour Front in Madrid), and for the S.L. the spirit of victory was pervading the workers of Spain, who were impatient to carry out the Popular Front programme.[ix]

By June 1936, the League of Nations had proved futile; collective security had

---

[i] A. J. P. Taylor, 'Confusion on the Left', *The Baldwin Age*, p.79.

[ii] Graves and Hodge, *The Long Weekend*, 1941, p.337.

[iii] G. Orwell, *Looking Back on the Spanish War*, 1943, p.194.

[iv] Ibid, p.188. For Orwell's crude caricature, see p.388.

[v] Ibid, p.196.

[vi] 'World Front', *Socialist Leaguer*, No. 6, November–December 1934.

[vii] D. N. Pritt, forward to Leah Manning, *What I Saw in Spain*, reviewed in *Socialist*, No. 1, September 1935.

[viii] B. A. Betts, 'Opportunities in Spain', *Socialist*, No. 6, April 1936.

[ix] B. A. Betts, 'Spanish Workers Alert', *Socialist*, No. 7, May 1936.

broken down, Fascist and Nazi-controlled countries were triumphing; British policy towards war in Spain was one of non-intervention. The S.L. was convinced events in Spain were part of a Fascist plan for the conquest of Europe, but if democratic principles could triumph on the Spanish battlefields, the progressive cause could be reinvigorated throughout Europe. I.L.P. member Brockway reflected: 'My contact with the Spanish Civil War compelled me to revise my thought about fundamental things. It made me face up squarely to the pacifist philosophy, which I continued to cherish despite my rejection of reformism... How could I regard myself as a pacifist when I desired so passionately that the workers should win the civil war?'[i] S.L. members were close to this perspective, for the conflicts in Spain would have widespread international effects; a victory for Franco and his armies, aided by German and Italian armaments, would mean defeat for anti-Fascists. Support for the Republicans by the S.L. began to make the war a symbol of 'resistance to Fascism'. The idea of the *Unity Campaign* grew from the outbreak of the Spanish Civil War.

Summarising the activities of the Left, A. J. P. Taylor surmised that it had failed to decide what it meant by 'Socialism' or *how* to achieve a new kind of society, it had been romantic, idealistic, unworldly, yet *the General Strike and support for the Spanish Republic* were two honourable causes of which any political movement could be proud.[ii] Social and political awareness had never been so stimulated, and the impact of the Civil War upon the S.L. made more evident the S.L.'s proximity to the I.L.P. and the C.P. Naturally, the S.L. outlook was shaped by the Government's dismissal of Spain's Civil War as a purely internal matter (or even a Communist conspiracy). To the S.L., international law, class solidarity, with the Soviet Union as an ally, fitted into the same strategy,[iii] the Spanish Republican cause was *the last hope for defeating Fascism*, instead of waiting until the whole Movement had to fight for nothing but national survival: '*Spain was the first and last crusade of the British Left-wing intellectual. Never again was such enthusiasm mobilised nor did there exist such a firm conviction in the rightness of a cause*'.[iv] For the S.L. the Spanish Civil War substituted action for ideas, but the action was not directed into political parties so much as Left-wing collaboration. Public opinion, mobilised outside parties, was also transformed, S.L. members taking an active part in numerous semi-political organisations or 'fronts'.[v]

The N.C.L. supported the *Non-Intervention Agreement* of the French and British Governments with an embargo on arms and munitions of war to Spain, because that Agreement might lessen international tension. Bevin, Citrine and Dalton endorsed the policy of non-intervention; Lord Parmoor wrote to Cripps that there should be no Labour compromise, and the Party should urge the Government to declare what it intended to do in the Spanish crisis, but the war rolled on, with Britain in retreat all along the line'.[vi] The S.L. assessed the issue as whether Spain had to remain a backward, impoverished land under the autocratic rule of priests and army; the war represented part of a class struggle, because 'the democracies face the dictatorships – it

---

[i] F. Brockway, *Inside the Left*, p.338.
[ii] A. J. P. Taylor, 'Confusion on the Left', op. cit., p.79.
[iii] M. Foot, op. cit., p.218.
[iv] N. Wood, op. cit., p.57.
[v] Cf. Friends of Spain, London Committee for Spanish Medical Aid, National Joint Committee for Spanish Relief, The Basque Children's Committee, Committee of Inquiry into Breaches of International Law, and the International Brigade.
[vi] E. Estorick, op. cit., p.151.

is a war of ideas. The workers face the owners – it is a war of classes'.[i] However, it was presented in the British press as if the Republicans were 'the rebels' and the Fascists were the 'defenders of legality', with Franco's crusade for Christianity by 'Loyalists' and 'Insurgent patriots' against Communism. Contrary to this predominant voice in the British media, the S.L. portrayed the struggle as between reactionary forces and a democratically elected Republican Government. The S.L.'s instincts were honourable.

In August, the S.L. published a manifesto *A Workers' or a Fascist Spain?* in which all Socialists, unionists and Co-operative members were invited to support Spanish workers: 'In a world driving towards war and the further crushing of the Labour Movement, the international consequences of the Spanish struggle cannot be over-emphasised'.[ii] The S.L. was convinced a Fascist victory would intensify the danger of war because it would encourage Conservative forces: 'The workers of Spain are fighting … a major engagement in the world; workers' fight against Fascist aggression and for Peace, Freedom and Socialism'. No Socialist could support neutrality or non-intervention pacts; it was not a war between rival States, but a civil war between classes; there could be no neutrality in the class war; to secure 'neutrality' enabled Fascist forces and Conservative Governments to prevent Left-wing Governments aiding Spanish workers, while permitting Fascist powers (like Germany and Italy) to send armaments to help Franco's supporters. The S.L. admonished the British Press which sympathised with Franco's cause, (and published stories *against* the Republican cause) but: 'It is the duty of Socialists to denounce neutrality as a cover for aiding reaction'. The S.L. had a coherent position this time.

An S.L. Manifesto declared the defeat of Franco's 'militarists' would be a preliminary to substantial economic and political power for Spanish workers: 'Every Socialist knows that behind the present conflict is the issue – *a Fascist or a Workers' Spain*'. The S.L. encouraged the Movement to agitate for freedom of working-class action in rendering aid to Spanish workers, to prevent supplies to Franco's forces, to oppose restrictions on provision of arms to anti-Fascist forces. Proposals were made to help Spanish workers; propaganda meetings, Press reports (explaining the real issues of the conflict); giving a day's pay, collecting money (in union branches, Co-operatives, local Labour parties) for the Spanish workers, and union action to prevent aid to 'the Rebels'. The Spanish workers were depicted as 'the front line fighters for World Labour" facing 'the combined Fascist and Tory attack'.[iii]

By September 1936, for the S.L., 'Fascism' had become crystallised in the symbolic struggle in Spain, but the thoughts of British political parties and the T.U.C. stayed negative: Conservatives and Labour were united, at home, in palliatives for unemployment, but 'abroad, of surrender to dictators, side-stepping or drift'.[iv] At the Plymouth T.U.C. (September 1936), neither the rank and file nor union leaders wanted to take a militant position on the Spanish Civil War, even though their sympathies were with Republicans. E. Bevin was his usual trenchant self: 'The question of collective security is in danger of becoming a shibboleth, rather than a practical operative fact … We are not going to meet the Fascist menace by mass

[i] *New Statesman and Nation*, August 1st, 1936.

[ii] S.L. Manifesto, *A Workers' or a Fascist Spain?*, August 1936.

[iii] *New Statesman and Nation*, August 1st, 1936.

[iv] Michael Wharton, 'A Few Lost Causes', *The Baldwin Age*, p.81.

resolutions. We are not going to meet it by pure pacifism'.[i] What was the S.L.'s stance? – it was a struggle between capitalism and socialism: 'Is it to be a dictatorship or democracy? … Is it to be barbarism or civilisation?'. B. A. Bagnari thrashed about linking the 'National' Government with 'Fascist tendencies…' 'A Government which in essence is Fascist, a Government which has brought up to a pitch of efficiency the militarisation of the police and has backed those police in batoning the people who dared to defend their rights; a Government that is prepared to put into operation a Bill for industrial conscription in the event of a war situation'.[ii] Yet the British Government was not "in essence Fascist", even if S.L. trade unionists urged the T.U.C. to declare for 'working-class unity against the menace of Fascism and War'.[iii] They were to be disappointed. Labour leader Attlee bluntly commented: 'The Conservative Party tended to regard Franco as a saviour of society'.[iv] Conscious of this, the S.L. organised meetings to raise funds to aid the Republican cause, and to publicise the six points of its *Manifesto on Spain*.

Ramos Oliveira (of the Spanish Socialist Party) contributed an article for the S.L. to clarify class confrontations in Spain (landowners, army officers, Church, bankers and some of the industrial bourgeoisie *versus* the democratic Republican Government supported by Liberals, Socialists, Communists and Anarchists); the Republican Government had been carrying out agrarian reforms against landowners who wanted to conserve monopoly control of the State; Franco would have already been defeated had he not received foreign aid. Oliveira pleaded with the British to help Spanish workers because: *'if fascism triumphs in Spain, this will precipitate the world war'.*[v] This was prophetic. Spain was a semi-feudal country in which 57% worked the land, yet the Popular Front had done little to alter the distribution of economic power or carry through agrarian reform.[vi] The S.L. jibed at Northcliffe's newspapers (for labelling Republicans 'atheistic Reds' and Franco's supporters 'Christian patriots'),[vii] deducing that neutrality of the 'National' Government was a diplomatic manoeuvre, and the N.C.L. should declare solidarity with the forces in Spain that battled against Reaction and Fascism.[viii]

The S.L. National Council launched prospects of intervention against Franco, and many cross-currents in the Party were aired at the Edinburgh Conference. A. Greenwood inquired if the Conference was prepared to have the battle between 'dictatorship and democracy' fought over 'the bleeding body of Spain' (which was what the S.L. intended). Aneurin Bevan attacked Labour and union leaders for not acknowledging Franco's armies were receiving German and Italian aid; he asked what would be the effect on 'Socialism' if Spanish comrades were slaughtered (as would happen if foreign armaments continued to be transported to Franco's armies?[ix] On such issues raised by the Spanish Civil War, Labour leaders remained ambivalent and

---

[i] T.U.C. Report, September 1936, p.358.

[ii] Ibid., p.379.

[iii] 'Trade Unionist', 'Will the T.U.C. Lead?', *Socialist*, No. 10, September 1936.

[iv] C. R. Attlee, *As It Happened*, 1954, p.93.

[v] R. Oliveira, 'The Fascists Shall Not Pass! Spanish Workers in Battle Array… Class v Class', *Socialist*, No. 10, September 1936.

[vi] B. A. Betts, 'The Spanish Movement', *Socialist*, No. 10, September 1936.

[vii] Editor, 'Matters of Moment', *Socialist*, No. 10, September 1936.

[viii] Ibid.

[ix] *Labour Party Annual Conference Report*, October 1936, p.177.

voted for the *Non-Intervention Pact*. S.L. frustrations found vent in humanitarian aid (food, clothing and medical supplies), and *Labour's Spain Committee* which consisted mainly of Left-wingers.[i] The S.L. now symbolised the clamour against 'Non-Intervention'; C. Trevelyan levelled with Labour leaders: 'You are beggared of policy at this moment. When the last great war that is looming comes, and when Japan and Germany crash in to try to destroy Soviet Russia, I hope then that the Labour Party will have some other policy to offer than their sympathy accompanied by bandages and cigarettes'.[ii] Tough words only. Cigarettes then were not deemed bad for your health!

The Italians and Germans had already intervened, and the 'supervision of cargoes' did not prevent men and munitions landing, so the policy of blockade showed the farce of inequality. (By 1937 there were 30,000 German and 80,000 Italian troops in Spain.) Now there was an S.L. proposal that Labour and union leaders should lead a procession of loaded lorries to one of the ports to stimulate a campaign for 'arms for Spain', but Jennie Lee unearthed a reason for their reticence: 'The Labour Party is afraid of the Catholic vote. Honest to God [sic], some of them would sooner see the whole of Spain go up in smoke than damage their election chances. That's what is at the bottom of it'.[iii] This was far from being proved. Labour leaders had a position: to supply armaments would escalate the civil war into a general European conflict (so the Movement's conscience was salved by organising relief measures and Red Cross services), but this attitude by Labour and union leaders again helped propel the S.L. towards the *Unity Campaign*. The Spanish Civil War was becoming 'a test of conscience and a symbol of protest'.[iv]

Support for unity against Fascist aggression was growing, and a form of People's Front began to take shape in the *Spanish Medical Aid Committee*. J. T. Murphy assessed Edinburgh Conference Labour leaders: 'All were occupying defensive positions with characteristic British stubbornness. It was pretty shadow-boxing with Socialist words as we drifted towards Armageddon'.[v] Meanwhile, Brailsford helped to organise the British contingent of the *International Brigade*, which provided a focus for popular feeling and international solidarity. (The S.L. asked its members for one day's pay to aid the Spanish workers' cause.) Bevan averred that Socialist forces everywhere would be devitalised if Franco's armies won the battle of Madrid: 'The Non-Intervention Agreement has failed in its main object and is now operating to deprive the Spanish workers from obtaining the arms with which to defend themselves'.[vi] The S.L. scenario was that if Fascists won in Spain, French Fascists would be stimulated (with allies on the Spanish and Italian frontiers); a triumph of Fascism in France would end the League of Nations, rupture the Franco-Soviet Pact, leave Russia exposed to the combined attacks of Japan and Germany: 'It is our duty to use every endeavour to force the British Government to allow the Spanish Government to purchase arms in this country... The actions and the opinion of British Labour will have a profound influence on French policy'.[vii] Unfortunately for Bevan, he was close to what transpired.

---

[i] H. N. Brailsford, A. Albu, G. D. H. Cole, F. Horrabin, N. Mitchison, H. W. Nevinson, J. Parker, R. H. Tawney, C. Trevelyan, D. Woodman, and L. Woolf.
[ii] *Labour Party Annual Conference Report*, October 1936, p.173.
[iii] J. Lee, op. cit. p.170.
[iv] A. Bullock, op. cit., p.586.
[v] J. T. Murphy, *New Horizons*, p.322.
[vi] A. Bevan, 'If We Desert Our Comrades', *Socialist*, No. 11, October 1936.
[vii] Ibid.

The S.L. attributed another important feature to the Civil War: Spain had entered the era of proletarian revolution, and the class struggle (typified in January 1933, October 1934 and now July 1936); there was no justification for any coalition between working-class parties and bourgeois republicans: 'The Spanish Revolution is on the march. The era begun in October 1917 is renewed – a torch has been lifted up to lighten the dark places of Europe'.[i] Such hopes! The S.L. believed that to discover the correct theoretical formulation *would* result in a 'revolutionary transformation'. It could not understand why the mass Labour Movement was uninvolved when there was a growing revolt in the rank and file against Non-Intervention, yet even after the appeal of La Pasionaria at Edinburgh, Labour leaders counselled caution and delay.[ii] The Spanish Government needed to purchase arms outside Spain, and on October 23rd, 1936, the S.L.'s Executive Committee formally asked the N.C.L. to proclaim the policy of removing the embargo placed on arms to the Spanish Government; to resist Government 'neutrality' (an act of support for Fascism); and proposed the union movement establish Vigilance Committees at docks and ports (on shipments to Portuguese or other Fascist ports).[iii]

The T.U.C. had been praised at the Conservative Party Conference: 'The wise attitude adopted by the T.U.C. over the Spanish crisis shows that in the ranks of Labour there is *a solid force of patriotic responsibility*'.[iv] However, on October 28th, 1936, a joint meeting of the N.E.C., the P.L.P., and the T.U.C. did request that the Government restore full commercial rights to 'democratic Spain', including purchase of munitions: 'For the next nine months, the official policy of the Labour Movement was one of pressing the National Government both to support the implementation of this demand and to take measures to make the Non-Intervention Agreement work'.[v] For the S.L., W. Mellor was apoplectic that action had been postponed until Franco's armies had advanced because of a divided Labour leadership and lack of a class approach; the N.C.L. had not abandoned non-intervention: 'its policy takes the form merely of an exhortation to the Government rather than a working-class demand for activity, protest, demonstration and trade union action'.[vi] Mellor suspected the Party N.E.C. preferred collaboration with the Government in preparation for an international crisis, as a safeguard against Hitler's Government. In S.L. terminology: *'events in Spain have exposed the British Government more clearly than ever as the enemy of the working-class movement at home and abroad'*.[vii] The N.C.L. refused to inaugurate any national campaign for the Spanish Republican cause, although the Party formulated motions protesting against maintenance of non-intervention, and protested against the Government ban on British volunteers in the Republican forces – but the Party was repeatedly voted down. The S.L. was even less significant in its effect.

S.L. leaders were becoming influenced by the C.P.'s aid to Spanish workers. The C.P. was organising, demonstrating, protesting and fighting in Spain, and it rose in the estimation of the S.L. because of the popularity of the Soviet Union, which was the leading active anti-Fascist Power by November 1936. The S.L.'s position was neatly

[i] J. Winocaur, 'Spain Has Lighted a Torch', *Socialist*, No. 11, October 1936.
[ii] B. A. Betts, 'Behind the Neutral Veil', *Socialist*, No. 12, November 1936.
[iii] S.L. National Council letter to National Council of Labour, October 23rd, 1936.
[iv] K. W. Watkins, op. cit., p.167. My emphasis.
[v] Ibid.
[vi] W. Mellor, 'Edinburgh Conference and After', *Socialist*, No. 12, November 1936.
[vii] Ibid.

encapsulated by H. N. Brailsford in his pamphlet *Spain's Challenge to Labour*,[i] which posited that the future of the working class in Europe was at stake in Spain; Hitler and Mussolini had supplied Franco with his bombing planes, while the Spanish Government had been 'progressing in a Socialist direction';[ii] if Fascist powers succeeded in placing their veto on the Spanish people, their pretensions would not end there; the Republic had achievements in political democracy, enfranchisement of women, religious toleration, minimum wages, and partitioning the grandees' estates.[iii] French and British Governments' 'neutrality' had ignored the Madrid administration as the lawful Government, and this retreat before the Fascist Powers abandoned principles of international law. Brailsford widened the issue for the S.L.: *Spain was 'in process of being conquered by the Fascist Powers as a base for future operations in the international class struggle'.*[iv] The Labour Movement should be mobilising to defeat Government policy: 'The Dictators wage war upon our class. Shall we sit neutral till we too go under?'[v] The only alternative was a United Front. The S.L. must enrol 'all Socialists who recognise the class struggle as the driving force of social change', remind the Labour movement of its objectives; unite the working class movement of wage and salary earners for an attack on the capitalist system by political and industrial activity. If nothing else, Brailsford's pamphlet showed that the Fascist 'International' was more active than the Workers' International!

The S.L. reviewed John Langdon-Davies' *Behind the Spanish Barricades*, Carlos Prieto's *Spanish Front, Spain in Revolt*, by Harry Gannes and Theodore Repard, and *Reporter in Spain* by Frank Pitcairn. The latter was 'a Scarlet Pimpernel of the International Workers' struggle. Wherever the class war is being waged, be it in America, Germany, Austria, the Far East or Spain, Pitcairn will be there...'[vi] Europe divided into Fascist and Anti-Fascist Internationals: 'our Government has done all it can to give comfort to the first and to embarrass the second'.[vii] The Government was introducing a Bill to make it illegal for British ships to carry any war material specified in the Non-Intervention Agreement from foreign ports to Spain and the S.L. denounced the *Daily Herald* for approving the Government's actions. W. Mellor (Chairman of the S.L.) and M. McCarthy (Secretary) wrote to the N.C.L. about Madrid's struggle and the Labour Movement's travesty of a policy. McCarthy elucidated: 'My Executive would be glad to know what steps, other than by Parliamentary debate, the N.C.L. proposes to take to arouse public opinion on the question of the Spanish Campaign. I am asked to say that we would do everything in our power to help in supporting actively demonstrations in the country, under the auspices of the N.C.L. in opposition to the Government's neutrality policy'.[viii] The reply coldly stated it would report the S.L.'s communication to the N.E.C.

S.L. members did not wait for instructions from Transport House for an agitation in support of Spanish workers. Meetings were organised, the S.L.'s headquarters inundated with requests for speakers. Aerial bombardment of Madrid prompted the

---

[i] November 1936.

[ii] H. N. Brailsford, *Spain's Challenge to Labour*, p.3.

[iii] Ibid., p.5.

[iv] Ibid., p.10.

[v] Ibid., p.12.

[vi] Books and Reviews, *Socialist*, No. 13, December 1936–January 1937.

[vii] B. Betts, *Europe's Two Halves*, ibid.

[viii] Quoted in S.L. Notes, *Socialist*,.ibid.

rank and file; for the S.L. there was no difference between reactionaries in Spain, Germany, Italy or Britain: 'the international policy of our present Government is leading them straight towards an alliance with international fascism ... they are indirectly encouraging the rebels [Franco's troops] in Spain ... and believe that the rebels are the only means of saving capitalism in Spain ... Do not let us wait until the methods of the Spanish Rebels are used against the British workers'.[i] This S.L. equation of Spanish 'Fascism' with that of the British Government (in its *Sedition Bill* and *Public Order Bill*) was unsubstantiated, especially since events in Spain prompted the question of unity.

The first issue of *Tribune* (January 1st, 1937) challenged the Labour Movement to become the vanguard in the conflict threatening the international worker, 'instead of evading this responsibility'; rank and file indignation had been met by bureaucratic rebuff or indifference; Labour leaders had evaded a moral obligation, an historic mission! *Tribune*'s evaluation concluded that Labour leaders had used French and Soviet Governments as screens, to hide its own lack of class understanding, but it was not too late to pressurise the Government: '*British Labour has been and still is on trial. Spain is a crucial test*'.[ii] S.L. leaders alleged that 'unity' was galvanising the Spanish working class behind the Republican cause,[iii] although the object of defeating Franco might be weakened 'if sectional effort developed into internecine strife'.[iv] An augury indeed. The Government's ban on volunteers was indefensible; H. N. Brailsford indicted Anthony Eden: 'You are murdering Democracy'.[v]

On January 18th, 1937, Cripps, Maxton and Pollitt launched the *Unity Campaign*. On Spain, the Campaign had four points; N.C.L. to summon an 'all-in' conference against Government policy; an end to the embargo on armaments to the Spanish Government, end to the ban on volunteers; support for volunteers and funds for their equipment; the N.C.L. to raise money to provide medical and food supplies for Republican troops: 'This N.U.C.C. demonstration calls upon the N.C.L. to place these demands before a Special Conference ... for a nationwide campaign of demonstration.[vi] One of the factors in creating the demand for 'unity' was, said Cripps in February 1937, 'the tragic treatment meted out to democracy, and the working-class movements of Spain'.[vii] The war in Spain was the most vital part of the international class struggle; fears of accommodation by the British Government with Hitler and Mussolini over Spain had motivated the cause of the *Unity Campaign* for the S.L.[viii]

By February 1937, the S.L., I.L.P., and C.P. had convinced themselves that a determined European stand against non-intervention would call Hitler's and Mussolini's bluff. (The latter were not bluffing.) Inability to change Government policy had led to increasing frustration at Labour and union leaders' hesitation and lack of zeal: 'There are moments when it is criminal for democrats to wait for General

---

[i] S. Cripps, 'The Frontier of British Democracy' speech, December 1936, Cripps Papers.

[ii] *Tribune*, January 1st, 1937.

[iii] Julius Deutsch, 'Our Hopes Are High on the Spanish Front', *Tribune*, January 8th, 1937.

[iv] 'Spain and Unity', *Tribune*, January 8th, 1937. On January 10th Britain banned volunteers from fighting in Spain and a two-year jail sentence for offenders was announced.

[v] *Tribune*, January 15th, 1937.

[vi] *The Unity Campaign* (pamphlet by Cripps, Maxton and Pollitt), January 18th, 1937. N.U.C.C. was the National Unity Campaign Committee.

[vii] Speech at Friends House, February 1937, Cripps Papers.

[viii] Cripps' speech at Tonypandy, February 14th, 1937, Cripps Papers.

Elections – moments when the fate of democracy is hanging in the balance. But the Labour Party seems only half-aware that this opportunity is here now'.[i] The new S.L. mouthpiece, *Tribune*, accused Labour leaders of having failed to give practical aid to the Spanish Government: vigorous intervention by Labour would have infused hope into the Movement: 'For 8 months, official British Labour has watched the death agony of Spanish democracy with polite expressions of sympathy'.[ii] Horrabin inevitably interpreted this as Imperialist interests struggling for strategic trade and war routes (vital to France and Britain); a war undertaken by France and Britain, even though ostensibly against Fascism, would necessarily be a war waged for the defence and maintenance of those Imperialist interests.[iii] So what was the choice? *Tribune* questioned whether the N.C.L. had ever attempted a coherent policy; had ever organised demonstrations or placed before workers the realities of Spanish struggles or the rôle of the Government; it had never effectively challenged the policy of non-intervention and had not supported volunteers for the International Brigade.[iv]

One of the major reasons for the dissolution of the S.L. evolved from its stance on the Spanish Civil War. By March 1937, serious divisions between the I.L.P. and the C.P. erupted over divisions on the Left in Spain (the I.L.P. supporting the P.O.U.M., the C.P. backing Soviet policy). Intimations of this conflict had begun in 1936, and the S.L. was hemmed between the two groups. Brockway (I.L.P.) wrote to W. Mellor on December 28th, 1936: 'I was disturbed by what H. Pollitt said at the end of one of our Unity Committee meetings about the P.O.U.M. in Spain … I did not want to say things which would impede our unity here…'[v] John McNair (I.L.P.) was writing from Spain about conflict between the P.O.U.M. and the Spanish Communists. The Communist International was identifying the P.O.U.M. with 'traitors' at the Moscow trials: 'I don't want you to become involved either on one side or the other in this dispute … Could not the S.L. send someone to Barcelona to try to prevent a conflict between the sections? … Possibly Brailsford could do the job, particularly in view of his support of the International Column'.[vi] But Brailsford was not going into that conflict as intermediary.

One condition for the I.L.P. *joining* with the C.P. in the Unity Campaign was that the I.L.P. could criticise Russian policies so long as those criticisms came to the Unity Campaign Committee. A private understanding effecting this was agreed by Brockway and Cripps on December 3rd, 1936.[vii] The S.L. played the rôle of mediator. On January 5th, 1937, R. Groves sent a letter to the S.L. Executive denouncing C.P. attacks on the Spanish Left Socialists (P.O.U.M.);[viii] but the C.P.'s *Daily Worker* denounced him as a "Trotskyist" attacking the Unity Campaign.[ix] Two days later, I.L.P.'er John McNair aired the conflicts in Spain in the *New Leader*.[x] Soon, the I.L.P. was exposing the

---

[i] *New Statesman and Nation*, February 1937.

[ii] *Tribune*, February 12th, 1937.

[iii] J. F. Horrabin, 'The Vultures Gather Around Spain', *Socialist Broadsheet*, No. 1, February 1937.

[iv] *Tribune*, February 19th, 1937.

[v] F. Brockway to W. Mellor, December 28th, 1936, Mellor Papers.

[vi] Ibid.

[vii] R. Groves Papers.

[viii] Ibid.

[ix] *Daily Worker*, January 20th, 1937.

[x] 'Charges Against the Spanish Workers' Party', *New Leader*, January 22nd, 1937.

Moscow trials, and announcing its support for the Spanish P.O.U.M.;[i] by March, dissensions among the I.L.P., C.P., and S.L. were irrevocable. For the I.L.P. the policy of the Spanish C.P. was a betrayal of conquests of the workers, because the C.P. had been determined to defeat any other 'Left opposition' in Spain; there was internecine strife within the Spanish working-class movement, lies and slander by one section against others, imprisonments, assassinations, extortion of 'confessions', abandonment of any moral code'.[ii] Doubts grew concerning the ethics of Socialist conduct in this struggle for power. A Socialist moral code no longer operated in Spain because for the I.L.P., Communists owed their first loyalty to the International and Russia, not to the working-class movement: 'The C.P. has no place for ethical considerations of fraternity, honour, truthfulness outside their own associates ... the C.P. approaches the working-class movement as something to be seized, as an organisation which must be manipulated and manoeuvred'.[iii] Naturally, the C.P. claimed the exact opposite.

Whether this was true, false or partly both, was not the matter; both parties were suspicious of the other. Policy clashes deepened, so these two partners in the *Unity Campaign* began to threaten the viability of the S.L. in the Labour Movement (which was probably intentional). Meanwhile, the Spanish Civil War was impinging upon all political and ethical ideas of democracy: 'Few wars, if any, were fought where so much unsullied personal idealism contended with such a morass of political depravity'.[iv] This was debilitating for the S.L. as sectionalist Left-wing politics gained ascendancy over the Republican cause: bitter in-fighting lessened the hopes of Spanish workers' victory or the *Unity Campaign*'s effectiveness: 'Instead of the oasis of escape from the wasteland which the British intellectuals believed they had discovered in communism, they found only a mirage concealing a desert of hatred, intolerance, deceit and conformity,'[v] concluded N. Wood. That way misery lies...

While Left-wing bickering was intensifying in Spain, the S.L. in March had been excommunicated/expelled from the Labour Party. The agitation for Spain continued, with the Government's *Merchant Shipping (Spanish Frontiers Observers) Bill* which side-stepped the problem of Fascist challenge in Spain. In *Tribune*, S.L. writers reiterated their belief that the *Unity Campaign* was crucial because Spanish workers had only been able to withstand Fascist armies because 'all the workers' parties united for common action'.[vi] The S.L.'s policy remained: to launch its campaign against Non-Intervention for the Republican cause,[vii] and get the N.C.L. to give the Spanish Government aid: 'Avenge Guernica! End Murder from the Skies Now by Challenging the Murderers'[viii] was the refrain.

In April, Sybil Wingate was reporting that 'Socialism' was becoming a reality in Spain! There was war, revolution, danger, distress, but she saw an environment being created worth fighting for, unlike the 'disillusionment in the capitalist world'. Her optimism was unbounded: 'Things which in England are topics of academic

---

[i] *New Leader*, February 5th, 1937.
[ii] F. Brockway, *Inside the Left*, p.341.
[iii] Ibid., pp.343–44.
[iv] R. Blythe, *The Age of Illusion*, p.213.
[v] N. Wood, op. cit., p.118.
[vi] 'Close the Ranks', *Tribune*, March 5th, 1937.
[vii] 'End the War', *Tribune*, March 25th, 1937 and *Tribune*, June 4th, 1937.
[viii] *Tribune*, April 30th, 1937.

discussion and definition have become in Spain the material of daily life'.[i] She admitted there *were* dissensions in the ranks, but averred there was *unity* for a common cause in face of a common danger. Her main fury was directed at British Labour leaders: 'To be a member of the British Labour Party is not a subject for pride in Spain today. *If it had been left to the official Party and trade union movement, there would not be one single English volunteer fighting in Spain'*.[ii] By May 1937, the Labour Party *was* condemning non-intervention and Labour's *Spain Campaign Committee* mobilised public opinion through demonstrations and meetings to pressure the Government into abandoning *its* non-interventionist approach … without Labour censure.

Two alternatives confronted Labour leaders; to pursue an anti-Fascist policy over Spain which would strengthen the leadership and lessen C.P. influence, or to use weapons of discipline and expulsion against dissident members. The second policy had been enacted for some months.'[iii] *Tribune* complained that the N.C.L. had refused to support united action: 'The National Council will bear full responsibility before history and the rank and file of the world movement for the continued martyrdom of the Spain it pretends to support'.[iv] Responsibility before history is a mighty burden, if anyone remembers. At last, in July 1937, the N.C.L. document *International Policy and Defence* abandoned non-intervention, and reaffirmed 'aid to Republican Spain'. Cripps celebrated the first 12 months of united struggle for Spanish workers; Labour had officially dissociated itself from 'the farce of non-intervention'.[v]

Spanish volunteers and the cause of the Civil War had been used in internal political struggle between Right and Left in the Labour Movement. This emerged at the Bournemouth Party Conference. C. Trevelyan put the resolution: 'That this Conference declares its solidarity with the people of Spain in their fight for Freedom and Democracy against Fascism'.[vi] It instructed the N.E.C. to launch a nationwide campaign to compel the Government to abandon the so-called Non-Intervention Agreement, and allow the Spanish Government to purchase arms: 'I hope the new Executive will not sit back content with general resolutions'.[vii] This was a C.P. policy as well. The N.E.C. speaker, G. Latham, replied: 'to ask for a nationwide campaign might impose upon us a responsibility which we should find ourselves unable to accept'[viii] and Labour leaders remained wary because the cause of Spanish Republicans had become dominated by the C.P. 'Arms for Spain' could only remain a slogan, since the Labour Party delegated the initiative to local organisations. The Spanish Government, meanwhile, was being compelled to give the C.P. too much power, because the Soviet Union alone was aiding the Republican cause. (Stalin by 1938 was unwilling to become too embroiled at the risk of losing some goodwill in the West.)

In February 1938, Cripps spoke in the House of Commons against withdrawal of volunteers from Spain: 'Whenever any restraint has been put nominally on both sides it has been effective against the Government of Spain, but never effective against the Rebels … they decide to stop munitions, but they stop them for the Government and

---

[i] S. Wingate, *Socialist Broadsheet*, No. 2, April 30th, 1937.

[ii] Ibid. On April 26, 1937, Guernica was destroyed by German bombers.

[iii] 'War Peril Grows: Labour Must Challenge Hitler and His Allies Here', *Tribune*, June 4th, 1937.

[iv] 'Labour's Chance', *Tribune*, June 18th, 1937.

[v] Cripps' speech at Oldham, July 18th, 1937, Cripps Papers.

[vi] *Labour Party Annual Conference Report*, October 1937.

[vii] Ibid.

[viii] Ibid.

not for Franco. They decide to stop volunteers, but they stop them for the Government, and not for Franco... We urgently desire the Spanish Government to be victorious... the other side anxiously desire to see the victory of General Franco'.[i] Attempts had been made before by the S.L to pressurise the N.E.C. to summon an Emergency Conference on the Spanish situation, but the decisions of Bournemouth were not revised. In 1938 the N.E.C. was anxious to avoid a Conference in which the Left in the Party might gain an opportunity to impose its policies and in March 1939, Cripps spoke of how to save 'a now defeated Spain' to save British democratic freedoms: *The tragedy of Spain has been the indecision of the Democracies of Europe...* Food ships and medical supplies allow the National Government to enjoy a vicarious humanitarianism... In a British plebiscite for sending arms to Spain we would have an overwhelming majority'.[ii] At the Southport Conference, the N.E.C. was accused of failing to utilise the resources of the Movement to bring effective aid to Spain or challenge the Government's betrayal of the Spanish Republic.[iii] All too late.

For the S.L., what was disillusioning was that the immense *yearnings for unity* around the issue of the Spanish Civil War ignited the historical divisions between Left groups and Labour's leadership. Instead of resolving differences, the Civil War exacerbated divisions. To the S.L., searching for a cause to revitalise the Movement, the Civil War had appeared a gigantic conflict between 'Good' and 'Evil', uncertainties and disappointments of the early 1930s replaced by hope and faith. An elected Spanish Government was fighting Fascism and opposing German and Italian dictators at last! The war brought all Socialist aspirations to the forefront: ideals of international working-class solidarity, class struggle, battles against the Fascist menace, could be realities. The S.L. gleaned from the Spanish experience a *Unity Campaign* in Britain which could sweep away all those years of Conference resolution defeats. It had forecast the collapse of capitalism; the opportunity had to be taken; conditions in Spain suggested a worthy setting for the *ultimate* conflict. The S.L. could not bear to admit there were intricacies, ambiguities and power struggles which were working contrary to those exhilarating ideals of brotherhood, liberation and a future Socialist society. Honi soit qui mal y pense, or as Stephen Spender ruminated:

> The 1930s, which seemed so revolutionary, were in reality the end of a Liberal phase in history. They offered Liberal individualists their last chance to attach Liberal democracy to a people's cause.[iv]

---

[i] Quoting E. Estorick, op. cit., p.160.
[ii] Cripps' speech at Queen's Hall, London, March 1939, Cripps Papers.
[iii] *Labour Party Annual Conference Report*, May 1939, p.260.
[iv] S. Spender, *World Within World*, 1951, p.290.

Chapter Eleven

The Socialist League and Origins of the 'United Front' (1932–1936)

It was a Saul Bellow character who remarked that history was a nightmare during which he was trying to get some sleep. The apparently radical belief in perpetual change, mobility, plasticity, is a fantasy largely in the service of the status quo. It is capitalism which arrogantly imagines that everything is possible and socialism which acknowledges in its more modest, materialist way the heavy ballast of legacy and circumstance ... Materialists ... are aware of how narrow our margin for manoeuvre really is. If change were just down to the will, it might never come about at all. The will is as much an historical product as whatever it struggles to transform.

> Terry Eagleton, *The Gatekeeper – A Memoir*, 2001, p.51

The bourgeoisie... has left remaining no other bond between man and man than naked self-interest and callous 'cash payment'. It has drowned the most heavenly ecstasies of religious fervour, of chivalrous enthusiasm, of philistine sentimentalism, in the icy water of egotistical calculation. It has resolved personal worth into exchange value.

> Karl Marx, qu. in *Marx: A Biography*, Robert Payne, p.167

"Winning seats in Parliament won't ever bring us Socialism, not even if we was to win a majority. The ruling class'll see to that. Parliament may look democratic, but after all it's only an organ of the bourgeois state, like the law courts, or the civil service or the police or the armed forces. What they call democracy is really disguised dictatorship."

> Edward Upward, *The Thirties*, 1969 edn., p.53.

Labour's 1930s' rank and file remembered the end of the War of 1914–18 with a Government which promised ab initio a future of opportunities. As a result, Labour Left supporters formulated the future in Messianic terms (until the economic depression from 1929). Pacifism had been rooted in Labour thinking but this became less practical with the growth of Fascism, and suppression of Labour and union political opposition in Berlin, Moscow, Tokyo, Madrid and Rome. In the S.L.'s logic, 'capitalism meant war', the chaos of war was bound up with private enterprise, and exemplified a lack of orderliness in a 'free-for-all' (in practice, 'free for a few') society: 'Can we believe that all those who make profits out of the traffic in *armaments* – manufacturers, exporters, bankers and shippers – are as anxious to stop war in Manchuria as they would be if the war were resulting in a loss to their enterprise?'[i]

---

[i] Sir S. Cripps, 'War on War – and Capitalism', *Social Democrat*, February 1932.

The S.L. believed this aspect of capitalist society increased national confrontations.

'Unity' in the Labour Movement was a vibrant concept with the formation of the S.L., since by October 1932, four political bodies (the C.P., I.L.P., S.L. and official Labour) claimed to be the 'pure apostles of Socialism', competing for the allegiance (and subscriptions) of the confused and often non-politically-minded public'.[i] L. L'Estrange Malone perceptively judged that the C.P., I.L.P. and S.L. would be engaged in attempting to make the Labour Party toe three separate lines of Socialist policy instead of attacking the Government! It was always more difficult to apply Socialist principles to foreign affairs or have a 'moral foreign policy' (echoes of the Labour Government 1997–2001) but the S.L. would demonstrate *constructive resistance to totalitarian ideologies* and relate that to undemocratic features in British society.[ii] Despite ideological differences, there were emotional ties for 'working-class unity' after the Labour Government's collapse in 1931.

(A) I.L.P./C.P. 'United Front' and the Labour Party (1933–1934)

The main stumbling block, before Hitler's accession to power gave urgency to Left unity appeals, was C.P. denunciation of the 'reformist nature' of the S.L. and I.L.P., both of which sought a 'militant class struggle' *within* a Parliamentary framework. All three groups yearned to extend their influence in the Labour Movement, and gradually sought each other's company to counteract the Fascist menace abroad. All three groups attempted to break out of their own isolation by poaching Socialists from each other, which lessened the possibility of creating formal relations between their own parties, until Hitler's triumph in January 1933, and disintegration of Social Democracy, unions and the C.P. in Germany. The Nazi Government was interpreted (by the C.P., I.L.P. and S.L.) as a form of 'capitalist reaction'. At first, only the C.P. and I.L.P. were willing to co-operate given the implications of this Nazi victory, while the mass of working people, grateful for the easing of unemployment, ignored the danger signs from Germany and Italy.

Attempts to create a 'united Left' against 'Fascist doctrines' were an expression of impatience at Government policy, a tactic for C.P. penetration into the Labour Party, and a traditional aspiration. The Bureau of the Labour and Socialist International hailed 'united working-class action' to challenge Fascism, as early as February 1933, and the C.P. and I.L.P. held a series of meetings on the Fascist danger. In March, they sent a letter to the Labour N.E.C. inviting participation in a 'United Front Against Fascism'.[iii] Labour leaders evaded this, and issued *Democracy and Dictatorship,*[iv] which indicated that *disunity* of the working class had brought Fascism to power in Germany (because electors were divided between Communism and Social-Democracy, and had fallen victims to Fascism). This did not imply the need for 'unity'; it was condemnation of Fascist and Communist dictatorships on equal terms: 'There was a strangely ambivalent attitude … which enabled both the Party and union leaders to call

---

[i] *New Statesman and Nation*, October 15th, 1932.
[ii] Cf. Letter from C. Allen to H. N. Brailsford, December 15th, 1932, quoting A. Marwick, *Clifford Allen*, p.126. (My italics.)
[iii] R. E. Dowse, *Left in the Centre*, p.186.
[iv] *Labour Party Annual Conference Report*, 1933, pp.220–221.

for resistance against undemocratic ideologies on one hand and to declaim about defence measures on the other'.[i] The N.J.C. prided itself on having successfully resisted attempts at disruption from the Right and the Left, and reiterated the historic task of British Labour to uphold the principles of Social Democracy against dictatorship of every kind.[ii] So far, the Labour Opposition had clarified *its* position. What did the new S.L. think?

The S.L. rebuffed *Democracy and Dictatorship*, resenting the equation of Nazism and Soviet Communism, and the N.E.C.'s inability to give a Socialist lead in this critical situation. In March, the S.L., stirred by the events in Germany and activities of the I.L.P. and C.P., passed a resolution for united action in the Labour Movement, although some S.L. members were demonstrably not enthusiastic about joining former I.L.P. colleagues or collaborating with the C.P. When Labour's N.E.C. intensified its measures against those 'acting under Communist influence', S.L. leaders backtracked on their bold statements (at the Derby S.L. Conference). Like all other issues which could have united the Movement, suspicions and mutual recriminations surfaced. (G. Orwell concluded: 'Fear! We swim in it. It's our element. Everyone that isn't scared stiff of losing his job is scared stiff of war, of Fascism or Communism').[iii]

The S.L. had begun to make its position apparent. L. Elvin wrote about the urgency for a United Front against Fascism and War;[iv] even if 'Left groups' disagreed with a United Front in method, they could all work for it in aim.[v] The S.L. co-operated with the *New Clarion* Youth Campaign, the Labour League of Youth and the University Labour Federation in an Anti-War position, but was wary of joining the *Anti-War Congress*, which *was* allied with Communist organisations.[vi] Yet, the S.L. denounced the pusillanimity of the German Social Democrats, and deduced from their collapse a justification for criticisms of Labour leaders' gradualist policies, but not to the point of eviction from the Party. Brockway wrote to Cripps that all groups needed to secure working-class united action, regretted the attitude of the Labour N.E.C. and T.U.C. leaders, and pleaded: 'Stop inter-Party attacks during the course of co-operation and act with the one purpose of organising effective resistance to war, Fascism and Capitalism.'[vii] He asked if Cripps would express his aspiration for united action in a 100-word statement. Cripps replied that, however much he desired a rapprochement between Left-wing groups: '*I must remain perfectly loyal to the decisions of my own Party Executive... I want to make my influence within the Labour Party as effective as possible*'.[viii] If he took the action suggested by Brockway, it would increase difficulties, rather than help remove differences between Labour groups. This was the S.L.'s 1933 stance.

The I.L.P. and C.P. co-operated in the anti-Fascist campaign, the Anti-War Movement, Hunger Marches, agitations against the Unemployed Assistance Board (U.A.B.) cuts, rent disputes and unofficial strikes. The United Front at this stage was specifically against war and Fascism, against a break with the Soviet Union, and against

---

[i] E. Shinwell, *Labour Story*, p.145.

[ii] *Labour Party Annual Conference Report*, October 1933, pp.220–21.

[iii] G. Orwell, *Coming Up for Air*, 1939 (1967 edn.), p.19.

[iv] *New Clarion*, March 25th, 1933.

[v] 'Dangle', 'I Am For War Against War... Now', *New Clarion*, April 8th, 1933.

[vi] *New Clarion*, April 29th, 1933.

[vii] Brockway to Cripps, April 3rd, 1933, Cripps Papers.

[viii] Cripps to F. Brockway, April 7th, 1933, Cripps Papers.

attack on workers' conditions.[i] Although the C.P.'s R. P. Dutt posited that the I.L.P. should visualise the struggle as one between revolutionary policy and parliamentary democracy, rather than training workers to use democratic machinery,[ii] Brockway was convinced the scope of co-operation between the two groups had extended far enough.[iii] The S.L.'s position was awkward. Committed to the Labour Party, it had uttered statements which suggested different aspirations: 'The penalty for lack of unity in the British Labour Movement is chains heavier than any before.'[iv] A. L. Rowse stated in '*The One Way to a United Front*', it was essential to build unity in the main movement of workers; '*that Mass Movement is the Labour Party*'.[v] At its Derby Conference, the S.L. judged issues raised by the United Front of the I.L.P. and C.P. Here, the S.L., in conformity with the Party, revised its March statement by asking the T.U.C. and Labour N.E.C. to formulate a policy which would rally the whole Movement against Fascism and Capitalism[vi] – a generality which committed the S.L. to nothing in particular. E. F. Wise pointed to the importance of a United Front since small unattached parties were a source of weakness (as proved in Germany), but he concluded tamely that 'it is for the Labour Party itself to take the initiative in suggesting a basis of common action'.[vii] The S.L. was enjoined to see it was doing its part to maintain the United Front by applying its policy by permeation of the Labour Party.

The S.L. did pass an *anti-war pledge* at Derby: 'Believing that war between nations arises directly from the necessities of Capitalism and Imperialism, we pledge ourselves neither to fight nor in any way to help in such a war'.[viii] A General Strike would be proposed in opposition to war. There was a rejection of the Hendon S.L. branch amendment for recruitment of the whole working class 'in support of a revolutionary Socialist policy on the basis of the United Front.'[ix] An S.L. statement diagnosed that it did not want to commit itself to any united front which was not 'fair, frank and open', although the I.L.P. denounced the S.L. for not being prepared to join with the C.P. and the I.L.P. and. Brockway criticised the S.L.'s procrastination and equivocation. (In March the S.L. had passed a resolution urging the Labour Party and T.U.C. to arrange a meeting with the Co-operative Movement, I.L.P. and C.P. proposing a basis for United Action'. Such a resolution was not put before the delegates): 'The S.L. has definitely retreated on this point… its Executive is content with a vague declaration … its Conference rejects an amendment for united action. This is repeating the very timidity which it condemns in the Labour Party Executive'.[x] At this time, the S.L. was taking no chances.

Tragically, for the whole Labour Movement, nothing was done to buttress united working-class action, which each political group on the Left had professed. The problem was that the C.P., I.L.P. and Labour Party wanted their own exclusive

[i] *New Leader*, May 12th, 1933.
[ii] R. Palme Dutt, 'The United Front and Revolutionary Unity', *Labour Monthly*, Vol. 15, No. 4, April 1933.
[iii] F. Brockway, *Inside the Left*, p.249.
[iv] S.L. News, 'Unity in Chains', *New Clarion*, May 6th, 1933.
[v] *New Clarion*, May 27th, 1933.
[vi] J. F. Horrabin moved this resolution, June 4th, 1933.
[vii] The S.L. Derby Conference, June 3rd, 1933.
[viii] *Derby Evening Telegraph & Derby Daily Express*, June 5th, 1933.
[ix] S.L. News, 'Unity in Chains', *New Clarion*, May 6th, 1933.
[x] F. Brockway, *New Leader*, June 9th, 1933.

leadership; there was not even a common struggle against Fascism, which did not augur well for future solutions to disunity. Nevertheless, the S.L. was gradually formulating its policies on foreign affairs, and had made considerable progress by September 1933, when G. D. H. Cole explained how recent events in Germany (and Italy) had illustrated the disastrous consequences of division of the working class into rival groups and parties (more active in fighting one another than for Socialism): 'Unity must not be purchased at the price of abandoning Socialist policies, for it is the unity for Socialism that is required'.[i] The S.L. maintained it was essential for them to remain in the Labour Party, to work for working-class unity and adoption of a Socialist policy and programme. It had to answer: *'How far is a "united front" desirable or possible, and on what conditions?'*[ii] Its ideal was 'reorganisation of the world as a federation of autonomous but closely co-operating Socialist republics', advocating economic and political relations with the U.S.S.R., reduction of armaments, pacts of non-aggression and inclusive arbitration (with all countries), mutual agreements for collective exchange of products, and abolition of protective tariffs: 'The S.L. calls upon all sections of the British working-class movement to affirm their solidarity with the workers in other countries to refuse their taking part in any war levied by a capitalist State, and to use every opportunity created by war to end the capitalist system, and to set up Socialism'.[iii] Fat chance in the twentieth century.

H. N. Brailsford propounded the S.L. critique of the last Labour Government's foreign policy (which had not been rooted in Socialist thinking, but in the Liberal tradition); any future Socialist foreign secretary would have to act with capitalist and Fascist Governments, and might have to use conventional diplomacy to buy off the instinctive hostility of capitalist Powers. What was vital was a perception of Socialist objectives: 'It is even easier in the foreign field to succumb to the temptations of reformism than it is in the domestic field'.[iv] Brailsford worried that 'short-term pacifism' seeking to prevent war might be ultimately opposed to long-term interests of Socialism: 'Disarmament ... brings us no nearer to the conditions required for the creation of a true international society'.[v] A Socialist foreign policy could not respect claims to national supremacy or a balance of power; capitalist treaties would have to be terminated, as would 'national sovereignty': 'We are more concerned to render frontiers unimportant than to redraw them'.[vi] So, a Socialist policy would sap national sovereignty, recognise cultural autonomy, surrender the national military machine and liberate weaker States from Imperialist pressure. Brailsford's idyll.

By the time of the Labour Conference 1933, it was obvious to Labour leaders that the I.L.P. and C.P. aspired to their own independence *and* influence within the Labour Party; their own distinctive organisations but use of Labour platforms; their own 'ideology' yet participation in the Labour Movement.[vii] At the Conference, 'war resistance' emerged, and 'a general strike' (if war was declared) was discussed, although the main activity was not with the new international menace, but development of a

---

[i] G. D. H. Cole, *A Study Guide on Socialist Policy*, S.L. pamphlet, August 1933, pp.1–3.
[ii] Ibid.
[iii] Ibid., p.18.
[iv] H. N. Brailsford, 'A Socialist Foreign Policy', *Problems of a Socialist Government*, 1933, p.254.
[v] Ibid., p.263.
[vi] Ibid., p.267.
[vii] Cf. H. Pollitt, 'Class Unity in the Struggle Against Reformism', *Daily Worker*, June 14th, 1933; 'It is Time all Revolutionary Socialists United', *New Leader*, Sept. 1st 1933.

Labour programme. After S.L. pressure, the Conference upheld collaboration with Russia to form a nucleus for international Socialist co-operation.[i] 'War resistance' was a feature, the high tide of pacifist influence. This resolution had been put by Sir C. Trevelyan, and was deemed by the S.L. a 'success for its own policy'; 'the General Strike had been accepted by the Party as part of the workers' weapons to defeat war'[ii] (not yet used), but Labour and union leaders regarded 'a United Front' as a weapon which would be utilised by Communists to draw the S.L. into vituperative attacks on their leaders, so the N.E.C. revised its list of banned organisations!

Two letters from Cripps show how the S.L. was to be circumscribed. He claimed that he could not take part in the *British Anti-War Movement* according to the Labour Party.[iii] Concerning a proposed Round Table Conference between leading politicians, Cripps replied it was too late for this programme, "collective security with agreements with Governments" was the short-term answer; 'Labour policy in the new circumstances has not been worked out, and consequently I do not think I could sign any such statement'.[iv] Before Labour policy could be worked out, the S.L. rallied behind the 'mass resistance to war' slogan, as proposed by Trevelyan for the S.L.: ('one of immediate and immense importance to the Labour Movement').[v] He stated in 1933 there was a *likelihood* of another World War, and the difference between the political parties was in their reactions to war danger; the Labour Party unanimously opposing war, Conservatives demanding increases in armaments.[vi] The S.L. was naïve, but the Left's position was clear: 'The majority preferred a simplified picture of the World, in which the Soviet Union stood as the champion of peace, freedom and progress against the fascist menace – while the democratic (or 'imperialist') powers hovered uneasily between appeasement of the fascist aggressors and preparation to fight them'.[vii]

This is illustrated in Cripps' pamphlet for the S.L., *The Choice for Britain*, a dogmatic, neo-Marxist position against existing international arrangements, founded on the *'iniquities and economic impossibilities of the Versailles Treaty'*.[viii] He conceived each State adhering to economic nationalism to maintain its international markets (wage levels and social services sacrificed in this economic competition); the weapon used by capitalist interests was economic warfare, competing nations to capture raw material supplies or markets by force of arms; the 'choice for Britain' to struggle on under capitalism *or* peaceful co-existence.[ix] He was pessimistic about co-operation between capitalist nations in the fields of industry, finance or disarmament, and expressed the S.L. mantra that pooled security in a nucleus of nations was unattainable *until major States had 'Socialist Governments'*. This was remote, but to rely on particular alliances, Britain's disarmament or rearmament, would solve nothing.[x]

Since the Hastings Conference, the S.L. stance had remained an uncompromising

[i] G. D. H. Cole, *History of the Labour Party Since 1914*, pp.287–88.
[ii] S. Cripps, S.L. Notes, 'Our Part', *New Clarion*, October 14th, 1933.
[iii] Cripps' letter, November 6th, 1933, Cripps Papers.
[iv] Cripps' letter, November 29th, 1933, Cripps Papers.
[v] S.L. Notes, *New Clarion*, December 2nd, 1933.
[vi] S.L. Notes, *New Clarion*, December 9th, 1933.
[vii] N. MacKenzie, *Socialism – a Short History*, 1966 edn., p.159.
[viii] S. Cripps, *The Choice for Britain*, (Capitalism in Crisis Forum Series No. 4), p.1. (My italics.)
[ix] Cf. ibid., pp.2–3.
[x] Cf. ibid., pp.9–11. W. Churchill stated in a radio broadcast: "We have never been so defenceless as we are now," (January 16, 1934).

opposition to war preparations, to organise working-class opposition in the event of war; 'War' was the test of Socialist conviction; S.L. policy to distrust capitalist governments in use of armaments for 'liberating purposes' and after 1933 to campaign in local Labour and union parties for working-class unity against War and Fascism. Recognising economic anarchy and unwillingness of national governments to disarm, the S.L. was wary of involvement in a United Front with the I.L.P. or C.P. For the S.L. Caitlin wrote to Cripps in January 1934: 'Lord Allen (I.L.P.-er) wanted some action against Fascism ... I believe in no coalition whatsoever, or any fusion of policy, but possibly, on specific issues, parallel lines of policy might be detectable'.[i] The *United Front National Congress of Action* (Bermondsey, February 24th, 1934) was organised mainly by the National Unemployed Workers' Movement, with I.L.P., C.P. and local Labour and union support. Criticised by the official Labour Party and T.U.C., the Congress did not include S.L. members.

The following day, Cripps at a Bristol meeting, relating the Austrian situation to Britain, stated how vital it was to meet similar attacks on British democracy. Only united support of workers could save democracy: 'Now more than ever it is essential to close up the ranks in the great working-class movements. Whatever our comparatively minor differences or views may be, we shall all agree on this vital necessity for unity'.[ii] Two days later, the National Joint Council (N.J.C.) met at Transport House to discuss resolutions moved at Hastings to organise opposition to war (including a General Strike).[iii] Union leaders killed this last suggestion, and the N.J.C. concluded there might be occasions when the Movement would assist an action to preserve the nation and democratic institutions.[iv] This *War and Peace* document prompted S.L. opposition to the N.E.C. assumption that the Government could be relied on to defend democracy and working-class interests in a war. (The document was a victory for union leaders.) As regards S.L. hopes for a General Strike: '*The trade union delegates effectively smashed this outdated, woolly minded and unrealistic proposal*'![v] This did not deter J. T. Murphy aiming for a debate on this at the Leeds S.L. Conference in 1934.[vi]

Opposition groups do most creative thinking because they do not have (or have lost) power. While the I.L.P. accepted a new constitution at its Conference (a 'centrist' strategy providing common ground on which Communist and 'reformist' movements could be brought together in support of a militant policy), the S.L. was beginning to move to the Left with its Leeds Conference manifesto *Forward to Socialism*. Zilliacus wrote to Cripps to enunciate Labour's international policy, to clarify the difference between the Socialist position and that of other Parties; while every Party supposedly supported peace through the League of Nations, Socialists' aim was a Co-operative World Commonwealth: 'Get the S.L. to put forward some fairly substantial pamphlet on Labour's foreign policy, for, hitherto, it has produced nothing except some pretty thorough tripe by Brailsford'![vii] Instead of the latter's 'tripe', Zilliacus offered Russia's impending entry into the League as sufficient reason for the S.L. to question Labour's

[i] G. E. G. Catlin to S. Cripps, January 24th, 1934, Cripps Papers.
[ii] S. Cripps' speech at Bristol, February 25th, 1934, quoted in *Daily Herald*, February 26th, 1934.
[iii] *Labour Party Annual Conference Report*, 1933, p.185.
[iv] *Labour Party Annual Conference Report*, 1934, p.17.
[v] E. Shinwell, *Labour Story*, p.147.
[vi] J. T. Murphy, 'If War Came', *New Clarion*, March 10th, 1934.
[vii] K. Zilliacus to S. Cripps, April 4th, 1934, Cripps Papers.

foreign policy! One of the resolutions (on foreign policy) embodied in the S.L.'s *Forward to Socialism*, proclaimed a Socialist Government would look to those States where workers were 'in control' as its natural allies: 'Instead of a fettered Trade Agreement with the Soviet Union, limited in objective and purpose, enshrining old quarrels of Capitalism and private interests, there should be a new and wider treaty of friendship'.[i] With the Soviet Union, a British Socialist Government could aim at security by pacts of non-aggression, backed by sanctions, with countries prepared to join, using the League of Nations, because the opposition to international war had to be waged on more than one front. Mellor put the S.L.'s position: 'The foreign policy of a Socialist Government with the existing situation must be similar to that now being pursued by the Soviet Union'.[ii] "Must be"? But why? Campaigners were about to discover.

S.L. procrastination regarding the United Front emerged at Leeds. There were amendments to the *Forward to Socialism* document, some branches still urging a General Strike if the Government deprived workers of democratic rights, Holborn S.L. regretting the Party had turned down United Front discussions with the I.L.P. and C.P.[iii] The S.L. urged the National Joint Council to take the lead in uniting workers behind a militant programme: 'It is the duty of all working-class organisations to subordinate their theoretical differences and tactical methods and to agree to joint action for immediate purposes, which can be entered upon without any group being required to abandon its distinctive outlook'.[iv] H. L. Elvin argued the S.L. was willing to achieve unity and the Party ought to have said, 'they desired unity and laid down certain conditions'.[v] Moving the S.L. resolution, J. Marcus (Holborn S.L.) proclaimed *'group dogmatism is poisoning the Movement'*,[vi] but then, dogmatism poisons everything.

Yet, as in other S.L. campaigns (to change Party policy), this elicited recriminations in the Party towards the C.P. and I.L.P. Susan Lawrence (not an S.L. member) spoke *against* the United Front, "because the C.P. despised Parliamentary Government"; she asked delegates to remember earlier difficulties with the I.L.P. in search of unity with the C.P.: 'When we were penetrated by C.P. members [sic], every meeting was turned into a bear-garden ... the pet name of the Communists for those societies which typify the United Front is the Innocents Club'.[vii] The S.L. would disintegrate if the united front and connection with Communists became one of the S.L.'s tenets: 'You will bring into great difficulties, if not to an end, one of the most promising movements in the Labour Party'[viii] – she was proved right! W. Horrabin (for the S.L.) warned if there was to be no United Front, the S.L. had to see the Party's Executive 'took up the fight' instead of letting the Communists take the lead, make the Party more militant, not just a respectable Party (that merely wanted office): 'If the Labour Party maintains its present attitude towards the United Front, it must organise demonstrations, hunger

---

[i] 'Forward to Socialism', S.L. document, May 22nd, 1934.

[ii] W. Mellor, 'The Menace Today', *Socialist Leaguer*, No. 2, July–August 1934.

[iii] 'If There Is No 'Next Election' – A Problem for the S.L.', *New Leader*, May 18th, 1934. That 'problem' was solved in 1935.

[iv] *Leeds Weekly Citizen*, May 25th, 1934.

[v] *New Leader*, May 25th, 1934.

[vi] *Manchester Guardian*, May 22nd, 1934.

[vii] *Leeds Weekly Citizen*, May 25th, 1934.

[viii] 'S.L. and C.P. – Miss Lawrence in Lively United Front Debate' (this confrontation was the only aspect of the conference reported by *Morning Post*, May 22nd, 1934); *Daily Herald*, May 22nd, 1934.

marches, etc., instead of leaving that work to the C.P.[i] Subordinating theoretical differences and tactical methods was not going to be easy. W. S. Watkins (of Stepney S.L.) expressed amazement at the attention the Party N.E.C. gave to the C.P. (when Communists never polled 1,000 votes in any by-election). Cripps pointed out the resolution did not say the S.L. was going to *have* a United Front with any group, but it was an invitation to Communists to change their tactics.[ii] T. Howard reiterated that the resolution, as S.L. delegates saw it, was a vote of censure on Labour's N.E.C. for failure to agree to approaches made by the C.P. for a United Front, but the S.L. would not commit itself to any resolution which implied association with the C.P.,[iii] a factor which triggered *The Times* heading 'S.L. and Unity: Communist Tactics'.[iv] The outrage over the United Front which the press seized on was of little significance, since the S.L. had no intention of working with Communists in 1934. The S.L. accepted the argument that the Labour Party would have no trouble with the Communists if its own policy and tactics were sufficiently inspiring – an S.L. approach to all issues, until its dissolution!

By July 25th 1934, Labour leaders had rejected a United Front.[v] This brought an immediate rejoinder from the C.P. and I.L.P.;[vi] *'Who was splitting the workers' ranks?'*[vii] The S.L. looked to the policy adopted by the Labour Movement in face of 'a capitalist war' and sought a pledge of resistance should any war be threatened or declared by the Government, and now *advocated* the General Strike to defeat the Government.[viii] Cripps confirmed the S.L. line that if war and armaments build-ups were to be opposed, preparations had to be made to 'change the economic system': 'The real fight against war must be the fight against Capitalism'.[ix] All very well, but with the Fascists' meeting at Olympia and a Labour Party ban on the Anti-Fascist Hyde Park rally on September 9th, 1934, J. Strachey sent to the S.L. his *Memorandum on Anti-Fascism*; Fascism could be combated only by mobilisation and organisation of working-class counter-activity;[x] he criticised the N.J.C. for its conviction that 'Anti-Fascist' activity *advertised* Fascism: this view stifled working-class opposition and created disunity; Labour supporters who opposed Fascism should contact the C.P. or I.L.P., regardless of differences: *'Prevent the disunity of the British workers before Fascism by presenting a practical lead for anti-Fascist work... this will make it quite impossible for the National Joint Council to continue its present line of policy'.*[xi] As it was, J. T. Murphy was doubtful about T.U.C. policy because it was retreating from its decision concerning industrial action against Fascism in the event of war preparations.[xii]

Preparing its resolutions on War and Peace, problems of unity, and a Socialist foreign policy for the Southport Party Conference, the S.L.'s efforts to make a United

[i] *New Leader*, May 25th, 1934.

[ii] Cf. *Leeds Mercury*, May 22nd, 1934.

[iii] *Manchester Guardian*, May 22nd, 1934.

[iv] *The Times*, May 22nd, 1934.

[v] 'United Front Rejected by Labour', *Daily Herald*, July 25th, 1934.

[vi] *Daily Herald*, July 27th, 1934.

[vii] *Daily Worker*, August 10th, 1934.

[viii] Cf. W. Mellor, 'The Menace Today', *Socialist Leaguer*, No. 2, July–August 1934.

[ix] S. Cripps, 'War Talk!', *Stoke Newington Leaguer*, May 1934, Cripps Papers.

[x] J. Strachey, *Memorandum on Anti-Fascism*, September 1934.

[xi] Ibid.

[xii] J. T. Murphy, 'What Will Congress Do About Fascism?', *Socialist Leaguer*, No. 3, August–September 1934.

Front plausible were boosted by French and Spanish United Fronts. The S.L. formulated an amendment on War and Peace for the Party's *For Socialism and Peace* but this confirmed it distrusted the Government![i] European nations announced programmes of expenditure on armaments in 1934; there was an exultation of war spirit in Germany, Japan and Italy, while the S.L. proclaimed it impractical and unjust to defend the Versailles Treaty or the British Empire. A Socialist Government's 'war and peace' policy might consist of remaining in the League (if Russia joined), if international disputes were submitted to arbitration, there were pacts of mutual defence; socialising the armaments industry, economic and political relations with Socialist countries, Britain accepting arbitration of other States in dealings with Ireland, India, and Kenya.[ii] The Executive's *War and Peace* document (presented to the Southport Conference) supported collective security and economic co-operation in the League's framework, but a 'General Strike against war' was opposed because the onus ought not to be placed on the union movement![iii] As in *Forward to Socialism*, the S.L. sought political and economic relations with the Soviet Union, workers to prepare resistance to war.[iv] The Conference upheld the *War and Peace* policy,[v] despite contradictions between resisting aggression and opposition to armaments; the official Labour position for League support and pacifism, the S.L. for war resistance (a war 'utilised by Socialists against the capitalist forces which created it').[vi]

The crucial issue was the *United Front*. An attempt by the S.L. to move the reference back of sections of the Executive's report dealing with the *United Front* was defeated,[vii] although many Labour members were sympathetic to anti-Fascist unity, and were only deterred by C.P. influence. The C.P. was disappointed with the Southport Conference on *United Front* proposals and S.L. tactics; C.P.'er Dutt considered decisions raised issues for the working-class movement and for the S.L.: 'The Labour Executive has reinforced last year's rejection of the United Front by new and intensified discipline against any form of association *between revolutionary and reformist workers*'.[viii] Put like that it was hardly likely to tempt the S.L.! Dutt was adamant the S.L. had to choose between 'daydreams' of a future Parliamentary Socialist transformation or the building of the united working-class front. Which would one choose – 'daydreams' or 'unity'? Southport decisions represented 'the extreme offensive of the ruling Right wing in the Labour Party ... to erect a dam against the rising united front demands'. Labour leaders had followed a tactical policy against any militancy by its *For Socialism and Peace* programme, the *War and Peace* resolution (which scotched the Hastings resolution), and disciplinary regulations against association by any Labour group with the *United Front* or the C.P.

The Labour Party had rejected the *United Front*,[ix] but S.L. leaders continued to consider it. Cripps wrote to Lord Parmoor: 'The one thing that is essential above all

---

[i] Editorial, 'Forward to Socialism', *Socialist Leaguer*, No. 3, September–October 1934.
[ii] Cf. G. D. H. Cole, 'A Socialist Peace Policy – Is 1914 Near Again?', *Socialist Leaguer*, No. 4, September–October 1934.
[iii] 'War and Peace' document, *Labour Party Annual Conference Report*, Appendix 2, pp.242–246.
[iv] S.L. statement in *Labour Party Annual Conference Report*, October 1934, pp.175–6.
[v] *Labour Party Annual Conference Report*, October 1934, p.178.
[vi] B. A. Betts, 'Youth & Peace', *Socialist Leaguer*, No. 5, October–November 1934.
[vii] *Labour Party Annual Conference Report*, October 1934, p.136.
[viii] R. P. Dutt, 'The United Front and the Labour Party', *Labour Monthly*, Vol. 16, No. 11, November 1934.
[ix] 'Labour Rejects Latest United Front', *Daily Herald*, October 25th, 1934.

others at the present moment is unity'.[i] Not until the November Special S.L. Conference did it commit itself to this, and even then, its adherence was veiled. For the C.P., William Rust presented the choice starkly: 'Will the S.L. boldly organise a fight against the Southport decisions and join in the *building up of the United Front of action against Fascism, war and hunger,* or will it toe the line?'[ii] Couched in these terms, there seemed no choice if the S.L. could only accept the logic of Southport decisions and make a decisive break with past vacillations. Rust interpreted the S.L. efforts as a retreat, especially since the Labour Party at Hastings had passed resolutions on emergency powers and a General Strike against war, and the S.L. had advocated an alliance of Socialist States to prevent war: 'The S.L. has never acted according to the conclusions stated in *'Forward to Socialism'*, that 'events in Europe have shown that a policy of reformism and trade union and Socialist Movements have not availed to stem the tide of Fascism'.[iii] What *had* stemmed this tide?

After the 'National' Government posed as the champion of the League of Nations and Labour had been defeated, 'unity' became the slogan of the Left, from November 1935. There had been a gradual alteration in S.L. policy to reveal 'faith in mass activities', which had played a vital part in the C.P.'s approach; some S.L. leaders recognised common traditions and principles which the C.P. and I.L.P. held with the S.L., particularly Marxist terminology and a critique of Parliamentary reformist modes of action. From November 1934, the S.L. waived its primary research work and policy amendments, and began to consider *tactics against unemployment and localised capitalism.*[iv] At the S.L.'s *Special National Conference*, November 24th and 25th, 1934, two (or four) questions posed were 'War or Peace?' and 'Fascism or the Making of a Genuine Democracy?' The S.L. was thinking, in the event of Capitalist or Imperialist war, the General Strike could be made effective, while internationally it would maintain contact with foreign Socialists: 'By the establishment of socialism alone can the menace of War and Fascism be averted ... without constant agitational effort and organised resistance the Will to Power on which the coming of Socialism depends, cannot be created'.[v] Possibly. The S.L. declared that power to defeat war and Fascism lay in working-class unity by implementation, politically and industrially, of a *policy based on the class struggle.*[vi] Extremely unlikely, but the S.L. linked war, poverty and Fascism. J. F. Horrabin at least put the S.L.'s stance: 'Work if you will for the success of a Peace Ballot... but *do not emasculate Socialism by pretending that its attitude to War is indistinguishable from that of capitalist Liberalism'.*[vii] What if 'capitalist Liberalism' was the right approach? Basing its agitation on threats of unemployment, Fascism and War, the S.L. was moving into C.P. territory, because until now anti-war and anti-Fascist committees were Communist-led; the S.L. could only take effective action through *some* kind of association with the I.L.P. or C.P., a situation which could not improve its relations with Labour and union leaders.

---

[i] Cripps to Lord Parmoor, October 17th, 1934, Cripps Papers.

[ii] W. Rust, 'The S.L.: What Next?', *Labour Monthly*, Vol. 16, No. 11, November 1934. (My italics.)

[iii] Ibid.

[iv] Reviewed in *Socialist Leaguer*, No. 6, November–December 1934.

[v] S.L. editorial, 'On the Basis of a Policy of Class Struggle (The S.L.'s New Tasks)', *Socialist Leaguer*, No. 7, December 1934.

[vi] S.L. Special Conference, November 24th–25th. (My italics.)

[vii] J. F. Horrabin, 'Class – Rule and War', *Socialist Leaguer*, No. 7, December 15th, 1934.

(B) The S.L., the C.P. and the I.L.P. on Unemployment, Fascism and War (1935)

'1935' brought a decisive volte-face in Labour foreign policies. A year in which only in Britain did Conservatives remain in power in Europe. From the beginning of 1935 the united front (C.P., I.L.P. and N.U.W.M.) began to branch out into a popular front.[i] A. Austen, for the S.L., traced the danger of world war to victories of Fascism, only to be opposed by the Socialist working-class movement and the Soviet Union: 'The united power of the Soviet Union and the Comintern combined with that of the Social-Democratic Parties could become a force not only capable of preventing War and Fascism, but which might achieve out of its common strength the aim of us all: the building of Socialism'.[ii] The gulf between the S.L., C.P. and I.L.P. centred around the *tempo and means of change*, and possibility of bringing constitutional change as against a 'violent revolution'.[iii]

Individual S.L. members became involved in Peace Pledge groups and the *Peace Ballot* of February 1935, but ineffectuality of this form of protest further encouraged a *United Front* campaign.[iv] Inability to influence the Government swayed the S.L., which believed that lip-service to 'collective security' was used as a cloak for old diplomacy; it was critical of Party policy: 'The Party's peace policy rests on the argument that war threatens because the National Government refuses to make genuine use of international machinery now available. The Party is making a wide "national" appeal and rejecting the class basis of Socialist policy'.[v] Labour's rejection of non-Party members regarding unity "was a mistake", because the experience of Italian, German, Austrian and Spanish workers warned against disunity (and uncertainties in policy). Cripps kept his main critique for the Government's armaments policy, which could create a war situation as in 1914: 'It is typical of the technique of the propaganda of the capitalist Party that when they have no arguments to support their case, *they attempt to create a feeling of fear in the electorate* by threatening to use their economic power... against the interests of the country and the workers.'[vi] Horrabin's front-page cartoon in the *Socialist Leaguer* offered a similar perspective: a picture of Asquith in 1913 and MacDonald in 1935 both stating 'To ensure peace, we must be strongly armed. Other nations are etc., etc.'[vii]

The Labour Movement objected to the *Anglo-German Naval Agreement* because it would undermine the League and divide Britain and France; Britain seemed to be returning to policies preceding 1914, with new alliances, to re-enforce the case for increasing armaments: 'If one believes in economic competition, Empire, social inequalities, national sovereignty, then the Government's White Paper (on Defence) is

---

[i] 'Pollitt Shows Way Forward', *Daily Worker*, January 1935.

[ii] A. Austen, 'The Internationals and the Problem of Unity', *Socialist Leaguer*, No. 8, January 15th, 1935.

[iii] Cf. Cripps' arguments in a letter, January 22nd, 1935, Cripps Papers.

[iv] B. A. Betts, 'Socialist Youth Day', *Socialist Leaguer*, No. 9, February 15th, 1935.

[v] The Price Will Be Paid in Blood (Labour Must Resist War)', *Socialist Leaguer*, No. 10, March–April 1935.

[vi] Cripps in letter, March 12th, 1935, Cripps Papers.

[vii] *Socialist Leaguer*, No. 10, March–April 1935 and 'Government Starts New Arms Race', *Balham and Tooting Citizen*, April 1935.

the true exponent of the inescapable consequences.'[i] The S.L. noted Germany and Japan rearming, the 'European Powers' searching for profitable investment in undeveloped territory, clamouring for raw materials/markets, highlighting economic and political nationalism, fomenting class conflicts. The S.L. sought a Conference of the Labour Movement which could oppose the Government's war psychology and war preparations. These views were put to a *London Area Committee Conference*.[ii] Labour members drew a distinction between force used in support of collective security and as an instrument of *national* policy; Labour leaders *were* suspicious of reluctance to force an issue with Mussolini over Abyssinia and the Stresa Conference: 'Stresa has ended. With it has demonstrably gone all pretence of an 'all-in' system of collective security. The world is back into a pre-war era of ententes and alliances... Can it still be maintained that the situation in Europe after Stresa is any other than *a lining-up of military alliances?*'[iii] Unfortunately, the S.L. wished it wasn't so, but it was.

When the world was regarded as too small to contain both the U.S.S.R. and the states of the capitalist world,[iv] France and Russia signed a treaty of mutual assistance: in France and Spain, C.P. members and other Socialists were beginning to work in Popular Fronts and the S.L. campaigned for a Labour-led unity through '*mass resistance against war*'.[v] The Party at Southport had advocated war resistance against a Government which defied the League Covenant, and the T.U.C. instructed its General Council to call a special Congress should war threaten: 'It is now the duty of the Labour Movement's leaders to call a special joint conference to consider anew its policy in the light of the present menacing situation'.[vi] Participation of the S.L. in a *United Front* with the C.P. and I.L.P. became the central question at the S.L.'s Bristol Conference, but opposition to this recognised the C.P. and I.L.P. as factional groups dissipating the Movement's force, which could only lead the S.L. to disillusionment. One criticism from an S.L. member came two years before the reality: '*The dangerous tendency behind some quite influential support for the United Front is the hidden desire for a split in the Labour Party which shall take a large portion of the Left-wing elements out*'.[vii] This section should be titled 'casus conscientiae'; who benefitted from the S.L.'s dissolution in 1937?

Criticism of involvement in a 'United Front' brought retorts. The very same A. Austen accused United Front supporters of harnessing agitation efforts to factional groups. Were demonstrations against the *Unemployment Act* merely 'agitation efforts'? Had not the Leeds S.L. Conference passed a resolution declaring it 'the duty of all working-class organisations to subordinate theoretical differences and tactical methods in favour of joint action for immediate purposes which could be entered upon *without any group being required to abandon its distinctive outlook*'?[viii] One United Front activist declared Labour and union members regarded 'unity' as the major issue, which, far from splitting the Party, would create a Socialist attitude;[ix] another thought flexibility could *only* be

---

[i] 'The Price Will Be Paid in Blood (Labour Must Resist War)', *Socialist Leaguer*, No. 10, March–April 1935.

[ii] Conference at Caxton Hall, April 6th, 1935.

[iii] S.L. Notes & Comments, *Socialist Leaguer*, No. 11, May 1935.

[iv] Robert Briffault, *Breakdown (The Collapse of Traditional Civilisation)*, 1935, p.276.

[v] H. L. Elvin, 'Looking Back on May Day', *Socialist Leaguer*, No. 11, May 1935.

[vi] S.L. Notes & Comments on Foreign Policy, *Socialist Leaguer*, No. 11, May 1935.

[vii] A. Austen letter to *Socialist Leaguer*, No. 11, May 1935.

[viii] Quoting *Daily Herald*, May 22nd, 1934 in letter from A. Philippa Grimshaw, *Reverse the Ban! Socialist Leaguer*, No. 12, June 1935.

[ix] A. J. Scroggie, 'The United Front', *Socialist Leaguer*, No. 12, June 1935.

secured by unity among Socialist forces: 'A great social change cannot be brought about by the splendid isolation of democratic principles'.[i] R. George, a detractor from the United Front, envisaged no room for new organisations; a 'United Front' would confuse people (between working-class unity and proposals of the C.P. and I.L.P.), the C.P. opposed Labour's 'reformist' Parliamentary politics, so it was not wise for the S.L. to highlight rival bodies, because 'United Front' activities were *recruiting drives*. R. George posited the S.L. should question Labour leaders, and the value of demonstrations (which the official leadership was not prepared to organise), but a greater consciousness amongst Labour members *within* the existing Party would be the most effective way to achieve unity: 'It is the stirring of the workers as a movement that is our main task, and not the leadership of fractions; it is the maximising of working-class power that we must set as our objective, and not the satisfaction of our own desires for immediate action'.[ii] In these letters to the S.L. journal were the first arguments within the *United Front* (rather than presentation of divergent views as at the Leeds S.L. Conference).

On 'a *United Front*', there was a distinct set of opinions recorded in the agenda to the Bristol S.L. Conference. Enfield branch wanted the S.L. to redouble its agitation in the Party to induce a United Front; for Marylebone and Paddington branch: 'the S.L. must agitate for the raising of the ban on Left-wing organisations'; Uxbridge S.L. wanted the 2nd and 3rd Internationals to co-operate (but was uncertain about the C.P.); Stepney S.L. branch opposed organisations whose acknowledged policy was inimical to the Labour Party; and Kensington S.L. sought disciplinary action against any S.L. branches which acted contrary to the spirit of the Stepney resolution.[iii] At the Conference, the proposed United Front was not faced directly. The S.L. was deemed an integral part of the Labour Party, with a declared objective, to assist the Movement to become the 'united front' against Capitalism and war.[iv] The Conference reaffirmed the position taken by the S.L.'s National Council, which (in a circular to branches) stated S.L. members must not be diverted into activities condemned by the Party, which would jeopardise S.L. affiliation: 'We should create the temper of militant socialism within the trade union and Co-operative Movements, without whose support no Labour Party will gain power in this country or be able to accomplish Socialism'.[v] So far, so reasonable.

In the S.L. resolution on '*International Affairs*', a Socialist Government was envisaged as founded on economic and political alliance with Soviet Russia (and other Socialist States); the N.C.L. should summon a conference on the international situation and danger of war, and decide on methods of mass resistance to the aims of the Government.[vi] No support should be given to an 'Imperialist' Government, nor should the Movement assist in a war waged "under capitalist rules" (Difficult to get out of this one, or, as the I.L.P. contended, if the S.L. carried out this policy it would not remain in the Labour Party in a war situation).[vii] S.L. leaders affirmed that economic forces controlled foreign and domestic policy, and the Movement had to

[i] Letter from R. V. Sturgess, *Socialist Leaguer*, No. 12, June 1935.
[ii] R. George letter on 'United Front', *Socialist Leaguer*, No, 12, June 1935.
[iii] Agenda for S.L. branch resolutions to Bristol S.L. Conference, June 1935.
[iv] 'S.L. Bans Communist Alliance', *Daily Herald*, June 10th, 1935.
[v] Cripps quoted in *Bristol Evening Post*, June 10th, 1935. Or 'temperata socialismi ratio' – a *moderate* form of socialism!
[vi] Quoted in *Daily Herald*, June 11th, 1935 and 'Resistance to War', *Manchester Guardian*, June 11th, 1935.
[vii] 'Labour Party: 'Lefts' Crippled – Want To Take Socialist Action, but the Labour Party Says "No"', *New Leader*, June 14th, 1935.

decide *how* to counter the Government's nationalist, Imperialist and militarist propaganda. What could the S.L. recommend the Party to benefit the workers' cause?[i] The resolution on *Mass Resistance to War* stated the necessity for action: 'It is and must be something more than a *scrap of paper*. We are pledging ourselves to our fellow workers... to speak and act to the utmost of our power to keep from them the horror and tragedies of Armageddon'.[ii] Fatal would be a lack of leadership and direction for workers from Labour leaders.[iii] In hindsight, these acquire tragic proportions as pleas of their time.

So the S.L. voted against involvement in the United Front in 1935 and for a more 'radical policy' in the Labour Movement. The main topics for discussion at Bristol remained 'Peace and War', Imperialism and colonial exploitation, inability of the Government to deal with causes of war, and the S.L. hoping the Movement would base its policy/tactics on class objectives (as the U.S.S.R. based its policy on the need to defend the Soviet system); S.L. members were to prepare *'mass resistance to war' conferences* in their districts, with Trades Councils as centres of action. C. Trevelyan, in his pamphlet *Mass Resistance to War*,[iv] favoured the close co-operation of Britain with the United States and the Soviet Union[v] (and so it eventually transpired during the latter part of the War), but the lead had to come from the rank and file and Labour's political organisation;[vi] The only road to security was through mass resistance to any war: 'Supposing there was ... a definite avowal by the responsible conferences of the industrial and political sections of our Movement that they intended to resist war ... Supposing it was known that mobilisation or definite moves towards war would be met by a general strike ... What Government, in spite of any war fury, would care in these days to call down war on such an utterly divided nation?'[vii] Yet talk of 'general strikes' was unrealistic in a situation where Germany and Italy would have none.

The message from the S.L. was: *'Fight Now Against War: A Call to Action'*, to strengthen mass resistance. This manifesto was a compendium of resolutions passed at Conference: 'In every branch and area by conference, by speech, by literature, by canvass, we can help to create that public opinion which will support mass resistance when it comes'.[viii] The S.L.'s position was summarised: 'To co-operate in a war which, whatever its declared objectives, was *serving capitalist ends*, would be to forfeit the right to such development and to do a disservice to Socialism'.[ix] Its appeal to 'mass resistance to war' replaced a 'united front'. This could not remain for long. In August 1935, there was a C.P. change in tactics, when it reneged on criticisms of Labour's 'Social Fascist' policies. In an address to the closing session of the Communist International, Dimitrov replaced a policy of 'the United Front of equals' with that of 'peace at almost any terms with Social Democracy'.[x] The only conditions for united action would be

---

[i] Quoting *Manchester Guardian*, June 10th, 1935.

[ii] Quoting Cripps, 'Mass Resistance to War', *Morning Post*, June 11th, 1935. The 'scrap of paper' arrived in 1938 from Chamberlain in Munich.

[iii] Quoted in *Western Daily Press* and *Bristol Mirror*, June 11th, 1935.

[iv] *Capitalism in Crisis*, S.L. Forum Series, No. 2, December 1935.

[v] Ibid., p.5.

[vi] Ibid., p.7.

[vii] Ibid., p.8. The answer in 2003 would be: "a Labour Government".

[viii] 'Fight *Now* Against War: A Call to Action', S.L. manifesto by the S.L. National Council', June 1935, p.3.

[ix] Ibid., p.8. (My italics.)

[x] *Communist International*, August 1935, *Labour Monthly*, September 1935 and *Imprecorr*, August 24th, 1935.

the offensive against fascism and war danger. The C.P. (in each country) was instructed to conclude pacts with Labour or Social Democratic Parties for joint action, but accession of the U.S.S.R. to the League and conclusion of the Franco-Soviet Pact created confusion. Shrewdly, B. A. Betts asked: 'Has not the Comintern, in moulding its tactics upon the necessities of the Soviet Union's foreign policy, postponed the day when the workers in other countries will win through to Socialism?' No one answered, but the answer was in the affirmative.

While the C.P. transmogrified from offensives against 'bourgeois democracy' to defence against Fascist regimes, it became less urgent to label the British system 'a dictatorship over the working class',[i] and more compelling for the C.P. to seek support for measures to secure victory of 'democracy over Fascism'.[ii] The S.L. did not change its decision to follow the tactic of *'mass resistance to war' conferences* and on August 19th, 1935, there was an *S.L. London Conference against War*, to prepare mass conferences for September, to debate Abyssinia and League sanctions (in which the S.L. majority opposed the C.P. supporting sanctions as part of Soviet policy, the U.S.S.R. now a member of the League of Nations by September). The S.L. arranged for a week of *conferences against war* with representatives of the Labour, Co-operative and union movement, S.L. speakers introducing the resolutions: 'Discussions were to be over ways and means by which the masses could resist war'. Idealistic, but noble.

The resolution before the 17 *Anti-War Conferences* read: 'Realising the strength of the forces making for war in the Capitalist and Imperialist system, the members of the Conference pledge themselves to take immediate action within their own organisation to mobilise every available force for the mass resistance to war'. J. T. Murphy proclaimed the urgency of these Conferences, which could increase S.L. membership and funds,[iii] and the S.L. explained that *'mass resistance to war'* was the only way to prevent economic exploitation and political enslavement: 'Every worker who is a member of the Labour and industrial organisations throws away the hopes and efforts of a lifetime by accepting hypocritical slogans [sic!] such as "democracy", "The League of Nations" or the "sanctity of treaties"'! The S.L.'s *Anti-War Conferences* were held between September 14th and September 21[st][iv] with all the leading S.L. members, nationally and locally, as speakers.[v]

Opening the first Conference, Cripps set the scene: Germany, Japan, Britain, France, the U.S.A. and Russia were rapidly increasing their armaments, which could not be suppressed by dealing with the individual case of Italy in Abyssinia; Germany and Japan required Imperialist expansion which had been typical of British industrialisation in the 19th century; the World Economic Conference had failed because each country was intent on preserving its armaments; the crux was whether

---

[i] J. Strachey, *Theory and Practice of Socialism*, 1936, p.154.
[ii] H. Pollitt, *How to Win the War*, p.3. The Liberal position was Violet Bonham Carter's: "war can be prevented now, if every nation still within the League of Nations is prepared to carry out its obligations." *The Times*, 29 August 1935, qu. M. Pottle, *Champion Redoubtable: The Diaries and Letters of Violet Bonham Carter 1914–45*, 1999 edn., p.184.
[iii] J. T. Murphy, 'Campaign to Fight War Menace', *Socialist*, No. 1, September 1935.
[iv] London (1400 delegates), Leeds (311), Newcastle (300), Cardiff (285), Manchester (205), Hull (200), Birmingham (182), Swansea (133), Sheffield (No. n.k.), Bristol (130), Brighton (120), Durham (108), Nottingham (90), Luton (70), Norwich (61), Reading (60), Eastleigh (36), *Socialist*, No. 1, September 1935.
[v] Speakers included, S. Cripps, A. Bevan, D. N. Pritt, W. Mellor, Sir C. Trevelyan, J. T. Murphy, G. R. Mitchison, John Lewis, H. L. Elvin, C. Borrett, Ithel Davies, J. Boggis, John Cripps, J. F. Danby, D. R. Davies and T. Howard.

Imperialism was supported or not: 'Once we have committed ourselves to the support of Imperialism in the form of a British Conservative Government, it will become impossible for us to convince the people that on some other occasion such support should be withheld'.[i] Energy should be directed towards replacing the Government, which could not deny Mussolini the right to seize Abyssinia, when it had itself seized the Transvaal by force of armaments. In 1914 the 'war resisters' had been isolated, unable to concentrate their opposition to influence public opinion; but now, in 1935, the attempt had to be to build *mass opinion against war*: "Every kind of device must be used to make the workers realise that they are not isolated cranks opposing the will of the nation... Create within the working class a strong and determined resistance to those false cries of patriotism".[ii] Noble thoughts, once more, but of marginal significance in dealing with Nazism and Fascism.

One omen for the future relations between the S.L. and the official Party emerged at this London '*Mass Resistance to War*' *Conference*. The London Trades Council withdrew from involvement because the S.L. did not follow an official Party line. The Brighton Conference would be crucial for the S.L. The struggle between the S.L. and Party policy appeared over 'Abyssinia, sanctions and pacifism'. At the T.U.C. at Margate, union leaders sought approval for sanctions against Italy, and the T.U.C. voted in favour, with an understanding that sanctions might mean war.[iii] While Party leaders recognised the causes of war as dictators' ambitions, nationalism, capitalist and imperialist rivalries, and pursuit of private profit, *they* stood for the collective peace system. The S.L. analysed the international conflict with Abyssinia as the signal for an Imperialist drive, waged by economically hard-pressed capitalist powers (Italy, Germany and Japan) for a redistribution of colonial territories: '*The "menace of Fascism" is a powerful lever to force the working masses of the satisfied empires to support war and war preparations, for it supplies capitalist politicians with a war-cry*'.[iv] It was not a question of the Government supporting Abyssinian freedom. It was a case of protecting British conquests, especially in Africa. The S.L. had no alternative to that vulgata opinionum commenta.

On September 22nd, 1935, the S.L. issued a statement to all branches about the Italo-Abyssinian War, denouncing Government sanctions' intentions, and proposing union action at ports and an oil embargo against Italy. Bevan extolled: 'If I am going to ask workers to shed their blood, it will not be for medieval Abyssinia or Fascist Italy, but for making a better social system'.[v] Not all S.L. leaders agreed; S.L. General Secretary, J. T. Murphy, supported the Party's official policy. He was busy organising anti-war conferences and popularising the S.L.'s Bristol policy, which opposed a British Imperialist war under slogans 'War for the Covenant and the League' and 'War Against Fascism'. So long as S.L. propaganda was of a general and abstract character (dealing in war in general) Murphy could comply, but when the S.L. *opposed* sanctions against Italy... 'I found myself sending out documents over my signature urging the S.L. members to use all their influence to reverse Party policy with which I agreed'![vi]

---

[i] Cripps on 'Mass Resistance to War', September 14th, 1935, Cripps Papers.

[ii] Ibid.

[iii] T.U.C. Report, September 1935, p.349.

[iv] S.L. editorial, 'War or Socialism: Choice that Faces Workers – Get Ready Now', *Socialist*, No. 1, September 1935.

[v] M. Foot quoting A. Bevan, op. cit., p.211. Not very PC!

[vi] J. T. Murphy, *New Horizons*, p.317.

The issue of 'Pacifism' arose in the Brighton Conference, and created further divisions just when agreement seemed to have been reached on methods of resisting Fascist aggression. (Lord Ponsonby resigned from Labour in the Lords, Cripps resigned from the N.E.C. and Lansbury publicly stated his disagreement with Party policy); the Labour Party seemed nearer to a major split than since I.L.P. disaffiliation, and divided along three lines; the Christian pacifism of Lansbury, the Socialist anti-Imperialist pacifism of the S.L., and union leaders' unequivocal support for action against Italian aggression.

At the Brighton Conference, Lansbury reaffirmed his renunciation of force, and the Conference knew he could no longer remain leader.[i] As averred, Bevin feared a repetition of 1931 when the Party leader had one policy, his lieutenants another, the rank and file bewildered, so he discredited Lansbury and Cripps under the banner of 'unity and loyalty' in a Party facing an Election: 'The crime of these people is that they have sown discord at the very moment when candidates want unity to face an election... I have lived through three splits in the Movement and I do not want any more'.[ii] Historians quote Bevin's words, but ignore Cripps' response: 'So long as a capitalist Government is in power, I am not prepared to trust them to use their military power for other than Imperialist and capitalist aims. The League is nothing but the tool of the Imperialist Powers'.[iii] Not very pragmatic, but the S.L. majority voted against the Party's League of Nations' resolution. The S.L. refused to accept the need for rearmament, and was blinkered about the League of Nations, 'which in its existing state would commit working people to the capitalist military machine'.[iv] If a Socialist Government controlled foreign policy, the S.L. saw no risk of Imperialist bargains, but that was a long way ahead. The difficulty with the S.L.'s position was it would make the Movement ineffectual in the international field, unable to prevent the surge to war, or to stem a war once begun. What the S.L. did not appreciate (until too late) was that the malaise which affected the Government was *not* that of Imperialist ambition but of weakness and vacillation'.[v]

The S.L. did not make a great impact in the Brighton Party Conference. Unlike the 75 amendments to 'For Socialism and Peace' at Southport, the S.L. submitted only two crucial resolutions for the Brighton Conference; for suspension of Standing Orders to allow the Conference to debate the issue of 'Peace and War' (ruled out of order); the second, on 'Armaments' was included; the S.L. refrained from any campaign against the Party's decision to support sanctions against Italy. J. T. Murphy considered this a lost opportunity for Cripps to challenge for the Party leadership: 'Had he on this occasion cut clear of pacifism and boldly declared himself in favour of sanctions against Italy and stood firmly for collective security, which would have included ... alliance with the U.S.S.R., he could have swept the Conference with him. But he was tied to the S.L. policy'.[vi] Yet, the S.L. policy resulted in one outcome when the *Hoare-Laval Pact* a few months later exposed the lack of confidence which the Government possessed in the League of Nations.

'United Front' ideas were fermenting. Allan Young warned of the dangers of

[i] E. Estorick, op. cit., pp.143–4.
[ii] Bevin in *Labour Party Annual Conference Report*, October 1935, p.243.
[iii] S. Cripps, ibid, p.158.
[iv] *Labour Party Annual Conference Report*, October 1935, pp.156–7.
[v] F. Williams, *Ernest Bevin*, p.199.
[vi] J. T. Murphy, *New Horizons*, p.317, which meant Attlee became Labour Party leader.

fragmentation in the working-class movement: 'In the problems now confronting the Labour Movement, there is none more important and urgent than to mobilise all progressive opinion on its side in a wide united front against the intellectual, moral, political and cultural darkness of Fascism'.[i] The S.L. was aware of the signs of war, and with a General Election in sight, members wanted to make sure the P.L.P. was fully represented,[ii] J. T. Murphy proposed a People's Front (a coalition of all parties and organisations against Fascism), but other S.L. leaders, such as W. Mellor, proposed the 'united working class' front of the Left, a campaign for C.P. affiliation to the Labour Party, a common platform with the I.L.P. After the General Election, the majority of the S.L. became attracted to the prospect of ending feuds within the Left (despite policy differences over Abyssinia), and sought meetings between the C.P., I.L.P. and S.L. about co-operation in a Unity Campaign.[iii] The S.L. had failed to represent a source of rival policies to Labour leaders, but it could hope to reinvigorate the Party through a Unity Campaign which might challenge the control of the N.E.C. Suppositions, but worth a try.

The S.L. was helping to shape one significant aspect of public opinion on foreign policy, in its assessment of Fascist characteristics in Germany, Italy and Austria; plus visualising the 'defence of London' in 'the defence of Madrid', although it was difficult to follow the tortuous paths and mixed motives[iv] of the various S.L. members' positions during the Abyssinian crisis and United Front agitation. The problem was to work out a policy which would obstruct Mussolini's imperialist aggression without identifying the S.L. with the warlike preparations or 'imperialist aims' of British capitalism. This was improbable unless there was a *United Front* on the Left, instead of national unity behind 'imperialist' Governments.[v] The S.L.'s message remained couched in neo-Marxism: 'The British workers' main fight must be concentrated upon defeating British capitalism and imperialism in British constituencies and in the fields of industry'.[vi] It wasn't to be the 'main fight' for the S.L. for much longer.

By November 1935, the prospect of peace had diminished, Labour's hesitation and search for alternatives to force had disappeared, the Brighton Conference left a confusion of views, but began a readjustment in Labour and union thinking in face of international aggression. The embodiment of the Party's belief in the League (A. Henderson) died on October 20th, 1935, and Cripps became a Labour back-bencher. No longer an N.E.C. member, he now spoke for himself (or the S.L.) which enabled Party leaders to dissociate themselves from his pronouncements. While the S.L. attempted to enlist unionists for a recruiting campaign in new industries in London, against military preparations,[vii] E. Bevin hoped if Labour could win the Election it would demonstrate it was capable of accepting responsibility and that 'individualism

---

[i] Allan Young, 'The Political Problems of Transition', chapter 8 in *New Trends of Socialism*, 1935, ed. G. E. G. Catlin.

[ii] J. T. Murphy to S. Cripps, October 9th, 1935, Cripps Papers.

[iii] R. Miliband, op. cit., p.245.

[iv] David Carlton reviewing M. Krug's *A. Bevan: Cautious Rebel*, for *Society for Study of Labour History*, No. 6, May 1963.

[v] 'Balham and Tooting Citizen', *For a Socialist Government*, November 1935.

[vi] S. Cripps, 'Your Enemy Is at Home! Win Battle at the Polls: Forward to Socialism!', *Socialist*, No. 2, November 1935.

[vii] 'Balham and Tooting Citizen', *The War and the Workers*, October 1935.

such as that which has characterised certain persons in the past must be checked"[i] – a barb directed at Cripps and other recalcitrant S.L. leaders. Labour lost, so Bevin had to stick the knife in later.

The Labour Party acknowledged that potential enemies were arming vigorously, but was not convinced Britain intended to go to war, and argued that rearmament was unnecessary for a policy of appeasement; 'opposition to rearmament' was a tactical weapon against Government foreign policy, but wistful optimism and absence of a realistic approach did the Party no service in the 1935 campaign[ii] (the N.C.L. supported collective security, the P.L.P. opposed the Defence Estimates). Labour played into Baldwin's hands in the Election and he had qualities for leading the coalition Government; he acted like a Conservative, spoke like a Liberal, and was a representative of the British middle class![iii] The Election results brought back Clynes, Morrison, Dalton, Alexander, Shinwell, Pethick-Lawrence and Chuter Ede, which strengthened the Party's debating power, and propelled the S.L. opposition 'Unity-bound'. In 1936, the *Unity Campaign* would become the dominant question in the S.L., while a national ostrich-like reaction to war festered.[iv] The Hoare-Laval episode did nothing to check Italian aggression and hardened the British Government's unwillingness to oppose the Fascist menace.

The S.L. began planning campaigns on behalf of the miners,[v] and a resolution for S.L.-directed conferences stated: 'every economic struggle of the workers for higher wages or better conditions is in reality part of the struggle for political power … there is needed a concentration of all the forces of the Labour Movement … to create the political power and understanding necessary to bring down the "National" Government'.[vi] By February 1936, incentives were drawing the S.L. towards a United Front, especially the influence of international events. Growing pessimism in the S.L. caused by Fascist successes merged with C.P. willingness to abandon its hard-line against Labour policies in favour of *mobilisation of anti-Fascist opinion*. Many in the S.L. remained wary of the C.P., particularly submission to the Soviet Union, while Gallacher for the C.P. unjustly chastised Cripps who, he said, 'was for the League of Nations when it was a den of imperialist war intrigue, [but] is now against it when the first Socialist State is bending all its energies with the support of workers everywhere, to make it a real centre against aggression and war'.[vii] This was a projection or transference on Gallacher's part, since it was the C.P. which had made the volte-face on the League. Not surprisingly, with C.P. accusations of 'individual diversions' of S.L. members, it took long for United Front approaches to be taken seriously. G. E. G. Catlin interpreted the United Front as precisely the reason why the S.L. should *not* follow the I.L.P. into secession from the Labour Party.[viii] He would be proved right.

The S.L. now criticised the *Daily Herald*: 'We are getting politically inept leadership

---

[i] General Secretary's Quarterly Report, December 1935.

[ii] E. Shinwell, *Labour Story*, p.152 and H. Pelling, 'Short History of the Labour Party', chapter 5, p.81.

[iii] K. Martin, *The Editor*, pp.187–88. Precisely the qualities of Mr Blair from 1997.

[iv] M. George, *Hollow Men*, p.37.

[v] Minutes of London Area Committee Meeting, January 1st, 1936, R. Groves Papers; Minutes of London Area Committee Meeting, January 23rd, 1936, R. Groves Papers; Report of West London S.L. Branches Co-ordinating Committee Meeting, January 6th, 1936, Groves Papers.

[vi] S.L. Resolution for 55 Conferences, *Socialist*, No. 4, January–February 1936.

[vii] W. Gallacher, 'The Fight for Unity in Parliament', *Labour Monthly*, Vol. 18, No. 2, February 1936.

[viii] G. E. G. Catlin, 'Problems of Labour Policy', *Labour Monthly*, Vol. 18, No. 2, February 1936.

from the official organ of the Labour Movement ... just at the time when the fight against the "National" Government should be driven home on all fronts',[i] while Labour leaders had to be persuaded not to offer any support to the Government in its foreign policy, because it professed to work through the League of Nations. As it unfailingly did, the S.L. pointed out the vices of the Imperialist system and its incompatibility with peace or justice.[ii] Reoccupation of the Rhineland (March, 1936) jolted the Labour Movement into further opposition against Government foreign policy; Labour leaders now claimed the latter's policy was leading Britain into a probable war, and could not resist European Fascism: 'Here you can hear the volcano sizzling, immense military preparations and no sense of what they are for. Literally, the Cabinet hasn't a foreign policy'.[iii] With the *Government's White Paper on Defence* and the P.L.P. opposing the Defence Estimates, H. Dalton expressed anxiety about Labour: 'The Party won't face up to realities. There is still much more anti-armament sentiment and many are more against our own Government than against Hitler'.[iv] This was also a criticism of the S.L. with its policy of opposing war and armaments because 'Fascism' could come into Britain under the guise of 'war necessity', patriotic fervour, demagogic promises, by inflation or high wage levels in munitions factories.[v] Cripps began to posit 'unity' of the Left; the S.L. should associate 'with those professing an equally strong desire to achieve the same end ... in the face of these essentially Capitalist dangers, unity in the working class is becoming daily more urgent.'[vi] Laski went further; it was 'morally obligatory' on the Labour Party to enter discussion with the C.P. to see whether an adequate common basis of action could be found.[vii]

(C) The S.L.'s Seven-Point Resistance Plan to Rearmament (April 1936)

While the S.L. received sceptical responses about its anti-war crusade,[viii] it set out an immediate policy, a *Seven-Point Resistance Plan to Rearmament*, a charter of action, in April 1936. In this, the S.L. opposed all preparations for waging war in support of British Imperialism or Capitalist 'collective security'; such were designed to check workers in their struggle for political and industrial power: 'If a foundation is to be laid for world peace it must be upon the firm basis of international working-class unity and not upon the shifting sands of Imperialist rivalry'. Thus the S.L. retained its mantra to widen the struggle against the Government and 'its war organisation', and secure adhesion of all sections of the Movement to the 'plan'. R. Groves attempted to link the fight against war and the daily class struggle, which had been by-passed by the urgency of war danger: 'The elaborate legal systems for the settlement of disputes leave the cause of disputes untouched. Wars are judged by courts as wars of aggression or as

---

[i] S.L. editorial, 'Some Matters of Moment', *Socialist*, No. 4, January–February 1936.

[ii] Cripps, 'Fight Imperialism – The Enemy of Peace and Justice', *Socialist*, No. 4, January–February 1936.

[iii] K. Martin, *Harold Laski*, quoting Laski, p.103.

[iv] H. Dalton, *The Fateful Years*, pp.88–90.

[v] R. George, 'How to Fight Fascism', *Socialist*, No. 5, March 1936.

[vi] S. Cripps, 'Weld the Workers Together', *Socialist*, No. 5, March 1936.

[vii] H. Laski, 'Problems of Labour Policy', *Labour Monthly*, Vol. 18, No. 3, March 1936.

[viii] R. Hardine to Cripps, March 11th, 1936, Cripps Papers.

wars of defence … teaching the masses to put their trust in peace machinery'.[i] This was the conundrum for Labour leaders who recognised the need for 'national defence' and 'adequate defence forces' and only differed from the Government as to what *was* an 'adequate defence force'.

Groves developed his ideas in *Arms and the Unions* issued by the S.L. in its resistance to Government war preparations. His was a predictable S.L. analysis; war purposes were for property-owners, working people would pay in the end for the armaments programme; Conservatives had a choice between a policy of disarmament, social reform, financial rehabilitation and heavy expenditure on armaments,[ii] but the Government *increased* expenditure on armaments, and reduced social services, until industry would be drawn to equip the country for war.[iii] In this scenario, workers shifted from one industry to another, unskilled labour would be used to reduce rates of skilled workers (and weaken the union movement), with Socialist workers excluded from war industries: 'Trade unions are faced with the choice: to co-operate with the Government's measures, to accept the inevitable blows at conditions and rights which will follow, or to seize this opportunity to build a powerful movement of resistance'.[iv] Groves argued that work in connection with Government war plans should be treated like any other employers' proposals; unions had to retain freedom of action (no concessions to patriotic appeals),[v] full recognition of shop stewards, a shop movement in all factories, union recruiting in potential war industries, a 40-hour week (and higher wages) and close contact between the shop movement through Trades Councils. With the Government's war drive, he concluded that 'large-scale war preparations involves inevitably the curtailment and eventual suppression of the rights won by organised labour over a hundred years of bitter struggle'.[vi] The final battle for the S.L. had begun.

In April 1936, negotiations began (at Cripps' invitation) between representatives of the C.P., I.L.P. and S.L. in his chambers in Middle Temple. All three groups believed their own interests could be served by united action, yet the unconscionable time it took to make headway illustrated incompatibility in their objectives. Despite differences over practical details of the campaign, each group hoped to reinvigorate itself through the United Front. S.L. leaders were themselves not united on this, and were in disagreement as to implications for its future, of any decision to create a common front. Now it sought to enrol within its ranks 'all socialists who recognise the class struggle as the driving force of social change'. Its objects were to unite the organised working-class movement of wage and salary earners by means of political and industrial activity; rally the masses by aiding them in their day-to-day struggles; and make the Movement fully conscious not only of its power to achieve Socialism, but the means by which that power should be exercised,[vii] whatever that might entail. Maybe this was also moonshine.

In May, Mussolini proclaimed Italy's annexation of Abyssinia. The Labour Party issued *Labour and the Defence of Peace*, a manifesto upholding collective security as a

---

[i] R. Groves, 'A Marxist Looks at War and its Causes', by "Jacques"', *Socialist*, No. 6, April 1936.

[ii] Quoted in *The Times*, March 10th, 1936.

[iii] R. Groves, *Arms and the Unions*, S.L. pamphlet, April 1936, p.2.

[iv] R. Groves, ibid., p.8.

[v] Ibid., p.10.

[vi] Ibid., p.11.

[vii] S.L. National Council objectives (attached to S.L. pamphlets, April 1936).

deterrent, but avoiding what was to be done now the League had failed, while the S.L.'s *'Seven-Point Resistance Plan to Rearmament'* was, according to J. T. Murphy, well received in local party and union organisations,[i] and the S.L.'s May Day message to workers was *'Win Your Way to Security and Peace by Winning Class Power – Unity Is Strength'!*[ii] The probability was that armaments would replace social needs but the S.L. noted the Party Executive had now renounced any formal collaboration with the Government in the Commons,[iii] and the Government, in its rearmament plans, had not mentioned legal measures necessary to facilitate Britain's achievement of military parity, type of weapons to be manufactured, nor social consequences of large-scale armament plans. It remained a predominant S.L. assessment that the Government had a 'Fascist tendency', witnessed in the *Sedition Bill*, the *Trade Disputes Act*, political and legal discrimination against Socialist newspapers, threats of newspaper censorship, and semi-militarisation of the police.[iv]

The notion of 'national unity' was regarded as a trap by S.L. leaders, who wanted to save the British worker from the tragedy of another World War: 'What can we do NOW? Nothing – unless you are prepared to utilise the present circumstances and the past events to destroy capitalism and imperialism with the Government that is their tool'.[v] Not much chance of that but the division between the S.L. and official Labour was now on *foreign policy* (and willingness of the Party to support the Government in imposition of sanctions under the League). At its Stoke Conference, the S.L. stood for a decisive challenge to this. In the S.L.'s resolution on foreign affairs, the Party was criticised for remaining on the defensive in the Election: 'The S.L. should assist in transforming the existing Labour Movement into a movement whose mass loyalty to Socialism could be depended upon at all times'.[vi] The resolution was passed (by 74 votes to 17), *opposing* the Government's rearmament programme and industrial mobilisation. The S.L. aimed to stay in the Labour Party, but another resolution endorsed support for C.P. application to affiliate to the Party (with only one dissentient).[vii] Moving this, W. Mellor spoke of the urgency to secure unity in policy and action by the working class, all sections to 'modify their attitudes' to secure this (whatever that implied). Promoting a class struggle, Cripps supported a United Front but opposed the suggested Popular Front of all Parties: 'With an almost negligible Liberal Party and no second ballot ... it would be suicidal for the workers to enter into such a coalition. The experience of the years 1929 to 1931 should be strong enough warning'.[viii] Those lessons haunted the S.L. throughout its existence.

'Unity in working-class action and policy' was the crucial resolution passed at Stoke. The object of a Unity Campaign would be a sustained attack on the Government by combined forces of the Left, and (the big one) replacement by a Labour Government.

---

[i] J. T. Murphy, 'Anti-War Fight Wins Support', *Socialist*, No. 7, May 1936.

[ii] *Socialist*, No. 7, May 1936.

[iii] Editor, 'Matters of Moment', *Socialist*, No. 7, May 1936.

[iv] Louis Borrill, 'Fascism for Defence', *Socialist*, No. 8, June 1936.

[v] S. Cripps, 'National Unity A Delusion (What Abyssinia Should Teach Labour): Class Struggle Paves the Way to Peace', *Socialist*, No. 8, June 1936.

[vi] 'Labour and the Defence Programme – Opposition to any Collaboration', *Manchester Guardian*, June 2nd, 1936.

[vii] 'Staying in Labour Party: But Want the Communists in too', *Daily Herald*, June 1st, 1936. L.P. rejected C.P. affiliation in October 1936, L.P.A.C.R. pp.257, 296.

[viii] Cripps' Presidential Address, quoted in *Stoke on Trent City Times*, June 6th, 1936.

A new combination of the C.P., I.L.P. and Labour Party could somehow achieve this: 'The Labour Party must receive a transfusion of blood by an understanding and an alliance with the Communists and I.L.P. It is no use arguing that these bodies are so numerically small that they don't count. Numbers are of little importance; assimilation of the I.L.P. and C.P. into the Labour Party would be futile. It is the alliance which is of importance, not the assimilation',[i] argued A. Bevan. The I.L.P., in decline since 1932,[ii] was keen to re-establish connections with the official Movement, but angled to be the organisation leading the Unity Campaign, despite its suspicions of the C.P. In the *New Leader*, the I.L.P. queried: 'Socialists in the Labour Party – Should They Leave It?' and answered by documenting 'The Case for Joining the I.L.P.'![iii] All three parties, preparing for a United Front, were interpreting politics from the 'class struggle' point of view, even though the histories of such Socialist groups were of unsuccessful little combinations, Popular Fronts, United Fronts, Seven Point Plans, People's Charter Groups, National Petition Groups, all trying to create *some* common resistance to Fascism, all collapsing after the refusal of leaders of established parties to have anything to do with them,[iv] and internecine squabbles.

When the Government abandoned sanctions in June 1936, those who were reluctant to relinquish Labour's programme of disarmament and opposition to war were furnished with an admirable reason. Events had now vindicated the S.L.'s views on national and international events: 'We have urged that those who relied on capitalist governments to translate into real action the desire for peace or to operate the principles of collective security, would be betrayed. They have been'.[v] The Government's recruiting campaign was part of the consequences of a policy of power politics, heavy armaments, and abandonment of the League. It was essential to try to defeat the Government, but this would be impossible if Labour supported rearmament,[vi] but did the average voter comprehend the argument that a vote against provisions for the Army, Navy and Air Force was not really a vote against all defence, but only against Government foreign policy? Dalton was sure it was impossible to win an Election unless the Labour Party ceased symbolic opposition to all rearmament.[vii] (Dalton as N.E.C. Chairman in October 1936, and Bevin as T.U.C. Chairman collaborated on foreign policy and defence matters, in opposition to the S.L.).

By July 1936, the S.L. National Council of 18 members had lost the services of its General Secretary, J. T. Murphy and Sir C. Trevelyan.[viii] The Unity question grew with the S.L.'s desire for collaboration on particular issues. Mellor stated the S.L.'s move towards a United Front (integrated in the Labour, union and Co-operative Movements, with working-class sanctions and Socialist collective security)[ix] although

---

[i] A. Bevan, *Labour Monthly*, Vol. 18, No. 6, June 1936.

[ii] H. Pelling, *The British Communist Party*, p.77.

[iii] *New Leader*, June 5th, 1936.

[iv] M. Cole, *Story of Fabian Socialism*, p.217.

[v] Editor, 'Matters of Moment', *Socialist*, No. 9, July–August 1936.

[vi] Cripps' letter, July 28th, 1936, Cripps Papers.

[vii] Dalton, op. cit., July 26th, 1936. A U.K. mass production of gas masks began on July 14, 1936.

[viii] July 1936, S.L. National Council consisted of W. Mellor (Chairman), B. Betts, C. Borrett, H. N. Brailsford, S. Cripps, Ruth Dodds, H. L. Elvin, R. George, R. Groves, Gwyn Hopkins, J. F. Horrabin, G. E. Humphreys, G. R. Mitchison, H. Palmer, Trevor Pugh, M. Waters, M. Wigglesworth, and L. A. Fenn (Treasurer).

[ix] W. Mellor, 'Here Is a Popular Front!', *Socialist*, July–August 1936.

no one had yet attempted to *define* a platform on which 'unity' could be realised. Cripps suggested a 'short programme of action', which represented the S.L.'s tentative steps to a United Front, under the guise of opposition to the Means Test and Unemployment Regulations; Brailsford was thinking in terms of a United Parties Popular Front and a defensive alliance of Britain, France and Russia (with smaller 'Left States') and a People's Front as a startling 'event' to interest the apathetic elector, win by-elections, and shake the Government with the stipulation for some measures of socialisation: 'Would you and/or the S.L. be bound to oppose it? Or is your mind also moving in the same direction?'[i] he asked Cripps. The latter was moving towards a restatement of Labour's principles. In *The Struggle for Peace* he returned to causes of war as inherent in a system based on economic competition;[ii] and supporters of a peace initiative with dictators failed to acknowledge the cardinal importance of economic power.[iii] Because he saw this simple conflict of Capitalist and Socialist interests, he believed it possible to combine all parties opposed (in general principles) to capitalist society; it would make the S.L. influential in the Labour Party or would break it. There was no middle path. '*United Front*' would carry inspiring associations of the French and Spanish Popular Fronts, and G. R. Strauss explained that the C.P., I.L.P. and S.L. should not regard a 'United Front' as a manoeuvre: 'It will be the mission of the United Front ... to transform the Left from a negative force into a positive one'.[iv]

While the I.L.P. rejected a Popular Front on the grounds of the ineffectiveness of the Labour Party to create working-class unity,[v] it did desire a 'Workers' Front'.[vi] C.P. member, W. Rust, noted the clash between Communists and the Labour Party and the 'complacency of Transport House' and was unsympathetic to H. Morrison's argument that a Labour/Communist alliance would lose millions of votes[vii]; 'a People's Front in Britain meant the banding together of all opponents of the National Government,[viii] espoused Rust. The struggle for unity, for reorganisation of the Labour Movement, became the central quest.[ix] R. P. Dutt (also for the C.P.) hoped every delegate to the Edinburgh Conference whould forget prejudices from past controversies, and support 'unity',[x] but the N.C.L. replied with *The British Labour Movement and Communism – an Exposure of Communist Manoeuvres*, a bitter attack against C.P. tactics; the Labour Executive distrusted the C.P., because it was a disruptive force and had abused the Labour Party as 'Social Fascists'.[xi]

---

[i] H. N. Brailsford, Letter to Cripps, July 31st, 1936, Cripps Papers.

[ii] Cripps, *The Struggle for Peace*, p.108.

[iii] Ibid., pp.114, 118–119.

[iv] G. R. Strauss, 'Problems of a Labour Policy', *Labour Monthly*, Vol. 18, No. 8, August 1936.

[v] *New Leader*, July 24th, 1936.

[vi] N.A.C. Circular, *Workers' Front*, July 1936.

[vii] *News Chronicle*, July 17th, 1936. A Popular Front in France from June 1936 brought major changes for workers: "For the first time in history an entire class has won improved conditions," claimed union leader Leon Jouhaux.

[viii] W. Rust, 'Problems of Labour Policy', *Labour Monthly*, Vol. 18, No. 8, August 1936.

[ix] Ibid.

[x] R. P. Dutt, 'To the Delegates of the L.P. Conference at Edinburgh', *Labour Monthly*, Vol. 18, No. 10, October 1936.

[xi] *Labour Party Annual Conference Report*, October 1936, p.297.

(D) Edinburgh Conference Decisions

Before the Edinburgh Conference, there had been some support in the S.L. for a Popular Front representing *all* parties and groups, such as the *Next Five Years' Group*, *the Councils of Action*, and the *League of Nations Union*. The majority of the S.L. endorsed C.P. affiliation to the Labour Party,[i] as F. Brockway (secretary of the I.L.P.) wrote to Cripps about a method of bringing about common action 'between all Socialists': 'We (in the I.L.P.) realise the difficulties of those who are in the Labour Party and certainly do not want to intensify them, but we feel that in this crisis we must somehow overcome all organisational differences'.[ii] Cripps agreed, but thought the S.L. could not commit itself until after the Edinburgh Conference.[iii] The S.L. drafted its resolution in support of the Spanish Republicans (which brought the C.P., I.L.P. and S.L. members onto the same platform). The Spanish Civil War had, as noted, stirred the conscience and quickened the political understanding of those hitherto not particularly interested in politics';[iv] to the S.L., C.P., and I.L.P. it now provided an opportunity to enhance the case for a '*United Front*' in opposition to the indecisive, compromised and delaying tactics of the Movement in the past. The S.L. position was now for Labour support for the Spanish Republicans in their 'class struggle', opposition to the Government's rearmament policy, and support for a United Front.[v]

The T.U.C. rejected unity links with the C.P. (which Citrine denounced as subsidised and directed from Moscow, insincere and dictatorial) while Labour could only tolerate 'increased armaments' as buttressing collective security (not as a game of alliances based on the balance of power).[vi] Cripps made the anti-rearmament case for the S.L., and queried who was to control British armaments and for what purpose: 'If once the workers get drawn into support of the rearmament and security measures of this Government, the Labour Movement as an effective opposition and fighting force is doomed'.[vii] If there was a war, 'workers would use it [like Russia in 1917?] for the purpose of revolution'. He supported every effort to prevent recruitment for the armed forces.[viii] (A subversive position.) The S.L. would not support a policy of putting armaments into the control of a Government implicated in the existing world crisis (that presumably ruled out all Governments, except one), or likely to use armaments, not against Fascist powers, but against the Soviet Union. (Here, the S.L. had again failed to discriminate between the British Government and Fascist powers.) Denying the Government armaments could solve nothing, and the N.E.C.'s resolution on the issue was adopted.[ix] Added to Conference decisions on non-intervention in Spain, defeat for the 'United Front', and for C.P. application for affiliation, the S.L.'s position

---

[i] Minutes of National Council Meeting, September 20th, 1936, R. Groves Papers.

[ii] F. Brockway to S. Cripps, September 23rd, 1936, Cripps Papers.

[iii] S. Cripps to F. Brockway, September 25th, 1936, Cripps Papers.

[iv] John Lewis, *The Left Book Club*, pp.34–35.

[v] S. Cripps, 'Unity Now for Action! (No Truce with Baldwin)', *Socialist*, No. 11, October 1936.

[vi] *Labour Party Annual Conference Report*, October 1936, p.193.

[vii] Cripps' speech at Leeds, October 1st, 1936, Cripps Papers and Cripps at Glasgow, October 4th, 1936, Cripps Papers.

[viii] Cripps in Glasgow, 'Forward' (used in L.P.'s 'Unity: True or Sham?'), October 3rd, 1936.

[ix] *Labour Party Annual Conference Report*, October 1936, p.207.

was precarious, but the *Unity Campaign* grew, in defiance of Conference decisions; the S.L. had nothing to lose – or so it seemed in October 1936. A draft resolution for the S.L. on the *Unity Campaign* was drawn up and Cripps was writing about the need to get 'a hot and strong movement going in the country to overcome the apathy': 'I am so heavily engaged in trying to do something to galvanise the Labour Party into activity on the international situation'.[i]

W. Mellor interpreted the Edinburgh Conference as one of uncertainty. On the issue of rearmament, not even the Party's N.E.C. knew whether the Government was receiving Labour support, because the decision had been transferred to the P.L.P. and Spanish Republican support was postponed: 'On the issues of working-class solidarity abroad in the fight against Fascism and War, and in the fight against British Imperialism at home, Labour must not be content to watch the National Government at work'.[ii] Hunger Marches and South Wales industrial struggles epitomised the practicability of unity; the C.P. concluded that Labour's decisions on Spain, 'arms' and 'unity' were subordination of the Movement to the Government:[iii] Laski drew the lesson as 'the need to redouble our efforts for unity'.[iv] But for Labour leaders, C.P. support would repel more than it would bring, the I.L.P. was negligible, and a Popular Front was unreliable: 'Whom is it to include? How is it to work? What, if it wins power, is it to do?'[v] Good questions. No definite answers.

To buttress opposition to Fascism, an East London Conference was organised by the S.L. on October 31st, 1936. Groves wrote for the S.L., *East End Crisis: Socialism, the Jews and Fascism*, in which he annotated low wages, sweat shops, poverty, bad housing in East London (caused, he claimed, by rival capitalist groups for markets, colonies and investment, keeping their own power and profit, restricting production, closing workshops and factories). He explained capitalists' divisive policies of setting Gentile against Jew, Catholic against Protestant, Labour against Communist, when those responsible for low wages and unemployment were not 'Jews' or Communists but financiers and employers who had closed down factories and concentrated production to increase their own profits: 'The common struggle of the world's workers against poverty and war is greater than the divisions and barriers of boundary, race and colour'.[vi] Fascist propaganda had been successful because of weaknesses in the Labour Movement, and this could only be altered by combined union, Co-operative, Labour and Left-wing campaigns against low wages, long hours, sweat shops, bad housing, the Means Test... Or a Unity Campaign?

The other event stimulating a united front was the unemployed *Hunger March* of November 1936. This achieved a *united platform* of the C.P., I.L.P., S.L., Co-operative Party, union and Labour members, *for the first time in the history of the Movement*, and proved Labour also required a united leadership. In its Annual Report for 1936 the

---

[i] S. Cripps to Mrs. P. F. Barrass, October 27th, 1936, Cripps Papers.

[ii] W. Mellor, 'Edinburgh Conference and After', *Socialist*, No. 12, November 1936.

[iii] R. P. Dutt, 'Notes of the Month: After Edinburgh', *Labour Monthly*, Vol. 18, No. 11, November 1936.

[iv] H. Laski, 'The Labour Party Conference at Edinburgh', ibid.

[v] H. Dalton, 'The Popular Front', *Political Quarterly*, October–December 1936.

[vi] R. Groves, *East End Crisis: Socialism, the Jews and Fascism*. The S.L. joined the East London Anti-Fascist Unity Committee. The idea of fighting anti-Semitism by opposing Fascism and defeating both by working towards a socialist society, removed the stigma of being preoccupied with self-defence, and allied Jewry to a seemingly progressive movement, advocating peace and social reforms. qu. G. C. Lebzelter, op. cit., 1978, pp.152,155.

London Trades Council observed the most significant feature of that March was support given *by people of all classes, creeds and politics,* an impetus to the Movement to seek ways and means of harnessing public opinion.[i] Just as the East End Conference was represented by numerous working-class organisations, United Front committees were created during the Hunger March, with members from all sections of the Movement. Party leaders had been compelled to accept the lead of the rank and file under the banner of the very United Front turned down at Edinburgh. Bevan believed: 'success such as the Hunger March has been able to achieve is evidence that given the right lead there is a real desire for struggle among the rank and file of all working-class parties'.[ii]

While Transport House was preoccupied with Party discipline, the S.L. looked to unofficial sources for encouragement. They required a channel of communication and inspiration to widen the appeal of the S.L.[iii] After Edinburgh, Cripps, Bevan, Mellor, Strauss and E. Wilkinson formed the editorial board of *Tribune* 'to advocate vigorous Socialism and active resistance to Fascism at home and abroad'.[iv] When *Tribune* began on January 1st, 1937, the question was how it would affect the paper's policy, now the S.L. had allied itself with the C.P. The initiative for the *Unity Campaign* came from the S.L.; it remained the conciliator between the C.P. and I.L.P. On November 7th and 8th, 1936 there was an S.L. National Council meeting which considered a United Front, but did not commit itself. On November 20th, there was an Emergency Executive Committee Meeting, because I.L.P. differences with the C.P. had arisen over the I.L.P. decision to criticise Russian foreign policy, but the following day a circular was issued to all S.L. National Council members stating the *Unity Campaign* was going ahead,[v] although a minority of S.L. leaders supported I.L.P. reservations about joining with the C.P.[vi]

Cripps' dissatisfaction with Labour's lack of objectives or strategy and its impotence in Parliament led him to this *Unity Campaign.*[vii] By November 17th, he acknowledged, 'I am all in favour of a United Front and against the People's Front';[viii] (This was when he unfortunately uttered that he did not think it would be disastrous for the British working class if Germany defeated Britain in a war, because it could create a revolutionary situation as in Russia in 1917).[ix] This was symptomatic of Cripps' thinking. The '*Unity Campaign*' was supposed to unify diverse elements on the Left, consolidate it organisationally and intellectually as a symbol of protest against Fascism, the Government, and dilatoriness of Labour leaders. Mellor exclaimed: '*Get Together, Comrades! Working-class Unity on Workers' Issues – Stop the Drift to a "National" Front'.*[x] On December 1st, Cripps maintained the struggle had to be in the Party, although: 'There

---

[i] Quoting A. Hutt, *Post-War History of the British Working Class,* October 1936, pp.282–83.

[ii] A. Bevan, 'Challenge of the Hunger March (Banners of the United Front Point Road to Victory)', *Socialist,* No. 12, November 1936.

[iii] H. N. Brailsford, 'Unity Can Only Come by Action. The Hunger March supplies the Perfect Model, What Next After Edinburgh?', *Labour Monthly,* Vol. 18, No. 12, December 1936.

[iv] Cripps' reply to letter, December 1st, 1936, Cripps Papers.

[v] Circular to all National Council of S.L. members, November 21st, 1936, Groves Papers.

[vi] Deborah Barker to R. Groves, November 24th, 1936, Groves Papers.

[vii] Obituary of S. Cripps, 'Selfless Devotion to Public Duty', *The Times,* April 22nd, 1952.

[viii] Cripps Papers, November 17th, 1936.

[ix] Cripps quoted in *Manchester Guardian,* November 16th, 1936. This statement has been analysed earlier in the book.

[x] W. Mellor, *Socialist,* No. 13, December 1936–January 1937.

may come a time when some other course will be rendered necessary'.[i] He believed failure of Labour to take the lead in militant opposition had led the rank and file to seek 'unity', with local Labour Parties and Trades Councils joining C.P. and I.L.P. members in committees against the Means Test and 'Fascist tendencies' in Government legislation.

The *'Unity Campaign'* faced major obstacles. The I.L.P. was keen to end its isolation but did not want too firm a commitment. Maxton and Brockway insisted the I.L.P. remain distinct, with its own newspaper, literature, and right to criticise any other section of the Movement *and* the Unity Campaign! On December 3rd, 1936, a private understanding between Brockway and Cripps was arrived at; the I.L.P. could publicly criticise Russian foreign policy but had to bring any issue before the *Unity Campaign* to discuss it, the S.L. playing the rôle of mediator.[ii] Compared with the rôle of 'prophet for Unity', Cripps found association with the S.L. an embarrassment, although this did not emerge at the December 3rd S.L. Executive Committee meeting, or in the December 7th circular from the S.L. National Council to all S.L. branches. Later, Brockway blamed the S.L.'s urgency to create a *United Front* for enabling the C.P. to smooth over differences with the I.L.P.! He also blamed Cripps, with justification, for lack of Socialist fundamentals or any awareness of policy differences between the P.O.U.M. and the C.P. in Spain. While the I.L.P. sought new organisational forms, the S.L. and C.P. concentrated on the Labour Party; while the I.L.P. hoped for a restricted programme, the C.P. submitted a full 'Popular Front' document. The I.L.P. was in a vulnerable position when it had been experimenting in tactics; one time approaching the Communist International, another moving to the Trotskyist position, attaching its hope to united fronts, reverting to purism, preparing for Soviets, then recognising the value of Parliament'...[iii] The I.L.P. had its contradictions, as did the S.L. and the C.P.!

S.L. leaders were at last aware they had more in common with the I.L.P. and C.P. than the Labour Party, to which they were affiliated. Ex-I.L.P. leader, Clifford Allen, envisaged an association in politics on the Left,[iv] and what he pronounced in 1934 in *Britain's Political Future* was now pertinent; manifestos could make it easier in all parties to speak with one voice on immediate policy: 'It is clear that many... wish to do so, but are naturally restrained by loyalty to party machinery.'[v] George Cadbury wrote to Cripps on the value of *Tribune*, whose theme would be *'Peace and Anti-Fascism'*,[vi] although Sidney Webb (who had written an article for the first issue) decided he should withdraw it since it had not anticipated a Unity Campaign![vii] Cripps reiterated the S.L.'s faith in unity to be accomplished within the Labour Movement, the Labour Party the only effective political instrument, unions the only effective industrial movement in their struggle for economic freedom and against War and Fascism,[viii] yet the S.L. maintained a United Front *could* be the only way to ensure a Socialist victory in Parliamentary elections, through an immediate anti-Fascist crusade.

---

[i] Cripps reply to letter, December 1st, 1936, Cripps Papers.

[ii] December 3rd, 1936, Groves Papers.

[iii] F. Brockway, *Inside the Left*, p.237.

[iv] Memorandum in Allen Papers, December 15th, 1936.

[v] Quoting A. Marwick, *Clifford Allen – The Open Conspirator*, p.129.

[vi] G. Cadbury to S. Cripps, December 18th, 1936, Cripps Papers.

[vii] S. Webb to Cripps, December 22nd, 1936 and S. Webb to W. Mellor, December 26th, 1936, Cripps Papers.

[viii] Cripps at Bristol Meeting, December 21st, 1936, Cripps Papers.

Writing in the *Political Quarterly*, G. D. H. Cole considered it to be poor Labour tactics to follow a process of *gradual persuasion* in a world of arming Fascist nations: 'The reason for desiring a People's Front in Great Britain is to be found abroad, and not mainly at home'.[i] This Front could prevent war through supporting creation of a 'Left' bloc and a triple pact between Britain, France and Russia. Domestically, the Popular Front policy could include improved treatment for the unemployed, regional economic planning (in depressed areas), public control of new industrial enterprises, public works (to increase economic activity), a minimum wage, revision of the *Sedition Act*, repeal of the *Trade Disputes Act*.[ii] What emerged was that it was *organisational* rather than purely *political* considerations which divided the C.P. from other Labour groups, because the C.P. also knew the People's Front could only be effective *within* the Labour Movement.[iii]

All three groups in the *Unity Campaign* believed it would reinvigorate their own organisation. The S.L. majority hoped it could be used in S.L. conflicts with the Party's N.E.C., as a struggle for 'freedom of action for the rank and file' to participate in political activities, without prior approval of the N.E.C. Unfortunately, the *Unity Campaign* lasted too short a time for the S.L.'s challenge to become effective. Since the S.L. was internally divided over the Campaign, it could only perform the balancing act between demands made by the I.L.P. and the C.P. This was not a strong bargaining position, but in December 1936 this seemed of minor importance compared with the constructive aspects involved. To the S.L., a radical campaign could reveal more than anything else the failure of the existing political structures to represent the political needs of a supposedly democratic society. Like later campaigns which focussed on a single issue (colonial freedom, racial equality, nuclear disarmament, up to mass opposition to the war in Iraq in 2003) the S.L.'s unity campaign against War and Fascism could possibly create a *political consciousness* which would make the official Party programmes appear limited and out of touch with the conscience of the Labour Movement. Although, as Eric Hobsbawm assesses:

> In the 1930s we on the Left were campaigning against Fascism, and I remember being convinced we were mobilising the people against war. But, with the benefit of historical perspective, I can see we were a total failure, merely rallying people already sympathetic to our cause[iv]

Nevertheless Fascism was defeated – and the S.L. played a part in that struggle. It was 'crackpot realism' to ascribe to the assertion that war rather than peace was the natural character of humans, that national paranoia, suspicion and ill will were permanent and unalterable characteristics of society, that it was simpler and 'more realistic' to prepare for war than prepare for peace, that military solutions were the simplest, or that it was "hardheaded business realism to profit in the manufacture of the means of violence".[v]

---

[i] G. D. H. Cole, 'A British People's Front', *Political Quarterly*, October–December 1936.

[ii] Ibid.

[iii] H. Pollitt, *Communist International*, November 1936.

[iv] E. Hobsbawm, qu. in D. Snowman, *The Hitler Emigrés: the Cultural Impact on Britain for Refugees from Nazism*, 2002, p.328.

[v] C. Wright Mills, qu. Greg Dening, *Readings/Writings*, 1998, p.193.

Chapter Twelve

The Socialist League and the Unity Campaign (1937)

The need for absolute goodies and absolute baddies runs deep in us but it drags history into propaganda and denies the humanity of the dead: their sins, their virtues, their efforts, their failures to preserve complexity, and not flatten it under the weight of anachronistic moralizing, is part of the historian's task.

> Robert Hughes, *Culture of Complaint: The Fraying of America*, 1999 edn., pp.103–104

In their pursuit of political correctness the party leadership not only sacrificed much of their own credibility but sapped the raison d'être of the party itself. For dissent is as much the legacy as the life force of socialism, and unless it acknowledges the right to challenge received opinions as well as to advance alternative strategies, Labour is in danger of losing both its character and its ideological dynamism... Both realism and dissent are the prerequisites of an effective Labour Party.

> David Powell, *What's Left? Labour Britain and the Socialist Tradition*, 1998, p.13

Spalding: The capitalist economic system is cracking, though it won't go to pieces until it's pushed. There have been cyclical crises ever since early in the last century, but now after the '14 to '18 Imperialist war we've reached the general crisis from which capitalism will never recover... The ruling class naturally tries to solve its problems by directing its main attack against those whom it thinks least able to defend themselves – the unemployed.

> Edward Upward, *The Thirties*, 1969 edn., p.46

Moves towards a *United Front* gave a positive energy to Left-wing groups. Carpe diem! Instead of internal squabbling, they were not only attacking social inequality but challenging the conduct of the Government. *Tribune* was founded to represent a broader viewpoint (not served by S.L. journals) with W. Mellor its first editor, and Cripps, Bevan, Laski, E. Wilkinson and Strauss on board;[i] it was 'a paper of Unity, of the Class Struggle; a paper for all who fight Fascism and war'.[ii] Cripps and Strauss supplied most of the capital (£20,000), a fact used by Labour's N.E.C. to disparage the *Unity Campaign*, but S.L. influences continued in *Tribune*, where its views were propagated by ex-S.L. members after May 1937 (when the S.L. was dissolved). In charming editorial fashion Cripps wrote to Mellor after the first issue: 'I must congratulate you upon a very first-rate production... my main criticism would be of the comparative weakness of the non-political part of the paper... The next thing we

---

[i] Co-opted onto the Board were H. N. Brailsford, Ben Greene, James Griffiths and G. R. Mitchison.
[ii] *Tribune*, first edition and publicity advertisement, January 1st, 1937.

must tackle is circulation in selected areas'.[i]

In this first *Tribune*, Cripps himself assessed "weak Labour leadership", and confusion and apathy in the rank and file: 'The Edinburgh Conference had led to a great deal of heart-searching in our ranks',[ii] to the point of searching for outside affiliations! He recognised the crucial part played by C.P. and I.L.P. members in working-class activities, and the need for self-belief in the Labour Party. He sought mobilisation of opposition to the Government through unity and Mellor wrote of the first step to Socialism as a united Movement, the spirit in the 1920 Councils of Action, the General Strike and Hunger Marches. Defeat of the General Strike, the *Trade Disputes Act*, the 1936 *Public Order Act*, these were caused by divisions in the Movement: 'No Government would have dared to impose a Means Test upon a *united working class*. No Government would have allowed the distressed areas to stagnate if a united working class had willed it otherwise'.[iii] The struggle had to be extended *beyond Parliament*, if the deadlock (in which the S.L. found itself) was to be broken. To be achieved was the autonomy of a political campaign, rousing public opinion against the Government's foreign policy, however anathema this protest might appear to Labour leaders. A *United Front* would bring enthusiasm, devotion and also political education into the centre of political struggle.

The *Unity Campaign* could satisfy that urge to belong, the need to act, which the S.L. felt was in the heart of every class-conscious worker. Equipped with *Tribune* and the Left Book Club, (which was itself becoming a political 'movement', with its Left Book News, discussion groups, centres of propaganda rallies and speaking tours for unity), a gap was filled.[iv] The *Unity Campaign* was not only to express opposition to Government policies and draw attention to the implications of Fascism; it was to agitate *in* the Labour Movement since the S.L. believed the Party was not near winning a Parliamentary majority. Even G. D. H. Cole, who had left the S.L., insisted the way to get a United Front meant '*confronting the official Labour Party with a movement in the country too powerful and spirited for them to resist … we must go on demanding the United Front but let us set to work to build up the People's Front*'.[v]

There was an enduring sense, even in atrophied form, of being a distinct community which appealed in the creation of the United Front, a most ambitious attempt to unite pressure in and outside the Labour Party. *Unity Campaign* supporters saw themselves as champions against union bureaucracy, as the S.L. queried *why* Citrine was on the same platform with Churchill at the Albert Hall on December 3rd: 'Why do you seek your allies with the Churchills and not with the Pollitts and Maxtons?'[vi] (Within three years Citrine would have a perfect answer!) Joint meetings with the C.P. were a challenge flung by the S.L. at Party leaders, and heightened dissatisfaction of a substantial part of the Party with union domination. The *Unity Manifesto* marked the closest contact up to 1937 between the C.P. and any substantial section of the Labour Movement: 'The time is never more opportune than now for building effective unity within the framework of the Labour Party… All of us must be

[i] Cripps to Mellor, January 2nd, 1937, Cripps Papers, Mellor Papers.

[ii] Cripps, 'Unity – the Power Way', *Tribune*, January 1st, 1937.

[iii] W. Mellor, 'What We Stand For in the Struggle for Socialism', *Tribune*, January 1st, 1937. (My italics.)

[iv] *Tribune*, January 15th, 1937: 'In the 300 Left Book Clubs every kind of person who hates Fascism and War – Socialists, Liberals, Communists, I.L.P. members, Progressives – meet and hammer out their differences.'

[v] G. D. H. Cole, 'The United Front and the People's Front', *Labour Monthly*, Vol. 19, No. 1, January 1937.

[vi] 'We Ask Sir Walter Citrine', *Tribune*, January 1st, 1937.

prepared to reconsider our tactics and strategy in this dangerous world position', announced *Tribune*.[i]

The action of the S.L. was symptomatic of the temper of active Party workers who held that any campaign which sought to rescue the Movement from 'impotence or defections' needed unity as its centre. Dalton (for the Party Executive) was prompted to refer to the 'windy verbiage' of the United Front.[ii]) At the inaugural meeting of the Bristol Committee for the *Unity Campaign*, the object was stated to be revitalisation of the working-class movement, an end to apathy and defeatism, unity of all sections of the working-class movement in the struggle against Fascism, Reaction and War.[iii] However, on January 12th, 1937, the Party's N.E.C. circularised affiliated organisations to refrain from any co-operation with the United Front,[iv] and used danger of alliance with 'non-Socialists' as its principal objection rather than pre-1936 arguments about an 'undemocratic C.P. philosophy'. The N.E.C. was aware of preparations for the Campaign, had issued its *'Appeal for Party Loyalty'*, in which united action with the C.P. was incompatible with Labour membership, and, as for the I.L.P., individual members were invited to apply for re-admission to the Labour Party if they wished to work in the Movement! The N.E.C. based its decision on a Party that was *the most democratic party in British politics* and the only effective force whereby 'Socialism' could be achieved. Despite a desire to secure 'unity within the Labour Party', the C.P., I.L.P. and S.L., were misrepresented, with the N.E.C. quoting the 'overwhelming majorities' against the United Front at Edinburgh, concealing that the minority had substantially increased for 'unity' since then.

The argument that unity with Communists would alienate 'millions of middle-class people' and create internal dissensions, had been constantly levelled at the S.L.;[v] as Sidney Webb insisted, the Labour Party had to avoid anything that militated against unionists or Co-operative Party members; the Party would not allow 'orders from Moscow'; Webb could justify a Popular Front, if it increased numbers at demonstrations, but regarded it as unsuited to British political conditions at Election time.[vi] To the S.L. the mere whisper of 'unity in action' was met by threats of discipline,[vii] but this did not influence S.L. leaders: 'This spirit is gathering strength and momentum among Labour's rank and file and it is hoped that the decisions of the S.L. will give it voice'.[viii]

On January 13th, 1937, National Council S.L. member, Reg Groves, sent a confidential circular to branch secretaries, asking about consequences for the S.L. of a *Unity Campaign*. This circular was passed on, by G. Allighan, to the Political Correspondent of the *Daily Herald,* and printed! The circular stated the S.L. National Council was *not* unanimously in support of the *Unity Campaign*; the S.L. had not met since November 7th, 1936, and had only considered a preliminary draft to which Council members had several objections. Even the S.L. Executive had not met to

---

[i] 'Unity in Britain', *Tribune*, June 8th, 1937.

[ii] A. Hutt, *Postwar History of the British Working Class*, p.303.

[iii] January 9th, 1937, for the inaugural meeting of February 13th with Cripps, Maxton and Pollitt as speakers, Cripps Papers.

[iv] *Labour Party Annual Conference Report*, October 1937, p.26.

[v] J. Morris, 'Unity and the Middle Class', *Tribune*, January 15th.

[vi] S. Webb, 'Unity: Labour's Future, the Popular Front, and the Communists', *Tribune*, January 15th.

[vii] 'United Front – Labour Executive's Warning', *Daily Herald*, January 15th.

[viii] S.L. Statement, 'Our Unity', *Tribune*, January 15th.

discuss the resolution which had been issued to branches for the S.L. Conference on January 16th–17th. Groves continued: 'The consequences of agreement for united action on the lines of the document have not been discussed by the S.L. National Council, and it has never considered the possibility of the S.L.'s dissolution in the event of Transport House action, although certain members of the Executive Committee visualise such a situation. No decision on the future of the S.L. has been taken. The Conference is to be confronted with an accomplished fact'.[i] The Unity document, signed by S.L. representatives and public members of the Unity Campaign, showed contempt for S.L. members: 'I am confident that the National Council as a whole would never have agreed to such procedure' (to which statement Cripps wrote 'quite false' on his own copy).[ii] Groves believed a straight choice of an 'accept' or 'reject' document made it impossible for the Conference to come to a decision which would allow forms of united action without destroying the S.L.: 'I hope the Conference will not allow itself to be hustled into decisions without insisting on full opportunity to formulate the kind of policy which will preserve and strengthen the Socialist League'.[iii]

(A) The S.L. Special Conference (January, 1937)

The Special S.L. Delegate Conference in London on January 16th and 17th, met to discuss S.L. participation in the *Unity Campaign* (on the basis of agreement with the Unity Committee). The lengths to which S.L. negotiators had gone to secure agreement caused disruptions; some S.L. leaders shared with the Party N.E.C. suspicions about co-operating with the C.P., although the main issue was the future of the S.L., and possibility of sacrificing its position in the Labour Party, rather than with ideological implications of working with C.P. members. The S.L. did not endorse participation without a serious internal conflict, and a substantial secession from the organisation once a vote had been taken. What emerged was a long-term puzzle: '*Socialist Leaguers worried about Communist Party aims to destroy the Socialist League as a competitor*'.[iv] However, the persistence and persuasion of Cripps, Mellor and Bevan pushed the project forward under the guise of a campaign to revitalise and transform the Movement by seeking unity within the framework of the Labour Party.

56 S.L. leaders voted for the *Unity Campaign*; 38 opposed, 23 abstained. There should have been another Conference and more time to consider the implications, but the opposition did not capitalise on the fact that less than 50% of the S.L. leadership had voted in favour of the *Unity Campaign*. The opposition should have pressed the point that the S.L. could continue on the basis of *individual affiliation*, thus dissociating the organisation from the *Unity Campaign*. The S.L. had joined the Campaign only at the expense of losing a proportion of its membership which would not tread this path. In fact, the *Unity Campaign* was born at this Conference. With Cripps in the chair, the purpose was to urge C.P., I.L.P. and Labour Party to co-operate, and not that the three

---

[i] R. Groves, circular to branch secretaries, January 13th, 1937.

[ii] R. Groves, ibid., Cripps' copy, Cripps Papers.

[iii] Ibid.

[iv] M. Foot, *A. Bevan*, p.244.

Hitler

ANVIL WEDDINGS ARE MORE ROMANTIC

January 25, 1937

Nazi economic plans were announced which made it clear to all that the parties in Europe were at cross purposes – that while the economics of the democracies aimed at peace, those of Hitler aimed at war.

Eden   Blum   Delbos

"STICK TO IT, LADS! WE'VE NEARLY GOT ONE FOOT IN!"

February 3, 1937

Hitler from time to time made nebulous "peace efforts" but efforts to bring him down to detail were invariably futile.

Eden Blum   Hitler   Litvinov

THERE'S ANOTHER SIDE TO IT

March 15, 1937

Hitler made a "gesture" to Britain and France jointly: if France would cancel her pact with Soviet Russia, he would guarantee to keep peace in the West. He would give no undertaking concerning the East.

THE CONFERENCE EXCUSES ITSELF

May 23, 1937

Circumstances became too much for the Disarmament Conference which had come down to arguing about the number of bolts and nuts on a tank. It adjourned.

parties should affiliate, only that they would form a loose alliance and cease attacking one another.

On January 18th the National Unity Campaign Committee (N.U.C.C.) published its pamphlet, *The Unity Campaign*, by Cripps, Maxton and Pollitt. The Campaign was presented for strengthening the Labour Party and unions in the class struggle, and mobilising workers for action against the Government, Fascism and War. Cripps claimed the demonstration at the Free Trade Hall, Manchester, had shown determination to defeat the Government; unity within the Movement was precursor to winning political power: 'If ever the Labour Party is to become more than a tolerated reformist party within a capitalist democracy, we must concentrate within it every available element of working-class political activity'.[i] He predicated this on relinquishing theoretical differences for immediate practical objectives; since 1931 the Movement had failed to galvanise workers; the Party was just an opposition; Maxton claimed the S.L., C.P., and I.L.P. had played an energetic part in 'building the working class', now they had to work against the largest armaments race in history. He anticipated reprisals: 'There will be strenuous efforts to discredit Cripps, to depreciate his undoubted capacity and his unquestionable character'.[ii] H. Pollitt deduced that the *Unity Campaign* had been formed because of the Fascist offensive, and confusions in the Labour Party: 'the Campaign is not in any way directed *against* the Labour Party',[iii] but was to infuse a spirit of urgency and he urged unions to support this: 'Unity in Britain… strikes the heaviest blow against Hitler, Mussolini and Baldwin… Tonight opens the mightiest campaign for splendid unification the Labour Movement of Britain has ever seen'.[iv] (Not difficult, if one analysed the previous 37 years.)

The *Unity Manifesto* embodied the decisions of the Unity Committee. It was the first and last product of representatives of the British Left, the most ambitious bid made to end the rigidities of Party alignments,[v] until the S.D.P. in the 1980s. The *Unity Manifesto* differed from Labour in its accent against Imperialism in India and the Colonies, insistence on not waiting for a General Election but embarking (by means of a pact with France and the Soviet Union) for the defence of Peace; it advocated democratisation of the Labour and union Movement; repudiated class collaboration, labelled the Government the 'agent of British Capitalism and Imperialism' (no surprise there) and recorded its opposition to rearmament. It encouraged demonstrations for abolition of the Means Test, upheld national work of social value for the Distressed Areas, the 40-hour week, union action for higher wages, nationalisation of key industries, control of banks and stock markets, and 'to make the rich pay for social amelioration',[vi] all signed by Cripps, Mellor, G. R. Mitchison, J. F. Horrabin, H. N. Brailsford and A. Bevan, for the S.L.[vii]

This *Manifesto* was a hotchpotch, and in stressing 'the defence of the Soviet Union', the C.P. was using the United Front for its own aims.[viii] The alliance was uneasy from

---

[i] Cripps, 'Define the Campaign's One Purpose', *The Unity Campaign* pamphlet, January 18th, 1937.

[ii] J. Maxton, 'Cell for Democracy and Struggle', ibid., January 18th, 1937.

[iii] Pollitt, 'Raises Standard of United Advance', ibid.

[iv] Ibid., Free Trade Hall Meeting, January 24th, 1937.

[v] M. Foot, op. cit., p. 243.

[vi] *Unity Manifesto*, January 18th, 1937 (published in *Tribune*, January 22nd, 1937).

[vii] It was also signed by H. Pollitt, W. Gallacher, R. Palme Dutt, A. Horner, J. Tanner, T. Mann, J. Strachey, F. Brockway, F. Jowett, J. Maxton and H. Laski.

[viii] M. M. Krug, *A. Bevan: Cautious Rebel*, 1961, New York, p.52.

the beginning because of disagreements over the nature and extent of the United Front. As the C.P. developed moderate tactics, it yielded its position on the extreme Left to the more uncompromising I.L.P., as differences of principle (arising from policies of the Soviet Union) made the I.L.P. and C.P. rivals. The C.P. aspired to Labour affiliation without conditions; the I.L.P. was not prepared to enter the Labour Party except to advocate 'a revolutionary socialist programme'.[i] (It also had reservations about the *Unity Manifesto*, which included refusal to consider affiliation to the Labour Party until its Constitution had been democratised, and opposition to any reliance on the League of Nations and Soviet policy on this). For the *Unity Campaign*, its prospects of a calm voyage were nil. Two of the three sponsors were opposed to each other's policy[ii] from the outset.

For Cripps, this could be his prophetic mission as he presided over Unity discussions: 'He had the earnestness of a crusader, and when deadlocks between the I.L.P. and C.P. threatened to bring all his efforts to nought, he refused to give up until his purpose was achieved'.[iii] Cripps' efforts were aided by his disinterest in any ideological disputes compared to his appeal to Christian Socialist values and fundamental liberties (a refreshing alternative from the conflicts of political theory and sectionalism in the I.L.P. and C.P.). He suffused the whole enterprise with his own optimism, and had become the symbol of the Left. He wrote to Professor Bryn Jones on January 19th 1937: 'The Labour Party is not taking a vigorous lead ... we have been compelled to try to stimulate its socialist outlook by forming a United Front ... which may temporarily have the effect of putting me outside the Labour Party, but we shall not do anything to set up any alternative party or to weaken the Labour Movement'.[iv] To work within the Movement remained the object of the *Unity Campaign* and Cripps' conviction.

J. T. Murphy had a particular grievance against the *Unity Campaign*; it diverted all 'Left-wing' forces from his People's Front Propaganda Committee.[v] Meanwhile, the *Daily Herald* began a 'Cripps Must Go' campaign on January 19th, and a circular on Campaign decisions was sent by the S.L. to all its branches. Although the Unity Agreement had stated the three groups would not attack each other or its personnel, Groves had already been vilified in the *Daily Worker* for his circular. On January 5th, he had sent letters to the S.L.'s Executive on the Campaign and C.P. attacks on P.O.U.M. in Spain. On January 20th the *Daily Worker* stigmatised him: 'Attack on Unity by Trotskyist'. He wrote a reply which was partially published, to which the *Daily Worker* retorted in 'A Denial and a Reply'.[vi] The attack on this S.L. National Council member was made because he had supposedly given information to the *Daily Herald*, (which he denied). Whatever the truth, Cripps' reaction was unusual. He stated the S.L. National Council had already expressed its views 'as regards the very undesirable and unauthorised action taken by Comrade Groves', and added: 'Groves only has his own actions to blame for what has occurred and I hope that now we shall all go forward working on the *Unity Campaign*'.[vii] The unconscious irony of this would have not gone

---

[i] F. Brockway, op. cit., p.267.

[ii] R. E. Dowse, 'Left in the Centre', op. cit., p.198.

[iii] F. Brockway, op. cit., p.264.

[iv] Cripps to Professor B. Jones, January 19th, 1937, Cripps Papers.

[v] J. T. Murphy, *New Horizons*, p.319.

[vi] *Daily Worker*, January 23rd, 1937.

[vii] Cripps' letter, January 27th, 1937, Cripps Papers.

unnoticed by I.L.P. leaders in the process of exposing C.P. activities against the P.O.U.M. in Spain.

Lord Passfield (S. Webb) wrote to Lord Parmoor (Cripps' father) to say how perturbed he was by Cripps' action in defiance of Labour's ruling: 'Alliance with the C.P. [can only] lessen the S.L.'s effect on a hostile Cabinet or on employers or other classes prejudiced against Communism as being unChristian.'[i] Labour leaders were alleging the *Unity Campaign* was a 'Communist trick' to capture the Movement. What irked them more was the growing popularity of the *Campaign*, the *Left Book Club*, and *Tribune*, which might result in more vigorous elements in the Labour Party challenging control of the Party machine: 'Not only had the S.L. started the *Unity Campaign* ... it was an organisational link through which the local Labour Parties could take joint action'.[ii] **Cripps, Maxton and Pollitt** provided an unrivalled attraction to politically-minded audiences and after the January 24th Free Trade Hall, Manchester opening of the Campaign, demonstrations with leading S.L., I.L.P. and C.P. speakers took place throughout Britain. Cripps stated the *Campaign* was for everyone who recognised the class bases of existing divisions in society, but he knew the N.E.C.'s position: 'As the Labour Party leadership moves more and more in the direction of class collaboration over the rearmament programme, so the tendency to ban association with socialist or communist bodies will strengthen'.[iii] The Party was accused of 'bureaucratic formalism',[iv] but Pollitt for the C.P. reassured Labour leaders that the Campaign was not directed against the Labour Party, and Maxton for the I.L.P. believed the agreement 'ought to mark a *turning-point in the political history of Britain*'.[v] How many of those have there been?

On January 22nd, 1937 it came to pass. The *Daily Herald* carried the headline *'The S.L. To Be Disaffiliated Next Week?'*, while P. Gordon Walker wrote to Cripps expressing sympathy with his efforts to revitalise the Labour Party, and unite the Left, concentrate attention on Spain and the armaments issue: 'but I do not wish to go out of the Party, nor to become divorced or isolated from it... it might happen if the National Council of Labour banned as well as disaffiliated the Socialist League'.[vi] At the same time as the Manchester Free Trade Hall Conference Campaign meeting (which Cripps regarded as *'the most remarkable experience of my short political career'*[vii]), the *Daily Herald* rebuked the S.L. for its breach of the anti-*United Front* resolution passed at Edinburgh. (Dalton thought Cripps was interfering with the Executive's steadily constructive work.[viii]) In fact, Cripps was only nominally connected; control of the Campaign was passing out of S.L. hands. All that had been important was the formal agreement with S.L. signatories to give the Campaign a closer connection with the Labour Party. The S.L. was a pawn in a larger political game, its function submerged by the time of the Party's pronouncements on January 27th.

As a theme in the S.L.'s history, the result of this Campaign was to reopen old divisions. Banishing Cripps and the S.L. would lose some of the younger generation

---

[i] Quoting E. Estorick, op. cit., pp.155–56.

[ii] P. Strauss, op. cit., p.93.

[iii] S. Cripps, 'Unite Now in Class Struggle – Rank and File Eager for Action', *Tribune*, January 22nd, 1937.

[iv] Ibid.

[v] H. Pollitt and J. Maxton, 'Worthy of Supreme Effort', *Tribune*, January 22nd.

[vi] P. Gordon-Walker to S. Cripps, January 23rd, 1937, Cripps Papers.

[vii] Quoting M. Foot, op. cit., p.246, from *Tribune*, January 29th, 1937.

[viii] 'United Front Parties Challenged', *Daily Herald*, January 25th, 1937.

and some of the most enthusiastic workers in the Labour Party, but Bevin thought S.L. activities since its inception justified the Executive's warnings: 'You talk about driving Cripps out. He is driving himself out. The Annual Conference came to certain decisions'.[i] Bevin was convinced the Communists were out to destroy unions. As for the *Unity Campaign*: 'We shall have the storm, the large meetings, the enthusiasm and the cheering, and then just as in the case of Abyssinia, Germany, Spain and all the other big problems, it will be the trade unions who will have to do the practical work'.[ii] He did not say what 'practical work' unions had achieved hitherto on these issues.

On January 27th the Executive sent a circular to Labour branches disaffiliating the S.L.: 'The N.E.C. regrets that the S.L. has taken action which its National Council must have known would be contrary to the cause of unity in the ranks of Labour, and would render the S.L. ineligible for continued affiliation to the Labour Party. The N.E.C. resolves that the S.L., having acted at a Special Conference (January 16th–17th) on the recommendations of its National Council in defiance of the Labour Party Conference decisions, be disaffiliated from the Labour Party, nationally and locally'.[iii] The Party N.E.C. prompted the S.L. to work for Socialism through the Labour Party, while the N.E.C. denounced the *Unity Campaign* in a document: *The Labour Party and the So-called Unity Campaign*.[iv] The S.L. had been brought to book for its defiance of an N.E.C statement, but Bevin unfairly compared the *Unity Campaign*'s ringleaders with MacDonald, Snowden and Thomas![v] Labour leaders had always regarded the Campaign as Communist-inspired and the personal machine of a few wealthy men (G. R. Strauss, J. Strachey, S. Cripps, and V. Gollancz), and the *real United Front* was in the Labour, union and Co-operative Movements.[vi] For flouting its Conference decisions, the Labour Executive broke the S.L. on the Party Constitution, voting 23 against 9 for S.L. disaffiliation.

S.L. leaders protested that the S.L. National Council decision on the Campaign had been inspired by unity in the ranks of Labour. Had not the Labour Party's rules been broken over Spain, the Means Test, Rearmament and Peace?: 'The S.L.'s purpose has been and remains, the strengthening and revitalising of the Labour Party and Labour Movement. *The Unity Campaign is no campaign of disruption: it is a campaign of healing, of comradeship. It has opened the way to building a Labour Party, all-embracing, democratic in its workings, bold in its policy, courageous in action*'.[vii] The S.L. would work for the Party regardless of its disaffiliation and hoped there would be no heresy-hunting. (One of the weakest aspects of the *Unity Campaign* had been its inconsistency between demand for armed intervention in Spain, yet active resistance to Fascist expansion[viii] *and* adherence to outdated pacifist slogans). The Labour Party had offered the S.L. a choice – remaining effective in the Labour Party or being swallowed up in the *Unity Campaign*.[ix] The C.P.'s *Daily Worker* expressed 'shock' at the intolerance of Labour's

[i] G. D. H. Cole letter from E. Bevin, January 25th, 1937, quoted by A. Bullock, op. cit., p.596.
[ii] Ibid.
[iii] *Labour Party Annual Conference Report*, October 1937, p.27.
[iv] *Labour Party Annual Conference Report*, ibid, pp.268–270.
[v] Bevin at Bristol, 'Cripps' Tactic an Echo of Mosley's', *Daily Herald*, February 13th, 1937.
[vi] C. R. Attlee, 'A Call for Real Unity', *Daily Herald*, January 30th, 1937.
[vii] 'On Discipline: L.P. Executive Attitude to Unity', *Tribune*, January 29th, 1937.
[viii] 'National Unity Campaign Committee' decision at Manchester, January 24th, 1937.
[ix] 'The Choice Is Theirs', *Daily Herald*, January 28th, 1937.

Executive,[i] while S.L. National Council member, R. Dodds, wrote to Cripps: 'I am anxious that we maintain our *Unity Campaign* on a basis of advocating unity within the Labour Movement, and that we shall not be side-tracked by disaffiliation into more denunciation of the National Executive … This is not a United Front but a United Campaign'.[ii] G. D. H. Cole dedicated his book *The People's Front* to Cripps, stating that faction-fighting weakened the struggle for Socialism, strengthened Fascist influences, and entrenched the Government; if Britain was to be for a democratic defence against Fascism and war, the Left had to have a victory in British politics, which could not be achieved without unity: *'Transport House is afraid of struggling too hard for Socialism lest it provoke the reactionaries to hit back'*.[iii]

Mellor's message to the Labour Party was to offer the S.L. to heal the Movement and end infighting (armaments for the Spanish Republicans, action for the unemployed, trade unionism fighting the class struggle?): 'We are loyal to the spirit and declared purpose of the Labour Party; we challenge the bureaucracy which seeks to drive the Party into the paths of class collaboration and national unity'.[iv] S.L. members were asked to resist efforts by Transport House to destroy the *Unity Campaign*, but what could they do? Sir C. Trevelyan claimed that in Cripps' activity lay the hope of the Movement, but he himself thought the Campaign and Manifesto had been strategic mistakes.[v] By February 5th, 5,000 signed peace pledge cards for unity had been gathered from seven *Unity Campaign* meetings; Lansbury appealed for tolerance for the S.L. (and loyalty by the S.L.) and could find 'no reason for driving members of the S.L. out of the Labour Party … Our Movement cannot afford to become a party of "yes men"'.[vi] *Tribune* editors asked Arthur Greenwood (President of the University Labour Federation) whether he was aware that the U.L.F. contained C.P. members, and if he was aware when he castigated the S.L. in the *Unity Campaign*, while Laski could not see why a United Front (which had saved France and was saving Spain) was such a danger to the Labour Party: 'Is it heresy in the Labour Party to believe in the class war? … As principles, *the Unity Manifesto statements are an integral part of the Socialist faith* … The N.E.C. denounces as disloyalty a passionate faith in socialism, a zeal for ending the differences that, in the past 12 years, have done the working class so grave an injury.'[vii] Labour's N.E.C. was unmoved.

Controversy between the S.L. and the Party Executive was over rights of a minority to carry on propaganda to persuade the Party to change its views *after* official policy had been laid down at the Party's Conference. The issue was complicated by controversy between unions and Divisional Labour Parties as to *their* relative importance in the Labour Party and the justifiability of the block vote. Labour's N.E.C. ruled it was undesirable for *minorities* in the Party to pursue meetings in favour of policies opposed to majority decisions, if non-Labour people were involved. The controversy led to the adoption by the Party of a doctrinaire discipline, curbing new ideas and new policies. The exasperation of Left-wing members was elucidated: 'Labour leaders had never led

---

[i] 'Labour Expels S.L.', *Daily Worker*, January 28th, 1937.

[ii] R. Dodds to S. Cripps, January 28th, 1937, Cripps Papers.

[iii] G. D. H. Cole, *The People's Front*, p.7.

[iv] W. Mellor, 'Our Message to L.P. Members', *Socialist Broadsheet*, No. 1, February 1937.

[v] Sir C. Trevelyan to S. Cripps, February 3rd, 1937, Cripps Papers.

[vi] G. Lansbury, 'Tolerance and Loyalty: 'Let Left and Right Wings Unite for Socialism', *Tribune*, February 5th, 1937.

[vii] H. Laski, *What Is This Crime of Unity?*, *Tribune*, February 5th, 1937.

a single mass campaign … had behaved at every critical moment of those tragic years like spinsters terrified lest their skirts should brush against a Red, [revealing analogy for a lawyer] and spent their time and energy … in a virulent witch-hunt against those within their own ranks who dared to suggest a policy of combined sanity to save the world from war'.[i] Cripps was quoted as saying 'reactionaries' in the Movement were preventing Socialists from joining: 'J. Maxton and H. Pollitt should be the leaders in the Labour Movement today',[ii] Cripps averred! He complained that the University Labour Federation had a 'United Front' with many Communists and was permitted to remain an affiliated organisation, but J. Middleton (Party Secretary) replied that the 'Appeal for Loyalty' was issued and addressed to all sections of the Labour Party.[iii] However, because local constituency parties were not mobilised in the Party, the *Unity Campaign* gained much of its support from these members.

Tribune denounced the sectarian policy of the N.E.C.; when thousands of Socialists were laying down their lives for the cause in Spain, the Labour hierarchy was mounting a heresy-hunt against *Unity Campaign* supporters: 'Those in the Labour Party who do not want a United Front will soon be reduced to an army of generals deserted by the rank and file'.[iv] In a speech at Tonypandy, Cripps declared the *Unity Campaign* a reaction to 'Fascist' characteristics of the Government; a rank and file expression of opinion, a symbol of militancy: '*Something has to be done to try and break into the self-satisfaction of the Party control*'[v] (this would resonate into the 21st century). At Middlesbrough and Stockton he spoke of class and economic interest as the basis of struggle, "not theories, policies or programmes of Parties". Unfortunately, 'unity' was not the only discussion in February 1937. The conflict opened up by Groves' circular was extended. There was an exchange between Mellor and Pollitt over the lack of publicity given to an S.L. leader to refute the charges made against him in the *Daily Worker*.[vi] This confrontation was emerging when Cripps was quoted: 'Unity means comradeship, a forgetting of differences, a new approach to one another, a sinking of our personal vanities and views for the common good'.[vii] So no chance there, then.

(B) The C.P., the S.L. and the Labour Party

As noted, Cripps could not fathom the policy differences between the P.O.U.M. and the C.P. in Spain. He was impatient with controversy about such issues as 'social revolution' versus 'capitalist democracy'. When approached on the question of the Moscow Trials, he argued that it was an internal matter for Russia and could not perceive that vital principles for the international socialist movement were involved.[viii] Yet, working-class unity remained a desired end; there was no hope of removing the Government so long as divisions continued, but events in the Spanish Civil War had

---

[i] D. N. Pritt, *From Right to Left*, 1965, pp.102–103.

[ii] *Manchester Guardian*, February 15th, 1937.

[iii] Cripps to Middleton, February 16th and Middleton to Cripps, February 17th, Cripps Papers.

[iv] 'Unity Campaign', *Tribune*, February 12th, 1937.

[v] Cripps in Tonypandy, February 14th, 1937, Cripps Papers.

[vi] Mellor to Pollitt, February 12th and C.P. to Mellor, February 17th, R. Groves Papers.

[vii] *Daily Worker*, February 24th, 1937.

[viii] F. Brockway, op. cit., p.264.

sharpened tensions between the C.P. and I.L.P. C.P. member Gallacher opposed the I.L.P.'s 'ultra-Left' attitude, and S.L. members 'in a sort of political daze, would gaze from one side to the other with little or no appreciation of what was going on'[i] Gallacher recounted how he, Cripps and Brockway were billed for meetings in Eastleigh and Southampton: 'We travelled from Waterloo in the same train, but in different carriages. What an exhibition of unity!'[ii] At least they were in the same train!

The *Unity Campaign* raised questions about the working-class movement, but what should have been a democratic discussion of policy turned into questions of discipline and disruption. The *Daily Herald* caricatured the Campaign as the formation of a Triple Alliance, with a 'thick smokescreen of unity talk', 'a lining up against Labour',[iii] but the vote in the Labour Party for 'unity' had risen in three years from 89,000 to 592,000 and unity in action had been partially achieved in the campaign against unemployment regulations in 1935, the Hunger March 1936, and defeat of Mosley in the East End. ('Disaffiliation of the S.L.' dated back to the 1935 Conference when 'doctrinal exclusion' of Socialists was first established as a system. Before that, the S.D.F. had the same rights as the Fabian Society and I.L.P., while preaching Marxist doctrines of class war and social revolution).[iv]

For the S.L., the *Unity Campaign* was achieving isolation. Labour leaders, having shed one set of leaders, were busy threatening to expel S.L. members who could not sit down and do nothing at the orders of Transport House. A boycott could only impoverish and narrow the Movement, but Cripps hadn't finished: 'Once this unity has been achieved and a strong and virile working-class party has been built up and has taken the political lead of the country, then it will be time enough to consider tactical associations with progressive groups... for electoral purposes'.[v] He seemed oblivious to frictions in the *Unity Campaign* at every level. His agent, H. Rogers, was exasperated about animosity towards the *Unity Campaign* in Bristol East because the C.P. had disrupted the union movement. Astoundingly, Cripps replied: 'This sort of friction is pretty widespread now, I am glad to say, and is considerably waking up the Movement ... we must avoid personal vituperation'.[vi] What about vilifications, invective, aspersions and denunciations? They continued.

By February 1937, the *Left Book Club* was running a monthly bulletin, *Left News*, local discussion groups, rallies against Fascism and War, lectures, and weekend and vacation schools: 'It provided the one forum in which activists of different tendencies and of diverse social origin were able to meet and engage in common political activity',[vii] a vital requisite for a propaganda literary organisation. The *Left Book Club* rejuvenated one function of the S.L. – to link Labour, Communist and middle-class intellectuals – who would not otherwise have exchanged views in an organised manner: 'In the L.B.C. we are creating the mass basis without which a true Popular Front is impossible'.[viii] It was an educational and propaganda outlet and, unlike the S.L.'s 3,000 members, it could boast 50,000 members (by 1938). The *Left Book Club*

[i] W. Gallacher, *The Rolling of the Thunder*, 1947, pp.147–148.
[ii] Ibid.
[iii] *Daily Herald*, December19th, 21st and 29th, 1936.
[iv] Cf. R. P. Dutt, 'The Unity Campaign', *Labour Monthly*, Vol. 19, No. 2, February 1937.
[v] S. Cripps, 'United Front', *Labour Monthly*, Vol. 19, No. 2, February 1937.
[vi] Rogers to Cripps, February 26th and Cripps to H. Rogers, March 2nd, 1937, Cripps Papers.
[vii] R. Miliband, op. cit., pp.243–244.
[viii] V. Gollancz, February 7th, 1937, *Left News*, March 1937.

helped in 'the struggle for World Peace', for a more egalitarian social and economic system, and came into existence when hopes were increasing there could be a planned economy, a Popular Front (as in France and Spain), and successful propaganda against Fascism and armament increases. Its object was 'to enlighten, to educate, to supply relevant information and theoretical analysis of the problems of the day'.[i] The L.B.C. moved to the centre when the S.L. disbanded.

Curiously and significantly, the *Left Book Club* began at a meeting (called by Cripps) to discuss the future Socialist weekly (*Tribune*). On February 26th, 1937, Gollancz wrote to Cripps: 'The *Left Book Club* is no more in competition with the *Tribune* than the *Tribune* is with the *New Statesman and Nation*. I see the problem as a two-fold one: how to get across immediate propaganda, and how to give fundamental education. The *Tribune* is doing the former: the *Left News Weekly* aims at doing the latter... Education for working-class unity ... is the very essence of the Left Book Club... It is simply and solely a movement of political education'.[ii] He continued in as enthusiastic a vein as Cripps' commitment to the *Unity Campaign*: 'Trade unionists write that when they started with the L.B.C. they were completely passive, but now they are militant fighters for unity; middle-class people say that they were Liberals and are now Left Socialists; everywhere there is the same atmosphere of *eagerness, hope and enthusiasm*... We are preparing the minds of the people of this country for the message which you, H. Pollitt and others give them from your platforms'.[iii] Mellor (editor of *Tribune*), wrote later to Cripps to say that Gollancz would complicate the *Tribune* position if he went ahead with a weekly![iv]

The *Left Book Club*, through its local groups and regular circulation of books of Left-wing appeal (chiefly on international affairs) began to exert a widespread influence, especially among younger Labour members and the intelligentsia, but the existence of the Club embittered the controversy between Labour and the Left.[v] Its books played a part in awakening social conscience to the poverty of the 1930s, as few of the S.L.'s pamphlets and books had done, and its rallies drew larger audiences than *any* political party, but the Labour Party opposed the L.B.C.'s policy of a common platform for all groups in the *Unity Campaign*, officially denounced publication of books by Communists (e.g. Dutt, Hannington and Strachey), *and* the Popular Front agitation by the L.B.C. Typically, Bevin attacked the L.B.C. for trying to undermine and destroy unions and the Labour Party as an effective force (which certainly was not on the L.B.C.'s agenda), while H. Morrison believed it was interfering with the Party's '*consistent ordered work*'.[vi] How similar were *their* criticisms of the L.B.C. to their denunciations of the S.L.! Although A. J. P. Taylor sceptically viewed the *Left Book Club* as 'a safety valve', acting as a substitute for action, not a prelude to it; and L.B.C. members 'worked off their rebelliousness by plodding through yet another orange-coloured volume';[vii] the striving was to create a *new political awareness* which expressed aspirations, indignations, questioning and convictions'[viii] of the time: 'We were the

---

[i] John Lewis, *The Left Book Club*, 1971, p.13.
[ii] Gollancz to Cripps, February 26th, 1937, Cripps Papers.
[iii] Ibid.
[iv] Mellor to Cripps, March 3rd, 1937, Cripps Papers. (My italics.)
[v] Graves and Hodge, *The Long Weekend*, p.334.
[vi] John Lewis, op. cit., p.94.
[vii] A. J. P. Taylor, 'Confusion on the Left', *The Baldwin Age*, edited by J. Raymond, p.76.
[viii] J. Lewis, op. cit., p.132.

voice of the times'.[i] Certainly the L.B.C. expressed the S.L.'s Marxist/Labour mélange and anti-Fascism, and provided unprecedented demand for a committed political literature, which had only partially emerged through the S.L. at the time.

(C) Labour's Immediate Programme

Throughout its existence the S.L. had been angling for concise statements of Labour policy. On March 7th, 1937, the S.L. got one – the Labour Party's *Immediate Programme* published to counteract the *Unity Campaign's Manifesto*. It was to be as 'Socialist' as the Manifesto, although G. Strauss considered it was in such general terms as to conceal deep divisions in the Labour leadership on foreign policy and rearmament, and vague enough to permit a wide range of interpretations should a Labour Government be called to put it into operation'.[ii] Since its domestic policy was virtually the same as the Manifesto, the N.E.C. had partially renounced its case against co-operation with the C.P. and I.L.P., but foreign policy and rearmament declarations were different from those of the Manifesto (except for agreement on 'nationalisation of the armaments industry'). The Programme maintained such armed forces as were necessary to defend Britain and fulfil obligations as a member of the British Commonwealth and League of Nations.[iii] The *Unity Campaign Manifesto* had inquired what obligations there were to the British Commonwealth and the League; declaring its opposition to the rearmament and recruiting programme of a Government that used arms 'only in support of Fascism, Imperialist War, Reaction and Colonial Suppression'.[iv] While the *Programme* aimed to be carried out during a full term of office, the *Manifesto* preferred 'active demonstrations now'.

These were essential differences between *the Manifesto* and *the Programme*. The *Manifesto* was for immediate policies in the workshops, for the unemployed and this was opposed in the *Immediate Programme*. To the Labour Party's N.E.C., Communism was a disruptive force threatening Labour's constitutional advance to power, liable to provoke Fascist reprisals (and frighten off voters);[v] to union leaders, Communism was an irresponsible, provocative nuisance, inspiring unionists to flout machinery of conciliation; political and industrial Labour had learnt their lesson, the unions in the General Strike of 1926, Labour leaders in the débâcle of 1931. The S.L. could not acquiesce in the status quo, and could not accept a *Programme* which made no mention of Fascism, the Soviet Union or Spain. Admittedly, Labour and union leaders had acquired a more consistent policy on defence and foreign affairs, but that consistency replaced any acceptable Socialist principles – for the S.L.

The S.L. returned to one of its major themes – armaments. S.L. leaders hoped the *Immediate Programme* would build 'an increasingly militant opposition to the Government 'principally today in its armament programme',[vi] while the National

---

[i] Graves and Hodge, *The Long Weekend*, p.334.
[ii] G. R. Strauss, 'Labour's Short Programme and the Unity Campaign', *Labour Monthly*, Vol. 19, No. 6, June 1937.
[iii] Labour's Immediate Programme, March 7th.
[iv] 'Unity Manifesto', January 18th.
[v] G. D. H. Cole, *The People's Front*, p.341.
[vi] *Tribune*, March 5th, 1937.

Unity Campaign Committee (N.U.C.C.) stated that, by its decision to raise £400 million by loans and spend £1,500 million in five years on war preparations, the Government was making an arms race *inevitable*.[i] Exposure of the Government's armament increases temporarily concealed painful differences in the S.L.'s relationship with Labour leaders. On March 9th, Groves and Mellor wrote to the S.L. Executive about Government armaments plans, which the S.L. National Council discussed on March 13th and 14th. Cripps explained how the P.L.P. had decided not to vote against the Government's armament estimates, but to criticise them by proposing a reduction in estimates and noted the N.U.C.C.'s Manifesto against rearmament and recruitment: 'To attain peace, Socialists must insist upon working-class control of the Government, a co-operative economic basis for international commerce and finance, and a definite line of opposition to the National Government's rearmament proposals'.[ii] But war was on the horizon.

In a speech in Hampshire in March 1937, Cripps queried: 'You manufacture arms. To what end? ... For imperialist purposes, for the extinction of your liberties by Fascism? What guarantees has the working class that British rearmament will not be turned against itself ... Refuse to make armaments, the only way you can keep this country out of war and obtain power for the working class'.[iii] The Labour Movement had virtually caved in to the Government's armaments policy, but the *Daily Herald* utilised Cripps' speech to damn him in *Unity, True or Sham?* What the S.L. yearned for was socialisation of the armaments industry: 'expose the arms racket... turn the weapons of destruction into the tools of the workers of the world'.[iv] Highly unlikely, but the S.L. issued a statement: '*Oppose Re-Armament! Death Warrant of Working-class Freedom*', illustrating how the Government prepared for war to defend and extend profits of the rich, while the S.L. had no quarrel with workers in other lands. Believing the Government supported Fascist powers abroad (in Abyssinia and Spain), the S.L. feared a military dictatorship in Britain (utilising the *Incitement to Disaffection Act* and *Public Order Act*); Labour and Co-operative Movements *should* unite in resistance to Government war preparations, unionists to oppose any truce between employers and unions (or any surrender of union rights and conditions), the Labour Party take the lead against Government war preparations, and mobilise mass resistance to the 'Arms Plan'.[v] The dying flame for the S.L.

Cripps convinced himself that through the *Unity Campaign*, the S.L. had prevented the possibility of the C.P. and I.L.P. opposing the Labour Party and had actually managed to get them to support it: 'The C.P. have given up their plans for dictatorship and are now working for the return of the Labour Party'.[vi] This would have been news to the C.P.! Low drew a cartoon for the L.C.C. Elections with Herbert Morrison wearing a 'Vote for the severely respectable light pink Morrison' tag. 'A Red' and 'Anti-Red' are fighting over a scarecrow (Cripps) who has notices pinned on him announcing 'Hooray for Stalin Morrison; Vote for Red Morrison and the dictatorship

---

[i] 'Fight Now Against War Plan: Unity Campaign's Call', *Tribune*, March 5th, 1937.
[ii] S. Cripps, 'Arms for What? Beware Menace of the National Front', *Tribune*, March 12th, 1937.
[iii] Quoted in the *Daily Herald*, March 15th, 1937.
[iv] Frank Stonham, 'Arms and the Money', *Socialist Broadsheet*, No. 2, April 1937. In 1935–36, £129½ million had been spent on armaments.
[v] S.L. Executive Committee Statement, *Socialist Broadsheet*, No. 2, April 1937.
[vi] S. Cripps letter, March 2nd, 1937, Cripps Papers.

of the Proletariat'. The caption is *'The Outsider'*.[i] (An apposite description by March 1937.) With the result of the L.C.C. Elections (the C.P. having taken a prominent part), the S.L. lauded the *Unity Campaign* even more. Strauss' article was headlined: *'Laying the Red Bogey: London's Answer to All This Talk of Disruptive Forces'*.[ii] The following week there was an exposé on the refusal by Westminster council for the Albert Hall to allow a meeting for Cripps and the *Unity Campaign*. Cripps pleaded to leading politicians, Baldwin said the matter was outside his province, MacDonald that it was impracticable for him to write to the trustees; Churchill accused Cripps of working with Communists, but Lloyd George said the trustees' conduct was monstrous, Sir A. Sinclair believed in the right of free speech, and Attlee protested at an action which appeared to be dictated by political prejudice.[iii] Cripps failed to reverse the decision. At the same time, G. Starr of the East London Socialist Front wrote to Groves that the East End Campaign had terminated. One of the united front movements against Fascism had come to an end, when the S.L. faced a decision on its own future.

When the Party N.E.C. disaffiliated the S.L. from the Labour Party on January 27th, there was an ex cathedra circular *The Labour Party and the So-called Unity Campaign* which relayed S.L. misdemeanours: 'The Labour Party has never exercised an iron discipline nor does it demand unthinking loyalty. It encourages free discussion and it has been tolerant in its fellowship. It seeks a loyalty to its general principles, based on an understanding of democratic consent. The N.E.C. has not acted hastily, but only after its appeal for loyalty has been completely disregarded... It calls for a real and not a sham unity'.[iv] Real, sham – always tricky in politics. The result was that the S.L. immediately lost much of its support, and remaining members involved themselves purely in the *Unity Campaign*, no pronouncements being made officially by the S.L., no pamphlets, journals or bulletins being produced. Laski and G. D. H. Cole (by then neither S.L. members) put the S.L.'s position succinctly at the Battersea Town Hall Labour Monthly Conference; Laski stated the life-blood of the Movement was "a healthy freedom of discussion"; he did not believe there was 'unity in the Movement' because it lacked a coherent philosophy, had not analysed 'capitalist democracy', nor had it *coherently examined the dynamics of power in a capitalist state*: 'Unless the philosophy of the British Labour Movement is built upon a full acceptance of Marxism, there can be no real hope for its survival'.[v] (It depended on what one understood by 'philosophy', 'Labour Movement' or even 'Marxism'!); G. D. H. Cole accused Labour leaders of muddling along without any concept of the class struggle, or comprehensive definition of objectives or methods: 'The Labour Party is thinking only of its strictly constitutional task as H.M.'s Opposition in Parliament'.[vi] This was the S.L.'s view.

---

[i] Low, *Manchester Guardian*, March 3rd, 1937.

[ii] *Tribune*, March 12th, 1937.

[iii] 'Free Speech Battle: National Leaders Line Up in Defence and Attack', *Tribune*, March 19th, 1937.

[iv] N.E.C. Circular, January 27th, 1937.

[v] H. Laski, 'Unity and the Labour Party', *Labour Monthly*, Vol. 19, No. 3, March 1937 (Battersea, February 14th Meeting).

[vi] G. D. H. Cole, *The People's Front*, *Labour Monthly*, Vol. 19, No. 3, March 1937 (Battersea, February 14th Meeting).

(D) The N.E.C. Disaffiliates the S.L. (March 1937)

Dalton for the N.E.C hit back: the S.L., he reiterated, was little more than 'a rich man's toy'; the 'so-called *Unity Campaign*' was 'financed by one or two rich men who were using their private wealth in constant attacks on the policy and the leadership of the Party';[i] as for the S.L.'s United Front it was 'a most exasperating diversion of the Party's mind and energies',[ii] (wherever 'mind' and 'energies' were diverted to), and worse, it was a form of 'splitting tactics'.[iii] March 25th, 1937, was dies irae for the S.L.; the N.E.C. decreed that membership of the S.L. would be *incompatible* with membership of the Party. The rôle of a body affiliated to the Labour Party, which was itself primarily a propaganda body, was at an end; this was the ultimate lex talionis. Mellor responded; the importance of the S.L. was as an organised Left in the Party and, if the S.L. were dissolved, it would be playing into the hands of the Right wing of the Party, who wished to get rid of separately organised Left organisations.

The S.L. did not want to give the N.E.C. the opportunity to stamp on Left-wing dissidents. If it dissolved, it would have to announce that its adherents could continue in individual capacities to support the *Unity Campaign*. The S.L.'s interpretation was that the issue had come to a head because the *Unity Campaign* seemed to the N.E.C. to be having too much success *outside* the confines of the Party, although it was using Party platforms. The last thing the S.L. wanted was to further divide the ranks of Labour; they had been campaigning for *unity,* not splits. That is why the S.L. majority decided to disband *voluntarily*, the members remaining in the Labour Party as individuals. J. T. Murphy interpreted the event: 'The S.L. had now to face a complete climb down or expulsion. It decided to face expulsion, but at the last moment performed a somersault in Communist fashion. It decided not to face expulsion but to die. The S.L. was no more, but its members remained Labour Party members. Thus the Left was spread-eagled. The I.L.P. and C.P. went their respective ways, as did the ex-members of the S.L., having secured neither the unity of the workers nor the unity of the people'.[iv] A tragic outcome for the S.L. but it had been a death wish.

Thus ended Part One of the Labour Party's suppression of the United Front campaign. Instead of improving the bargaining position of the S.L., with the N.E.C., the S.L. had been defeated by the choice of submission or expulsion. S.L. leaders who led the S.L. into the *Unity Campaign* had put organisational factors above principles to cement an alliance with the C.P. and I.L.P., instead of keeping the possibility of voluntary secession from the Labour Party to the forefront. A new resolution for Campaign meetings was formulated: 'This mass meeting protests against the action of the Labour Party N.E.C. in disaffiliating the S.L. and in declaring that, after June 1st, membership of the S.L. will be held incompatible with membership of the Labour Party; and calls upon all members of the Labour Party to register their protest with the N.E.C.'. *Tribune* concluded the N.E.C.'s action was motivated by fear of association with Communists; counteracting N.E.C. accusations of S.L. disruption, *Tribune*

---

[i] Dalton, *The Fateful Years*, p.130.

[ii] Ibid., p.129.

[iii] Ibid.

[iv] J. T. Murphy, *New Horizons*, p.321.

continued: 'The Labour Party must make sure that its own constitution and practice are democratic… Does not unrest in the political constituencies and the industrial field give reason for the N.E.C. to pause before it acts in the formal, soulless manner of an autocracy?'[i] No chance! Suppression was no remedy; *tolerance* was the hallmark of a Movement's confidence.

W. Ebenstein remarked that in Britain, Fascism was destroyed by the Conservative Party, Communism by the Labour Party.[ii] Who was to blame for the dissolution of the S.L.? It was on the advice of the Communist Party that the S.L. was 'invited' to disband; it was on C.P. advice that joint meetings between Labour Unity supporters, the I.L.P. and the C.P. were terminated. There were discussions in the Unity Campaign Committee as to S.L. tactics, and C.P. leaders urged the S.L. to prove the sincerity of its desire for unity 'within the framework of the Labour Party' by accepting the ultimatum of the N.E.C. and voluntarily dissolve itself. Brockway commented: 'As one of the I.L.P. representatives, I opposed the C.P.'s advice, backing those who contended that if the S.L. liquidated itself, it would be surrendering in advance the claim of the I.L.P. and C.P. for the right to enter the Labour Party as independent parties… [However] as a tactical move in the interests of the *Unity Campaign*, the S.L. was dissolved and joint meetings went on, with Cripps [etc.] appearing … as individual Labour Party members'.[iii] A divided S.L. and a united C.P. gave Pollitt and Cripps a majority on the U.C.C.: Did the C.P. deliberately destroy the S.L.?' I do not know, but I learned later that the opponents within the S.L. of any campaign associated with the C.P. had forecast that it would lead to this very result',[iv] concluded Brockway. The rhetoric which had poured from the S.L., particularly Cripps, matched in style the perpetual exhortations of career politicians. The crisis of the S.L. was related to ferment among Labour and union leaders, but there was a critical choice for the S.L.; whether to go on working in Labour institutions, or to make a break to a new organisation and campaign: 'There was an enduring suspicion that the Labour leaders were more concerned to assert party discipline than to conduct "the fight against Fascism";[v] but one of the S.L.'s problems was that political initiative was directed, not down to the grass-roots, but upwards, attempting to influence career politicians.

On April 3rd and 4th the National Council of the S.L. met, which, despite resolutions on S.L. tactics, proceeded on the assumption that nothing would happen to the S.L. organisation. No decision was produced to put before the S.L. Conference (to be held in May), although a letter was drafted to the Labour N.E.C. replying to the disaffiliation order and asking for an appeal to the Bournemouth Conference in October. Many S.L. members had departed, but a resolution for the S.L.'s Conference was put by the Balham and Tooting S.L. branch to enable the S.L. to continue.[vi] R. St. John Reade (of Bristol S.L. branch) wrote to Cripps, suggesting the 'sit-down strike' for Socialists in the Labour Party: 'If the S.L. is taboo, let us form the Socialist Federation and then the Socialist Association'![vii] (Cripps thought this was quite a

[i] 'Unions for Unity!' Swift Rebuffs to Inquisitors of Transport House', *Tribune*, April 2nd, 1937.

[ii] W. Ebenstein, 'Today's Isms', op. cit., p.174.

[iii] F. Brockway, *Workers' Front*, pp.225–26.

[iv] F. Brockway, *Inside the Left*, p.268.

[v] A. J. P. Taylor, *English History (1914–45)*, p.397.

[vi] National Council of S.L. Meeting, April 3rd–4th, Groves Papers.

[vii] R. St. John Reade to Cripps, April 4th, Cripps Papers. And the SDP in the 1980s!

worthy idea!)[i] The S.L. in Bristol was, in fact, dissolved by 19 votes to 8, only to discover that the S.L. National Council had agreed to continue until the Bournemouth Conference in October 1937, but the Party Executive had decided that S.L. members could not remain Party members after June 1st. H. Rogers wrote to Cripps: 'It would be far more spectacular to have cheated the Labour Party by the dissolution of the S.L. than to wait and find that the Annual Conference support the N.E.C.'s decision'.[ii] Cripps replied that if the S.L. dissolved itself it could be interpreted by those opposed to the Campaign that the S.L. was running away, that it had withdrawn from the Campaign; the I.L.P. and C.P. should issue a statement deploring the action of Labour's N.E.C. in its tactics of disruption of the workers' Movement.[iii] As it was the N.E.C. was delaying endorsement of candidates because of their support of the *Unity Campaign* and S.L. membership.

Cripps was convinced there was no other reason for the S.L.'s disaffiliation except its participation in the *Unity Campaign*: 'Given a proper system of democracy within the Labour Party, the Communists and I.L.P. members would be perfectly willing, if affiliated, to accept the majority decision'.[iv] The N.E.C.'s response to the *Unity Campaign* had been calculated to prevent any autonomy of any one section of the Party, and to sap the S.L.'s sense of identity. Yet, of 2½ million Labour members, the 'opposition' by the I.L.P. was only 19,000 with the C.P. membership. If the active membership in the Movement was 450,000, the Left appealed to about 110,000 Labour supporters, while the S.L. membership was only 3,000.[v] Cripps' determination to arrive at any agreement with the C.P. and I.L.P. had surrendered the S.L.'s distinct contribution before the Party Executive sealed its fate.

The intellectual's dilemma reflected that of the S.L. in 1937: 'Every Party intellectual has a breaking point beyond which he will not go. If he has no such point, he has ceased to be an intellectual. He ceases to be a creator of ideas and becomes a retailer of the ideas of others and a manufacturer of slogans. He no longer searches for the truth; he begins with the truth as revealed in the pronouncements of the Party leaders',[vi] as N. Wood had commented. S.L. leaders were not all intellectuals by any means, but they were misfits searching for a political home and in the pages of *Tribune* in April, they continued to call for 'Unity': 'There can be no real advance of the working class as a whole towards higher wages and better conditions so long as the Labour Movement fights sectional battles'.[vii] They pleaded with the N.E.C. to 'think again', since constituency parties and union branches had condemned its decision: 'The *Unity Campaign* is not undertaken out of caprice or pique against the N.E.C. of the Labour Party ... It is a spontaneous movement, a determination to accelerate politically the brotherhood of man through the agency of the Labour Party'.[viii] The brotherhood could wait a little longer.

Unfortunately, there was distaste for individual rebels in the Labour Movement;[ix]

---

[i] Cripps to R. St. John Reade, April 13th, 1937, Cripps Papers.

[ii] H. Rogers to Cripps, April 5th, 1937, Cripps Papers.

[iii] S. Cripps to H. Rogers, April 7th, 1937, Cripps Papers.

[iv] S. Cripps in letter, April 9th, 1937, Cripps Papers.

[v] Cf. J. Jupp, op. cit., pp.555–59.

[vi] N. Wood, op. cit., pp.219–220.

[vii] 'World Strike Wave', *Tribune*, April 9th, 1937.

[viii] *Tribune*, April 16th 1937, letter 'Comradeship in Unity'.

[ix] Ibid., 'Red Gold Again: Truth about U.C.'s Finances – and a Challenge'.

critics in the Party were subjected to *vitriolic personal abuse* from Labour and union leaders, especially by Dalton and Bevin, who had a distinctive voice in the Party. This emerged in a confrontation over the *Unity Campaign*'s finances. The N.E.C. was obsessed by 'Moscow Gold' and J. S. Middleton (for the Party N.E.C.) had spoken of large sums of money (the sources of which were not disclosed), being spent on the *Unity Campaign*.[i] The *Daily Herald* upheld the Executive's innuendo, and Dalton sneered: 'the *Unity Campaign* was financed by rich men using their wealth in attacks on the Labour Party,' setting at defiance decisions of the Labour Conference regarding joint action with Communists: 'If the U.C. were deprived of these plutocratic props, the whole agitation would speedily collapse'.[ii] *Tribune* denounced Middleton's and Dalton's "lies" as disgraceful in common decency as in political tactics: 'The only possible explanation of such perversions of truth is the absolute inability of the N.E.C. to refute the policy and programme of the *Unity Campaign* on political grounds'.[iii] (The Campaign had received £1,907.19s.10d up to April 13th of which £1,600.7s.5d had come from the 44 public demonstrations; £277.12s.5d[iv] from tickets for the demonstrations and £10 each from the S.L., I.L.P. & C.P.)

The peculiar feature of Dalton's stance was that he regarded anyone putting money into the *Unity Campaign* as conclusive proof against it as a legitimate expression of opinion within the Labour Party. Yet every campaign needed financial backing, and since the S.L. was not entitled to a share of the financial resources of the Labour Party, in what other way could an organisation run such a campaign? The reality was that Labour leaders discredited the Campaign to avoid a discussion of its merits; Dalton was evading real issues by irrelevancies, since if no 'rich man' had helped Labour newspapers and Party, the Movement would have found it impossible to continue. As a postscript to this controversy, the finances of the L.C.C. Elections showed that £2,785 for the Labour Party came from 'anonymous sources'. *Tribune* exclaimed: 'Dr. Dalton, do your duty!'[v] and asked him 'to admit that he sought, by making unfounded charges on U.C.'s finances – charges now being used in the constituencies by agents of the Executive – to avoid discussing the purposes of the Campaign'.[vi] There was no reply.

On April 19th a circular was sent to all S.L. branch secretaries, enclosing S.L. recommendations for '*the future of the S.L.*'. The initial decision had been to disband. There was to be no break with the Party, because differences with Party leaders were not on principles but on methods and immediate aims. Since the Party had proscribed the S.L., the latter met to dissolve itself and disappear as an organised body. S.L. members were to continue in the *Unity Campaign* as individuals. On April 21st a reply to the S.L. National Council's circular came from three members of the London Area Committee, G. Allighan, Donald Barber and A. G. Bennett, entitled *Our Future of the S.L.*, but Cripps admitted in a letter (April 21st), 'I do not think at the present time that it is the right policy to build another Party outside the Labour Party. The Trade Union position makes this impossible and inadvisable';[vii] R. St. John Reade thought it good

---

[i] Ibid., 'Red Gold Again: Truth about U.C.'s Finances – and a Challenge'.

[ii] H. Dalton, *The Fateful Years*, p.130.

[iii] *Tribune*, April 16th, 1937.

[iv] Ibid.

[v] *Tribune*, May 7th, 1937.

[vi] *Tribune*, May 21st, 1937.

[vii] Cripps letter, April 21st, 1937, Cripps Papers.

tactics to tone down the *Unity Campaign* in public and concentrate on it in the Party, especially in the constituency parties, where opinion was 50–50 in favour of Unity and where the *Left Book Club* could possibly help the Unity cause.[i] Cripps received a response from J. F. Horrabin, who was wholly in favour of continuing the *Unity Campaign*, not simply as a fight *for* unity, but as a demonstration *of* unity for specific issues. He was convinced that if S.L. leaders had identified the Campaign with a demand for a more militant policy on Spain, rather than with the demand for 'Unity' per se, the S.L. would have been in a stronger bargaining position.[ii] S.L. disaffiliation was discussed by another correspondent: 'It will be a fatal error to disband the S.L. after all the work expended on building it. The S.L. can be built into a numerous and effective organ, by the attraction of professional men … It is necessary to get good, snappy and well-informed articles for *Tribune*; then to get them quoted in professional journals … When you have an S.L. numbering 20,000 good professional men, you can talk effectively at Congress and in Parliament.[iii] The attempt of the Party Executive to *outlaw* well-known Socialists was causing consternation in the Movement's rank and file. Was the Labour Party too respectable to shout its wares from the market place? Deborah Barker suggested in April 1937 that to challenge Transport House, each centre (such as Bristol and Manchester) had to act at the same time, dissolving their S.L. branches and forming Labour Unity Committees, so that every S.L. member had to be dealt with at the same time: 'We must manage to stick inside the Labour Party right up to October next, and continue with our Unity agitation, while winning the support of those who will hate the heresy hunting'.[iv]

The S.L. in the Labour Party could not act as a united group in the Unity Campaign or question its final existence. In trying to preserve its intellectual and propagandist nature, it had fractured into a faction of agitators with no roots and a compromised integrity as a distinct organisation. The question of 'Unity' continued to figure before its final Leicester Conference of May 15th, 16th and 17th, and judging the history of the *Unity Campaign*, Cripps focussed on the weakness of Opposition tactics: 'The S.L. has made various abortive attempts to swing the Party back to a more challenging and less compromising line of action'.[v] He nailed the Party's irresolution – evasion of the class struggle: 'The S.L. decided, after Edinburgh, that something would have to be done if the Labour Party was to be saved from a slow death',[vi] since there had been examples of united activities in Hunger March protests, Spanish committees, French and Spanish Popular Fronts, and the C.P., I.L.P., and the S.L. had launched the *Unity Campaign*. Now, in May, 'the National Council of the S.L. recommended **dissolution of the S.L.**'[vii]

Cripps intended to continue the Campaign, and widen its influence to bring in unorganised local unionists. The problem was in the clash between Strauss and Morrison over Campaign funds; Morrison replied to Strauss' denunciation of Dalton's accusations that some 'rich Labour members' felt they had to go 'farther to the Left, talk more about the "working class" than anybody else, emphasise the authenticity of

---

[i] R. St. John Reade to Cripps, April 23rd, 1937, Cripps Papers.

[ii] J. F. Horrabin to Cripps, April 25th, 1937, Cripps Papers.

[iii] Letter to Cripps, April 26th, 1937, Cripps Papers.

[iv] Deborah Barker to Cripps, April 27th, 1937, Cripps Papers.

[v] Cripps on 'New Masses', May 9th, 1937, Cripps Papers.

[vi] Ibid.

[vii] Ibid.

their proletarian loyalty; Morrison claimed there would be danger if Party policies could be 'bought', money should be freely contributed to the Party funds controlled by the Party itself; when well-to-do Socialists financed publications or activities which were critical of the Party itself they were open to the accusation of using money-power to impose on the Party a policy which it had rejected, etc.[i] Strauss retorted that the implication of Dalton's attack was that a political movement was suspect because 'rich people' were prepared to support it by financial contributions: 'The Labour Party's staunchest supporters are entitled to criticise the adopted line on a certain issue, or the general lack of initiative of the Party leadership, without being accused of attacking the Party'.[ii] (Rich supporters for Labour post-1997 fared a little better.) Morrison responded that he had opposed the Party's non-intervention policy in Spain, but stated his views so that the minimum of friction in the Party would result, and he had refused to speak with the Communists – the exact opposite of the S.L. in the *Unity Campaign*.[iii] Morrison would soon be promoted.

At the S.L.'s Leicester Conference, the Minutes of the S.L. National Council meeting were delivered. There were no public announcements, but suggestions of winding-up the S.L., and the *Leicester Evening Mail* of May 15th headlined its report of proceedings: 'S.L.'s Sacrifice Hint'. On May 16th the Minutes of the S.L. National Council's emergency meeting were discussed, and the following (and final) day, the *Daily Worker* headed its description: 'The S.L. to Dissolve', stating the S.L. was 'sacrificing itself for unity', and the news-stand poster for the *Daily Herald* announced '*Exit S.L.*' On May 20th, Low's cartoon in the *Manchester Guardian* showed Cripps and Mellor rushing to Transport House with the coffin of the S.L.; the caption: '*Hopeful Funeral*'.

May 21st brought an article by Cripps in *Tribune* explaining why the S.L. had dissolved, and why the Campaign would go forward; the Leicester S.L. Conference had been 'first class', despite 'a small minority' [who] put forward highly theoretical and 'revolutionary Left views'. By 56 votes to nil, the S.L. had declared to go forward with the *Unity Campaign* 'even at the price of the sacrifice of its own organisation'. If the S.L. had done nothing else than inaugurate the Campaign, it would have justified its formation. The resolution passed by the Conference stated: 'This Conference, recognising the urgent necessity for attaining unity for the whole working class of this country within the Labour Party, recognising also that the multiplication of parties or organisations outside the Labour Party will not assist in furthering that objective, and being determined to do its utmost to prevent any split or breakaways from the Labour Movement, is prepared to sacrifice its own organisation rather than allow its continued separate existence to be made an excuse for further disunity in the ranks of the workers'.[iv]

A decision was made to appeal to the Labour Conference in October to reverse the disaffiliation decision of the Party's N.E.C. Cripps praised the 'fine fighting spirit'[v] of the S.L.'s Conference, and saw it as a happy omen; fresh energies could now be channelled into the Campaign. He denied the 'wholly inaccurate and intentionally

[i] H. Morrison to G. R. Strauss, May 26th, 1937.

[ii] G. R. Strauss to H. Morrison, May 29th, 1937.

[iii] H. Morrison to G. R. Strauss, June 1st, 1937.

[iv] S.L. National Council resolution, May 16th, 1937.

[v] S. Cripps, 'Unity Is Now the Issue: Why the S.L. Came to its Decision to Dissolve', *Tribune*, May 21st, 1937.

misleading reports"[i] of the private sessions of the Conference, communicated to the Press by 'disloyal members of the S.L.' His logic on the dissolution was: 'We have cleared out of the way what might have been a dangerous argument for misleading the rank and file of the Movement. Had we continued with the S.L. it would have been said that its members had been given the choice between membership of the S.L. or of the Labour Party, and had chosen the former.' Fortunately for him, the possibility of appearing disloyal to the Party had been prevented by sacrificing the S.L. 'in the interests of the Movement', the death knell of the S.L.

(E) Dissolution of the Socialist League

There were suspicions that Cripps had for some time found the S.L. an embarrassing encumbrance; he had argued that the S.L. was no longer 'appropriate to the times', whereas the *Unity Campaign* was the one hope for a militant opposition to the Government. He acknowledged that, because he 'wanted the challenge to come on this basis, I was in favour of winding up the S.L.'[ii] By May 21st, there had been over 100 local Unity Committees, 65 mass meetings, 36,000 pledge cards signed, £1,673 collected.[iii] A year later, in reply to an American inquiry about the S.L., Gwendoline Hill (Cripps' secretary) answered: 'The S.L. was wound up ... owing to the hostility of the official Labour Party to the S.L. and its activities. It did serve a very useful purpose while it existed in the way of forming *a concentration point of Left-wing opinion* and its recent members are almost entirely present members of the Labour Party and are carrying on such Left-wing propaganda within the Labour Party as they can'.[iv] Not irrelevant, then.

Cripps' circuitous and tortuous arguments for the S.L.'s dissolution appeared in notes for a speech at Greenock on May 22nd; he claimed the S.L. had not been dissolved because any of its members had gone back on their political outlook or had changed their views, but because 'in the circumstances of today it was felt that it was wiser and better for the working-class movement as a whole – to close it down'.[v] He added that it was no longer possible to carry on the S.L. inside the Labour Party, and there were already too many organisations outside the Party to warrant another. Sacrificing the S.L. had demonstrated members' sincerity on the Unity issue and differences around the S.L. had not ended, since the *Unity Campaign* had 'sharpened those conflicts'. Cripps interpreted that the Labour Party was anxious to rid itself of the 'more extreme elements of class opinion', so the Party would appear respectable and safe to the middle class (and attract more votes) and the issue had boiled down to the choice: 'class collaboration or class struggle?'[vi] The former won.

In the Minutes of the last meeting of the S.L.'s Executive Committee on May 24th S.L. belongings were disposed of in a perfunctory manner. The Left in the Labour Party, robbed by its own effective organisation, found itself hopelessly pitted (as

---

[i] Ibid.

[ii] S. Cripps, *Tribune*, May 21st.

[iii] 'Going Ahead for Unity', *Tribune*, May 21st.

[iv] G. Hill letter, May 4th, 1938, Cripps Papers. (My italics.)

[v] Cripps' notes on Greenock speech, May 22nd, 1937, Cripps Papers.

[vi] Cripps at Greenock, May 22nd, 1937, Cripps Papers.

individuals) against the Executive machine. On May 26th the N.E.C. issued a circular requiring Labour members 'refrain from any further activities with the C.P. or I.L.P.', members to concentrate on Labour's constructive proposals;[i] M. Foot remarked laconically: 'In dealing with the "rebels", the leadership had shown itself *more purposive and effective* than for some years'![ii] Lansbury looked forward to a 'United Party', although not bound by 'cast-iron formulas or vain efforts to establish uniformity either in thought, speech or action'[iii] and hoped Labour leaders would not consider themselves 'a kind of infallible hierarchy', and the S.L.'s gesture would be met by an equally friendly gesture from the Party Executive. Direct challenge to the official Labour leaders by the S.L. had failed, as had the attempt to combine official and unofficial pressure on the Executive in the *Unity Campaign*. The S.L. had proved incapable of prosecuting a vigorous campaign in isolation or in unity.

In June 1937 the Party's N.E.C. challenged *Unity Campaign* initiators' sincerity. Women's sections and constituency parties were forbidden even to discuss 'unity'; divisional party officers were told to ensure the U.C.'s defeat; Party membership refused to applicants whose *husbands* were Communists, yet 'Not once has the Executive attempted to argue the practical case for Unity'.[iv] Heresy-hunts were necessary because the Party was not whole-hearted in its attacks on the Government.[v] *Labour's National Unity Committee* (L.N.U.C.) now organised the campaign in the Labour Party, while the C.P. and I.L.P. carried on separate agitations. Cripps, Strauss and Mellor led the L.N.U.C., with Bevan and Laski. This 'Committee of Labour Members Sympathetic to Unity' had Cripps as Chairman and *Tribune* its official organ, and was based on the constituency Labour Parties. It organised meetings with C.P. and I.L.P. speakers.[vi] Opening a rally for Labour's National Unity Committee in Hull on June 6th, Cripps inferred there was room for agreement between *Labour's Immediate Programme* and the *Unity Manifesto*: 'We are concerned with the temper and spirit in the Movement behind whatever programme it has'.[vii] He welcomed Labour's propaganda drive as 'showing signs of a new spirit and a new desire for leadership',[viii] but was perturbed by the Executive's continuing heresy hunt, now that all Unity meetings had to be manned by Labour speakers only. This pronouncement was signed by Cripps, Mellor, Mitchison, Strauss, Brockway, Jowett, Maxton, Palme Dutt, Gallacher and Pollitt.

Lionel Elvin (ex-S.L. National Council) thought this a humiliation because at the Leicester Conference the purpose of dissolving the S.L. had been to challenge discipline against Unity Campaigners. Then S.L. leaders had agreed to continue the U.C. regardless of Party expulsion: 'If it was intended to fold up like this under the first threat from Transport House and we were not going to fight it, then we might have made that clear at first and kept on the S.L.'[ix] He found it painful that the I.L.P.

---

[i] *Labour Party Annual Conference Report*, October 1937, p.27.

[ii] M. Foot, op. cit., pp.267–268. And Neville Chamberlain became PM as Baldwin resigned.

[iii] 'Heresy Hunts', *Tribune*, June 4th, 1937.

[iv] Ibid.

[v] Cf. A. B. White, *The New Propaganda*, p.367.

[vi] H. Rogers to S. Cripps, May 30th, Cripps Papers, Bristol ex-S.L. branch would not invite C.P. or I.L.P. speakers.

[vii] Cripps' Hull Speech, June 6th, *Tribune*, June 11th, 1937.

[viii] Ibid.

[ix] L. Elvin to Cripps, June 7th, Cripps Papers.

and C.P. had brought about this state of affairs. Cripps replied that Labour members of the U.C. were divided, Strauss, Mellor and himself anxious to continue, the C.P. 'very insistent on taking the line that has now been taken'.[i] (The C.P. view was supported by Laski and G. R. Mitchison.) After Pollitt's speech at the C.P. Congress, 'it was a little difficult to proceed, added to which the increasing friction over Spain between the I.L.P. and the C.P. did not hold out very good prospects. ...After a very full discussion, we practically unanimously came to the point of view that the line we took was a wise one'.[ii] Otherwise, Cripps expected expulsions of Labour Party members, and Elvin remained disappointed the view held by Mellor, Strauss and Cripps had not prevailed.[iii] (H. Rogers regarded the decision as 'the only practical way out, although in some respects 'it is disappointing'.)[iv]

Deborah Barker had received no reply from Cripps when she asked if the I.L.P. was intending to back out of the Unity agreement because of the conflict between the C.P. and the P.O.U.M. but she noted that the *New Leader* and *Daily Worker* were, as usual, attacking one another's tactics.[v] Civil War in Spain and the Moscow trials had created more conflict because, while leaders of the I.L.P. and C.P. kept the letter of their agreement, their second rank of speakers had not been so disciplined. The irony of Unity meetings (when I.L.P. and C.P. canvassers were selling literature *exposing* each other's heresies!) did not go unnoticed. The disintegration of the U.C. led not only to the end of the S.L. but disillusionment of the rank and file: 'The real lesson of the *Unity Campaign* was the need to limit united action to specific issues'.[vi] This action had succeeded locally in industrial disputes, and nationally in unemployment agitations, in opposition to Mosley's Fascist groups, in Hunger Marches and withdrawal of U.A.B. regulations.

J. R. Campbell fanned the flames of the antagonism between the I.L.P. and C.P. when he dubbed I.L.P. Conference resolutions as 'a guide to abstract criticism of the C.P.'[vii] He lambasted I.L.P. 'hysterical clamour' over Spain, and accused P.O.U.M. of possessing 'a policy of resistance to the formation of a united army, break-up of the Popular Front, and ... a wedge between the C.P. and the Anarchists'.[viii] Meanwhile, ex-S.L. members held their first meeting of the new *Labour's National Unity Committee* on June 10th, with Cripps (Chairman), Strauss (Treasurer), Mellor (Honorary Secretary), and Entwhistle (Secretary).[ix] Provided the L.N.U.C. carried on without association with Communists there would be no victimisation by Head Office, but 'this does not mean that there will not be victimisation in an underground way'.[x] For example, the N.E.C.'s threat of expulsion made to Strauss was if he appeared at a meeting with C.P. or I.L.P. leaders. (Another Low cartoon depicted Attlee and Morrison in bed, and E. Bevin out of bed, taking the cat (called 'United Front') out of the room, while Cripps

---

[i] Cripps to L. Elvin, June 9th, Cripps Papers.

[ii] Ibid.

[iii] L. Elvin to S. Cripps, June 11th, Cripps Papers.

[iv] H. Rogers to S. Cripps, June 8th, Cripps Papers.

[v] Deborah Barker to Cripps, May 30th, 1937, Cripps Papers.

[vi] F. Brockway, *Inside the Left*, p.270.

[vii] J. R. Campbell, 'Left Socialism and the People's Front', Notes on I.L.P. Conference, *Labour Monthly*, Vol. 19, No. 5, May 1937.

[viii] Ibid.

[ix] 'Unity Drive's New Phase', *Tribune*, June 18th, 1937.

[x] Cripps to Robert Young (later Lieutenant), June 21st, 1937, Cripps Papers.

and Pollitt look on, from underneath the bed. Bevin says to the cat: 'How can anyone sleep with you stamping about the room'.)[i] At a meeting in Oldham to celebrate six months of the *Unity Campaign*, Cripps denounced the Labour Movement's ineffectiveness: 'If anything were necessary to confirm the need for Unity, that confirmation would be provided by the propaganda in favour of disunity in all the Capitalist Press';[ii] he noted the heresy hunting and exclusion of the Left, although convinced the *Campaign* would have to be wound up after the Bournemouth Conference. Mellor regretted this, hoping the primary reason was financial, since 'the only future for the Left in the Movement seems to be to rest in the *Unity Campaign*'.[iii] Even Pollitt believed the C.P. should back the L.N.U.C. because there was 'too much defeatism about, too great a belief that it is hopeless to attempt to defeat the aims of the Bevins, Daltons, Citrines and Middletons'.[iv] Ignore the Jeremiahs.

Throughout June and July a particular conflict between the Labour Right and Left occurred. In *International Policy and Defence*,[v] the N.C.L. concluded that war could be prevented, the arms race stopped, the League of Nations made strong (again), provided there was a Labour Government. Party leaders accused the Labour Left of discrediting the Party and jeopardising its chances of electoral success; the Left opposed rearmament on doctrinal grounds.[vi] Belief in pacifism, disarmament and collective security without rearmament had been undermined for the Labour Party by events abroad. In July 1937, the P.L.P. abandoned opposition to the Estimates of the Service Departments and, with the winding up of the S.L., opposition to the Party to rearmament lessened. The Party's decision on armaments and the Defence Estimates was carried at the Bournemouth Conference of 2,169,000 to 262,000. In April 1937 the principal question on which there had been disunity in the Movement was Armaments policy.[vii] No longer did the Party feel (by the end of July) that by abstaining or voting for the Defence Estimates, there would be a threat to its identity. On July 28th, the N.E.C. made any association with a *Unity Campaign* incompatible with membership of the Labour Party.[viii] The L.N.U.C. was banned and the *Unity Campaign* ceased to exist.

This was not the end of the S.L.'s influence. On September 5th, Cripps complained to J. Middleton (Party Secretary) that there had been action by the N.E.C. against Mellor (who was not endorsed as an MP candidate for Stockport because he had been Secretary of the L.N.U.C.). Cripps, Laski and Strauss refused to speak on Labour's *Crusade Week* as a result. Cripps disentangled it: 'This is victimisation, while the N.E.C. are using my services for their propaganda campaign';[ix] a Mr Gower wrote to Cripps: 'Victimisation is swinging many who have hitherto been neutral, or even hostile, to our side'.[x] Cripps maintained there was an N.E.C. intention to get rid of

---

[i] *Evening Standard*, July 14th, 1937.
[ii] Cripps' speech at Oldham, July 18th, 1937, Cripps Papers.
[iii] Mellor to Cripps, July 24th, 1937.
[iv] H. Pollitt, 'The C.P. Congress and the Next Stage in the Fight for Unity', *Labour Monthly*, Vol. 19, No. 7, July 1937.
[v] July 26th, 1937.
[vi] K. W. Watkins, *Britain Divided*, p.186.
[vii] J. R. Campbell, *Labour Monthly*, Vol. 19, No. 4, April 1937.
[viii] *Labour Party Annual Conference Report*, pp.27–28.
[ix] Cripps to Middleton, September 5th, 1937, Cripps Papers.
[x] Gower to Cripps, September 20th, 1937, Cripps Papers.

"uncompromising Socialists" from unions and Party, especially those who were preaching the class struggle (shock horror!) as the basis of action in the political field: 'We want unity as the essential pre-condition to waging the class struggle with efficiency'.[i] Unity is strength.

43 resolutions on 'Unity' from affiliated organisations came to the Bournemouth Conference (compared with 26 resolutions on war and peace), but the N.E.C. decided the Conference would not discuss 'Unity'! 'For a party that boasted its democratic constitution, the Labour Party was a highly successful practitioner of the art of stifling discussion'.[ii] (The author of these comments, R. P. Dutt, knew a thing or two about stifling discussion in the C.P.) The Executive banned resolutions on the *United Front* and 'the position of the S.L.' from affiliated organisations under the '3 years' rule' (by which the Executive held that the issue had been settled at Edinburgh). Cripps pointed out that the ban imposed on association with the C.P. and I.L.P. was not extended to those who associated themselves with members of opposing 'capitalist parties'[iii] (The *Next Five Years' Group* and the *National Peace Council*), that the L.N.U.C. had been set up in the Labour Party and the ban on this was unconstitutional. Laski seconded Cripps. Morrison replied that it was not possible to have disunity spread in the Party 'in the name of unity', Cripps answered at the final L.N.U.C. meeting on October 5th: 'It is far better to face the risks and difficulties which are inherent in working-class unity than to accept the dangers which are bound to follow from a disunited working class. Our *Unity Campaign* was initiated as a *campaign*; it was neither our intention or desire to bring into being any permanent organisation either without or within the Labour Party ... our purpose is to achieve a policy for the Labour Movement based upon the class struggle and the Socialist conception of national and international problems ... From the tragedies suffered by the workers abroad we must surely learn ... the lesson of unity.[iv]

Pleading for 'greater democracy' in the Party, Cripps stated that the minority opinions of today *might* become the majority of opinions tomorrow; this could be achieved only through *public discussions*, otherwise the Party would remain a 'mechanical automaton'. Organisations alone could not give the outlet necessary for sincere conviction on particular issues. What the N.E.C. distrusted was the political judgement of the rank and file; this was expressed by anxiety to crush 'unorthodox' opinion in the Party. G. Strauss augmented this: 'We are always being told that we are being disloyal to the Party ... Do they mean that we are being disloyal to the *leadership* of the Party?'[v] He quoted Dalton, when the latter had written that the second Labour Government had missed opportunities and Party members 'should have kicked up more row, been less loyal to the leaders and more loyal to principles'.[vi] Morrison had little difficulty convincing Conference that persistent attacks on Party members were not the best way to promote working-class unity!

When the votes were cast, the Executive's resolution to ban the *Unity Campaign* was

---

[i] Cripps speech at Norwich, September 6th, 1937, Cripps Papers.

[ii] R. P. Dutt, 'Norwich, Bournemouth and After', *Labour Monthly*, Vol. 19, No. 10, October 1937.

[iii] Cripps at Bournemouth Conference, October 5th, 1937 (speech used in L.P.'s 'Unity! True or Sham?', February 1st, 1939).

[iv] Cripps at L.N.U.C. Meeting October 5th 1937 (Cripps' Papers)

[v] Ibid.

[vi] Quoted by P. Strauss, *Cripps – Advocate and Rebel*, p.97.

passed and the S.L.'s disaffiliation carried,[i] although the M.F.G.B. support for the U.C. was only narrowly lost at its own Conference by 285,000 to 259,000.[ii] (Support from the M.F.G.B. would have added 500,000 to the *Unity Campaign* vote at Bournemouth.) The result was that *Labour's Immediate Programme* and implicit rearmament were.[iii] The decision left ex-S.L. members as Party members, so long as they were prepared to abide by Conference decisions, while the Party launched *Labour's Immediate Programme*. There was encouragement which emerged from Bournemouth in the decision to increase Constituency parties' membership/ representation on the N.E.C. from 5 to 7, for it had been through local Labour Parties that the S.L. had sought to increase its influence. (Pritt, Laski and Cripps (all ex-Unity supporters) were elected to the N.E.C. as a result.) Constituency parties were allowed to elect their representatives separately from union voting and it was hoped constituency parties could perform the rôle which the S.L. had sought to fill, since the election of Pritt, Laski and Cripps indicated a desire by local Parties for a *Socialist leadership*. The *Manchester Guardian* observed of Cripps: 'He has some of the higher qualities of leadership – character, disinterestedness, courage, sincerity and a certain aloofness. He is a thoroughly unskilful politician; he has been in politics for 8 years and is still inexperienced; he has made more "gaffes" than any of his contemporaries'.[iv] Promotion beckoned.

Cripps now believed in 'transparent propaganda' through the Labour Party[v] *for unity*, and the first step was to review Mellor's candidature at Stockport: 'If we are to heal effectively the dissensions of the past year, it is important that in matters such as this we should, if possible, make a new start … I am most anxious to avoid any acrimonious discussion as to the past at the beginning of our new effort at co-operation'.[vi] Cripps' renaissance, without the S.L., was interpreted by a Low cartoon called 'Ready for the Motor Show' with Cripps in a '1938 Labour' model of a million horse power 'runabout', reading the *Daily Worker*. A man is uttering the following: *'The fellow should be prosecuted for cruelty to machinery'*![vii]

George Strauss gleaned from the Bournemouth Conference that the militancy of the Left had not been in vain. The outstanding event of the Conference had been the concession to the Constituency Parties (of their demand to elect their own delegates to the Executive)[viii] because the Constituency Parties' Movement had been an organisational expression of the dissatisfaction voiced by the *Unity Campaign*.[ix] Dutt (for the C.P.) deduced that the weakness in the U.C. had been its 'abstract approach to unity', the disruptive I.L.P., and contradictions vis-à-vis rearmament and peace policy,[x] but he thought it *had* revitalised the Movement by pressurising the Executive, (which had resulted in changes towards democratisation in the N.E.C.). Nevertheless, the Left wing of the Labour Party failed to maintain its hold on Labour opinion after October 1937, partly because of the revelation of the Moscow show trials, adoption of *Labour's*

[i] *Labour Party Annual Conference Report*, October 1937, p.164.

[ii] *New Leader,* July 30th, 1937.

[iii] *Labour Party Annual Conference Report*, October 1937, p.212.

[iv] Quoting P. Strauss, op. cit., p.98.

[v] Cripps letter, October 8th, 1937, Cripps Papers.

[vi] Cripps to George Dallas, October 12th, 1937, Cripps Papers.

[vii] Low cartoon, *Evening Standard*, October 13th, 1937.

[viii] G. R. Strauss, 'Bournemouth and After', *Labour Monthly*, Vol. 19, No. 11, November 1937.

[ix] Ibid.

[x] R. P. Dutt, Bournemouth Conference, *Labour Monthly*, Vol 19, No. 11, November 1937.

Immediate Programme, and traditional Labour union antagonism to 'intellectuals'. Optimism in the Labour Left diminished. Any future campaign would have to be made on the N.E.C.'s terms. With the S.L.'s dissolution, Socialists in the Labour Party lost some faith in the ability to acquire a *voice* in the formulation of Labour policies. Retrospectively, to have sacrificed independence, and then been cheated of a United Front could only result in disillusionment, but problems with the N.E.C. faded into insignificance with the immediacy of the threat of Fascist expansion. There was no time for ex post facto reassessment then.

Cripps' activities were mentioned by the N.E.C. at the Southport Conference (May 1939) in relation to his *Popular Front* and *Petition Campaign*. Reviewing Cripps' record, the N.E.C. noted he had been largely responsible for a series of *campaigns* which sought to change the Party's Constitution, Programme, Principles and Policy. These had covered such a wide territory that the N.E.C. felt it impossible to believe he adhered to Labour Party terms of membership! He was the S.L. leader (an organisation which utilised its privileges as an affiliated organisation to promulgate rival policies to those of the Party); in 1935, he had resigned from the N.E.C. (because he opposed Party policy on the Italo-Abyssinian War); he had made a number of 'irresponsible' speeches during seven years; had presented political opponents with many opportunities to attack the Party, and was a leader of the *Unity Campaign* (for an alliance on the class-war basis of the C.P. which 'stood for Dictatorship')! After Bournemouth, such controversies were to cease with *Labour's Immediate Programme*, but Cripps (according to the N.E.C.) had backed the proposed Peace Alliance initiated by the *Reynolds News* (in March 1938), had publicly indicated his view that the Party was incapable of returning a Labour Government, had peremptorily demanded an N.E.C. meeting to discuss his Memorandum in January 1939, had not informed his N.E.C. colleagues the Memorandum had been publicly printed, and was now preparing a campaign to change the Party's direction. The N.E.C. decided to expel him from the Party![i]

The background to the post-S.L. Cripps' expulsion[ii] formed part of the struggle between the divisional parties and union officials controlling Party policy. Divisional parties carried out Party's propaganda but had little influence in deciding Party policy; their dissatisfactions appeared after Edinburgh, and Cripps had become chairman of the *Constituency Party Association* (for reform of the Constitution to enable divisional parties to elect their own N.E.C. members and increase representation). At Bournemouth, these hopes had borne fruit, and the N.E.C. now contained seven members. In his address dissolving the *Petition Campaign* on June 11th 1939, Cripps claimed: 'Every step we have taken in the last three or four years has been to try and adapt the political tactic of the working class to the fight against Fascism. When we have failed in one course we have tried another ... I hope *Tribune* will be able to play its part in the future, serving as a guide of information and inspiration to all those who accept our approach to the political problems'. The quarrel within the Party was that critics of policies and tactics of Party leaders had been deprived of a voice. Summarising Labour leaders' work, C.P.'er Pollitt provided an example of the different approaches of Labour leaders and the Labour Left: 'On its present basis and policy, the Labour Party cannot successfully organise the type of mass campaign which is now required ... the response from its own membership has not come; there has

---

[i] Report of the N.E.C. to 38th Annual Conference of L.P. at Southport, May 29th–June 2nd, 1939.
[ii] *Labour Party Annual Conference Report*, May 1939, voted 2,100,000 to 402,000, pp.226–29.

been no heart, no burning enthusiasm, no sustained drive, no confident leadership, inspiring, rousing and stimulating the whole drive forward ... but a policy of suppression and exclusion of genuine sections of the working-class movement from the Labour Party'.[i] But then, the C.P. *would* say that!

S.L. leaders did not appreciate that N.E.C. hostility was not essentially based on any objective principles; failure to relate S.L. proposals and aims to the realities of power in the Party was the S.L.'s Achilles heel; it was not so much the *methods* of opposition which were attacked by the N.E.C. as dissent itself. The search by 'loyal critics of the Labour Party' for acceptance of their position in the Party proved fruitless, and S.L. leaders exacerbated their difficulties by denying the N.E.C.'s unassailable authority was the *source* of the S.L.'s lack of influence. The S.L. had diagnosed wrongly that British capitalism was likely to lead to 'Fascist dictatorship and attacks on working-class living standards', and the S.L. was crippled by its own leaders' determination not to repeat I.L.P. mistakes and allow the N.E.C. to force the organisation to secede. The result was constant change in the form of S.L. agitations. By 1937, the N.E.C. implied that it alone was entitled to make or reconstruct Party policy because any attempt to challenge the Party's 'Constitution, Principles, Programme and Policy' was *incompatible* with membership.

Another feature of the S.L.'s existence was its members' sense of imminent political, economic and social catastrophe. One of the obstacles to the success of any Socialist movement was this reliance on economic impediments, rather than a widening awareness of irrational fears of working people to *any* change, which made them deaf to the appeal of Marxist 'facts'. Areas of radical experience were locked in a limited demonstration against 'the Party machine'. The S.L. held to a simplistic philosophy that *only* a change in economic structure could initiate the introduction of Socialist planning, could 'cure' society of its problems: 'We were right in saying that given a better educated society, not over-populated and reasonably homogeneous, a more egalitarian civilisation was possible, but 'we did not attach enough importance to colour differences or ancient national traditions or understand how limited would be the effect of good laws, and how overwhelming the social results of world communications would be... *Where we went wrong was in not realising the complexity of human motives and the universality of aggressiveness.* We assumed that the Affluent Society would be a satisfying one'.[ii] A massive assumption.

Clear-cut political issues were diminishing. Social changes and economic opportunities were no longer only moulded by politicians through manifestos and programmes. Scientific advances and technical changes were altering peoples' habits and ways of living. Party in-fighting was no longer the *key* to controlling and liberating; the new language was technical, of questions of *efficiency* and *technological innovation*. The Labour Party enveloped the Left in State-sponsored planning and politics became a process of alternating Conservative and Labour Governments which were agreed on fundamentals and sparring over incidentals. (By the early 1950s, Keynesian capitalism eliminated 'mass unemployment' and allowed a steadily increasing material standard of living for the working class; this somewhat annulled the 1930s' case for Socialism (that a capitalist society was *unable* to prevent cyclical slumps and economic disintegration). For the non-politicised public, the negative

---

[i] H. Pollitt, *Labour Monthly*, July 1939.
[ii] K. Martin, *The Editor*, p.325. My emphasis.

identification of socialism had begun when the C.P. (and to a lesser extent, the S.L.) paraded Soviet economic achievements, but dismissed the Moscow trials as 'capitalist propaganda'. Full employment and rising incomes would later render the classic Socialist solutions temporarily redundant, in particular social ownership of the means of production. This created an ideological barrier which blocked the Movement's political advance, and was traced to the S.L.'s ideological confusions and sterility of *most* of its debates with Labour and union leaders in the 1930s. The Labour Left had to offer a fresh moral authority. The Socialist 'ideal' had been in a vision of a more liberating environment, but the S.L. viewed the world through materialist eyes (economic exploitation) as if there was no mental, spiritual, sexual and psychological exploitation worth debating.

Jennie Lee reviewed the approach: 'When cynics try to cut the ground from under my feet by claiming that all our efforts to build a friendlier, gayer world are worthless, that people everywhere are too narrowly self-regarding, too much the prisoners of prejudice and greed ever to respond, I am not impressed ... I have the final argument. And it does not depend on the changing whims of abstract political dogmas. It is rooted in the concrete reality of everyday experience. More than all else it draws its strength from the family and friends ... The urge to serve is as strong as the will to dominate. The impulse to share is as much a part of our make-up as the temptation to exploit'.[i] It had to be a *vision* of a society beyond the focus by the S.L. on the production side of the economic system, and devotion to one aspect of social progress. The S.L. was an educational and research organisation, but did not formulate principles on the *cultural* tasks of education (to distribute knowledge of constructive possibilities of human welfare), nor offer to Labour members how to replace defective social mechanisms which prevented people from taking advantage from opportunities. To draw encouragement from active, committed groups in the local community could engage the Movement in a wider disclosure of the incompatibility between Socialist and capitalist priorities, and could provide local initiatives and more self-confidence in the rank and file.

It may be true that people 'aim at projecting their own inward unease onto as large a screen as possible',[ii] but the S.L.'s history was not the history of its leaders, nor a chapter of accidents, nor an organisation engulfed in a bureaucracy. It was a school of *practical experience* in a rapidly-changing international, economic, social and political environment. Although the impulse of 1930s Socialism, 'nationalisation plus social security', has waned, the success of the Welfare State resulted in a new source of Socialist aspirations, (unforeseen by the S.L.). The 1930s struggles (between capitalist and socialist economic systems, Parliamentary and authoritarian political systems[iii], Imperialist and indigenous national systems, technologically-advanced nations arming against each other) are recognised today, but the preoccupations of the Left have moved to the environment; formalism of education; saturation of new communications network with trivia; monopoly of media control, and new conformities resulting from that.

---

[i] J. Lee, *This Great Journey*, 1963, p.230.

[ii] M. Muggeridge, *The Thirties*, p.23.

[iii] Stefan Zweig spoke for a generation: 'Against my will I have witnessed the most terrible defeat of reason and the wildest triumph of brutality ... Never ... has any generation experienced such a moral retrogression from such a spiritual height...' qu. P. Singer 'Unus Multorum', in ed. M. V. Bukiet, *Nothing Makes You Free: Writings by Descendants of Jewish Holocaust Survivors* (2002).

However, to put the S.L. into perspective, while it was disappearing in 1937, 20 million people were attending cinemas each week. *Hollywood* was providing the main consolation and escape for the dissatisfaction of millions, and many of the stars most beloved by British film-goers – Garbo, Boyer, Dietrich – had foreign accents and exotic names to make them even more glamorously remote from the world of the Depression. Very few Hollywood films touched on the workers and the underpaid (except '*Mr Deeds Goes to Town*', '*Dead End*' (with Bogart), '*Grapes of Wrath*' and Chaplin's '*City Lights*' and '*Modern Times*') yet American domination of the screen dream-world was *one* factor which indirectly helped to weaken respect for the old British ruling-caste values – titles, hereditary wealth, Oxford accents, public school manners – among the working class.[i] Not that the Socialist League could compete with Hollywood! A more serious addendum, which illuminates the world of the Labour Left in the 1930s comes from Isaiah Berlin:

> Once people say: 'I am the agent of history – we shall do this or that because history demands it, because the route we take is a kind of progressive autostrada, along which we are driven by history itself, so that anything which gets in the way, must be swept aside'; once you are in that kind of frame of mind, you tend to trample on *human rights and values*. There is a need to defend basic decency against the kind of passionate, often fanatical, faith.[ii]

I have endeavoured to rescue the 3000 S.L. members from George Orwell's contemptuous approach to Marxism ("the usual jargon of 'ideology' and 'class-consciousness' and 'proletarian solidarity' … the intellectual tract-writing type of Socialist, with his pullover, his fuzzy hair and his 'Marxian quotation' … the prim white-collar Nonconformist intent on professional status … the 'Snob-Bolshevik'")[iii]. That caricature of representative Socialists (and Orwell's loathing of working-class intellectuals) only illuminates his sour resentments, prejudices and snobbishness. When Orwell presented his blueprint of the new Socialist Britain in his 1941 essay, 'The English Revolution', it included nationalisation of major industries – coal, railways, banks, utilities; creation of a democratic, classless education system, dominion status to India (with full independence once the War was over), and abolition of the House of Lords – all S.L. policies.[iv]

---

[i] Qu. From N. Branson. M. Heinemann, op. cit., 1973 edn., pp.275–277.

[ii] Isaiah Berlin, *Conversations with Isaiah Berlin*, by Ramin Jahanbegloo, 1993 edn., p.147. (My italics.)

[iii] And Orwell's homophobia ("the pink Nancy-boys of the 'left'"), qu. F. Gloversmith, 'Changing Things: Orwell and Auden', in *Culture and Social Change: A New View of the 1930s*, 1980 edn., pp.115–123.

[iv] Simon Schama, 'A History of Britain 3. 1776–2000. The Fate of the Empire', 2003 edn., p.404.

Conclusion

Gorbachev said: 'Politics needs to be nourished by the intellectual in each country because he is more likely to keep the human being at the centre of his examination.'

qu. Arthur Miller, *Timebends*, 1987, p.563.

Faith in universally-valid formulas and goals was an attempt to escape from the unpredictability of life into the false security of fantasy.

Aileen Kelly, qu. in *The First and the Last*, by Isaiah Berlin, 1999, p.135.

Sigmund Freud in *The Future of an Illusion* writes that we may insist as much as we like that the human intellect is weak in comparison with human instincts, and be right in doing so. But nevertheless there is something peculiar about this weakness. The voice of the intellect is a soft one, but it does not rest until it has gained a hearing. Ultimately, after endlessly repeated rebuffs, it succeeds. This is one of the few points in which one may be optimistic about the future of mankind.

qu. Jonathan Glover, *A Moral History of the 20th Century*, 2001, p.224.

The events of 1931 presented the Labour Left with an opportunity to challenge Party leaders and perhaps radicalise the Party. The formation of the S.L. was a reaction to the disappointing record of the Labour Government, economic depression, and the 'crisis in capitalism'. Initially, the strategy was to present the S.L. as a heterogeneous pressure group seeking a prominent place in Labour counsels through the formulation of Conference resolutions. Inherent in this was the attempt to combine an inquiry organisation (with locally active political groups) and a determination to work in the Labour Party, to inculcate precision and definition in Party programmes. Offsetting the anti-theoretical and anti-doctrinal basis of the Party, the S.L. extended traditions of the S.D.F., Fabian Society and I.L.P., from which it inherited its structure, leaning towards propaganda and research, and a programme of activities to adapt Party policies.

Aiming to fill the I.L.P.'s position as the major propagandist influence in the Movement, the S.L. continued the I.L.P.'s political approach, belief in 'direct action', call for a General Strike (if war arose), extra-Parliamentary associations, exposure of Party 'inadequacies', and an anti-Imperialist analysis. In justifying its separate existence (by formulating a radical programme, acting as a catalyst and focal point, possessing what it perceived to be the 'advanced' policies in the Party), the S.L. searched for a position between the Moscow-orientated C.P., and Labour's social democratic empiricism; but, the S.L. never developed a cohesive political standpoint or firm organisational structure to withstand criticisms. Rebuffed as a propagandist body *and* as a political action group, the S.L. acknowledged the dichotomy between Labour's educational and political functions. Having interpreted the concerns of any Labour Government, the S.L. became an irritant, exhibiting principles muzzled by the Party

389

Executive. Presented with the choice of accepting discipline or gaining more independence *outside* the Party, the S.L.'s conflict evolved into battles with Party leaders over international issues and particular activities *within* the Party. Its structural position in the Party gave it little room for manoeuvre, so the N.E.C. could dismiss it as 'a Left-wing smokescreen' alienating the marginal voter. Ensconced as a safety valve for Party critics, it became isolated as a political misfit.

S.L. assessments of the 1929–1931 Labour Government coloured its activities and intra-Party relationships, and its judgements on the Party originated from that Government's failures, from which Left-wing members distanced themselves. Exposing the P.L.P.'s vacillation, confusion, economic orthodoxy, and failure to rectify the unemployment problem, S.L. critics castigated Party leaders for 'moral bankruptcy' in bolstering a capitalist crisis. From this critique evolved mutual suspicions and recriminations of Labour Right and Left. By analysing the Party's helplessness in the face of economic dislocations, insufficiencies in proposed remedies, and limitations of social reforms, S.L. leaders implied a disbelief in 'Parliamentary gradualism'. Its own remedies included a comprehensive plan for the transition to a Socialist society, a definitive policy of nationalisation (implemented through Parliament!), and a determination to clarify details and implications of Party policy and especially political tactics.

Reacting to the 1931 financial crisis, the S.L. became entrenched in a 'sabotage' theory, in which there was 'a bankers' conspiracy', the Crown's 'constitutional manoeuvrings', Labour leaders' 'betrayal', exaggerated 'Press alarms', all of which had undermined the Labour Government. These perceptions were extended by the overwhelming odds against the Labour Party in the Election campaign, and mystification of a 'National' Government appeal. Profoundly affecting the S.L.'s subsequent positions, it made the organisation wary of Parliamentary 'democracy' per se, reliance upon electioneering, or possible 'peaceful transition' towards a Socialist society. The S.L. became preoccupied with intrigues of power politics, political, economic and constitutional privileges which would keep capitalist interests entrenched and closure of most media to propagation of Socialist views. These criticisms entailed one-dimensional attitudes to 'capitalist economics', a conviction and expectation of unconstitutional resistance (to any future Socialist measures), a policy to safeguard measures through Emergency Powers or the threat to use them, to offset disadvantages under which a Labour Government would operate.

This response was intensified in the unique conditions of 1930s' mass unemployment and threats of Fascism and war, with concurrent ineffectual Labour Opposition to the Government and lacklustre alternatives promulgated by the Party's Executive. In explaining rank and file disillusionment [by inspecting the diminished significance of the Party], the S.L. instigated its own ostracism and intractable conflicts of personality and policy, which subsumed it. It hoped there was room for a pressure group propounding Socialist views in the Labour Party, that economic slump was propitious for working-class political initiatives but there remained contradictions in the S.L.'s analysis between fundamental social changes yet attachment to Labour's gradual processes. Faith in 'political education' proved illusory (it had little effect on the Party's praxis), while the S.L.'s agitatory style grew more irksome to the N.E.C. as elections drew near, whether local or the national Election of 1935.

From the outset, the S.L. exhibited its characteristics – its desire for a planned society, a simplified Marxist economic analysis, concentration on an *economic* diagnosis of political and social events, impatience with the N.E.C.'s tentativeness, yet an optimistic confidence in a Socialist future, mixed with an intense wariness of financial influences on Government decisions. As a result of the economic crisis, many soi-disant intellectuals were motivated and prompted by the indignity of 'starvation in the midst of plenty', a revolt of social conscience reviving Socialist theories to counteract the Party's anti-theoretical prejudices and pragmatism. The gap between the intellectual and the politician was slightly bridged as professional radicals, advocating Socialist alternatives in the Labour Party, stirred latent suspicions of some Labour and union leaders (who estimated intellectuals' pretensions as dogmatism, unreliability, impatience with practicalities, devaluing of Party loyalties, and vagueness of their proposals as "hindrance"); confrontations were endemic between intellectuals and the Party and union hierarchy, epitomising the inability of intellectuals 'to fit into' Labour politics; such groups were less susceptible to Parliamentary respectability and had a history of pressurising the Party to adopt more radical proposals which had proved counter-productive.

The intellectual element in the S.L. was exaggerated by Party and union leaders in the latter's accusations against the S.L.'s supposed pedantry, dilettantism or indecisions. Nevertheless, there *were* contradictions in the rôle of the S.L. intellectual. Hostile to the Party's perceived 'bureaucracy', he (or she) hailed an authoritarian ideology imported from another country; while the search for definitive answers to British problems (such as mass unemployment) contrasted with necessary Party pragmatism, compromises and opportunism (the *currency* of Parliamentary politics). The S.L. intellectual extended the assumptions of State Socialism, the application of Marxist thinking to British conditions (and analysis in Party programmes); the motivation was the need for action in an era of economic, political and social chaos. Hence, the S.L.'s recognition that "professional workers" were rarely reached by Labour propaganda, and should be, because they held a position of strategic importance and were as much divorced or alienated from the existing ownership of the means of production as industrial workers. Since the professional's vocational self-respect was also shattered by economic waste and narrow considerations of profit, the S.L. lauded not only a planned economic system, but worries that middle-class professionals might accept Fascism as an answer to economic and industrial problems, hence the important rôle for professional technician and administrator in a potentially Socialist society.

Assessing the European political situation as an extended class struggle, the S.L. formed a unique approach in the Labour Party. Utilising the Party platform, it envisaged that class distinctions had forced *the class struggle* into the open. This inspiration to re-invigorate the Labour Party was gleaned from a Marxist analysis which supplied a logic, relevance and 'answer' to the economic depression and S.L. leaders' allegiance to neo-Marxism evolved from a recognition of Soviet economic achievements, disappointments of two Labour Governments, 'endless' economic depression, and mass unemployment, Socialists' exclusion from power, thwarting of industrial action and triumphs of European Fascism in 'solving' their countries' crises. This Marxist adherence was a guide to an analysis of capitalist crisis, a formula for unmasking 'democratic inconsistencies', a method of human change venerating the vitality in changing society radically. Marxism justified the S.L.'s cultivation and simplification of 'the class struggle' and gave credence to an optimistic belief never fully annotated in the 'collapse of capitalism', because the S.L. had no faith that prosperity was coming soon or that capitalism was being reformed, and only saw signs of a sinister Fascist menace in Government legislation.

The attractions of Marxism in the 1930s were that people were viewed as *active agents* in the historical process, a strategic rôle was assigned the working-class and the radical intellectual. This intensified friction between the S.L. and the Party and union leaders, the latter alienated by Marxist bourgeois-baiting and pessimistic view about Parliamentary 'reformism'. No practical bridge existed between the class struggle thesis promulgated incessantly and existing social democratic policies in the Labour Party; S.L. leaders' Marxist analysis exhibited a stultifying approach to British politics, because it did not develop a theory of Socialist transformation beyond the ideas of socialisation/nationalisation which might not fundamentally affect differences in power, status, or privileges; Marxist attachments prevented opportunity to analyse possibilities of a *mixed economy*, thus under-estimating the regenerative powers of the capitalist system to overcome crises. The S.L. had a static interpretation of Marxism, and the theme of 'class struggle' became the final illusion for the Party hierarchy and ultimate reality to the S.L. Never again could an affiliated organisation base its strategy so clearly on such a bald thesis.

With Labour intellectuals attached to Marxism, S.L. leaders were emboldened by a particular attachment to the Soviet Union, which coloured their relationships with Labour leaders, I.L.P. and C.P. The S.L. was fascinated by the Russian example, especially Lenin's method, theory, organising élite, persistence, grasp of essentials, refusal to compromise. Sustained by a belief in Soviet experimentation, application of Marxism, conversion of representative institutions and the Soviet Union's supposed *'solution'* of conflicts between economic planning and political liberty, S.L. leaders expounded enthusiastically on Soviet practical demonstrations of rational planning and full employment, 'Socialist principles in action', and supposed elimination of the differences between 'worker' and 'intellectual'. Although many S.L. members were critical of contradictions between a supposedly Soviet egalitarian economic structure and a dictatorial political system, no serious analysis was undertaken into the reality of 'proletarian dictatorship', Soviet 'democracy' or 'workers' control of industry'. The 'ideal of the Soviet Union' was a framework from which to criticise Labour's reformism; as a result, the N.E.C. was sceptical of S.L. faith in 'an alliance with the Soviet Union' as the only way to defeat Fascism. Gradually internally divided over the patent absence of 'workers' democracy' in Russia, the S.L. was further split when the Soviet Union joined the League of Nations; the S.L. became victim of its own projected vision of Soviet achievements, since Soviet experimentation *had been* replaced by enforced industrialisation, and it was in social policy and education, not material wealth and production, that the Soviet Union actually offered a little inspiration. Revelations in the Spanish Civil War and the Moscow Trials (of the Soviet C.P. in action) came too late to jolt the S.L. out of its faith.

The S.L. sought to represent 'the active' in the Labour Party, but epitomised the Party's complex intellectual, empirical and working-class representation. Restating the Party's fundamental tenets, the S.L. was opposed by leaders whom it needed to influence, and had to act within a framework chosen by that leadership. The S.L. incorporated every shade of Left-wing opinion, upholding flexibility in the Party's thought and proclamation of Socialist alternatives. In the circumstances, such a pressure group could not create *new* political perspectives, could not alter the N.E.C.'s focus on Parliament, could be disregarded for proposing generalities without practical experience, criticising without inside knowledge, suggesting actions without responsibility for consequences. Held strictly to account for the leaders it presented, its position was precariously balanced. These leaders were controversial, eloquent debaters whose published lectures exhibited a principled (if Messianic) style. Impatient as resolution-formulators and programme-makers, they remained aloof, unsuccessful in gaining sufficient support from the rank and file; their protests brought them notoriety in the Press because of their bluntness; this candour (in dramatising public issues) was refreshingly independent but was labelled 'reckless' by the Party Executive.

In a time of stocktaking and reformulation of Party programmes and policies, the S.L. had a unique base for a Socialist organisation in the Party. Its initial critique was directed at the Party's lack of a cohesive programme, and there the S.L. provided the sustenance of educational propaganda to revitalise Party programmes, from miscellanies to plans of campaign and schemes of priorities. From its inception, the S.L. began by working out detailed solutions to problems for a future Socialist Government, but this evaded the difficulties of influencing the whole Movement and countering the N.E.C.'s image of the S.L. as 'irresponsible'. Determination to be publicly honest about Socialist intentions had a hollow basis, since, in debating every controversial issue *publicly* as a tactic to challenge Party and union leaders, the S.L. was attempting to establish answers before political power was anywhere near being achieved. However, the S.L. managed to reduce Party leaders' freedom of action sufficiently to reveal the value of divergent political opinion within the Movement, and utility of a pressure group to stimulate discussion and argument.

Attracting Labour members starved of political thought, S.L. publications on a broad range of topics affecting the Labour Movement were a forum for viewpoints and debate (rather than the presentation of a coherent policy). One of its assumptions was that *thoroughly explained* Socialist policies and tactics could gain support and dispel unwarranted fears. (This again originated in reaction to the shrouded events of 1931.) Pamphlets were used as a basis for discussion, to help Labour members recognise an element of choice in action, but, under-estimating problems of applying pressure on the Executive, the S.L. placed too much hope in a dramatic conversion in the rank and file, while pressure was focussed on Party leaders rather than on unions. As a propagandist fulcrum in the Party, the S.L. expressed dissatisfactions of Labour dissidents with the unprecedented political and economic problems, but Nazism nullified the S.L.'s hopes of revivifying the Labour Party in a more Socialist direction. What it achieved was a confirmation that totalitarianism of the Right and Left was not Labour's way. By 1934, the S.L.'s open debates on abolition of the Lords, questions of sabotage, and seizure of power, were embarrassing the N.E.C. After October 1934, the S.L. was compelled to re-channel its energies locally to salvage a rôle as a pressure group.

From 1935, the S.L. initiated immediate local activities, organising conferences and demonstrations on the *Unemployment Act*, the Means Test, industrial nationalisation, and dangers of Fascism, the Corporate State and War. Here the S.L. attempted to supply a practical context for its previously theoretical approach, but its alleged 'reformation in function' was not substantial; its tactics remained ill-defined through increasing internal disagreements; S.L. leaders failed to comprehend that Party and union leaders could affect the rank and file more through appeals to immediate interests than clearly-defined arguments. Although the S.L. operated as the safety-valve for Socialist sentiment (fostering a pseudo-conflict against the Party's N.E.C.), it had a coherent analysis of capitalist society, and was the last vigorous movement for Socialist education, research and propaganda in the institutionalised Labour Party before subordination to the electoral machine proved successful.

The S.L. desire to create an independent image can be seen in its national conferences and policy resolutions. Its basic tenets included State ownership, workers' control in industry, social welfare through a Welfare State, full employment through economic planning, and appropriation of property incomes. This did not become apparent until 1934, for, at its Derby Conference in 1933, the S.L. had drawn up a programme of action which dealt with generalities. In 1934, the S.L. had its own programme, *Forward to Socialism*, and an election manifesto with a five-year plan (haunted with fears of Fascism and armed Powers). This heralded the first confrontation with Party and union leaders. Intended to translate principles into practice and offer Party delegates a coherent programme, *Forward to Socialism* was more a popular *leaflet* than a detailed *plan*. Replacing its original research function, it proved the S.L. could only concentrate on the general tempo of Party policy. Defeat of its recommendations at Southport compelled the S.L. to alter its perspective in 1935. Its Bristol and Stoke Conferences dealt with foreign affairs and proposals for strengthening Trades Councils and local Labour Parties as the foci for S.L. activities. Press coverage of its activities diminished until the S.L. considered a *United Front* in mid-1936. Once the S.L. sought more independent action, there were no more wordy resolutions or neat plans, and the S.L. found its platform inspiring agitations rather than developing Party programmes.

In its policy recommendations and specific obsessions, the S.L. reflected many of the broader Movement's apprehensions about Parliamentary democracy, free speech, the Press and monarchy, dictatorships and Fascism, and problems of mass unemployment. The S.L. acted out for the whole Movement the fears and fantasies associated with these issues. They urged the Party Conference to incorporate preparations to combat any future obstruction from financial interests and to implement Emergency Powers. Here, the S.L.'s hysterical tone was a response to an impotent political situation for the Labour Left, yet it was impossible for the Party to centre *any* Socialist campaign on these constitutional issues, however relevant it might be to explain that political capital was being extracted from them by the Government. The S.L.'s questioning of the realities of democratic values (at a time of overt Nazi oppressions) was ill-judged and bound to be misinterpreted by the Press. Evincing analogies between British and German Governments and potential threat to a Socialist future was to evade immediate threats to democratic values. It is not surprising that the Party's N.E.C. was alarmed and feared a Conservative backlash if S.L. priorities were promoted; it was a tactical error to consider the question of 'dictatorship', since emotional connotations of the word allowed for misinterpretation and supplied further reason for the N.E.C. to discipline 'irresponsible declamations', however much the latter might excite the rank and file. Placing private thoughts into the public political arena had to be very carefully prepared. Sometimes the S.L. gave the impression it just wanted to make a big noise.

The S.L. was far more constructive on the issue of *unemployment*, contributing directly to unemployed agitations, and presenting this as the major issue for the Movement; this became the emotional, political and social fulcrum for the S.L. Reacting to the unemployment problem was the main theme until 1936, and it focussed on the failure of the capitalist system, and made it difficult to tolerate

Labour's gradualist remedies, while Government treatment of the problem strengthened S.L. conviction that it was impossible to cure when it represented a failure of the system of wealth production. While demanding immediate panaceas (a 25% increase in unemployed maintenance pay, abolition of transitional benefit and the Means Test, a four year slum clearance scheme), the S.L. supplemented local agitations by exposing the divisive *Unemployment Act*. Tensions mounted between the S.L. and union leaders' respective methods of protest against U.A.B. demands, so that by 1937 the S.L. was calling for one national unemployed movement (inevitably to involve the C.P.) to replace local agitations. On the issue of unemployment, the S.L. proved its case against the market economy, although it did not anticipate Keynes' diagnosis nor the potential demand created by the advance of technology in production. Government remedies to counter economic depression were rejected as by-products of the retention of private ownership, while a Socialist pressure group such as the S.L. confronted economic nationalism, recurrence of crises, and waste of resources in unplanned production. The S.L.'s alternative economic ideas were directed at removing inefficiencies of capitalist distribution through nationalisation, investment boards, planning authorities, regional development councils, redistributive taxation, and new social services, most of which *were* implemented during the 1940s.

In terms of its relations with Party leaders, the S.L. considered that conflicts arose in the interpretations of the use of the block vote, affiliated groups' representation in the Party, and what Party 'loyalty' entailed. A struggle raged over Party policies and programmes but, with each successive debate, the S.L. grew more fragmented, while the Executive's fear of unorthodox opinions, crippling the Party in a time of crises, disguised the Party's successful function as the agent for the institutionalisation of the working class. The economic slump was *the* moment of choice for Party leaders; was the Party to work towards State welfare economics or a fundamental change in the economic system? (The S.L. worked for a radical restatement of Party objectives and methods, and in 1932 and 1933 gained resolution successes at Party Conferences, but by 1934 it was obvious Party leaders only tolerated divergent opinions so long as they were insignificant.)

Consistently translating political issues into questions of leadership, the S.L.'s verbal victories had little influence on the N.E.C., which labelled the S.L. disloyal, confused, fragmentary, diverting attention from its own cautious policies over rearmament and unemployment. The crunch with the N.E.C. was postponed, and contributed to bitter debates on discipline, C.P. affiliation to the Party, and the *Unity Campaign*. Underlying the N.E.C.'s attitude was a purposeful discouragement of any unconventional methods of protest, but buttressing S.L. militancy was the rôle of a pressure group. Although the S.L.'s *Forward to Socialism* was nebulous and contradictory, objections to the absence of an immediate programme and reliance on Parliamentary agitations were submerged in the N.E.C.'s *For Socialism and Peace*; the decision to give more time to policy reports at Conference and less time to affiliated bodies nullified effective criticism of the Party platform, and by-passed most controversial issues. The Southport Conference decisions elucidated the S.L.'s complex position, of challenging the Executive through Conference resolutions; to avoid canalising its discontents into harmless channels, the S.L. had to concentrate on immediate action, polarising a possible confrontation between 'Fascism and Socialism', and warning of the danger of a Corporate State.

The Party's N.E.C. rejected a '*programme of mass activity*' and juxtaposed differing functions of political and industrial activities in the Movement to strengthen the unifying agency of its leadership. By failing to alter the Party's Election programme, the S.L. acknowledged that debate (and organisation) was only possible on N.E.C. terms. The Election defeat of 1935 reaffirmed S.L. criticisms of the Party, and justified S.L. reorientation towards local agitations, but in 1936, the S.L. worried that Party leaders would co-operate with the Government in its defence programme. This seemed to be confirmed by ambiguous policy statements and S.L. defeats at Edinburgh, propelling the S.L. further to a United Front campaign to counteract Party dilatoriness. *Labour's Immediate Programme* completed the emasculation of S.L. protests, proving irreconcilable contradictions between Socialist principles and the practical politics of Labour, while N.E.C. demands for 'loyalty and discipline' lessened the Movement's diversity and potential vitality. While the Party's organisation was tightened, immediate objectives clarified, a programme of reforms developed, the S.L. failed to generate *a philosophy of action* for Labour and union leaders, since manifestos, pamphlets and radical programmes could alter nothing without involvement in immediate causes and campaigns.

From its formation, the S.L. lost much union support when E. F. Wise was preferred to E. Bevin as the S.L.'s Chairman, and although the S.L. was most influential when union membership had temporarily diminished, the T.U.C. increased its influence in the Labour Movement through the National Council of Labour. Between the S.L. and union leaders grew resentments, suspicions and non-communication, exhibited in confrontations over the block vote and the S.L.'s plans for 'workers' control'. Among specific S.L. disappointments was union work for a greater share in economic concessions and wage negotiations to the detriment of involvement in unemployment struggles, union leaders' assurance the economy would recover and their institutionalised co-operation with management and the State. Questioning the T.U.C.'s functions on socialised industries, the S.L. proposed direct industrial action and extended backing for Trades Councils and local unemployed organisations. Challenging the structure and function of existing unions, S.L. leaders viewed the T.U.C. as 'saturated with a capitalist outlook', but the S.L.'s economic analysis was grossly impractical (especially for union leaders permanently and constantly committed to raising the *status* of organised Labour).

By 1935, the S.L. became more committed to the unemployed, local unions, supporting unofficial strikes, and Trades Councils for strike action. At the Brighton Conference, union leaders reasserted their control, so the S.L. turned its attention to miners' struggles (and visions of workers' control of industry) in the resolution of the 55 Conferences. Doubts were expressed as to the T.U.C.'s acceptance of the Government's armament programme; would the T.U.C. resist dilution of labour? The S.L. hoped conditions of labour sought by unions would become inimical to the capitalist economy, but the T.U.C. rejected the *Unity Campaign* and condemned the hunger marchers for 'unconstitutional' protests. The S.L.'s case for industrial unionism remained unanswered, but was far from involving the mass of unionists in the conviction that wage movements could become a method of 'class advance'. Similarly, the Co-operative Movement was viewed as the potential consumption aspect of a Socialist society, which *had to* lessen its dependence on private manufacturers, if it wished to offer workers experience in the management of productive and distributive enterprises. Such hopes remained dormant.

The N.E.C.'s opposition to the C.P. widened the gap between the S.L. and Party leaders, who feared C.P. infiltration and disruption and resented the 'Social Fascist' label applied (by the C.P.) to Labour's reformism. With the economic crisis and emergence of Nazism, the S.L. underplayed historical antagonisms between the Labour Party and C.P., and always regarded the latter as a potential ally. United unemployed agitations appeared, led by the N.U.W.M., C.P. and I.L.P., but the Labour Executive denounced any connections with the C.P. in *Democracy and Dictatorship,* and vetoed any collaboration by Labour members in anti-Fascist groupings linked with the C.P. By 1935, with a volte-face in Soviet foreign policy, the C.P. haggled for co-operation with the Labour Party against 'Fascism and War', and withdrew most of its election candidates, re-applying for affiliation to the Labour Party. This was supported by the S.L., which sought help in its own struggles with the Party Executive. The N.E.C. threatened disciplinary action if any attempt was made to bury ideological differences in united actions with the C.P. and mutual suspicion of each other's motives and tactics restricted co-operation. By the Edinburgh Conference defeat of the C.P.'s application for affiliation to the Labour Party, too many S.L. leaders had become committed to a *Unity Campaign,* to resolve S.L. difficulties vis-à-vis Labour's N.E.C. Links with the C.P. and I.L.P. precipitated the S.L.'s demise.

Since the S.L. promoted local branch activities so zealously in its first two years, it is surprising there was less mention of those activities when S.L. leaders turned their attention to them after S.L. impact in Party Conferences had been thwarted (by November 1934). There is no evidence that S.L. local influence was *extended* outside ex-I.L.P. strongholds; S.L. branch members agitated on behalf of local grievances; based on research projects into local conditions and existing facilities, developed a knowledge of local difficulties, branch work consisting of surveys, lectures, study groups, collation of facts for speakers' classes, S.L. pamphlets, plays, outings, fundraising and recruitment campaigns. This work was a *unifying* medium, a means to constructive local action, an emotional therapy, a training in local government – clear messages conveyed in a time of mass unemployment and fears of a future war.

Head Office tended to exaggerate local branch achievements when the initial fervour had waned by the end of 1934. The dominating feature of local branch work was for funds, donations, pamphlet finances, membership campaigns. Branch dissatisfactions emerged at the S.L. Leeds Conference; Southport Party Conference decisions nullified much of branch work. The special S.L. Conference in November 1934 rectified little, apart from urging local branches to help Trades Councils in unemployed agitations, strengthen local unions' protests against the Sedition Bill, demonstrate against Fascism (and a possible war). The S.L.'s *'Mass Resistance to War'* conferences, miners' campaigns, and demonstrations against the *Unemployment Act,* occupied local branches, with reminders from Head Office of fundraising and membership campaigns. Henceforth, S.L. leaders attempted to harness the constituency parties in their struggle for more representation in the Party, with local activities against the *Unemployment Act,* support for the Labour League of Youth and the *Unity Campaign,* since S.L. criticisms of the Party structure found favour in the constituency parties. Contacting the Labour League of Youth as an ally receiving similar treatment from the Executive was a typical S.L. tactic. As an assertion against the Executive, the S.L. promoted the League of Youth offering flexibility in policy discussions, through resolutions against stifling the League of Youth, its right to discuss policy, and to have representation on the Executive. A battle ensued for the support of the youth organisation, resolved when the Executive reduced the League of

Youth's age limit to 21 and compelled it to concentrate on recreational, educational and electoral work; its membership declined drastically! The S.L. colluded with constituency parties in their struggle for more representation on the N.E.C., and a decentralisation of union funds; this justified the S.L.'s work. Envisaging the constituency parties as local action groups, the S.L. was given a new lease of life. The *Constituency Party Association* (with Cripps as Chairman), and the effort to attach it to the *Unity Campaign*, proved abortive. Past S.L. disappointments could not be re-channelled into the C.P.A.'s interests, although local debates (on Fascism, Abyssinia, the Soviet Union, Spanish Civil War, rearmament and working-class unity) eased the S.L.'s path into the *Unity Campaign*. Nevertheless, there is little evidence that local branches were transformed *'from research groups into active political units'*, since local activities were largely uncoordinated, S.L. Head Office could only diffuse influence, not organise it, and branch members could not overcome general lack of interest in the provinces.

The S.L. evolved a complex foreign policy on the *British Empire, Nazi Germany, the League of Nations, the Spanish Civil War, and Unity Campaign*. Anti-Imperialism was the central theme; British Imperialism was denounced more than Nazi aggression. In its publications, the S.L. viewed Imperialism as the ultimate phase of capitalist, national economic rivalries, the solution in national self-determination and renunciation of overseas territories (which transpired from the late 1940s). It feared a 'patriotic war' would divert working-class opposition into support for Empire, especially since the Government seemed to have no intention of supporting a Socialist France, a Soviet Russia, or Popular Fronts. In relation to Indian self-government, the S.L. criticised the imposed Indian Constitution, which left the armed and financial power of the Empire intact, made India safe for British investments, did not solve Indian poverty, and denied civil liberties. Disappointed that the Party had no mass campaign against the India Bill, the S.L. was spared later Socialist disillusionment witnessing those suffering under Imperialist rule primarily fighting for nationalist, not Socialist, ends.

Reacting against the N.E.C.'s official support for the League of Nations, the S.L. majority viewed the League of Nations as the sheet-anchor of British Imperialism, which could *not* cure political or economic maladjustments, and would only legislate and administer in the capitalist interest, so could never be a vehicle for a future Socialist foreign policy. This majority S.L. position noted the illusory nature of pacts and covenants; instead, a treaty with the Soviet Union and 'mass resistance to war' (through a General Strike) were promoted, until the Soviet Government joined the League of Nations! By 1935, the S.L. was further divided over sanctions against the Italian Government in Abyssinia, the S.L. majority wary that sanctions could be used by any Imperialist Power, and would not deter Mussolini's war preparations. The S.L. was more interested in *who* controlled the doing than *what* could be done, which was not a practical alternative to the N.E.C.'s policy. Perhaps no Socialist anti-war position was viable, but no practical means for workers to counteract war were offered. While Party leaders retained faith in the League of Nations, the only outcome for the S.L. was indecision, self-contradiction, and internal dissension.

The emergence of Nazi Germany confirmed to the S.L. necessity for Socialist alternatives proclaimed in the Labour Party, but each section of the Party drew different conclusions from this new German threat, and divisions in the Movement were exacerbated over the precise response. The S.L. interpreted Nazism as the result of economic chaos, mass unemployment, wrongs of the Treaty of Versailles, weaknesses of Social Democratic parties and their struggle with the C.P. Recognising dangers inherent in a rearmed Germany, the S.L. grew more wary (when the German Government left the League of Nations and the Disarmament Conference), and believed Nazism fed on the caution of the union movement and respectability of Social Democrats – a lesson for the British Labour Movement to heed. By 1935, the S.L. was assessing Germany as an exploited colony of finance capital in which war production was the only method of solving contradictions in the economy; therefore, re-occupation of the Rhineland appeared the 'logical consequence of rearmament', while German workers suffered diminishing wages, and lessening bargaining power and legal rights. Looking to a Popular Front as the force to check Nazism and Fascism, the S.L. was stimulated by a *Unity Campaign* with the example of the French Popular Front.

The Spanish Civil War produced the first and last crusade of the Left intellectual; substituting action for ideas, offering conviction, inspiration and justification for anti-Fascist policies; a battleground for rival ideologies enervating class-consciousness; the complex issues divided the Left, illustrated in the wrangling between I.L.P. and C.P. (which precipitated the end of the S.L.). Initially, events in Spain added impetus for a *Unity Campaign*, since the whole Left viewed Franco's fight as a Fascist plan for conquest of Europe. The claims of international law and class solidarity (and the Soviet Union as an ally) made the S.L. more conscious of its proximity to the I.L.P. and C.P. Counter-acting the N.C.L.'s non-intervention stance, the S.L. sought a campaign to aid Spanish workers and prevent supplies to Franco's forces; the war appeared as one between democracy and dictatorship (workers versus owners). By October 1936, the Germans and Italians aiding Franco justified the S.L.'s denunciation of the N.E.C.'s caution and its association with the unofficial movement for intervention. With the Government's ban on British volunteers, S.L. leaders were more influenced by Soviet aid to Spanish workers; united platforms appeared, with the S.L. as the vanguard of the Labour Party. The S.L., I.L.P. and C.P. were certain a determined stand against Hitler and Mussolini would call the latter's bluff, but irrevocable dissensions between I.L.P. support for P.O.U.M. and C.P. support for Soviet policy threatened the S.L.'s mediatory rôle in the *Unity Campaign*. Underlying a characteristic in the S.L.'s history, its hopes for unity on the Left in the Spanish Civil War brought to surface historical divisions between the Left and Right in the Movement, creating more conflicts. The uncertainties and disappointments of the early 1930s could have been replaced by a united struggle against Fascist influences, but the S.L. could not afford to admit the intricacies, ambiguities and political intrigues in Spain, so contrary to international brotherhood and a possible Socialist future.

Ties for unity in the Labour Movement should have been strengthened by European Fascism and disintegration of a Social-Democratic Government, the union movement and C.P. in Germany, but only the I.L.P. and C.P. initially conferred in united demonstrations against Fascism. Labour leaders, presenting the choice of '*Communism or Social Democracy*', refused to give a lead, so the S.L. abstained from any limited united action (other than co-operation in an anti-war campaign with the Labour League of Youth and University Labour Federation). At its Derby Conference the S.L. passed an anti-war pledge but rejected any united front. Typically, after a rebuff, the S.L. rallied behind a slogan (for Mass Resistance to War), a feature of the S.L.'s strategy for survival. While the T.U.C. defeated the S.L.'s resolution for 'a general strike if war', the Leeds S.L. Conference exhibited divisions on the United

Front, some members urging subordination of theoretical differences and tactical methods in joint action (with the C.P., and I.L.P.), the majority echoing N.E.C. suspicions of I.L.P./ C.P. motives. Returning to its theme of war resistance, the S.L. did not associate itself with the *Memorandum on Anti-Fascism* in September 1934, and the Southport Conference passed the Executive's *'War and Peace'* formula, defeating the S.L's tentative United Front resolution for limited objectives.

By now, the S.L. recognised its common interests with the I.L.P. and C.P. in local activities, tactics on unemployment, and opposition to Mosley's British Union of Fascists, while Peace Pledge groups and the Peace Ballot encouraged the possibility of a Unity Campaign. At the S.L.'s Bristol Conference, the S.L.'s *Mass Resistance to War Conferences* could be interpreted as efforts to keep inside Party rules. Long before the Unity Campaign the S.L. was divided over diversion into activities condemned by the Executive, but after the Brighton Conference, S.L. interest returned to a United Front and dangers of working-class fragmentation. S.L. interest in a United Front was now bound up with its need to break the hold of the Party and this explanation is offered for the S.L.'s tortuously mixed motives and outlook in the Abyssinian crisis, and why the Hoare-Laval episode propelled the S.L. majority to a Unity Campaign as a *solution* to its predicament inside the Party, because the N.E.C. failed to expose the Government's refusal to oppose Mussolini's ventures.

In April 1936 the S.L. returned to its theme of opposing increased armaments and war (rather than commitment to a United Front) in the *Seven-Point Resistance Plan to Rearmament*. Negotiations between the C.P., I.L.P. and S.L. were also now promoted. While the S.L. demanded a decisive challenge to Government rearmament and plans for industrial mobilisation, suggestions for a *Unity Campaign* divided the S.L. (especially over definitions of a 'united platform', which would carry inspirational associations of French and Spanish Popular Fronts rather than appear as a mere manoeuvre). The Labour Party's negative vote at the Edinburgh Conference on the Spanish Civil War and a United Front enhanced the links between the C.P., I.L.P. and S.L. Events such as the Hunger March, the Spanish Civil War, South Wales' industrial struggle and the East London Conference against Fascism, proved the validity of united platforms. By 1937, the *Unity Campaign* was projected to consolidate and reinvigorate the diverse Left (intellectually, organisationally and emotionally) as a symbol of protest against Fascism, although the S.L. planned to utilise the Campaign in its struggle with the N.E.C. for freedom of action to participate in activities not designated by the latter.

The *Unity Campaign* was a reaction to the ambivalence of Party leaders and apathy of the rank and file. Equipped with *Tribune*, the Left Book Club, I.L.P. and C.P. publications, the Campaign filled a gap in propaganda against Government policies. It highlighted dissatisfaction with T.U.C. domination, and marked the closest contact the C.P. had with any section of the Labour Party. Insisting on no such connections, the N.E.C. forwarded *Labour's Immediate Programme* to counteract the *Unity Campaign*, which it condemned as unsuited to British political conditions. Inside the S.L. leadership, questions were asked about the consequences of a Campaign for which there was less than majority support. Dissolution of the S.L. was not contemplated, although some members were wary of the C.P.'s possible aim to limit the S.L. as a competitor for a unique position in the Labour Party. The Campaign remained a loose alliance blurring theoretical differences for immediate practical objectives.

Infusing a spirit of urgency, the *Unity Manifesto* was the first and last product of representatives of the British Left in the 1930s, the most ambitious bid to break the Labour Party's strict alignments. Labour's N.E.C. became impatient with the growing popularity of the Left Book Club, *Tribune* and the *Unity Campaign*, rebuking the S.L. for ignoring its veto on the latter, control of which was evaporating daily from the S.L. As in all attempts at joint action, the *Unity Campaign* reopened old divisions and recriminations, and the N.E.C. disaffiliated the S.L. for opposing a Conference decision, the principal controversy being the *limits of a minority* to persuade the Party to change its views. This confirmed the S.L.'s isolation, since any debate on policy was translated into a question of 'discipline and disruption'. The Campaign raised questions as to the future of the Labour Movement, but was a focus of dissent which evolved into that safety-valve and emotional release, while the Executive was convinced the Campaign was a splitting tactic and C.P. infiltrations would provoke Fascist reprisals.

Thwarted by the N.E.C. in the direct question of united action, the S.L. returned to the issue of control of the armaments industry and mobilisation of mass resistance to war. Although the S.L. had put organisational factors above everything, its suppression was not a remedy, since the choice for S.L. members was one of working in established Labour formats (however diluted), or making a break into a new organisation. Acceptance of any slogan to keep the S.L. in existence was no answer nor was determination to arrive at any agreement with the C.P. and I.L.P., yet the S.L. could not contemplate a direct challenge to the Executive, because individual rebellion would be scapegoated. Inadequate reasons were given for the S.L.'s dissolution. Supposedly it was to demonstrate the S.L.'s sincerity about Party 'unity', or was the purpose of dissolving the S.L. to challenge the question of discipline? The S.L. was incapable of prosecuting a campaign in isolation or in the *Unity Campaign*, its remedies for international problems had been vaguely formulated, its analysis of current issues blinkered by neo-Marxist preconceptions, and the Executive was never sufficiently pressurised to discuss the practical case for or against the *Unity Campaign*. Future Left Labour groups learnt to limit united action to one issue, such as an industrial dispute or opposition to specific reactionary Government legislation, such as the poll tax.

Although Unity Campaign committees activated constituency Labour Parties to demand increased representation on the N.E.C., pressure groups' influence could now be minimised. Despite 43 resolutions on the *Unity Campaign* sent from affiliated branches to the Bournemouth Conference, the Executive shelved the question. The Campaign had been too broad, too abstract in practice, the S.L. only posed short-term objectives, and had been enmeshed in the complex relationship between the C.P., I.L.P. and Labour Party. The S.L. had formed part of the struggle between divisional parties and union officials for representation on the N.E.C., had campaigned to change the Party's constitution, programme, principles and policy, had utilised its privileges as an affiliated organisation to promulgate rival policies, and presented Labour's political opponents with juicy opportunities for attacking Labour's already vulnerable image. Defining itself as a series of *'short-term campaigns'* to crystallise unrest in Labour ranks, the S.L. became a counter-balancing group in the Movement. It had to change the form and direction of its agitation and propaganda to avoid disbandment (or secession from the Party); in attempting to keep open channels between itself and other Left groups, its position became untenable. It tried to offset N.E.C. bureaucratic tendencies while utilising the platform from which such tendencies originated, until, increasingly disciplined, its balancing act foundered, revealing the illogicality of its position.

Enigmatic in its teachings, cryptic or bald in its pronouncements, contradictory in its aims, it embraced the kaleidoscope of political attitudes in only five years – Parliamentarianism, class struggle, social democracy, revolutionary socialism, anti-Fascism, pacifism, nationalisation – all found favour at different times. Bridging the chasm between the Labour Party and the aspirations of a militant class struggle, the S.L. was attacked from all sides.

The S.L. set out to analyse, enlighten, educate, and inform. It produced intelligently written pamphlets, perceptive monthly journals, ran stimulating and provocative lectures, which helped keep the Left lively. Its well-dramatised activities, cavalier approach to Party traditions (and official responsibilities) and public style of agitation, were refreshing. It led the Party's 1930s' propagandist education, mirrored dissatisfactions of Socialists in 'an age of crises', exemplified great diversity of opinion in the Party, but it was at a disadvantage when calls were made for Party *loyalty* and reasonable Party *discipline*. Its successful Conference resolutions of 1932 and 1933 were later muted or ignored, and after 1934, *it did not win a single resolution.* Here was proof that the 'Leftward swing' after 1931 had been exaggerated, especially in relation to strengthening the Party and union bureaucracy. This helps explain how the S.L. was galvanised by *international affairs* (after 1934), so that it transferred European events to assess British politics. Such prognostications proved onerous, since Labour leaders refused to see in the Government a neo-Fascist counterpart to European dictatorships; the S.L. itself became more divided over foreign policy than domestic policy as a result of its own flexible mixture of Marxist and Fabian tenets.

The S.L. did not appreciate that the Executive's hostility was not based on intellectual principles; it was not able to make adequately apparent the leadership's evasions, and found it difficult to relate its proposals to realities of power in the Party; it never possessed freedom of action to develop alternative policies, denying the Executive's unassailable authority as a main source of its own lack of direction. The S.L.'s appeals for 'anti-Fascist unity' and 'Party democracy' had little influence on Party leaders, and S.L. leaders were crippled by the conviction not to repeat the I.L.P.'s mistakes, despite the constant changes in form and content of S.L. agitations, which weakened the potency of its message. The Party in the 1930s proved not a practical field of action for a Left-wing Socialist since any influence was deemed disruptive. The S.L.'s conviction of imminent political, social and economic *catastrophe* should have encompassed an analysis of fears for working people about losing the little security they had, but the S.L. was locked into strict demonstration against the Party machine and an assumption that an 'affluent society' would supply answers. Party in-fighting could not liberate people; State-sponsored planning and 'automation' would not automatically result in fundamental changes. The S.L. advanced the negative identification of 'Socialism' with Soviet economic achievements, augmenting an ideological confusion and sterility in debates with Labour leaders. It concentrated on economic exploitation as if mental, spiritual, and psychological oppressions were non-existent, and this devotion to the economic side of social progress resulted in a paucity in S.L. research and propaganda.

The 1930s witnessed an increasing awareness of local participation in politics, diffusion of power and responsibility (to incorporate local initiatives), creation of more local self-confidence; the S.L. extended local community work, kept up local morale and modified British prejudices towards minorities. The Left Book Club helped with the dissemination of Socialist ideas, Constituency parties grew in authority with the help of S.L. local work, and those who formed the Popular Front extended the unification process of progressives, which underlay S.L. interests in stimulating the non-Parliamentary militant. In a struggle between capitalist and Socialist economic systems, and authoritarian political systems, Imperialist and indigenous populations, and technically advanced nations arming against each other, the S.L.'s rôle was essentially *informative*. Its kind of pressure group continued in the Labour Movement, alongside extra-Party pressure groups with specific causes, a new development in opposition tactics to the prevailing Government. Labour's 1945–50 mixture of social concern, policies of full employment, welfare and budgetary control of the economy, owed a great deal to the groundwork of the S.L. Much of the S.L.'s thinking had won acceptance a decade after its demise, even among those who had been its harshest critics.

Bibliography

Primary Sources

(A) MANUSCRIPT

C. Allen Papers (L.S.E.)
E. Bevin Papers (Churchill Coll., Cambridge)
G. D. H. Cole Papers (Nuffield, Oxford)
Sir S. Cripps Papers (Nuffield, Oxford)
R. Dodds Papers (Gateshead)
R. Groves Papers (Battersea)
J. F. Horrabin Letters (Hendon)
G. Lansbury Papers (L.S.E.)
W. Mellor Letters (Dagenham)

(B) PRINTED

S.L. Publications (Books and Pamphlets)

Problems of a Socialist Government (1933)
Problems of a Socialist Transition (1934)
Forward to Socialism (Leeds S.L. Conference 1934)
Fight Now Against War: A Call to Action (Bristol S.L. Conference 1935)
S.L. Conference Reports (1932–1937)

S.L. Pamphlets

Rt. Hon. Dr. C. Addison, *Socialist Policy & the Food Supply*, 1933
C. R. Attlee, *Local Government & the Socialist Plan*, 1933
F. B., *Socialism for the Small Town*, 1934
H. N. Brailsford, *A Socialist Foreign Policy*, 1933
H. N. Brailsford, *The Nazi Terror*, 1933
H. N. Brailsford, *India in Chains*, 1935
H. N. Brailsford, *Spain's Challenge to Labour*, 1936
H. Clay, *Workers' Control*, 1933
H. Clay, *Trade Unionism: Some Problems & Proposals*, 1934
G. D. H. Cole, *Socialist Control of Industry*, 1933
G. D. H. Cole, *A Study Guide on Socialist Policy*, 1933
G. D. H. Cole, *The Working-class Movement & the Transition to Socialism*, 1934
G. D. H. Cole & G. R. Mitchison, *The Need for a Socialist Programme*, 1932
S. Cripps, *Can Socialism Come by Constitutional Methods?*, 1933
S. Cripps, *The Choice for Britain*, 1934
S. Cripps, *Democracy: Real or Sham?*, 1934

S. Cripps, *'National' Fascism in Britain*, 1935
L. A. Fenn, *What of the Professional Classes?*, 1934
R. Groves, *Trades Councils in the Fight for Socialism*, 1935
R. Groves, *Arms & the Unions*, 1936
R. Groves, *East End Crisis! Socialism, the Jews & Fascism*, 1936
J. F. Horrabin, *The Break with Imperialism*, 1933
J. F. Horrabin, *The Class Struggle*, 1934
J. F. Horrabin & G. D. H. Cole, *Socialism in Pictures & Figures*, 1933
W. Horrabin, *Is Woman's Place the Home?*, 1933
H. Laski, *The Roosevelt Experiment*, 1933
H. Laski, *The Labour Party & the Constitution*, 1933
W. Mellor, *The Claim of the Unemployed*, 1933
W. Mellor, *The Co-operative Movement & the Fight for Socialism*, 1934
G. R. Mitchison, *Banking*, 1933
J. T. Murphy, *Fascism: The Socialist Answer*, 1933
J. T. Murphy, *Trade Unions & Socialism*, 1936
H. B. Pointing, *A Countryman Talks About Socialism*, 1933
Sir C. Trevelyan, *The Challenge to Capitalism*, 1933
Sir C. Trevelyan, *Mass Resistance to War*, 1935
R. H. Tawney, *The Choice Before the Labour Party*, 1932
E. F. Wise, *The Control of Finance & Financiers*, 1933
E. F. Wise, *The Socialisation of Banking*, 1934

Other Pamphlets and Articles

Clifford Allen, *Labour's Future at Stake*, I.L.P., 1932
P. Anderson, 'The Left in the 1950s', *N.L.R.*, No. 29, January–February 1966, pp.3–18
P. Anderson, 'Socialism & Pseudo Empiricism', *N.L.R.*, January–February 1966
R. P. Arnot, 'From Right to Left', *Labour Monthly*, No. 48, 1936, pp.89–92
R. Aronson, 'The Movement & Its Critics', *Studies on the Left*, Vol. 6, No. 1, January–February 1966
P. N. Backstrom, 'The British Labour Movement: A Challenge to the Young Historian', *Historian 24*, 1962, pp.415–422
R. Barker, 'The Labour Party & Education for Socialism', *International Review of Social History 14*, 1962, pp.22–53
Frank Bealey, review of Miliband's *Parliamentary Socialism* in *3rd Bulletin of Society for Study of Labour History*
S. Bernstein, 'Notes on Recent Literature on Socialism', *Science & Society*, No. 28, 1964, pp.48–63
A. Bevan, 'Problems of Labour Policy', *Labour Monthly*, Vol. 18, No. 6, June 1936
H. N. Brailsford, et al., *The Living Wage*, I.L.P., 1926
H. N. Brailsford, 'What Next After Edinburgh?', *Labour Monthly*, Vol. 18, No. 12, December 1936
F. Brockway, *The I.L.P. & the Crisis*, I.L.P., 1931
F. Brockway, *The Coming Revolution*, I.L.P., 1932
F. Brockway, *Socialism at the Crossroads*, I.L.P., 1932
E. Burns, *Communist Affiliation*, C.P.G.B., 1934
E. Burns, *The People's Front*, C.P.G.B., 1937

J. R. Campbell, 'The I.L.P.: Has it Really Changed?', *Labour Monthly*, Vol. 14, No. 9, September 1932

J. R. Campbell, 'Next Steps in the "United Front"', *Labour Monthly*, Vol. 19, No. 4, April 1937

J. R. Campbell, '"Left" Socialism & the Popular Front', *Labour Monthly*, Vol. 19, No. 5, May 1937

J. R. Campbell, '"Left" Socialism & the Crisis', *Labour Monthly*, Vol. 20, No. 11, November 1938

G. E. G. Catlin, 'Problems of Labour Policy', *Labour Monthly*, Vol. 18, No. 2, February 1936

Colin Clark, 'What's Wrong with Economics', *Encounter*, April 1958

G. D. H. Cole, 'Chants of Progress', *Political Quarterly*, October–December 1935

G. D. H. Cole, 'A British People's Front: Why & How', *Political Quarterly*, Vol. 7, No. 4, October–December 1936

G. D. H. Cole, 'The United Front & the Popular Front', *Labour Monthly*, Vol. 19, No. 1, January 1937

G. D. H. Cole, 'The People's Front', *Labour Monthly*, Vol. 19, No. 3, March 1937

M. Cole, 'In the Past', *Political Quarterly*, Vol. 40, No. 4, October–December 1969

M. Cole, Letter to *Society for Study of Labour History*, Spring 1971, Bulletin No. 22, pp.25–26

Communist Party Conference Report, 12th Congress, Battersea 1932, 'Road to Victory'

Communist Party Conference Report, 13th Congress, Manchester 1935, 'For Soviet Britain'

Communist Party Conference Report, 14th Congress, 1937, 'It Can Be Done'

J. Coombes, 'British Intellectuals and the Popular Front', in *Class, Culture and Social Change: A New View of the 1930s*, ed. F. Gloversmith, 1980

S. Cripps, *Are You a Worker?*, L.P. 1933

S. Cripps, 'The Next Election', *Political Quarterly*, Vol. 3, No. 1, January–March 1932

S. Cripps, Preface to *Problems of a Socialist Government*, S.L., 1933

S. Cripps, 'Democracy & Dictatorship: The Issue for the Labour Party, *Political Quarterly*, Vol. 4, No. 4, October–December 1933

S. Cripps, 'United Front', *Labour Monthly*, Vol. 19, No. 2, February 1937

S. Cripps with Maxton & Pollitt, *The Unity Campaign*, National Unity Campaign Committee, January 1937

R. H. S. Crossman, 'Labour & Compulsory Military Service', *Political Quarterly*, July–September 1939

H. Dalton, 'The Popular Front', *Political Quarterly*, Vol. 7, No. 4, October–December 1936

P. Derrick, 'Class and the Labour Party', *Twentieth Century 173*, Spring 1965, No. 1025, pp.121–126

G. W. Ditz, 'Utopian Symbols in the History of the British Labour Party', *British Journal of Sociology 17*, 1966, pp.145–150

R. E. Dowse, 'The P.L.P. in Opposition', *Parliamentary Affairs XIII*, 1960, pp.520–259

R. E. Dowse, 'Left-wing Opposition During the First Two Labour Governments', *Parliamentary Affairs XIV*, No. 2, pp.80–93, 229–243

R. E. Dowse, A comment on 'The Second Labour Government', by D.E. Loone, *Society for Study of Labour History*, Bulletin No. 8, Spring 1964, p.16

E. F. M. Durbin, 'Democracy & Socialism in Britain', *Political Quarterly*, July–September 1935

R. Palme Dutt, 'The United Front & the Labour Party', *Labour Monthly*, Vol. 16, No. 11, November 1934

R. Palme Dutt, 'The Popular Front', *Labour Monthly*, Vol. 18, No. 6, June 1936

R. Palme Dutt, 'The United Front & Revolutionary Unity', *Labour Monthly*, Vol. 15, No. 4, April 1933

R. Palme Dutt, 'The Burning Question of Working-class Unity', *Labour Monthly*, Vol. 14, No. 7, July 1932

R. Palme Dutt, 'The I.L.P. & Revolution', *Labour Monthly*, Vol. 14, No. 9, September 1932

R. Palme Dutt, 'Notes of the Month', *Labour Monthly*, Vol. 14, No. 10, October 1932

R. Palme Dutt, 'Notes of the Month', 'The Labour Movement & Fascism', *Labour Monthly*, Vol. 15, No. 10, October 1933

R. Palme Dutt, 'The Unity Campaign', *Labour Monthly*, Vol. 19, No. 2, February 1937

R. Palme Dutt, 'Norwich, Bournemouth & After', *Labour Monthly*, Vol. 19, No. 10, October 1937

R. Palme Dutt, 'Labour & the People's Front', *Labour Monthly*, Vol. 20, No. 6, June 1938

S. Elliott, 'The Peace Alliance & the Future', *Labour Monthly*, Vol. 20, No. 6, June 1938

G. Elton, 'The Future of the Labour Party', *Political Quarterly*, January–March 1932

G. Fanti, *The Resurgence of the Labour Party*, N.L.R., No. 30, March–April 1965

J. F. Finlay, 'John Hargrave: the Green Shirts & Social Credit', *Journal of Contemporary History*, Vol. 5, No. 1, 1970, pp.53–71

M. Foot, *Credo of the Labour Left*, interview in N.L.R., No. 49, May–June 1968, pp.19–34

Paul Foot, 'H. Wilson & the Labour Left', *International Socialism*, No. 33, Summer 1968, pp.8–26

Robert Fraser, 'The Front Against Fascism', *New Trends in Socialism*, 1935

W. Gallacher, 'The Fight for Unity in Parliament', *Labour Monthly*, Vol. 18, No. 2, February 1936

J. Gollan, 'Muzzling the League of Youth', *Labour Monthly*, Vol. 16, No. 12, December 1934

P. Gordon-Walker, 'The Attitude of Labour & the Left to the War', *Political Quarterly*, Vol. 11, No. 1, January–March 1940

John Grieve-Smith, 'Matters of Principle', *Labour's Last Chance*, 1968

E. Hobsbawm, on D. Marquand's 'The Dilemma of Gradualism (1929–1931), *Society for Study of Labour History*, Bulletin 21

J. A. Hobson, 'The Economics for a Popular Front', *Labour Monthly*, Vol. 19, No. 1, January 1937

A. Horner, *Trade Unions & Unity*, C.P.G.B. 1937

A. Horner, *Towards a Popular Front*, C.P.G.B. 1938

A. Hutt, 'Labour & the Cripps Campaign', *Labour Monthly*, Vol. 21, No. 4, April 1939

An ex-I.L.P.'er, 'The Future of the I.L.P.', *Labour Monthly*, Vol. 14, No. 9, September 1932

Storm Jameson, 'To a Labour Party Official', *Left Review*, November 1934, pp.32–33

G. S. Jones, 'History in One Dimension', *N.L.R.*, No. 36, 1966

Fred Jowett, *The I.L.P. Says No to the Present Standing Orders of the Labour Party*, I.L.P., 1932

M. Karson, 'H. Laski and the Soviet Union', *New Politics 4*, 1964–65, pp.104–109

A. Kettle, 'The Future of the Left', *Marxism Today*, No. 10, 1966, pp.5–9

J. M. Keynes, 'The Dilemma of Modern Socialism', *Political Quarterly*, Vol. 13, No. 2, April–June 1932

F. Kingsley Griffith, 'Political Parties & the Next Election', *Political Quarterly*, April–June 1935

Labour Party pamphlet, *Labour and the New Social Order*, 1918

Labour Party pamphlet, *Labour and the Nation*, 1928

Labour Party pamphlet, *Two Years of Labour Rule: Why a Labour Party?*, 1931–32

Labour Party pamphlet, *The L.P. and the I.L.P.*, 1932–33

Labour Party pamphlet, S. Cripps, *The Ultimate Aims of the Labour Party*, 1933–34

Labour Party pamphlet, G. Lansbury, *Immediate Steps Towards the New Order*

Labour Party pamphlet, *The Communist Solar System*, 1933

Labour Party pamphlet, *Labour and the Unemployment Bill*

Labour Party pamphlet, *For Socialism and Peace*, 1934

Labour Party pamphlet, *Local Government and the Depressed Areas*

Labour Party pamphlet, L. A. Benjamin, *The Position of the Middle-class Worker in the Transition to Socialism*

Labour Party pamphlet, *British Labour and Communism*, 1935

Labour Party pamphlet, *Labour and the Defence of Peace*

Labour Party pamphlet, *Victory for Socialism*

Labour Party pamphlet, C. R. Attlee, *The Betrayal of Collective Security*, 1936

Labour Party pamphlet, H. Morrison, *Labour and Sanctions*

Labour Party pamphlet, *Labour's Immediate Programme. Party Loyalty: an Appeal to the Movement*, 1937

Labour Party pamphlet, *Labour Party and the So-called 'Unity' Campaign*, 1937

Labour Party pamphlet, *The Agony of Spain*

Labour Party pamphlet, *Unity: True or Sham?*, 1937

H. J. Laski, 'Some Implications of the Crisis', *Political Quarterly*, Vol. 2, No. 4, October–December 1931

H. J. Laski, 'The General Election of 1935', *Political Quarterly*, January–March 1936

H. J. Laski, 'Problems of Labour Policy', *Labour Monthly*, Vol. 18, No. 3, March 1936

H. J. Laski, 'S. Cripps – Socialist Leader', *The Nation*, CXLIV, January 1937

H. J. Laski, 'Unity and the Labour Party', *Labour Monthly*, Vol. 19, No. 3, March 1937

Rt. Hon. H. B. Lees-Smith, 'Political Parties & the Next Election – Prospects for the Labour Party', *Political Quarterly*, January–March 1935

A. Lehning, 'Sources of Labour History', *Times Literary Supplement*, 66, 1966, pp.809–811

Robert Looker, 'The Future of the Left in Britain', *Studies on the Left*, Vol. 7, No. 2, March–April 1967

G. Lowes Dickinson, 'The Essential Issue', *Political Quarterly*, October–December 1931

R. W. Lyman, 'The Conflict Between Socialist Ideals & Practical Politics Between the Wars', *Journal of British Studies V*, 1965, pp.140–152

A. MacIntyre, 'Labour Policy & Capitalist Planning', *International Socialism*, Winter 1963, pp.5–9

D. I. Mackay, 'The Discussion of Public Works Programmes (1917–1935)', *International Review of Social History*, 11, 1966, pp.8–17

S. Mallet, 'Socialism and the New Working Class', *International Socialist Journal*, Vol. 2, No. 8, April 1965, pp.152–172

D. Marquand, 'The Liberal Revival', *Encounter*, July 1962

D. Marquand, 'The Politics of Deprivation', *Encounter*, April 1969

K. Martin, 'This Crisis', *Political Quarterly*, October–December 1931

A. Marwick, 'Middle Opinion in the 1930s', *English Historical Review*, Vol. 79, April 1964

A. Marwick, 'Labour Party and the Welfare State in Britain', *American Historical Review* 73, 1967, pp.380–403

A. Marwick, 'Youth in Britain (1920–60): Detachment & Commitment', *Journal of Contemporary History*, Vol. 5, No. 1, pp.37–51, 1970

R. B. McCallum, 'The Future of Political Parties', *Political Quarterly*, April–June 1932

R. Miliband, 'Labour's Framework of Policy', *I.S.J.*, 1964, pp.282–292

R. Miliband, 'Socialism and the Myth of the Golden Past', *Socialist Register*, 1964, pp.92–103

R. Miliband, 'What Does the Left Want?', *Socialist Register*, 1965, pp.184–194

R. Miliband & J. Saville, 'Labour Policy and Labour Left', *Socialist Register*, 1964, pp.149–156

W. Milne Bailey, 'The Strategy of Victory', chapter 14, *New Trends in Socialism*, 1935

H. Morrison, 'Social Change: Peaceful or Violent?, *Political Quarterly*, Vol. 10, No. 1, January–March 1939

C. L. Mowat, 'The Mood of the 1930s', *Critical Quarterly*, Autumn 1961

C. L. Mowat, 'Ramsay Macdonald and the Labour Movement – Right-Left-Right', *Society for the Study of Labour History*, Bulletin 14, Spring 1967, pp.6–7

Lionel Munby, 'Studying and Writing Working-class History', *Marxism Today*, No. 8, 1964, pp.309–313

T. Nairn, 'The Fateful Meridian', *New Left Review*, No. 60, March–April 1970, pp.3–35

P. Noel-Baker, 'The Future of the Labour Party', *Political Quarterly*, Vol. 15, No. 1, January–March 1932

O. Oltis, 'The Labour Party and International Socialism', *Plebs*, No. 57, 1965, pp.488–489

John Parker, 'The Constitutional Background to the Cripps Controversy', *Political Quarterly*, Vol. 10, No. 2, April–June 1939

B. Pearce, 'The Establishment of Marx House – a Comment', *Society for the Study of Labour History*, Bulletin 16, Spring 1968, pp.20–22

H. Pelling, review of R.E. Dowse, 'Left in the Centre', *Society for the Study of Labour History*, Bulletin 14, Spring 1967

S. Pollard, review of D. Fauvel-Rouif ed., 'Mouvements Ouvriers et Depression Economique de 1929 a 1939', *Society for the Study of Labour History*, Bulletin 12, Spring 1966

S. Pollard, 'The Great Disillusion', a review of R. Skidelsky, *Politicians and the Slump*, *Society for the Study of Labour History*, Bulletin 12, Spring 1968

H. Pollitt, *Which Way for the Workers?*, C.P.G.B., 1932

H. Pollitt, *The Labour Party and the Communist Party*, C.P.G.B., 1935

H. Pollitt, *The Working Class Can Stop the War*, C.P.G.B., 1935

H. Pollitt, 'The Next Stage in the Fight for Unity', *Labour Monthly*, Vol. 19, No. 7, July 1937

H. Pollitt, 'Unity and the Popular Front', *Labour Monthly*, Vol. 20, No. 7, July 1938

H. Pollitt, 'The People's Movement', *Labour Monthly*, Vol. 20, No. 10, October 1938

Lord Ponsonby, 'The Future of the Labour Party', *Political Quarterly*, Vol. 3, No. 3, January–March 1932

W. A. Robson, 'The Past and the Future', *Political Quarterly*, October–December 1932

A. L. Rowse, 'Mr. Keynes on Socialism', *Political Quarterly*, Vol. 3, No. 3, July–September 1932

A. L. Rowse, 'The Present and the Immediate Future of the Labour Party', *Political Quarterly*, January–March 1938

W. Rust, 'The Socialist League – What Next?', *Labour Monthly*, Vol. 16, No. 11, November 1934

W. Rust, 'Problems of Labour Policy', *Labour Monthly*, Vol. 18, No. 8, August 1936

R. Samuels, 'The Left Book Club', *Journal of Contemporary History*, 1966, pp.65–86

R. Samuels, 'Intellectuals in the 1930s', *Society for the Study of Labour History*, Bulletin 14, Spring 1967

P. Sedgewick, 'The New Left', *International Socialism*, No. 17, Summer 1964

P. Sedgewick, 'Varieties of Socialist Thought', *Political Quarterly*, Vol. 40, No. 4, October–December 1969

P. Seyd, review of Janosik, *The Constituency Labour Parties in Britain*, *Society for the Study of Labour History*, Bulletin 18, Spring 1969

P. Seyd, review of Haseler, *The Gaitskellites 1951–1964*, *Society for the Study of Labour History*, Bulletin 21, Autumn 1970

P. Seyd, 'Factionalism Within the Labour Party: the S.L. 1932–1937', in *Essays in Labour History*, ed. A. Briggs et al., Vol. 3, 1977

H. Short, 'The Days of G. Lansbury: a Picture from Labour's Past', *Plebs*, 57, May 1965, pp.386–389

J. Silverman, 'Socialism and the Popular Front', *Labour Monthly*, Vol. 21, No. 5, May 1939

B. Simon, 'The Challenge of Marxism', *Marxism Today*, 8, 1964, pp.6–8

R. Skidelsky, '1929–1931 Revisited', *Society for the Study of Labour History*, Bulletin 21, Autumn 1970

'A Socialist', 'Working-class Unity and a Popular Front', *Political Quarterly*, October–December 1936

N. C. Soderland, 'Left Socialism and Communism', *Labour Monthly*, Vol. 14, No. 1, January 1932

J. Southall, 'The Position of the I.L.P.', *Labour Monthly*, Vol. 14, No. 10, October 1932

J. Strachey, 'Peace Alliance Holds the Field', *Labour Monthly*, Vol. 20, No. 7, July 1938

G. R. Strauss, 'Problems of Labour Policy', *Labour Monthly*, Vol. 18, No. 8, August 1936

G. R. Strauss, 'Labour's Short Programme and the Unity Campaign', *Labour Monthly*, Vol. 19, No. 6, June 1937

G. R. Strauss, 'Bournemouth and After', *Labour Monthly*, Vol. 19, No. 11, November 1937

A. J. P. Taylor, 'Looking Back at British Socialism (1922–1939)', *Encounter*, Vol. 10, No. 3, March 1958

A. J. P. Taylor, 'Confusion on the Left', *The Baldwin Age*, ed. J. Raymond, 1960

R. H. Tawney, 'The Choice Before the Labour Party', *Political Quarterly*, Vol. 3, No. 3, July–September 1932

M. Thomas, 'Rearmament and Economic Recovery in the Late 1930s', *EHR*, November 1983

E. P. Thompson, 'Socialism and the Intellectuals', *Universities and Left Review*, Spring 1957

E. P. Thompson, 'Socialist Humanism: An Epistle to the Philistines', *New Reasoner*, 1957

E. P. Thompson, 'The Peculiarities of the English', *Socialist Register*, 1965, pp.311–362

T.U.C. Report/Pamphlet, *The Government Evades Its Responsibilities*, 1933

T.U.C. Report/Pamphlet, *The Menace of Dictatorship*, 1933

T.U.C. Report/Pamphlet, *Workers' Control*, 1933

T.U.C. Report/Pamphlet, *Workless – a Social Tragedy*, 1933

T.U.C. Report/Pamphlet, *United Against Fascism*, 1934

T.U.C. Report/Pamphlet, *Peace or War*, 1935

T.U.C. Report/Pamphlet, *Youth for Socialism*, 1935

T.U.C. Report/Pamphlet, *The Spanish Problem*, 1936

T.U.C. Report/Pamphlet, *No United Front with Communism*, 1936

C. Trevelyan, 'The Outlook of the Socialist League', *Political Quarterly*, Vol. 6, No. 2, April–June 1935

M. Warner, 'The Webbs, Keynes, and the Economic Problems in the Inter-war Years', *Political Studies*, 14, 1966, pp.81–86

S. Webb, 'What Happened in 1931: A Record', *Political Quarterly*, Vol. 3, No. 1, January–March 1932

Jeffrey Weeks, 'Foucault for Historians', *HWJ*, No. 14, 1982

James Weinstein, 'Socialist Intellectuals', *Studies on the Left*, Vol. 6, No. 5, September–October 1966

J. Wetherby, 'Some Notes on Changes in the British Working Class', *Marxism Today*, 6, 1962, pp.270–276

E. Wilkinson, 'Socialism and the Problem of the Middle Classes', *New Trends in Socialism*, 1935

R. Williams, 'The British Left', *New Left Review*, no. 30, March–April 1965, pp.18–26

E. M. Winterton, '"Left" Intellectuals and the War', *Labour Monthly*, Vol. 22, No. 6, June 1940

E. F. Wise, 'An Alternative to Tariffs', *Political Quarterly*, April–June 1931

L. Woolf, 'A Constitutional Revolution', *Political Quarterly*, October–December 1931

A. Young, 'The Political Problem of Transition', *New Trends in Socialism*, 1935

Alfred Zimmern, 'The Choice Before the Labour Movement: A Reply to Mr. Tawney', *Political Quarterly*, October–December 1932

B. M. Zweibach, 'The Political Thought of R. H. Tawney', Dissertation Abstract 25, 1964

Newspapers and Periodicals

Birmingham Town Crier
Bristol Evening Post
Bristol Evening World
Bristol Labour Weekly
Bristol Observer
Bristol Times
Challenge
Communist International

Daily Express
Daily Herald
Daily Mail
Daily Telegraph
Daily Worker
Derby Daily Express
Derby Evening Telegraph
Discussion
Fabian News
Foreign Affairs
Forward
Gateshead Herald
Hampstead Citizen
History Today
International Press Correspondence
Journal of Modern History
Kentish Independent & Kentish Mail
Labour Magazine
Labour Monthly
Labour News
Lansbury's Labour Weekly
Leeds Mercury
Leeds Weekly Citizen
Left Forum
Left News
Left Review
Manchester Guardian
Morning Post
New Age
New Clarion
New English Review
New Leader
New Left Review
New Nation
News Chronicle
New Statesman and Nation
Oxford Mail
Peace
Political Quarterly
Reynolds' News
Socialist (S.L.)
Socialist Broadsheet (S.L.)
Socialist Leaguer
Socialist Review
Spectator
Stockport Advertiser
Stockport Express
Stoke-on-Trent City Times

Sutton Times
The Times
Tribune
Twentieth Century
Western Daily Press
West Fulham Labour Magazine
World News
Yorkshire Post

Secondary Sources: Books Quoted or Consulted

H. B. Acton, *The Illusion of an Epoch (Marxism – Leninism as a Philosophical Creed)*, 1955
G. Aldred, *Essays in Revolt*, 1940
C. Allen, *Labour's Future at Stake*, 1932
C. Allen, *Britain's Political Future*, 1934
G. A. Almond, *The Appeals of Communism*, 1954
C. R. Attlee, *The Will and the Way to Socialism*, 1935
C. R. Attlee, *The Labour Party in Perspective*, 1937
C. R. Attlee, *As It Happened*, 1954
A. W. Baldwin, *My Father: The True Story*, 1955
G. Barraclough, *An Introduction to Contemporary History*, 1964
E. E. Barry, *Nationalisation in British Politics*, 1965
R. Bassett, *Nineteen Thirty-one*, 1958
H. L. Beales & R. S. Lambert, *Memoirs of the Unemployed*, 1934
F. Bealey, *The Social and Political Thought of the British Labour Party*, 1970
F. Bédarida, *A Social History of England 1851–1975,* 1979 edn.
F. Bédarida, *The Social Responsibility of the Historian*, 1994
D. Bell, *The End of Ideology*, 1965
Tom Bell, *Pioneering Days*, 1940
I. Berlin, *The First and the Last*, 1998
I. Berlin, *The Legacy of Isaiah Berlin*, 2001
A. Bevan, *In Place of Fear*, ed. J. Lee, 1952
C. Bloom, *Violent London: 2000 Years of Riots, Rebels and Revolts*, 2003
R. Blythe, *The Age of Illusion*, 1963
H. N. Brailsford, *Property or Peace?*, 1934
H. N. Brailsford, *Why Capitalism Causes War*, 1938
C. F. Brand, *The British Labour Party*, 1964
N. Branson, M Heinemann, *Britain in the Nineteen Thirties*, 1973 edn.
J. Braunthal, *In Search of the Millennium*, 1945
R. Briffault, *Breakdown: The Collapse of Traditional Civilisation*, 1935
V. Brittain, *Pethick-Lawrence – A Portrait,* 1963
F. Brockway, *Workers' Front*, 1938
F. Brockway, *Inside the Left*, 1942
F. Brockway, *Bermondsey Story*, 1949
V. Brome, *Aneurin Bevan*, 1953
A. Brown, *The Fate of the Middle Classes*, 1936

M. Bruce, *The Coming of the Welfare State*, 1961

M. V. Bukiet, ed., *Nothing Makes You Free: Writings by Descendants of Jewish Holocaust Survivors*, 2002

A. Bullock, *Life and Times of Ernest Bevin*, Vol. 1, 1881–1940, 1960

Tyrrell Burgess, ed., *Matters of Principle: Labour's Last Chance*, 1968

E. Burns, *Capitalism, Communism, and the Transition*, 1933

E. G. Carlston, *Thinking Fascism: Sapphic Modernism and Fascist Modernity*, 1998

E. H. Carr, *The Bolshevik Revolution (1917–1923)*, 1950

E. H. Carr, *From Napoleon to Stalin and Other Essays*, 1960

E. H. Carr, *What Is History?*, 1961

G. E. G. Catlin, ed., *New Trends in Socialism*, 1935

C. Caudwell, *Studies in a Dying Culture*, 1938

D. Caute, *The Left in Europe Since 1789*, 1966

Chester, Fay & Young, *The Zinoviev Letter*, 1967

N. Chomsky, *Understanding Power*, 2003 edn.

Lord Citrine, *Men and Work* (autobiography), 1964

A. Clinton, *The Trade Union Rank and File: Trades Councils in Britain 1900–40*, 1977

J. R. Clynes, *Memoirs (1924–1937)*, 1937

C. Cockburn, *In Time of Trouble*, 1956

P. Cohen, ed. *Children of the Revolution: Communist Childhood in Cold-War Britain*, 1997

G. D. H. Cole, *The Next Ten Years in British Social and Economic Policy*, 1929

G. D. H. Cole, *What Marx Really Meant*, 1934

G. D. H. Cole, *The Simple Case for Socialism*, 1935

G. D. H. Cole, *The People's Front*, 1937

G. D. H. Cole, *Socialism in Evolution*, 1938

G. D. H. Cole, *British Trade Unionism Today*, 1939

G. D. H. Cole, *A Plan for a Democratic Britain*, 1939

G. D. H. Cole, *History of the Labour Party Since 1914*, 1948

G. D. H. Cole, *A Short History of the British Working-class Movement (1789–1949)*, 1952

G. D. H. Cole, 'Socialism and Fascism (1931–39)', *A History of Socialist Thought*, 1959

G. D. H. Cole & M. Cole, *The Intelligent Man's Review of Europe Today*, 1933

G. D. H. Cole & R. Postgate, *The Common People (1746–1946)*, 1963 edn.

M. Cole, *Makers of the Labour Movement*, 1948

M. Cole, *The Story of Fabian Socialism*, 1961

R. Collins, ed., *The Discovery of Society*, 1993 edn.

C. Cooke, *The Life of Richard Stafford Cripps*, 1957

D. Cooper, ed., *Dialectics of Liberation*, 1968

P. Corrigan, ed., *Capitalism, State Formation and Marxist Theory*, 1980

Council of Action, *A Call to Action*, 1935

Council of Action, *Peace and Reconstruction*, 1935

Council of Action, *Peace and Social Justice*, 1936

Council of Action, *Social Justice and National Reconstruction*, 1938

S. Cripps et al., *Where Stands Socialism Today?*, 1933

S. Cripps et al., *Why This Socialism?*, 1934

S. Cripps et al., *The Struggle for Peace*, 1936

S Cripps et al., *Democracy Up-to-date*, 1939

C. A. R. Crosland, *The Future of Socialism*, 1956

C. Cross, *The Fascists in Britain*, 1961

R. H. S. Crossman, ed., *The God that Failed*, 1954
R. H. S. Crossman, ed., *Labour in the Affluent Society*, 1959
R. H. S. Crossman, ed., *The Politics of Socialism*, 1965
H. Dalton, *Twelve Studies in Soviet Russia*, 1933
H. Dalton, *Practical Socialism in Britain*, 1935
H. Dalton, *Call Back Yesterday (Memoirs 1887–1931)*, 1953
H. Dalton, *The Fateful Years (Memoirs 1931 1945)*, 1957
P. Davies, *A.J. Cook,* 1987
S. Davis, *British Labour and Foreign Policy (1933–1939)*, thesis 1950
H. A. Deane, *The Political Ideas of Harold Laski*, 1953
Greg Dening, *Readings/Writings*, 1998
I. Deutscher, *Marxism in Our Time*, 1972
C. H. Douglas, *Social Credit*, 1933
R. E. Dowse, *Left in the Centre*, 1966
E. F. M. Durbin, *The Politics of Democratic Socialism*, 1940
R. Palme Dutt, *Fascism and Social Revolution*, 1934
T. Eagleton, *The Gatekeeper – A Memoir*, 2001
W. Ebenstein, *Today's Isms: Communism, Fascism, Capitalism and Socialism*, 1970
H. W. J. Edwards, *Young England*, 1938
G. Elton, *Towards the New Labour Party*, 1932
G. Elton, *Towards a National Policy*, N.L.C., 1935
G. R. Elton, *The Practice of History*, 1967
E. Estorick, *The Life of Stafford Cripps*, 1949
J. N. Evans, *Great Figures in the Labour Movement*, 1966
L. Fischer, *Men and Politics*, 1941
M. Foot, *Aneurin Bevan*, Vol. 1, 1962
V. E. Frankl, *Man's Search for Meaning*, 2004 edn.
E. Fromm, *The Fear of Freedom*, 1960 edn.
B. Fuller, *The Life Story of J.H. Thomas*, 1932
W. Gallacher, *The Chosen Few: A Sketch of Men and Events in Parliament*, 1940
W. Gallacher, *The Rolling of the Thunder*, 1947
M. George, *The Hollow Men*, 1965
B. B. Gilbert, *Britain 1914–1945*, 1996
M. Gilbert & R. Gott, *The Appeasers*, 1963
M. Gilbert, *Auschwitz and the Allies*, 2001 edn.
J. Glover, *A History of the 20th Century*, 2001
V. Gollancz, *The Betrayal of the Left*, 1941
R. Graves & A. Hodge, *The Long Weekend*, 1941
H. R. G. Greaves, *Reactionary England*, 1936
M. Green, *Children of the Sun: A Narrative of Decadence in England after 1918*, 2001 edn.
A. Greenwood, *Why We Fight: Labour's Case*, 1940
W. Greenwood, *Love on the Dole*, 1933 (1967 edn.)
J. B. S. Haldane, *Heredity and Politics*, 1938
M. A. Hamilton, *Arthur Henderson*, 1938
M. A. Hamilton, *The Labour Party Today*, 1939
S. Hampshire, *Innocence and Experience*, 1992 edn.
W. Hannington, *Ten Lean Years*, 1940
W. Hannington, *Never on Our Knees*, 1967

R. F. Harrod, *The Life of J.M. Keynes*, 1951

M. Heinemann & N. Branson, *Britain in the Nineteen-thirties*, 1973 edn.

C. Hill, *Lenin and the Russian Revolution*, 1947 (1965 edn.)

E. Hobsbawm, *Interesting Times: A 20th-Century Life*, 2002

L. Hogben, *Dangerous Thoughts*, 1939

S. Hook, *Marx and the Marxists*, 1955

S. Hornby, *Left-wing Pressure Groups in the British Labour Movement (1930–40)*, M.A. thesis, Liverpool University, 1966

A. Horner, *Incorrigible Rebel*, autobiography, 1960

R. Hughes *Culture of Complaint: The Fraying of America*, 1999 edn.

A. Hutt, *This Final Crisis*, 1935

A. Hutt, *Postwar History of the British Working Class*, 1937

A. Hutt, *British Trade Unionism*, revised edition 1962

D. Hyde, *I Believed*, 1951

M. Ignatieff, *A Life of Isaiah Berlin*,

Caren Irr, *Cultural Politics in the US and Canada during the 1930s*, 1998

T. A. Jackson, *Sole Trumpet: Some Memories of Socialist Agitations and Propaganda*, 1953

R. Jahanbegloo, *Conversations with Isaiah Berlin*, 1993 edn.

S. Jameson, *No Time Like the Present*, 1933

E. G. Janosik, *Constituency Labour Parties in Britain*, 1968

D. Jay, *The Socialist Case*, 1936

R. Jenkins, *Mr. Attlee*, 1948

H. Johnson, *The Socialist Sixth of the World*, 1939, LBC

T. Johnson, *Memories*, 1952

J. Joll, *Intellectuals in Politics*, 1960

J. Jupp, *The Left in Britain*, M.Sc. thesis, 1956

H. Kemp et al., *The Left Heresy in Literature and Life*, 1939

D. Kirkwood, *My Life of Revolt*, 1935

V. Klemperer, *I Shall Bear Witness: The Diaries of Victor Klemperer (1933–1941)*, 1998 edn.

A. Koestler, *The Invisible Writing*, autobiography, 1954

M. M. Krug, *Aneurin Bevan: Cautious Rebel*, 1961

J. Kuczynski, *The Conditions of the Workers in Great Britain, Germany and the Soviet Union (1932–1938)*, 1939

J. P. Kyba, *British Attitudes Towards Disarmament and Rearmament (1932–35)*, Ph.D. thesis, L.S.E., 1967

D. P. F. Lancien, *British Left-wing Attitudes to the Spanish Civil War*, 1964 thesis, Oxford

G. Lansbury, *Looking Backwards, Looking Forwards*, 1935

G. Lansbury, *My Quest for Peace*, 1938

G. Lansbury, *My England*, 1964

H. J. Laski, *The Crisis and the Constitution*, 1932

H. J. Laski, *Democracy in Crisis*, 1933

H. J. Laski et al., *Where Stands Socialism Today*, 1933

H. J. Laski, *The State in Theory and Practice*, 1935

H. J. Laski, *The Rise of European Liberalism*, 1936

H. J. Laski, *Liberty in the Modern State*, 1936

G. C. Lebzelter, *Political Anti-Semitism in England 1918–1939*, 1978

J. Lee, *Tomorrow Is a New Day*, 1939

J. Lee, *This Great Journey*, 1942

H. Levy, *A Philosophy for Modern Man*, 1938

J. Lewis, *The Left Book Club*, 1970

D. Low, *Europe Since Versailles* (cartoons), 1940

R. W. Lyman, *The First Labour Government*, 1957

S. Macintyre, *A Proletarian Science: Marxism in Britain 1917–1933*, 1980

S. Macintyre, *Little Moscows*, 1980

N. MacKenzie, *Socialism: A Short History*, revised edition 1966

H. MacMillan, *Reconstruction*, 1935

J. MacMurray et al., *Aspects of Dialectical Materialism*, 1934

C. Madge & T. Harrison, *Britain by Mass Observation*, 1939

B. Magee, *The New Radicalism*, 1962

H. Marcuse, *One Dimensional Man*, 1964 edn.

H. Marcuse, *Eros and Civilisation*, 1969 edn.

H. Marcuse, 'Liberation from the Affluent Society', *Dialectics of Liberation*, 1970

K. Martin, *Harold Laski*, 1953

K. Martin, *The Editor (1931–45)*, Vol. 2

A. Marwick, *Clifford Allen: The Open Conspirator*, 1964

A. Marwick, *Britain in the Century of Total War*, 1968

A. Marwick, *The Explosion of British Society (1914–70)*, 1971

D. E. S. Maxwell, *Poets of the Thirties*, 1969

G. McAllister, *J. Maxton*, 1935

M. McCarthy, *Generation in Revolt*, 1953

C. McElwee, *Britain's Locust Years*, 1962

D. E. McHenry, *His Majesty's Opposition (1931–8)*, 1938

R. T. McKenzie, *British Political Parties*, 1958

J. McNair, *James Maxton: The Beloved Rebel*, 1955

R. Miliband, *Parliamentary Socialism*, 1961

A. Miller, *Timebends*, 1987

A. Miller, *Echoes Down the Corridor*, 2000

D. Mirsky, *The Intelligentsia of Great Britain*, 1935

G. R. Mitchison, *The First Workers' Government*, 1934

N. Mitchison, *The Moral Basis of Politics*, 1938

R. Monk, *Bertrand Russell: The Ghost of Madness*, 2000

H. Morrison, *Autobiography*, 1960

C. L. Mowat, *Britain Between the Wars*, 1955

M. Muggeridge, *The Thirties*, 1940, 1967 edn.

J. T. Murphy, *Preparing for Power*, 1934

J. T. Murphy, *New Horizons*, 1941

J. T. Murphy, *Labour's Big Three*, 1948

Nicholas Murray, *Aldous Huxley: An English Intellectual*, 2003 edn.

J. P. Nettl, *The Soviet Achievement*, 1967

Next Five Years Group, *An Essay in Political Agreement*, 1935

Next Five Years Group, *A Programme of Priorities*, 1937

F. S. Northedge, *The Troubled Giant*, 1966

G. Orwell, *Down and Out in London and Paris*, 1932, 1967 edn.

G. Orwell, *The Road to Wigan Pier*, 1937, 1966 edn.

G. Orwell, *Coming Up for Air*, 1939, 1967 edn.

G. Orwell, *Looking Back on the Spanish War*, 1943

R. Page-Arnot, *Forging the Weapon: The Struggle of the Labour Monthly (1921–41)*

J. Paton, *Left Turn!*, 1936

L. Paul, *Angry Young Man*, 1951

R. Payne, *Marx: A Biography*

H. Pelling, *American and the British Left: From Bright to Bevan*, 1956

H. Pelling, *The British Communist Party*, 1958

H. Pelling, *A Short History of the Labour Party*, 1968 edn.

F. W. Pethick-Lawrence, *Fate Has Been Kind*, 1943

P. Philip, *English Political Ideas (1918–39)*, Ph.D. thesis 1950

B. Pimlott, *Labour and the Left in the 1930s*, 1980

M. Polanyi, *The Contempt of Freedom: The Russian Experiment and After*, 1940

S. Pollard, *The Development of the British Economy*, 1962

H. Pollitt, *Serving My Time*, 1940

R. Postgate, *How to Make a Revolution*, 1934

R. Postgate, *Life of George Lansbury*, 1951

Mark Pottle, ed., Champion Redoubtable: The Diaries and Letters of Violet Bonham Carter (1914–1945), 1999 edn.

D. Powell, *What's Left? Labour Britain and the Socialist Tradition*, 1998

D. N. Pritt, *From Right to Left*, Vol. 1, 1965

F. Raphael, The Necessity of Anti-Semitism, 1997

J. Raymond, ed., *The Baldwin Age*, 1960

A. Rawnsley, *Servants of the People: The Inside Story of New Labour*, 2002

L. Robbins, *The Great Depression*, 1934

R. Rosenstone, *Romantic Revolutionary: A Biography of John Reed*, 1982

A. L. Rowse, *The Uses of History*, 1963

B. Russell, *Power*, 1938

W. Rust, *Britons in Spain*, 1939

J. Saville, *Democracy and the Labour Movement*, 1954

S.Schama, *A History of Britain 3, 1776–2000. The Fate of the Empire*, 2003 edn.

J. Scanlon, *Decline and Fall of the Labour Party*, 1932

L. Schapiro, *The Communist Party of the Soviet Union*, 1960

J. A. Schumpeter, *Capitalism, Socialism and Democracy*, 1942

E. Shinwell, *Conflict Without Malice*, 1955

E. Shinwell, *The Labour Story*, 1963

R. Skidelsky, *Politicians and the Slump*, 1967

P. Sloan, ed., *John Cornford: A Memoir*, 1938

P. Snowden, *Autobiography*, 1934

D. Snowman, *The Hitler Emigrés: The Cultural Impact on Britain of Refugees from Nazism*, 2002

S. Spender, *Forward from Liberalism*, 1937

J. Strachey, *The Coming Struggle for Power*, 1932

J. Strachey, *The Menace of Fascism*, 1933

J. Strachey, *The Theory and Practice of Socialism*, 1936

P. Strauss, *Bevin and Co.*, 1941

P. Strauss, *Cripps – Advocate and Rebel*, 1943

A. Sturmthal, *The Tragedy of European Labour (1919–1939)*, 1943

P. Sweezy, *Socialism*, 1949

Earl of Swinton, *Sixty Years of Power*, 1966

J. Symons, *The Thirties*, 1960

A. J. P. Taylor, *The Trouble Makers*, 1957

A. J. P. Taylor, *English History (1914–45)*, 1965

R. H. Tawney, *The Acquisitive Society*, 1921, 1966 edn.

R. H. Tawney, *Equality*, 1938 edn.

Lord Templewood, *Nine Troubled Years*, 1954

H. Thomas, *The Spanish Civil War*, 1961

J. H. Thomas, *My Story*, 1937

E. P. Thompson, *Writing by Candlelight*, 1980

Ian Thomson, *Primo Levi*, 2003

E. Upward, *The Thirties*, 1962

E. Varga, *The Great Crisis and Its Consequences*, 1934

W. H. Walsh, *An Introduction to the Philosophy of History*, 1967 edn.

K. W. Watkins, *Britain Divided: Effect of the Spanish Civil War on British Opinion*, 1963

B. Webb, *Diaries*, 1924–1932

F. Wheen, *How Mumbo-Jumbo Conquered the World: A Short History of Modern Delusions*, 2004

A. B. White, *The New Propaganda*, 1939

A. N. Whitehead, *Adventures of Ideas*, 1935

F. Williams, *Fifty Years' March*, 1950

F. Williams, *Ernest Bevin*, 1952

F. Williams, *Magnificent Journey*, 1954

F. Williams, *A Pattern of Rulers*, 1965

R. Williams, ed., *May Day Manifesto*, 1968

T. Wilson, *The Downfall of the Liberal Party*, 1966

N. Wood, *Communism and British Intellectuals*, 1959

L. Woolf et al., *Intelligent Man's Way to Prevent War*, 1933

C. Wright Mills, *The Marxists*, 1962

50 Labour Party Members Associated with the Socialist League Leadership (members, pamphleteers or sympathisers)

Austen Albu
J. B. Ashworth
A. Austen
Donald Barber
L. A. Benjamin
Barbara Betts
Aneurin Bevan
Constance Borrett
H. N. Brailsford
G. E. G. Catlin
Harold Clay
G. D. H. Cole
Sir S. Cripps
D. R. Davies
Ithel Davies
Ruth Dodds
Glyn Evans
H. L. Elvin
Max Elyan
Louis A. Fenn
R. George
H. R. G. Greaves
H. L. Grimshaw
Reg Groves
E. Hartley

F. C. Henry
Gwyn Hopkins
J. F. Horrabin
W. Horrabin
T. Howard
F. L. Kerran
Harold Laski
John Lewis
James Marcus
M. McCarthy
Krishna Menon
W. Mellor
G. R. Mitchison
J. T. Murphy
D. N. Pritt
Joseph Reeves
A. L. Rowse
F. Wilson Temple
Jean Thompson
Sir Charles Trevelyan
M. Wigglesworth
E. Wilkinson
Dorothy L. Wise
E. F. Wise
F. Wynne Davies

Printed in the United Kingdom
by Lightning Source UK Ltd.
103299UKS00002B/178-267